The Historical Archaeology Laboratory Handbook

Volume 2: Seventeenth, Eighteenth, and Nineteenth Century Materials

Edited by John M. Chenoweth

SOCIETY *for* HISTORICAL ARCHAEOLOGY

A Society for Historical Archaeology Publication

The Historical Archaeology Laboratory Handbook Volume 2: Seventeenth, Eighteenth, and Nineteenth Century Materials

© 2016 Society for Historical Archaeology
13017 Wisteria Drive #395
Germantown, MD 20874, U.S.A.

Edited by John M. Chenoweth

Library of Congress Control Number: 2016944270

Cover Design by Dylan Telerski and Knic Pfost.

www.sha.org

Contents

Preface: Citations to the Original Publications

The editor and the SHA would like to extend their deepest gratitude to the authors whose work has been collected here and to the original publishers who have given permission for the works to be reprinted. Full original citations to the reprinted chapters are included below.

ADAMS, WILLIAM HAMPTON, AND SARAH JANE BOLING
1989   Status and Ceramics for Planters and Slaves on Three Georgia Coastal Plantations. Historical Archaeology 23(1):69-96.

ANDERSON, ADRIENNE
1968   The Archaeology of Mass-Produced Footwear. Historical Archaeology 2:56-65.

BALLIN, TORBEN BJARKE
2012   'State of the Art' of British Gunflint Research, with Special Focus on the Early Gunflint Workshop at Dun Eistean, Lewis. Post-Medieval Archaeology 46(1):116-142.

BEAUDRY, MARY C., JANET LONG, HENRY M. MILLER, FRASER D. NEIMAN, AND GARRY WHEELER STONE
1983   A Vessel Typology for Early Chesapeake Ceramics: the Potomac Typological System. Historical Archaeology 17(1):18-43.

BELL, EDWARD L.
1990   The Historical Archaeology of Mortuary Behavior: Coffin Hardware from Uxbridge, Massachusetts. Historical Archaeology 24:54-78.

BINFORD, LEWIS R.
1962   A New Method of Calculating Dates from Kaolin Pipe Stem Samples. Southeastern Archaeological Conference Newsletter 9(1):19-21.

BRADLEY, CHARLES S.
2000   Smoking Pipes for the Archaeologist. In Studies in Material Culture Research. K. Karklins, ed. Pp. 104-133. Rockville, MD: Society for Historical Archaeology.

BUSCH, JANE
1981   An Introduction to the Tin Can. Historical Archaeology 15(1):95-104.

——
1987   The Second Time Around: A Look at Bottle Reuse. Historical Archaeology 21(1):67-80.

CHENOWETH, JOHN M.
2006   "What'll Thou Have": Quakers and the Characterization of Tavern Sites in Colonial Philadelphia. Northeast Historical Archaeology 35:77-92.

COHEN-WILLIAMS, ANITA G.
1992   Common Majolica Types of Northern New Spain. Historical Archaeology 26(1):119-130.

DETHLEFSEN, EDWIN, AND JAMES DEETZ
1966   Death's Heads, Cherubs, and Willow Trees: Experimental Archaeology in Colonial Cemeteries. American Antiquity 31(4):502-510.

DUNNING, PHIL
2000   Composite Table Cutlery from 1700 to 1930. In Studies in Material Culture Research. K. Karklins, ed. Pp. 32-45. Rockville, MD: Society for Historical Archaeology.

GLEICHMAN, PETER J., AND DOCK M. TEEGARDEN
2005   Cartridges, Caps, and Flints: A Primer for Archaeologists. Southwestern Lore 71(3):3-27.

GRIFFITHS, DOROTHY M.
1978   Use-Marks on Historic Ceramics. Historical Archaeology 12:68-81.

GUSSET, GÉRARD
2000   A Preliminary Annotated Bibliography on Electrical Artifacts In Studies in Material Culture Research. K. Karklins, ed. Pp. 134-140. Rockville, MD: Society for Historical Archaeology.

HARRIS, JANE E.
2000   Eighteenth-Century French Blue-Green Bottles from the Fortress of Louisbourg, Nova Scotia. In Studies in Material Culture Research. K. Karklins, ed. Pp. 233-258. Rockville, MD: Society for Historical Archaeology.

HILL, ERICA
1995   Thimbles and Thimble-Rings from the Circum-Caribbean Region, 1500-1800: Chronology and Identification. Historical Archaeology 29(1):84-92.

JONES, OLIVE R.
1971   Glass Bottle Push-Ups and Pontil Marks. Historical Archaeology 5(1):62-73.

——
1993   Commercial Foods, 1740-1820. Historical Archaeology 27(2):25-41.

——
2000   A Guide to Dating Glass Tableware: 1800 to 1940. In Studies in Material Culture Research. K. Karklins, ed. Pp. 141-232. Rockville, MD: Society for Historical Archaeology.

KARKLINS, KARLIS
1982   Guide to the Description and Classification of Glass Beads History and Archaeology. Histoire et Archéologie. [Parks Canada] 59:83-117.

KELLY, ROGER E., AND MARSHA C. S. KELLY
1977   Brick Bats for Archaeologists: Values of Pressed Brick Brands. Historical Archaeology 11:84-89.

KENMOTSU, NANCY
1990   Gunflints: A Study. Historical Archaeology 24(2):92-124.

KIDD, K. E., AND M. A. KIDD
1970   A Classification System for Glass Beads for the Use of Field Archaeologists. Canadian Historic Sites, Occasional Papers in Archaeology and History 1:45-89.

LIGHT, JOHN D.
2000   A Field Guide to the Identification of Metal. In Studies in Material Culture Research. K. Karklins, ed. Pp. 3-19. Rockville, MD: Society for Historical Archaeology.

LINDSEY, BILL
2006   Overview of BLM's Historic Glass Bottle Identification and Information Website. Technical Briefs in Historical Archaeology 1:16-20.

LOCKHART, BILL
2004   An Annotated Bibliography of Bottle Manufacturer's Marks. SHA Newsletter 37(4):10-13.

—
2006   The Color Purple: Dating Solarized Amethyst Container Glass. Historical Archaeology 40(2):45-56.

LORRAIN, DESSAMAE
1968   An Archaeologist's Guide to Nineteenth Century American Glass. Historical Archaeology 2:35-44.

MARTIN, ANN SMART
1989   The Role of Pewter as Missing Artifact: Consumer Attitudes Towards Tablewares in Late 18th Century Virginia. Historical Archaeology 23(2):1-27.

MAXWELL, D. B. S.
1993   Beer Cans: A Guide for the Archaeologist. Historical Archaeology 27(1):95-113.

MILLER, GEORGE L.
1991   A Revised Set of CC Index Values for Classification and Economic Scaling of English Ceramics from 1787 to 1880. Historical Archaeology 25(1):1-25.

—
2000   Telling Time for Archaeologists. Northeast Historical Archaeology 29:1-22.

MILLER, GEORGE L., AND CATHERINE SULLIVAN
1984   Machine-Made Glass Containers and the End of Production for Mouth-Blown Bottles. Historical Archaeology 18(2):83-96.

MYERS, ADRIAN T.
2010   Telling Time for the Electrified: An Introduction to Porcelain Insulators and the Electrification of the American Home Technical Briefs in Historical Archaeology 5:31-42.

NEWMAN, T. STELL
1970   A Dating Key for Post-Eighteenth Century Bottles. Historical Archaeology 4:70-75.

OLSEN, STANLEY J.
1963   Dating Early Plain Buttons by their Form. American Antiquity 28(4):551-554.

PRIESS, PETER J.
2000   Historic Door Hardware. In Studies in Material Culture Research. K. Karklins, ed. Pp. 46-95. Rockville, MD: Society for Historical Archaeology.

ROCK, JAMES
1984   Cans in the Countryside. Historical Archaeology 18:97-111.

ROSS, DOUGLAS E.
2009   Identification and Dating of Japanese Glass Beverage Bottles. Technical Briefs in Historical Archaeology 4:7-17.

ROSS, LESTER A., AND JOHN D. LIGHT
2000   A Guide to the Description and Interpretation of Metal Files. In Studies in Material Culture Research. K. Karklins, ed. Pp. 20-31. Rockville, MD: Society for Historical Archaeology.

SAMFORD, PATRICIA M.
1997   Response to a Market: Dating English Underglaze Transfer-Printed Wares. Historical Archaeology 31(2):1-30.

SCHARFENBERGER, GERARD P.
2004   Recent Evidence for Broad Window Glass in Seventeenth-and Eighteenth-Century America. Historical Archaeology 38(4):59-72.

SINGLEY, KATHERINE R.
1981   Caring for Artifacts After Excavation: Some Advice for Archaeologists. Historical Archaeology 15(1):36-48.

SOUTH, STANLEY
1964   Analysis of the Buttons from Brunswick Town and Fort Fisher. Florida Anthropologist 17(2):113-133.

—
1971   Evolution and Horizon as Revealed in Ceramic Analysis in Historical Archaeology. Conference on Historic Site Archaeology Papers 6(2):71-106.

—
1978   Pattern Recognition in Historical Archaeology. American Antiquity 43(2):223-230.

SPRAGUE, RICK
    2003   China or Prosser Button Identification and Dating.
            Historical Archaeology 36(2):111-127.

SPUDE, CATHY
            n.d. Common 20th Century Artifacts - A Guide to
            Dating, Society for Historical Archaeology Research
            Resources Website, http://www.sha.org/index.php/
            view/page/20thCent_artifacts, accessed August 12,
            2014.

STUART, IAIN
    2005   The Analysis of Bricks from Archaeological Sites
            in Australia. Australasian Historical Archaeology
            23:79-88.

SUSSMAN, LYNNE
    1977   Changes in Pearlware Dinnerware, 1780-1830.
            Historical Archaeology 11:105-111.

—
    2000   Objects vs. Sherds: A Statistical Evaluation. In
            Studies in Material Culture Research. K. Karklins,
            ed. Pp. 96-103: Society for Historical Archaeology.

TURNBAUGH, WILLIAM, AND SARAH PEABODY TURNBAUGH
    1977   Alternative Applications of the Mean Ceramic
            Date Concept for Interpreting Human Behavior.
            Historical Archaeology 11(1):90-104.

VOSS, BARBARA L., AND REBECCA ALLEN
    2000   Guide to Ceramic MNV Calculation Qualitative
            and Quantitative Analysis. Technical Briefs in
            Historical Archaeology 5:1-9.

WALL, DIANA DIZEREGA
    1991   Sacred Dinners and Secular Teas: Constructing
            Domesticity in Mid-19th-Century New York.
            Historical Archaeology 25(4):69-81.

WEILAND, JONATHAN
    2009   A Comparison and Review of Window Glass
            Analysis Approaches in Historical Archaeology.
            Technical Briefs in Historical Archaeology 4:29-40.

WELLS, TOM
    1998   Nail Chronology: The Use of Technologically
            Derived Features. Historical Archaeology 32(2):78-
            99.

WHITE, CAROLYN L.
    2009   Knee, Garter, Girdle, Hat, Stock, and Spur Buckles
            from Seven Sites in Portsmouth, New Hampshire.
            International Journal of Historical Archaeology
            13(2):239-253.

WHITE, JOHN R.
    1978   Bottle Nomenclature: A Glossary of Landmark
            Terminology for the Archaeologist. Historical
            Archaeology 12:58-67.

WILKIE, LAURIE
    1996   Glass-Knapping at a Louisiana Plantation: African-
            American Tools? Historical Archaeology 30(4):37-
            49.

—
    2000   Culture Bought: Evidence of Creolization in the
            Consumer Goods of an Enslaved Bahamian Family.
            Historical Archaeology 34(3):10-26.

Introduction to Volume Two: 17th, 18th, and 19th Century Materials

John M. Chenoweth

Volumes II and III of this collection focus on the identification of different kinds of archaeologically-recovered materials. The volumes are divided chronologically, because many historic sites have limited occupation ranges. Pieces on characterizing electrical artifacts will not be necessary for sites that are abandoned before the American Revolution, say, just as those working on most sites in the Western US will not encounter much in the way of 17th-century ceramics. This said, there is of course overlap between these two volumes, and the division of earlier and later material is not absolute, since many types have long histories.

Volumes II and III are internally organized by artifact type. This mirrors the workflow of many archaeological projects: when artifacts are first recovered, they are usually separated by material for conservation, analysis, and cataloging. Often it is not possible on an initial examination in the field to determine much more than a rough categorization: it is a ceramic, it is iron. This is where the identification process begins, and this collection is designed to help at this early stage.

Volume II focuses on earlier materials, primarily from the 17th and 18th centuries, but also extending into the early decades of the 19th century. Ceramics are one of the most useful categories of artifact to any archaeologist working in a time and place where they were in common use (the majority of the world for much of the last several thousand years) and Volume II begins with considerations of these. We focus both on vessels (pots for storage, cooking, eating) and also on other objects made from ceramic; especially important among this latter group are ceramic pipes, which are also considered here (Bradley 2000, II:5)[1]. During the earlier historic period considered in this volume, there was far less mass-production, mechanization, or standardization in material culture, at least compared to the time covered in Volume III. Ceramic vessels were often made and decorated by hand on a wheel, and this led to a wide variety in shapes and forms. This coupled with forms no longer in use means that archaeologists may encounter unfamiliar shapes, and so Beaudry et al's article on the "POTS" typological system (Beaudry et al. 1983, II:2) is an excellent starting-point for categorizing these objects and understanding their uses.

Glass windows were, for centuries, a relative rarity and so the identification of window glass can be an important piece of evidence in interpreting a site. Two articles (Scharfenberger 2004, II:6) and (Weiland 2009, II:7) discuss this material and ways of distinguishing between the two main methods of making such glass. Glass vessels in this period were manufactured most often by blowing molten glass freehand, and so they exist in a wide variety of forms. Nonetheless, archaeologists have identified patterns in these forms which are useful for talking about use and dating (Noël Hume 1970). The first step to this analysis is to learn the marks on the finished product of different production techniques, which are explained by Jones (1971, II:8).

Many other kinds of artifacts are uncovered by archaeologists besides ceramics and glass, of course: pins, beads, buttons, nails, thimbles, buckles, and the list goes on. As a shorthand, these are often called "small finds" and the remainder of this volume includes articles on these objects. Nails are among the most mundane objects around us, rarely noticed and yet integral to holding together our buildings and furniture. From the late 18th to late 19th century, nails were manufactured in several different ways, making them valuable chronological markers. Buildings can be studied by looking at the different nail types used in different parts, and Wells' (1998, II:10) chronology is the starting point to this type of work.

Glass beads were widely traded between Europeans and Native peoples during the colonial era. Beads were worn by people from all backgrounds as a form of adornment and some have argued for spiritual importance of beads as well. There has been a great deal of research on the manufacture, composition, trade, and meanings of these artifacts, which are found in many contexts, from where they are dropped in daily use to careful placement in burials. There exists a dizzying variety of bead types, colors, sizes, and styles, and two seminal pieces which have attempted to put these in order and which are still in use by bead experts today (Karklins 1982, II:15; Kidd and Kidd 1970, II:14) are included here. Other types

[1] References to works included in The Historical Archaeology Laboratory Handbook will be given to their original publication followed by a Roman numeral indicating the volume within the handbook and then an Arabic numeral giving the chapter within that volume.

John M. Chenoweth

of artifacts considered here include clothing fasteners (White 2009, II:13), particularly buttons (Olsen 1963, II:20; South 1964, II: 21), as well as gunflints (Ballin 2012, II:19; Kenmotsu 1990, II:18), cutlery (Dunning 2000, II:16), door hardware (Priess 2000, II:11), and thimbles (Hill 1995, II:12). Olive Jones' article on "Commercial Foods" (Jones 1993, II:17) is included here because the containers she discusses are of a wide variety of materials, including ceramic, glass, wood, metal, and even fiber or leather.

References

BALLIN, TORBEN BJARKE
    2012   'State of the Art' of British Gunflint Research, with Special Focus on the Early Gunflint Workshop at Dun Eistean, Lewis. Post-Medieval Archaeology 46(1):116-142.

BEAUDRY, MARY C., ET AL.
    1983   A Vessel Typology for Early Chesapeake Ceramics: the Potomac Typological System. Historical Archaeology 17(1):18-23.

BRADLEY, CHARLES S.
    2000   Smoking Pipes for the Archaeologist. In Studies in Material Culture Research. K. Karklins, ed. Pp. 104-133. Rockville, MD: Society for Historical Archaeology.

DUNNING, PHIL
    2000   Composite Table Cutlery from 1700 to 1930. In Studies in Material Culture Research. K. Karklins, ed. Pp. 32-45. Rockville, MD: Society for Historical Archaeology.

HILL, ERICA
    1995   Thimbles and Thimble-Rings from the Circum-Caribbean Region, 1500-1800: Chronology and Identification. Historical Archaeology 29(1):84-92.

JONES, OLIVE R.
    1971   Glass Bottle Push-Ups and Pontil Marks. Historical Archaeology 5(1):62-73.

    1993   Commercial Foods, 1740-1820. Historical Archaeology 27(2):25-41.

KARKLINS, KARLIS
    1982   Guide to the Description and Classification of Glass Beads History and Archaeology. Histoire et Archéologie. [Parks Canada] 59:83-117.

KENMOTSU, NANCY
    1990   Gunflints: A Study. Historical Archaeology 24(2):92-124.

KIDD, K. E., AND M. A. KIDD
    1970   A Classification System for Glass Beads for the Use of Field Archaeologists. Canadian Historic Sites, Occasional Papers in Archaeology and History 1:45-89.

NOËL HUME, IVOR
    1970   A Guide to Artifacts of Colonial America. New York: Knopf.

OLSEN, STANLEY J.
    1963   Dating Early Plain Buttons by their Form. American Antiquity 28(4):551-554.

PRIESS, PETER J.
    2000   Historic Door Hardware. In Studies in Material Culture Research. K. Karklins, ed. Pp. 46-95. Rockville, MD: Society for Historical Archaeology.

SCHARFENBERGER, GERARD P.
    2004   Recent Evidence for Broad Window Glass in Seventeenth-and Eighteenth-Century America. Historical Archaeology 38(4):59-72.

SOUTH, STANLEY
    1964   Analysis of the Buttons from Brunswick Town and Fort Fisher. Florida Anthropologist 17(2):113-133.

WEILAND, JONATHAN
    2009   A Comparison and Review of Window Glass Analysis Approaches in Historical Archaeology. Technical Briefs in Historical Archaeology 4:29-40.

WELLS, TOM
    1998   Nail Chronology: The Use of Technologically Derived Features. Historical Archaeology 32(2):78-99.

WHITE, CAROLYN L.
    2009   Knee, Garter, Girdle, Hat, Stock, and Spur Buckles from Seven Sites in Portsmouth, New Hampshire. International Journal of Historical Archaeology 13(2):239-253.

Part I:
Ceramics and Glass

MARY C. BEAUDRY
JANET LONG
HENRY M. MILLER
FRASER D. NEIMAN
GARRY WHEELER STONE

A Vessel Typology for Early Chesapeake Ceramics: The Potomac Typological System

ABSTRACT

A tentative scheme for classifying vessel shapes excavated in the Chesapeake region of Maryland and Virginia is presented. The result, dubbed "The Potomac Typological System" (POTS), links gradations of forms of vessels commonly excavated on Tidewater sites to terms used in inventories and other documents of the period. Although many of the colonial terms also belong to the modern lexicon, their connotations and referents were not always identical in the past. The aim is not to produce a standardized, all-purpose typology but rather a preliminary foundation for comparisons enabling the exploration of what sorts of functional variability exist within and between assemblages. The important role of data from documentary sources in the interpretation of excavated ceramic material is also discussed.

Introduction

This paper is the result of a general dissatisfaction with the way in which archaeologists working on colonial Chesapeake sites (including the authors) have typically analyzed their excavated ceramics. Historical archaeologists spend considerable time excavating, sorting and gluing together pots. Yet there is very little to show for it, save the contents of exhibit cases. While architectural data from a number of sites excavated in the Chesapeake are beginning to increase the understanding of the effects in daily life of demographic and economic instability (Carson et al. 1981) and of changing social relations between planters, their laborers and their neighbors (Neiman 1980; Upton 1979), it is impossible to cite any similarly systematic contributions based on ceramic analysis.

The failure to impart much analytical utility to ceramics is the product of a number of factors. Some of these infect the discipline of archaeology as a whole. The lack of general archaeological theory and the failure to be imaginative make convincing attempts to connect the things dug up with other areas of past experience very rare (Leone 1978). Others are related to the often unhappy way ceramic data are cast once the pots are out of the ground. Categories are employed which, despite frequent assertions of an interest in past behavior, poorly reflect functional variation. The variety of such schemes in use makes comparisons between assemblages excavated by different archaeologists impossible. Finally, there is the failure to make good use of the documentary record with which we are blessed (or cursed).

Antidotes for the fear and trembling engendered by the call to make interesting connections and to manufacture fascinating hypotheses are hard to come by—so too are remedies for archaeology's theoretical deficiencies. However, it may be useful to offer some suggestions about the categories used in the interpretation of excavated ceramics in the light of documentary evidence and about the use of the documentary record in archaeological research focusing on ceramics.

The immediate goal is to begin to systematize the chaos in the categories used to describe excavated ceramic vessels and the assemblages they comprise, in a way that will make the cultural dynamics behind them more accessible. The Potomac Typological System (POTS) is the result. It is a first attempt whose ultimate purpose will have been served if it provokes historical archaeologists to begin to think seriously and critically about the analytical utility of the pottery typologies they currently employ.

Vessel Typologies in Historical Archaeology

Discussions of typology have long had a central place in the archaeological literature. The importance of the topic is understandable for archaeology pivots upon the initial ordering of data. The disagreement that runs through the literature concerns how one brings about order. Does it exist in recoverable form in the data, or is it imposed by the investigator (Brew 1946; Spaulding 1953; Hill and Evans 1972; Doran and Hodson 1975)? Since these stump–infested fields have been plowed before, an extended discussion of the issues will not be undertaken here. However, let the cards be laid on the table at the outset. The authors sympathize with the second position: that all classifications are arbitrary. People impose categories, and hence order, upon objects to facilitate communication; this is as true of the archaeologist as much as it is of the people he or she studies.

The theoretical underpinnings of this view, which has found acceptance in a host of fields from physics to literary criticism, runs something as follows. Despite our everyday notions, our world does not consist of independently existing objects whose nature is immediately known to the observer. In fact, this sort of immediate knowledge is impossible since any object, from a white saltglaze mug to a suspension bridge, presents the observer with a potentially infinite array of sensory data. If persons are to make sense of this bewildering variety of experience, they must pick and choose, recognizing certain features as significant and disregarding others. Perception is a creative process. People of different groups construct reality in characteristically different ways. Thus, the "true" nature of the world is not to be found in the world itself but in the relationships which one chooses to perceive among the objects in it. An object is a mug and not a cup only because the observer chooses to recognize a rather limited number of features which make it so.

Obviously, from the researcher's point of view, there is no single best or true classificatory scheme for ceramics or for anything else for that matter. It is equally obvious that different classifications can and must coexist peacefully if we are to make the most of our data. Any system will have limitations which can only be remedied by the complementary use of other systems. For example, there has long been a working recognition of the fact that technological and stylistic attributes are best suited to the definition of units of temporal significance. *Termini post quem*, marker types, and the Mean Ceramic Date are all dating tools whose efficacy turns on the chronological significance of ceramic technology and decorative style. But if pots are to be used for more than dating sites and the features on them, some attention needs to be paid to function. Given the primitive state of research in this area, what is needed is a scheme which will allow the systematic description and comparison of assemblages and which, by attending function in even a crude way, will allow a preliminary appreciation of just what sort of functional variation exists between assemblages in time and space. Since direct evidence for past use of ceramic vessels (e.g., knife marks on a plate) is spotty, the criteria used to assess functional variation must be indirect. They must trade on the physical and traditional cultural constraints on possible use. There are of course several ways in which such a measurement device might be constructed.

Archaeologists working on the colonial Chesapeake have long used shape to describe their ceramic finds. All of these workers have written about cups, mugs, pitchers, bowls and who knows what else. By giving these items names, some sense is made of them (Tyler 1969:6). The names are of course English, and, more important, the categories which they represent are those unconsciously employed in our own day-to-day transactions, often supplemented by notions inherited from late 19th and 20th century antiquarians and collectors. By naming objects from the past, they are made comprehensible in behavioral terms. They silently slip into our own familiar world so subtly that one feels little need for theoretical or methodological reflection. Problems can be expected.

The most glaring problem is consistency. The pages of even scholarly works on the pottery of a particular period show vessels that are given the same name even though they have significantly different shapes. Even worse, two identical vessels illustrated on different pages may be given different names. If individual authors have a hard time being consistent, there would appear to be little hope for a group of feisty archaeologists. One person's plate is another's charger and another's dish. If nothing else, this situation is embarrassing.

Complacency in the face of this situation may be a product of the way in which most archaeologists have until recently reported excavated ceramics. Either a few particularly complete or spectacular pieces are chosen for illustration, in which case the names given the vessels are unimportant since the vessels themselves are there on the page for public inspection, or sherd counts by ware are presented for each excavated context, in which case the question of shape is otiose. Occasionally the two approaches are combined.

The interpretive possibilities of data cast in either of these two forms are rather limited. It is difficult to imagine why one vessel which has by chance survived the passage of time relatively intact should possess more behavioral significance than one represented by only a few sherds. The relevance of sherd counts to the explication of past behavior is equally obscure. One needs to remember the obvious: the people whom archaeologists study worked with, ate from and drank from whole vessels, not the sherds the vessels

would eventually become. If archaeologists are interested, at the very least, in the systematic description of the way in which these folks lived, they need to consider every vessel represented in the archaeological record as well as some that are not.

When the desirability of a systematic morphological description of the entire ceramic assemblage from a given period at a given site is recognized, inconsistency in the classification and naming of vessels ceases to be simply embarrassing and becomes intolerable. On a practical level, since one cannot illustrate every vessel from a relatively complex site, some naming (and/or verbal description) becomes unavoidable. Under such circumstances, unless there is some standardization in vessel nomenclature, inter-assemblage comparison is impossible. The need for explicitness to facilitate functional interpretation is one of the primary motivations behind this paper.

The analytical morass attendant on such inconsistency has not gone unnoticed, and attempts have been made to rid the field of the problem. One solution has been to discard traditional names entirely in favor of two categories which at least have the virtue of being unambiguous: flatwares and hollowwares. This is the Stoke-on-Trent approach (Celoria and Kelly 1973). In justifying this solution, its authors plead ignorance and understandable dissatisfaction with the fact that in recent numbers of *Post Medieval Archaeology*, "a bewildering variety of vessels have been called dishes" (Celoria and Kelly 1973:16). The authors also suggest that the flat/hollow dichotomy is legitimate by virtue of its use by 17th century Staffordshire potters. Despite this historical validity, the wholesale acceptance of this two-term typology would send the baby out with the bath water. While the two terms may have served the potter's primarily technological concerns well, distinguishing those vessels which were usually press-molded from those which were thrown ("reckoned by their different breadths . . . or their contents [volume]'') and stacked or nested for firing and storage, by themselves they scarcely can be considered useful tools in the functional explication of an assemblage. In a behavioral context, cups and butter pots, both hollowwares, have little in common.

A second sort of remedy is to attempt to give everyday and antiquarian terms, along with the fuzzy notions behind them, a degree of precision. Many people, for example, have called any two–handled vessel, roughly square in profile, with pint or more capacity, a posset pot. The name of course implies a very specific use, and the term was used in the 17th century. Unfortunately, it did not then apply to the wide class of vessels often described as such today (see below). Small mistakes of this sort will inevitably distort the reading of individual excavated vessels, not to mention the interpretation of entire ceramic assemblages, especially when comparisons with documentary evidence are made.

Both the above approaches meet one criterion for typological adequacy. They allow the unambiguous assignment of new objects to their categories. In addition, the Stoke–on–Trent solution is adequate insofar as it accounts for the entire range of variability in the objects under study, and the second approach could be elaborated without much difficulty to the same end (and in fact has been by many). However, adequacy is not the sole basis on which a typology should be evaluated (Binford 1972:247). While any adequate typology allows the systematic description of similarities and differences between assemblages, not all are equally well equipped to make possible insights into the significance of this variability in the context in which the objects themselves were used.

POTS is one attempt to circumvent these problems. The distinctions made by colonial Virginians and Marylanders who named and described their neighbor's possessions in probate inventories were used as clues to where breaks of possible functional signifi-cance occur along the continuum of formal variation. The characterizations of contemporary terms which POTS offers were arrived at by considering variation in adjectives applied to the terms in a sample of Virginia and Maryland inventories and descriptions (verbal and pictorial) of the terms' referents in other contemporary sources. The categories used by inventory takers appear to have been based largely on three dimensions of formal variation: shape, size and ware. Since the categories resulting from the intersection of these dimensions successfully mediated people's everyday interactions (behavior) with the objects denoted, they can serve as a reasonable basis for the construction of a functionally sensitive typology. Descriptions of the categories which comprise POTS provide a glossary for terms encountered in inventories, making more accurate comparisons between excavated and inventoried ceramic assemblages possible.

The Use of Documents in Ceramic Analysis

In putting POTS together, documentary sources have served as texts. In these sources, the manner in which their authors categorized a small part of the material world (which happens to be ubiquitous on archaeological sites) could be approximated. The application of POTS to an excavated assemblage, or any other sort of explication of archaeological material from an historic period site, should also proceed with the documents in mind. Here, however, the archaeologist will be on more familiar ground, using the historical record, initially at least, as a source of data about the artifactual contents of the past. Doing history with objects is considerably easier and the results certainly more complete if the historical record is used to fill in the holes in the archaeological records and *vice versa*. Of more far–reaching importance however is the fact that, by using documents, one can ask more interesting questions about the things one excavates. These objects, in turn, can be expected to suggest more interesting questions about the documents. Documents do not provide archaeologists with a "telephone to Glory." However, ignoring the documents is at one's own peril. This point can be illustrated through several cautionary tales. Two widely held propositions, derived from archaeological sources, about the cultural significance of ceramics in 17th century Anglo–America suffer quite devastating defects which are the inevitable result of the failure to take full advantage of the historical record.

The attempt to define socioeconomic status through ceramic assemblages is a genre which has gained considerable popularity in recent years, as historical archaeologists have struggled with the challenge to impart some anthropological or social-historical significance to their work. While explicit written statements on this topic (and many others) are rare in the study area, the proposition that in the 17th century Chesapeake there was a strong correlation between the numbers and kinds of ceramics an individual possessed and his wealth appears to have some currency. Confronted with two ceramic assemblages from a pair of sites whose occupants are known through the historical record to have been of considerably different means, it is quite easy for one to attribute any quantitative or qualitative differences which he or she is able to define in the pottery to differences in the wealth of his owners, consider no other factors, and leave the matter at that.

This sort of analysis has been the bread and butter of prehistoric archaeologists for years. Whereas historical archaeologists are here treating assemblage variability as an index to wealth, prehistorians have traditionally treated it as an index to the presence of different tribes or cultural groups. In both cases percentage and/or empirical frequencies, calculated for a variety of artifact classes, are used as a measure of distance, cultural in one case and economic in the other, between the occupants of a number of sites. As Lewis

Binford (1968, 1972), among others, has pointed out, this kind of approach severely limits the interpretive possibilities of the archaeological record and its potential to inform us about the past. The problem is that in both cases it is simply assumed that the contents of the archaeological record and its determinants are unidimensional. It would be surprising indeed to discover that any set of phenomena for which human beings were responsible was attributed to the operation of a single variable.

Theory aside, this particular projection of our own ethnocentric notion that the rich will invariably possess lots of pretty pots has another shortcoming. A cursory examination of the inventories indicates that it simply does not fit the 17th century Chesapeake. Ceramics were optional for many of the early Chesapeake's wealthiest men. A case in point is Capt. John Lee, a Westmoreland County, Virginia, gentleman whose estate was probated in 1674. Lee was a quorum justice, the brother of a member of the Governor's Council, and with an estate valuation in excess of 200,000 lbs of tobacco and 24 laborers, the wealthiest decedent appraised in the county during the 17th century. Yet Lee's collection of ceramics was exceedingly limited. The six quarts of oil and an equal amount of honey which the appraisers found "In Capt. Lee's Chamber" may have been kept in a couple of earthen jars. Lee's kitchen contained the three chamber pots, two old close stool pans, two porringers and a chafing dish. But all these items, save the chafing dish, may well have been pewter, given their relatively high valuations. The chamber pots were worth 15 lbs of tobacco each, and the two close stool pans and porringers were valued at 40 lbs for the lot, this at a time when butter pots, typically one of the most common ceramic forms, were worth only 7 lbs each (*Westmoreland County, Virginia, Deeds, Patents and Accounts 1665–1677*: 180). But even if one assumes in the face of this evidence that all these objects were ceramic,

Lee's assemblage was modest indeed in terms of quantity as well as quality. Lee's inventory is characteristically detailed, containing specific entries for items as trifling as "a small parcell of twine." In addition, there are no non-specific entries like "a parcell of lumber," or "small things forgotten" for that matter, which might conceal ceramics. Nor was Lee married, so there are no pots hiding in an uninventoried widow's portion.

In Westmoreland County, Virginia, Lee was by no means unique. Mr. Robert Jadwin, who died in the same year with a hefty estate valued at 46,749 lbs of tobacco, had no ceramics at all (*Westmoreland County, Virginia, Deeds, Patents and Accounts 1665–1677*: 188). In fact, of the 19 pre–1677 Westmoreland County, Virginia, inventories valued at over 20,000 lbs of tobacco, ceramics are not mentioned in seven. Of the remaining 12, seven contain only coarse earthen and/or dairy–related forms. Typical of these for example is the inventory of Mr. Richard Sturman (d.1669), valued at 55, 015 lbs. Sturman's only ceramic possessions were "milke trays potts & panns" (*Westmoreland County, Virginia, Deeds, Patents and Accounts 1665–1677*: 54). Another example, slightly lower down the economic scale, is Mr. Daniel Hutt (d.1674), worth 20,820 lbs. whose inventory contained the following uninspiring ceramic entries: "crakd earthenware & a prcell of nales in it" and "In the Milke-house . . . a prcell old lumber" (*Westmore-land County, Virginia, Deeds, Patents and Accounts 1665–1677*: 194).

What one might consider fine ceramics appear with certainty in only three of the remaining inventories: Robert Nurses's "prcell painted earthen ware" (1672), Nathaniel Pope's "2 juggs" (1660), and John Roasier's "earthen porringer" (1661) (*Westmoreland County, Virginia, Deeds, Patents and Accounts 1665–1677*: 198; *Westmoreland County, Virginia, Deeds, and Wills 1660–1661*: 42; *Westmoreland County, Virginia, Deeds, Wills and Patents 1653–1659*: 8).

In Charles County, Maryland, settled like Westmoreland County, Virginia, in the 1650s, from 1658 to 1684 only 36% of the inventories of middling and wealthy planters list any ceramics (Walsh 1979: Table 2A).

On a practical level, these examples from the documents mean that a meager ceramic assemblage from a 17th century Chesapeake site does not guarantee that its occupants were of meager means. This is not meant to imply that the appearance of vast quantities of porcelain and delft, for example, on a site suggests nothing about the wealth of its occupants. Quite obviously it does. But once one realizes that ceramics were not *de rigeur* among the rich in the early Chesapeake, the interesting question is not whether rich people could afford more pottery than the poor, something anyone might have deduced without touching a trowel, but why some individuals chose to buy lots of fancy pots while many of their peers did not.

The second example is drawn from the work of James Deetz (1972, 1977). In attempting to develop a model for changing patterns of ceramic use in 17th and 18th century Anglo–America, Deetz noticed a dearth of nearly all but dairy–related wares on pre–1660 sites around Plymouth, Massachusetts. Drawing on Anderson's (1971) work on Tudor and Stuart English foodways he concluded, correctly, that eating and drinking vessels were generally not ceramic. Specifically, Deetz suggested that shared wooden trenchers and shared pewter and/or leather drinking vessels comprised the typical dining assemblage in early 17th century Anglo–America. Deetz outlined two phenomena visible in the archaeological data after ca. 1660. The first was a general scarcity of ceramic plates, the second a gradual increase in the absolute numbers of ceramic drinking vessels. He concluded that wooden trenchers continued to be the norm for food consumption, that ceramic plates served primarily as decorative items in lieu of costly pewter and that since trenchers do not survive in the ground, the increase in the number of drinking vessels might be taken as indicative of a general trend toward more individualized consumption of both liquids and solids.

While much of Deetz's (1972) article relies on documentary evidence and the companion piece by Marley Brown (1972) is based solely on inventories, both suffer a preoccupation with excavated ceramics. Apparently when the inventory data were assembled for comparison with information from the ground, only entries for ceramics were systematically collected, a procedure not uncommon in the field. As one of the present authors (Stone 1977:57) has pointed out elsewhere, because archaeologists excavate ceramics they wish also to "excavate" them from inventories. In the process, they often ignore the other forms listed there which comprised the larger context in which the ceramics had meaning.

Deetz's model was of course designed specifically for early New England. It may not be appropriate to attack it with data from the Chesapeake. Nevertheless, its applicability to all of Anglo–America is at least implicit throughout Deetz (1977). The criticisms offered below, however, can be supported with data from New England as well.

The claim that trenchers were standard eating vessels is difficult to support, once one looks beyond the ceramic entries in the inventories. In the earliest Potomac inventories, those taken in frontier St. Mary's County, Maryland, 1638–1650, wooden trenchers and dishes (other than Indian bowls used as utility vessels) were important only in newly established households—the households of recent immigrants or recently freed servants. In well–established households, even of tenants, pewter predominated (*Archives of Maryland* 1887; Stone 1977: 60).

On the Virginia side of the river, the same pattern prevailed. In Westmoreland County, Virginia, in 14 extant inventories taken during the decade following the county's incorporation in 1653, four contained *only* wooden eating vessels. Dishes and trays are mentioned

specifically. In the rest, eating vessels were of pewter: saucers, plates, dishes, among other forms. In 31 inventories taken between 1668 and 1677 in the county, again only four listed eating vessels of wood, to the exclusion of other materials. And again all the rest contained pewter saucers, plates, or dishes.

The number of eating vessels, either in pewter or wood, was considerable. In the earlier Westmoreland County, Virginia, sample, Nathaniel Pope, with an estate worth ca. £380, owned nine saucers, 12 plates, and 36 dishes, all of pewter. At the other end of the economic scale, George Poper, worth a paltry 1035 lbs of tobacco (ca. £5) had three pewter saucers and three pewter plates (*Westmoreland County, Virginia, Deeds, Wills and Patents 1653–1659*: 72). The pattern was the same in the later sample. Capt. John Ashton, with the second largest estate in the group, worth 94,000 lbs of tobacco (ca. £470) owned 51 pewter plates, two pewter dishes, and "40 pewter dishes basons and pye plates" (*Westmoreland County, Virginia, Deeds, Patents and Accounts 1665–1677*: 321–22). Francis Lewis, worth only 1,395 lbs of tobacco, the second poorest member of the sample, had three pewter plates and two pewter dishes. Men who owned smaller amounts of pewter typically supplemented their collection of eating vessels with wooden ones. Richard Sampson, a middling planter whose estate was not valued, had only three pewter dishes, but he also owned nine trenchers. Even the few planters who owned only wooden vessels owned them in quantities which suggest, given the small size of their households, that they were not shared. Henry Alday, for example, with an estate worth 5,840 lbs of tobacco (ca. £29), had seven wooden trays, and Thomas Baron, whose estate valued at 394 lbs of tobacco (ca. £2) made him the poorest individual in the sample, had four wooden dishes (*Westmoreland County, Virginia, Deeds, Patents and Accounts 1665–1677*: 72; *Westmoreland County, Virginia, Deeds, Wills and Patents 1653–1659*: 88). These examples could be extended, *ad nauseam*, from the St. Mary's County, Maryland, inventories.

Clearly, then, the great majority of the 17th century Virginians and Marylanders were eating from pewter plates and not wooden trenchers, and eating vessels in either material were not being shared at the table in all save perhaps the poorest households.

This apparently had been the case in the most economically advanced areas of England since the late 16th century. In 1587, William Harrison, commenting on the effects of the price revolution, included in his famous three things "marvelously altered in England within . . . sound remembrance" the appearance of quantities of pewter in the households of "inferior artificers and many farmers." The ordinary farmer had recently changed his "treen platters into pewter," providing himself with a "fair garnish of pewter for his cupboard" (Harrison 1968:200–01). According to Harrison, a "garnish" was comprised of 12 platters, 12 dishes and 12 saucers (Harrison 1968:367). Without doubt, the pewter vessels which proliferated in the houses of English yeomen were flatwares. It should not be surprising then to find Chesapeake planters following a pattern set by their ancestors in the previous century. Obviously the quantities of pewter plates in Chesapeake households make Deetz's suggestion that ceramic plates were commonly displayed in lieu of pewter ones questionable.

If pewter eating vessels were numerous in the 17th century Chesapeake, pewter drinking vessels were not. While the number of pieces of pewter a planter possessed was to some extent correlated with the size of his estate and household, the number of drinking vessels remained consistently small across the economic continuum. In Westmoreland County, Virginia, Nathaniel Pope had only four pewter drinking pots, and John Hiller, a planter of far more modest means (9, 529 lbs of tobacco, ca. £48), owned two drinking pots and three cups (*Westmoreland County,*

Virginia, Deeds and Wills 1660–1661: 16). Of the remaining six estates inventoried in the county between 1654 and 1661 in which pewter vessels were listed entirely by shape, none contained more than three pewter drinking vessels, although three of the individuals involved were more than twice as wealthy as Hiller. The pattern which emerges from the extant Westmoreland County, Virginia, inventories taken between 1668 and 1677 is similar. Capt. John Ashton, second wealthiest member of the group, had no pewter drinking vessels at all. Two middling planters had six each, and the remaining members of the sample owned three or less. Unless similar forms were present in ceramic or, in the wealthiest households, silver, the inevitable conclusion is that drinking vessels were being shared, if not with laborers, at least with neighbors when they came visiting.

It would seem that the increase in absolute numbers of ceramic drinking vessels noted by Deetz in the archaeological record toward the end of the 17th century might be taken to represent a trend toward more individualized consumption of beverages. But in social and religious ceremony, shared drinking vessels continued to be used as symbols of intimacy until the mid-19th century (Stone 1977:61–62).

Developing the Potomac Typological System

The method behind the construction of POTS was unabashedly democratic. The authors have attempted to assign excavated forms to common categories and names derived from a number of documentary sources, most importantly probate inventories taken in Maryland (St. Mary's County) and Virginia (Westmoreland and York counties) during the 17th and early 18th centuries. It appears that Englishmen in the Chesapeake took vessels from a wide variety of European potting traditions and applied relatively standardized uses and names to them. The functional significance of shape differences unique to a particular regional English folk culture may not have survived long on the Chesapeake frontier, where consumers could be less discriminating and where their needs were considerably altered. Similarly, some taxonomic distinctions with only regional distribution at home proved of little relevance to life in the Chesapeake, where they were discarded in favor of those which did.

In general, the process was akin to that by which Virginians and Marylanders developed a distinctive vernacular architecture by drawing on a variety of English forms to combine and alter them according to local requirements. The general impression is that, as with architecture, the ways in which Chesapeake planters and New England farmers categorized their food vessels differed considerably in some domains. While there seems to have been significant variation between communities with different subsistence orientations in New England (Yentsch 1977), such regional differences do not seem to have been characteristic of the Chesapeake (Beaudry 1980).

While many of the categories derived from the documents are fairly straightforward, some do require discussion.

Dish appears to have been used both as a specific and a generic term. Randle Holme, an English artist who between 1640 and 1680 attempted to record and illustrate all of the symbols employed in English heraldry, provided a valuable source of information about 17th century objects and their uses. Holme (1905:4) listed the following terms under "the several names of a dish":

A platter if large.
A dish, which [is] of a lesser sort.
A midleing dish
A Broth dish, deeper bottomed than flesh dishes.
A Bason, is almost half round in the concave, . . .
A sallet dish
A trencher plate or plate
A saucer

Holme's specification that a basin is "almost half round in the concave" suggests that the term denoted a vessel different from the others. Elsewhere he pictures a vessel, round in plan, and labels it "a dish, a platter, a saucer, a trencher plate." Leaving basins aside then, one can map "the several names of a dish" in a tree diagram in which the lower levels are related to the higher levels by inclusion:

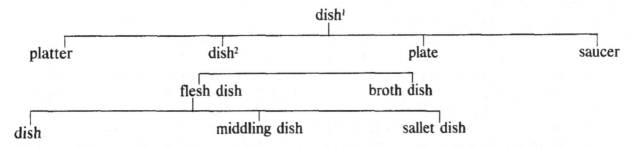

The arrangement of the terms in Holme's (1905) list is not accidental. They are given in order of decreasing size, a relation which obtains between the terms in the second row of the tree, from left to right. Depth was not a factor in distinguishing between terms at this level: *dish²* subsumes both *flesh dish* and *broth dish*. William Harrison looked at the matter in a similar fashion, noting in 1587 that "dishes and platters in my time begin to be made deep like basins" (Harrison 1968:367).

If the terms *platter, dish,² plate,* and *saucer* denote vessels differing primarily in size (diameter), where do the breaks come? The anonymous author of *The Complete Appraiser* (1770:42–43), published in the mid-18th century, provides a partial answer in a table detailing prescribed weights and diameters for pewter plates and dishes. Plates run from 7 ¾ in to 9 ¾ in. Dishes range from 10 ¾ in all the way up to 28 in (Montgomery 1973:135). Criteria similar to these were apparently in use in the 17th century Chesapeake. Corduroy Ironmonger's 1675 inventory, taken in Westmoreland County, Virginia, listed dishes weighing 5.4 lbs each and plates weighing 1.5 lbs each (*Westmoreland County, Virginia, Deeds, Patents and Accounts 1665-1677*: 243). The figures fit comfortably with *The Compleat Appraiser*'s listing of the smallest dish at 1 lb, 12 oz. One can infer that saucers, as the smallest members of the dish family, were of something less than ca. 7 in diameter and that platters were the largest members of the group. *Platter* may have had other referents as well. There is some evidence that it was on some occasions synonymous with *oval dish*. Holme makes the equation twice, noting that John the Baptist's head was served up to King Herod on an oval dish "although some call it a platter" (Carson 1970:44, 296; Holme 1905:4). It would seem then that platters were *dishes*[2] which were either very large, or oval, or both. As the distinction between *platter* and *dish* was even then unclear, *platter* has been excluded from the POTS typology. All flat vessels greater in diameter than 10 in are defined as *dishes*.

As indicated, Holme (1905) made a distinction, echoed by Harrison (1968), between *flesh dishes* and *broth dishes*. However, the distinction does not appear in the authors' inventory sample until the early 18th century when it applies to plates. In 1756, William Wallet advertised in the *Maryland Gazette* that he would recast "either flat or soup dishes or flat or soup plates" (Montgomery 1973:135). Surviving pewter pieces from the period suggest that soup dishes and plates ranged in height between 1 in and 2 in. Rather than offer absolute criteria for soup dishes and plates versus flat dishes and plates, it is suggested that the distinction in an excavated ceramic assemblage be based on the objects in it. If the excavated material exhibits a continuum of depths relative to diameters, the distinction might best be ignored. However, if the distribution of shapes exhibits a break, the

distinction may reflect functional differences and therefore be of utility.

Holme gives two functions for basins. He implies a food function by classifying basins as members of the dish family, and in this he was paralleled by many estate appraisers who grouped or found pewter basins with pewter dishes and plates. Holme also illustrates a barber's basin and a "stand . . : used for to set a Bason on whilest washing . . ." (Holme 1688:432, 438; 1905:18, 18a). Both food basins and a great (wash) basin on a stand are listed in Robert Slye's inventory (see Appendix). While some basins may have been used for both dining and washing, archaeologists should try to determine the functions of the vessels that they recover from the find contexts of the sherds. At the Clifts site in Westmoreland County, Virginia, one of the authors excavated sherds of decorated basins matching plate fragments from early 18th century contexts (Neiman 1980). At Rosewell, Noël Hume found undecorated wash basin fragments in a ca. 1763-1762 pit (Noël Hume 1962:203-07). In the Rosewell report, Noël Hume rightly grouped the wash basins with the chamber pots, while in the author's report on the Clifts site, the basins will be counted as dining vessels.

Apart from the problems presented by *platter* and *basin*, the sources used above describe a relatively straightforward typology for categorizing flat dining vessels. It is a comfortable typology as much of it remains in use today. But readers of 17th century documents should be aware that alternate taxonomies were in use during that century. Some appraisers recorded many dishes and few plates. Others listed "platters great & small" to the exclusion of both dishes and plates (*Archives of Maryland* 1887:93).

Drinking vessels presented fewer problems. *Pot* is the most troublesome form as well as the most common. Fortunately Holme illustrates one pot shape—a pitcher-like form (Carson 1970:14, 68, 196; Holme 1688:167).

The name also seems to have been applied to bulbous and squat cylindrical drinking vessels as probate and potters' inventories do not provide alternate designations. "Drinking bowl" seems to have been applied to metal vessels only. Except in silver, *cup* was restricted to small containers. "Pint cup" appears rarely in Chesapeake inventories, while (in pewter) drinking pots routinely appear in pint, quart, and pottle (2 qt) sizes.

The procedure of naming by plebiscite bypassed most of the problems of describing food preparation vessels. Thus, all large pans are typed as *milk pans*, although some were used as wash basins and cooking pans. All dairy pots will be considered as *butter pots* until someone defines—in Chesapeake terms—the difference in form between a butter pot and a cream pot. While excavated dairy pots vary in shape, the most important variable seems to be place of manufacture. Thus, most North Devon pots have constricted shoulders (Watkins 1960:45), while Flintshire pots are generally more cylindrical (Noël Hume 1976:135). In a similar fashion, a 17th century definition of *pipkin* has evaded these authors; it is assumed that the term encompassed most of the cooking pots excavated on Chesapeake sites. No other term identifiable as an earthen cooking pot appears in the inventories, and most excavated specimens are of one general shape.

Commonly used categories for summarizing excavated vessels have been too general. More gradations are needed to distinguish between shared and individual drinking vessels, and dining vessel groups oriented toward hominy and pottage versus boiled, baked, or roasted foods. The recommended categories are illustrated below. These are simplified groupings. It is realized, for example, that bottles were storage as well as serving vessels and that jugs of less that a pottle could be used for serving. In English America as well as in England, some families undoubtedly used pitchers as jugs and drinking pots as well as utility vessels. However, without some simplification, summary would be impossible, and these categories represent the best fit achievable between the multifarious uses suggested by the documents and employable archaeological categories (Table 1).

The logical conclusion of an article such as this would witness the application of POTS to several excavated assemblages. Presumably, this would demonstrate the virtues of the typology by comparing ceramic assemblages from successive periods at the same site and from the same period at different sites. At the present time, however, such comparisons cannot be undertaken. Analyses of the excavated materials from St. John's and the Clifts Plantation sites are still underway, although they both will be used as test cases for POTS, along with materials from sites on the James River. This typology is presented in its tentative form as a means of informing colleagues in historical archaeology of the direction this research is taking and in hopes of eliciting comments, suggestions and shared information from others concerned with the problems of ceramic typologies and functional interpretations based on archaeological assemblages from historical sites.

Chesapeake Ceramic Forms and Definitions

Ceramic forms discussed previously and listed in Table 1 are illustrated and defined below. Groupings are determined primarily on the basis of vessel shape and only secondarily by vessel function. These groupings are not necessarily those used in the course of ceramic analysis, and infrequently excavated forms are neither illustrated nor defined. Some of these forms are mentioned in the accompanying probate inventories, however (Appendix).

TABLE 1
A SUGGESTED FUNCTIONAL DIVISION OF VESSEL FORMS FROM 17TH CENTURY SITES

FOOD PROCESSING
(Cooking and Darying)
Pipkin
Pudding Pan
Bowl
Milk Pan
Collander

FOOD AND DRINK STORAGE
Storage Pot
Jar
Bottle

BEVERAGE CONSUMPTION

Individual

(1 pt or less)
Cup
Mug
Jug
Footed Bowls

Communal or Individual

(More than 1 pt)
Mug
Jug
Drinking Pot
Flask

Serving

Pitcher
Ewer
Punch Bowl
Large Jug
Sillabub Pot

FOOD CONSUMPTION

Stews/Pottages/Soups

Porringers
Soup Plates
Small Bowls

Solid Food Consumption and Serving

Caudle Pots
Basins
Plates
Dishes
Saucers
Salts

HEALTH/HYGIENE
Galley Pots- Large
            - Small
Chamber Pots
Basins- Plain
        - Barber's

OTHER
Chafing Dish
Candlesticks
Betty Lamp

Hollow Vessels for Liquids—1/8 size

CUP. A small, handled drinking vessel of less than a pint in capacity. In form, cups are closely related to drinking pots.

DRINKING POT. A one or multi-handled vessel, usually bulbous, but sometimes cylindrical in form, ranging in capacity from 1 pt to 2 qts or more. Cylindrical drinking pots are distinguished from mugs by being wider than tall and/or having two or more handles.

MUG. A single-handled, straight-sided drinking vessel, taller than wide, ranging from 1 gill (¼ pt) to 2 qts (or more).

JUG. A handled vessel of bulbous form with a cylindrical neck rising from a pronounced shoulder, with or without a gutter. In size, jugs range from small drinking vessels to large serving vessels. Jugs occur generally in refined earthenwares and stonewares.

PITCHER. A handled vessel with bulbous body, having a flaring neck with a gutter. In America, used primarily in the kitchen and dairy. Pitchers occur in coarse earthenwares.

EWER. A handled, bulbous–bodied serving vessel, similar in shape to a jug, but with a narrower, elongated neck with a gutter or spout. Ewers occur in refined earthenwares or stonewares.

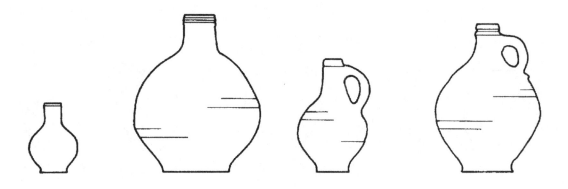

BOTTLE. A bulbous–bodied storage and serving vessel with a neck narrower than a jug or ewer, with or without a handle.

FLASK/COSTREL. A bulbous–bodied vessel with a very narrow neck, similar in form to a bottle, but having two ears or strap handles rising from the shoulder. A drink container carried by travelers and field workers.

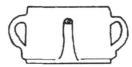

SILLABUB POT. A pot with a spout, two handles, and sometimes a cover, for drinking and serving sillabub, posset, and wassail.

Hollow Vessels for Liquids and Semi-solid Foods—1/8 size

CAUDLE CUP/POT. A two–handled, covered cup, for making and serving fermented gruel. The appearance of the term caudle pot suggests that it occurs in sizes larger than that illustrated.

PORRINGER. A vessel usually hemispherical in shape and shallower in relation to its diameter than a cup or a pot. Porringers have at least one and sometimes two handles, either horizontal or vertical. Used for eating porridge, pottage (stew), soup, etc.

PUNCH BOWL. A hemispherical vessel with a plain rim. Punch bowls occur in refined earthenwares, stonewares, and porcelain. They range in capacity from ½ pt to several gallons. The smallest sizes were used by individuals for drinking punch and perhaps eating semi-solid foods. The larger sizes were used for making and serving punch.

BOWL. An open vessel with convex sides terminating in either a plain or everted rim or brim. Bowls have no footrings and occur only in coarse earthenwares. Bowls were used primarily in the kitchen and dairy.

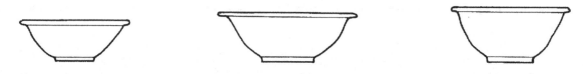

BASIN. An open vessel with convex sides, of greater width than depth, having a brim or everted lip. Basins occur with or without footrings but only in refined earthenwares and porcelain. These forms were used for washing, shaving and for dining.

Flat Vessels for Food—1/8 size

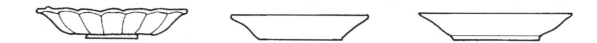

DISH. A serving vessel larger than 10 in either in diameter or in length, with or without a footring. Dishes were made in shallow and deep forms.

PLATE. An eating vessel from 7 in to 10 in in diameter, with or without a footring. Plates were made in shallow and deep (i.e., soup) forms.

SAUCER. A vessel less than 7 in in diameter, with or without a footring. Saucers were used for serving condiments (hence: sauce–r) and perhaps as small plates.

Miscellaneous Dining Forms—1/8 size

SALT. A pedestaled serving vessel in refined earthenware or stoneware with or without supports at the rim.

CHAFING DISH. A coarse earthenware vessel on a pedestal with supports around the rim. Chafing dishes held coals used to warm food at the table.

Cooking Vessels—1/8 size

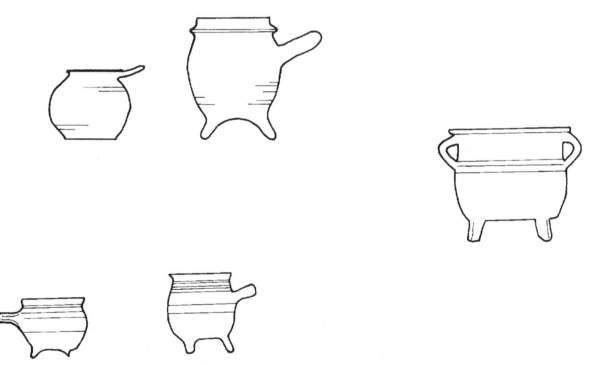

PIPKIN. An earthen cooking pot. Two varieties of pipkins have been excavated in the Chesapeake. The handled pipkin (above left) is a small, bulbous cooking pot, frequently with a rod handle. The pot/flesh pot (above right) is a cooking vessel with two ears and three legs. While the form is a metal one, it was occasionally copied in coarse earthenwares.

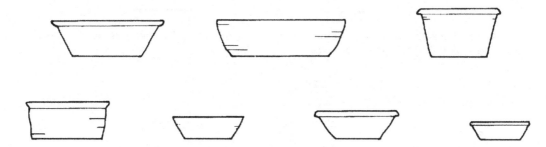

PAN/PUDDING, PASTRY, PATTY, ETC. A coarse earthenware cooking vessel, roughly in the shape of an inverted, truncated cone, less than 10 in in diameter.

Dairy and Kitchen Vessels—1/8 size

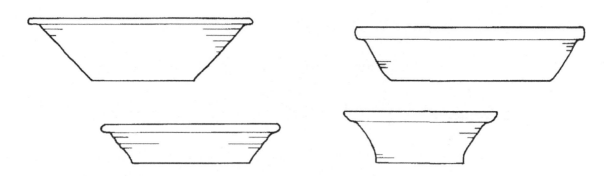

MILK PAN. A vessel roughly in the shape of an inverted, truncated cone, 10 in or more in diameter. Used for cooling milk, as a wash basin and probably for cooking.

COLANDER. A pan–like, handled utensil with a perforated bottom. Colanders were used for making cheese, washing vegetables, etc.

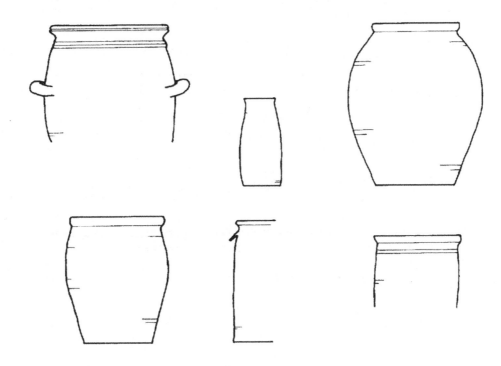

POT/BUTTER POT. A large, cylindrical or slightly convex-sided vessel, taller than wide, used for souring cream or storing butter, fat (lard), etc.

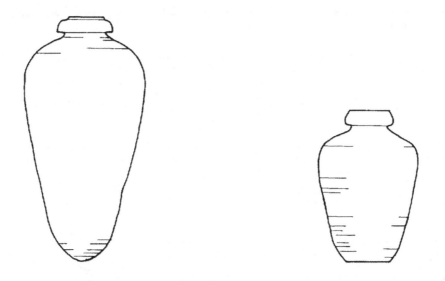

JAR. A large vessel, taller than wide, with pronounced shoulders and constricted neck, bearing a heavy, rounded lip. Jars were used for storing water, oil, beer, etc.

Hygiene-related Forms—1/8 size

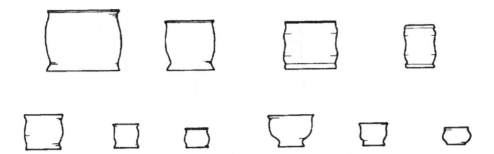

GALLEY POT. A cylindrical tin–glazed vessel with slightly flared rim and base. Large and small sizes may be distinguished. Used for drugs, ointments, cosmetics and, occasionally, condiments.

CHAMBER POT. A handled vessel with convex sides and a sturdy flared rim or brim. The eventual repository of the contents of all of the above.

CANDLESTICK. A lighting device consisting of a hollow tube, a foot and/or a drip tray.

ACKNOWLEDGMENTS

The authors would like to thank the following people for taking time to comment on this manuscript: John Austin, Norman Barka, Barbara Carson, James Deetz, William Kelso, Ivor and Audrey Noël Hume, Alain and Merry Outlaw, and C. Malcolm Watkins. All of the drawings in the text are by Janet Long. An earlier version of this manuscript was presented at the Jamestown Conference on Archaeology, Jamestown, Virginia, April 1979.

REFERENCES

ANDERSON, JAY
1971 *A Solid Sufficiency: An Ethnography of Yeoman Foodways in Stuart England*. Ph.D. dissertation, University of Pennsylvania, University Microfilms, Ann Arbor.

ANONYMOUS
1770 *The Compleat Appraiser* (fourth edition). London.

ARCHIVES OF MARYLAND
1887 *Archives of Maryland*. Judicial and Testamentary Business of the Provincial Court, 1637–1650 (Vol. 4). Edited by William Hand Browne. Maryland Historical Society, Baltimore.

BEAUDRY, MARY C.
1980 *"Or What Else You Please to Call It": Folk Semantic Domains in Early Virginia Probate Inventories*. Ph.D. dissertation, Brown University. University Microfilms, Ann Arbor.

BINFORD, LEWIS R.
1968 Archaeological Perspectives. In *New Perspectives in Archeology*, edited by Sally R. Binford and Lewis R. Binford, pp. 5–32. Aldine Publishing Company, Chicago.
1972 Model Building-Paradigms, and the Current State of Paleolithic Research. In *An Archaeological Perspective*, edited by Lewis R. Binford, pp. 244–294. Seminar Press, New York.

BREW, JOHN OTIS
1946 Archaeology of Alkali Ridge: Southeastern Utah. *Papers of the Peabody Museum of American Archaeology and Ethnology* 21. Harvard University, Cambridge, Massachusetts.

BROWN, MARLEY R. III
1972 Ceramics from Plymouth, 1621–1800: The Documentary Record. In *Ceramics in America*, edited by Ian M. G. Quimby, pp. 41–74. University of Virginia Press, Charlottesville.

CARSON, BARBARA G.
1970 Illustrations and Extracts from the Text of Randle Holme's *The Academy of Armory*. Ms. on file, Plimoth Plantation, Plymouth, Massachusetts.

CARSON, CARY, NORMAN F. BARKA, WILLIAM M. KELSO, GARRY W. STONE AND DELL UPTON
1981 Impermanent Architecture in the Southern Colonies. *Winterthur Portfolio* 16(2/3):135–196.

CELORIA, F. S. C. AND J. H. KELLY
1973 A Post Medieval Pottery Site with a Kiln Base Found Off Albion Square, Hanley, Stoke–on–Trent, Staffordshire, England SJ 885 474. *City of Stoke–on–Trent Museum Archaeological Society Report* 4.

DEETZ, JAMES
1972 Ceramics from Plymouth, 1635–1835: The Archaeological Evidence. In *Ceramics in America*, edited by Ian M. G. Quimby, pp. 15–40. University of Virginia Press, Charlottesville.
1977 *In Small Things Forgotten: The Archaeology of Early American Life*. Anchor Books, Garden City, New York.

DORAN, J. E. AND F. R. HODSON
1975 *Mathematics and Computers in Archaeology*. Harvard University Press, Cambridge, Massachusetts.

HARRISON, WILLIAM
1968 *The Description of England*. Edited by George Edden. The Folger Shakespeare Library. Cornell University Press, Ithaca, New York.

HILL, H. N. AND R. K. EVANS
1972 A Model for Classification and Typology. In *Models in Archaeology*, edited by David L. Clarke, pp. 231–274. Methuen and Company, London.

HOLME, RANDLE
1688 *The Academy of Armory*. Chester, England.
1905 *The Academy of Armory, Part 2*. Edited by I. H. Jeayes. Printed for the Roxburghe Club, London.

LEONE, MARK P.
1978 *Archaeology's Relationship to the Present and the Past*. Paper Delivered to the American Anthropological Association Symposium, "The Archaeology of US." Los Angeles, California, November, 1978.

MARYLAND PROVINCIAL RECORDS (St. Mary's County)
Testamentary Proceedings 5. Hall of Records, Annapolis.
Testamentary Proceedings 6. Hall of Records, Annapolis.

MONTGOMERY, CHARLES F.
1973 *A History of American Pewter*. Weathervane Books, New York.

NEIMAN FRASER D.
1980 *The "Manner House" before Stratford (Discovering the Clifts Plantation)*. Robert E. Lee Memorial Association, Stratford, Virginia.

NOËL HUME, IVOR
1962 Excavations at Rosewell, Gloucester County, Virginia, *United States National Museum Bulletin 225*. The Smithsonian Institution, Washington, D.C.
1977 Early English Delftware from London and Virginia. *Colonial Williamsburg Occasional Papers in Archaeology* 2. Colonial Williamsburg Foundation, Williamsburg.

SPAULDING, ALBERT C.
1953 Statistical Techniques for the Discovery of Artifact Types. *American Antiquity* 18:305–313.

STONE, GARRY WHEELER
1977 Artifacts Are Not Enough. *The Conference on Historic Site Archaeology Papers 1976* 11:43–63.

TYLER, STEPHEN A.
1969 *Cognitive Anthropology*. Holt, Rinehart and Winston, Inc., New York.

UPTON, DELL
1979 *Early Vernacular Architecture in Southeastern Virginia*. Ph.D. Dissertation, Brown University. University Microfilms, Ann Arbor.

WALSH, LORENA
1979 *A Culture of "Rude Sufficiency": Life Styles on Maryland's Lower Western Shore Between 1658 and 1720*. Paper Delivered to the Society for Historical Archaeology, January 1979.

WATKINS, C. MALCOLM
1960 North Devon Pottery and Its Export to America in the Seventeenth Century. *Contributions from the Museum of History and Technology*, Paper 13. Smithsonian Institution, Washington, D.C.

WESTMORELAND COUNTY, VIRGINIA
Deeds, Wills and Patents 1653–1659. Westmoreland County Courthouse.
Deeds and Wills 1660–1661. Westmoreland County Courthouse.
Deeds, Patents and Accounts 1665–1677. Westmoreland County Courthouse.

YENTSCH, ANNE E.
1977 *Farming, Fishing, Trading, and Whaling: Subsistence Patterns Revealed by Probate Inventories for Eighteenth Century Cape Cod Towns*. Paper Delivered to the Society for Historical Archaeology, January 1977.

MARY C. BEAUDRY,
ARCHAEOLOGICAL STUDIES PROGRAM,
BOSTON UNIVERSITY,
232 BAY STATE ROAD, BOSTON, MASSACHUSETTS, 02215

JANET LONG,
DEPARTMENT OF ANTHROPOLOGY,
UNIVERSITY OF WASHINGTON,
SEATTLE, WA, 98195

HENRY M. MILLER,
ST. MARY'S CITY COMMISSION,
ST. MARY'S CITY, MD, 20686

FRASER D. NEIMAN.
DEPARTMENT OF ANTHROPOLOGY,
YALE UNIVERSITY,
NEW HAVEN, CT, 06520

GARY WHEELER STONE,
ST. MARY'S CITY COMMISSION,
ST. MARY'S CITY, MD, 20686

Appendix: Probate Inventories

The following inventories were selected to provide a sample of the vessel types found in 17th century Chesapeake households. Examples have been taken from various wealth groups in the society including slave or servant quarters (in Slye and Lee inventories), poor and middling planters and extremely wealthly planter-merchants. Vessels and other food–related items have been extracted from the inventories, edited and the spelling modernized. Of particular interest in these examples in the variability in ceramic frequencies and the often minor portion of the total assemblage they comprise. Iron, pewter, tin, leather, and wooden wares are more common than ceramics. This low frequency of ceramic forms is apparently not related to their being overlooked because of low value, since many seemingly inconsequential items, such as remnant of cloth or a "staple for the spring lock," are noted.

The first inventory represents a small planter of limited means. When Francis Lewis died, he left his orphans five barrels of corn and eight cattle.

Inventory of the estate of Francis Lewis (*Westmoreland County, Virginia, Deeds and Wills 1665–1677*: f. 241, 1677):

2 pewter dishes, 3 plates, 2 porringers, 3 spoons
2 iron pots, 1 frying pan
1 candlestick
5 earthen pans, 2 trays, 3 earthen pots, 1 pan

Thomas Thomas was a planter of modest means with an estate valued at 7,140 lbs of tobacco. He owned no servants. He left his heirs 12 cattle and a simple collection of household possessions which included no ceramics.

An Inventory of the Chattles and Goods belonging to the estate of Thomas Thomas (*Maryland Provincial Records, Testamentary Proceedings* 5: f. 126–127, 12 August 1671):

4 iron pots, 1 iron kettle
4 new pewter dishes
Half a dozen of plates

10 pewter porringers
2 old pewter dishes, two old basins, 20 pewter spoons
1 pewter chamber pot
2 old frying pans
9 wooden trays, 2 platters

Robert Cole, a St. Mary's County planter, inventoried his own estate prior to his departure for England in 1662. He left his family with movable goods valued at over 28,887 lbs of tobacco. They included four indentured servants and numerous cattle and hogs. Cole was a successful planter of better than average wealth.

An Inventory of the estate of Robert Cole (*Maryland Provincial Records, Testamentary Proceedings* 6: f. 121–124, 25 April 1662):

5 iron pots, 2 small iron kettles, 2 skillets
1 copper kettle of 18 gallons, 2 frying pans
15 milk trays, 5 cedar tubs for the dairy, 1 cedar cheese tub, 1 oaken milk tub, 1 oaken milk tub
1 great round bowl, 5 pails
2 dozen trenchers, 18 spoons
1 collander of tin, 3 tin drip pans, 1 tin funnel, 5 tin candlesticks
2 wyar candlesticks, 1 pewter bottle, 1 pepper box of tin, 1 pepper grinder
1 straining dish, 1 chafing dish, 1 tin skimmer, 2 wooden platters
2 lifting trays, 1 gridiron, 1 iron ladle
5 pewter platters, 1 pewter basin, 4 pewter porringers, 2 small pewter dishes
5 wooden spoons, 3 wooden ladles
2 pewter pint pots, 1 pewter quart pot, 1 tin quart pot
1 salt box, 2 great butter pots, 5 smaller earthen;
1 earthen frying pan, 1 three legged cream pot of earthen
3 large stone jugs
1 iron bound case with six bottles with pewter screws
1 earthen pitcher, 1 earthen jug, 2 gallons of sweet oil
1 butter tub, 2 cases of quart bottles
5 speckled Dutch pots to drink in, 9 other like pieces but they are butter pots, dishes and porringers
Some gunpowder in a bottle left for use, 2 round glass bottles
10 quarts of rum in bottles
2 tin pudding pans

The inventory of Nathaniel Pope represents the estate of a wealthy Potomac planter with his total value approximately 76,000 lbs of tobacco. Pope owned 15 servants, 40 cattle, 40 swine and extensive lands.

A true and perfect inventory of the personal estate of Mr. Nathaniel Pope (*Westmoreland County, Virginia, Deeds and Wills 1660–1661*: f. 8, 14 May 1660):

3 dozen knives
1   silver bowl and 12 silver spoons
1   dram cup
1   two quart pot and 1 three pint pot
36 dishes and a basin of pewter
12 plates and 9 saucers
3   candlesticks, 12 spoons and 2 quart pots
1   knife and 2 frying pans
6   old chamber pots, 2 salts
4   iron pots, a skillet
3   great kettles and 2 small ones
2   jugs
6   porringers
2   wooden bowles
1   stew pan
1   frying pan
2   trays, a bowl and 1 iron pot

At his death, Captain John Lee was the richest man in Westmoreland County. His estate, appraised at more than 200,000 lbs of tobacco, included 13 indentured servants, 15 slaves, 88 cattle, 32 sheep, and eight horses. Lee was a merchant–planter with a well–stocked store. His servants and slaves grew tobacco on several plantations, tanned hides, and made shoes. He owned few or no ceramic vessels.

An Inventory of the estate of Captain John Lee (*Westmoreland County, Virginia, Deeds, Patents and Accounts 1665–1677*: f. 180, 2 March 1673/4):

In the Hall Chamber
2   frying pans
In the Parlor
Silver Plate valued at 4000 lbs. tobacco
In Capt. Lee's Chamber
6   qts honey
6   qts oil
In the Kitchen
1   frying pan
1   iron pot
115 lbs of pewter
1   gallon flagon
3   old chamber pots
2   close stool pans and 2 porringers
1   chafing dish and a skillet
2   brass kettles
4   brass candlesticks

In the loft over the store
Some empty bottles
In the English Quarter
2   pots
At the New Plantation
2   iron pots
1   frying pan

Robert Slye probably was even wealthier than Lee. (The goods listed in Slye's inventory were not appraised.) A merchant, Slye had extensive contacts in England, the West Indies, and New England. In addition to merchandise and several plantations, Slye owned 11 indentured servants, 14 slaves, 43 horses, 23 sheep, 83 cattle, 124 hogs, and three bee hives. Slye's inventory includes one of the largest and most detailed listings of vessels to survive from the 17th century Chesapeake.

An Inventory of the Goods, Chattles and Debts belonging to the Estate of Mr. Robert Slye of St. Mary's County, Merchant (*Maryland Provincial Records, Testamentary Proceedings 5*: f. 152–190, 19 December 1671):

In the Kitchen
3   great brass kettles
2   smaller kettles
4   iron pots
4   brass skillets
1   stew pan
1   frying pan
1   brass chafing dish
1   iron chafing dish
1   small brass skillet
1   iron kettle
4   pewter dishes
3   pewter basins
12 pewter plates
1   pewter porringer
12 alchemy spoons
3   iron bound pails
4   wooden trays
3   wooden bowls
5   old earthen pans
1   latten pudding pan
In the Dairy
12 great pewter dishes
7   small pewter dishes
2   pewter basins
1   pewter collander
12 pewter plates
9   pewter porringers

9	pewter saucers
2	small pewter salts
1	pewter flagon
1	pewter tankard
1	great pewter basin
2	latten collanders
1	latten watering pot for a garden
2	latten pudding pans
2	latten sauce pans
1	latten fish place
1	latten pie plate
1	latten covering plate
2	great milking pails
3	small milking pails
5	kimmels
13	milk trays
1	butter bowl
2	cheese tubs
1	wooden pail
16	earthen milk pans
4	large earthen dishes
4	small earthen dishes
6	white earthen porringers
8	large gallypots
1	earthen chamber pot
25	earthen butter pots
1	cream pot
5	small earthen jugs
4	small earthen flower pots
11	quart glass bottles
1	latten pepper box
2	earthen pitchers

In the Beer Room

4	empty jars
7	small earthen jugs
1	earthen chamber pot

In the Beer Room Loft

2	iron candlesticks
1	great copper kettle
1	frying pan
8	earthen butter pots
5	earthen honey pots
2	earthen drinking cups

In the Hall

1	iron bound case of bottles
1	pewter salt
1	white earthen salt
1	great earthen basin
1	basin stand
1	white earthen sillabub pot
1	case with 6 knives

In the Hall Chamber

2	pewter chamber pots

In the Parlor

1	silver flagon

1	silver bowl
1	silver caudle cup
1	large silver tumbler
1	silver salt
1	silver porringer
1	silver sack sup
2	silver dram cups
22	silver spoons
1	pewter flagon
1	pewter cup
1	pewter quart pot
1	pewter wine pot
1	latten broad candlestick
2	great stone jugs
2	small stone jugs

In the Parlor Closet

1	small box full of vials with chemical biles
13	small earthen painted dishes
1	earthen chamber pot
4	small earthen jugs
8	gallypots
6	beer glasses
6	wine glasses
2	great glass bottles
4	quart glass bottles
2	horn cups
4	vials with chemical biles
6	earthen pots

In the Parlor Chamber

1	pewter chamber pot

In the New House Hall Chamber

23	earthen butter pots
22	earthen milk pans
1	earthen pitcher

"In the Said Hall remaining of a Cargo received last voyage by the Constant Friendship, Captain Benjamin Cooper, Comander from London"

9	dozen and 4 alchemy spoons
3	latten stew pans
39	latten sauce pans
1	latten pail
17	latten funnels
3	latten collanders
10	latten pudding pans
8	latten pottle pots
9	latten quart pots
4	latten pint pots

In the Store

12	latten saucepans
2	iron bound cases and bottles
1	pewter gallon pot
1	latten pottle pot
1	latten quart pot
1	latten pint pot
1	latten funnel

30   gross of tobacco pipes
431 earthen porringers
10   butter pots
31   milk pans
3   small jugs
4   small painted dishes
3   iron chafing dishes

In the Tobacco House store
6   iron pots
9   stone jugs

In Clanse the Negro's Quarters
1   iron bottle
1   iron pot
1   frying pan

In Dockey the Negro's Quarter
1   old brass kettle
1   brass skillet

In Tony the Negro's Quarter
1   great iron pot
1   brass skillet

At Lapworth Plantation
3   iron pots
1   old brass kettle, 1 frying pan
4   latten pudding pans
1   latten pail
1   latten quart pot
1   latten sauce pan
1   milk pan
2   butter pots
8   alchemy spoons
a iron bound pail

ANITA G. COHEN-WILLIAMS

Common Maiolica Types of Northern New Spain

ABSTRACT

Since 1984 the author has been involved in a series of investigations of sites located in areas that were once part of northern New Spain. The information produced by these studies has been combined to reconstruct the succession of maiolica types and varieties for the period dating from 1550 to 1900. This essay offers a summary description of this sequence.

Introduction

One of the characteristic types of ceramics found on Hispanic sites in the New World is maiolica, a tin-glazed earthenware. Sherds of this variety represent a particularly significant class of artifacts because changes in style make it possible to establish dates for associated deposits (Caywood 1950; Goggin 1968). Shifts in types and varieties of maiolica provide a handy reference for controlling a diverse array of chronological variables within, and between, sites. Because of maiolica's demonstrated value in temporal control, the author became interested in establishing a general sequence of the major types and varieties that were utilized on the northern frontier of New Spain. Earlier research by John Goggin (1968:218–221) indicated that such a study would be difficult because of the general scarcity of maiolica in the region. He noted that:

> Archaeological excavations in sites of the Spanish-Indian period in this region (the Southwest) are probably more extensive than in any New World area. Yet the total number of majolica sherds recovered from many of the sites is less than that obtained in a single day's surface collecting at comparable Florida sites with no impressive architectural remains (Goggin 1968:220).

Work undertaken by Barbolla-Roland (1983), Barnes (1983), Barnes and May (1972), Di Peso et al. (1953), and Gerald (1968) established that impressive quantities of maiolica were present in at least some sites. Data from the locations with larger collections could provide information relevant to identifying various kinds of changes in ceramic styles.

Since 1984 the author's interest has led her to become involved in a series of investigations of Spanish colonial and Mexican Republic sites in what was once northern New Spain. Initially these investigations were pursued under a research program sponsored by the Colegio del Bajio, located in the State of Guanajuato, Mexico. This project was directed by Jorge Olvera. During 1987 and 1988 additional studies were undertaken in connection with dissertation research being conducted by Jack Williams. In 1989 the research goals described here were formally incorporated into those of the Center for Spanish Colonial Archaeology, a not-for-profit research institute headquartered in Tubac, Arizona.

Study Methods

The author's goal of establishing a general sequence of changes in maiolica in northern New Spain required that several obvious tasks be accomplished. First, there was a need to compile data from a site, or series of sites, that spanned the entire period in which maiolica was used. Second, sites with relatively abundant deposits of maiolica would have to be found to avoid the problems noted by Goggin. Finally, the sites selected would need to include a variety of locations to avoid the possible consequences of uneven geographic distributions of maiolica types within the larger study area. Table 1 summarizes the sites eventually investigated in connection with these efforts, and Figure 1 illustrates their locations.

Sites that were investigated but that did not produce at least a dozen pieces of maiolica have not been included in Table 1. The major excavation projects specifically undertaken in connection with this research included endeavors at Tucson (3,244 sherds of maiolica), Tubac (1,160 sherds of maiolica), the Cerro del Cuarto (5,602 sherds of maio-

Anita G. Cohen-Williams

TABLE 1
SITES WITH COLLECTIONS USED IN THIS ARTICLE

Sites	Collection Type	Site Type	Dates	Key on Map
Sonora				
Arizpe	SC	C/M	1644–present	a
Bacoachi	SC	M	1784–present	b
Bisanic	SC	M	1700–1770?	c
Cochari	SC	H	1810–1865	d
Dolores	SC	M	1687–1767	e
Fronteras	SC	P	1692–1900	f
Guevavi	SC	M	1730–1777	g
Tucson (Mission)*	E	M	1770–present	h
San Bernardino*	SC	P	1775–1780	i
Santa Cruz de Terrenate*	SC & E	P	1776–1780	j
Tubac*	SC & E	P	1752–present	k
Tucson (Presidio)*	E	P	1776–present	l
Unidentified site near Guevavi	SC	O	1800–1830?	m
Nueva Vizcaya				
Aldama	SC	P/C	1787–present	n
Carrizal*	SC	P/C	1757–present	o
Casas Grandes*	SC & E	M/P	1650–1700	p
Coyame	SC	P	1780–present	q
Guajoquilla	SC	P	1752–1900	r
Janos*	SC	P	1690–present	s
Mapimí	SC	P	1714–present	t
Pilares*	SC	P	1774–1782	u
San Buenaventura (Galena)*	SC	P	1778–present	v
San Carlos*	SC	P	1772–1782	w
San Francisco de Conchos	SC	P	1685–1751	x
San Francisco de Conchos	SC	M	1590–present	y
San Miguel de Cerro Gordo	SC	P/C	1646–present	z
San Pedro de Gallo	SC	P/C	1685–present	aa
Sauz	SC	H	1800–present	bb
Coahuila				
Agua Verde	SC	P	1773–1780	cc
San Vicente*	SC	P	1773–1781	dd
San Fernando de Austria	SC	P	1753–present	ee
Other regions				
Cerro del Cuarto, Guanajuato	E	O	1800–present	ff
Plaza de Los Fundadores, León	E	P/C	1570–1820	gg
El Fuerte del Sombrero, Guanajuato/Jalisco	SC	O	1817–1817	hh
San Diego, Zacatecas	SC	H	1729–present	ii

Notes. C = civil settlement; E = excavation; H = hacienda; M = mission; O = other; P = presidio; SC = surface collection; lower-case letters in column labelled "Key on Map" refer to Figure 1.
* = sites with previously recovered collections that were incorporated in this analysis.

lica), and the Plaza de Los Fundadores (526 sherds of maiolica). Of particular importance was the last named project, as fortunate circumstances preserved an unusually well stratified sequence dating from the 16th through early 19th centuries. The number of maiolica sherds recovered in surface collections varied widely. The largest assemblage (from San Francisco de Conchos) tallied over 300

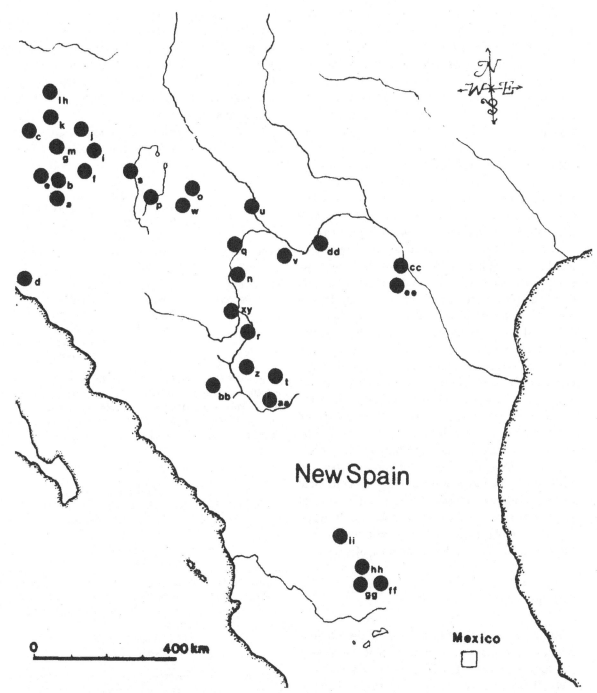

FIGURE 1. Map of northern New Spain showing distribution of sites discussed in the text. The key to individual site locations is provided in Table 1.

pieces. Most of the efforts described above focused on sites that had served as presidios (military colonies) or civilian settlements. Although relatively small collections of maiolica have been recovered from some civil/military outposts (Howard 1971; Arthur et al. 1975; Leon Quintana and Snow 1980; Benté et al. 1982; Huckell and Huckell 1982; Benté 1984; Olson 1985), work by Di Peso et al.

(1953) at Santa Cruz de Terrenate, Shenk and Teague (1975) at Tubac, Barnes (1983) at Tucson, and Barbolla-Roland (1983) at San Diego had already suggested that presidios might be more productive than their mission counterparts. As one might predict on the basis of previous work, results from the few missions that were explored were disappointing. Once assembled, data from the individual sites, and discrete components within sites, were listed on a series of charts. By linking chronological units, such as periods of occupation, with the presence and frequencies of various types, it was possible to create a master chart—a seriation—of the general changes occurring over time.

The data produced by the author are flawed by a number of significant limitations. Although the collections recovered did include materials ranging from the 16th through 20th centuries, the largest number of sites had maiolica produced between 1750 and 1850. While sites were widely distributed, entire regions were not included. Behavioral factors related to systems of commerce, ethnicity, and socio-economic status, that may have affected archaeological contexts, were not taken into account. Thus, it can be argued that the study did not recover a sample which was representative. The value of the data remains high only if one accepts that the consumption and use of various types and varieties of maiolica followed highly consistent patterns within northern New Spain. The general validity of such a view will be upheld only when the patterns observed here are confirmed by collections drawn from a larger number of sites.

Results

In an attempt to counter some of the obvious limitations of the data, a number of features were incorporated into the tabular presentation of results that follow. Since the counts of sherds of the listed types and varieties of maiolica sometimes numbered less than 200, no attempt was made to establish absolute date ranges for individual wares. Instead, the approach followed was to include items whose presence could be consistently established for sites in terms of 50-year chronological

units. Because estimates of absolute percentages of wares based on relatively small counts can easily be misleading, frequencies were generalized into three categories. These are common types (over 40%), standard types (10%–40%), and rare types (less than 10%). The resulting presentation is, at best, a general picture.

Tables 2 through 8 summarize conclusions based on the data assembled by the author. Space

TABLE 2
COMMON MAIOLICA TYPES OF NORTHERN NEW SPAIN, 1550–1600

Common Types 40%+	Standard Types 10–40%	Rare Types <10%
Mexico City Green/Cream	San Luís Blue/White Valle Ware Columbia Plain	San Juan Polychrome (Fig Springs Polychrome) Mexico City White San Luís Polychrome La Traza Polychrome

Note. Snow (1965) also lists Puebla Blue/White, Lacy Puebla Polychrome, Abó Polychrome, Mount Royal Polychrome, Aucilla Polychrome, Puaray and Castillo Polychrome, and San Luís Blue/Cream as dating to 1598–1725 (early wares), based on New Mexico and Chihuahua data.

TABLE 3
COMMON MAIOLICA TYPES OF NORTHERN NEW SPAIN, 1600–1650

Common Types 40%+	Standard Types 10–40%	Rare Types <10%
Puebla Blue/White	Mexico City Green/Cream Castillo Polychrome Mexico City Blue/Cream Valle Ware	San Luís Polychrome San Juan Polychrome Puaray Polychrome

Note. Indigena ware occurs in contexts dated to pre-1625. Snow (1965) also lists Abó Polychrome, Mount Royal Polychrome, Lacy Puebla Polychrome, Aucilla Polychrome, and San Luís Blue/Cream as dating to 1598–1725 (early wares), based on New Mexico and Chihuahua data. Plowden (1958) recorded a single sherd of Ichtucknee Blue/White at Hawikuh, Mt. Royal Polychrome at Pecos and in the Tesuque Valley site LA 16/740, and Tallahassee Blue/White at Santa Fe and Quari in New Mexico.

TABLE 4
COMMON MAIOLICA TYPES OF NORTHERN
NEW SPAIN, 1650–1700

Common Types 40% +	Standard Types 10–40%	Rare Types <10%
Puebla Blue/White	Abó Polychrome	Puaray Polychrome
Lacy Puebla Polychrome		Castillo Polychrome

Note. Florence Lister, quoted in Deagan (1987), considers Puaray Polychrome to be a variant of Castillo Polychrome.

limitations prevent the inclusion of more detailed information about sherd counts and distributions at the sites listed in Table 1. Descriptions of types and varieties that have not been previously identified are provided in Appendix A. Figures 2 through 6 illustrate some of the wares listed in the tables. The sizes of vessels shown in Figures 2 through 5 have been standardized for comparative purposes; their actual diameters ranged from 20–30 cm.

Conclusions

The work described here confirms the presence of reasonably large quantities of maiolica at civil and military sites in northern New Spain. The occurrence of the ware makes it possible for researchers to reconstruct changes in ceramics in a manner similar to that used by archaeologists in other regions of the Spanish empire (Goggin 1968; Deagan 1987). No easy answer can be formulated to account for the comparative scarcity of maiolica at frontier missions (cf. Williams 1987). Distance alone seems an inadequate explanation, since presidios with abundant sherds can be found in the same remote regions where missions have little, if any, maiolica. Perhaps the decisive factor was consumer preference. Maiolica may not have been found desirable by Indian people who had their own well-developed ceramic traditions. Barnes (1983) has argued that wealth was the decisive factor. While the price of maiolica seems relatively reasonable in terms of presidio wages, the cash-poor mission Indians may still have found imported glazed wares to be prohibitively expensive (Cohen-Williams 1986). The role of central planning in mission economics may also have contributed to scarcity. Frontier missionaries may have limited the supply of what they considered to be luxury goods to their Indian wards. The civil/military settlement's system of individual purchases was unaffected by similar constraints. It is hoped that future investigations will provide insights into why Southwestern ecclesiastic sites lack the concentrations of maiolica that characterize similar Hispano-Indian settlements in other regions. It is also interesting to note that the excavations at the Plaza de Los Fundadores suggest that maiolica was already present in significant quantities at frontier military sites by the era of the Chichimec Wars (1550–1600). This situation stands in sharp contrast with that noted by Charlton (1972) and Seifert

TABLE 5
COMMON DIAGNOSTIC MAIOLICA TYPES OF NORTHERN NEW SPAIN, 1700–1750

Common Types 40% +	Standard Types 10–40%	Rare Types <10%
Puebla Blue/White	San Agustín Blue/White	Puaray Polychrome
Lacy Puebla Polychrome	Castillo Polychrome	Mexico City Blue/Cream
		San Luís Polychrome (before 1650)
		Huejotzingo Blue/White
		San Antonio variant Puebla Blue/White

Note. Snow (1965) dates Abó Polychrome through 1780. The San Antonio polychrome definition used here was supplied by Jake Ivey (unpublished manuscript). It is essentially similar to San Elizario Polychrome, except that it lacks black accent lines.

TABLE 6
COMMON MAIOLICA TYPES OF NORTHERN NEW SPAIN, 1750–1800

Common Types 40%+	Standard Types 10–40%	Rare Types <10%
Puebla Blue/White	San Agustín Blue/White	San Diego Polychrome
	Huejotzingo Blue/White	Tucson Polychrome
	San Elizario Polychrome	San Ignacio Polychrome*
	Aranama Polychrome	Orangeline Polychrome
	(general category)	Robertos Polychrome*
		Wavy Rim Blue/White
		Castillo Polychrome
		San Antonio variant Puebla Blue/White
		Monterey Polychrome (Nopaltapec Polychrome)
		Other Aranama Polychrome varieties with blue

* = new type

TABLE 7
COMMON MAIOLICA TYPES OF NORTHERN NEW SPAIN AND NORTHERN MEXICO, 1800–1850

Common Types 40%+	Standard Types 10–40%	Rare Types <10%
Aranama Polychrome (general category)	Puebla Blue/White	Tucson Polychrome
	San Elizario Polychrome	Dolores Hidalgo Fine Line Polychrome*
	Monterey Polychrome	Guanajuato Fine Line Polychrome*
	(Nopaltapec Polychrome)	Tumacacori Polychrome
		Amarillo Polychrome*
		Ventura Polychrome
		Wavy Rim Blue/White
		Green and Yellow variants of Huejotzingo and Wavy Rim
		Tubac Polychrome*

Note. White or cream slipped pseudo-maiolica becomes the equivalent of a standard type in Sonora. Imported European wares become common during this era, representing up through over half the assemblage.
* = new type

(1977) in the Teotihuacán Valley of Central Mexico, where maiolica did not occur with frequency until the later colonial era. The presence of significant quantities of maiolica at the Plaza de Los Fundadores also suggests potential problems for the argument offered by Lister and Lister (1987: 229) that the large-scale importation of maiolica to presidios did not occur until after the end of the 16th century.

The tentative results of the author's analysis have been offered to serve as a general model which she expects will be the subject of continuing revisions. At present a more detailed analysis reporting specific counts for all the sites considered here, and including color illustrations of whole vessels, is being prepared for publication at the Center for Spanish Colonial Archaeology (Williams and Cohen-Williams 1992). It is hoped that these contributions will prove useful to researchers working on sites or site components where chronological control needs to be established through the study of ceramics.

TABLE 8
COMMON MAIOLICA TYPES OF NORTHERN MEXICO, 1850–1900

Common Types 40% +	Standard Types 10–40%	Rare Types <10%
Later Guanajuato Polychrome Tradition* (general category)	Later Guanajuato Bichrome Tradition* (general category)	Puebla Blue/White
		Dolores Hidalgo Polychrome*
Later Puebla Polychrome Tradition (general category)	Later Puebla Bichrome Tradition (general category)	Aguas Calientes Polychrome
	Guanajuato White*	Guanajuato Polychrome Green variety*
		Guanajuato Polychrome Brown variety*
		Guanajuato Polychrome Zoomorphic var.*
		Guanajuato Blue variety*
		Green/White*
		Guanajuato Blue/Brown banded*
		Guanajuato Blue/White*
		Guanajuato Brown/White*
		Sayula Polychrome
		Oaxaca Polychrome
		Guanajuato Flown Blue*
		Guanajuato Wavy Linear*

Note. Maiolica usually represents a minority of the decorated wares in collections from this era.

* = new type

Appendix A: Proposed Maiolica Types (not previously identified)

PUEBLA WARES

AMARILLO POLYCHROME
Dates: 1800–1850
Paste: white
Colors of glaze: orange and yellow on creamy white
Decoration: a single orange band highlighted by two broad, thick, yellow accent lines
Probable point of production: Puebla

FIGURE 2. Patterns from maiolica plates commonly found on 18th-century presidio sites: *a*, Puebla Blue on White; *b*, San Antonio Blue on White; *c*, Puebla Polychrome (Lacy Polychrome); *d*, San Elizario Polychrome.

Forms: *soperas* (soup plates)
Sites: Tubac Presidio
Notes: This type is probably related to later variants of Huejotzingo Blue and Green on White

SAN IGNACIO POLYCHROME
Dates: 1750–1810
Paste: white to pink
Colors of glaze: blue and orange with black accent lines on creamy white
Decoration: San Ignacio Polychrome is identical to Gerald's (1968) San Elizario Polychrome, except the blue band is replaced by orange, as is seen in various Aranama polychromes. It differs from Barnes and May's (1972) Orange-line Polychrome in that the accent dots that are perpendicular to the blue band are blue and not green.
Probable point of production: Puebla
Forms: *soperas* (soup plates)
Sites: Presidio of Santa Cruz de Terrenate, Presidio of Tubac, Presidio of Tucson

ROBERTOS POLYCHROME
Dates: 1750–1800

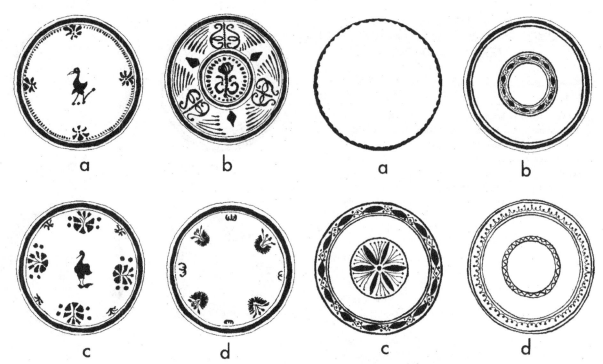

FIGURE 3. Patterns from Aranama Tradition maiolica plates commonly found on late 18th-century presidio sites: *a*, Orangeline Polychrome; *b*, Monterey Polychrome; *c*, Tucson Polychrome; *d*, Tucson Polychrome.

FIGURE 4. Common patterns from maiolica plates produced in Guanajuato and Puebla dating to the first half of the 19th century: *a*, Wavy Rim (Puebla Blue on White); *b*, Dolores Hidalgo Fine Line Polychrome; *c*, Guanajuato Fine Line Polychrome; *d*, Guanajuato Fine Line Polychrome.

Paste: white to pink

Colors of glaze: orange, yellow, green, black, and blue on creamy white

Decoration: Robertos Polychrome is similar to other Aranama Tradition wares. It has a yellow orange band near the rim, enclosed by three black accent lines. Its central medallion is a symmetrical floral design encircled by a ring of orange that has been accented with three black lines and six blue dots. At the very center of the medallion is a single blue dot encircled by a black accent line. In between the rim and the base the same basic design elements are repeated, with some reversal of green and yellow. Some cups are known, but as of today, the examples are too fragmentary to be described in comparable detail.

Probable point of production: Puebla

Forms: *soperas* (soup plates), *tazas* (cups)

Sites: Tubac Presidio

TUBAC POLYCHROME

Dates: 1800–1850

Paste: white to pink

Colors of glaze: dark green and bright yellow on creamy white

Decoration: No plates representing this type have been found.

Tubac Polychrome vessels have a style of decoration that is similar to that found on some Puebla Blue on White bowls and jars dating to the 18th century. Tubac Polychrome's design elements consist of a series of yellow bands that alternate with rows of green dots. When compared to similar, earlier, Puebla Blue on White vessels, Tubac Polychrome differs in having green dots instead of dark blue, and bright yellow encircling bands instead of light blue.

Probable point of production: Puebla

Forms: *platos* (bowls), *jarras* (jars), *tazas* (cups)

Sites: Tubac Presidio, Tucson Presidio

GUANAJUATO AND RELATED WARES

DOLORES HIDALGO FINE LINE POLYCHROME

Dates: 1800–1820?

Paste: pink to terracotta

Colors of glaze: These include black, green, yellow, and brown on white (the white glaze of this type has subtle green coloration). The glaze is thick and uniformly applied.

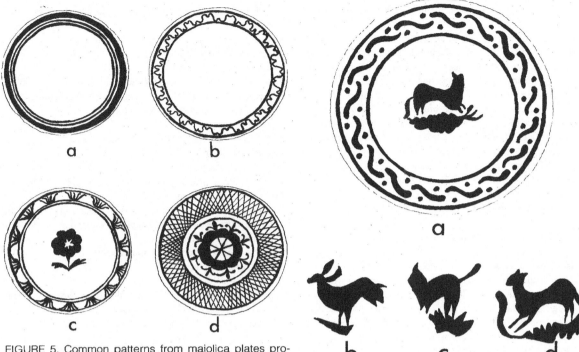

FIGURE 5. Common patterns from maiolica plates produced in Guanajuato dating to the second half of the 19th century: *a*, Guanajuato Blue and Brown Banded Polychrome; *b*, Guanajuato Blue on White; *c*, Guanajuato Polychrome (Green variety); *d*, Guanajuato Polychrome (Blue variety).

FIGURE 6. Later 19th-century Guanajuato Polychrome (Zoomorphic variety): *a*, plate pattern; *b–d*, zoomorphic medallions. The diameter of the plate is 27 cm.

Decoration: The decoration of Dolores Hidalgo Fine Line Polychrome is similar to Guanajuato Fine Line Polychrome with fine black and brown accent lines. Other decorative elements include encircling accented bands, alternating flowers on a vine, and interwoven vine decorative motifs. Flower clusters may be brown, green, or yellow. The favored motif involves a green rim band with black or brown accent lines. One sherd collected had brown in place of green as a rim band color. The central medallion is decorated by encircling brown bands and floral motifs. Black accent lines have a dispersed appearance resembling the marks of a wax crayon.

Probable point of production: Dolores Hidalgo

Forms: *soperas* (soup plates)

Sites: Fuerte de el Sombrero

Notes: The type site was built and destroyed in 1817. See Figure 4b.

GUANAJUATO BLUE ON WHITE

Dates: 1850–1900

Paste: pink to terracotta

Colors of glaze: blue on creamy white

Decoration: Two styles are known. In the first, two parallel bands of cobalt blue enclose a third irregularly undulating line (see Figure 5b). The other style has a similar blue banded panel, but an alternating checkerboard of light and dark blue replaces the undulating third line. A series of miniature crosses are fixed as pendants to the inner blue band. A single blue band delineates the basal area.

Probable point of production: Guanajuato

Forms: *soperas* (soup plates)

Sites: Cerro del Cuarto

GUANAJUATO BLUE AND BROWN BANDED POLYCHROME

Dates: 1850–1900

Paste: pink to terracotta

Colors of glaze: blue and coffee brown on creamy white

Decoration: Near the rim two narrow coffee brown bands encircle a broad cobalt blue band.

Probable point of production: Guanajuato

Forms: *soperas* (soup plates)

Sites: Cerro del Cuarto

GUANAJUATO FINE LINE POLYCHROME

Dates: 1800–1850

Paste: pink to terracotta

Colors of glaze: black, green, yellow, and brown on creamy white

Decoration: Guanajuato Fine Line Polychrome is similar to Dolores Hidalgo Fine Line Polychrome and early 19th-century Puebla wares with fine black and brown accent lines. Basic design elements include encircling accented bands, alternating flowers on a vine, and interwoven vine decorative motifs. Flower clusters may be brown, green, or yellow. The favored motif involves a green rim band with black or brown accent lines. The central medallion decorated by encircling brown bands and floral motifs.

Probable point of production: Guanajuato

Forms: *soperas* (soup plates), *platos* (bowls)

Sites: Cerro del Cuarto, Plaza de Los Fundadores

Notes: See Figure 4c and d.

GUANAJUATO FLOWN BLUE

Dates: 1850–1900

Paste: pink to terracotta

Colors of glaze: blue, and muddled blue on creamy white

Decoration: Guanajuato Flown Blue represents an imitation of English produced flown blue. The ware uses various floral elements that imitate flown blue in style and execution. As in flown blue, figures appear with diffuse color.

Probable point of production: Guanajuato

Forms: *soperas* (soup plates), *tazas* (cups), *platos* (bowls)

Sites: Cerro del Cuarto

Notes: This ware is a clear imitation of a European import and probably represents an attempt by Guanajuato regional potters to keep up with overseas competitors.

GUANAJUATO POLYCHROME (Blue variety)

Dates: 1850–1900

Paste: pink to terracotta

Colors of glaze: blue, coffee brown, and yellow on creamy white

Decoration: In the blue variety of Guanajuato Polychrome two blue bands enclose a broad panel. This panel is crosshatched with alternating blue and yellow lines that form a diamond-shaped pattern. The central medallion is enclosed by two cobalt blue bands. The center is composed of a stylized floral element in yellow brown and blue.

Probable point of production: Guanajuato

Forms: *soperas* (soup plates)

Sites: Cerro del Cuarto

Notes: See Figure 5d.

GUANAJUATO POLYCHROME (Brown variety)

Dates: 1850–1900

Paste: pink to terracotta

Colors of glaze: dark brown, yellow, coffee brown on creamy white

Decoration: In a typical example of the brown variety of Guanajuato Polychrome two sets of alternating coffee brown and yellow accent lines enclose a yellow panel with undulating dark brown lines. In the medallion a simple coffee brown and

dark brown central medallion is enclosed by a dark brown band.

Probable point of production: Guanajuato

Forms: *soperas* (soup plates)

Sites: Cerro del Cuarto

Notes: Guanajuato Green on White sherds and Brown on White sherds probably represent fragments of Green variety and Zoomorphic Guanajuato Polychromes.

GUANAJUATO POLYCHROME (Green variety)

Dates: 1850–1900

Paste: pink to terracotta

Colors of glaze: green and coffee brown on creamy white

Decoration: In the green variety of Guanajuato Polychrome a double set of narrow green bands encloses a panel of coffee brown floral elements. A simple green stylized flower fills the center of the medallion.

Probable point of production: Guanajuato

Forms: *soperas* (plates)

Sites: Cerro del Cuarto

Notes: Guanajuato Green on White sherds and Brown on White sherds probably represent fragments of Green variety and Zoomorphic Guanajuato Polychromes (see Figure 5c).

GUANAJUATO POLYCHROME (Zoomorphic variety)

Dates: 1850–1900

Paste: pink to terracotta

Colors of glaze: green, yellow, coffee brown, dark brown, and creamy white

Decoration: The zoomorphic variety of Guanajuato Polychrome has a central motif representing an animal in two or more colors. The creatures depicted include cats, birds, rabbits, and possibly deer. A few birds shown in profile have black accent lines. Two green bands near the rim border a yellow panel. On the yellow pattern a twisted broken coffee brown line is alternated with green dots.

Probable point of production: Guanajuato

Forms: *soperas* (plates)

Sites: Cerro del Cuarto

Notes: In style and execution the zoomorphic figures are reminiscent of some naturalistic Puebla depictions (see Figure 6).

GUANAJUATO WAVY LINE

Dates: 1850–1900

Paste: pink to terracotta

Colors of glaze: green, black, brown, and white

Decoration: Plates exhibit a series of parallel runny lines in a repeated pattern of green, black, brown, and white.

Probable point of production: Guanajuato

Forms: *soperas* (soup plates)

Sites: Cerro del Cuarto

GUANAJUATO WHITE

Dates: 1850–1900

Paste: pink to terracotta

Colors of glaze: creamy white to greenish white

Decoration: none

Probable point of production: Guanajuato

Forms: *soperas* (soup plates), *tazas* (cups—including tea cup varieties), *tarros* (mugs), *lavabos* (wash basins/chamber pots), *candeleros* (candlesticks)

Sites: Cerro del Cuarto

Notes: This ware is an apparent crude imitation of the undecorated Ironstone, or Hotel Wares. More recent examples show increasingly less tin content, and poor, irregular, glaze surfaces.

HUEJOTZINGO BLUE ON WHITE (Guanajuato variant)

Dates: 1770–1900

Paste: pink to terracotta

Colors of glaze: blue on creamy white

Decoration: The same decoration is used as is found on Huejotzingo blue on white vessels from Puebla. This consists of a single blue band without accent line or central motif. The Guanajuato variant differs in having a terracotta paste.

Probable point of production: Guanajuato

Forms: *soperas* (soup plates), *tazas* (cups)

Sites: Plaza de Los Fundadores, Cerro del Cuarto, San Pedro del Gallo

Status: new variant

SAN ELIZARIO POLYCHROME (Guanajuato variant)

Dates: 1770–1810

Paste: pink to terracotta

Colors of glaze: blue with black accent lines on creamy white

Decoration: The same technique as described by Gerald (1968) for the other San Elizario Polychrome vessels. The blue bands of the Guanajuato variant show somewhat less intense cobalt color. Some experiments with green (in place of blue) were noted in the Cerro del Cuarto collection.

Probable point of production: Guanajuato

Forms: *soperas* (soup plates)

Sites: Cerro del Cuarto

Status: new variant

Notes: Gerald stated his suspicion that a non-Pueblan point of production existed for San Elizario Polychrome. Current work confirms his suspicion.

Later Guanajuato Bichrome tradition refers collectively to Guanajuato Blue on White, Guanajuato Green on White, and Guanajuato Brown on White.

Later Guanajuato Polychrome tradition refers collectively to the various variants of Guanajuato Polychrome (Green variety, Blue variety, and Brown variety) as well as Guanajuato Blue and Brown Banded Polychrome.

ACKNOWLEDGMENTS

The author would like to thank Jorge Olvera, the late Wigberto Jimenez-Moreno, and Jack S. Williams. The illustrations were prepared by Jack S. Williams. The maiolica type definitions were also formulated in cooperation with Williams. The analysis described here was made possible through grants from the City of Tucson, the Colegio del Bajio, and the Instituto Nacional de Antropología e Historia office in Guanajuato. Additional support was provided by Tubac Presidio State Historic Park.

REFERENCES

ARTHUR, DON, JULIA COSTELLO, AND BRIAN FAGAN
1975 A Preliminary Account of Majolica Sherds from the Chapel Site, Royal Spanish Presidio, Santa Barbara, California. *The Kiva* 41(2):207–214.

BARBOLLA-ROLAND, DIANE
1983 Maiolica at the San Diego Presidio Gateway Search Excavation: A Preliminary Analysis. *Journal of San Diego History* 29(3):193–211.

BARNES, MARK R.
1983 Tucson: Development of a Community. Unpublished Ph.D. dissertation, Department of Anthropology, Catholic University of America, Washington, D.C.

BARNES, MARK R., AND RONALD V. MAY
1972 Mexican Majolica in Northern New Spain. *Pacific Coast Archaeological Society Occasional Paper* No. 2. Costa Mesa.

BENTÉ, VANCE
1984 *Santa Barbara Presidio Archaeological Field Work Summer 1983*. Bellephron Books, Santa Barbara, California.

BENTÉ, VANCE G., JUDITH D. TORDOFF, AND MARY HILDERMAN-SMITH
1982 *Phase VIII: Archaeological Excavations of the Chapel Site CA-SBA-133*. Santa Barbara Trust for Historic Preservation, Santa Barbara, California.

CAYWOOD, LOUIS R.
1950 Hispanic Pottery as a Guide to Historical Studies. In *For the Dean: Essays in Anthropology in Honor of Byron Cummings on His Eighty-ninth Birthday*, edited by Eric K. Reed and Dale S. King, pp. 77–97. Hohokam Museums Association and the Southwestern Monuments Association, Tucson, Arizona.

CHARLTON, THOMAS
1972 Post-Conquest Developments in the Teotihuacán Valley, Mexico. Part 1, Excavations. *Report* No. 5. Office of the State Archaeologist, Iowa City, Iowa.

COHEN-WILLIAMS, ANITA G.
1986 The Presidio as Trading Post: Some Notes on the Commercial Records of Don Francisco Guizarnotequi, Merchant-Contractor for the Presidios of Nueva

Vizcaya, 1787–1790. Paper presented at the 19th Annual Meeting of the Society for Historical Archaeology, Sacramento, California.

DEAGAN, KATHLEEN
1987   *Artifacts of the Spanish Colonies of Florida and the Caribbean 1500–1800.* Vol. 1, *Ceramics, Glassware, and Beads.* Smithsonian Institution Press, Washington, D.C.

DI PESO, CHARLES, ARTHUR WOODWARD, REX GERALD, AND M. VIRGINIA GERALD
1953   The Sobaipuri Indians of the Upper San Pedro Valley of Southeastern Arizona. *The Amerind Foundation Publication* No. 6. Amerind Foundation, Dragoon, Arizona.

GERALD, REX
1968   Spanish Presidios of the Late Eighteenth Century in Northern New Spain. *Museum of New Mexico Research Records* No. 7. Santa Fe.

GOGGIN, JOHN M.
1968   Spanish Majolica in the New World. *Yale University Publications in Anthropology* No. 72. New Haven, Connecticut.

HOWARD, DONALD
1971   Archaeological Investigation of the Royal Presidio. *Monterey County Archaeological Society Quarterly* 1(2). Monterey, California.

HUCKELL, BRUCE B., AND LISA W. HUCKELL
1982   Archaeological Test Excavations at Tubac State Park, Arizona. In Archaeological Test Excavations in Southern Arizona, compiled by Susan Brew. *University of Arizona Archaeological Series* No. 152: 63–104. Cultural Resource Management Division, Arizona State Museum, Tucson.

LEON QUINTANA, FRANCES, AND DAVID H. SNOW
1980   Historical Archaeology of the Rio Colorado Valley, New Mexico. In *Spanish and Mexican Land Grants in New Mexico and Colorado*, edited by John R. and Christine M. Van Ness, pp. 40–50. Colorado Humanities Program, Boulder.

LISTER, FLORENCE C., AND ROBERT H. LISTER
1987   Andalusian Ceramics in Spain and New Spain: A Cultural Register from the Third Century B.C. to 1700. University of Arizona Press, Tucson.

OLSON, ALAN P.
1985   Archaeology of the Presidio of Tucson. *The Kiva* 50(4):251–270.

PLOWDEN, WILLIAM W., JR.
1958   Spanish and Mexican Majolica Found in New Mexico. *El Palacio* 65(6):212–219.

SEIFERT, DONNA
1977   *Archaeological Majolicas of the Rural Teotihuacán Valley, Mexico.* Unpublished Ph.D. dissertation, Department of Anthropology, University of Iowa, Iowa City.

SHENK, LYNETTE O., AND GEORGE TEAGUE
1975   Excavations at Tubac Presidio. *University of Arizona Archaeological Series* No. 85. Arizona State Museum, Tucson.

SNOW, DAVID H.
1965   The Chronological Position of Mexican Majolica in the Southwest. *El Palacio* 72(1):25–35.

WILLIAMS, JACK S.
1987   Non-indigenous Artifacts from Feature 5, a Mid to Late 19th-Century structure. In *Archaeological Assessment of the Mission Road Extension: Testing at AZ:BB:13:6 (ASM)* (Technical Report 87–6), edited by Mark D. Elson and William Doelle, pp. 76–83. Prepared by Archaeological Institute of America. Submitted to the City of Tucson, Tucson, Arizona.

WILLIAMS, JACK S., AND ANITA G. COHEN-WILLIAMS
1992   *A Maiolica Key for Northern New Spain.* Center for Spanish Colonial Archaeology, Tubac, in press.

ANITA G. COHEN-WILLIAMS
CENTER FOR SPANISH COLONIAL ARCHAEOLOGY
TUBAC, ARIZONA 85646

LYNNE SUSSMAN

Changes in Pearlware Dinnerware, 1780–1830

ABSTRACT

Information concerning changes in style and execution of pearlware has been neglected in modern published sources on ceramic history. This paper attempts to put together changes in decoration and manufacturing methods in pearlware dinnerware from 1780–1830. Datable archaeological contexts for Fort Beauséjour, a military site in New Brunswick, Canada, provided the data.

In 1779, Josiah Wedgwood introduced a new earthenware that he called pearl white. It is a tribute to his business acumen that he successfully introduced a product that did not personally appeal to him. His cynical but accurate assessment of the buying public indicated that a change from "creamcolor" was due. In a letter to Thomas Bentley on 6 August 1779 he states:

> . . . You know what Lady Dartmouth told us, that she and her friends were tired of creamcolor, and so would be of Angels if they were shewn for sale in every chandlers shop through the town. The pearl white must be considered as a *change* rather than an *improvement*, and I must have something ready to succeed it when the public eye is palled (Finer and Savage 1965: 237).

Pearlware, as it is now called, was created by the simple expediency of covering a creamware fabric with a blue-tinged glaze. Although Wedgwood and other manufacturers claimed to have used a whiter, harder fabric, comparisons have failed to reveal any differences in either density or color between creamware and the early pearlware fabrics. The effect of the blue-tinged glaze, especially in combination with blue painted decoration, was, however, to give the appearance of a seemingly whiter fabric.

As with most of Wedgwood's inventions and innovations, his new ware was not pat-ented. For this reason, and because its production required no major changes in manufacturing methods, pearlware was being manufactured by many British factories soon after its introduction. Contemporary references to pearlware are remarkably sparse, considering the 50 years' popularity that this ware enjoyed. It seems to have been consistently referred to by the popular types of decoration used on it, such as blue- or green-edged, blue painted and blue printed (Cruickshank 1929: 150). Several manufacturers, notably Spode and Davenport, called it "White ware," thereby causing some confusion for ceramic historians studying 19th century white earthenware (Shaw 1968: 215).

Unfortunately, pearlware is similarly neglected in modern published sources on ceramic history and in museum collections. Most of the information concerning changes in style and execution is derived from archaeological specimens. Since very little pearlware was marked, it is necessary to rely upon datable archaeological contexts. Most of the conclusions outlined in this paper concerning changes in decorative and manufacturing methods are based on the analysis of the large quantities of pearlware retrieved in excavation of Fort Beauséjour, a military site in New Brunswick, Canada (Sussman 1975).

Fort Beauséjour, built by the French in 1751, was captured in 1755 by the English who changed the name to Fort Cumberland and who continued to occupy it until 1768. After a temporary abandonment, it was reoccupied by the British between 1776 and 1793. The fort was again abandoned, then reoccupied from 1812 to 1833 (Nadon 1968). As pearlware was in common use from shortly after 1780 until about 1830, the break in occupation between 1793 and 1812 facilitated the sorting of this ware into 18th and 19th century types. The following observations are primarily a comparison of the characteristics of the early (pre-1793) pearlware and the later pearlware deposited after 1812.

Eighteenth century pearlware, in general, is characterized by a light, cream-white fabric covered with a thin, soft, blue- or blue/green-tinged glaze. The walls of the objects tend to be thinly potted and the edges especially at the foot ring, are sharply defined. The 19th century pearlware is heavier and whiter with a harder, more brilliant glaze that may vary from deeply blue-tinged to almost colorless. The walls are thicker and the edges softer and more rounded. These 19th century traits are more noticeable after about 1810.

Decoration

By far the most common decoration on excavated 18th century pearlware is the molded shell edge pattern with blue or green underglaze painting (Figures 1–4). Shell edge appears as early as 1775 on creamware (Meteyard 1963: 330) and was probably one of the first patterns used to decorate pearlware. It continued to be manufactured in great quantities during the 19th century although the occurrence of green painting diminishes towards the end of the pearlware period.

The molded relief on early shell edge dinnerware is most frequently an intricate ruffle that is presumably intended to represent naturalistic shell rims (Figure 1). Another frequently occurring early version of the shell edge pattern consists of a series of closely spaced im-

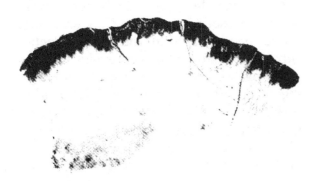

FIGURE 1. Eighteenth century pearlware, shell-edge decoration

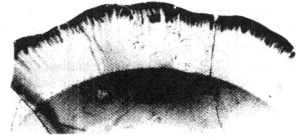

FIGURE 3. Eighteenth century pearlware, shell-edge decoration.

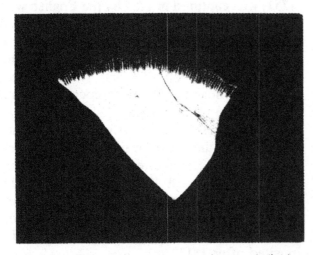

FIGURE 2. Eighteenth century pearlware, shell-edge decoration.

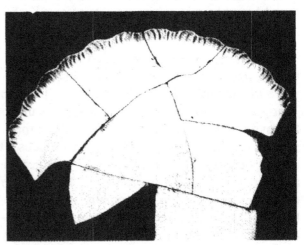

FIGURE 4. Late 18th or early 19th century pearlware, shellware decoration.

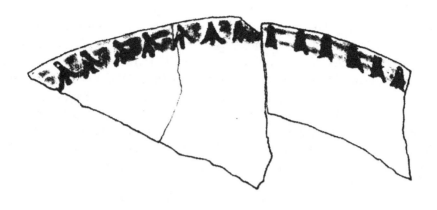

FIGURE 5. Nineteenth century pearlware, shell-edge decoration.

pressed vertical lines (Figure 2). The introduction of this simple, highly stylized version undoubtedly post-dates that of the more elaborate shell edge. No examples have as yet been found on creamware. However, its presence on 18th century pearlware contradicts a commonly held belief in the gradual "decadence" or stylization of the shell edge pattern throughout the 19th century. The most elaborate and naturalistic versions of this pattern do eventually disappear in the 19th century, but simple, stylized versions were apparently manufactured at the same time as the intricate versions and at an earlier date than has been heretofore acknowledged.

A group of shell-edge variations that has been found only on 19th century pearlware and white earthenware is the "chicken foot (Figure 5)" regularly spaced clusters of two or three curved lines.

Many variations employing irregularly spaced impressed curved lines and evenly spaced curved lines appear on both 18th and 19th century pearlware (Figures 4 and 6). A

FIGURE 6. Nineteenth century pearlware, shell-edge decoration.

study of edge-decoration motifs is currently being carried out by George Miller of Canadian National Historic Parks and Sites Branch in Ottawa. It is hoped that this study will enable him to trace the development of several ubiquitous motifs such as the 'peacock feather" or "bud" that are associated with these curved line shell edge variations (Figure 3).

The degree of sharpness of the molded relief was not helpful in dating the shell edge dinnerware. Many objects had obviously been made from worn molds, and the molded designs of some are discernible only by touch. Differences in the manner of painting were likewise unhelpful for dating. Simple banding, fine feathery painting, and combinations of both were found on both 18th and 19th century pearlware. Although cobalt was used as the coloring agent throughout the entire pearlware period, the blue on 18th century pearlware is a dark rather grey-toned color with a Munsell reading of 5PB3/6-3/10, whereas the blue or pearlware after about 1820 is a brighter purple-toned color with a Munsell reading of 7.5PB3/8-3/10. The green painted shell edge occurs in various shades ranging from blue-toned to yellow-toned, but the shade differences do not appear to be chronologically significant.

A considerable number of edge-decorated patterns other than shell edge occur in much smaller quantities on dinnerware. The molded relief consists of floral, leaf, scroll, or geometric motifs and the painting, almost always in blue, is applied underglaze in a band along the rim (Figure 7). These patterns have been found only on 19th century pearlware and on white earthenware. The only non-shell edge dinnerware pattern found on excavated examples of early pearlware is a simple pattern of narrow banding in underglaze blue (Figure 8). Banded decoration of this type was popular in brown or red on creamware during the late 18th and early 19th centuries. The same pattern in underglaze brown was found at Fort Beauséjour on a Davenport creamware dinner service dated 1793–1810.

During the 19th century, blue underglaze transfer printing became the favored method for decoratng pearlware. As this subject has been quite thoroughly covered in the published literature, only a few observations based on the material retrieved from Canadian archaeological sites will be mentioned. Although blue underglaze prints had been used as decoration on earthenware since 1780 (Meteyard 1963: 330), very little pearlware has been found on Canadian sites that can definitely be dated to the 18th century. The blue color used for prints, like that used for painting edge-decoraton, changed from a grey-toned blue on pearlware made before about 1820 to a brighter royal blue. No excavated examples were found on pearlware printed in any color other than blue.

The decorative methods and patterns used on pearlware can be divided roughly into two groups, those used for dinner services, that is, a set of plates and matching serving pieces,

FIGURE 7. Nineteenth century pearlware, edge decoration.

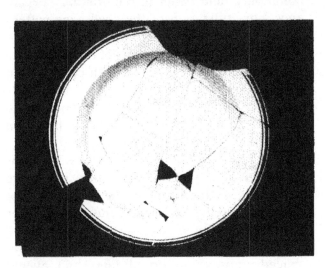

FIGURE 8. Late 18th or early 19th century pearlware, banded decoration.

and those found only on plates. Since one serving piece such as a covered dish costs as much as a dozen plates and a large dinner service could include as many as 20 serving pieces, the acquisition of a dinner service involved considerably more expense than the acquisition of a set of plates. A dinner service including such articles as sauce boats, condiment containers, and salad bowls implies, moreover, a diet and style of dining that requires some expense to maintain. Some indication of the status of a pattern can thus be determined by its occurrence or non-occurrence on elaborate serving pieces. The shell edge pattern on early pearlware is found on a great variety of serving pieces while toward the end of the pearlware period the occurrence of shell edge serving pieces other than platters is quite rare. The other 19th century edge-decorated patterns, even though they are more elaborate than the shell edge, fare no better. They have been found only as decoration on plates. Late pearlware serving pieces are almost always decorated with blue transfer-print. Edge-decoration in general suffered a fall in status during the 19th century probably due to the widespread acceptance of transfer printing.

Differences in size and shape in the following discussion will apply primarily to plates as they are the only dinnerware objects found in great quantity on archaeological sites. Dinnerware serving pieces such as tureens, sauce boats, covered serving dishes, bakers, etc. have been found in too few quantities for us to be able to determine chronological changes in their size and shape.

Size

In general the early pearlware plates are ½ inch smaller in diameter than those made after about 1820. The usual size for creamware and early pearlware dinner plates is 9½ inches, whereas the usual size for later pearlware and white earthenware dinner plates is 10 inches.

Plates

Dinnerware shapes in pearlware initially exhibited many of the same features as those of its predecessor, creamware. The following traits are characteristic of 18th and early 19th century pearlware. Brims are totally flat or flat with an upturned rim (Figures 9–11). They are narrow by modern standards (not over 1¼ inches wide on dinner plates) with a sharply defined brink or brim edge (cf. Figures 9 and 14). Bases are flat, countersunk, or are given a very small round foot ring (Figures 9–11).

Nineteenth century pearlware shapes, especially after 1810, exhibited many of the same traits as were found on white earthenware. The following traits have been found only on 19th century pearlware. Brims are highly concave or S-shaped with rounded brinks (Figures 13–14). Foot rings are (in cross section) truncated wedges or double low ridges (Figures 12, 15–16). Traits characteristic of the 18th century ware did not suddenly disappear in the 19th century; often 19th century pearlware objects were a mixture of old

FIGURE 9. Pearlware plates with 18th century traits.

FIGURE 10. Pearlware plates with 18th century traits.

FIGURE 11. Pearlware plates with 18th century traits.

FIGURE 12. Pearlware plates with 19th century traits.

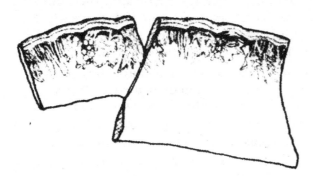

FIGURE 13. Pearlware plates with 19th century traits.

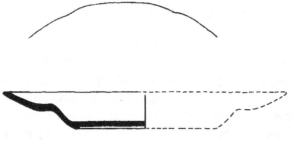

FIGURE 14. Pearlware plates with 19th century traits.

FIGURE 15. Pearlware plates with 19th century traits.

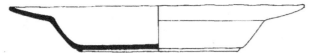

FIGURE 16. Pearlware plates with 19th century traits.

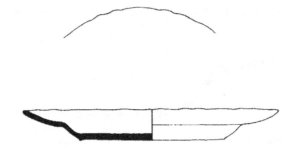

FIGURE 17. Pearlware plates with 19th century traits.

and new traits (Figures 14, 16–17). For this reason, 19th century pearlware seems more varied in shape than 18th century pearlware and creamware.

During the 18th century, plates were trimmed with a hand-held knife after being jiggered. This procedure made it possible to carve the rim in the irregular fashion associated with the ruffled shell-edge pattern. The rim treatment most frequently found on pearlware plates is a series of regular scallops. Even on the scalloped rims hand-trimming can be identified. The upper edge of the rim tends to be sharply defined while the carved lower edge will be rounded or bevelled. The trimming is often on several planes, a phenomenon that occurs when the cutting angle alters and is only possible using hand-held tools.

During the 19th century, the hand-trimming step was eliminated by improving the jiggering process so that forming and trimming were performed simultaneously. The mechanical trimming can be recognized by the sharper edge along the bottom of the rim and the rounded molded edge along the top. A raised line resembling a mold line can sometimes be seen along the edge of the rim. All mechanical trimming is, of course, on a single plane. The differences between mechanical and hand-trimming techniques apply only to circular objects. Non-circular objects such as platters and serving dishes were press-molded, then hand-trimmed.

Plain rims were used throughout the entire pearlware period, but because they were the preferred rim type on transfer-pearlware, they are more common in the 19th century. Rims with indentations at alternately short and long intervals (Figures 7 and 17) have been found only on 19th century pearlware after about 1810. This type of rim was later very popular on transfer-printed white earthenware.

No ware type changed so drastically in the course of its production as did pearlware. During the 50 years that this ware was manufactured, almost every trait underwent change including fabric, glaze, decorative method, decorative color, shape and size. It is one of the very few ceramics to form a link between two distinct ware types. At the time of its introduction it was identical to creamware in all traits except glaze color. By the time the blue-tinged glaze was abandoned, pearlware was indistinguishable from white earthenware. Pearlware is thus a unique phenomenon, a formally introduced and marketed ceramic that quickly sank into anonymity and yet one that succeeded in permanently changing the accepted standards of appearance for 19th and 20th century tableware.

REFERENCES

ANONYMOUS
1783   Price List Agreement for British Manufacturers of "Queen's Earthenware." Newcastle, England.
1833   Price List Agreement for Staffordshire Potteries. W. Rowley, Hanley, England.

CRUIKSHANK, E. A.
1929   A Country Merchant in Upper Canada, 1800–1812. *Ontario Historical Society Papers and Records* 35: 150.

FINER, ANN AND GEORGE SAVAGE (EDITORS)
1965   *The Selected Letters of Josiah Wedgwood.* Cory, Adams and Mckay, London.

METEYARD, ELIZA
1963   *The Wedgwood Handbook.* Timothy Trace, Peckskill, (Reprint of 1875 edition).

NADON, PIERRE
1968   Fort Beauséjour (1755–1833), a Technical Study. Manuscript on file, National Historic Parks and Sites Branch, Parks Canada, Ottawa.

SHAW, SIMEON
1968   *History of the Staffordshire Potteries.* Beatrice C. Weinstock, Great Neck. (Reprint of 1829 edition).

SUSSMAN, LYNNE
1975   Pearlware from Fort Beauséjour, N.B. Manuscript on file, National Historic Parks and Sites Branch, Ottawa.

LYNNE SUSSMAN
PARKS CANADA
OTTAWA, ONTARIO
CANADA K1A OH4

CHARLES S. BRADLEY

Smoking Pipes for the Archaeologist

Introduction

Tobacco consumption had become firmly entrenched in most Western industrial societies by the late 16th century. The popularity of the activity is evidenced by the abundance of smoking pipe remnants which frequent the artifact assemblages of most historical sites. The cheap, fragile, and expendable nature of clay pipes, the standard of the early pipe industry, coupled with the character of the smoking activity which generally deposited discarded pipes where they were consumed, have combined to produce an extensive record from which to draw valuable insight into the social lifeways and material consumption patterns of past cultures. Pipe attributes such as maker's marks, decorative elements, stem–bore diameter, and bowl size, style, and configuration, can help date the contexts from which the artifacts were recovered. Although a clay tobacco pipe can be considered a fragile commodity as a unit, pipe stems, once fragmented, provide an ideal, durable index for dating archaeological contexts prior to the 1760s. The quality and source of the pipes can also reflect the status of the user as well as current trade networks.

This work is not meant to be the definitive word on pipe manufacture, but is designed to provide a succinct and practical field guide for cataloguing and dating smoking pipes from archaeological contexts. It attempts to establish consistent terminology and a rudimentary, yet accurate, descriptive framework for recording the attributes of various types of pipes. The report also discusses the reworking of pipes, and use/wear marks on its various components, as well as such strategies as minimum object counts and bowl-to-stem ratios, and the significance of such analysis.

This study is a compilation of the contributions made by a number of material culture researchers who have worked on smoking pipe artifacts in the Parks Canada National Reference Collection over the past thirty years. Consequently, emphasis is on the European pipe tradition in Canada. Aboriginal pipes are beyond the scope of this paper.

Pipe Attributes and Characteristics

"Smoking pipe" is the general functional term employed when referring to this artifact class. Labels such as "tobacco pipe" are restrictive in that they represent specific smoking pipe types, and non-tobacco pipes have been encountered in the archaeological record (Figure 1). Furthermore, smoking pipes did not always consume tobacco, especially during times of scarcity; e.g., scraped willow root (Greenhous 1987:140).

Regarding orientation, a pipe should be described from the perspective of the smoker; the portion referred to as the bowl "back" is that section of the bowl that faces the smoker when the pipe is being smoked (Figure 2).

The terminology presented here applies to both clay and component pipes. These can be classified as single- or multiple-unit pipes. Single-unit pipes are of one-piece construction as exemplified by the common molded white clay pipe. Multiple-unit pipes, composed of two or more parts, can be further subdivided into two-unit (two parts) and multi-unit (three or more components) forms (Figure 3). A composite pipe

FIGURE 1. Pipes for substances other than tobacco: **a**, reproduction of an opium pipe bowl recovered from an 1850s context, San Juan Islands, Washington. Note the Chinese characters on the side identifying the maker; **b**, ceramic "toke stone" used in the consumption of marijuana, recovered from the sod layer during excavation of the Ottawa Lock Station, Ottawa, Ontario. (Photo by Rock Chan.)

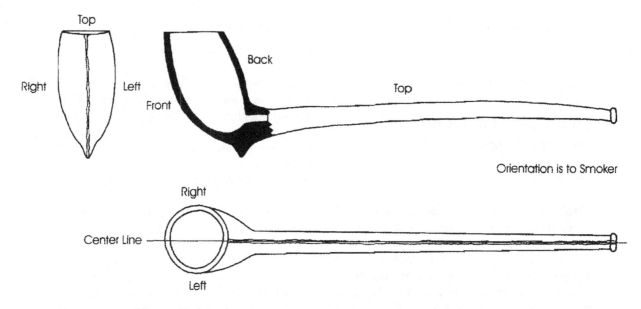

FIGURE 2. Pipe orientation. (Drawing by C. F. Richie.)

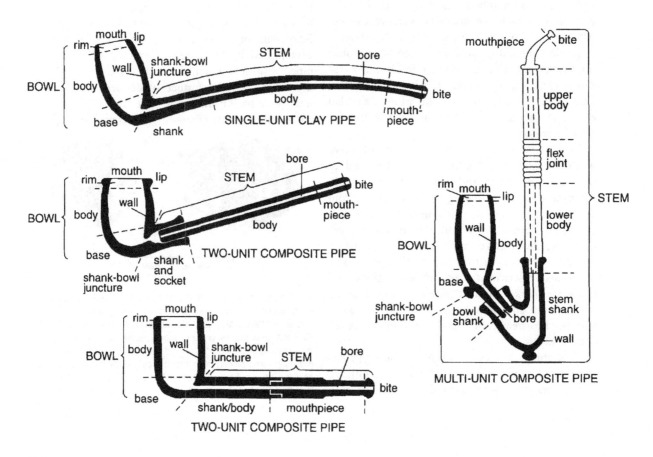

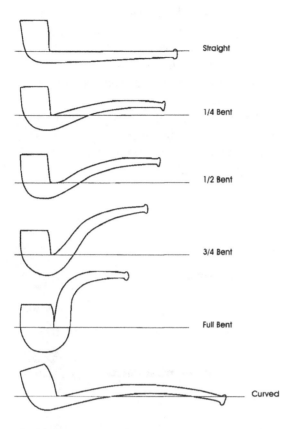

FIGURE 4. Stem configurations. (Drawing by C. F. Richie.)

reflecting a Central European tradition, which also became a prevalent form in the United States industry, incorporates a socket-shank that was designed to accept a separate stem of a different material.

A functional pipe consists of a bowl that holds the substance to be smoked, and a stem which transports the smoke to the mouth. The bowl is comprised of several parts which are identified in Figure 3. The point where the bowl and stem meet is the shank/bowl juncture. Feet and spurs are often found at the juncture of the shank and the base of the bowl. On clay pipes, maker's marks may appear on the shanks, bowls, spurs, and feet, while bowl decoration may also extend onto the shank and the stem of some models. The stem (or stem body), which generally tapers toward the bite on white clay pipes, connects the shank to the mouthpiece, the end of which is called a bite or bit. The hole running through the stem is called the bore.

Figure 4 illustrates the standard stem configurations of smoking pipes. Stems range from straight to curved, and include several degrees of bent forms. Although many of these stem styles are generally associated with composite pipes, molded clay imitations of fashionable composite designs were also manufactured. Fragmentary stems may not always conform to the standard. The specimen in Figure 5 is a section of a coiled pipe. Such smoking curios were fashionable novelties during the Victorian era and periodically appear in the archaeological record.

The condition of smoking pipe material can be an important factor in identifying the cause of deposition. For example, the presence of the relatively complete specimens in Figure 6 in latrine fill likely represents accidental loss. Condition encompasses the degree of completeness of the artifact by trait and attribute. Parts of a multi-component pipe should be considered as separate artifacts and described in degrees of completeness relative to the artifact and not to the pipe from which they came. A multi-component pipe is entered as a single artifact, and described as a whole prior to describing each component separately. A *complete* pipe is one with all elements intact as originally manufactured; a *functionally complete* pipe has been reworked to completeness or shows signs of use after breakage. Figures 7 and 8 illustrate the various levels of completeness that may be

FIGURE 5. Section of a coil pipe from a mid- to late-19th-century context at Fort Wellington, Prescott, Ontario. The presence of a bore indicates that this came from a functional pipe. (Photo by Rock Chan.)

FIGURE 6. Exploded view of two complete composite pipes. The specimen on the left is identified as a half-bent billiard with a military-style mouthpiece. The bowl is not briar but possibly of pearwood. The exterior surface was originally coated with black filler paint, typical of non-briar bowls or briars of inferior quality. The silver-plated brass shank ferrule was secured in grooves on the shank with an interior spring clip mechanism. The hard rubber mouthpiece and the metal tenon jacket were inserted into the ferrule spring clip which is forced over the end of the jacket, securing the mouthpiece to the ferrule. The case (a remnant of which is situated below the pipe) was black leather with a red felt lining and brass furniture. The pipe on the right is a traditional bent wooden style. The short, round briarwood bowl curves into a carved shank to accept the half-bent saddle style, hard-rubber mouthpiece. Elements of a nickel-plated brass ferrule were detected as were remnants of a spark cap. The threaded tenon was incorporated into the mouthpiece design. The mouthpiece is marked NRCo., identified as the mark of the Novelty Rubber Company, a firm that manufactured rubber products in New Brunswick, New Jersey, from 1855 to 1870 (Richie 1981:15). The recovery of these two pipes from 1870 to 1880 latrine fill at Fort Walsh, Saskatchewan, accounts for their relatively intact state. (Photo by Rock Chan.)

encountered within a pipe assemblage. The categories are:

1. Complete pipe: A complete bowl and stem, though the bowl may have portions of less than one major attribute missing.

2. Incomplete pipe: Specimens that do not meet the "complete pipe" criteria. This term should precede the categories listed below:

    a. Whole bowl: The complete bowl without any portion of the stem beyond the shank/bowl juncture. The bowl may have portions of less than one major attribute missing.

    b. Whole stem: The complete stem without any portion of the bowl beyond the stem/bowl juncture.

    c. Incomplete bowl: Any portion of a bowl less than a whole bowl as defined above.

    d. Incomplete stem: Any portion of a stem less than a whole stem as defined above.

Combinations of the whole and incomplete categories can be used except "whole bowl, whole stem" which should be subsumed under "complete pipe."

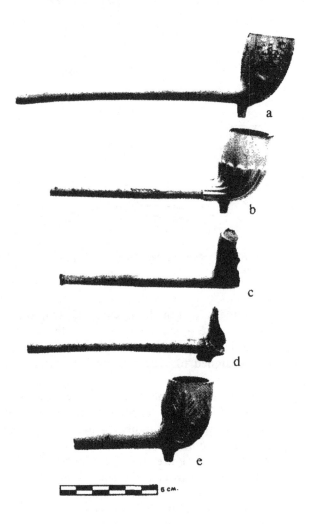

FIGURE 7. Levels of pipe condition: *a*, complete pipe (20th century; Fort Wellington, Prescott, Ontario); *b*, whole bowl/stem fragment (late 19th-early 20th century; Fort Wellington); *c*, bowl fragment/whole stem (mid to late 19th century; Lower Fort Garry, Selkirk, Manitoba); *d*, bowl fragment/whole stem (late 19th century; Fort Wellington, Prescott, Ontario); *e*, functionally complete, incomplete pipe (late 19th-early 20th century; Red Bay, Labrador). (Photo by Rock Chan.)

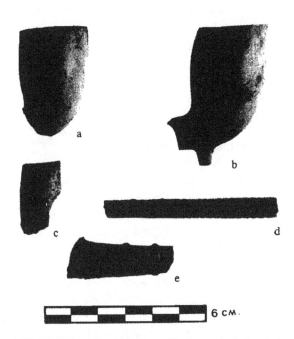

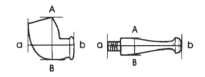

A-B   overall height
a-b   overall length

FIGURE 9. Measuring the overall dimensions of a smoking pipe: top, single-unit pipe; bottom, two-unit composite pipe bowl and stem. Debate exists over the merit of "the overall height" measurement as shown here. Some researchers feel that this should be measured perpendicular to the plane of the bowl rim, similar to bowl dimensions A-B in Figure 10. Either measurement is acceptable, but indicate which*ru are recording. (Drawing by C.F. Richie.)

FIGURE 8. Levels of pipe condition: *a*, whole bowl; *b*, whole bowl/stem fragment; *c*, bowl fragment; *d*, stem fragment; *e*, bowl fragment/stem fragment, classified as a bowl fragment because the shank/bowl juncture is represented. The specimens are from late-19th-century contexts at Fort Wellington, Prescott, Ontario, except for *d*, which dates to the 1840s-1850s. (Photo by Rock Chan.)

Properly recording the dimensions of a pipe is important as they can prove useful in determining the date of manufacture. Figures 9 and 10 show how to record bowl and stem dimensions as well as the angle of the bowl to the stem.

Clay Smoking Pipes

Most smoking pipes encountered on historical sites were made of clay. Its light, porous properties, coupled with its malleability prior to firing, made clay an ideal medium for pipe manufacture. Various clays were employed, the most common being a white ball clay, erroneously referred to as "kaolin" in the North American archaeological literature. A range of red to buff to orange clays, as well as occasional dark varieties, were also used. Although the majority of clay pipes were plain, they may also possess polished or glazed finishes.

Manufacturing Marks

A description of the complex process of clay pipe manufacture is beyond the scope of

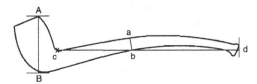

BOWL & STEM DIMENSIONS
A-B   bowl height
a-b   stem

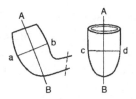

BOWL DIMENSIONS
A-B   plane of bowl mass
a-b   bowl length
c-d   bowl width

ANGLE OF THE BOWL
A-B   plane of bowl mass
a-b   plane of stem
x   angle of the bowl mass away from plane of stem

FIGURE 10. Proper orientations for recording bowl and stem dimensions, as well as the angle of the bowl to the stem. (Drawing by C. F. Richie.)

Charles S. Bradley

this report and has been well documented by a number of other researchers (Walker 1971b, 1977; Ayto 1994:19-24). In brief, the prepared clay was placed in a mold, the bowl was reamed with a plunging tool, and a wire was pushed through the stem to form the bore. The latter process usually left a small indentation or scar on the interior of the bowl opposite the bore.

Most clay pipes encountered in archaeological collections were made in two-piece molds, with each piece forming a longitudinal half of the pipe. Seams extend along the top and bottom of the stem and up the front and back of the bowl. The marks were usually removed after the molding process and prior to firing. Trimming marks appear in the form of facets left by the trimming knife. The application of decorative floral sprigs or fronds along the seams was a popular method of masking the mold marks to reduce the labor required to produce a pipe.

Mold marks could also be obliterated by polishing, a burnishing process that applied a uniform, smooth, hard finish to the entire pipe. This step generally identifies better-quality pipes associated with continental, specifically Dutch, manufacture. Evidence of polishing consist of numerous thin striations that follow the contours of the pipe and the resultant dense, smooth surface (Figure 16).

Manufactured Bites

The identification of manufactured bites, also referred to as "bits" in the United States (Weber 1965:169), is important as these can help establish a minimum object count for the pipes in a collection. At least six bite configurations have been encountered at archaeological sites: flared lip, raised lip, plain flat lip, beveled lip, rounded, and rounded flat (Pfeiffer 1982:125). Two types of mouthpieces are generally encountered: in-mold and cut-made; a third type, termed salvaged, appears occasionally:

1. In-mold: Perhaps the most obvious bite style is that which consists of a raised lip around the end of the stem in imitation of the mouthpiece of a composite pipe. A second, more common type of in-mold bite consists of a bulbous or convex contour at the tip, often with a small cylindrical projection at the opening which was created while drawing out the bore wire during production.

2. Cut-made: A flush, cut-made mouthpiece may not be as readily detected. Performed prior to firing, this process involved cutting off the rough end of the stem, usually at an angle so that the very end is tapered. Careful examination of the bite may reveal the cut mark and often a very small projection caused by residual clay adhering to the pipe when the excess material is pulled away.

3. Salvaged: A third type of mouthpiece consists of a pipe stem with a broken end that has been glazed. Broken pipes were glazed and marketed in an attempt to salvage batches of damaged or substandard pipes. Since this was done by the manufacturer, such pipes constitute manufactured bites.

Glazing was one way of treating the bite to keep the smoker's lips from sticking to its surface. The pipe ends were simply dipped in a glaze prior to firing, producing a smooth finish over the porous clay surface. Evidence suggests that yellow/brown and green glazes were employed to a minor degree towards the end of the 1700s, rising dramatically in popularity during the 1800s (Noël Hume 1969:302). Mouthpieces treated with paint and sealing wax, which became popular during the last quarter of the 1800s, have also been recovered archaeologically (Figure 11).

Heels, Feet, and Spurs

Heels and feet were usually associated with early pipes, being replaced by spurs as the pipe form evolved. While the heels and feet on earlier styles enabled the pipe to stand upright on a flat surface, spurs allowed later pipes to be held comfortably while being smoked as the bowl would become very hot. Spike and peg-shaped spurs, located at the base of the bowl at the shank/bowl juncture, were the two principal styles. Some bowl styles did not possess these features.

Decoration and Design

The shape of a pipe bowl may sometimes be considered as decorative, as in the case of effigy pipes (Figure 12) and imitations of meerschaum, calabash, and woodstock styles (Figures 13-14). When describing decorative elements, the method by which they were imparted should be noted.

FIGURE 11. Pipe stem bites exhibiting various finishes designed to prevent the smoker's lips from sticking to the porous material: *a*, glazed (Signal Hill, St. John's, Newfoundland); *b*, glazed—note the wear marks where teeth have abraded the glaze (Fort Temiscamingue, Quebec); *c*, red wax (Castle Hill, Placentia, Newfoundland); *d*, red wax (Signal Hill, St. John's, Newfoundland); *e*, black paint (1870s-1880s; Fort Walsh, Saskatchewan). (Photo by Rock Chan.)

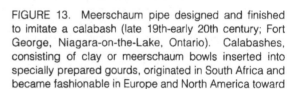

FIGURE 13. Meerschaum pipe designed and finished to imitate a calabash (late 19th-early 20th century; Fort George, Niagara-on-the-Lake, Ontario). Calabashes, consisting of clay or meerschaum bowls inserted into specially prepared gourds, originated in South Africa and became fashionable in Europe and North America toward the end of the 1800s. (Photo by Rock Chan.)

FIGURE 12. Examples of effigy bowls: *a*, sometimes referred to as a hussar effigy, there are several varieties of this decorative style ranging from very military-like to an obscure to civilian likeness. Variations are sometimes referred to as a sultan effigy. In the hussar style, a military cap forms the rim and mouth of the bowl. Close inspection may reveal a chin strap indicating the base of a helmet or possible pillbox cap with a puggaree and badge at the front. A high military style of collar can be detected at the junction of the bowl and stem (Fort Coteau du Lac, Coteau du Lac, Quebec); *b-d*, standard variations of a male effigy from post-1840s contexts (Le Vieille Maison des Jesuites, Sillery, Quebec; Fort Wellington, Prescott, Ontario; Signal Hill, St. John's, Newfoundland); *e*, fragmented bowl decorated with a lady's effigy. The fine craftsmanship coupled with remnants of painted detail indicate a pipe of probable French manufacture. The clothing style is suggestive of the latter half of the 1800s (Colonel By House, Ottawa, Ontario); *f*, knight with mailed hood, ca. 1870s. This specimen is unusual in that the effigy faces the smoker (Fort Wellington, Prescott, Ontario); *g*, lady effigy in a socket-stemmed style of probable U.S. manufacture (probably mid 1800s; non-archaeological specimen). (Photo by Rock Chan.)

FIGURE 14. Clay imitations of wooden pipe bowl styles: *a*, red clay panel style with a raised ring around the stem simulating the junction of the wood shank and the straight stem (late 19th-early 20th century; Fort Wellington, Prescott, Ontario); *b*, white clay billiard style (Signal Hill, St. John's, Newfoundland); *c*, white clay pipe with a half-bent stem, imitating a popular wooden style (Signal Hill); *d*, white clay bite fragment designed to resemble an articulated bite from a multi-component pipe (1870-1884; Lower Fort Garry, Selkirk, Manitoba). (Photo by Rock Chan.)

FIGURE 15. Some decorative elements on bowls dating from the mid to late 19th century: **a**, crossed lacrosse sticks and ball (Rideau Canal, Ottawa, Ontario); **b**, bowl fragment finished with an egg and claw motif (1870-1884; Lower Fort Garry, Selkirk, Manitoba); **c**, acorn bowl, 1857-1877; Lower Fort Garry); **d**, terra cotta urn bowl with a glazed finish of probable U.S. manufacture (ca. 1860; Fort George, Niagara-on-the-Lake, Ontario); **e**, knob-decorated bowl, sometimes referred to as an imitation corncob style; corncobs were softwood pipes that were developed initially for local consumption in the central United States (Fort George Military Reserve, Niagara-on-the-Lake, Ontario); **f**, thorn-decorated stem (1857-1877; Lower Fort Garry); **g**, scalloped bowl (Signal Hill, St. John's, Newfoundland). (Photo by Rock Chan.)

Furthermore, decoration applied during the manufacturing process should be distinguished from that applied afterwards by the purchaser. Such alteration should be identified as *reworking*.

DECORATIVE CATEGORIES

Seventeenth-century pipes were generally plain, with decoration being restricted to rouletted lines or grape patterns (Figures 22-23) and a Tudor rose design (Figure 22*e*) on the bowl. Bowl decoration became more common during the 18th century, and by the mid-19th century, pipe manufacturers were able to provide innumerable decorative themes to accommodate the great diversification in taste as far as pipe decoration is concerned. The diversity of designs can prove challenging in cataloguing pipe collections (Figures 15-16). The various designs can be documented and classified according to the principal subject of the decoration. Specimens

may be assigned to categories based on broad themes. The perceived themes may change as recording progresses, the researcher finding that what looked like a main decorative theme on a small bowl fragment is actually only a minor theme when seen on a more complete example. Most decorative themes fall into the following five categories:

1. Naturalistic: A realistic, or attempted realistic, representation of an object or scene.

2. Stylistic: A conventionalized representation of an object or scene. This includes abstract and geometric renderings of natural phenomena.

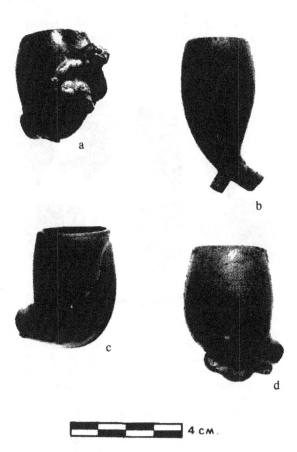

FIGURE 16. Decorative motifs on finer-quality 19th-century pipe bowls of probable continental manufacture (note the fine polishing marks on all of the examples that clearly follow the lines of the pipe): **a**, painted cherub erupting from the bowl front (late 19th century; Fort Wellington, Prescott, Ontario); **b**, plain bowl showing distinct striations as a result of burnishing/polishing (late 19th-early 20th century; Rideau Canal, Ottawa, Ontario); **c**, lotus leaf extending along the front of the bowl axis (early 20th century; Rideau Canal, Ottawa, Ontario); **d**, beaver effigy on the underside of the bowl (1870s-1880s; Fort Walsh, Saskatchewan). (Photo by Rock Chan.)

3. Free-form: The design elements are not representative of natural phenomena and are characterized by non-geometric free forms.

4. Geometric: The design elements do not represent natural phenomena and are characterized by straight lines, circles, triangles, and similar forms (Figure 17).

5. Symbolic: The design elements (including letters, numbers, emblems, etc.) have, or are suspected of having, a meaning derived from their integrated whole. Some examples are:

    a. Ethnic/Patriotic: This category (Figure 18) became a popular form of decoration as pipe manufacturers began to cater to ethnic and national sentiments, which was particularly fashionable throughout the 19th century.

    b. T.D.: The initials "TD" situated on the back of the bowl (Figure 19)

comprise one of the most common decorative categories on clay pipes. There are numerous variations, with the letters raised or impressed on a plain bowl, or within ovals and rounded cartouches, rope wreaths, shields, sunbursts, circles of stars, etc. The significance of the lettering is uncertain. The letters are believed to have appeared in the mid to late 1700s, and are thought to have been the initials of a maker of quality pipes. Through widespread plagiarism, they evolved into a popular symbolic decorative element. By the early 20th century, the firm of Duncan McDougall of Glasgow, Scotland, possessed 22 mold variations of the TD design (Walker 1977:88).

    c. Masonic: Modern Freemasonry was established in England in 1717, and the society had become popular in the United States by the 1730s. The movement was firmly entrenched in the

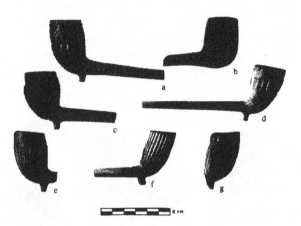

FIGURE 17. Typical geometric decoration encountered on 19th-century pipes: *a*, raised, wide vertical ribbing encircling the bowl, beginning at the halfway point of the bowl body and continuing down the base and curving towards the stem (late 19th century; Fort Wellington, Prescott, Ontario); *b*, a series of raised vertical ridges within a U-shaped border which covers the bowl sides from the rim to the base (late 19th-early 20th century; Fort Wellington); *c*, raised, beaded paisley decoration around the base of the bowl (1870s-1890s; Fort Wellington); *d*, a series of raised, wide, vertical rectangles encircling the upper portion of the bowl, combined with raised crosshatching on the base (post-1850s; Lower Fort Garry, Selkirk, Manitoba); *e*, pattern of raised panels following the contour of the pipe bowl from the base and extending approximately ¾ of the way up the sides; the panels are crosshatched and alternate with raised ridges (post-1865; Fort Wellington, Prescott, Ontario); *f*, fine raised ribbing which covers the entire bowl and follows its contours (Fort St. Joseph, Ontario); *g*, a series of raised, vertical ridges and facets which alternate around the bowl and follow its contours (Fort Wellington). (Photo by Rock Chan.)

FIGURE 18. Clay pipes decorated with ethnic and patriotic motifs: *a*, flag of Scotland/thistle on bowl sides (late 19th-early 20th century; Fort Wellington, Prescott, Ontario); *b*, crossed flags–Red Ensign and Stars and Stripes–on bowl sides (late 19th-early 20th century; Fort Wellington); *c*, crossed flags, British Flag of the Union and Stars and Stripes, on bowl sides (late 19th-early 20th century; Ottawa Lock station, Rideau Canal, Ottawa); *d*, fleur-de-lis/thistle on bowl sides (1870s-1890s; Fort Wellington, Prescott, Ontario); *e*, Scottish thistle/ Irish effigy harp on bowl sides (1870s-1890s; Fort Wellington, Prescott, Ontario); *f*, maple leaf on bowl sides (late 19th-early 20th century; Ottawa Lock station, Rideau Canal, Ottawa); *g*, Irish effigy harp on the bowl front (post-1840s; Signal Hill, St. John's, Newfoundland); *h*, Wolfe Tone and Irish effigy harp on the bowl sides (late 19th-early 20th century; Fort Wellington, Prescott, Ontario). (Photo by Rock Chan.)

Charles S. Bradley

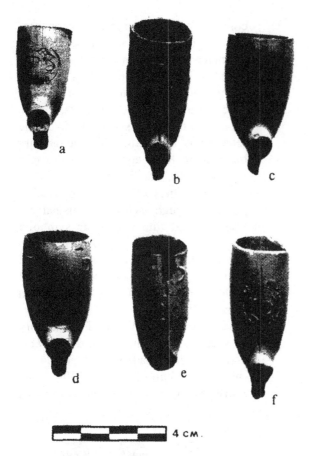

FIGURE 19. A selection of white clay "TD" bowls: *a*, impressed TD within a circular cartouche (ca. 1810; Fort George, Niagara-on-the-Lake, Ontario); *b*, raised TD within a shield with sprigs (ca. 1820s; Fort George); *c*, impressed TD (ca. 1870s; Fort Wellington, Prescott, Ontario); *d*, raised TD (1870s-1890s; Fort Wellington); *e*, raised TD on bowl rim (Fort George); *f*, raised TD within a sunburst (Fort Coteau-du-lac, Quebec). (Photo by Rock Chan.)

British military by the early 1800s. The decoration on Masonic pipes can be quite abstract as it often consists of a number of obscure symbols of fraternity and other devices relevant to the organization (Figure 20). One of the more common is the letter "G" set within dividers and a square.

TYPES OF DECORATION

Decorative elements fall into four principal categories, depending on how they were applied to the pipe:

1. Raised: Applied by molding, the design elements appear in relief.

2. Impressed: Also applied by molding, the design elements are sunk into the pipe. An effigy pipe bowl is an example of impressed decoration.

3. Incised or Abraded: The design elements are abraded or cut into the pipe with an instrument during the manufacturing process. As mentioned above, this does not include designs added after the pipe has been fired.

4. Color contrast: The design elements are defined by color.

Dating Clay Pipes

Pipes are seldom marked with absolute dates. Specimens do occasionally depict commemorative themes which imply absolute dates and enable the determination of at least a *terminus post quem* for the pipe (Figure 21). Such instances are relatively rare, however, and dates and ascriptions generally need to be determined on the basis of a pipe's attributes. Examination of stem bore diameter, stem thickness, and bowl size and shape should supply a gross assessment of a pipe fragment's chronological position.

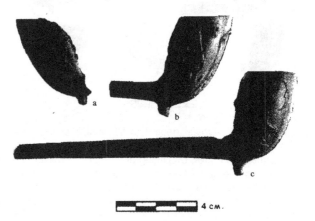

FIGURE 20. Examples of Masonic motifs on pipe bowls: *a*, standard Masonic symbol/bird decorative motif with elk head on the bowl back (Signal Hill, St. John's, Newfoundland); *b*, Masonic symbol consisting of the letter G within a cartouche formed by dividers and a set square. This appears on the bowl side opposite the bird shown in a. The bowl back exhibits the Prince of Wales plumes (early 1840s to early 1850s; Fort Wellington, Prescott, Ontario); *c*, another Masonic pipe style marked W. White, Glasgow. This pipe illustrates a variety of symbols associated with the Order. The design on the bowl back is a sunburst within a Masonic cartouche (late 19th century; Fort Wellington, Prescott, Ontario). (Photo by Rock Chan.)

FIGURE 21. Pipes commemorating events (dating by association): *a*, pipe commemorating Daniel O'Connell, leader and organizer of the Irish Catholic emancipation movement. His election to British Parliament in 1828 led to the passing of the Emancipation Bill of 1829 (Signal Hill, St. John's, Newfoundland); *b*, white clay pipe bowl exhibiting the two sides of a five-franc coin of the Second Republic of France, dated 1849 (Fort Wellington, Prescott, Ontario); *c*, reproduction of a Franklin Pierce presidential campaign pipe. Pierce, elected 14th president in 1852, was in office from 1853-1857 (San Juan Islands, Washington); *d*, temperance motif commemorating the work of Reverend Theobald Mathew, a leader in the British Temperance Movement (Signal Hill); *e*, white clay pipe bowl commemorating Queen Victoria's 75 years on the throne in 1897 (Ottawa Lock Station, Ottawa, Ontario); *f*, presidential campaign pipe bearing the effigy of Zachary Taylor, elected 12th president of the United States in the 1848 presidential election (non-archaeological specimen); *g*, coronation pipe marking the accession of Edward VII, and dating to the beginning of the 20th century (Fort Wellington). (Photo by Rock Chan.)

Other attributes such as finish, maker's marks, and decoration, if any, are also helpful for this purpose. Comparing the data recovered from pipe analysis with that derived from other material in an archaeological assemblage will generally also prove useful in dating pipe material.

THE EVOLUTION OF ATTRIBUTES

Clay smoking pipes of British manufacture underwent numerous changes from the 16th to the 20th century. The following sections highlight the more prominent changes apparent in the evolutionary progression.

17TH-CENTURY PIPES

Figures 22 and 23 illustrate examples of early bowl shapes from the 17th century. The bowls, bulbous or barrel-shaped, are squat and very small at the beginning of the century but increase in size as the century progresses. The plane of the lip of the bowl slopes away from the smoker and is at a very acute angle to the stem. Many styles possess flat feet or heels at the base of the bowl which are often large enough for the pipe to rest on in an upright position. Spurs are rarely present during this period. Decoration is also rare and generally consists of a rouletted line encircling the rim of the bowl. A maker's mark, if present, usually consists of a symbol, initials, or a full name, sometimes within a cartouche, impressed in the foot or heel. Toward the end of the century, marks also appear on the side or back of the bowl, as well as on top of the shank.

18TH-CENTURY PIPES

Typical bowl shapes of the 18th century are shown in Figure 24. The plane of the lip of the bowl is parallel to the stem. The rouletted line encircling the rim has disappeared by this time. The standard of manufacture has improved. Spurs become fashionable, and many makers begin applying their raised, mold-imparted initials to the sides of these projections. During the second half of the century, the angle of the axis of the bowl to the stem tends to become less obtuse (more nearly a right angle). Toward the end of the 18th century, the baroque, heavy style of decoration which would come to dominate the Victorian period begins to appear; fluting and leaves belong either to the end of this century or the beginning of the next.

19TH-CENTURY PIPES

The mass production of clay pipes carried out in many countries–such as England, Scotland, France, Canada, and the United States–resulted in innumerable types and styles (Figure 25). Pipes from this period are heavily decorated, for the most part. The popularity of meerschaums and briars led to imitations in clay. Clay bowl shapes, bites, and stem configurations, imitating those of meerschaums or briars, date from the

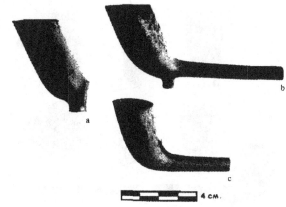

FIGURE 22. Pipe bowl shapes, ca. 1640s-ca. 1690s: *a,* ca. 1650-1680 (Fort Anne, Annapolis Royal, Nova Scotia); *b,* ca. 1640-1660 (H.M.S. *Sapphire*, Bay Bulls, Newfoundland); *c,* ca. 1640-1700 (*Sapphire*); *d,* ca. 1670-1690 (*Sapphire*); *e,* ca. 1670-1690; this bowl also has a raised Tudor-style rose on both sides of the bowl base (*Sapphire*). (Photo by Rock Chan.)

FIGURE 24. Bowl shapes typical of the mid to late 1700s: *a,* ca. 1760 (H.M.S. *Sapphire*, Bay Bulls, Newfoundland); *b,* ca. 1720-1780 (Riviere Richelieu underwater survey to, St-Jean Cantic, Quebec); *c,* a style typical of the North American export trade, a pipe by R. Tippet of Bristol, ca. 1720-1760 (wreck of *Le Machault*, Chaleur Bay, Quebec). (Photo by Rock Chan.)

second half of the 19th century. Effigy pipes had become popular by the beginning of the century. They are certainly represented on sites dating to the first half of the 1800s, as are heavily decorated bowls and stems. Mold-imparted names and ascription on the sides of the shank are also typical of the period. Peg and spike-style spurs are still encountered, many

with marks as before. Old features reappear, such as the plane of the bowl lip once again becoming moderately slanted away from the smoker. On machine-made pipes, the finish of the bowl may be careless (mold lines may not be smoothed off), even though the clay may be

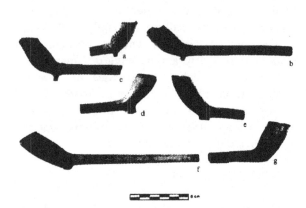

FIGURE 23. Pipe bowl shapes, ca. 1680s-ca. 1740s: *a,* ca. 1680-1710; "mulberry" or "grape" decoration (Castle Hill, Placentia, Newfoundland); *b,* ca. 1680-1710; single rouletted band around bowl back rim (this and the following specimens are all from the 1696 wreck of the H.M.S. *Sapphire*, Bay Bulls, Newfoundland); *c,* ca. 1680-1710; *d,* ca. 1680-1730; *e,* ca. 1680-1730; *f,* ca. 1680-1720; *g,* ca. 1690-1720, with an ambiguous impressed linear decoration extending along the back rim of the bowl (Castle Hill, Placentia, Newfoundland). (Photo by Rock Chan.)

FIGURE 25. Pipe bowl shapes typical of the 1800s. The complete pipe is a short cutty style that became popular during the 1800s. The whole bowl and stem fragment in the lower right is a "woodstock" style which became popular during the latter half of the 19th century. Provenience: *a,* mid to late 19th century (Fort George, Niagara-on-the-Lake, Ontario); *b,* late 19th-early 20th century (Fort Wellington, Prescott, Ontario); *c,* post-1840 (St. Andrew's Blockhouse, St. Andrew's, New Brunswick); *d-e,* mid to late 19th century (Signal Hill, St. John's, Newfoundland). (Photo by Rock Chan.)

smoother and purer than in earlier pipes. Bore-stem diameter is not helpful for dating during this period.

Bowl Shapes

The size and shape of the bowl of a clay pipe and its relationship to the stem can also provide reliable dating clues as these attributes experienced numerous recognizable changes throughout the historic period. The best source for distinguishing English bowl types is Oswald (1961; 1975). A simplified version of his bowl-shape chronology, which is more applicable to North American researchers as it is based on pipes recovered from American sites, appears in Noël Hume (1969:303). It should be noted that as with most typologies, allowances must be made for variations in bowl shape. Departures from the norm will be encountered and should, therefore, be expected throughout any period. The presence, style, and location of the foot or spur may also provide a relative date since spurs begin to appear on the bowl around the early 1700s.

The Dutch clay-pipe industry was initiated around 1600, largely by immigrant English pipemakers, thus, basic similarities in style between English and Dutch pipes are present throughout the 17th century. By the end of the century, bowl shape had changed to one where the mouth became as wide as or wider than the middle of the bowl. This conical shape, referred to as conoidal by Walker (1966a:4), continued until the end of the 19th century in the Netherlands, the size of the bowl and the obtuseness of its angle to the stem tending to increase with time, while the cross section of the bowl changed from circular to oval. Dutch pipes usually exhibit a much finer finish than English ones, frequently having a glossy, well-polished surface and milling along the rim of the bowl (Walker 1971a:90). Dutch bowls often appear to be smaller than English ones. An excellent study of early Dutch pipes in North America is by McCashion (1979). Atkinson and Oswald (1972) and Duco (1976) present more information concerning the identification and dating of Dutch clay pipes.

MAKER'S MARKS

Identifiable maker's marks provide the most dependable means to date clay pipes. These include all marks (such as symbols, names, initials, and numbers) put on a pipe to identify the maker and the place of manufacture, as well as the style and mold number of the pipe. It should be noted that there was a degree of plagiarism within the industry, in that the marks of firms associated with better-quality products were copied by others. These include Peter Dorni pipes, as well as certain Dutch marks synonymous with finer pipes. The ubiquitous "TD" mark, perhaps the most common decorative element on clay pipes, is thought to have originally represented a British maker who manufactured quality pipes (Walker 1966b). There are three types of marks:

1. Raised: The mark appears in relief.
2. Impressed: The mark is sunk into the surface.
3. Incised or abraded: The mark is cut or ground into the pipe with an instrument during the manufacturing process (before firing in the case of clay pipes).

Early pipe marks (dating from the first half of the 1600s) appeared on the base of the foot, the top of the shank or around it, or on the back or sides of the bowl. The marks consisted of initials, a full name, or a combination of the two. Symbols were also employed. With the advent of spurs in the early 18th century, English pipemakers began placing their initials on these features. It was customary to put the initial of the maker's first name on the left side of the spur and the initial of the last name on the right side. It should be pointed out that in these marks, the letter "I" also represents "J" in some cases. Who the initials represent can frequently be determined by consulting Oswald (1975). Cartouches enclosing maker's marks on the sides and backs of bowls persisted throughout this period. One of the more prominent firms to employ this form of identification was the Ford pipemakers of the Stepney area of London. The Fords were principal suppliers to the Hudson's Bay Company and pipes bearing their names within oval cartouches on the bowl back have been excavated at numerous fur trade sites in Canada and the United States. Walker (1983:65) illustrates some typical marks associated with these prominent London makers. Mold-imparted maker's names, usually accompanied by the name of the city where the factory was located, generally began appearing on pipes of British manufacture during the early 1800s, and continued into the 20th century.

Around the middle of the 1800s, a number of British manufacturers began putting marks on the bowls, shanks, or in some cases, the spurs of their pipes. These codes are believed to have identified specific mold patterns or decorations, and could be used to order the desired pipe pattern.

Most Dutch bowls exhibit maker's marks. Unlike the English who tended to use their initials as marks, Dutch makers employed various devices. Their marks were extremely well defined and consisted of very small numbers and letters, often surmounted by crowns, as well as various heraldic and symbolic devices such as windmills, mermaids, milkmaids, etc. These marks were usually located on the base of the foot or heel, and later on the peg-style spur. Dutch pipemakers continued to put their marks in these locations until the end of the 1800s. In the case of a pipe with no spur, the mark was placed on the base of the bowl where the spur would have been or, occasionally, on the back of the bowl. Research on pipe marks registered in the city of Gouda, the major center of the Dutch clay-pipe industry, has resulted in an illustrated catalogue (Helbers 1942). More recently, Don Duco (1976) has conducted extensive research into the identification of Dutch clay pipes and their marks. Although Dutch marks are superbly made with meticulous detail, their use to identify makers and date pipes can be problematic. As these marks could be bought, sold, or inherited, they can be difficult to associate with an individual maker or firm. Nevertheless, the presence of the coat of arms of the city of Gouda on pipes is indicative of manufacture after 1739/1740, when authorization to use this device was granted. The letter "S" for the Dutch word *slegte*, which denotes lesser-quality pipes, was placed above the city's arms shortly thereafter (Walker 1971a:62).

PROMINENT PIPE MANUFACTURERS

CANADA

The Canadian pipemaking industry began in earnest in the 1840s, and lasted into the 20th century. The pipes were produced in the British tradition. Consequently, the maker's name and city of manufacture appeared on the left and right shank sides, respectively, in keeping with the trend in Britain during this period. A list of Montreal pipemakers has been compiled by Robin Smith who is currently researching the clay pipe industry in that city. This listing, "Montreal Clay Tobacco Pipe Makers, 1846-1902," is accessible through the Internet (Smith 1998).

Maker	Location	Date
R. Bannerman	Montreal	1858-1888
Bannerman	Montreal	1888-1907
T. Doherty	Montreal	1850-1857
W. H. Dixon & Co.	Montreal	1876-1894
D. Ford	Montreal	1857-1873
Henderson	Montreal	1847-1876
Henderson's	Montreal	1849-1876
Murphy	Montreal	1859-1886
W&D Bell	Quebec City	1862-1881

SCOTLAND

Five Scottish pipe manufacturers—Alexander Coghill, William Murray, William White, Duncan McDougall, and T. Davidson—monopolized pipe exports during the 19th century.

Maker	Location	Date
Alex. Coghill	Glasgow	1826-1904
Davidson, T & Co.	Glasgow	1861-1910
Duncan McDougall & Co.	Glasgow	1847-1967
Wm. Murray & Co.	Glasgow	1830-1861
John Nimmo	Glasgow	1834-1846
W. White	Glasgow	1805-1955
Thos. White & Co.	Edinburgh	1823-1876
Thos. Whyte	Edinburgh	1832-1864

ENGLAND

As pipe smoking was practiced in England as early as the 1570s (Oswald 1975:4), Great Britain has a long tradition of clay pipe manufacture with thousands of individuals having been associated with the industry. An exhaustive listing was compiled by Adrian Oswald (1975:128-207) which covers pipemakers from the various parts of England as well as Scotland, Ireland, and Wales. When combined with temporal data provided by a pipe's attributes, these lists can be most helpful in identifying the maker of a pipe and its probable date.

Maker	Location	Date
Ford	London (Stepney)	1805-1865
Michael Martin	London (Woolwich)	1847
Posener	London	1866-1899
Swinyard	London	1836-1853
John Williams	London	1828-1842
William Williams	London	1823-1864
Ring	Bristol	1803-1883
Robert Tippet	Bristol	1660-ca.1720
T. Pascall	Dartford	1839-1851
J. Braithwaite	Liverpool	1816-1864
R. Morgan	Liverpool	1790-1845
W. Morgan	Liverpool	1767-1796, 1803
Edward Higgins	Salisbury	ca.1680-1710
C. Carter	Southampton	1720-1750
Reuen Sidney	Southampton	1687-1748

FRANCE

Although this industry has a long history, French pipes only came into their own between the 1850s, and the beginning of the 20th century. French pipes were generally of superior quality, with many of the bowls displaying finely molded effigies and designs. Many of the effigies possessed painted features, such as eyes, hair, hats, scarves, etc., and the clay used for some pipes was dyed red or black, attributes that may help to identify French pipes in a collection (Pfeiffer 1985:117, 1999:personal communication). French pipes were usually marked with the name and place of manufacture on the top of the shank. Two references which illustrate the styles of pipes produced by French pipemakers are Jean-Léo (1971) and Augustin (1980-1981).

Maker	Location	Date
Peter Dorni	St. Omer	ca.1850-ca.1880
Dumeril	St. Omer	1844-ca.1885
L. Fiolet	St. Omer	1746-1920
Nihoul	Nimy	1766-1914
Gambier	Paris	1780-1926
Gisclon	Paris (Lille)	ca.1820-ca.1880

NETHERLANDS

In North America, Dutch pipes appear on sites associated with Dutch and French settlement. One of the principal manufacturers was J. & G. Prince, Gouda (1773-1898).

UNITED STATES

Although Euroamerican smoking pipes have been manufactured in the United States since the 1600s, their production generally constituted a minor portion of a potter's trade and pipes were generally manufactured to fulfill local demand (Sudbury 1979:215). Consequently, few American pipes possess any identifiable maker's marks. The first pipes were crude copies of European designs made in a variety of colored clays, apparently in Virginia and New England (Noël Hume 1969:308). A style of pipe produced in the United States since at least the mid-1700s was the socket-shanked pipe, a two-unit pipe in which the clay portion, consisting of a bowl and shank, was designed to accept a separate stem. Considered the most dominant pipe form manufactured in the United States from the 1840s into the early 1900s, these pipes became synonymous with the later American clay pipe industry (Pfeiffer 1981b:109). This pipe style is believed to reflect a central European tradition (Walker 1971c:30, 1983:40).

Many American pipes were made of terra cotta, a red to orange clay. As with the Aust pipe illustrated in Figure 26, the investigation of pottery and kiln waster sites in the United States is slowly providing information concerning the products of specific pipemakers (South 1964, 1967). Consequently, it is important to record the finish on terra cotta pipes, whether plain or glazed (numerous glazes were used, the most common being salt, or fly ash glaze) and, if glazed, whether the glaze covers only the exterior or both the interior and exterior of the bowl. Sudbury (1979, 1980, 1983, 1986) provides an essential starting point to the very complex problem of identifying American pipemakers. Industrialization within the American pipe industry by the middle of the 19th century prompted large-scale production in areas such as Point Pleasant, Ohio and Pamplin, Virginia.

THE U.S. MCKINLEY TARIFF ACT

The McKinley Tariff Act of 1891 stipulated that all goods imported into the United States henceforth had to bear the name of the country of origin. Often used in dating ceramics, this act also applied to the pipe industry as foreign pipemakers had to comply if they were to compete in the lucrative U.S. market.

STEM-BORE-DIAMETER DATING

Some years ago, North American archaeologists concentrated their efforts on determining the utility of stem-bore diameters to date clay smoking pipes in archaeological assemblages. They concluded that the bores of pipes, measured in increments of 1/64 of an inch, progressively decreased in size until about 1770. Harrington (1954, 1990) gives specifics. The reduction was gradual with the result that three different diameters were often manufactured simultaneously during any given period. Consequently, the mean of the bore diameters derived for a collection of pipe stems provides the probable date for the assemblage, except in the case of the last (1750-1800) period defined by Harrington. The erratic results for samples from sites of this period reveal that the trend towards smaller bores no longer prevailed and demon-

strates the futility of using stem-bore-diameter dating on material postdating the 1750s or 1770s.

As more data were collected, a number of regression formulae were devised in an attempt to date archaeological assemblages. Although it is beyond the scope of this work to describe their mechanics (Harrington 1954, 1990; Binford 1962; Heighton and Deagan 1971) or to assess the accepted dating techniques (Omwake 1956; Noël Hume 1963, 1979:5-7; Walker 1965, 1967; Pfeiffer 1978), some considerations should be raised. The application of the formulae should be restricted to pipes manufactured in England, specifically London and Bristol. Assemblages with a heterogeneous composition tend to provide erratic dates, as do assemblages that predate the 1680s and postdate the 1760s (Noël Hume 1969:300). Therefore, the formulae are not applicable to sites dating from the latter half of the 18th century where a variety of pipes from a number of countries may be present.

A statistically significant sample is needed to obtain good results in stem-bore-diameter dating. Harrington, as the principal proponent of stem-

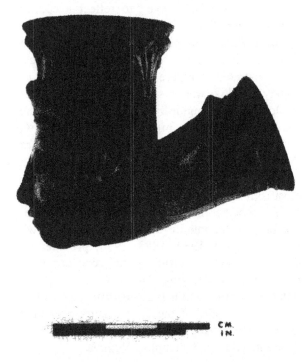

FIGURE 26. A stylized, anthropomorphic effigy pipe attributed to the Moravian Potter Gottfried Aust of Bethabara, North Carolina. Once considered a post-18th-century phenomena, it is now known that such pipes were in production prior to 1800. The pipe is a bent-elbow socket-stemmed style with a half-bent shank. The bowl is cylindrical and flared at the top; it portrays the face of a mustached man wearing a flared, visored shako. Raised floral rococo scrollwork decorates the cap. Recovered from the 1760 wreck of the French privateer *Le Machault*. (Photo by Rock Chan.)

bore-dating, recognized this and the potential for misuse: "I had hoped that no one would be uncritical enough or so literal-minded, that they would attempt to date a single pipe stem fragment, or even a limited number from my chart" (Harrington 1955:12). The formulae also require an even temporal distribution of pipe material. This may not be the case at some sites as samples may be skewed by intermittent occupation. The greatest misuse of the regression formulae, however, has occurred as a result of a researcher's inherent tendency to assign a mathematically derived, absolute date to a pipe sample. Caution must be taken when employing bore diameters to calculate dates for an archaeological assemblage. Considering the non-regulated nature of the pipe industry, coupled with the extremely gradual evolution of the bore-reduction phenomenon, considerable variation may be expected in stem-bore diameters throughout any given period. The finding of two distinct stem-bore diameters in a wrecked ship's cargo reveals that different-size bore tools were being used simultaneously by a single manufacturer (Higgins 1997:131). Nevertheless, a nominal date for a pipe assemblage can be established in some cases through analysis of the bore diameters of the recovered pipe stems, especially when combined with data derived from other attributes such as bowl configuration and maker's marks.

There is a correlation between time and bore-stem diameter, thus measuring the bore diameters of clay pipe fragments should be a standard cataloguing procedure even though there may be no immediate practical application. As both Pfeiffer (1981a) and Cranmer (1990:73) noted, attributes such as the shape and diameter of stem bores, as well as their frequency in deposits, may prove more useful than for simply determining a mean date. Analysis of these characteristics may provide critical insight into the spatial distribution of a specific site, as well as its occupational phases and their intensity.

Drill bits are ideal for measuring stem-bore diameters. Bits ranging from 4/64 in. to 9/64 in. can be embedded in a rubber stopper, thus forming a handy little measuring device. Another popular tool for measuring bore diameters is the step gauge which incorporates all the required measurements into one implement (Lenik 1971:100-101).

Metal Pipes

Occasional fragments of metal pipes have been recovered from North American sites (Noël Hume 1969:308). One- and two-piece pipes were manufactured from various metals, including silver, iron, brass, and copper. Even some pewter examples are known from Jamestown (Noël Hume 1969:308) and Sainte-Marie among the Hurons (Jeanie Tummon 1990:personal communication). Believed to have been most popular towards the end of the 1700s, these pipes were employed during more robust activities, such as traveling and hunting, where fragile clay pipes might not survive. The forms of the metal pipes mirrored those of contemporary clay pipes. Iron pipes covered with brightly colored enamel are also known, and smokers in remote areas sometimes fashioned pipes from such objects as tin cans (Figure 27).

c m

FIGURE 27. Smoking pipe fashioned from a tin can by a member of Franklin's 1845-1848 Arctic Expedition (Eden Point, Devon Island). (Photo by Rock Chan.)

Charles S. Bradley

Composite Pipes

Composite smoking pipes possess several components which are frequently composed of different materials such as porcelain, stone, and wood. In addition, composite pipes can also be composed of several clay components, or consist of reworked clay pipes fitted with homemade elements, such as whittled wooden stems. Ehwa (1974) gives a description of various types of composite pipes and their manufacture.

Porcelain

Although documented in the 1700s, porcelain pipes came into fashion around the 1850s (Figures 28-29). Many excavated examples can be identified as the "coffee house" style which consists of a porcelain bowl, usually with a metal spark cap, a porcelain reservoir which connects the bowl to a straight cherry-wood stem of varying length, and a horn, bone, or possibly amber mouthpiece (Figure 30). These pipes were designed for a sedentary, relaxed setting.

Stone

Most European stone pipes are composed of meerschaum, a German term meaning "sea surf" as it was originally thought to be petrified sea foam. The material is, in reality, a metamorphic rock composed of a hydrous magnesium

FIGURE 29. Artist's reconstruction of the porcelain lion effigy pipe bowl shown in Figure 28**a**. The spark cap representing the animal's head is based on a similar animal effigy pipe illustrated by Fairholt (1859:201). (Drawing by Dorothea Larsen.)

silicate (Weber 1965:76). The best meerschaum came from Asia Minor, specifically Turkey. It has been carved into pipe bowls since the early 1700s, and such pipes were very much in fashion with the very rich by the 1750s. The discovery of new deposits of meerschaum made this form more affordable and, by the 1850s, meerschaum pipes were a popular smoking medium of the middle classes. Fragile and expensive, meerschaum pipes are occasionally encountered in archaeological contexts.

Meerschaum pipes are composite or multicomponent pipes in that the bowl was attached to an amber or horn mouthpiece by a bone tenon and ferrule, or the pipe had a socket style of shank with a tapered hole which accommodated a cork or leather-tipped stem, usually of cherry wood. The bite was generally composed of amber or horn. Pipe bowls of carved meerschaum can be plain or highly decorated (Figure 31). A peculiar quality of meerschaum is that its color changes from chalk white or

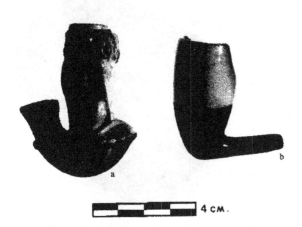

FIGURE 28. Glazed and painted porcelain pipe bowls: **a,** lion effigy of possible German manufacture (1830-1860; Fort George, Niagara-on-the-Lake, Ontario); **b,** two-tone decorated bowl (late 19th-early 20th century, Rideau Canal, Ottawa, Ontario). (Photo by Rock Chan.)

FIGURE 30. Porcelain pipe bowl fragments from ca. 1860s-1880s archaeological contexts in relation to an intact coffee house specimen. (Photo by Rock Chan.)

creamy yellow to a rich amber or golden brown as the tars and oils from the tobacco interact with the waxed surface of the bowl.

Fashioned from siltstone, steatite, and catlinite, fragments of stone pipes similar in form to clay pipes have also been encountered on archaeological sites. These generally represent an indigenous pipe industry and probably reflect a Euroamerican pipe tradition (Figure 32).

Wood

Briar pipes, fashioned from the burl of the white heather tree, became popular around the 1850s. As a result, a number of briar-bowl styles came into being during the latter part of the 19th century. Figure 33 illustrates some of the more common forms; billiard, panel, and apple are three of the earlier styles that may be encountered in archaeological collections. Pipe bowls were also made of apple, cherry, and

pear wood. Mouthpieces were also occasionally fashioned from wood (Figure 36c).

Other Materials

Composite pipes frequently have components fashioned from such materials as metal, bone and ivory, amber, horn, and synthetic substances.

1. Metal: Metal pipe components were generally in the form of spark caps, ferrules, and filters. *Spark caps*, usually made of copper alloy with a nickel finish, were found on some models of porcelain and wooden pipe bowls (Figure 34).

Ferrules, metal bands or sleeves that covered the join between the pipe shank and mouthpiece, occasionally provide very useful information concerning the origin and date of a pipe. Many better-quality British briar and composite pipes of the 19th century had hallmarked sterling-silver

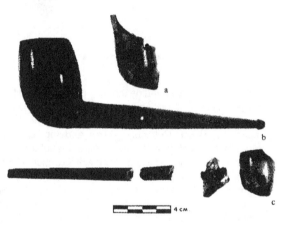

FIGURE 31. Meerschaum pipes and a white clay meerschaum imitation (late 19th-early 20th century): *a,* plain meerschaum bowl fragment. The light color suggests that the pipe was not heavily smoked, despite attempts to prolong the life of the piece by reaming out the broken shank to accept a makeshift stem (Fort Walsh, Saskatchewan); *b,* complete composite meerschaum pipe. The color of the plain bowl indicates that the piece was well-smoked. The pipe possesses a straight-stemmed amber mouthpiece. Note the hallmarks on the silver pipe stem ferrule (non-archaeological specimen); *c,* four fragments of a white clay pipe manufactured by Fiolet of France, and finished with a baked varnish finish to imitate a well-smoked meerschaum. Note the uniform color on the stem, the same amber-colored hue as a meerschaum, and the darker color of the rim and base of the bowl fragment in imitation of the well-smoked pipe in the center. The detailed figure on the bowl back is typical of the style encountered on meerschaums (Fort Wellington, Prescott, Ontario). (Photo by Rock Chan.)

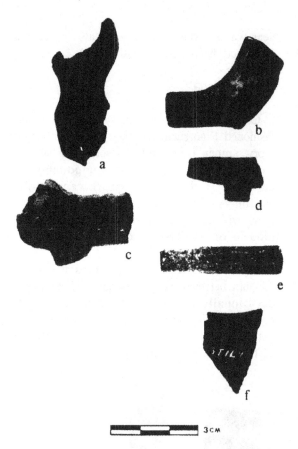

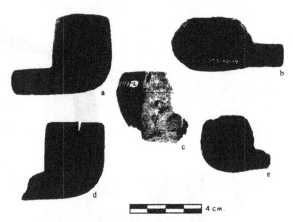

FIGURE 33. Wooden bowl styles: **a,** billiard bowl (probably 20th century; Fort Wellington, Prescott, Ontario); **b,** undesignated squat, panel, or faceted bowl style (Lower Fort Garry, Selkirk, Manitoba); **c,** bulldog bowl (Fort Anne, Annapolis Royal, Nova Scotia); **d,** panel bowl (1870s-1880s; Fort Walsh, Saskatchewan); **e,** small "prince" bowl (ca. 1848-1911; Lower Fort Garry, Selkirk, Manitoba). (Photo by Rock Chan.)

2. Bone and Ivory: These materials usually appear in composite pipes in the form of mouthpieces or tenon inserts in pipe shanks (Figure 36*a-b*, *e*; 38*a-b*).

3. Amber: Mouthpieces were also made from amber (Figures 36*f*, 37), and it was also periodically employed as a decorative element.

4. Horn: This substance was usually used for mouthpieces.

FIGURE 32. Fragmentary stone pipes: **a,** traditional indigenous style (Fort Amherst, Prince Edward Island); **b,** unfinished siltstone whole bowl/stem fragment (Fort St. James, British Columbia). This and the remaining fragments reflect Euroamerican pipe manufacture; **c,** siltstone bowl fragment/stem fragment (Yuquot, Nootka Island, British Columbia); **d,** steatite bowl fragment/stem fragment which includes the stem/bowl juncture as well as a rectangular spur (Fort St. James); **e,** steatite stem fragment, note the teeth marks (Fort St. James); **f,** bowl fragment, unidentified stone (Fort St. James). (Photo by Rock Chan.)

ferrules. The marks consisted of a maker's mark, a mark indicating the guild/city, and, most importantly, a date mark. By comparing these marks to references on the subject (Bradbury 1927), it is possible to determine the year of manufacture. Less expensive pipes with plated copper-alloy ferrules often had the maker's initials stamped within a number of cartouches that were reminiscent of hallmarks (Figure 35).

Filters, small metal fittings found within some stems, served to remove tars, oils, and other substances from the smoke. As the volatized material encountered the filters, it was trapped on the fittings which absorbed the heat, causing the substances to condense on the metal.

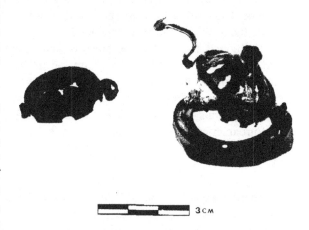

FIGURE 34. Metal spark caps, also known as wind caps or pipe-bowl covers, from component pipes. Note the hinge which allows the cap to swivel and the curved metal clips which secure it in the closed position. Both specimens appear to be nickel-plated brass and date to the 1870s-1880s (**left**, Lower Fort Garry, Selkirk, Manitoba; **right**, Fort Walsh, Saskatchewan). (Photo by Rock Chan.)

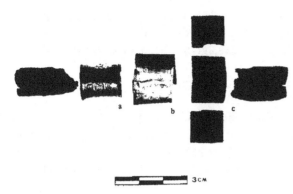

FIGURE 35. Marked metal pipe ferrules from the Fort Wellington latrine, Prescott, Ontario: **a,** cylindrical silver ferrule with a remnant of a briar shank. The marks include the maker's initials "HF," the mark designating Birmingham, and the date code for 1903; **b,** cylindrical silver ferrule with marks including the maker's initials "HM," the mark for Chester, and the date code for 1903; **c,** fragmented diamond-faceted ferrule with remnants of an associated wooden shank (late 19th-early 20th century). Maker's marks appear within a series of cartouches in imitation of hallmarks on a better-quality pipe. "EP" within the diamond-shaped cartouche indicates a silver, electro-plated finish on copper alloy. (Photo by Rock Chan.)

5. Synthetics: Vulcanite, a form of hard sulfurized rubber, was made into mouthpieces for briar and several other component pipes (Figures 36d, 38). Although Walker (1983:39-40) stated that Vulcanite mouthpieces came into use around 1878, a small number of pipe stems recovered from the 1865 wreck of the steamboat *Bertrand* possessed poorly molded, hard-rubber mouthpieces (Pfeiffer 1986:86), indicating that they were in use at least thirteen years prior to that date. Pfeiffer (1986) goes on to say that the use of Vulcanite mouthpieces on a variety of composite pipes had been firmly established by 1875. Plastic has also been used to manufacture mouthpieces since at least the 1950s.

Tenon Styles

The tenon united the shank with the stem component of a composite pipe. There are three principal types:

1. Threaded Tenon: This consists of a carved insert, generally of bone, that threads into the stem/mouthpiece and the shank body. It can also be molded into the mouthpiece as in the case of Vulcanite, or carved as in the case of some wooden examples.

2. Push Tenon: These generally consist of a smooth tube projecting from the mouthpiece which slips into the wooden shank and is held in place by a combination of friction and expansion caused by the heat generated during smoking.

3. Military Tenon: Sometimes termed a military stag tenon, the military tenon consists of a tapered form of push tenon, and was held in place by the same forces. The style's name derives from the fact that it was easier for a soldier to repair it rather than a threaded tenon in the field.

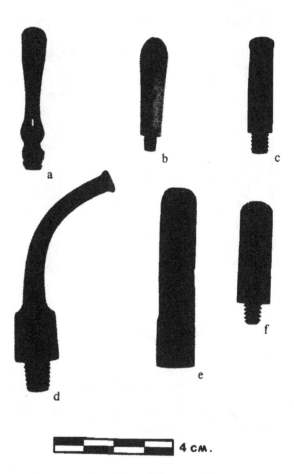

FIGURE 36. Mouthpieces from composite pipes: **a,** bone mouthpiece held in place by a crimped copper-alloy ferrule. It was probably for a multi-unit coffee-house style pipe (1870-1884; Lower Fort Garry, Selkirk, Manitoba); **b,** ivory example with a carved tenon extension (1870-1884; Lower Fort Garry); **c,** wooden mouthpiece with an integral carved tenon; **d,** Vulcanite, half-bent saddle-style mouthpiece with integral threaded tenon (1870s-1880s; Fort Walsh, Saskatchewan); **e,** ivory saddle-style mouthpiece (1870s-1880s; Fort Walsh); **f,** amber mouthpiece with threaded bone tenon insert (Fort St. James, British Columbia). (Photo by Rock Chan.)

Charles S. Bradley

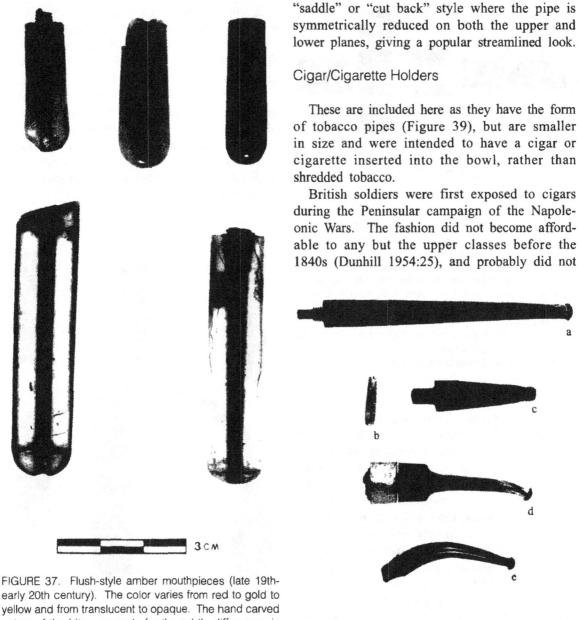

"saddle" or "cut back" style where the pipe is symmetrically reduced on both the upper and lower planes, giving a popular streamlined look.

Cigar/Cigarette Holders

These are included here as they have the form of tobacco pipes (Figure 39), but are smaller in size and were intended to have a cigar or cigarette inserted into the bowl, rather than shredded tobacco.

British soldiers were first exposed to cigars during the Peninsular campaign of the Napoleonic Wars. The fashion did not become affordable to any but the upper classes before the 1840s (Dunhill 1954:25), and probably did not

FIGURE 37. Flush-style amber mouthpieces (late 19th-early 20th century). The color varies from red to gold to yellow and from translucent to opaque. The hand carved nature of the bites accounts for the subtle differences in form. (Photo by Rock Chan.)

FIGURE 38. Hard rubber mouthpiece styles: *a,* straight-tapered flush stem with a threaded bone tenon insert (late 19th-early 20th century; Fort Wellington, Prescott, Ontario); *b,* threaded bone tenon from a composite mouthpiece (late 19th-early 20th century; Rideau Canal, Ottawa, Ontario); *c,* diamond-sectioned straight stem with a push-style tenon. Note the pattern of teeth marks (1870s-1880s; Fort Walsh, Saskatchewan); *d,* bent saddle-style mouthpiece. The threaded tenon is integral with the mouthpiece. Note the electro-plated ferrule with imitation hallmarks (late 19th-early 20th century; Fort Wellington); *e,* tapered, half-bent, military-style mouthpiece pared down to fit snugly into a pipe shank (late 19th-early 20th century; Rideau Canal, Ottawa). (Photo by Rock Chan.)

Composite-Pipe Bites

The weight of composite pipes necessitated a change from the traditional round clay-pipe style mouthpiece to a wider and flatter one which enabled the smoker to better clench, balance, and support the heavier pipe in his teeth (Walker 1983:39). The two most common mouthpieces used with composite pipes are known as "flush," where the mouthpiece is flush with the adjoining shank, gradually tapering to the bite, and the

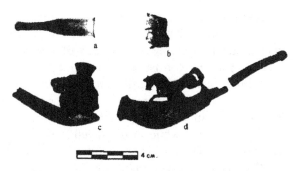

FIGURE 39. Typical forms of cigar/cigarette holders, latter half of the 19th century: *a,* glass cigar holder (1870s-1880s; Fort Walsh, Saskatchewan); *b,* small grenadier effigy white clay cigarette pipe. The cigarette was inserted in the bowl and smoked in a vertical position (late 19th-early 20th century; Fort Wellington, Prescott, Ontario); *c,* fragmented meerschaum cigarette pipe in the form of a woman's head. Worn features on the example indicate that the pipe was subjected to heavy handling (non-archaeological specimen); *d,* fragmented cigarette pipe with a more horizontal orientation of the bowl, indicating the direction of evolution (non-archaeological specimen). (Photo by Rock Chan.)

achieve a degree of popularity until the 1860s or 1870s. Cigarette smoking, a legacy of the Crimean campaign, also became very popular in Great Britain.

As in Britain, cigars became popular in North America during the early 1800s (Pfeiffer 1983:43), and cigarettes came into fashion around mid-century (Pfeiffer 1985:114). Certainly, both practices were well-established by the late 19th century, and cigar/cigarette holders co-existed with the many types of smoking pipes available during this period.

Analyzing Pipe Material

Examination of such physical attributes as bowl shape, maker's marks, decoration, and stem-bore diameter should reveal information concerning a site's overall temporal placement. The second phase of analysis is to examine the pipe material collectively in order to place the assemblage within the cultural context of the site, identifying the nature of the occupation as well as activity areas, thereby shedding light on the lifeways of the occupants.

Once the recovered pipe material has been sorted by material (clay, stone, porcelain, etc.), the fragments should be sorted and counted by provenience. The number of bowl frag-

ments, stem fragments, shank/bowl junctures, and manufactured bites should also be tallied. The amount and nature of use/wear exhibited by the fragments, as well as any evidence of reworking, should also be noted.

Crossmends

To determine distribution and discard patterns, crossmends should be recorded. Although straight mending of any pipe assemblage may prove labor-intensive and provide only minimal returns, mending is still useful to determine maker's marks and decorative motifs represented within a collection, and possibly associating a specific maker with a particular decoration.

Minimum Object Count

When counting fragments, the number of shank/bowl junctures and manufactured bites should be recorded in addition to the total number of bowl fragments and stem fragments. Since conventional pipes have only one shank/bowl juncture and one manufactured bite, a tally of these attributes will provide a minimum object count for an assemblage, the highest number of either attribute determining the population. Any fragment containing the shank/bowl juncture should be considered a bowl fragment, regardless of the amount of stem that is present, as the integral portion of the pipe is represented. Conversely, any portion of the stem which does not include the shank/bowl juncture should be classified as a stem fragment.

Bowl-to-Stem Ratio

Determining the bowl-to-stem ratio of a clay-pipe assemblage may provide insight into the nature of pipe use on site, indicating where smoking took place, and possibly identifying disposal patterns (Richie 1978:136). The ratio is based on the premise that a pipe can still be functional even after the stem has been broken. A pipe's stem can be reduced through breakage several times during its life, resulting in a higher recovery of stem fragments than bowl fragments at most sites. Theoretically, the longest clay pipe style of the first half of the 18th century had a 12-inch stem which will produce a ratio of one bowl fragment to four stem fragments

(Richie 1978:135). The bowl to stem ratio for pipes manufactured after 1780, which had shorter stems, should not be less than 1 bowl fragment to 1.5-2 stem fragments for a typical distribution. This reduced ratio is based on the regulated and relatively short "Virginia" pipe style which was exported to North America in an attempt to alleviate the high rate of stem breakage in transit (Jackson and Price 1974:83, 85).

Pipe assemblages from sites with highly transient populations and no nearby source of pipes should have a low number of bowls in proportion to stems because functional bowls were removed from the site in spite of attrition in the form of stem breakage. Conversely, a site with a population close to its source of pipes should exhibit a higher proportion of bowl fragments as the probability of bowls being discarded would be higher. For example, statistics approaching a 1:1 ratio of bowls to stems indicate a somewhat restricted smoking population close to its source of pipes, a typical distribution expected in, for example, military garrisons.

As with stem-bore diameters, caution should be exercised in determining bowl-to-stem ratios. The presence of pipe stems may not necessarily represent smoking activity. Some fragments may represent merchandise damaged in transit, or possibly some form of reuse. Since the ratios are based on postulated stem length, adjustments need to be made to the formula because stems shortened over time. Also, variations in stem length will be encountered throughout any given period. Only an approximate size can be reflected in archaeological material. An ideal assemblage for such analysis would be English pipes, especially those made in Bristol, representing isolated events or limited occupations during the latter half of the 18th century.

Use/Wear Marks

Clay pipe fragments should also be examined for use/wear marks and evidence of reworking as such information will help to determine the nature of the material and consumption patterns. For example, a lack of teeth marks and smoking stains on broken pipes may be indicative of damaged cargo, rather than personal possessions, and extensively repaired and reworked pipes might suggest that pipes were not readily available.

Teeth marks on pipe stems are caused by clenching them between the teeth, an activity that gradually abrades the surface of the stem. Classic patterns consist of an upper bite which is a little further forward than the lower bite. Evidence of idiosyncratic behavior can also be defined on occasion, such as chewing or twirling the pipe while in the mouth. Finding a relatively intact pipe which exhibits the reverse of the classic pattern indicates that the owner either smoked or held the pipe upside down. Teeth marks on the end of a clay stem fragment indicate that the owner either intentionally shortened the stem of his pipe to suit his needs, or continued to smoke a pipe after its stem broke accidentally (Figure 40). Such stems often exhibit score marks or rings which helped to snap the stem at the desired location (Figure 41).

Smoking stains found within the bowl and, in some cases, radiating out from the bore of the stem are clear evidence that a pipe was used. The degree of staining can reveal how much a pipe was smoked. The stains can range from a light gray color to blue to black, depending on how much the pipe was smoked. This dark discoloration is caused by the oils and tars being absorbed by the clay. On extremely heavily smoked specimens, the outer rim of the pipe–especially the area around the back of the rim–can become quite black from use. The staining substances are water soluble so care must be taken not to remove them when washing pipe material after excavation. It should also be noted that some types of soil and exposure to sunlight can eradicate smoking stains, as can burning.

Other use/wear marks noted primarily on clay pipes include:

1. Charring/burning: Exposure to high heat, as in a house or trash fire, can cause clay pipes to become semi-vitrified, approaching a near-porcelain-like state. This can also cause slag/cinders to adhere to the fragments (Figure 42).

2. Chipping: Found on the bowl interior and resulting from ash extraction.

3. Spalling: Pock marks caused by exposure to fire, salt, or freeze/thaw (Figure 43).

4. Abrasion: Marks imparted to a pipe fragment after being discarded, as gouged surfaces caused by grinding underfoot.

FIGURE 40. Classic teeth-mark patterns on the stems of mostly 19th-century smoking pipes. The lower examples reflect idiosyncratic habits. The patterns on the lower-most stem fragments, in particular, indicate habitual chewing and twirling of the pipe while in the mouth. The other examples demonstrate the range of wear, from slight abrasion to pronounced teeth marks indicative of hard use. (Photo by Rock Chan.)

5. Trowel marks.

When recording such evidence, the main objective should be to determine whether the artifact was deposited as the result of loss or discard and, in the case of the latter, whether primary or secondary deposition is involved.

Reworking

Reworking marks found on pipe fragments indicate purposeful alteration after the manufacturing process. This was done for three reasons: (1) to customize an individual pipe; (2)

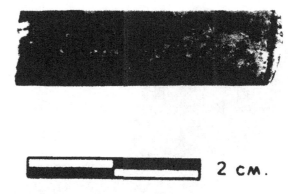

FIGURE 41. Pipe stem scored to facilitate snapping at the desired point (1750-early 1800s; Beaubassin, New Brunswick). (Photo by Rock Chan.)

to prolong the life of a pipe; and (3) to adapt the pipe or pipe fragment for alternative uses. Instances of reworking tend to be higher on sites where the populace has limited mobility or is some distance from a source of pipe supply, such as remote military and fur trade posts. With the advent of more-expensive composite pipes, instances of reworking components to prolong the life of a pipe would be expected to be higher. Some of the most common examples of reworking include: (1) stems fashioned into bites (Figure 44); (2) stems and bowls altered to accommodate reed or wooden stems (Figure 45); (3) repairs to such components as ferrules (Figure 46); (4) initials and/or designs applied by the owner (Figure 47); and (5) pipe stem fragments reworked into such objects as beads

FIGURE 42. Evidence of charring and exposure to extreme heat on smoking pipe fragments: *a,* charred bowl; *b,* charred stem; *c-f,* burned bowl and stem fragments. (Photo by Rock Chan.)

FIGURE 45. Broken pipes reworked by abrasion in an attempt to extend their life. Although the majority of these appear to have been altered to friction-fit in a wooden or reed stem, the bowl fragment in the top right has been reamed out to accept a stem insert. (Photo by Rock Chan.)

FIGURE 43. White clay bowl/stem fragment exhibiting classic evidence of frost spalling (mid-1800s; Mount Beaufort, Devon Island, Northwest Territories). (Photo by Rock Chan.)

and hairpipes (Figure 48) (Walker 1976:124-127; Sudbury 1978:105-107).

Conclusion

Smoking became so rapidly entrenched after its mid-16th-century introduction into European

FIGURE 44. Examples of bites fashioned on clay pipe stems. The two uppermost specimens have definite carved bites. The other examples have been altered into mouthpieces by abrasion. The one in the lower right was carved prior to abrasion and could also represent alteration to accommodate a makeshift stem. (Photo by Rock Chan.)

society that few other artifacts are as indicative of occupation by Northern Europeans. Consequently, fragmented smoking pipes invariably occur on most historical sites in North America. Large-scale industrialization in the pipemaking industry in both Europe and North America, coupled with recognition of pipes as a medium of decorative expression, resulted in the production of an innumerable variety of styles and designs, many of which can help to date and interpret their archaeological contexts.

Although smoking could be described as a highly social activity, it is also very personal, as evidenced by variations in use, the idiosyncrasies of wear, ingenuity in repair, and acts of personalization detected on many pipe fragments. An apt statement in the frontispiece of Iain Walker's monumental work on the Bristol pipemaking industry was an observation made by Sir Arthur Conan Doyle's fictional detective, Sherlock Holmes: "Pipes are occasionally of extraordinary interest–nothing has more individuality save, perhaps, watches and bootlaces" (Walker 1977:iii). The researcher should document any details of use and wear in pipe assemblages as they may prove helpful in expanding a record of past lifeways.

The advent of composite-pipe styles during the latter half of the 19th century fostered a radical change in smoking habits as smoking

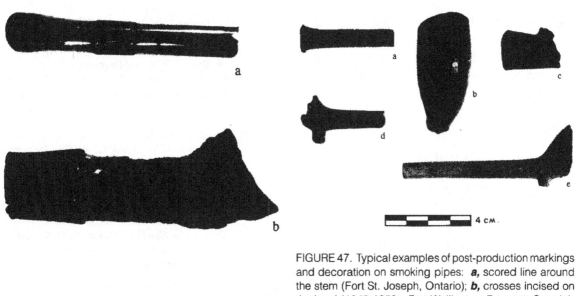

FIGURE 47. Typical examples of post-production markings and decoration on smoking pipes: **a**, scored line around the stem (Fort St. Joseph, Ontario); **b**, crosses incised on the bowl (1840-1850s; Fort Wellington, Prescott, Ontario); **c**, the letter "A" incised on the socket shank (Fort Walsh, Saskatchewan); **d**, painted decoration on the bowl (Fort St. Joseph, Ontario); **e**, series of intermittent incised lines encircling the pipe shank (Fort St. Joseph, Ontario). (Photo by Rock Chan.)

FIGURE 46. Reworked pipe stem fragments illustrating the range of makeshift ferrules: **a**, this homemade stem and mouthpiece represents a lot of effort to repair a pipe. The stem body was fashioned from a hollow bird bone, while the mouthpiece was carved from more dense bone. The two components are joined by a silver ferrule crimped around the juncture. The success of this repair is revealed by the dense pattern of teeth marks on the mouthpiece (1870s-1890s; Fort Wellington, Prescott, Ontario); **b**, shank of a wooden pipe with an improvised ferrule fashioned from the base of a .410-gauge shotgun shell (1870s-1880s; Fort Walsh, Saskatchewan); **c**, remnant of an amber mouthpiece with a decorated white-metal ferrule crimped around one end (1870s-1880s; Fort Walsh). (Photo by Rock Chan.)

unit pipe elements that are recovered archaeologically often exhibit evidence of reworking, showing that the owner attempted to prolong the life of his pipe.

Other forms of tobacco consumption during the latter half of the 19th century must also be considered by the researcher. Cigars, cigarettes, and chewing tobacco represent expressly expendable tobacco products which have left only a very subtle trace in the archaeological record.

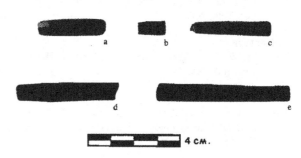

FIGURE 48. White clay pipe stem fragments reworked into beads: **a**, definite bead, tapered at both ends; **b**, possible wampum-style bead; **c**, possible bead preform consisting of the manufactured bite and a scored and snapped opposite end; **d-e**, long beads or possible hairpipes. All specimens are from H.B.C. Nottingham House, Lake Athabasca, Alberta (1802-1806). (Photo by Rock Chan.)

pipes were no longer considered a cheap and expendable commodity. The increasing popularity of composite forms should be reflected in late 19th-century disposal patterns, as the more-durable and expensive composite pipes were kept for longer periods than were traditional clay forms, often lasting throughout the occupation of a site and leaving very little trace. Those multi-

Although much has been learned about smoking-pipe assemblages, the potential to learn more is incredible as archaeologists have really only just begun to appreciate the potential of this artifact class.

REFERENCES

ATKINSON, D. R., AND ADRIAN H. OSWALD
1972   A Brief Guide for the Identification of Dutch Clay Tobacco Pipes Found in England. *Post-Medieval Archaeology* 6:175-182.

AUGUSTIN, NIELS
1980-81 *The European Picture Book of Clay Pipes*. Icon-Ceramisch Museum, Willemstad, Netherlands.

AYTO, E.G.
1994   Clay Tobacco Pipes. *Shire Publication* 37. Shire Publications, Aylesbury, Bucks, England.

BINFORD, LEWIS R.
1962   A New Method of Calculating Dates from Kaolin Pipe Stem Samples. *Southeastern Archaeological Conference Newsletter* 9(1):19-21.

BRADBURY, FREDERICK
1927   *Bradbury's Book of Hallmarks*. Reprinted 1988, J. W. Northend, Sheffield, England.

CRANMER, LEON E.
1990   Cushnoc: The History and Archaeology of Plymouth Colony Traders on the Kennebec. *Occasional Papers in Maine Archaeology* 7. Augusta.

DUCO, DON H.
1976   *Gouda Pipemakers' Marks*, L. T. Alexander, translator. Privately printed, Amsterdam, Netherlands.

DUNHILL, ALFRED H.
1954   *The Gentle Art of Smoking*. G. P. Putman's Sons, New York, NY.

EHWA, CARL, JR.
1974   *The Book of Pipes & Tobacco*. Random House, New York, NY.

FAIRHOLT, FREDERICK W.
1859   *Tobacco: Its History and Associations*. Chapman and Hall, London, England. Reprinted 1968, Singing Tree Press, Detroit, MI.

GREENHOUS, BRERETON
1987   *Guarding the Goldfields: The Story of the Yukon Field Force*. Dundurn Press, Toronto, Ontario.

HARRINGTON, J. C.
1954   Dating Stem Fragments of Seventeenth and Eighteenth Century Clay Tobacco Pipes. *Quarterly Bulletin, Archeological Society of Virginia* 9(1).

1955   A Comment on "A Critique and Rebuttal of the Paper Dating Stem Fragments of 17-18 Century Clay Tobacco Pipes" by John F. Chalkley. *Quarterly Bulletin, Archeological Society of Virginia* 9(4):11-12.

1990   Dating Stem Fragments of Seventeenth and Eighteenth Century Clay Tobacco Pipes. *Quarterly Bulletin, Archeological Society of Virginia* 45(3):123-128.

HEIGHTON, ROBERT F., AND KATHLEEN A. DEAGAN
1972   A New Formula for Dating Kaolin Clay Pipestems. *The Conference on Historic Site Archaeology Papers 1971* 6:220-229. Columbia, SC.

HELBERS, G. C.
1942   De Merken en het Merkenrecht van de Pijpmakers te Gouda. In *Goudsche Pijpen*, by G. C. Helbers and D. A. Goedewaagen. *Monographiae Nicotinae* 4. Gouda, Netherlands.

HIGGINS, DAVID A.
1997   The Identification, Analysis and Interpretation of Tobacco Pipes from Wrecks. In Artefacts from Wrecks: Dated Assemblages from the Late Middle Ages to the Industrial Revolution, Mark Redknap, editor, pp. 129-136. *Oxbow Monograph* 84. Oxford, England.

JACKSON, R. G., AND R. H. PRICE
1974   Bristol Clay Pipes: A Study of Makers and Their Marks. *Bristol City Museum Research Monograph* 1. Bristol, England.

JEAN-LEO
1971   *Les pipes en terres Françaises du 17me siècle à nos jours*. Les Grenier du Collectionneur, Brussels, Belgium.

LENIK, EDWARD J.
1971   The Step Gage: A New Tool for Measuring Pipestem Bore Diameters. *Historical Archaeology* 5:100-101.

McCASHION, JOHN H.
1979   A Preliminary Chronology and Discussion of Seventeenth and Early Eighteenth Century Clay Tobacco Pipes from New York State Sites. In The Archaeology of the Clay Tobacco Pipe: II; The United States of America, Peter Davey, editor, pp. 63-150. *British Archaeological Reports International Series* 60. London, England.

NOËL HUME, AUDREY
1963   Clay Tobacco Pipe Dating in Light of Recent Excavations. *Quarterly Bulletin, Archeological Society of Virginia* 18(2):22-25.

1979   Clay Tobacco Pipes Excavated at Martin's Hundred, Virginia, 1976-1978. In The Archaeology of the Clay Tobacco Pipe: II. The United States of America, Peter Davey, editor, pp. 3-36. *British Archaeological Reports International Series* 60. London, England.

NOËL HUME, IVOR
1969   *A Guide to Artifacts in Colonial America.* Alfred Knopf, New York, NY.

OMWAKE, H. G.
1956   Date-Bore Diameter Correlation in English White Kaolin Pipe Stems, Yes or No? *Quarterly Bulletin, Archeological Society of Virginia* 11(1).

OSWALD, ADRIAN H.
1961   The Evolution and Chronology of English Clay Tobacco Pipes. *Archaeological Newsletter* 7(3):55-62.
1975   Clay Pipes for the Archaeologist. *British Archaeological Reports* 14. London, England.

PFEIFFER, MICHAEL A.
1978   The Utility of Clay Tobacco Pipes and Stems as a Time Marker in the Pacific Northwest. Paper presented at the 31st Northwest Anthropological Conference, Pullman, WA.
1981a Clay Tobacco Pipes from Spokane House and Fort Colvile. *Northwest Anthropological Research Notes* 15(2):221-235.
1981b Notes on Unusual Clay Tobacco Pipes Found in Seattle. *Historical Archaeology* 15(1):109-112.
1982   The Clay Pipes. In Kanaka Village/Vancouver Barracks 1975, by David Chance, et al., pp. 113-127. Office of Public Archaeology, Institute for Environmental Studies, University of Washington, *Reports in Highway Archaeology* 7. Seattle.
1983   Clay Tobacco Pipes from Five Archaeological Sites in Nebraska. *Historic Clay Tobacco Pipe Studies* 2:39-47. Bryon Sudbury, Ponca City, OK.
1985   Tobacco. In Archaeological Investigations at the Cabinet Landing Site (10BR413), Bonner County, Idaho, by Keith Landreth, Keo Boreson, and Mary Condon. *Eastern Washington University Reports in Archaeology and History* 100-45:114,116-120. Cheney.
1986   Tobacco Pipes from the Arrowtown Chinese Settlement, Central Otago, New Zealand. *Historic Clay Tobacco Studies* 3:79-88. Bryon Sudbury, Ponca City, OK.

RICHIE, CLARENCE F.
1978   Nineteenth-Century Clay Tobacco-Pipes from the High Arctic. *Canadian Journal of Archaeology* 2:123-137.
1981   Tobacco Pipes from Fort Walsh, Saskatchewan: A North-West Mounted Police Post, 1875-1883. Manuscript, Parks Canada, Ottawa, Ontario.

SMITH, ROBIN
1998   Montréal Clay Tobacco Pipe Makers 1846-1902. <http://www.virtlogic.ca/pipe/mtlmake.html>29 January 1998.

SOUTH, STANLEY
1964   Eighteenth Century Clay Pipes from the Kiln Waster Dumps in the Moravian Town of Bethabara, North Carolina. *North Carolina Department of Archives and History Newsletter.*
1967   The Ceramic Forms of the Potter Gottfried Aust at Bethabara, North Carolina, 1755 to 1771. *The Conference of Historic Site Archaeology Papers 1965-1966* 1:33-52. Columbia, SC.

SUDBURY, BYRON
1978   Additional Notes on Alternative Uses for Clay Tobacco Pipes and Tobacco Pipe Fragments. *Historical Archaeology* 12:105-107.
1979   Historic Clay Tobacco Pipemakers in the United States of America. In The Archaeology of the Clay Tobacco Pipe: II. The United States of America, Peter Davey, editor, pp. 151-340. *British Archaeological Reports International Series* 60. London, England.
1980   *Historic Clay Tobacco Pipe Studies*, Vol. 1. Byron Sudbury, Ponca City, OK.
1983   *Historic Clay Tobacco Pipe Studies*, Vol. 2. Byron Sudbury, Ponca City, OK.
1986   *Historic Clay Tobacco Pipe Studies*, Vol. 3. Byron Sudbury, Ponca City, OK.

WALKER, IAIN C.
1965   Some Thoughts on the Harrington and Binford Systems for Statistically Dating Clay Pipes. *Quarterly Bulletin, Archeological Society of Virginia* 20(2):60-64.
1966a Identification and Dating of Clay Tobacco Pipes. Manuscript, Parks Canada, Ottawa.
1966b TD Pipes: A Preliminary Study. *Quarterly Bulletin, Archeological Society of Virginia* 20(4):86-102.
1967   Statistical Methods for Dating Clay Pipe Fragments. *Post-Medieval Archaeology* 1:90-101.
1971a An Archaeological Study of Clay Pipes from the King's Bastion, Fortress of Louisbourg. *Canadian Historic Sites, Occasional Papers in Archaeology and History* 2:55-122. Ottawa, Ontario.
1971b The Manufacture of Dutch Clay Tobacco-Pipes. *Northeast Historical Archaeology* 1(1):5-17.
1971c Note on the Bethabara, North Carolina, Tobacco Pipes. *The Conference on Historic Site Archaeology Papers 1969* 4:26-36. Columbia, SC.
1976   Alternative Uses for Clay Tobacco Pipes and Tobacco Pipe Fragments: Some Notes. *Historical Archaeology* 10:124-127.
1977   Clay Tobacco-Pipes, with Particular Reference to the Bristol Industry. Parks Canada. *History and Archaeology* 11. Ottawa, Ontario.
1983   Nineteenth-Century Clay Tobacco-Pipes in Canada. In The Archaeology of the Clay Tobacco Pipe: VIII; America, Peter Davey, editor, pp. 1-87. *British Archaeological Reports International Series* 175. London, England.

Charles S. Bradley

WEBER, CARL
   1965   *Carl Weber's The Pleasures of Pipe Smoking*. Bantam
          Books, New York, NY.

CHARLES S. BRADLEY
MATERIAL CULTURE RESEARCH
ONTARIO SERVICE CENTRE
PARKS CANADA
1600 LIVERPOOL COURT
OTTAWA, ONTARIO K1A 0M5
CANADA

Gerard P. Scharfenberger

Recent Evidence for Broad Window Glass in Seventeenth- and Eighteenth-Century America

ABSTRACT

Window glass is a common artifact found on many historic archaeological sites. Until now, some researchers have believed that crown window glass was used exclusively during the colonial period and early postcolonial period (Tunis 1965; Pepper 1971; Louis Berger and Assoc. 1996; LeeDecker et al. 1997; Bedell et al. 2002). Broad window glass had been assigned a *terminus post quem* of 1820, eventually replacing crown window glass by around 1840 (Louis Berger and Assoc. 1996). However, recent excavations at the First Baptist Church and Old Scots Meetinghouse sites in Monmouth County, New Jersey, past excavations at St. Mary's City, Maryland, and historic documentation indicate that broad glass was manufactured and used in America during the colonial period, possibly as early as the 17th century. This paper will examine the production processes for both crown and broad window glass as well as the physical evidence for the use and production of broad window glass alongside crown window glass during the early colonial period.

Introduction

Window glass is a common artifact found on the majority of historic archaeological sites. As an analytical tool for 17th- and 18th-century deposits, window glass has been largely overlooked by archaeologists in the past. In many studies, window glass is not distinguished as being either "broad" or "crown." Some researchers identify it as simply "window glass" and others, "flat glass" (Moran et al. 1982; Middle Atlantic Archaeological Research Assoc. 1986). The examination of window glass as an indicator of economic status, regional access to goods, architectural design, construction preference, or temporal manufacturing modes, to name a few, is rarely undertaken.

Glassmaking in America can be traced back to 1608 in the fledgling colony of Jamestown, Virginia. This glassworks was operated by the London Company and was staffed by European continental glassblowers. Rather than producing glass for the colonies, this venture was designed to exploit the vast sources of fuel available in the New World as a replacement for exhausted resources in England (Wilson 1972:3; McKearin and Wilson 1978:26). This first venture, however, lasted only until fall 1609. A second attempt at glassmaking in Jamestown occurred in 1622. It, too, failed within two years, mainly because of undercapitalization and a paucity of skilled glassblowers (McKearin and Wilson 1978:27). In general, the strength of the English glass industry kept glass blowers from emigrating to America (Davis 1949:23). Also, the poor transportation network in the colonies limited the market for domestic products to the area in the immediate vicinity of the glasshouse, which was often sparsely settled and unable to consume the quantities of goods needed to support a glassmaking operation (McKearin and Wilson 1978:27). Between the years 1639 and 1725, only four other attempts were made in three American locations to establish a glassworks in the colonies. However, the chronic shortage of imported window and vessel glass in the colonies still made domestic glass manufacturing an attractive proposition. One colonist even wrote back to England in 1675 that "... glass was among the best commodities for any to carry with them" (White 1964:2). In 1629, the Reverend Francis Higginson of Salem was more direct when he wrote to friends in England, "Be sure to furnish yourselves with glass for windows" (Wilson 1969:11). The demand for glass was so high that many colonies ignored the English ban on colonial manufactures that competed with English goods and openly supported domestic glassmaking enterprises (White 1964:2; McKearin and Wilson 1978: 29). Although reports were made to the mother country regarding the unlawful manufacture of glass by American glassworks, the quality was purported to be so poor that the products of these operations were deemed not to be a serious threat to English exports. Even the wares of the famous Stiegel factory were described as "... very ordinary quality ... to ... supply the small demands of the villages and farmers in the adjacent country" (McKearin and Wilson 1978:

29–30). New Jersey's ardent Tory Governor William Franklin summed up the Crown's ambivalence toward domestic glassmaking when he reported to his father:

> The Profits made by this Work (Wistarburgh Glass Works of New Jersey) have not hitherto been sufficient it seems to induce any Persons to set up more of the like kind in this Colony ... It seems probable that notwithstanding the Duty, Fine Glass can still be imported into America cheaper than it can be made here (cited in Pepper 1971:22).

However tepid the English government's response was to the breach of the ban on domestic glass manufacturing, glass remained (alongside tea, paper, and painters' colors) as the material catalyst for fostering patriot sentiment against the growing oppression of the Crown (McKearin and Wilson 1978:30).

Other early attempts at glassmaking in America occurred at New Amsterdam during the 1650s in factories run by Everett Duycking and Johanas Smedes—in a factory near Philadelphia in 1682 under the direction of Joshua Tittery, described as a "broad glass maker" and at Salem, Massachusetts, in 1639 at a factory run by Obadiah Holmes (Watkins 1950:23; McKearin and Wilson 1978:27–28). Coincidentally, it was the aforementioned Holmes who was one of the original patentees of Monmouth County, New Jersey, and a founding member of the First Baptist church in Middletown, one of the sites included in this study (Ellis 1885:65).

By the middle of the 18th century, American glass production accelerated as a result of an increased native and immigrant population and the resultant expansion of local markets. The increased demand spurred by the growing colonial population made glassmaking once again an attractive proposition to investors toward the middle of the 18th century (Davis 1949:24). Glassmaking monopolies were granted by Connecticut (1747) and Rhode Island (1752), although the petitioners never followed through with their ventures. In 1771, the Provincial Council of Pennsylvania gave William Stiegel £150 to underwrite his glass factory located outside of Philadelphia. The sparse documentary record regarding the product lines of these factories indicates that most lines produced at least some window glass along with a wide variety of bottles (McKearin and Wilson 1978:28–30). The paucity of detailed records of production lines and quantities also impedes a determination of the broad versus crown glass output of individual glasshouses. Moreover, surviving 18th- and early-19th-century advertisements do not always indicate which type of window glass was being offered. Rather, it is just described as being window glass of a particular quality (Wilson 1976:157; McKearin and Wilson 1978:34). Although the later wave of American glasshouses was longer lived than the earlier attempts, they too failed. In 1763, Massachusetts Governor Bernard stated that "... nails, glass, lead, locks, hinges and many other materials for houses are wholly imported from Great Britain" (cited in Davis 1949:25). Thus, it was not until after the Revolution that American glassmaking became a force in the market (Davis 1949:25).

Taxes, Tariffs, and Regulations

Any discussion of the value of window glass to the evaluation and interpretation of archaeological sites must consider the legislative context of the colonial and early postcolonial period and the control exerted by England over the manufacture and importation of goods into the colonies. These regulations and taxes created an intricate web of restrictions that dictated everything from who could produce glass to what type of glass was produced (Charleston 1984:74–75). These myriad taxes and regulations illustrate that glass was recognized early as a valuable commodity that was both a luxury and a necessity, thus a perennial target of governmental tax levies. In fact, window glass was so coveted that when pirates broke into the Virginia home of Thomas Cornwall in 1652, they took all of the windows (Wilson 1976:163).

Control over the manufacture and sale of window glass extends back to medieval times. A guild of glaziers existed in London as early as 1328 and possibly before (Charleston 1984:40). The licensing of window glass factories by the Crown began in the latter part of the 16th century. One of the more prominent glassmaking families was the de Henzell family, which was producing both broad and crown glass by 1568 (Charleston 1984:71). In 1567, a member of the de Henzell family was granted a monopoly for making window glass. Part of the agreement called for the manufacturer to compensate the government for lost excise taxes on imported window glass. After 1600, this arrangement, combined with the increasing scarcity and rising costs of fuel, severely impacted the glassmakers' profits (Charleston 1984:72–73). It was around this time, that Parliament placed restrictions forbidding glasshouses from being built within a certain distance of large urban centers that were severely deforested (Charleston 1984:73). These conditions in England intensified the appeal of the resource-rich territory of the newly colonized United States.

The crisis that resulted from the dwindling supplies of wood for fuel, however, would be somewhat eased after 1612. Tests on coal-burning glass furnaces provided favorable results. In 1618, Sir Robert Mansell acquired the entire English glassmaking monopoly and began producing both broad and crown glass using furnaces fired by coal (Davis 1949:15; Charleston 1984:75). Nevertheless, Mansell was still required to pay compensation to the Crown at the rate of £1,000 per annum, which kept his operating costs prohibitively high (Charleston 1984:75). Contemporaneous with the rise of coal-burning glass furnaces in England were the nascent glasshouses of the New World. These, however, would have little or no impact on the English window glass industry. Thus, most of the window glass used in America prior to the Revolution was manufactured in England (Davis 1949:22–25). A nominal amount of window glass was imported from other European countries, namely Holland, France, and Germany (Wilson 1969:11, 1976:158). However, English tariffs, importation restrictions, and the popularity of English glass kept their share of the market small (Charleston 1984:72).

The first in a long line of excise taxes on glass was instituted in England in 1645. This called for a duty of twelve pence on every twenty shillings worth of glass produced in England (Roenke 1978:27). A century later, a duty was placed on each hundredweight of glass manufactured (Roenke 1978:27; Charleston 1984:142). By 1777 the war in America had put a tremendous strain on the English government's finances. To offset these deficits, the excise tax on glass was doubled (Wilson 1969:11). Contemporaneous with this was the tariff placed on imported glass designed to protect the English glass industry (Roenke 1978:27).

The inherent form of window glass produced by the crown method was more favorable with regard to the amount of duty being paid than glass produced by the broad method. The normally thinner crown windowpanes weighed less than the thicker broad glass panes; therefore, they were taxed less (Roenke 1978:28). Meanwhile, glass imported into America also became the target of severe taxation. British officials felt that the growing wealth of Americans was a heretofore-underutilized source of revenue for the Crown and should be exploited to help defray the costs of maintaining a military and governmental infrastructure in the colonies (McKearin and Wilson 1978:30). In 1767 the Townsend Act was passed, mainly to fill the depleted government coffers resulting from the French and Indian War (McKearin and Wilson 1978:30). The Townsend Act imposed a duty on certain goods imported into the colonies, including paper, paint, tea, and glass (Henretta et al. 1993:146). This tax was met with fierce resistance from the colonies, resulting in a very effective boycott of English goods (Henretta et al. 1993:149). The growing patriotic sentiment also helped to renew the interest in establishing glasshouses in the colonies (Davis 1949:24). The resistance eventually paid off: the Townsend Act was repealed in 1770 (Henretta et al. 1993:150).

During the 18th century, in an effort to ensure the primacy of English products in the colonies and abroad, the government imposed a ban on colonial manufactures that might compete with goods produced in the mother country. Glass was among the goods affected by the ban, which stayed in effect until the outbreak of the Revolutionary War. Enforcement of the ban, however, was sporadic at best. England simply did not have the labor or the resources to police the activities of a growing population in a vast territory 3,000 miles away (McKearin and Wilson 1978:28–29). During the Revolutionary War, the British blockade kept all imported glass from reaching American shores (Davis 1949:25–26). This was devastating to the American glass supply, as many of the existing domestic glasshouses were faced with the difficulties of cash flow and the loss of workers to the war effort (Pepper 1971:26–27; McKearin and Wilson 1978:41).

The postwar period saw the most aggressive campaign to jumpstart the lethargic domestic glass industry. The monopoly granted to the Boston Glass Manufactory was backed up with the threat of a £500 fine for any transgressions (Davis 1949:28). The State of Massachusetts went even further by paying the owners a bounty on the glass they produced as a countermeasure to the bounty paid by England on its exported glass (Davis 1949:28–29). In 1797 the State of New York devised its own procedures for aiding the local glass industry by providing a five-year exemption from taxes for the Hamilton Manufacturing Company and its workers (Davis 1949:30).

After the war, the new colonial government also instituted a number of taxes to support the national infrastructure. High taxes to pay off the wartime debt of the states led to resistance similar to that organized against England during the Revolution. Shay's Rebellion and the Whiskey Rebellion were two of the armed uprisings that responded to the new taxes (Henretta et al. 1993: 200). In 1798 the federal government became increasingly alarmed at the worsening relations with France, which appeared to be leading the two countries toward war. To prepare the country's defenses, congress authorized the Direct Tax, which also came to be known as the "glass tax" or "window tax" (O'Herron 2003:3). The Direct Tax, as it relates to glass, called for the assessing of property values based on structural measurements, building materials, the number of windows, and even the number of panes or lights in each window (Lanier and Herman 1997:347).

Colonial Window Glass

Research has demonstrated that two types of window glass were used during the colonial period: crown glass and broad, or cylinder, glass (Wilson 1969:27). Both types had been used in Europe from the 16th century into the 19th century (Dodsworth 1996:8). Although both were contemporaneous, crown glass fell out of use early in the 19th century, and broad glass remained the preferred type until the advent of flawless modern window glass during the first quarter of the 20th century (Persson 1969:4; Pepper 1971:65). Michael Owens, owner of the Toledo Glass Works, acquired the patent for and perfected the mechanized process for producing window glass during the first quarter of the 20th century (Davis 1949:184–185). The last

"handmade" sheet of window glass was produced by the Lefevre Glass Works of Bridgeton, New Jersey, in 1926 (Pepper 1971:65).

Historic documentation indicates that crown glass was the predominant type of window glass used during the colonial period in England and her colonies. Broad glass has been found in 18th-century archaeological contexts, however, and was apparently manufactured in the United States, where it is mentioned in the period documents of several American manufacturers. One reference to the production of broad glass in the U.S. comes from this excerpt from a letter written in 1754 by the clerk of the Germantown Glassworks to the proprietors: "We have about eight hundred foot of glass, stretched and cut, which I shall pack and send to Boston per the first opportunity" (Wilson 1972:44–45). "Stretching" refers to the flattening of the cylinder into window glass. This indicates that window glass was produced at Germantown using the broad or cylinder method. In fact, most window glass manufactured in the United States prior to 1780 was made using the broad or cylinder method (Wilson 1969; Starbuck 1986:9). Toward the end of the 18th century, advertisements for crown glass became more frequent throughout the colonies. However, a letter from Boston merchant Thomas Bannister to his London agent in 1701 indicates that crown glass was available earlier in the colonies. Bannister wrote that he had seen "some curious clear glass" which someone had reportedly told him was "crown glass" (cited in Carson 1994:636). He went on to say that it looked "exceedingly well" and that he had "a great mind to have one room or two glazed with that glass" (Carson 1994: 636). Factories specializing in the production of crown glass were more common in America by the end of the century, such as the Crown Glass Company, which began production in 1790. Their products were of such high quality and so well received by consumers that a second factory was erected in South Boston in 1811 to meet the demand (Wilson 1969:27–31). Although the crown method did not produce as much finished product as the broad method, it evidently was in great demand simply because of its superior clarity and durability. A glassblower who worked at the Boston Crown Glass Company stated, "the company made good and brilliant glass of a light, bluish white color that was quite thick and strong" (cited in Wilson 1976:158).

The preference for crown glass may be the result of several factors. First, the crown process produced clearer, more brilliant panes (Davies 1973:80; Starbuck 1986:9; Noël Hume 1991:235). Second, although there was technically more waste in crown glass, even the more opaque "bull's eye" panes could be used in areas where less light was required (Tunis 1965:139; Wilson 1976:152). Thus, a disk of crown glass could produce more expensive, first quality panes and less expensive, but saleable, lesser quality pieces. Finally, the demand for crown glass was apparently greater among those who could afford glass windows (Wilson 1976:156).

The broad glass method was introduced into the American glassmaking community by German glassblowers during the 18th century (Wilson 1971:12). In addition, broad glass has been identified in deposits associated with the James Wray house (1732–1750) in Williamsburg, Virginia (Davies 1973:84). Moreover, a property list from the sale of the Wistarburgh Glassworks in Allowaystown, New Jersey, in 1780 included ovens for annealing glass and flattening ovens, both essential in the production of broad glass (McKearin and Wilson 1978:33). The markets for Wistarburgh window glass were primarily Philadelphia and the Pennsylvania-German areas, surrounding New Jersey villages and, near the end of the company's existence, New York City (McKearin and Wilson 1978:33). Governor William Franklin, son of Benjamin Franklin, described the window glass produced at Wistarburgh as being, " ... a very coarse Green Glass used only in some of the houses of the poorer Sort of People ... ," suggesting that different grades of window glass were utilized by people from various economic backgrounds (Pepper 1971:22; McKearin and Wilson 1978:30).

Identifying Window Glass

The identification of window glass as to whether it was produced by the broad or crown method can only be undertaken with any degree of certainty by examination under a microscope. The processes for manufacturing crown and broad glass produce different physical attributes on the finished products, which can be identified in the

archaeological record. The process of making crown glass (Figure 1) is described by glass historian Kenneth Wilson (1972:56):

> A large bubble was blown, a pontil rod was attached opposite the blowpipe, and the blowpipe was cracked off, leaving a hole in the bubble. The bubble was then

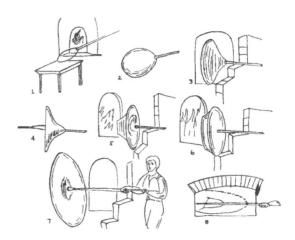

FIGURE 1. Method of crown glass production: (1) a gather is drawn onto a blow pipe; (2) the gather is blown into an elongated shape; (3) the gather is heated and spun into a bubble; (4) a punty iron is attached opposite the blow pipe; (5) the blow pipe is cracked off; (6) the bubble is reheated and rotated; (7) the rotating motion creates a disk; (8) the disk is cooled in an annealing oven (Wilson 1969:21).

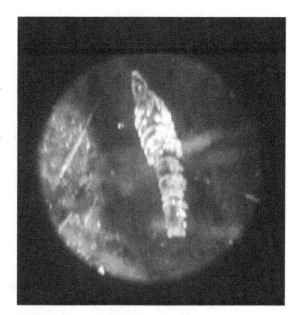

FIGURE 2. Crown glass bubble.

reheated and twirled several times so that it became flat and disk-shaped. The disk was cooled and cut into panes of glass.

The crown method resulted in imperfections, such as a "bull's eye," a raised scar where the pontil was attached, and worm-shaped bubbles shown in Figure 2, or curved stress marks, which are often only detectable under a microscope. The curved nature of the stress marks is a result of the circular spinning motion of the disk during production (Noël Hume 1991:234–235).

The cylinder or broad glass method (Figure 3) is described by Wilson (1972:46): "A cylinder about five feet long and one foot in diameter was blown; then the end was cut off, the blowpipe was cracked off, and the cylinder was slit and opened out into a flat sheet." Once opened, broad glass had to be ground and polished to smooth the surface. Fragments of broad glass often exhibit elongated, "rice-shaped" bubbles (Figure 4) that are generally oriented in the same direction, parallel to the edge of the sheet (Noël Hume 1991:234–235).

A third type of window glass, plate glass, was available as early as the late-17th century. However, plate glass was only occasionally used in windows and was more commonly used in coaches and for mirrors. The initial technique for manufacturing plate glass involved the opening of large, thick-walled cylinders. Towards the end of the 17th century, French glassmakers devised a method of casting plate glass (Charleston 1984:196). Plate glass only came into use on a significant scale in the 1830s, mainly to satisfy an increased demand for larger display windows in commercial establishments (Wilson 1976:161). Plate glass only began to be manufactured domestically in 1856 (Tunis 1965:140).

Identifying window glass without the presence of crown or broad bubbles is difficult. Given the fragmentary nature of much of the window glass recovered archaeologically, smaller fragments will not always possess discernable imperfections (Noël Hume 1991:233). In cases where no imperfections are visible, fragments from the same context that directly mend to fragments with bubbles or share other identifiable attributes, such as color or relative thickness, can safely be assigned a type/subtype designation. Otherwise, a default designation of "crown/broad" is preferable.

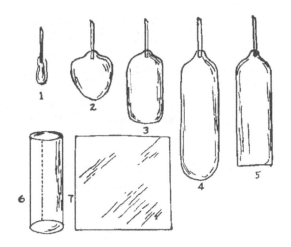

FIGURE 3. Method of broad glass production: (1) a gather is drawn onto a blow pipe; (2) the gather is blown into an elongated shape; (3–4) swinging gradually elongates the gather into an oblong cylinder; (5) the ends of the cylinder are cut off; (6) the open-ended cylinder is cut lengthwise; (7) the resulting sheet is opened (Wilson 1969:21).

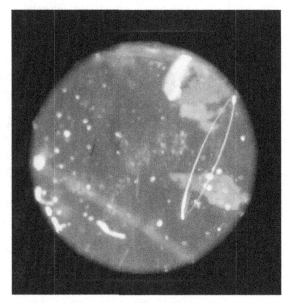

FIGURE 4. Broad glass bubble.

Color has mistakenly been used by archaeologists as an identifying characteristic for both crown and broad glass (Davies 1973:80; Noël Hume 1991:233–234). The color of glass, as illustrated by the fragments of glass scrap shown in Figure 5, is a result of impurities in the materials or the deliberate addition of metallic oxides to the batch, not a consequence of the manufacturing process (Watkins 1950:9; Tunis 1965:138;

FIGURE 5. Glass scrap fragments.

Starbuck 1986:6). In fact, the color of historic window glass may have been an indicator of the economic standing of the consumer. The quote by Franklin mentioned earlier suggests that differing grades of window glass were utilized by people on varying ends of the economic spectrum, with dark green or thicker opaque panes with poor visibility used by the lower classes, and clearer, thinner panes with better transparency used by those of more substantial means.

The thickness of window glass has also been thought to be an indicator of the method by which it was produced and the date range of its manufacture. However, the sheets produced by both the crown and broad methods will exhibit a great deal of size variability, with panes of differing thickness originating in the same sheet. This is particularly evident with crown glass, where the extreme thickness of the "bull's eye" and the relative thickness of the edge will be in marked contrast with the thin panes cut from the inner section (Noël Hume 1991:234). The inherent size variability in early window glass made the manufacture of panes of consistent, reliable thicknesses virtually impossible (Plumb 1989:995; Neumann 1996). Taphonomic conditions may also distort the size of glass in the archaeological record, with the surface exfoliating over time, often accelerating after excavations. While a number of studies have attempted to use thickness as a datable attribute (see Roenke 1978; Schoen 1990), the wide variability and unpredictability of depositional environments precludes thickness as a useful dating tool. The variability in window glass thickness is illustrated by this passage from an order sent by Thomas Hancock

of Boston in 1737, asking for "380 squares of best London crown glass, all Cutt (sic) Exactly 18 Inches long and 11 Inches wide of a Suitable Thickness to the Largeness of the Glass ..." (Wilson 1972:6). This suggests that consumers could choose from a range of glass thicknesses to suit their particular needs.

The clarity or cloudiness of a window glass fragment has also been thought to be the result of its mode of manufacture (Davies 1973:80). However, the soils and associated elements in which glass is buried will ultimately determine the condition and degree of devitrification present after recovery. The determination of which method was used to produce the glass fragments in this study was based upon the presence/absence of either rice-shaped or worm-shaped bubbles under a microscope.

Production of Window Glass

Indications of the production of broad window glass may be found in the layout of a glassmaking complex. The glassmaking operation during the 18th and early-19th centuries required the processing of large quantities of raw materials through a series of specialized structures and features encompassed in a relatively expansive manufacturing compound. Each building within the glassworks served a particular function. The pot house was where the raw materials for glass were melted down and stored for slow drying, sometimes for as long as six months. The lime shed was a simple structure used to house the lime needed as a base for the batch. The melting furnace was the center of the production process and consisted of several ovens with the melting furnace in the center. Small pots positioned under openings in the side of the furnace held the molten glass. Through these holes, the glassblower would draw a "gather" on his pipe and swing the pipe back and forth in an area at the end of the furnace called the "swing pit." This would stretch the glass into a long cylinder. For hollow wares, the glassman would blow a bubble into a mold located in the pit. Other, smaller ovens located in this building were used to dry the wood and sand or to bring pots about to be used in the furnace up to the proper temperature. Wood ash was routinely gathered and stored in a pit at the end of the building and eventually thrown into the batch.

Gerard P. Scharfenberger

The manufacture of broad window glass called for a complex different from that which produced crown glass. Glass historian Adeline Pepper (1971:60) states that a glasshouse designed to produce broad glass had to be two stories high, which was unnecessary for bottle or crown glass. At least one additional structure was also needed. A flattening house was constructed for the sole purpose of manufacturing individual window lights. This building would be needed only if window glass was produced using the broad glass method (New Jersey Pinelands Commission 1983:30). Here, cylinders produced in the melting furnace were cut lengthwise and gently rocked back and forth until the piece was flat. The finished pane was then taken to a cutting house, where the panes were cut into individual lights and packed into crates for shipment (New Jersey Pinelands Commission 1991:78–79).

Archaeological Evidence

In an effort to confirm the presence of broad glass on 17th-century sites, the following collections were analyzed. These sites are 17th- and/or 18th-century sites that have produced broad glass fragments, which were examined by the author, or, in the case of the St. John's site, data was generously provided by Henry Miller of St. Mary's City. A very conservative identification strategy was employed, resulting in the use only of fragments that possessed the visible, internal imperfections of broad and crown glass.

The Old Scots Burying Ground

The first site in this study is the Old Scots Burying Ground (28-Mo-294), located in Marlboro Township, Monmouth County, New Jersey. The site is a one-acre cemetery, owned and maintained by the Old Tennent Church of Freehold. It was settled by Scottish emigrants who were banished by the English government on religious grounds during the second half of the 17th century. The settlement of the Marlboro area of Monmouth County, which encompasses the Old Scots Burying Ground, was the result of an exodus by Scottish Presbyterians who were fleeing brutal persecution at the hands of the British monarchy. The Scottish settlers had a profound effect on the colonization and culture of New Jersey as well as on the entire middle

Atlantic region. By 1750, Scots comprised one-fifth of the central Jersey population (Landsman 1985:101). The congregation that built the Old Scots meetinghouse arrived in New Jersey in 1685. Many came as indentures and were settled in the area by John Reid, surveyor general of the state. The meetinghouse they built was purported to have been a log structure, no more than 20 ft. square. Church records indicate that the congregants arrived with few possessions and little money, which is reflected in the structural austerity of the meetinghouse (Symmes 1904).

The Old Scots Burying Ground site is notable for a number of reasons. It was the site of the first Presbyterian meetinghouse erected in the New World (ca. 1692) and was the scene of the first ordination of a Presbyterian minister in the New World—the Reverend John Boyd in 1705. Services were held at the meetinghouse until around 1750, when a larger structure, known as the Old Tennent Church, built in 1730 and renovated in 1751, became the sole house of worship for the Presbyterian congregation.

The meetinghouse was either demolished or left to decay around 1750. While there is evidence of prehistoric occupation, there were no known historic structures on the site prior to the meetinghouse. Moreover, aside from the construction of a commemorative stone monument in 1898, there were no architectural additions made to the site after the meetinghouse was abandoned. Recent excavations at the site uncovered part of the foundation of the original meetinghouse, along with a number of architectural and personal artifacts related to the structure and the congregation.

Among the recovered artifacts were several fragments of window glass. A total of 20 window glass fragments have been recovered from the site thus far. All are aqua or light green-colored broad glass. Also, all of the fragments exhibit superior clarity and show no signs of devitrification. The relatively small amount of window glass, found thus far, may be an indication of the small number of windows in the structure or the possibility that many of the windows were removed prior to the structure's demise.

The relatively short occupancy of the site precludes the existence of deeply stratified deposits. However, other diagnostic nonarchitectural artifacts were recovered from around the foundation and floor area, including fragments of a ca. 1720 glass bottle, clay pipe stem and bowl fragments, European gunflint fragments, English buff-bodied slipware, and several bone fragments. These artifacts cannot help to distinguish 17th-century contexts from 18th-century contexts but offer only relative dating for the period of use of the meetinghouse. Excavations are still ongoing; therefore, any discussion of window design or placement cannot be undertaken at present.

St. John Site, St. Mary's City

The second site in this study is the St. John's site, located in St. Mary's City, Maryland. The site was occupied from 1638 to about 1720. The building was occupied until about 1647 by Secretary John Lewger, who used it as a dwelling and office. The structure was determined to have been a substantial brick and timber building that was large by colonial standards. The exact number or form of the windows are unknown, but numerous diamond-shaped panes and square "quarrels" were recovered, indicating a lattice design with possible later repairs or a possible intricate decorative pattern formed by a combination of the two (Stone 1974:155–162). Excavations during the early 1960s exposed the foundation of a center chimney farmhouse measuring 52-ft. long by 20.5-ft. wide. Four of the features from the site, including a dairy, privy, trash pit, and cellar, produced nearly 5,000 window glass fragments. All of these are broad glass (Henry Miller 2001, personal communication). An in-depth study of the window glass by Miller (1978: 24), which included the reconstruction of numerous panes determined that the windows from the early occupation of the site were set in geometric patterns, including triangles and pentagons, while those from the later period were diamond-shaped quarrels and rectangular panes.

The occupants of the St. John's sites were obviously individuals of higher means. The substantial size of the building and the numerous windows illustrate the relatively easy access to materials that were in chronic short supply during the late-17th to early-18th centuries, particularly in areas away from urban centers. Also, when Lewger first arrived in Maryland in 1637, he brought his wife, son, and seven servants (Stone 1974:153). Other artifacts

recovered from the site, such as nonfunctional brass escutcheon plates, paste-inlaid clasps, and hand-painted delft tiles indicate an ability to acquire goods beyond mere utilitarian items (Stone 1974:162,164; Stone 1986:1).

The Old First Church

The third site in this study is the Old First Church (28-Mo-253), located in Middletown, New Jersey. The structure shown in Figure 6 was constructed in 1832. Prior to that, two previous structures stood on the site: one constructed ca. 1735 and the other dating to ca. 1688. The latter building represented the first Baptist meetinghouse erected in New Jersey. The founding members of the congregation were among the 18 Baptists who were the patentees of the Monmouth Patent land grant of 1665. Most were large landholders and several served in various capacities in the local and state governments (Scharfenberger 2000).

FIGURE 6. The present-day Old First Church, built in 1832. This is the third church structure on the site, with the first built ca. 1688 and the second built ca. 1734.

Recent excavations at the site uncovered physical evidence of the early meetinghouse, confirming its previously uncertain location. Shovel testing and unit excavations at the site, particularly in the church basement, demonstrated a clear stratigraphic chronology for the construction and subsequent demolition of the two early structures. Stratum A contained artifacts associated with the 1735 and 1832 structures, while Stratum B was determined to date prior to 1735, which encompassed the period of the first meetinghouse. Carbon-14 testing was performed on a sample of architectural wood from the site. This specimen was one of four fragments of architectural wood recovered from Stratum B in Shovel Test 13 from the church basement. This wood was found directly overlying several fragments of broad window glass and is determined to be from a context that predates the 1735 structure. In addition to the window glass and architectural wood, two sherds of English buff-bodied slipware (1670–1795) were recovered from the same context (Scharfenberger 2000).

The wood sample was tested using Radiometric-Standard delivery and provided plenty of carbon for reliable measurements. A two-sigma calendar calibration age range was calculated for this sample. Sigma, in relation to carbon dating, is the standard deviation (plus/minus) of dates for a given sample. In the case of our sample, the two sigma ranges are AD 1395 to 1530, and AD 1545 to 1635. This indicates that the wood sample is likely no younger than AD 1635 and may be substantially older. Based on this early date, it can be assumed that this wood originated in the first meetinghouse and was deposited before the second structure was erected in 1735. The result of the radiocarbon analysis is significant in that it provides a possible 17th-century date for the church basement Stratum B, using a scientific dating-method with a 95% probability rate. It should be noted that although the wood sample was dated to the early-17th century, it was likely deposited in the early-18th century when the first meetinghouse was taken down (Scharfenberger 2000).

The distribution of window glass types and quantities also differed from the western to eastern halves of the basement (Table 1). Broad glass constituted over 90% of the window glass in the western half, Stratum B, and just under 42% in the eastern half, Stratum B. Perhaps one type of better (or lesser) quality glass was preferred over the other for one side of the building. In addition, a larger quantity of window glass, 81 fragments, was recovered from Stratum B in the western half than from Stratum B in the eastern half, where 21 fragments were recovered. This may be an indication that there were a greater number of windows along the west side of the 17th-century structure than along the east side, possibly to exploit the east/west exposure (Scharfenberger and Baugher 2000).

Evidence from the Old First Church indicates that broad glass was present in substantial quantities in Stratum B, a context determined to date prior to 1735. The broad glass recovered from Stratum B came in a variety of colors, including a dark aqua (Figure 7) and various shades of green (Figure 8). All of the fragments were well preserved and exhibited superior clarity. The crown glass fragments from the same stratum, however, were characterized by a high degree of devitrification and cloudy green coloration (Figure 9). Both the broad and crown glass fragments were recovered from the church basement and were not subject to the type of harsh weather conditions and climatic extremes that would affect external deposits. Therefore, the state of the fragments in this case was likely

TABLE 1

VERTICAL DISTRIBUTION BY QUADRANT OF BROAD AND CROWN WINDOW GLASS FROM CHURCH BASEMENT, OLD FIRST CHURCH SITE

Type	SW Quadrant Stratum A	SW Quadrant Stratum B	SW Quadrant Stratum A	SE Quadrant Stratum B	Total	%
Broad	88	19	11	34	152	69.0
Crown	12	2	7	47	68	31.0
Total	100	21	18	81	220	100.0

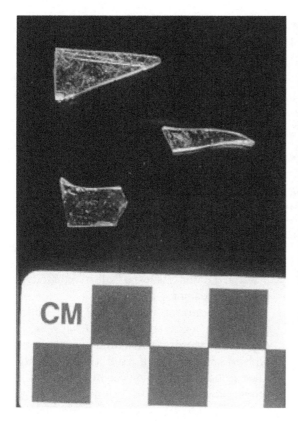

FIGURE 7. Aqua broad glass fragments from the Old First Church Site.

FIGURE 8. Green broad glass fragments from the Old First Church Site.

the result of the impurities in the batch prior to manufacture, rather than the taphonomic conditions of the basement.

Conclusion

The documentary and archaeological evidence presented in this study indicates that broad window glass was used on early-18th and possibly late-17th-century sites throughout the colonies. The sites discussed in this study have one common thread: all of the occupants had access to and utilized broad window glass during the late-17th and early-18th centuries. Interestingly, their social status ran the gamut from religious refugees and indentured servants, to upper-middle class landowners, to a wealthy public official.

The confusion over when broad window glass was available in the United States appears to stem mainly from two circumstances: the scarcity of reliable, detailed records from glasshouses during the 17th and 18th centuries and erroneous and/or ambiguous information

embedded in the documentary record. Ivor Noël Hume points out that in one early reference book, Ephraim Chamber's *Cyclopedia* published in 1728, the author describes the process for making broad glass and incorrectly calls it the crown glass process (cited in Noël Hume 1991:234). Further, it is virtually impossible to distinguish domestic window glass from European window glass in the archaeological record without chemical analysis (Starbuck 1986: 127–129) or the presence of a form known to be exclusive to one source.

Window glass production during the colonial period was not only an important component of the nascent architecture of the colonies but of the developing social and economic structure as well. The processes of manufacturing both broad and crown window glass required the services of glassblowers who were among the most sought after and well-paid artisans of their day. These individuals, many of whom were immigrants from Europe, particularly Germany and France, formed a sort of elite group of

FIGURE 9. Heavily devitrified crown glass fragments from the Old First Church Site.

artisans whose occupational structure was modeled after the craft guilds of Medieval Europe. They enjoyed a degree of autonomy rare for employees in colonial America and often moved from factory to factory as higher wages would dictate. Thus, glassmakers themselves formed a small but prominent economic force capable of deciding the ultimate success or failure of a glasshouse operation. Their products were essential to every aspect of life, from containers to tableware, to personal adornment, and, perhaps most important, to architecture. While glass products such as bottles, stemware, glass beads, and buttons have proven to provide invaluable archaeological information about a site and its occupants, the extent to which window glass can fill in the gaps of past behavior and social conditions has never been fully explored. As an analytical tool, window glass may be useful in determining the preference of the builders, the access to certain goods within a region, and possibly even the economic status of the occupants. During the 18th century, window glass in the homes of wealthy Americans was numerous and of fine quality, usually being the preferred imported window glass (Sweeney 1994:17–18). This was further evidenced by the Direct Tax (commonly called the "window tax") that was instituted in 1798, which determined that windows were a luxury item subject to taxation. Conversely, homes of the lower classes, including slaves, often had little or no window glass (Chappell 1994: 192–193). Further study into the price lists of local and foreign glass factories, the quantities and types of window glass imported into the United States, and the distribution of domestic products may provide information not only on practical issues of architectural design and material but on issues of class, ethnicity, and colonial economies as well.

Most important will be the data collected through the excavation of historic sites. The dearth of records related to many early glasshouses has created a void that can only be filled through archaeological research. With the proper identification of historic window glass and the quantification of both broad and crown window glass in archaeological assemblages, answers to questions once taken for granted or thought to be too unimportant to pursue may finally be answered.

ACKNOWLEDGMENTS

Special thanks are extended to Henry Miller and Silas Hurry of St. Mary's City for data related to the St. John's site, Garry Wheeler Stone for articles and information on the St. John's excavations, Sherene Baugher for her assistance during the Old First Church excavations, Marie-Lorraine Pipes and Nadia Maczaj for the glass bubble images, Mallory A. Gordon for reading an early draft, Rob Tucher for the spectacular artifact photos, Rick Vernay for help with the graphics, and Richard Veit for reading and commenting on the rough draft of this article. Any mistakes or omissions are of course, my own.

REFERENCES

BEDELL, JOHN, INGRID WUEBBER, META JANOWITZ, MARIE-LORRAINE PIPES, GERARD P. SCHARFENBERGER, AND CHARLES LEEDECKER
  2002   An Ordinary Family in Eighteenth-Century Delaware: Excavations at the Dawson Family Site. *Deldot Archaeology Series*, No. 161. Delaware Department of Transportation, Division of Highways Location and Environmental Studies Office, Dover.

CARSON, CARY
1994 The Consumer Revolution in Colonial British America: Why Demand? In *Of Consuming Interests: The Style of Life in the Late-Eighteenth Century,* Cary Carson, Ronald Hoffman, and Peter J. Albert, editors, pp. 483–697. University of Virginia Press, Charlottesville.

CHAPPELL, EDWARD A.
1994 Housing a Nation: The Transformation of Living Standards in Early America. In *Of Consuming Interests: The Style of Life in the Late-Eighteenth Century,* Cary Carson, Ronald Hoffman, and Peter J. Albert, editors, pp. 167–232. University of Virginia Press, Charlottesville.

CHARLESTON, R. J.
1984 *English Glass and the Glass Used in England, circa 400–1940.* George Allen and Unwin, London.

DAVIES, ISABEL
1973 Window Glass in Eighteenth-Century Williamsburg. In *Five Artifact Studies,* Ivor Noël Hume, editor, pp 78–99. The Colonial Williamsburg Foundation, Colonial Williamsburg, VA.

DAVIS, PEARCE
1949 *The Development of the American Glass Industry.* Harvard University Press, Cambridge, MA.

DODSWORTH, ROGER
1996 *Glass and Glassmaking.* Shire Album 83. Shire Publications, Ltd., Buckinghamshire, England.

ELLIS, FRANKLIN
1885 *History of Monmouth County.* R. T. Peck & Co. Philadelphia.

HENRETTA, JAMES A., W. ELLIOT BROWNLEE, DAVID BRODY, AND SUSAN WARE
1993 *America's History: Vol. 1 to 1877.* Worth, New York.

LANDSMAN, NED C.
1985 *Scotland and Its First Colony 1683–1765.* Princeton University Press, Princeton, NJ.

LANIER, GABRIELLE M., AND BERNARD L. HERMAN
1997 *Everyday Architecture of the Mid-Atlantic.* Johns Hopkins University Press, Baltimore, MD.

LEEDECKER, CHARLES H., RICHARD J. DENT, META JANOWITZ, MARIE-LORRAINE PIPES, INGRID WUEBBER, MALLORY A. GORDON, HENRY M. R. HOLT, CHRISTY ROPER, GERARD P. SCHARFENBERGER, AND SHARLA AZIZI
1997 Archaeological and Historical Investigation of the Metropolitan Detention Center Site (36 PH 91) Philadelphia, Pennsylvania. Volume I: Technical Report. Report to the U.S. Department of Justice, Federal Bureau of Prisons, Washington, DC, from Louis Berger and Associates, East Orange, NJ.

LOUIS BERGER AND ASSOCIATES, INC.
1996 *Analytical Coding System for Historic Period Artifacts.* The Cultural Resource Group, Louis Berger & Associates, Inc., East Orange, NJ. [Prepared by Sharla Azizi, Diane Dallal, Mallory A. Gordon, Meta F. Janowitz, Nadia N.S. Maczaj, and Marie-Lorraine Pipes.]

McKEARIN, HELEN, AND KENNETH M. WILSON
1978 *American Bottles and Flasks and Their Ancestry.* Crown Publishing, New York.

MIDDLE ATLANTIC ARCHAEOLOGICAL RESEARCH ASSOCIATES
1986 Data Recovery at 28-Ca-50 Gloucester City, New Jersey. Report prepared for the National Park Service, Philadelphia, PA, from the Middle Atlantic Archaeological Research Associates, Newark, DE.

MILLER, HENRY
1978 An Analysis of Window Glass and Turned Lead from the St. John's Site. Manuscript, The Department of Research, Historic St. Mary's City, St. Mary's City, MD.

MORAN, GEOFFREY P., EDWARD F. ZIMMER, AND ANNE E. YENTSCH
1982 Archaeological Excavations at the Narbonne House. *Cultural Resources Management Study,* No. 6. National Park Service, Denver Service Center, CO.

NEUMANN, FLORIN
1996 Glass: Liquid or Solid: Science vs. an Urban Legend. University of Alberta, Canada <http://www.ualberta.ca/~bderksen/florin.html>.

NEW JERSEY PINELANDS COMMISSION
1983 *Pinelands Cultural Resource Management Plan for Historic Period Sites* [Draft]. New Jersey Pinelands Commission, New Lisbon, NJ.
1991 *Pinelands Cultural Resource Management Plan for Historic Period Sites* [Final]. New Jersey Pinelands Commission, New Lisbon, NJ.

NOËL HUME, IVOR
1991 *A Guide to Artifacts of Colonial America.* Alfred A. Knopf, New York.

O'HERRON, SEAN
2003 *The 1798 Direct Tax in New Jersey as a Study in Local Architecture.* Manuscript, Monmouth University, Long Branch, NJ.

PEPPER, ADELINE
1971 *The Glass Gaffers of New Jersey and Their Creations from 1739 to the Present.* Charles Scribner's Sons, New York.

PERSSON, RUNE
1969 *Flat Glass Technology.* Plenum Press, New York.

PLUMB, R. C.
1989 Antique Windowpanes and the Flow of Supercooled Liquids. *Journal of Chemical Education,* 66(12): 994–996.

ROENKE, KARL G.
1978 Flat Glass: Its Use as a Dating Tool for Nineteenth-Century Sites in the Pacific Northwest and Elsewhere. *Northwest Anthropological Research Notes,* Memoir No. 4. University of Idaho, Moscow.

SCHARFENBERGER, GERARD P.
2000 The Baptists of New Jersey: An Ethnoarchaeological Study of New Jersey's Earliest Congregation. Masters Thesis, Hunter College, New York.

SCHARFENBERGER, GERARD P., AND SHERENE BAUGHER
2000 Preliminary Archaeological Report on the Old First Church Site, Middletown, New Jersey. *Bulletin of the Archaeological Society of New Jersey,* 55:44–56.

SCHOEN, CHRISTOPHER M.
1990 Window Glass on the Plains: An Analysis of Flat Glass Samples from Ten Nineteenth-Century Plains Historic Sites. *Central Plains Archaeology,* 2(1):57–90.

STARBUCK, DAVID R.
1986 The New England Glassworks: New Hampshire's Boldest Experiment in Early Glassmaking. *The New Hampshire Archeologist,* 27(1):6–129.

STONE, GARRY WHEELER
1974 St. John's: Archaeological Questions and Answers. *Maryland Historical Magazine,* 69(2):146–168.
1986 Seventeenth-Century Wall Tile from St. Mary's City Excavations 1971–1986. *St. Mary's City Research Series,* No. 3. Historic St. Mary's City, MD.

SWEENEY, KEVIN M.
1994 High-Style Vernacular: Lifestyles of the Colonial Elite. In *Of Consuming Interests: The Style of Life in the Eighteenth Century,* Cary Carson, Ronald Hoffman, and Peter J. Albert, editors, pp. 1–58. University of Virginia Press, Charlottesville.

SYMMES, WILLIAM
1904 *History of the Old Tennent Church.* George W. Burroughs, Cranbury, NJ.

TUNIS, EDWIN
1965 *Colonial Craftsmen and the Beginnings of American Industry.* World Publishing Co., New York.

WATKINS, LURA WOODSIDE
1950 *American Glass and Glassmaking.* Cracker Barrel, Southampton, New York.

WHITE, MARGARET E.
1964 *The Decorative Arts in Early New Jersey.* D. Van Nostrand Co., New York.

WILSON, BUDD
1971 The Batsto Window Light Factory Artifacts. *Bulletin of the Archeological Society of New Jersey,* 27:11–18.

WILSON, KENNETH M.
1969 *Glass in New England.* Old Sturbridge Booklet Series. Old Sturbridge, Inc., Sturbridge, MA.
1972 *New England Glass and Glassmaking.* Thomas Y. Crowell Co., New York.
1976 Window Glass in America. In *Building Early America,* Charles E. Peterson, editor, pp. 150–164. Astragal Press, Mendham, NJ.

GERARD P. SCHARFENBERGER
THE LOUIS BERGER GROUP
120 HALSTED STREET
EAST ORANGE, NJ 07019

A Comparison and Review of Window Glass Analysis Approaches in Historical Archaeology

Jonathan Weiland

ABSTRACT

The measurement of the thickness of window glass to determine relative dates for historic-structure sites has been practiced by historical archaeologists for 40 years, yet much could be done to understand this research technique better. A number of different approaches to analysis exist, each with its own strictures, date ranges, and regions of application. For this study six of these methods were reviewed, compared, and tested on eight historic window glass collections in an attempt to reduce confusion on the topic and provide researchers with a tool for choosing the most appropriate method.

Introduction

Window glass, by its shear ubiquity at historic sites, deserves attention as a potential source of valuable dating information. Window glass analysis constitutes a serious attempt to make use of that resource. Despite the long application of this technique, the results of window glass analyses are often considered to have dubious legitimacy. Much of the problem stems from a lack of information or an investigator not knowing more recent and sophisticated methods. In recognition of these challenges, this article has three goals: first, to explain briefly the premise of window glass analysis and why it is believed to work; second, to compare concisely six methods developed for conducting window glass analysis; and third, to present the practical insights gained by testing those methods so that archaeologists can evaluate the utility of window glass analysis, or at the very least, better understand the results of window glass analyses they find in the reports of other investigators.

Window Glass Analysis

Window glass analysis is a process of determining a *relative* initial construction date for historic structures in North America by recording the thickness of the window glass—produced by the cylinder glass manufacturing technique—found on location and then analyzing the resulting data in modes, or by inserting the mean of the thickness data into a regression formula. The process of conducting window glass analysis involves using a micrometer to measure the thickness of a sample of window pane fragments and recording other information pertinent to the method of window glass analysis being employed.

This dating method is thought to work because during the first part of the 19th century the process of window glass production called cylinder glass became the predominant method of window glass manufacture (Davis 1949), and this form of window glass became gradually thicker over the next 70 to 100 years.

Although there were variations in the process, in general these steps were followed: A skilled laborer produced a long cylinder of glass by blowing a molten ball of glass, or "gather," into a sphere and "swinging" the molten glass into a cylinder shape. The ends of the cylinder were cut off and the cylinder was cut along its length while the glass was still semi-malleable. The resulting large curved pane was then flattened, cooled, and cut into smaller panes (Douglas and Frank 1972). What later proved serendipitous for archaeologists was that this manufacturing technique produced glass of highly uniform thickness. The manufacturing technique popular immediately prior to cylinder glass, often referred to as crown glass, does not produce a pane of glass uniform in thickness across a sheet.

As the 19th century progressed, Americans wanted larger and larger window panes. Larger windows necessitated thicker glass (Roenke 1978). As a result, cylinder glass increased in thickness steadily, if not uniformly. This thickening continued until as late as the first few decades of the 20th century. After that time, skilled laborers were almost completely replaced by machine production (Douglas and Frank 1972) and the thickness of glass was

Table 1. Flat Glass Method Comparison.

	Walker 1971	Chance & Chance 1976	Roenke 1978	Ball 1982	Moir 1983	Schoen 1990
Mean/Mode	Mode	Mode	Mode	Mean	Mean	Mean
Increment of Measure	1/64 in.	1/1000 in.	1/1000 in.	1/2 mm	1/100 mm	1/1000 in.
Region of Application	Undefined	Kanaka Village	Pacific Northwest	Ohio Valley	South and Northeast U.S.	U.S. Plains
Number of Sites	10	1	15	5	45	10
Minimum Sample Size	Undefined	37	78	256	15–20 minimum, >30 suggested	50
Date Range	Pre-1820 post-1845	1830–1900	1810–1915	1800–1870	1810–1920	1800–1900

more or less standardized at 3.0 to 3.3 mm (Walker 1971; Moir 1987).

A side-by-side comparison reveals a great deal of variation among the approaches to window glass analysis (Table 1). The time period for which window glass analysis is useful is not free of variation, but the time frame roughly mirrors the adoption of cylinder glass as the dominant form of window glass manufacturing until the technique's ultimate replacement by lubber machines in the first quarter of the 20th century. Table 2 illustrates that employing different window glass techniques with identical thickness data will produce different initial construction dates. Archaeologists studying window glass recognized the difference in thickness-to-date correlation and attributed the slight variations in thickness to regional differences (Chance and Chance 1976; Moir 1987; Schoen 1990) in the glass industry and site socioeconomic factors (Moir 1987; Schoen 1990). Different regions had cylinder glass introduced and popularized at different times, architectural styles in some areas possibly lagged in the adoption of larger window panes, and glass manufacturing did not develop at set rates or uniformly across North America.

Window Glass Dating Methods

An extensive search for methods of window glass analysis found six approaches. The methods considered in this study can be divided into two groups, the earlier "modal methods" and the later "mean methods." The modal methods were developed by Walker (1971), Chance and Chance (1976),

and Roenke (1978). Modal methods utilize a histogram compiled by assigning each sample to a mode determined by a range of thicknesses; each mode then correlates with a range of dates. The mean methods, by Ball (1982), Moir (1987), and Schoen (1990), insert the mean value of all viable samples into a regression formula and produce a number that represents a relative date for site construction.

The six methods are in many respects unique, but they can all be compared by their general criteria: the number of sites used to develop the method, how the data were collected, and how that data were used to provide an initial construction date. It should be noted that the window glass analysis methods reviewed here do not represent every window glass analysis technique; at least three others exist.

Associated with each brief description of the methods are tables that help describe the methods. The intention of these tables is to provide a straightforward means of evaluating the methods side by side according to a number of attributes.

Testing the Methods

To test the six methods for window glass analysis, glass assemblages from eight sites were evaluated according to each method's instructions, with the goal of better understanding the techniques and potentially eliminating unnecessary methodological steps and strictures. The collections from eight sites (Table 3) were selected on the basis of their previously determined dates, the availability of the collections, and because they represent a diversity of geographic and cultural contexts. Rather than conduct-

Table 2. Arbitrary Dating Results of Methods by Thickness.

0.01mm	0.001 in.	1/64 in.	Walker 1971	Chance & Chance 1976	Roenke 1978	Ball 1982	Moir 1983	Schoen 1990
0.75	0.030	2	<1845					
0.80	0.031	3	<1845					
0.85	0.033	3	<1845					
0.90	0.035	3	<1845					
0.95	0.037	3	<1845					
1.00	0.039	3	<1845			1800.0		
1.05	0.041	3	<1845			1801.7		
1.10	0.043	3	<1845			1803.5		1799.9
1.15	0.045	3	<1845	1830–1840	1820–1835,1835–1845	1805.2	1809.6	1803.3
1.20	0.047	4	>1845	1830–1840	1820–1835,1835–1845	1807.0	1813.8	1806.6
1.25	0.049	4	>1845	1830–1840	1820–1835,1835–1845	1808.7	1818.0	1810.0
1.30	0.051	4	>1845	1830–1840	1820–1835,1835–1845	1810.5	1822.2	1813.4
1.35	0.053	4	>1845	1830–1840	1820–1835,1835–1845	1812.2	1826.4	1816.7
1.40	0.055	4	>1845	1835–1845	1810–1825,1820–1835,1835–1845	1814.0	1830.6	1820.1
1.45	0.057	4	>1845	1835–1845	1810–1825,1820–1835,1835–1845	1815.7	1834.8	1823.5
1.50	0.059	4	>1845	1835–1845	1810–1825,1820–1835,1835–1845	1817.5	1839.0	1826.9
1.55	0.061	4	>1845	1835–1845	1810–1825,1820–1835,1835–1845	1819.2	1843.2	1830.2
1.60	0.063	5	>1845	1835–1845	1810–1825,1820–1835,1835–1845	1821.0	1847.5	1833.6
1.65	0.065	5	>1845	1840–1850	1845–1855	1822.7	1851.7	1837.0
1.70	0.067	5	>1845	1840–1850	1845–1855	1824.5	1855.9	1840.3
1.75	0.069	5	>1845	1840–1850	1845–1855	1826.2	1860.1	1843.7
1.80	0.071	5	>1845	1840–1850	1845–1855	1828.0	1864.3	1847.1
1.85	0.073	5	>1845	1840–1850	1845–1855	1829.7	1868.5	1850.5
1.90	0.075	5	>1845	1850–1860	1850–1865	1831.5	1872.7	1853.8
1.95	0.077	5	>1845	1850–1860	1850–1865	1833.2	1876.9	1857.2
2.00	0.079	6	>1845	1850–1860	1850–1865	1835.0	1881.1	1860.6
2.05	0.081	6	>1845	1850–1860	1850–1865	1836.7	1885.4	1864.0
2.10	0.083	6	>1845	1850–1860	1850–1865	1838.5	1889.6	1867.3
2.15	0.085	6	>1845	1855–1885	1855–1885	1840.2	1893.8	1870.7
2.20	0.087	6	>1845	1855–1885	1855–1885	1842.0	1898.0	1874.1
2.25	0.089	6	>1845	1855–1885	1855–1885	1843.7	1902.2	1877.4
2.30	0.091	6	>1845	1855–1885	1855–1885	1845.5	1906.4	1880.8
2.35	0.093	6	>1845	1855–1885	1855–1885	1847.2	1910.6	1884.2
2.40	0.094	7	>1845	1855–1885	1855–1885	1849.0	1914.8	1887.6
2.45	0.096	7	>1845	1870–1990	1870–1990	1850.7	1919.0	1890.9
2.50	0.098	7	>1845	1870–1990	1870–1990	1852.4	1923.3	1894.3
2.55	0.100	7	>1845	1870–1990	1870–1990	1854.2		1897.7
2.60	0.102	7	>1845	1870–1990	1870–1990	1855.9		1901.0
2.65	0.104	7	>1845	1870–1990	1870–1990	1857.7		
2.70	0.106	7	>1845		1900–1915	1859.4		
2.75	0.108	7	>1845		1900–1915	1861.2		
2.80	0.110	8	>1845		1900–1915	1862.9		
2.85	0.112	8	>1845		1900–1915	1864.7		
2.90	0.114	8	>1845		1900–1915	1866.4		
2.95	0.116	8	>1845			1868.2		
3.00	0.118	8	>1845			1869.9		
3.05	0.120	8	>1845			1871.7		
3.10	0.122	8	>1845					
3.15	0.124	8	>1845					
3.20	0.126	9	>1845					

Jonathan Weiland

Table 3. Tested Sites.

	Location	Total Pieces of Glass (n)	Documented Occupation Dates	Site Type
Bailey Brick House	Chesterton, Indiana	1,717	1800–present	Domestic structure
Boston House (33SU270)	Boston County, Ohio	1,747	1836–present	General store
Burch Lot (13SG1328)	Springfield, Illinois	161	1840–1900	Domestic structure
Carrigan Lot (13SG1327)	Springfield, Illinois	115	1840–1880	Domestic structure
Freeman School (25GA90)	Gage County, Nebraska	13	1870–present	School
Freeman Cabin (25GA91)	Gage County, Nebraska	29	1800–?	Homestead cabin
Lawnfield	Mentor, Ohio	1,045	1800–present	Domestic structure
Miller House (11SG1318)	Springfield, Illinois	215	1800–present	Domestic structure

Table 4. Thickness Analysis Results.

	Walker 1971	Chance & Chance 1976	Roenke 1978	Ball 1982	Moir 1983	Schoen 1990
Bailey Brick House	Post-1845	1870–1900	1870–1900	1854.93	1903.95	1883.87
Boston House (33SU270)	Pre-1845	1850–1860	1850–1865	1850.94	1909.05	1889.45
Burch Lot (13SG1328)	Post-1845	1850–1860	1850–1865	1853.90	1902.34	1877.55
Carrigan Lot (13SG1327)	Post-1845	1835–1845	1850–1870	1831.92	1857.71	1839.07
Freeman School (25GA90)	Post-1845	1870–1900	1870–1900	1804.69	1869.79	1866.63
Freeman Cabin (25GA91)	Post-1845	1855–1885	1855–1885	1864.27	1903.64	1900.97
Lawnfield	Post-1845	1870–1900	1870–1900	1843.99	1888.15	1861.65
Miller House (11SG1318)	Post-1845	1870–1900	1870–1900	1834.59	1855.69	1843.69

ing six tests on each of the eight sites, the data from all the methods were collected in a database once, and that database was filtered according to the strictures for each of the six methods (Table 4).

A problem is immediately obvious to anyone familiar with this dating technique. As previously mentioned, most window glass analysis methods are explicitly designed for certain non-overlapping regions of the United States. Some of the sites used in this comparison also violate other strictures, such as the Schoen and Moir method requirement to exclude structures from upper socioeconomic-class sites. Such violations are unavoidable, as the site selection criteria for these methods make it impossible for a single site to be viable for all methods. This means that the results from this testing of dating techniques have questionable legitimacy when it comes to reviewing the overall accuracy of the methods. Nonetheless, this approach allowed for a comparative review of how the methods differ in a number of aspects,

such as sample size, the effectiveness of strictures, and to a certain extent, how time-consuming the methods are.

In addition to the brief discussion of each method, a table is supplied to present pertinent information in order to provide an easy basis for comparisons of how each method of window glass analysis is conducted. In some cases, especially with older methods, it is entirely possible that all the details of the investigation were not explicit in the original study. Nevertheless the studies were presented in identical format even if they were written in a way that did not lend them to this process. These tables are no substitute for reviewing the entire reports by the various authors.

Walker

Published in 1971, Walker's window glass study (Table 5) is the earliest reviewed in this article, and is referenced by later investigators as the original attempt to create a

Table 5. Walker Method, 1971.

Mean/Mode	Mode	
Applicable Date Ranges	1800 to post-1845	
Number of Sites Used to Produce Method	10	
Location of Sites	Arkansas, Arizona, North Dakota, South Dakota, Texas, Virginia	
Increment and Number of Measurements	1/64 in.; 1 measurement per piece assumed (unstated)	
Region of Application	Southeast Arkansas (Arkansas Post Bank), thickness data taken from 8 sites around the country (North Dakota, South Dakota, Virginia, Arizona, Texas)	
Sample Sizes	Arkansas collection, 384 pieces; The sample sizes from the additional sites are not listed	
Strictures and Exclusions	Window glass 6/64 in. and thicker was considered too thick to be window glass; Modern window glass was determined to be 8/64 in. (3.175 mm) and thicker; Partially melted and warped glass was still measured for thickness	
Data Processing	Take the thickness data collected from each piece of glass and compile histogram; Take the first major mode of thickness and evaluate that mode according the Walker timescale	
Dating Scale	**2/64 in. (0.794 mm)**	Sites occupied by 1820 and no longer occupied by 1840
	3/64 in. (1.191 mm)	Sites built or occupied prior to 1845
	4/64 in. (1.587 mm) or greater	Sites dating after 1845
	6/64 in. (2.381 mm)	Thickness exceeds historic context
	8/64 in. (3.175 mm) or greater	Modern glass thickness

window glass dating method (Roenke 1978; Moir 1983; Schoen 1990). The analysis is only a small part of a larger report on the excavations at the Arkansas Post Branch Bank in southeast Arkansas; in fact the topic of window glass is covered in just two pages. Due to the brevity of the write-up, many details found in other window glass studies are not available in Walker's study.

Little can be stated specifically about the Walker method as a result of the present study. In every test the dating scheme accurately showed a great deal of activity after 1845, but the modal distribution of glass for all eight of the tested sites was more complex than the sample collected by Walker, and there are no clear directions on how to adjust for this complexity. The Walker method also includes glass that would almost certainly be excluded by later methods of window glass analysis. Half the samples were partially melted or warped by fire to an undefined degree. Melted and warped glass was measured for thickness while evaluating the methods, and those pieces of glass varied in thickness noticeably as a result of being burned.

The significance of Walker's work is not in the sophistication of his techniques, but the pioneering aspect of his investigation. His three-mode scale was groundbreaking work upon which other archeologists expanded.

Chance and Chance

David and Jennifer Chance published a window glass dating method in 1976 as an appendix to an excavation report, *Kanaka Village Vancouver Barracks 1974*. The Chance and Chance method (Table 6) is also a modal method describing one large site, Fort Vancouver/Kanaka Village, which is split into 12 assemblages from both structures and strata within the site. This site provided an excellent opportunity to illustrate the gradual increase in glass thickness over time because of two factors: the site's strata were relatively undisturbed, and the large multistructure site probably received most of its glass through bulk orders from distant manufacturers, resulting in considerable continuity in glass thickness across the site.

Table 6. Chance & Chance Method, 1976.

Mean/Mode	Mode	
Applicable Date Range	1830 to 1900	
Number of Sites Used to Produce Method	1 site (12 assemblages)	
Location of Sites	Kanaka Village, southwest Washington	
Increment and Number of Measurement	1/1000 in.; 1 measurement (assumed)	
Region of Application	Pacific Northwest	
Sample Sizes	Sample sizes range from 37 to 378 pieces of window glass	
Strictures and Exclusions	Smallest sample size given is 37 pieces, the largest is 378 pieces; Test the entirety of smaller collections; It is acceptable to subsample larger collections, no specific area (i.e., structure outline, privy, etc.) is mentioned as most valuable for subsampling	
Data Processing	Distribute glass measurements into 0.005 in. modes and compare with dating scale; The primary mode is the likely date of construction; Secondary and tertiary modes may represent repairs or modification	
Dating Scale	0.045 in. (1.143 mm)	1830–1840
	0.055 in. (1.397 mm)	1835–1845
	0.065 in. (1.651 mm)	1840–1850
	0.075 in. (1.905 mm)	1850–1860
	0.085 in. (2.159 mm)	1855–1885
	0.095 in. (2.413 mm)	1870–1900

One of the strengths of the Chance and Chance modal method is that the results are based on the primary mode. The use of a primary mode to determine a site construction date results in a "built-in" filter for the occasional piece of misidentified bottle glass, mirror fragment, or any window glass of unusual thickness. This study provides clear evidence that glass does indeed get thicker over time at a fairly consistent rate, but given that window glass analysis is a regional dating method and this is a study of one site, later window glass analysis methods probably represent more viable options for archaeologists.

Roenke

Roenke's 1978 method (Table 7) was developed as the focus of an extensive study of window glass, with sections describing historical methods of window manufacturing, and explanations of glass color and chemical composition. This method was developed on a much larger scale then

prior investigations, using 21,965 pieces of glass from 15 different sites. The Roenke method and the Chance and Chance method bear strong resemblances to one other. This is unsurprising since Roenke included the data from Kanaka Village in developing his chronology and often references the work of David and Jennifer Chance in his publication.

Roenke's report also gave extensive instruction on conducting window glass analysis, and was the first to have a complex sampling strategy. The Roenke method is also the first to advocate the analysis of means and median values—dealing with every collected piece of window glass—as a tool for evaluating a site's reuse.

The assemblages tested by the Roenke method showed modal distributions nearly identical to those of the Chance and Chance method. This similarity is probably due to the two methods use of the same relatively broad increments of measurement and modal divisions. The strong similarity also indicates that measuring each piece three times,

Table 7. Roenke Method, 1978.

Mean/Mode	Mode	
Applicable Date Range	1810 to 1915	
Number of Sites Used to Produce Method	15	
Location of Sites	13 in Washington, 2 in the Idaho panhandle	
Increment and Number of Measurements	1/1000 in., with a Fowler dial gauge micrometer; 3 for each piece, once at each end, and once in the middle; The middle value was used in the modal representation	
Region of Application	Pacific Northwest	
Sample Sizes	Sample sizes range from 78 to 5,819 pieces of glass	
Strictures and Exclusions	Sampling approaches will be dictated by site: Small collections should be sampled entirely whenever possible; Larger collections can be subsampled by randomly selecting glass from each arbitrary or stratigraphic level; Largest collections can be sampled by testing all pieces excavated from specific structures, and selection should consider the excavation techniques employed at those structures	
Data Processing	Distribute glass measurements into 0.005 in. modes and compare with dating scale; The primary mode is the likely date of construction; Secondary and tertiary modes may represent repairs or modification; Augment dating with research into other cultural material, and historical research; Use mean and median with mode and distribution of thickness to consider difference between sites; Means can be used as a single number value for sites with smaller collections	
Dating Scale	0.055 in. (1.397 mm)	1810–1825
	0.055 in. (1.397 mm)	1820–1835
	0.045 in. (1.143 mm)	1830–1840
	0.045–0.055 in. (1.43 mm –1.397 mm)	1835–1845
	0.065 in. (1.651 mm)	1845–1855
	0.075 in. (1.905 mm)	1850–1865
	0.085 in. (2.159 mm)	1855–1885
	0.095 in. (2.413 mm)	1870–1900
	0.105 in. (2.667 mm)	1900–1915

as opposed to just once for the Roenke method, does not have a significant impact on the results. This was the only example of a method's strictures being ignored without skewing the final results. The dates that the two approaches produced are not similar, however, because Roenke adjusted the chronological scale *after* adding the data from 14 other sites.

The Roenke method subsampling criteria for large collections is to select opaque bags of window glass from each stratigraphic layer rather than testing the entire collection of glass. This method could not be reproduced, since collections for this study were sorted and stored in transparent bags, and Roenke based his random selection approach on the fact that his window glass was stored in opaque bags. It was possible, however, to use a random selection function in the measurement database to reduce the sample size of each stratigraphic layer by roughly 75%, and the results from the reduced sample were virtually unchanged.

Ball

Ball's work is a more recent approach to window glass analysis (Table 8), in which the mean value of window glass thickness is inserted into a regression formula to produce a relative date. His study also touched on dating glass by color and published the BASIC program code for applying the method's regression formula.

No great insights resulted from the testing of the Ball method; it does not have a complex sampling model or any strictures, aside from suggesting that 3 mm thick glass is modern glass. Given the previously mentioned problems with cross-testing the accuracy of the various methods, the Ball method often produced dates significantly different from the other methods.

The Ball method, like the Walker method, represents an early attempt at a new process. Ball, in his report, welcomed further development of window glass analysis and accurately predicted that both modification and refinement were inevitable.

Moir

Moir, who has written extensively on this topic (Moir 1982, 1983, 1987), in producing his method of window glass analysis, utilized the largest number of sites, two regions with "essentially the same relationship between thickness and time" (Moir 1987), and a rigorous set of strictures. The Moir method (Table 9) places emphasis on reducing the sample size to include only glass that is reliably window glass. Another important aspect of the Moir method is that it was intentionally developed to exclude sites containing upper-class structures, since those sites tended to have thicker window glass due to larger window panes and were more likely to use more expensive "double thickness" glass. The higher level of sampling complexity stipulated by the Moir method reflects the greater necessity with mean window glass analysis methods of efforts to eliminate samples that would produce erroneous results.

The many strictures of the Moir method permit a large reduction in the amount of glass measurement necessary for analysis, which in turn reduces the time investment for conducting the experiment. Also, the testing showed that the strictures set forth in the Moir method are reliable ways to exclude flat glass that is not window glass. The collections used to conduct the current test were already separated into bags by artifact type, but the Moir method strictures still identified many pieces of glass that were not window glass. Two strictures were specifically useful: laying the glass on a flat surface and attempting to "rock" it to determine if the glass is actually slightly curved, and closely inspecting glass that is pink and perfectly clear for signs the artifact is not window glass.

Table 8. Ball Method, 1982.

Mean/Mode	Mean
Applicable Date Range	1800 to 1870
Number of Sites Used to Produce Method	5 sites, 1 thickness date estimate borrowed from the Roenke method (Ohio site used to establish modern glass thickness)
Location of Sites	2 in Kentucky, 1 in Alabama, 1 in Arkansas, 1 in Ohio
Increment and Number of Measurements	0.5 mm; Number of measurements unreported, assumed to be 1
Region of Application	Ohio Valley
Sample Sizes	1 sample reported (Linville Kentucky), 256 pieces
Strictures and Exclusions	No stated exclusions; 3.0 mm thickness represents modern glass
Data Processing	Averaged thickness data from each piece of measured glass and inserted value into Ball regression formula
Dating Equation	Date $= [(M - 1.00 \text{ mm}) / 0.0286] + 1800$ where $M =$ mean thickness in 0.5 mm

Table 9. Moir Method, 1982.

Mean/Mode	Mean
Applicable Date Range	1810 to 1920
Number of Sites Used to Produce Method	45
Location of Sites	South and northeast U.S., Texas
Increment of Measurement	0.01 mm; 1 measurement (assumed)
Region of Application	South and northeast U.S., many sites in Texas
Sample Sizes	15 to 20 pieces of glass can produce viable results, above 30 pieces is recommended for reliable results; Largest sample noted was 659 pieces

Strictures and Exclusions	Select best possible context of glass from site, as opposed to seeking larger samples:
	     Foundation lines are best;
	     Scatters immediately next to walls are acceptable;
	 Only when glass from foundation lines or in scatters next to walls is not available should other glass be used;
	 Exclude glass from trash pits;
	 Confirm the structure was built after 1800 and before 1920;
	 Confirm the glass is flat by placing the glass on a flat surface and attempting to "rock" it back and forth by placing light pressure on opposite edges;
	 Confirm the glass is flat by letting light play across it;
	 Make sure the sample is window glass by eliminating potential bottle glass, mirror, or decorative glass shards:
	     Confirm glass is actually flat on both surfaces;
	     Confirm that glass bears no ripple marks which would indicate it was made in a bottle mold;
	     Confirm glass shards do not have beveled edges which would indicate the glass was decorative;
	     Confirm glass does not have silver backing indicating it is from a mirror;
	     Closely inspect glass that is pink or perfectly clear as it has a high probability of not being window glass;
	 Discard data when all pane thicknesses are greater than 3.2 mm

Data Processing	Collect measurements from a subsample of site according to sampling criteria, average all the values and insert that value in place of the *TH* variable in Moir's regression formula
Dating Formula	$ID = 84.22\,(TH) + 1712.7$ where ID = date of site construction (± 7 years) TH = thickness in 0.01 mm

Schoen

The final and most recent study explored is a mean method of window glass analysis for the Plains region of the U.S. The Schoen method (Table 10) was developed with the advantage of access to already-established window glass analysis techniques, as the methodology of the Schoen method reflects. The Moir method specifically was crucial in developing Schoen's method, as one of the Schoen's stated goals was to test Moir's research.

Testing Schoen's method with the additional data collected for this research provided valuable insights. Schoen's method dictates that only pieces with an edge longer than one inch be measured, and that those pieces be measured three times. These strictures reduce the size of the sample and have a profound effect on the final mean of the glass samples. Of the 5,032 window glass samples measured in the research for the current study, only 45% of those samples (2,283) were greater than one inch in diameter. Pieces larger than 1 in. were also thicker, by about 0.011 in.

Table 10. Schoen Method, 1990.

Mean/Mode	Mean
Applicable Date Range	1800 to 1900
Number of Sites Used to Produce Method	10, all thickness data was collected for this investigation
Location of Sites	6 sites in Nebraska, 3 in North Dakota, 1 in South Dakota
Increment of Measurement	0.001 in., with Starett micrometer
Region of Application	"Plains Region"
Sample Sizes	Schoen used no sample smaller than 100 shards; Samples that were large (large, e.g., is 3,000 pieces) were sampled by arbitrarily selecting opaque bags from each stratigraphic layer at a site; Bags selected from each arbitrary or stratigraphic level randomly; 50 shards is suggested as a viable minimum sample

Strictures and Exclusions	Four site selection criteria:
	     Sites must be from the central and northern Plains;
	     Sites must represent lower- or middle-class occupations, or be utilitarian in nature (trading posts, forts, stage stations);
	     Sites must have been a short-term occupation;
	     Sites must be 19th century;
	 Whenever possible, collect sample from foundation lines associated with the initial construction and occupation of a site;
	 Measure pieces of glass that are longer than 1 in. along the longest axis;
	 Three measurements are made for each piece of glass;
	 Measure thickness to 0.001 in.;
	 Exclude trash dumps and privies as sources of window glass if at all possible

Data Processing	Take three thickness measurements along the longest axis of artifact, then average them into a single value; Average the mean value of each piece of glass into a single value for the entire assemblage; Insert the assemblage mean value into the Schoen method linear regression formula to predict the date of the initial construction/occupation of the site; Also record and consider the mode and median data from the site data as a means of evaluating reconstructions and refurbishments
Dating Equation	$Y = 1725.7 + 1713.0 \,(X)$ where X = thickness in 0.001 in. Y = initial occupation date (± 6.2 years)

This seemingly small difference in thickness would result in a dating difference of 18.22 years if applied to Schoen's formula. Consequently, Schoen's formula should not be applied to samples with an edge less than one inch in length.

Discussion

The investigation into the various window glass analysis methods produced a number of insights that should help historical archaeologists conduct similar research, or at the very least better understand and evaluate the results of window glass analysis if they are present in older investigation reports.

There are many situations in which window glass analysis, if done properly, can make a useful contribution to an archaeological investigation. Window glass is a common and durable artifact type, and in the event of a paucity of other chronological indicators window glass analysis can provide some results inexpensively. The process is especially useful on low-income, short-occupation structure sites, but can provide valuable data in other circumstances, such as providing a relative construction date for small structures at sites that lack documentation, or for out-buildings (of historic structures) that may not be noted in records. Also, while the dating accuracy of window glass analysis is less reliable on sites outside a region where a study took place, the methods provide excellent criteria for identifying window glass and collecting glass thickness data. Thickness data can be used to help determine the temporal relationships between closely related sites or structures without the benefits of a dating scheme.

Properly assessing the results of window glass analysis requires an understanding of the weaknesses inherent in this research technique. It became evident to many of archaeologists who studied window glass that thickness varied slightly by region (Roenke 1978; Moir 1987; Schoen 1990). There are several possible explanations for this regional variance but no present technique for how to adjust the methods or results from those methods so that utilizing a dating method outside of the region where it was developed will not skew the results.

The length of time a site was occupied is another serious consideration for window glass analysis. Short occupations are best since they are less likely to result in replacements of panes and the introduction of thicker glass to the site. Sometimes introduction of new window glass caused by renovation events can be seen in modal distributions, but the gradual replacement of windows as they are broken under normal circumstances would result in glass of multiple thicknesses with no clear second mode. The mean methods are not designed to cope with these later introductions of window glass.

Window glass can also be easily confused with a number of other sources of flat glass: mirrors, decorative glass, flat panel bottles, etc. Identifying and excluding flat glass that is not window glass is especially important for methods that rely on mean measurements rather than modes. Chance and Chance took time to mention in brief that their dating technique was developed and dependent on the assumption that the glass used on the Kanaka Village site was not recycled from earlier structures, but manufactured and purchased at a date very contemporary with the construction of Fort Vancouver. The likelihood of recycled window panes is difficult to estimate but certainly possible. This problem can be understood as a form of deposition lag. Finally, window glass analysis is, like many other relative dating methods, best used in concert with other dating

methods such as bottle manufacturing methods, ceramic styles, dated marks, and documentary information, rather than by itself.

Time consumption should be a serious consideration when choosing a method of window glass analysis. It is suggested that a mean method be employed as long as it is possible to meet the mean-method strictures. The sample sizes required by Moir's and Schoen's methods can be honed to the point that from start to finish the process should take only a few hours and the data still be considered reliable, while other methods that suggest using an entire collection could, by contrast, take days of commitment.

A valuable piece of information that resulted from testing the analysis methods is that with few exceptions, the strictures have such a significant effect on the resulting data that failing to observe them would most likely cause erroneous results. Collecting data from the same collections according to each method's strictures produced different average thicknesses and slightly different modal distributions, with the exception of the Chance and Chance and Roenke methods, which are very closely related. This also means that attempting to use thickness data gathered according to one methodology with a different dating scheme or regression formula will often produce poor results. The investigators employed different sampling methods, measurements, and strictures to gather the data that were used to construct their methods. As a result, the methods are dependent on their specific methodology. This is especially true in mean-based methods (Table 2).

Conclusion

The study of window glass can produce valuable information about historic sites, and if approached correctly these studies can be conducted in an efficient fashion. That being stated, one single method of window glass analysis does not represent the best choice in every circumstance, especially given regional constraints, and the results should be contextualized by other types of dating methods whenever possible.

After reviewing and testing each method on eight sites and over 5,000 pieces of glass, the three methods that stood out as the most thorough and well researched are conveniently the three most easily accessible. These are the Roenke, Moir, and Schoen methods. When the context of the glass is very reliably from a specific structure, the mean methods by Moir and Schoen can be employed in a small amount of time to produce good results. If the context of the glass is less reliable, the archaeologist should consider Roenke's modal method. It is strongly recommended that in conducting window glass analysis the researcher obtain the article describing the method to be employed. Each has been published in some form of serial. The details can be found in the references to this article.

ACKNOWLEDGMENTS

I would like to thank Erin Dempsey, Jeff Richner, Christopher Schoen, Kathryn McBride, and most of all Doug Scott, for their guidance, feedback, and editorial work on this article. Also, this study could not have occurred were it not for the willingness of the Midwest Archaeological Center staff to let students work with the extensive collections housed there.

REFERENCES

Ball, Donald B.
1982   Chronological Implications of Window Glass Thickness and Coloration at the Linville Site (15BK12), Bracken County, Kentucky. Manuscript, Office of State Archaeology, University of Kentucky, Lexington.

Chance, David H., and Jennifer V. Chance
1976   *Kanaka Village Vancouver Barracks 1974*. Office of Public Archaeology, University of Washington, Seattle.

Davis, Pearce
1949   *The Development of the American Glass Industry*. Harvard University Press, Cambridge, MA.

Douglas, Ronald W., and Susan Frank
1972   *A History of Glassmaking*. Whitefriars Press, London, UK.

Moir, Randall W.
1982   Windows and Pane Fragments: Sources of Chronological Data for Historic Archaeologists. Manuscript, Department of Anthropology, Southern Methodist University, Dallas, TX.

1983   Windows to Our Past: A Chronological Scheme for the Thickness of Pane Fragments from 1635–1982. Manuscript, Corning Museum of Glass, Corning, NY.

1987   Socioeconomic and Chronometric Patterning of Window Glass. In *Historic Buildings, Material Culture, and People of the Prairie Margin: Architecture, Artifacts, and Synthesis of Historic Archaeology*, Richland Creek Technical Series, Vol. 5, David H. Jurney and Randall Moir, editors, pp. 73–81. Southern Methodist University, Dallas, TX.

Roenke, Karl G.
1978   *Flat Glass: Its Use as a Dating Tool for Nineteenth Century Archaeological Sites in the Pacific Northwest and Elsewhere*. Northwest Anthropological Research Notes, Memoir No. 4, Moscow, ID.

Schoen, Christopher M.
1990   Window Glass on the Plains: An Analysis of Flat Glass Samples from Ten Nineteenth Century Plains Historic Sites. *Central Plains Archaeology* 2(1):57–90.

Walker, John W.
1971   Excavation of the Arkansas Post Branch of the Bank of the State of Arkansas: Arkansas Post National Memorial, Arkansas. Manuscript, Southeast Archeological Center, National Park Service, Tallahassee, FL.

Jonathan Weiland
770 N. Dodge Avenue
Apartment 20
Tucson, AZ 85716

GLASS BOTTLE PUSH-UPS AND PONTIL MARKS

OLIVE JONES

INTRODUCTION

Originally this study started as an attempt to explain the varied markings on bottle bases found in the National Historic Sites Service collection. These markings appeared to have been left on the glass by glassmakers during the formation of the base and while holding the bottle on the pontil. In the process of identifying the marks, some relationships between the marks and certain types of bottles and their country and date of manufacture became apparent.

Because most modern authors, with the exception of Dr. Julian Toulouse, have not discussed in detail the question of base formations and empontilling techniques, I have had to concentrate on bottles excavated by the Canadian National Historic Sites Service. I have also looked at some local private collections and the "wine" bottles in the Bristol City Museum and the Guildhall Museum in London. In general, these collections corroborated some of the conclusions in this paper.

The National Historic Sites Service collection has a built-in bias because very few of our excavated sites predate the 1720s and from that date to 1760, the predominant trading influence was French. After 1760, when New France passed into British control, the trading emphasis shifted to Great Britain. This means that there are few English bottles in the collection from before 1760, and after that date, very few French bottles. Because of this situation, the attempt to assign the different tools and techniques to specific countries and dates should be regarded by the reader as a question and a challenge, rather than as an immutable fact.

Although there are many variations in technique, a bottle is made in the following basic manner (Figure 1). A sufficient amount of glass is gathered on the end of a blowpipe. The glass is given a preliminary shape, called a parison, by marvering (turning) on a flat stone or metal slab and by preliminary insufflation. The parison is then usually inserted in a mould which may form only the body or almost the whole bottle. After the partially formed bottle is removed from the mould, if the base has not already been mould-formed, the base is pushed up. A tool, such as a pontil or a sabot, then holds the bottle at the base while the blowpipe is detached from the bottle. Extra glass is added at the mouth and then the glassmaker forms the finish (Figure 9). The completed bottle is carried to the annealing oven where it is slowly cooled to remove the stresses in the glass.

The two stages of the bottle-making process that are discussed in this paper are the formation of the base and the techniques used to hold the bottle while the finish is being made.

FIGURE 1. *Interior of a 19th century French bottle factory (Peligot 1877:299).*

PUSH-UPS

One of the familiar aspects of bottles is the base that has been pushed up into the body cavity. This formation is called a "push-up" (Toulouse: personal communication; Moody 1963:303) or "kick". Several explanations have been given for its presence:

1) Because glassmakers had difficulty making a bottle base flat enough for a bottle to stand upright without wobbling, they partially solved the problem by indenting the base.

2) A push-up helped to produce a stronger bottle. Part of the reason was that the glassmaker, while the bottle was being made, often rested the bottle on its base which allowed the glass to flow towards the basal area (Bontemps 1868:510). In pushing up the base, the glass was redistributed and thinned. If glass is too heavily concentrated in one place the annealing process is less effective and stresses are set up in the bottle which make it weaker. It is also possible that the push-up is structurally useful in helping the bottle withstand great internal pressure from contents such as sparkling wines.

3) Many authors suggest that push-ups were made deliberately deep, particularly in dark green glass bottles, so the bottles looked much larger than they actually were.

4) Many people also believe that the push-up assists in the sedimentation of wines (Mendelsohn 1965:51).

The practice of making a deep push-up probably continued long after its need was over because of conservatism on the part of the glassmakers and the consumers.

The push-up seems to have been formed by a variety of tools. In Diderot's *Encyclopédie* (1967:109), the base was formed by a mollette, *"morceau de fer plat, d'environ un pié de longueur"* (Figure 2). As forming the push-up could cause distortion in the body of the bottle, it was rolled again on the marver. Although there were no really distinguishing marks left by this process, bases which were formed in this way probably resemble those in Figure 3. This type of base is found on the familiar French "flower pot" wine bottles (Noël Hume 1970:71; Diderot 1772: Pl. V, VI) which have been excavated on many sites in Canada that were occupied by the French. The bases are normally very regular, with symmetrical, rounded conical profiles and a small pontil mark, usually between 25 mm. and 35 mm. in diameter, in the top of the push-up.

FIGURE 2. *The glassmaker forming the bottle base with the mollette and then remarvering the bottle to restore its symmetry (Diderot 1772: Pl. V).*

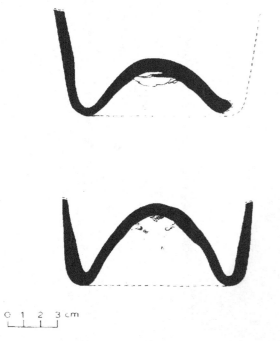

FIGURE 3. *Two bases, probably formed by a mollette, showing the regular, rounded conical profile and the pontil mark in the tip of the push-up.*

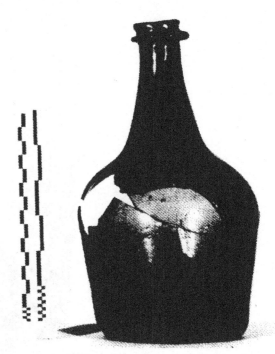

FIGURE 4. *An 18th-century French "flower pot" wine bottle excavated from a site dating from 1732 to 1745.*

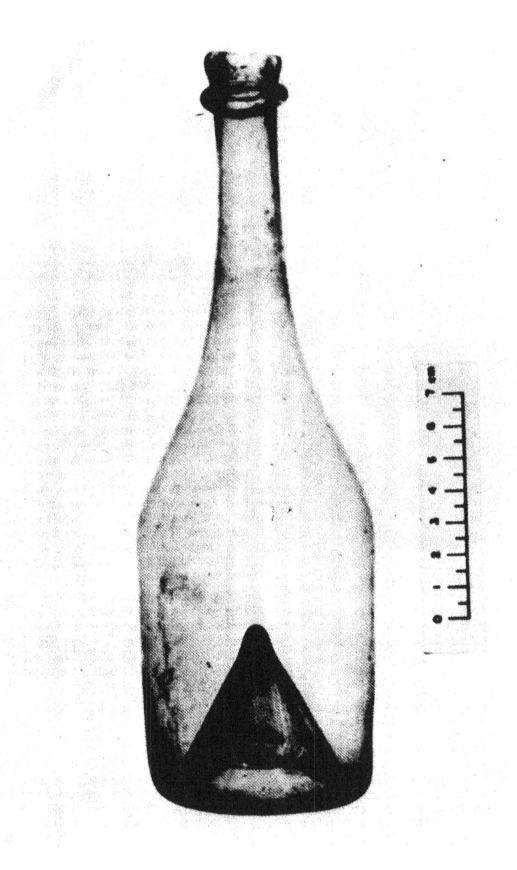

FIGURE 5. *A bottle showing how the base has been indented by a sharply pointed rod and the position of the pontil mark partway down the push-up.*

Another tool used to form the push-up appears to have been a thin, sharply pointed rod of wood or metal. As shown in Figure 5, the tip of the push-up often has a distinct, sharp point, visible on both the exterior and interior surfaces. The pontil mark is visible about two-thirds of the way down from the tip. On some small bottles, the push-up was so narrow that the pontil had to be applied on the resting surface. These sharply pointed push-ups appear primarily on medicine bottles and vials, occasionally on small rectangular bottles with chamfered corners and on olive oil bottles. Push-ups formed in this way are never found on the "wine" bottles. The use of this tool appears to have become less common during the 19th century as it was replaced by moulding techniques.

FIGURE 6. *The basal view of a bottle showing the quatrefoil impression in the tip of the push-up. The pontil mark can be seen as rough chips of glass.*

A third type of tool used to form push-ups appears to have been a circular iron rod, like a pontil, with the working end split into quadrants. The Canadiana Gallery of the Royal Ontario Museum, Toronto, has such a rod about 34 in. long with a working end about 7/8 in. in diameter. The separated quadrants left a quatrefoil impression in the top of the push-up. On some kicks the mark can barely be felt and on others, as in Figure 6, it is unmistakeable, even to the extent of distorting the profile. Occasionally iron oxide deposits from the iron tool are found in the impres-

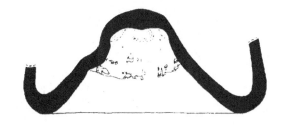

0 1 2 3 cm

FIGURE 7. *The same base as Figure 6 showing the relationship of the quatrefoil impression and the pontil mark. Note the distortion in the profile.*

sion (Toulouse 1968:140, 141). From above, on the interior surface, the push-up top often looks roughly square. In 75 examples from one Canadian site, the diameters of the impressions ranged from 16 mm. to 51 mm. In addition to the quatrefoil impressions, there is invariably a pontil mark consisting of an area of rough glass which encircles the push-up towards the resting surface. The pontil mark diameters range from 38 mm. to 64 mm. Figure 7 illustrates a base in which the push-up profile was distorted both by the forming tool and by the application of the pontil. Although split iron rods are still used today as pontil rods, the presence of both a distinct pontil mark and the quatrefoil impression on the same base suggests that the quatrefoil mark is logically explained if the split rod was used to indent the base.

The quatrefoil marks have been appearing almost exclusively in dark green glass "wine" bottles manufactured in the English shapes, such as Noël Hume's types 12, 15, 21, 22 (Noël Hume 1961:100-101). The earliest bases in the National Historic Sites Service collection with these marks date from the 1720s and they continue throughout the 18th and into the 19th century. Generally speaking, as the diameters of the bottles decreased towards the end of the 18th century, the quatrefoil marks also became smaller.

A fourth way of forming the push-up was by using a specially designed mould part which fit into the bottle mould. An example of this method was developed by the H. Ricketts Company of Bristol in 1821. The patent included a lettered ring which could be placed close to the circumference of the base and "according to the thickness or

```
0   1   2   3 cm.
```

FIGURE 8. *The base of a bottle formed in the Ricketts mould showing the marks left by the device.*

thinness of the said ring is the body of the mould shortened or increased, and the various sizes of bottles produced" (Ricketts 1821: 3). On the ring could be cut such information as the address of the manufacturer or the volume of the bottle.

As the Ricketts "three-piece" mould formed only the base, body and shoulder, the neck and finish were completed in a separate operation by hand. After a bottle was withdrawn from the mould, therefore, a pontil was attached to the base while the neck was finished. The base in Figure 8 illustrates the different markings left by the manufacturing process. The speckled area is the pontil mark and the raised ridge inside the lettering is the edge of the removable lettered plate. There is also a raised mould line on the resting surface which is not visible in the draw-

ing. Incidentally, these bottles negate a popularly held belief (Kendrick 1968:138) that basal lettering and pontil marks cannot be found on the same bottle.

Originally the Ricketts mould was "An Improvement in the Art or Method of Making or Manufacturing Glass Bottles, such as are used for Wine, Porter, Beer, or Cyder;" (Ricketts 1821:1) in other words, it was used to make the dark green glass "wine" bottle. Later in the 19th century and even in the early 20th century, however, this mould type was used for bottles holding other products, including solids. The Ricketts mould was used very widely. The French writers De Fontonelle and Malepyre (1854:272) recommended the Ricketts mould because it made bottles of exact capacity and was easy to use, saving of both time and fuel. As well as in France, the Ricketts type of mould appears to have been used in the United States by several companies (McKearin 1970:106-7).

In Figure 12,*d* is another example of a base formed in what appears to be a special multipiece conical tool which may have been part of the mould or which may have been used separately. This type of base has distinctive characteristics. A distinct mould line is visible as a slight projection at the base of the body. A rounded ridge is visible on the push-up close to the resting surface. A small but distinct impression is located in the tip of the push-up. This mark is usually dome-shaped, as in Figure 12,*d*, but may be slightly square or pointed and will sometimes have an iron oxide deposit caused by being formed by a hot bare iron tool. All these marks have obviously been made deliberately but why this somewhat complicated arrangement was chosen is not known. In addition, the glass distribution is often very uneven and, if a pontil mark is present, it is usually large and consists of many sharp bits of embedded glass or sand. These bases, found mainly on dark green glass "wine" bottles, were probably manufactured during the second and third quarters of the 19th century. Their country of origin is not known.

Obviously the above discussion does not include all of the tools or moulds that have been used to form bases. For example, Bontempts (1868:509) mentions that the glassmakers used the handle of the battledore (see McKearin and McKearin: 1948, xv) or "*un crochet special*", and Peligot (1877:301) writes, "*il comprime le fond plat de la bouteille avec un crochet en fer.*" The bases made with these tools may or may not be

Fig. 1

FIGURE 9. *The bottle is being held on the pontil while additional glass is added to the neck (Diderot 1772: Pl. VI).*

identifiable. Toulouse, in his article on mould seams, mentions other types of moulds used to form bases (Toulouse 1969:526-35, 578-87).

PONTIL MARKS

The pontil is a long iron rod used to hold a glass article during the finishing process after it is detached from the blowpipe (McKearin and McKearin 1948: xvi). In Figure 9, from the Diderot *Encyclopédie*, the bottle is empontilled while the bottlemaker adds additional glass to the neck to form the finish. When the pontil is detached from the bottle, usually by a sharp tap on the rod, there is a scar left in the base which is called a pontil mark. Figure 10 illustrates four empontilling techniques: (a) the plain glass-tipped pontil; (b) the sand glass-tipped pontil; (c) the blowpipe as pontil, and (d) the bare iron pontil. Each of these processes leaves a characteristic pontil mark.

The plain glass-tipped pontil (Fig. 10,*a*), hereafter called a "glass-tipped" pontil, con-

sists of a solid iron bar with a slightly widened end which is dipped in molten glass. The glass on the pontil rod adheres to the glass of the base. The mark left by the glass-tipped pontil is comparatively small, usually no larger than 30 mm., although this will vary according to the size of the vessel being held. Usually there is evidence within the pontil mark that the whole area has been in contact with other glass, either because there is excess glass left when the pontil is detached (Figure 11) or because bits of glass are torn out of the base. This empontilling technique was commonly used on tableware, medicine and toiletry bottles, and on flasks. The small glass-tipped pontil mark in the centre of the push-up is not found after the 1720s on dark green glass "wine" bottles manufactured in the English tradition (see Noël Hume 1961:100-101, Types 12-16, 19-22). Some of the French "flower pot" wine bottles discussed in the push-up section do appear to have been empontilled in this way (**Figure 3**). The technique is still used for objects manufactured by hand.

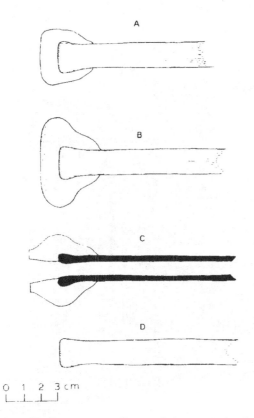

FIGURE 10. *Four empontilling techniques: a) the glass-tipped pontil; b) the sand pontil; c) the blowpipe as pontil; d) the bare iron pontil.*

FIGURE 11. *Tumbler base showing excess glass left on the base after removal of the pontil.*

The sand glass-tipped pontil (Figure 10,*b*), hereafter called a "sand" pontil, consists of a gather of glass on the pontil which has been shaped to conform to the basal profile and then dipped in sand (Toulouse: personal communication; Larsen, Riismøller and Schlüter 1963:397). The sand prevents the glass on the pontil from adhering too closely to the bottle.

The sand pontil mark is larger than the glass-tipped one, although again the size varies according to the size of the bottle. It consists of a thin line of glass chips encircling the push-up and enclosing a pebbled surface caused by the grains of sand (Figure 12). Some of the sand may also be embedded in the base (Toulouse: personal communication). Toulouse also points out that this type of pontil will conform to the shape of the already formed base without distorting it.

Sand pontil marks are very common on English dark green glass "wine" bottles, octagonal bottles and occasionally case bottles. The four "wine" bottle bases in Figure 12 have sand pontil marks (Toulouse: personal communication). In the upper two, dating from the 18th century, the pontil has been applied closer to the top of the push-up, which is usually hemispherical or dome-shaped. In 128 examples from one Canadian site, the diameters of the sand pontil mark ranged from 40 mm. to 71 mm., but 86 per cent were between 50 mm. and 64 mm. Sometimes one can feel a quatrefoil mark in addition to the pontil mark, but more often there is a pinch mark or wrinkle in the centre of the push-up which may be indicative of the tool used to form the push-up. In the lower pair (Figure 12, *c,d*), dating from the late 18th and 19th centuries, the sand pontil mark is less distinctive. Almost the entire basal surface is disturbed and is frequently roughened by embedded grains of sand or glass chips. The pontil mark usually begins close to the resting surface. In 76 examples from the same site, the pontil mark diameter ranged from 46 mm. to 71 mm., but 80 per cent were between 50 mm. and 60 mm. Sand pontils are still used on glass manufactured by hand (Toulouse: personal communication).

The third type of empontilling technique (Figure 10,*c*), probably no longer in use, consisted of using the glass left on the blowpipe after the bottle had been snapped off. In other words, the blowpipe itself was used as a pontil. The bottle was laid on a V-shaped structure (Figure 13) while the glass-

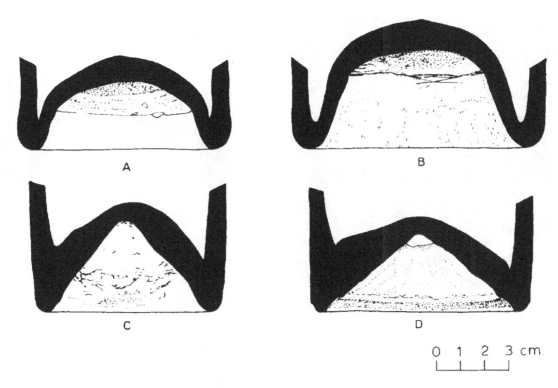

FIGURE 12. "Wine" bottle bases with sand pontil marks: a) and b) 18th century; c) late 18th, early 19th century; d) 19th century.

FIGURE 13. Bottle lying in a V-shaped structure while the blowpipe is attached to the base (Diderot 1772: Pl. V).

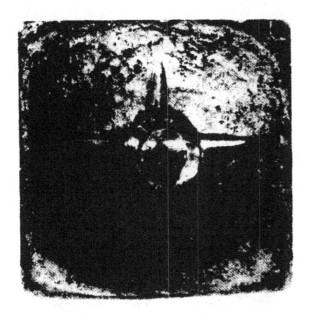

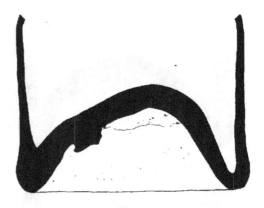

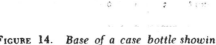

FIGURE 14. *Base of a case bottle showing the ring-shaped mark characteristic of the blowpipe used as a pontil. The embossed moulded cross is as undisturbed inside the ring as outside.*

FIGURE 15. *"Wine" bottle base showing distortion which may have been caused by using a bare iron pontil.*

maker applied the blowpipe with its excess glass to the base of the bottle. The pontil mark is a distinct ring-shaped mark about the same diameter as the neck (Toulouse 1968:139). When the blowpipe was removed from the base it either tore glass out with it or left extra glass behind. As the only area of contact is the ring of glass, any mould lines, embossed markings, and distinctive surface textures remain as undisturbed inside the ring as they do outside (Figure 14) (Toulouse 1968:139).

These ring-shaped marks are found on case bottles, champagne bottles, flasks, medicine bottles and other small vials, but they are not found after 1720 on the dark green glass "wine" bottles manufactured in the English tradition illustrated by Noël Hume (1961:100-101). This empontilling technique, described by Diderot (1772: Pl. V), was used for the French "flower pot" wine bottles, although the distinctive ring shape is not always obvious. Bottles of this type have appeared on a Canadian site occupied by the French be-

tween 1732 and 1745. The French writers Peligot (1877:300) and Bontemps (1868:509) described this technique, but whether this was straight copying from Diderot or whether the practise was still common has not been determined. Certainly it was still being used in the United States in the 19th century (Mc-Kearin 1970:89-91).

The fourth empontilling technique (Figure 10,d), probably discontinued, consisted of using a bare iron pontil with a suitably shaped end, usually a shallow arch, which was heated red hot and applied directly to the base of the bottle (Toulouse 1968:140). The pontil mark is a distinct circular mark covered with a reddish or black deposit which, when tested, indicated the presence of ferric oxide and occasionally ferrous oxide (Toulouse 1968:141). Toulouse (personal communication) also suggests that the bare iron pontil tended to distort the push-up more than any of the glass-tipped pontils (Figure 15). Some of the marks that I have seen on bottles in local collections are unmistakeable, but others in the National Historic Sites Service collection have iron oxide deposits spread unevenly over the pontil mark area (Figure 15). The deposit could be explained in a number of ways. Possibly a bare iron pontil was used to hold the bottle; the push-up may have been formed by a bare iron tool, or the bottle may have been buried next to an iron object.

The distinct form has been found in American flasks, fruit jars and carbonated beverage bottles dating from about 1845 to 1870 (Tou-

FIGURE 16. *Moulded lettering in the centre of the base, a position formerly occupied by the pontil mark.*

louse 1968:141-2). The indistinct marks in the National Historic Sites Service collection occur in 18th- and early 19th-century dark green glass bottle bases. Obviously further investigations will have to be carried out on this technique.

The pontil was gradually replaced by other tools, such as the sabot (Figure 1) and the snap case (Kendrick 1968:128), which held the bottle around the body and did not leave disfiguring scars in the base. These tools were introduced sometime between the late 1840s and the 1850s (Bontemps 1868:511; Larsen, Riismøller, and Schülter 1963:389; McKearin 1970:107; Scoville 1948:17), and by the 1870's had superceded the pontil for holding bottles during the finishing process (Toulouse 1968: 204). With the disappearance of the pontil mark, the glassmakers began to use the centre of the base for moulded lettering and numbers (Figure 16).

CONCLUSIONS

Several relationships became obvious during the course of this study. Different empontilling techniques and methods of form-

ing push-ups were used for different types of bottles. Possibly these differences can be related to the size of the bottle.

A regular, rounded, cone-shaped push-up, probably made with a mollette, as described by Diderot, in combination with a small pontil mark, either from a glass-tipped pontil or from a blowpipe used as a pontil, occurs on 18th-century French wine bottles. I have seen the same combination on 18th-century European spa water bottles and suspect that the Belgian wine bottles illustrated in Chambon (1955: Pl. T, facing p. 113) were formed in a similar way. The combination, therefore, should probably be regarded as Continental rather than strictly French in origin.

The glass-tipped pontil or the blowpipe as a pontil appear to have been favoured by the French, and possibly the Continental glassmakers, for holding all bottles, even those of larger capacity (about 26 oz.). The English, however, favoured these two methods for their smaller bottles and used the larger sand pontil for bottles of larger capacity (about 26 oz.).

A separate mould part designed specifically to form the push-up appears to have been first introduced in England in the 1820s for the dark green glass "wine" bottles. Afterwards, however, this technique was used in many countries for most types of bottles.

The bare iron pontil appears to have been used in the 19th century. Iron oxide deposits on the bases of earlier bottles may be from the use of this type of pontil or from a tool used to form the push-up.

Obviously there are a great many questions left unanswered by the above study. The relationships between different bottle types, techniques, country and period of manufacture are very complex. Often the different types of marks are difficult or impossible to identify, and available literature on glass has, with few exceptions, not covered this aspect in detail.

In combination with other criteria such as body shape, size, and finish formation, the formation of the push-up and the empontilling techniques can be used as additional evidence in determining bottle types made during the 18th and 19th centuries.

ACKNOWLEDGEMENTS

My appreciation and thanks are extended to Dr. Julian Toulouse, retired glass Consulting Engineer, for his inestimable help and comments in the preparation of this article. I would also like to thank the National Historic Sites Service for permission to publish the information relating to the archaeological collections made by the Service. The photographs were done by Georges Lupien and the drawings by Mrs. Jane Moussette, both of the National Historic Sites Service.

REFERENCES

BONTEMPS, GEORGES
1868 *Guide du verrier, traité historique et practique de la fabrication des verres, cristaux, vitraux.* Librairie du dictionnaire des arts et manufactures, Paris.

DIDEROT AND D'ALEMBERT
1967 *Encyclopédie, ou dictionnaire raisonné des sciences, des arts, et des métiers.* Facsimile reprint of 1765 ed. of Vol. 17, text. Friedrich Fromann Verlag (Gunther Holzboog), Stuttgart.

1772 "Vetterie en bouteilles chauffée en charbon de terre." *Recueil de Planches sur les sciences, les arts libéraux et les arts méchaniques, avec leur explication.* Vol. 10. Briasson, Paris.

CHAMBON, RAYMOND
1955 *L'Histoire de la verrerie en Belgique du IIme siécle à nos jours.* Editions de la Librairie Encyclopédique, Bruxelles.

DE FONTONÉLLE, JULIA, AND F. MALEPEYRE
1854 *Nouveau manuel complet de verrier et du fabricant de glaces, cristaux, pierres précieuses factices, verres colorés, yeux artificiels, etc.* Vol. I. La librairie encyclopédique de Roret, Paris.

KENDRICK, GRACE
1968 *The Mouth-Blown Bottle.* Grace Kendrick, Fallon, Nevada.

LARSEN, ALFRED, P. RIISMØLLER, AND M. SCHLÜTER
1963 *Dansk Glas 1825-1925.* Nyt Nordisk Forlag Arnold Busck, Copenhagen.

McKEARIN, GEORGE, AND HELEN McKEARIN
1948 *American Glass.* Crown Publishers, New York.

McKEARIN, HELEN
1970 *Bottles, Flasks and Dr. Dyott.* Crown Publishers, New York.

MENDELSOHN, OSCAR A.
1965 *The Dictionary of Drink and Drinking.* Macmillan, Toronto.

MOODY, B. E.
1963 *Packaging in Glass.* Hutchinson and Co., London.

NOËL HUME, IVOR
1961 "The Glass Wine Bottle in Colonial Virginia." *Journal of Glass Studies,* Vol. 3, pp. 91-119. The Corning Museum of Glass, Corning, New York.

1970 *A Guide to Artifacts of Colonial America.* Alfred A. Knopf, New York.

PELIGOT, E.
1877 *Le verre: son histoire, sa fabrication.* G. Masson, Paris.

RICKETTS, H.
1821 *Ricketts' Specification: An Improvement in the Art or Method of Making or Manufacturing Glass Bottles, such as are Used for Wine, Porter, Beer, or Cyder.* British Patent, No. 4623.

SCOVILLE, WARREN C.
1948 *Revolution in Glassmaking: Entrepreneurship and Technological Change in the American Industry.* Harvard University Press, Cambridge, Mass.

TOULOUSE, JULIAN
1968 "Empontilling—A History." *The Glass Industry,* Pt. I (March), pp. 137-42; Pt. II (April), pp. 204-5. New York.

1969 "A Primer on Mold Seams." *The Western Collector,* Pt. 1, Vol. 7, No. 11, pp. 526-35; Pt. 2, Vol. 7, No. 12, pp. 578-87. San Francisco.

JANE E. HARRIS

Eighteenth-Century French Blue-Green Bottles from the Fortress of Louisbourg, Nova Scotia

Introduction

The work reported is primarily a descriptive analysis of 18th-century French blue-green glass containers found in the extensive Fortress of Louisbourg archaeological collection. Artifacts from the excavations are only partially mended or restored, but on the evidence of necks, bases, and complete bottles (in this report the word "bottle" is used generically to refer to a glass container and "jar," more specifically, to a wide-mouthed glass container), four distinctive container forms, one of which occurs in nine distinct types, could be isolated. The forms vary in size, ranging from a few milliliters to several liters. Many of the types share identical features such as neck, body, or base shapes, implying a relationship at the manufacturing level. By isolating the various forms and types and then using available literature, inventories, contemporary art, and the evidence from blue-green bottles found on other French historic sites in North America, it became possible to discuss the physical relationships between the groups, the closures used, their possible functions, their social significance, and their cultural origins.

The bottles occurred in contexts from both French occupation periods (1713-1745 and 1749-1758) with no apparent stylistic differences pertaining to date of manufacture. This lack of variation is consistent with observations made by both Scoville (1950:20) and Barrelet (1953:110), who stated that there were essentially no technological changes in the common glass industry nor did its products give any indications of regional distinctions during these periods.

Blue-Green Glass

A mixture of sand, calcium, and an alkali flux (potash or soda) to which no decolorizer has been added results in a greenish and sometimes yellow or brownish glass due to iron impurities in the sand. Such glass produced in wood-fired furnaces has been called *waldglas*, forest glass, *verre fougère*, or *verre commun*, depending on its country of origin. The two latter French terms usually refer to lightly tinted tablewares which were produced in the *petites verreries* or *verreries communes* of France. These were generally small glasshouses which often produced a wide variety of products including more utilitarian items such as bottles (Barrelet 1953:71). Besides the glass used for the clearer tablewares, a "common green" glass or *verre vert* was produced in the *petites verreries* for bottles (Scoville 1950), its blue tint being more noticeable according to Barrelet (1953:103) among the bottles produced in the forest areas of Grésigne in Languedoc.

The *petites verreries* used wood-burning furnaces and were located throughout the forests of France. They usually had only one furnace and four to six pots in which to melt glass (*Diderot-d'Alemert Encyclopédie* 1751-1765 [17]:113; Scoville 1950:72). They commonly employed no more than 20 people including part-time workers such as basket weavers and packers (Scoville 1950:72). Some *petites verreries* made only bottles while others specialized in tablewares or window glass and made bottles as a sideline (Scoville 1950:14n., 150-151). Bottle production was separate from that of tablewares or other items on two levels. First, there would have been a separate pot for bottle glass, usually one of green and sometimes one of brown glass (*Diderot-d'Alembert Encyclopédie* 1772a:Plate 3). Second, there were workers who specialized in bottle blowing, for goblet and drinking-glass blowers apparently rarely made bottles (Scoville 1950:71).

The *petite verrerie* industry neither flourished nor declined throughout the 18th century for the number of factories, employment rates, and output increased in some areas, decreased in others, and stayed the same in still others (Scoville 1950:13, 21, 72, 147). The demand for wine bottles had increased greatly with the new practice of storing wine in bottles and with the growing export trade in bottled wines (Scoville 1950:11, 111; Barrelet 1953:100). This demand was largely met by the heavy dark glass bottles being made in the new or converted coal-fired furnaces introduced from England early in the century and by the heavy green bottles from *grosses verreries* (Scoville 1950:11, 41). Further to the detriment of the *petite verrerie* industry, wood was scarce in France, which meant many factories were unable by law to keep their furnaces lit year round. This forced some entrepreneurs to close down for as many as six months or more each year, having an obvious effect on production (Scoville 1950:13, 21, 149). On the positive side, the *petite verrerie* industry already had a considerable market, built up in the 16th and 17th centuries, for their cheap and useful common bottles whose domestic use in France was traditional and so widespread that it involved "members of all social classes" (Scoville 1950:111, 167).

For their domestic market the *petites verreries* made "large and small bottles" as well as "bowls, condiment containers, decanters, tumblers, goblets, ink wells, lamps and lamp chimneys, pitchers, plates, urinals, vases and other similar [useful] items" (Scoville 1950:111). This list would presumably include items in clear and blue-green glass. They may have also supplied the perfumeries of southern France as well as the needs of the growing export trade in toilet waters (Scoville 1950:112). Then, too, a variety of other items were packed in glass to be shipped to the colonies: olives, anchovies, capers, marinated tuna, olive oil, vinegar, liqueurs, *eau de vie*, and toilet water (Barrelet 1953:103).

Bottles were also made in the *grosses verreries* of Normandy and northeastern France, but in a "coarse, heavy" green glass or *gros verre* favored by those in the mineral water, liquor, and wine trades (Scoville 1950:8, 11). These *verreries* also burned wood, but specialized in window glass, either crown or sheet (Scoville 1950:8). The crown glass factories of Normandy normally reserved one of six pots for bottles alone (Scoville 1950:11). Owned and operated by the *gentilshommes verriers*, a minor nobility who considered bottle blowing unbefitting to their rank, they employed common workers to manufacture bottles (Scoville 1950:71, 84). According to Scoville (1950:147-148), a typical Normandy factory in 1740 would produce 70 tons of common green glass for every 150 to 200 tons of window glass. Whether the bottles they produced resembled those of the *petites verreries* in form or color is difficult to say, but there seems to have been a definite distinction in weight. Scoville (1950:19, 41) referred to bottles from crown glasshouses as coarse and heavy and those from the *petites verreries* as light. Bosc d'Antic described Norman window glass thusly: "There is no pane glass, I believe, more imperfect than that from our large glass factories; it is full of flaws . . . and colored to the point that it is of little transparency, even as thin as it is" Barrelet (1953:99). Presumably their bottle glass was no better and if so, Bosc d'Antic's statement accurately describes most of the 18th-century glass bottles found at Louisbourg.

French bottle glass composition in the 18th century is a generally neglected area of study. Both soda and potash were being used as flux. Preliminary analysis of a blue-green bottle fragment (Charles Costain 1978:personal communication) indicates a glass of soda-lime composition. Soda was more easily available in the coastal regions of France where it was produced from the ashes of various seaweeds (Scoville 1950:49). Potash was more accessible in the interior and urban areas of France in the form of bracken and wood ash, and it therefore seems likely that the small glasshouses, particularly in northeastern France, would find the use of potash more economical than soda.

French Bottle Manufacture

Enough has been written about bottle manufacture that it is only necessary here to stress the techniques and tools that help to distinguish French bottles from others. Diderot, who maintained that items were made in the same manner whether in wood- or coal-fired furnaces, gave the following description of bottle-making using coal (*Diderot-d'Alembert Encyclopédie* 1751-1765[17]:109, 112, 113; 1772b:Plates 3-6). After the parison was marvered and blown, the bottle was placed in a copper dip mold having a truncated cone shape. It was blown, removed from the mold, and up-ended in preparation to pushing up the base. A *molette*, or shaping tool, was used for this function. It was a short piece of flat metal, one foot long, with a pointed end used to push the base up while the bottle was continuously turned. The bottle was again marvered to correct any bulges or distortions that might have occurred when the base was pushed up. The base was then empontiled with a glass-tipped rod or with the *meule*; that is, with the portion of the glass that remained on the blowpipe after it was cracked off the neck. The bottle rested on its side during this operation. The lip was then reheated or fire-polished and finished as desired. It was at this point that a string rim could have been added. The bottle was then complete except for annealing.

Ducasse (1970:393) discovered in a Panckoucke edition of the *Diderot-d'Alembert Encyclopédie* that *terre à pot* molds in several sizes were used in the *petites verreries*, rather than the lone copper mold Diderot had ascribed (*Diderot-d'Alembert Encyclopédie* 1751-1765[17]:109; 1772b:Plates 3, 4) to each bottle blower. It is conceivable that clay molds could impart a less smooth texture to the surface of a glass bottle than would a copper mold. The presence of many sizes of molds is to be expected given the variety of vessels known to have been produced in *petites verreries*.

Blue-Green Bottles in the Inventories

It was customary in Louisbourg to take an inventory of the possessions of a deceased person immediately following his death, usually for reasons of settling the estate (Adams 1972:1). The inventories varied from a simple list of the contents of a fisherman's trunk to lengthy documentation of the contents of a house and often included appraisals of the values of the items listed. After the items were inventoried they were often sold at public auction and the item listed along with its sale price. These lists frequently mentioned both filled and empty bottles and their values. The information used in this section was drawn from inventories found in France, Archives Nationales (1732-1757:Section Outre-Mer, Series G², Volumes 181, 182, 197, 199, 201-203, 205, 209.)

Blue-green bottles are a difficult group to subdivide for discussion due to the lack of a consistent relationship between shape and function of the bottles, but a preliminary study of the inventories indicated that French clerks made a distinction between *flacon, bouteille, fiole,* and *dame-jeanne* (e.g., *"dix flacons et quatre bouteilles de verre," "quatre bouteilles et douze fiolle de verre,"* and *"six flacons de verre six mauvaises foilles"*).

Flacon was the term used for containers filled with *"huille," "huille dolive," "huille de palma," "citron confits," "fruit à l'eau de vie," "enchois," "liqueur," "sirop de capilaire," "d'orgea," "capres," "sirop,"* and, infrequently, wine. Filled or empty *flacons* were often found in boxes or baskets: *"canevettes," "paniers," "caves,"* and *"caisses."* There were *"petits flacons," "flacons de pinte"* (approximately 900 ml), and *"flacons de cinq chopines"* (about 2,300 ml).

In the same documents *bouteilles* were almost invariably referred to as containers for wine and spirits (although in one instance a *bouteille* held tobacco, and *d'huille* in another) and were seldom found in *canevettes.* There were *"bouteilles de peinte et . . . de chopine"* (ca. 450 ml). The distinction between *flacon* and *bouteille* suggests that *flacon* generally referred to blue-green glass multipurpose containers and *bouteille* commonly referred to the dark green or black glass flowerpot-shaped bottles now popularly known as French "wine" bottles. *Bouteille* could also have been used to refer to English black glass "wine" bottles.

Fioles (phials) and *dames-jeannes* (demijohns), whose approximate sizes and general forms are implicit in the definitions of the terms themselves, may also refer to vessels with other than French origins. Both forms occur only rarely in the inventories. *Fioles*, when mentioned with their contents, contained *"elixir," "Sirop de Capilaire,"* or *"eau de lavande."* Only one *dame-jeanne* was mentioned with its contents, six *pots* (approximately 14 liters) of *eau de vie. Fioles* and *dames-jeannes* were likely blue-green, but could have occurred in other colors as well.

It appears, thus that the French *flacon* in Louisbourg was a multipurpose bottle which would have had to exist in a variety of shapes and sizes in order to accommodate such a variety of liquids and solids. *Fioles* and *dames-jeannes* were restricted by their sizes to more specific functions while *bouteilles* would have contained wine or spirits.

Although several different systems for measuring capacity were in use in France prior to 1840 (Ross 1983), the terms *pinte, chopine,*

Jane E. Harris

and *pot* are found throughout historical French inventories to describe the capacitiies of glass containers. Genêt, Decarie-Audet, and Vermette (1974) equate a *pinte* to a liter, and define a *pot* as two *pintes* and a *chopine* as a half *pinte*.

Blue-Green Bottles from the Excavations

Archaeological excavations conducted at Louisbourg since 1960 frequently unearthed glass containers distinguished by their blue-green bubbled glass. Most examples fall into the 10BG to 2.5G Munsell color range (Munsell Color 1957), but some continue through the GY hues, several are as yellow as 10Y, and a few as brown as 10YR. Bubbling in the glass varies from light to very dense and is sometimes so close to the vessel's surface as to have caused elongated surface pitting. Some of the glass is glossy and new-looking while some is subject to a heavy, chalky-white or gold iridescent patina.

Rather than construct an arbitrary typology, it seemed logical to adhere to the nomenclature established in the inventories: *fioles, flacons, bouteilles,* and *dames-jeannes.* There are single *fiole, bouteille,* and *dame-jeanne* types, but nine styles of *flacon* type, all often occurring in several sizes. Three of the *flacons* (types 1, 4, 9) have square bodies; the other six (types 2, 3, 5-8) have cylindrical bodies. Except for the *dame-jeanne,* all seem to have been mouth blown into plain cylindrical or square dip molds. The *flacon* types are often only distinguished from one another by their particular neck shapes. For example, a square-bodied *flacon* might have a short thin neck, a tall slim neck, or a short, very wide mouth (types 1, 4, and 9, respectively). For this reason the total blue-green sample of 1,200 vessels and resulting percentages of each form and type in the following descriptions are based on neck counts rather than on bases. Descriptive terms used throughout this article are based on *The Parks Canada Glass Glossary* (Jones and Sullivan 1989).

Volumes are included for purposes of comparison only and it is to be understood that they are at best approximate. A dry measure was obtained using rice as the medium because most of the bottles were too fragile to measure with a liquid. The volumes of less complete cylindrical bottles were measured geometrically using the formula $v=\pi r^2 h$, where r is the average of the

radii of base and shoulder, and h is the distance from the top of the push-up to the base of the neck. The formula v=lwh was used similarly for square-bodied bottles. Volumes were then expressed in approximate metric measure. English equivalents have intentionally been omitted.

Other bottle measurements were taken, most of which are self-evident, but it may help to explain that "lip diameter" and "lip height" indicate outer dimensions of the lip, whereas "bore diameter" indicates the inner lip diameter.

Fioles

Of the total blue-green sample, 20% consists of small bottles or *fioles,* making them, with 239 necks, 254 bases, and 1 complete bottle, one of the most common blue-green bottle forms at Louisbourg. They are characterized primarily by their small cylindrical bodies which taper toward the shoulder, and their tall, slim, concave necks which often bulge at the base. The bases have conical, domed, truncated-conical, or rounded-conical push-ups which display glass-tipped pontil marks. The lips were usually thickened, apparently by applying pressure to the top of the lip after it was cracked off and reheated, a process which occasionally left a crease encircling the bore.

Definite size, shape, and color variations among base diameters can be seen in Figure 1. The smallest bases, those less than 38 mm in diameter, tend to be distinctive (Figure 2). They have proportionally heavy bases with shallow, dome-shaped push-ups, distinct basal sag, and proportionally large glass-tipped pontil marks (14 to 23 mm in diameter). Only one of these heavier bases varies by having a higher, rounded-conical push-up.

Of the bases with diameters from 38 mm to 40 mm, two-thirds are yellow-colored with slightly higher push-ups in truncated cone or dome shapes. They also have slightly lighter bases with less evidence of basal sag. It is into this base size and color range that the one complete bottle falls (Figure 3). It has an overall height of 118 mm and an approximate volume of 60 ml.

Of all the *fiole* bases, 71% have diameters from 47 to 61 mm (Figure 1) and push-ups in the shape of cones, truncated cones, or rounded cones. The glass is generally very thin, approxi-

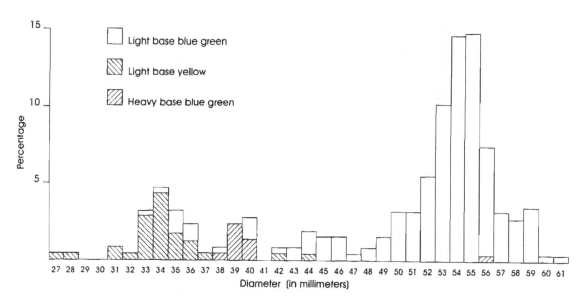

FIGURE 1. Percentage distribution of *fiole* base diameters. Total sample, 254 bases.

mately 1.0 mm thick, blue green, and distributed evenly throughout each bottle with usually no evidence of basal sag (Figure 4). Pontil marks for this large group are proportionally small (10 to 29 mm in diameter) when compared to those of the smallest *fiole* bases. Many of the push-ups have faint swirling impressions in the glass, possibly caused when the bases were pushed up by the *molette*.

Few *fiole* bases have complete body heights. At Louisbourg, two bases narrower than 38 mm in diameter have body heights extant to 70 and 74 mm, while the body height of the one complete bottle (Figure 3) is 67 mm, just over half its total height of 118 mm. The conjectural body height on the larger base in Figure 4 is at least 80 mm. A complete example from the Tunica Treasure with a 54-mm-diameter base

and 170-mm-overall height has a body height of approximately 90 mm (Brain 1979:92).

Neck dimensions vary more in height than diameter. Yellow neck heights vary from 40 to 50 mm, but 81% of all the *fiole* necks are taller than 50 mm, the tallest being 69 mm, and only two are shorter than 40 mm. On the whole, bore diameters vary from 10 to 18 mm with 88% between 12 and 15 mm, and lip diameters have a normal distribution from 15 to 24 mm.

The taper which occurs from base to shoulder on each of the restorable bottles is not a feature consistent with dip molding, but one that might be explained by the process of marvering after the base was pushed up and empontiled. During marvering such thin-glassed bottles could easily be changed from cylindrical to tapered. Another possibility is that the bottles were freeblown, the bases pushed up, and the bodies then marvered into a roughly cylindrical shape.

The *Dictionnaire universel françois et latin* (1743[3]:257) defined *fiole* as a little glass bottle used particularly by the apothecaries in dispensing their medicines, potions, and syrups to the ill. Governor Duquesnel's 1744 inventory (Adams 1978:126, 127, 131) tells us he had among his possessions "*une boette*" in which there were four "*fioles delixir nommé garrus*" in his wardrobe; two "*petites Fioles d'eau de lavande*" in his office, and five "*fiolles de Sirop*

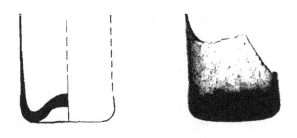

FIGURE 2. Small *fiole* base (35 mm maximum diameter).

Jane E. Harris

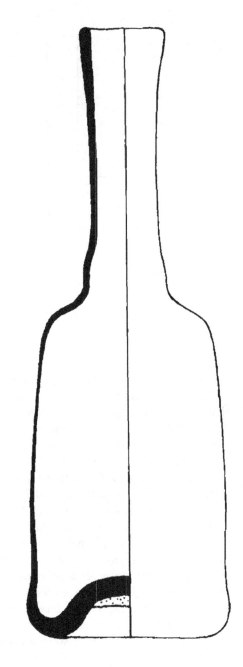

FIGURE 3. Middle-sized yellow *fiole*, approximate capacity of 60 ml (40 mm maximum diameter).

de Capilaire" in storage, but otherwise references to *fioles* in the inventories were rare. Perhaps they were too common for mention and those in Duquesnel's inventory were only important for their contents. No *fioles* were mentioned in conjunction with administered medicines in selected Louisbourg surgeon's bills (Hoad 1976:305-310), but various medicines and mixtures such as "*cordialles*," "*ptisannes pectoiralles*," "*sudorifiques*," and "*carminatives*" were dispensed in "*portions*," "*dragmes*," and "*bouteilles*." Perhaps it may be assumed that *portions* and *dragmes* of a particular medicine were administered in small bottles or *fioles*, and that *bouteilles* indicated a larger amount.

The use of *fioles* and wineglasses together was implied in two sources and may indicate a further use for *fioles*: the inventory of Pierre Lorant, *cabaretier* (Proulx 1972:107), listed six *fioles* with six *gobelets*, and a painting by Leonard de France (1735-1805) depicts a wineglass and small bottle sitting together on a plate, the aftermath of a meal (Faré 1962:437). Perhaps *fioles* were used on the buffet or table filled with oil, vinegar, or wine in place of *burettes* or cruets.

Fioles used as containers for medicines and toiletries necessitated some sort of closure. McKearin (1971:121) illustrated the use of a "spill of paper" for stopping small bottles. Whether this was the initial means of closure or merely a temporary one while the contents were being used is uncertain and the use of corks as closures is just as likely.

Flacons

Flacons occur in a variety of shapes and constitute 70% of the total sample. They have been divided into nine types based on combinations of shape elements. Closures are not dealt with at the end of each type discussion as those for types 1 to 7 were identical and are described once at the end of the discussion of short-necked square "case" *flacons* (type 1). Closures for types 8 and 9 were more varied and are discussed individually at the ends of those sections.

0   5
cm.

Page 132.

TYPE 1. SHORT-NECKED SQUARE "CASE" *FLACONS*

Square-bodied, short-necked "case" bottles (Figure 5) comprise 31% of the total blue-green bottle glass sample. There are 357 necks, 342 bases, and 13 complete bottles. These bottles usually have cracked-off and fire-polished lips, plain tubular necks, and horizontal shoulders. Occasionally the lips were thickened (Figure 14). The bodies generally widen 2 to 6 mm towards the shoulders and sometimes have vertical ridges left by the dip mold. The bases are not always true squares, are slightly arched and, as the surface texture of the bases mimics that of the bodies, would seem to have been formed in the mold. They usually bear glass-tipped pontil marks, but sometimes the glass adhered so lightly as to leave no mark at all. Glass distribution is quite even throughout these bottles, perhaps offsetting the inherent weakness in their square shape.

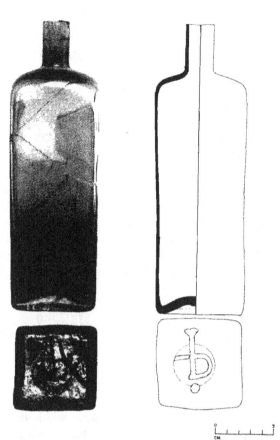

FIGURE 5. Type 1 *flacon*, approximate capacity 780 ml (70 mm maximum basal width).

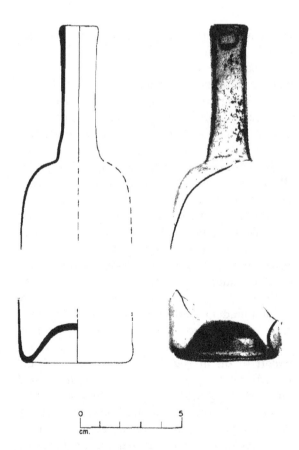

FIGURE 4. Neck and base of a common *fiole* (67 mm maximum diameter).

Embossed on some bases are very distinct letters or figures (Figure 6) that appear to have been part of the initial molding process. A lower case "b" is the most common letter found, occurring on at least 40 bases, often with a dot below its stem. The letter, usually placed to one side of the basal surface, was occasionally centered on the base, but was then only slightly distorted by empontiling (Figure 5). The lack of distortion is unusual and seems to indicate careful use of the glass-tipped pontil.

Short-necked square *flacons* appear to have been made in several sizes; four are suggested in Figure 7. They have respective base widths of 75, 55, 45, and 35 mm, dimensions about which type 1 basal widths (which vary from 33 to 88 mm) tend to cluster (Figure 8). The 65-mm range was omitted from the size categories as only nine square bases are spread over the 60 to 69 mm range; no short necks are attached to shoulders of a corresponding width; and the

TABLE 1

DIMENSIONS (IN MM) OF COMPLETE SHORT-NECKED SQUARE (TYPE 1) *FLACONS*

Provenience	Bottle Height	Bore Diam.	Lip Diam.	Neck Height	Shoulder Width*	Body Height	Pontil Diam.	Base Width*	Emboss.
1B.1J16		21	27	40	76/	130	35	72/76	
1B.1F2	231	19	26	43	77/77	184	29	74/75	
1L.34D4	231	17	24	39	78/79	190	33	71/74	
2L.18D2	211	17	22	40	74/74	165	31	70/72	
2L.19E3	215	21	30	39		175	38	73/75	
2L.53B4	198	20	26	40	76/78	164	31	74/74	
2L.53B4	212	21	28	38	77/77	190	35	71/73	
2L.53B4	218	18	24	34	81/	186	28	76/76	
2L.61E5	245	16	24	39	78/78	204	30	71/72	b
2L.61E5	238	16	24	37	78/	200	33	72/74	b
4L.52N18	231	20	28	36	73/75	182			
4L.55H3	215	20	27	40	80/80		27	76/77	
16L.92N16	212	25	31	38	76/76	152	30	73/74	

*Two sides were measured due to the asymmetry of these *flacons*.

one complete bottle with this base width has a different finish (Figure 13). Bases falling into this uncertain range, however, have been included in the following description.

By far the most common size of square *flacon* is represented by 270 bases (79% of square bases) in a range from 70 to 79 mm. This number includes 13 almost complete bottles whose measurements are given in Table 1. Their volumes vary from 570 to 900 ml. On the basis of the complete bottles and 30 other necks with extant shoulders wider than 70 mm, it was determined that neck heights for bottles of this size range from 32 to 47 mm, lip diameters from 22 to 32 mm, and bore diameters from 16 to 25 mm. There are only 10 necks with extant shoulders less than 60 mm wide and these present respective neck height and lip and bore diameter ranges of 20 to 39 mm, 15 to 22 mm, and 9 to 15 mm.

Pontil marks on square bases differ from those on cylindrical bases, generally having been applied in a manner that left the least amount of glass on the base. Pontil marks on bases wider than 70 mm have a 17 to 40 mm diameter range and a mean diameter of 33 mm. Marks on bases narrower than 70 mm wide have

the same diameter range but a mean diameter of only 28 mm.

As can be seen in Table 1, variations due to hand manufacture are ordinarily those of height, widths being controlled by the mold. There are only occasional deliberate variations among the square *flacons* and these have been illustrated. Figure 9 (*left*) depicts the only square-bodied bottle with a string rim and Figure 9 (*right*) illustrates an unusually short body which has begun to curve into the shoulder at a point only 40 mm above the base.

Aside from those *flacons* filled with food or condiments, most references to *flacons* in the inventories were to empty vessels and the next most common references were to those filled with oil (*flacons d'huile*). *Flacons* were very often found in *canevettes* or *caves* containing from 2 to 44 *flacons*, but most *canevettes* held 12 bottles. Barrelet (1953:103) mentioned the export of oil in "caves" and "cavenettes [sic]" containing 6, 9, or 12 *flacons* which he said were often squared. The frequency of *flacons d'huile* in the inventories and Barrelet's reference would imply that many of these square bottles did originally contain oil and the frequency of the reference to *canevettes* of empty *flacons*

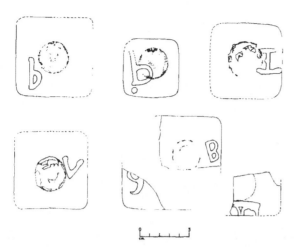

FIGURE 6. Type 1 *flacon* bases showing various embossed figures (the example in the upper left is 80 mm wide).

suggests as well their worth and reuse. Their large numbers from the excavations indicate their use for a variety of liquids other than oil, such as toilet water, vinegar, and, occasionally, spirits. Barrelet (1975:personal communication) has found blue-green bottles with labels indicating their use as containers for laboratory, apothecary, and household products as well as wine, oil, and perfumes.

Square *flacons* were most likely stoppered with plain corks. Corks have been found in situ in necks of square *flacons* and occur in large numbers in the inventories. Governor Duquesnel alone had over 1,200 *bouchons de bouteilles* (Adams 1972:187). Closures for other narrow-necked *flacons* (types 2-7) would have been the same.

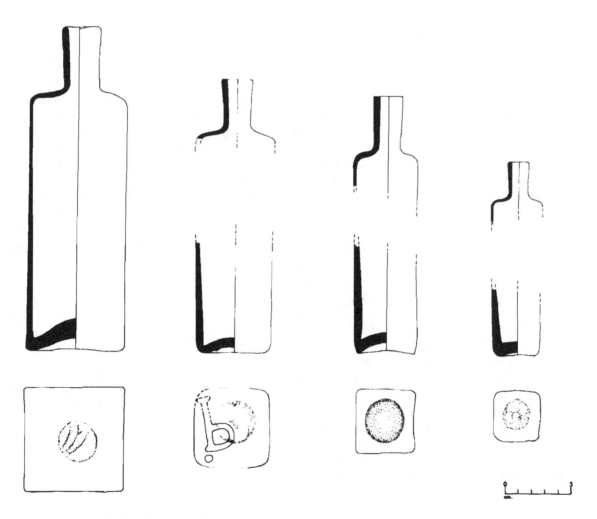

FIGURE 7. Type 1 *flacon* sizes (the example in the lower left is 75 mm wide).

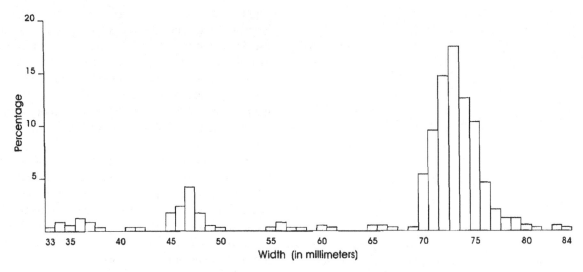

FIGURE 8. Percentage distribution of type 1 *flacon* base widths. Total sample, 342 bases.

TYPE 2. CYLINDRICAL "CASE" *FLACONS*

Cylindrical *flacons* exhibit the same profile as type 1 square *flacons*, having a plain cylindrical neck, horizontal shoulder, relatively straight-sided body, slightly indented base, and fairly uniform glass distribution. The neck is consistently longer, however, by approximately 20 mm than that of the type 1 *flacons*. There is one almost complete bottle in this group (Figure 10) as well as 11 necks and 11 bases. They constitute only 1% of the blue-green bottle sample.

The base of the nearly complete bottle is slightly ovoid–as though it had lain on its side for too long while still in its plastic state–with its diameter varying from 79 to 83 mm. The body rises 158 mm to the shoulder, widening only to a diameter of 83 to 85 mm at that point. Only the base of the neck remains and it is extant to a height of 48 mm. The neck height and finish are conjectural, based on dimensions of the other necks of this type. The bottle has a capacity of approximately 720 ml.

The 11 necks are distinguished from necks of other types by their true cylindrical shape, by their heights (47 to 60 mm) and plain, cracked-off and fire-polished lips (20 to 27 mm in diameter). The bore diameters range from 16 to 20 mm.

Bases vary from 79 to 83 mm in diameter, bear glass-tipped pontil marks 31 to 33 mm in diameter and can be distinguished by their shallow push-ups only 7 to 14 mm high. It would seem from the shallowness and surface texture of these bases that they were formed during dip molding and pushed up only slightly during empontiling. Perhaps the pontil was just pressed lightly to the base so as not to push it up any higher than necessary. This might account for the fact that so little glass adheres to the base in the case of both these bottles and the square *flacons*.

The relatively straight sides of this bottle type suggest it would fit snugly and securely into a case or *canevette*. Its shape also suggests modeling after the square *flacons* and its function would not vary from theirs.

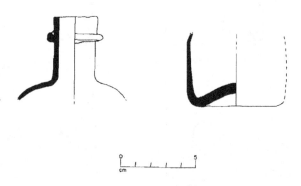

FIGURE 9. Occasional variations among type 1 *flacons*: **left**, string rim attached; **right**, extremely short body (68 mm maximum basal width).

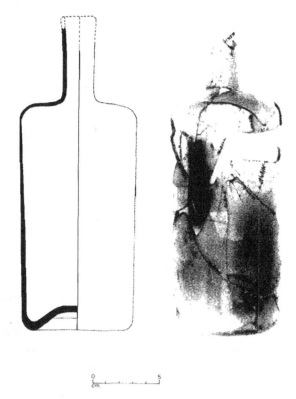

FIGURE 10. Type 2 *flacon*, cylindrical, approximate capacity 720 ml (85 mm maximum diameter).

TYPE 3. TALL CYLINDRICAL *FLACONS*

A type 3 *flacon* is defined primarily by its tall, slightly flaring neck and long thin body. The only complete example (Figure 11) is 317 mm high with a base diameter of only 60 mm and a capacity of approximately 690 ml. In addition to the one complete bottle, there are 99 necks and 3 bases, 8% of the blue-green sample. The disparity between the number of necks and bases is explained by the fact that bases of these bottles are identical to bases from two other types of *flacons*: cylindrical jars and short-necked cylindrical bottles (types 8 and 5). Bases of these three containers can only be differentiated from each other when most of the body is attached to them.

The container in Figure 11 has a neck 73 mm tall finished with a lip 27 mm in diameter and a bore 18 mm in diameter. The body narrows 8 mm over its height of 178 mm to a diameter of 52 mm at the shoulder. The smooth conical

push-up has a glass-tipped pontil mark 23 mm in diameter completely covering the push-up tip.

With the exception of neck heights, which varied from 57 to 84 mm, there is little variation in size or shape in this group of necks. Lips are usually thick, approximately 5 mm, and 90% of their diameters vary from only 25 to 30 mm; 93% of the bore diameters vary from 15 to 20 mm. The glass thins considerably towards the bases of the necks and tooling marks are often visible as horizontal impressions in those areas. The neck-shoulder junctions are usually distinct and the shoulders begin to curve immediately. The two necks in Figure 12 illustrate the few variations that did occur. The neck in Figure 12 (*left*) is excessively thick while the neck in Figure 12 (*right*) has been indented below its lip. There were two examples of the latter variation.

The three bases range in diameter from 65 to 70 mm and exhibit push-up profiles in two shapes: rounded-conical and dome-shaped. Push-up heights vary from 15 to 18 mm and the glass-tipped pontil used in each case left a mark varying in diameter from 21 to 25 mm.

Barrelet (1975:personal communication) included this bottle shape with those having varied functions as containers of spirits, oils, toiletries, or household products. The almost complete bottle (Figure 11) pours well and is a convenient size to hold, but with such a small base would seem impractical for everyday use. It seems possible that these bottles were placed in cases or *canevettes*.

TYPE 4. TALL-NECKED SQUARE *FLACONS*

One complete bottle, puzzling by its singularity and completeness, was found to represent another blue-green *flacon* shape. It combines the neck and body shape of two common *flacon* types for its neck belongs to the type 3 tall-necked cylinder and its body is identical to those of the type 1 short-necked squares. The bottle (Figure 13) has a base width of 60 to 61 mm and bears a glass-tipped pontil mark 22 mm in diameter. There is a tiny circular impression in the center of the basal area that indicates that a sharp instrument had been used to push the base up additionally after molding. The basal

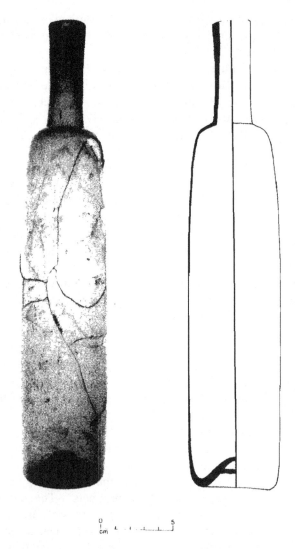

FIGURE 11. Type 3 *flacon*, approximate capacity 690 ml (62 mm maximum diameter).

one example of this bottle type occurs since its individual shape elements are both common. The fact that this bottle was excavated from the King's Bastion, even though from the end opposite that of the governor's wing, becomes interesting in the light of the bottle's uniqueness, for Governor Duquesnel's inventory (Adams 1978:124-132) included over 1,000 bottles containing a wide variety of liquids and solids. A *flacon* in an unusual type from this area is, therefore, less curious.

TYPE 5. SHORT-NECKED CYLINDRICAL FLACONS

Short tubular necks, either plain or thickened, are not limited to square-bodied type 1 *flacons*, but occur as well on round-shouldered cylindrical bottles (Figure 14). There are five necks (less than 0.5% of the total sample) with round shoulders attached. Two are plain cylinders as occur on most square *flacons*, and three are tapered from lip to shoulder with a narrow bore (Figure 14). The two tubular necks have lip

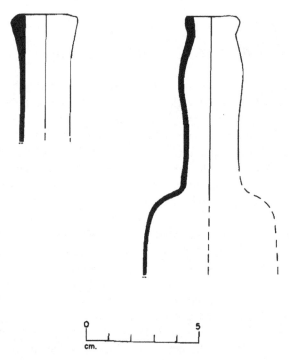

FIGURE 12. Occasional variations on type 3 *flacon* necks: **left**, flared lip (30 mm maximum diameter); **right**, constricted lip.

depression is only 8 mm high. The body is 184 mm high, a height similar to those of some of the large square *flacons* in Table 1. The shoulder is 64 mm square topped by a neck 60 mm high with a lip diameter of 24 mm and a bore diameter of 16 mm. The bottle's total height is 247 mm and it has an approximate capacity of 480 ml.

No other necks of this type were found with even the suggestion of a horizontal shoulder, but many were found with part of an unquestionably round shoulder attached, identifying them as type 3 *flacons*. Furthermore, among the short-necked squares are no shoulders in the 60-mm range attached to necks. It is surprising that only

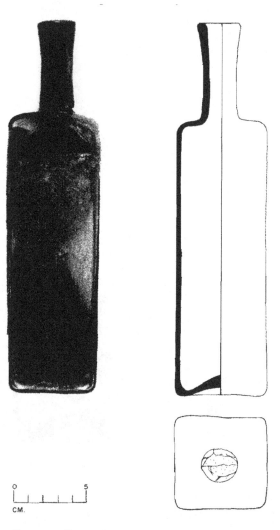

A similar bottle, corked and filled with a reddish liquid, is illustrated in a ca. 1756 Chardin still life entitled *Une orange, un gobelet d'argent et divers objects* (Chardin 1969:Plate 39). This bottle has straighter sides than do the tapered Louisbourg examples. Other similar short-necked bottles were found in a 17th-century archaeological context in Quebec City. One bottle was intact and contained wine (Lafrenière and Gagnon 1971:22, 68). In the 18th century these bottles would have likely had other functions, similar to those of any of the narrow-necked *flacons* already discussed, as well as being containers for wine.

TYPE 6. TALL-NECKED CYLINDRICAL *FLACONS*

Having a narrow body similar to *flacon* type 5 but a distinctive neck wider at its base than lip is the tall-necked round-shouldered cylindrical bottle illustrated in Figure 15. There are 23 necks, 2 bases, and 1 nearly complete bottle of this type, comprising 2% of the blue-green

FIGURE 13. Type 4 *flacon*, approximate capacity 480 ml (62 mm maximum width).

diameters of 30 mm and bore diameters of 22 mm. The three thicker necks have lip diameters of 31 to 32 mm and bores of only 17 to 20 mm. Neck heights of all five are comparable at 30 to 32 mm. Shoulder diameters could only be estimated as varying from 70 to 90 mm.

Only two bases can be definitely associated with the necks. The smaller one (Figure 14), 54 mm in diameter, has a truncated cone-shaped push-up profile with a glass-tipped pontil mark 23 mm in diameter securely placed in the tip. The larger base, 68 mm in diameter, exhibits a dome-shaped profile and a pontil mark 31 mm in diameter. These bases are identical to those associated with *flacon* types 3, 6, and 8.

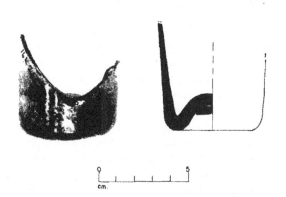

FIGURE 14. Type 5 *flacon* (54 mm maximum basal diameter).

sample. Few bases could be associated with this type because of their similarity to bases of *flacon* types 3, 5, and 8.

The bottle in Figure 15 is 269 mm high and would have held approximately 720 ml. It has a dome-shaped push-up 13 mm high with a pontil mark 30 mm in diameter. The diameter of the body widens to approximately 85 mm at the shoulder. The neck is a plain cylinder 40 mm wide at its base and 30 mm wide at its lip. The bore is 20 mm in diameter.

The base of this bottle is interesting for the area of the basal surface within the pontil mark is faintly corrugated as though the base had been pushed up with a rough flat-tipped tool rather than a *molette*. The pontil mark, a circle of glass chips, closely resembles that of a sand pontil (Jones 1971:69), but evidence from similar bases indicates that the mark is probably from a lightly applied glass-tipped pontil.

The only other base is domed, 68 mm in diameter, and had been pushed up 9 mm before the application of a glass-tipped pontil. The pontil mark is 35 mm in diameter.

The other 23 necks range in height from 45 to 64 mm, but 18 of these are in the 50 to 60 mm range. Lip diameters range from 24 to 31 mm; bores from 15 to 21 mm.

Lapointe (1981:28) reports finding a single type 6 *flacon* among the artifacts recovered from the Perthuis latrine at Place Royal, Quebec. It appears that there are no examples from other sites nor are there similar bottles in contemporary art. The function of this *flacon* type should parallel that of the other narrow-necked *flacons*.

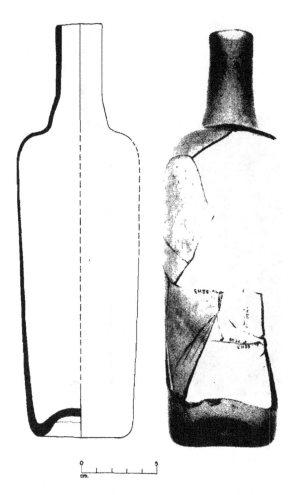

FIGURE 15. Type 6 *flacon*, approximate capacity of 720 ml (72 mm maximum basal diameter).

TYPE 7. LARGE STORAGE *FLACONS*

Bottles of the large storage type are unique among blue-green bottles from the fortress for they have distinct protruding lips (Figures 16, 17) and this neck/lip combination does not occur on any of the other *flacon* types. The bottle in Figure 16 is quite typical of the type, having a thick rounded lip; tall, slightly concave neck; broad rounded shoulder; tapered body; and a high conical push-up. Among the fragments are 76 necks (6% of the total sample) and a possible 24 bases as well as one complete but fragile bottle with an overall height of 355 mm and an approximate capacity of 2,400 ml.

There may have been two or more sizes of this bottle type, but the most common are set on bases 100 to 112 mm in diameter. Only two bases exceed these dimensions: one 127 mm in diameter and the other 160 mm in diameter. The latter is associated with the top portion of a large neck with a lip diameter of 50 mm and a lip height of 10 mm. This base and neck would appear to be representative of a deliberately larger size. Lip diameters range from 34 to 55 mm with 77% falling into a narrower range of 35 to 40 mm. Overall, lip heights range from 6 to 10 mm and bore diameters from 17 to 28 mm. Necks are from 90 to 120 mm tall.

Only two shoulder diameters are extant and they are 146 and 155 mm associated with bases 102 and 108 mm in diameter respectively. Their respective extant body heights are 192 and 206 mm.

Conical push-ups of the 24 bases are high, 22 to 37 mm, and bear relatively small (22 to

33 mm in diameter) glass-tipped pontil marks at or near the tips, often filling the tips or closing them over. Often a push-up mark could be seen as a flat circular impression in the tip about 8 mm in diameter. The marks appear to have occurred while the bottles were in the dip molds or when the bases were being pushed up.

This base type is shared with type 8 *flacons* (tall cylindrical jars). To date the largest jar reconstructed at Louisbourg has a base diameter of 94 mm and for this reason any larger conical bases of this style are described as large storage *flacon* bases. It should be kept in mind, however, that jars with bases as large as 100 mm in diameter do occur on other French historic sites, such as the Roma site on Prince Edward Island, occupied from 1732 to 1745 (Alyluia 1981). It appears likely, too, that jars this size did occur at Louisbourg, even though their large bases are not extant, on the evidence of the presence of jar necks exceeding 100 mm in diameter.

The protruding lips of large storage *flacons* seem to have been formed by tooling the cracked-off lip down and out, often leaving a crease around the bore. This is particularly evident on the neck in Figure 17 (*center*), one

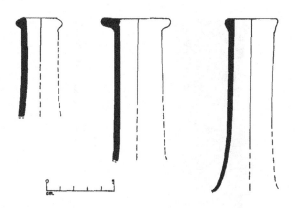

FIGURE 17. Lip variations which occurred on type 7 *flacons*: **left**, V-shaped lip; **center**, rounded lip (52 mm maximum diameter); and **right**, slightly protruding lip.

of the wider lips found. The finish would then be smoothed inside the bore and the lip given its final definition and distinctive shape: rounded (Figure 17 *center*), slightly uptooled (Figure 16), or V-shaped (Figure 17 *left*). Figure 17 (*right*) illustrates how little the lip protrudes on some examples.

Its size, relatively thin-glassed body, and heavy neck would seem to make this *flacon* type less practical as a container that would see daily or frequent use. The likelihood of its use as a storage container for a variety of liquids seems more probable. One inventory (MacLean 1974:139) listed a *canevette* containing six *flacons* of five *chopines*, or approximately 2,400 ml each, while a possible 1,440-ml size is cited in a 1684 Quebec inventory (Séguin 1973:525-6) which lists "*une cave de douse flacons de Trois chopines chacun plaine de Rossosel*." A large storage *flacon* of 1,800 ml capacity was excavated at Fort Michilimackinac (Brown 1971:109), and a 3,100-ml example is part of the Tunica Treasure (Brain 1979:92).

TYPE 8. WIDE-MOUTHED CYLINDRICAL FLACONS

At least 20% of the blue-green bottle sample consists of wide-mouthed cylindrical *flacons* or jars, which are, in effect, a horizontally expanded version of type 3 (tall cylindrical) *flacons*. In all there are 234 necks and 10 bases as well as

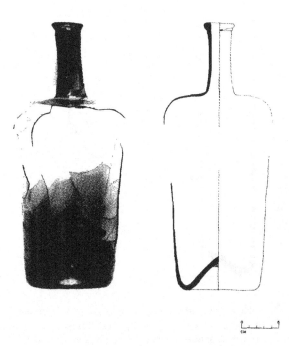

FIGURE 16. Type 7 *flacon* having a capacity of more than 1,800 ml (145 mm maximum diameter).

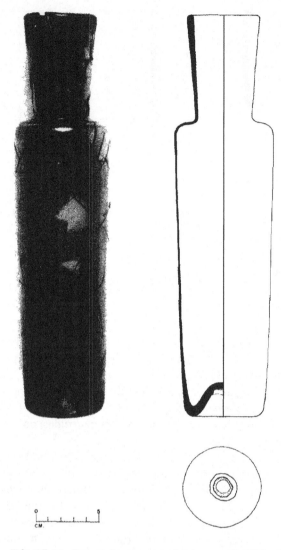

FIGURE 18. Type 8 *flacon*, approximate capacity 720 ml
(82 mm maximum diameter).

right). The illustrated example (Figure 19 *left*) is 307 mm high with an approximate capacity of 960 ml.

Diameters of 240 lips were taken and include those of the 6 complete bottles. The lip diameters cover a very wide range from approximately 35 to 110 mm (Figure 20), with bores from 30 to 97 mm, and tend to bunch at 5-mm intervals due to the rounding off of measurements which is inevitable when using a concentric semicircle gauge. By using the clusters as the center of each 5-mm interval, the distribution illustrated in Figure 21 occurs.

Of the 240 lips with diameters extant, 61 have complete neck heights; however, the diameter to height relationship is not always as expected.

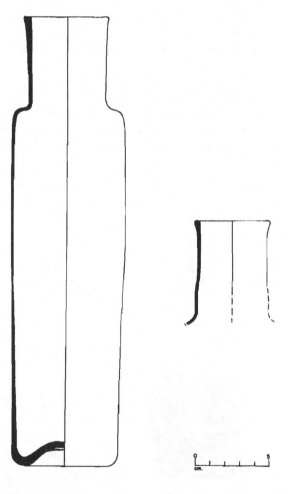

FIGURE 19. Variation of type 8 *flacons*: **left**, complete bottle (approximate capacity 960 ml) illustrating variations in overall shape (75 mm maximum diameter); **right**, neck illustrating occasional bulging.

6 complete bottles whose dimensions are given in Table 2.

Commonly cylindrical jars have thick lips, tapered necks, very short rounded shoulders, tall tapered bodies, and conical push-ups. Figure 18 illustrates a typical example, a jar 304 mm high with an approximate capacity of 720 ml. They occur most often in blue-green glass and occasionally in yellow or brown.

Significant variations from the norm do occur–in blue-green only–and the most extreme is illustrated by the jar in Figure 19 (*left*); it has straight sides, a shorter straight neck, relatively thin lip, and a shallow dome-shaped push-up. Occasionally the necks bulge slightly (Figure 19

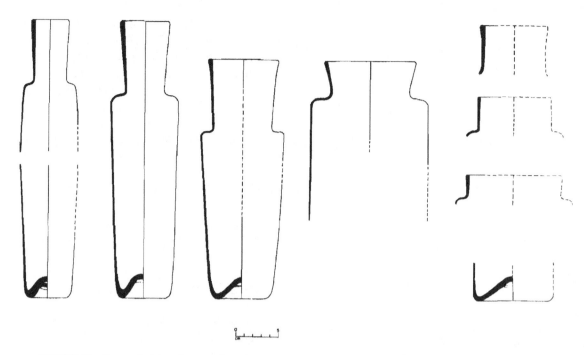

FIGURE 20. Size variations of type 8 *flacons* (the fourth example from the left has a lip 105 mm in diameter).

The narrowest lip diameters, from 40 to 70 mm, are associated with neck heights ranging from 22 to 80 mm (51 examples); in contrast, middle-sized diameters, from 76 to 84 mm, are associated with neck heights ranging from 74 to 82 mm (7 examples), and the widest diameters, from 90 to 110 mm, with neck heights ranging from only 23 to 39 mm (3 examples).

Including the bases from the complete bottles, there are only 16 definite cylindrical jar bases. Their numbers are low because of the usual confusion due to the similarity between these bases and those of types 3, 5, 6, and 7. The jar bases vary in diameter from 47 to 94 mm and all, with one domed exception (Figure 19 *left*), have conical or rounded-conical push-ups. Glass-tipped pontil marks vary in diameter from 20 to 31 mm, the diameter of the bases not always being determining factors in pontil diameter sizes.

The function of these jars was certainly to contain various foods, mainly fruits and condi-

TABLE 2

DIMENSIONS (IN MM) OF COMPLETE WIDE-MOUTHED CYLINDRICAL (TYPE 8) *FLACONS*

Proven.	Base Diam.	Push-Up Profile*	Push-Up Height	Pontil Diam.	Body Height	Shoulder Diam.	Neck Height	Lip Diam./ Base Neck Diam.	Bore Diam.	Total Height
1B.1B2	75	RC	16	25	196	94	79	84/71	76	276
2L.53B4	62	RC	21	22	224	74	80	58/44	45	304
2L.12H7	68	C	21	26	178	90	75	67/58	60	260
2L.12H7	70	C	20	25	181	98	78	82/70	74	265
1L.34D5	73	D	13	31	235	79	61	58/53	51	307
2L.12H8	71	C	20	26	182	97	75	82/70	75	262

*RC: rounded cibel; C: cone; D: dome.

Jane E. Harris

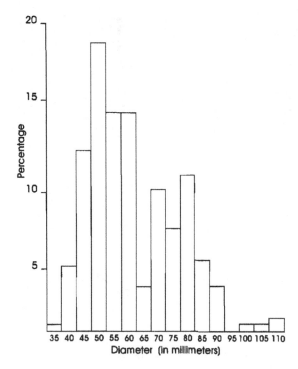

FIGURE 21. Percentage distribution of type 8 *flacon* lip diameters. Total sample, 240 lips.

ments, for storage and shipping. Governor Duquesnel's 1744 inventory indicates he had in storage 2 "*petits flacons de Citrons confits,*" 12 "*flacons d'Enchois,*" 5 "*flacons de Capres,*" and a case containing 6 "*flacons de capres*" and 4 "*d'Enchois*" (Adams 1978:131). The merchant Castaing (1756) had among his merchandise 3 cases of "*fruit à l'eau de vie*" containing 36 *flacons* each and a case "*danschoix*" (anchovies) containing 72 *flacons* (Thibault 1972:303). Chardin illustrates a jar of olives in his 1760 still life *Bocal d'olives* (Chardin 1969); Anne Vallayer-Coster, in the tapestry *La brioche ou le déjeuner*, modeled after a 1766 painting, includes a large jar of gherkins (Roland Michel 1970:No. 218), and de la Porte (1725-1793), in his still life *Une vielle et des fruits*, illustrates a jar of what could be apricots (Figure 22).

Narrow-necked *flacons* were stopped with corks, but wide-mouthed jars, by their size and the prohibitive cost of corks, necessitated a different means of closure. While the narrower jar necks could and did use corks, as illustrated by Chardin (1969) (Figure 23), the wider jars appear to have been usually closed by means

of some sort of cloth tied over the neck with string. McKearin (1971:120-121) cited 16th-century references to wax covered with leather or parchment, or sized cloth as covers. References in contemporary art to this practice are numerous; however, only one is illustrated here (Figure 22). A closure of this type would also provide a convenient space on which to note the contents, but the only illustrated example of this practice is from the first half of the 19th century (Richter and Härlin 1974:Figure 6). Labels could have been placed on the bodies of jars and such a practice is illustrated in a painting of the 18th-century *Ecole Française* (Faré 1962:Figure 401).

TYPE 9. WIDE-MOUTHED SQUARE *FLACONS*

Wide-mouthed square *flacons* make up only 2% of the blue-green sample with 25 necks, 2 bases, and 4 whole bottles. It is most likely that their numbers are somewhat larger as, like square type 4 *flacon*, they are a composite of parts of two other *flacon* types: square bottles (type 1) and cylindrical jars (type 8). As percentages are based on neck counts, should the percentage of square jars grow, the percentage of cylindrical jars would drop. In either case, over 20% of the blue-green sample consists of jars.

The jar in Figure 24 is typical in size and shape except that its lip is slightly everted. Most lips are quite straight, the necks narrowing slightly toward the shoulder. The illustrated jar is 235 mm high and has an approximate capacity of 810 ml. The base is 78 mm square with a slight arch 11 mm in height. The pontil has hardly marked the base, merely leaving a faint circle of chips and gouges 34 mm in diameter. The body has widened unevenly and measures 81 mm on one side and 85 mm on the other. The neck, 52 mm high with a lip 60 mm in diameter and a bore 53 mm in diameter, narrows to 51 mm at the shoulder.

From the remaining fragments it could be determined that the neck heights are quite variable (32 to 69 mm) as are their lip and bore diameters (46 to 90 mm and 39 to 60 mm, respectively). All necks with diameters over 70 mm have virtually no shoulders, as in Figure 25 (*right*), and the neck diameters are roughly equal to the body widths. Only one neck has a diameter as large as 90 mm and a correspond-

The Historical Archaeology Laboratory Handbook

FIGURE 22. *Une vieille et des fruits or Nature morte à la vielle,* still life by Henri Roland de la Porte (Musée des Beaux-Arts, Bordeaux.)

ingly large shoulder. The remaining shoulders are from 70 to 80 mm in width independent of their neck diameters which range from 47 to 60 mm.

Bases coincide in shape and style with those of the common type 1 *flacon,* but are limited to a width range of 72 to 78 mm. One base is embossed with a capital "B." Of the six bases, all have glass-tipped pontil marks varying slightly in diameter from 26 to 34 mm. Volumes of the other three complete jars are approximately of 750, 750, and 840 ml, respectively.

Even though there are no pictorial or written references to square jars, their functions and closures should, understandably, parallel those of cylindrical jars. They contained various foods and were stopped with large corks, or in the case of the wider mouths, possibly waxed and covered with cloth.

Bouteilles

Wine or spirits bottles in the typical French flowerpot shape in blue-green glass make up 7% of the total blue-green sample. There are 87 necks and 18 bases, but no complete bottles. Overall these bottles seem to be strong and while the glass is heaviest in their bases and necks, it is generally evenly distributed through their bodies, having a consistent thickness from 2 to 3 mm throughout the bodies and shoulders. The bottle in Figure 26, over 226 mm in height, has an approximate capacity of 780 ml. The base, 93 mm in diameter, has a rounded conical push-up 27 mm high. A glass-tipped pontil mark 28 mm in diameter is situated in the tip. The neck is extant to a height of 93 mm and bears a down-tooled string rim 35 mm in diameter and 8 mm high. The lip is 13 mm high with

FIGURE 23. *Canard sauvage avec divers objets or Rafraîchissements*, still life by Jean Baptiste Simeon Chardin, 1764 (The James Philip Gray Collection, Museum of Fine Arts, Springfield, Massachusetts.)

are often difficult to ascertain, but vary approximately from 85 to 120 mm.

Only 5 other bases have enough body extant to indicate flowerpot-shaped bodies, but 12 more could be tentatively attributed to the *bouteille* shape on the basis of their push-up shape and pontil mark diameters. *Bouteille* bases have push-ups that tend to be in the shape of a short broad-tipped cone, the pontil placed right in the tip and in some cases pushed up, causing the profile to become higher and almost bell-shaped. This action also resulted in push-up heights of considerable variety from 16 to 54 mm. The 18 *bouteille* bases (82 to 103 mm in diameter) have a mean diameter of 96 mm. Pontil marks range from 23 to 39 mm with a mean pontil diameter of 30 mm. By comparison, the bases of large storage bottles (type 7 *flacons*) and cylindrical jars (type 8 *flacons*) which could be included in this base diameter range generally have sharp conical push-ups and, as well, large storage bottles have a proportionally smaller mean pontil

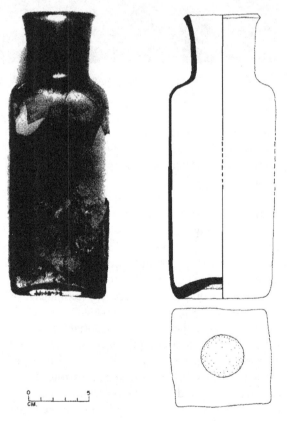

FIGURE 24. Type 9 *flacon*, approximate capacity 810 ml (85 mm maximum diameter).

a diameter of 24 mm and a bore diameter of 16 mm.

The necks generally present quite an elegant profile–tall and slim, gradually widening into broad rounded shoulders–and for this reason it is difficult to distinguish where the shoulders end and necks and bodies begin. All of the necks are finished with plain cracked-off and lightly fire-polished lips varying only slightly in outer diameter from 23 to 30 mm and bore diameter from 15 to 22 mm. A string rim from 3 to 9 mm in height was placed 1 to 18 mm below the lip. Almost 50% of the string rims are rounded, 33% had been tooled into a V-shape, and 20% had been down tooled (Figure 27). Many of the rounded string rims have some tooling above and below them to make them more uniform, but some are plain laid-on rings. Neck heights

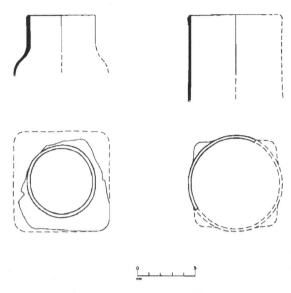

FIGURE 25. Variations in neck diameters of type 9 *flacons*: **left**, profile and cross-section (upper) and top view (lower) of a narrow neck (60 mm maximum lip diameter); **right**, profile and cross-section (upper) and top view (lower) of a wide neck.

mark diameter (27 mm) on a proportionally larger base (mean diameter, 105 mm).

Occasional push-up marks and possible *molette* marks occur on these bases, but most interesting are the two bases with a wide rectangular impression in the tip of each push-up. The marks appear to have been made by an implement in the shape of a 20-mm-wide slice through the center of a hemispherical object. They are both on slightly bell-shaped push-ups, implying that the tool was used to extend the height of the push-up before empontiling.

Barrelet (1975:personal communication) suggested that these bottles were undoubtedly used for wine. Chardin (1969:Plate 2) included one half full and corked in a still life ca. 1726-1728 entitled *Les apprèts d'un déjeuner*, while a short-necked example with a label on its body is depicted in *La théière blanche avec fruits*, ca. 1756 (Chardin 1969:Figure 246). Anne Vallayer-Coster (1744-1818) shows an addition to the usual cork and wire closure in *Fruits et bouteilles* (Roland Michel 1970:40) where cloth of some sort has been placed over the cork and tied down. It is difficult to say whether these *bouteilles* are *petite verrerie* attempts at copying black-glass bottles or whether French black-glass factories copied this already established wine bottle style.

Dames-Jeannes

Only in one style in blue-green glass, the extremely large fragile bottles comprise approximately 2% of the blue-green sample with 24 necks, 21 bases, and no complete examples. The bottles are quite plain and apparently free-blown and flattened into a flat onion or gourd shape. The necks are plain with slightly concave profiles and cracked-off, slightly everted lips (Figure 28). The lip on the illustrated example is 54 mm in diameter with a bore diameter of 42 mm on a neck 171 mm high. The base is decidedly ovoid and pushed up into a broad, almost bell shape. At the tip of the push-up is a circular protrusion or mamelon approximately 20 mm in diameter surrounded by a circle of glass chips, 42 mm in diameter, left by the pontil. Although the diameter of the base could not be taken, the distance across the resting point is 184 mm.

The remaining 20 bases have glass-tipped pontil marks although all that remains on each is a thin circle of glass. They vary in diameter from 34 to 49 mm with one extra large one of 59 mm. Only three of the bases are complete enough to measure the push-up height and these vary from 42 to 56 mm. Twelve of the bases each have a mamelon approximately in the center of the tip of the push-up.

FIGURE 26. Blue-green *bouteille*, approximate capacity 780 ml (108 mm maximum diameter).

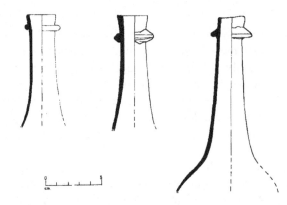

FIGURE 27. *Bouteille* string rim variations: **left**, rounded; center, V-shaped (28 mm maximum lip diameter); **right**, down tooled.

Lip diameters vary from 43 to 57 mm, but the most common size is 50 mm, a size represented by 5 lips. Bores vary from 34 to 42 mm in diameter. The 5 necks having complete heights vary from 131 to 171 mm.

It is impossible to estimate the volumes of any of these bottles but it is known that Governor Duquesnel had one which contained at least six *pots*, approximately 14 liters, which he had filled with *eau de vie* (Adams 1978:131). Another *dame-jeanne* with a funnel (Thibault 1972:308) was inventoried among merchant Castaing's goods, which would suggest that that vessel was used to carry smaller amounts of a liquid from storage to the house. Barrelet (1953:88) mentioned the use of demijohns in the 17th century as containers for oil. Scoville (1950:95) recorded that "appreciable quantities" of empty *dames-jeannes* were exported from France to the colonies. As with the other blue-green bottles, *dames-jeannes* seem to have been multipurpose containers.

Although there is no specific evidence pertaining to closures for *dames-jeannes*, the use of large corks, as used on narrow-mouthed *flacons* (type 8), as stoppers seems most probable.

Bases from Cylindrical Bottles

There are 242 bases from cylindrical bottles ranging in diameter from 41 to 98 mm which could not be definitely assigned to one particular *flacon* type, but could belong to types 2, 3, 5, 6, and 8, and even possibly to type 7 or to

the *fioles* or *bouteilles*. Since function was determined primarily by neck shape and since the enumeration of types was based on necks, the type attribution of these bases is unimportant; however, the bases do present interesting features pertaining to their manufacture.

Dark ferric oxide (Charles Saulnier 1974:personal communication) is deposited in the shape of a circle or a ring on the pontil marks on 47 bases, while many others show traces of the oxide. From this two things can be implied: (1) that the tips of the pontil rods used varied in diameter from 10 to 19 mm, and (2) that blowpipes were sometimes used as pontil rods. The iron oxide circles from the pipes vary in their outside diameters from 12 to 17 mm.

The base on the lower left in Figure 29 has a flat ring-shaped ferric oxide deposit with respective outside and inside diameters of 15 and 8 mm. In the same figure, the two bases on the right have flat circular ferric oxide deposits with respective diameters of 16 and 10 mm. The base on the upper left in Figure 29 has what at first appeared to be double empontiling, but what more likely is an example of over-zealous application of a glass-tipped pontil. This base has a circular slightly impressed area with traces of an iron oxide deposit covering an area 14 mm in diameter. Much lower on the push-up are adhering glass chips that form a rough circle 32 mm in diameter. It appears that the rod broke through the excess glass of the pontil, not

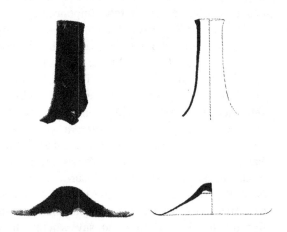

FIGURE 28. *Dame-jeanne* neck and base (220 mm maximum diameter). This bottle may have had a capacity of several decaliters.

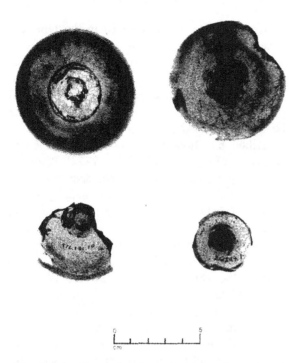

FIGURE 29. Pontil marks: **upper left**, glass-tipped (70 mm maximum basal diameter); **upper right** and **lower right**, glass-tipped with iron oxide deposit; **lower left**, glass-tipped blowpipe with iron oxide deposit.

stopping until it reached the tip of the push-up. The tip had then been slightly extended by the force of the rod.

By comparison, deposits of any sort on square-bodied *flacon* bases are rare. Usually the pontil appears to have been so lightly applied as to leave only the faintest trace of a pontil mark, other times leaving a circular area of excess glass and torn-out areas. It seems that ferric oxide deposits from the pontil rod or blowpipe could appear on any of the cylindrical *flacon*, *fiole*, or *bouteille* bases, but to date none have appeared on *dame-jeanne* bases.

Common occurrences on many bases are swirling striations or impressions from the base of the push-up towards the tip. These marks may have been left by the *molette* when the bases were formed. They are most noticeable on conical and rounded-conical push-ups and less evident on shallow domed push-ups which often have exceptionally smooth surfaces, possibly because the marks were obliterated by the pontil and possibly because the pontil may have been used in these cases as a push-up tool as well

as a pontil. If the pontil were used to push the base up farther after being shaped by the *molette*, the glass in the push-up would be extended and subsequently smoothed.

Conclusions

This study of blue-green bottles from Louisbourg has led to a definition of French 18th-century blue-green bottle forms, has provided additional manufacturing information, and has suggested possible uses and closures for the bottles. The sample of 1,200 blue-green bottles was divided for study into four distinct bottle forms based on terms used consistently in the inventories of the period: *fioles*, *flacons*, *bouteilles*, and *dames-jeannes*.

Fioles are small bottles, limited in size to a few milliliters and comprising 20% of the total sample. They were used primarily to contain medicines and toiletries, but may also have appeared on the buffet filled with oil, vinegar, or individual servings of wine.

Flacons, both narrow- and wide-mouthed, comprise 70% of the sample and occur in at least nine different types and several sizes. Wide-mouthed *flacons* held a variety of condiments such as preserved and pickled fruits, vegetables, and fish, and constitute 25% of the total sample. The primary purpose of narrow-necked *flacons* seems to have changed in the early 18th century with the advent of the black-glass "wine" bottle, from primarily containers for spirits to containers for a variety of liquids such as oil, toilet water, and, less often, spirits.

The flowerpot-shaped *bouteille* is the only bottle form in blue-green glass finished with a string rim. These bottles comprise 7% of the sample and were used for the storage or transport of wines and spirits.

Dames-jeannes, capable of containing several liters of a liquid, are the least common blue-green bottle form, comprising only 2% of the sample. They probably functioned as containers for a variety of liquids.

The usual form of closure, used on all the bottle forms above, was a cork, tied down with string or wire when practical. The very large-mouthed *flacons*, because of the size of their openings, were not corked, but covered with paper or cloth and tied down with string. These covers and corks could be retained while the bottles were in use, but occasionally sprays of paper stuffed into the necks served the same purpose.

The study of blue-green bottles from Louisbourg has revealed some evidence of the techniques used in the manufacture of these vessels and also evidence that the techniques used around wood-fired furnaces were not identical to those used around coal-fired furnaces.

According to Diderot (*Diderot-d'Alembert Encyclopédie* 1751-1765[17]:112; 1772a:Plate 18), there were two common empontiling techniques used in the manufacture of black-glass "wine" bottles; one used a glass-tipped pontil rod and the other used the *meule* or cylinder of glass left on the blowpipe after cracking-off. Both of these techniques are evident on common French black-glass "wine" bottles from Louisbourg; however, in the case of blue-green glass from Louisbourg, the former method, using the glass-tipped pontil, was by far the more frequently used and there are no examples of the characteristic ring-shaped pontil marks associated with the latter method. There is evidence of use of the blowpipe during empontiling, but in a manner rather different from that described by Diderot. This evidence is in the form of an occasional, iron-oxide-darkened, ring-shaped impression which occurs on the pontil mark itself, indicating the blowpipe had been cleaned off, a new gather added, and then the pipe pressed to the base of the bottle. With the exception of the incidental occurrence of this imprinted ring shape, the pontil marks left by this method of empontiling are identical to those of a glass-tipped pontil.

The pontil marks left on all the blue-green bottles are typically small (Jones 1971:68) in relation to the sizes of the bases on which they were placed, not exceeding 29 mm in diameter on *fiole* bases, 40 mm in diameter on *flacon* and *bouteille* bases, and not usually exceeding 50 mm on the huge *dames-jeannes*. Pontil marks are also generally much more prominent on cylindrical bottles than on square bottles, the pontil often appearing to have been more firmly attached to the former; however, in both cases, the pontil frequently adhered so lightly as to give the appearance of sand pontil marks.

In addition to the differences in the type and general appearance of pontil marks, there seems to be a difference in the formation of the bases of cylindrical and square bottles. Cylindrical bottles appear to have had their bases pushed up with a *molette* or other push-up tool after being removed from the dip mold, in the manner described by Diderot (*Diderot-d'Alemert Encyclopédie* 1751-1765, [17]:112; 1772b:Plate 5). Square bases, on the other hand, appear to have been formed in the mold, their usually slight basal concavity appearing to have been the result of empontiling.

The large number and variety of blue-green bottles in the Louisbourg collection are evidence that in the 18th century the *petites verreries* continued to play a significant role in the French glass industry by producing a wide variety of "large and small bottles" (Scoville 1950:111), many of which were being exported to the colonies throughout the French occupation periods at Louisbourg. Time has not allowed for a chemical analysis of the blue-green bottle sample; however, its future use, by determining the presence of significant quantities of either soda or potash in the glass, could help localize the origins of the containers to particular parts of France. At the very least this type of analysis could indicate whether a bottle is of a coastal or inland origin. Unfortunately, further precision in attribution is unlikely since both Scoville and Barrelet have noted the difficulty of identifying regional distinctions in form or shape among the wares of the *petites verreries*.

Certain general observations pertaining to the use and value of bottles in Louisbourg can be made. King's officers, merchants, *habitant-pecheurs*, innkeepers, and other middle and upper class members of Louisbourg society generally had the greatest variety and quantity of bottles in their inventories, while among those of the less well-to-do members of the community, such as the fishermen employed by the *habitant-pecheurs*, there was seldom any mention of glass items. This information, coupled with the knowledge of the kinds of luxury items often contained in bottles, bears out the contrast between the quality of life of the upper and lower classes. The apparent lack of blue-green bottles among the lower classes in Louisbourg is also in contrast to the situation in France where, according to Scoville, the use of common glass was widespread and included the lower classes. Transportation costs may have greatly increased the values of glass containers and their contents, making them less accessible to the poorer residents of Louisbourg.

The commercial value placed on bottled goods at Louisbourg is indicated by their very mention in the inventories and, while a systematic evaluation of prices for bottles and their contents has been excluded from this report, it may be of interest to include some examples. Among the estimated values from a 1756 merchant's inventory (Thibault 1972:299-310), a *flacon* of brandied fruit was worth 50 *sols*; a *flacon* of anchovies, 15 *sols*; a *"bouteille de frontignan,"* 40 *sols*; a *flacon* of oil, 30 *sols*; a *dame-jeanne* and funnel, 100 *sols*, and 100 empty *bouteilles* were worth 20 *livres* (400 *sols*). It is interesting, but not surprising in light of the less than ideal growing conditions in Louisbourg that the fruit was valued above both the wine and oil, and much above the anchovies.

Overall, Louisbourg's household inventories turned out to be a much richer resource than expected, resulting not only in the construction of the backbone of the present bottle typology, but also in defining the contents, sizes, prices, quantities, and uses of these distinctive containers. Because Louisbourg probably has the single best collection of blue-green bottle glass in North America, representing such a broad range of bottle types, archaeologists working on other French colonial sites should find this typology a useful tool in the interpretation of their own material.

ACKNOWLEDGEMENTS

There are several people I would like to thank for their professional assistance. The late Clarence Saulnier, assistant conservator of the Fortress of Louisbourg National Historic Park, conducted the analysis of deposits on container push-ups. Charles Costain, formerly of the Conservation Division, National Historic Parks and Sites Branch, Parks Canada, Ottawa, conducted an analysis of French glass in the collection of the Material Culture Research Division, Federal Archaeology Office, National Historic Directorate, Parks Canada, Ottawa. From Paris, James Barrelet offered helpful comments on blue-green bottle fragments and drawings sent to him from the Fortress of Louisbourg collection, and provided information about his own collection.

REFERENCES

ADAMS, BLAINE
1972 Domestic Furnishings at Louisbourg. Manuscript, Fortress of Louisbourg National Historic Site, Parks Canada, Department of Canadian Heritage, Louisbourg, Nova Scotia.
1978 The Construction and Occupation of the Barracks of the King's Bastion at Louisbourg. *Canadian Historic Sites: Occasional Papers in Archaeology and History* 18:59-147. Ottawa, Ontario.

ALYLUIA, JEANNE
1981 18th-Century Container Glass from the Roma Site, Prince Edward Island. Parks Canada, *History and Archaeology* 45:3-81. Ottawa, Ontario.

BARRELET, JAMES
1953 *La verrerie en France de l'époque Gallo-Romaine à nos jours.* Librairie Larousse, Paris, France.

BRAIN, JEFFREY P.
1979 Tunica Treasure. *Harvard University, Papers of the Peabody Museum of Archaeology and Ethnology* 71. Cambridge, MA.

BROWN, MARGARET KIMBALL
1971 Glass from Fort Michilimackinac: A Classification for Eighteenth Century Glass. *Michigan Archaeologist* 17(3-4).

CHARDIN, JEAN BAPTISTE SIMEON
1969 *Chardin*, revised edition, text by Georges Wildenstein, Stuart Gilbert, translator. Manesse, Zurich, Switzerland.

DICTIONNAIRE UNIVERSEL FRANÇOIS ET LATIN
1743 *Dictionnaire universel françois et latin [vulgairement appelé Dictionnaire de Trévoux], contenant la signification et la définition tant des mots de l'une & l'autre langue*, revised edition. Chez Delaune et al., Paris, France.

DIDEROT-D'ALEMBERT ENCYCLOPÉDIE
1751- *Encyclopédie, Ou Dictionnaire raisonné des sciences, des arts et des métiers. Mis en ordre et publié par m. [Diderot & quant à la*
1765 *partie mathématique, par m. d'Alembert].* Samuel Faulche & Compagnie, Neuchâtel, France.
1772a Verrerie en bois, ou petite verrerie à pivette. In *Recueil de planches, sur les sciences, les arts libéraux, et les arts mécaniques, avec leur explication*, Volume 10. Briasson, Paris, France.
1772b Verrerie, en bouteilles chauffée en charbon de terre. In *Recueil de planches, sur les sciences, les arts libéraux, et les arts mécaniques, avec leur explication*, Volume 10. Briasson, Paris, France.

Jane E. Harris

DUCASSE, BERNARD
1970   Anciennes bouteilles soufflées et marquées. In
        Vignobles et vins d'Aquitaine. Fédération historique
        du Sud-Ouest, Bordeaux, pp. 389-402. *Actes du XXe
        congrès d'études régionales, tenu à Bordeaux les 17,
        18 et 19 novembre 1967.* Bordeaux, France.

FARÉ, MICHEL
1962   *La nature morte en France: son histoire et son évolution
        du XVIIe au XXe siècle,* Volume 2: Illustrations et
        Planches. Pierre Cailler, Geneva, Switzerland.

FRANCE. ARCHIVES NATIONALES. SECTION OUTRE-MER.
1732-   G² Greffes des tribunaux de Louisbourg et du
1757   Canada, Conseil superieur et baillage de Louisbourg.
        Paris, France.

GENÊT, NICOLE, L. DECARIE-AUDET, AND L. VERMETTE
1974   *Les objets familiers de nos ancestres.* Les editions de
        l'homme, Montreal, Quebec.

HOAD, LINDA M.
1976   Surgery and Surgeons in Ile Royale. Parks Canada,
        History and Archaeology 6:207-361. Ottawa,
        Ontario.

JONES, OLIVE R.
1971   Glass Bottle Push-Ups and Pontil Marks. *Historical
        Archaeology* 5:62-73.

JONES, OLIVE R., AND CATHERINE SULLIVAN, WITH
CONTRIBUTIONS BY GEORGE L. MILLER, E. ANN SMITH, JANE
E. HARRIS, AND KEVIN LUNN
1989   The Parks Canada Glass Glossary for the Description
        of Containers, Tableware, Flat Glass, and Closures,
        revised edition. Parks Canada, *Studies in Archaeology,
        Architecture and History.* Ottawa, Ontario.

LAFRENIÈRE, MICHEL, AND FRANÇOIS GAGNON
1971   A la découverte du passé: fouilles à la place Royale.
        Série Place Royal, Ministère des Affaires culturelles
        du Québec, Québec.

LAPOINTE, CAMILLE
1981   Le verre des latrines de la maison Perthuis. Ministère
        des Affaires culturelles du Québec, *Dossier 52.*
        Québec, Québec.

MACLEAN, TERRENCE D.
1974   A History of Block 4, Louisbourg: 1713-1768,
        Fortress of Louisbourg. Parks Canada, Department
        of Canadian Heritage, *Manuscript Report Series*
        176. Ottawa, Ontario.

MCKEARIN, HELEN
1971   Notes on Stopping, Bottling and Binning. *Journal of
        Glass Studies* 13:120-127.

MUNSELL COLOR COMPANY
1957   *Nickerson Color Fan.* Munsell Color Company,
        Baltimore, MD.

PROULX, GILLES
1972   Aubergistes et Cabaretiers de Louisbourg 1713-1758.
        Parcs Canada, *Travail inédit* 136. Ottawa, Ontario.

RICHTER, ERNST L., AND HEIDE HÄRLIN
1974   A Nineteenth-Century Collection of Pigments
        and Painting Materials. *Studies in Conservation*
        19(2):76-82.

ROLAND MICHEL, MARIANNE
1970   *Anne Vallayer-Coster 1744-1818.* Comptoir
        international du livre, Paris, France.

ROSS, LESTER A.
1983   Archaeological Metrology: English, French, American
        and Canadian Systems of Weights and Measures
        for North American Historical Archaeology. Parks
        Canada, *History and Archaeology* 68. Ottawa,
        Ontario.

SCOVILLE, WARREN C.
1950   *Capitalism and French Glassmaking, 1640-1789,*
        reprinted 1968. Johnson Reprint Corp., New York,
        NY.

SÉGUIN, ROBERT-LIONEL
1973   *La civilisation traditionelle de l'"habitant" aux 17^e
        et 18e siècles.* Fonds matériel Collection "Fleur de
        Lys." Fides, Montreal, Québec.

THIBAULT, H. PAUL
1972   L'îlot 17 de Louisbourg (1713-1768). Parcs Canada,
        Travail inédit 99. Ottawa, Ontario.

JANE E. HARRIS
MILLTOWN CROSS
RR 1
MONTAGUE, PRINCE EDWARD ISLAND C0A 1R0
CANADA

Part II:
Metal and Small Finds

TOM WELLS

Nail Chronology: The Use of Technologically Derived Features

ABSTRACT

A technology-based nail chronology is presented. This chronology is derived from a typology based on a combination of general information about the historical developments of the technology applied by the nail manufacturing industry and the periods of actual use for each of twelve basic nail types presently identified as having been used in Louisiana. The author believes that the approach used to establish the Louisiana Nail Chronology can also be used to establish accurate nail chronologies in other regions.

Introduction

Nails are artifacts commonly found at historic sites. The frequency of their occurrence has encouraged archaeologists to use them as dating tools, supplementing chronologies based on ceramics, glass, and other artifacts. The nail chronologies in common use among archaeologists; however, have not been as reliable as the glass and ceramic chronologies. A reliable chronology is needed to make nails more useful as dating tools. To be reliable the nail chronology should be based on accurately dated nail types, and it should be useful for archaeologists in the field and in the laboratory. To answer this need the Louisiana Nail Chronology has recently been developed. This chronology is based on twelve basic types of nails, sampled from dated buildings. The nail types are readily identifiable and are based on the structure and the physical characteristics of the nails (here called features) that result from dateable technological developments in the history of nail manufacture. Each of the general methods of nail manufacture leaves readily identifiable features on nails. These features are indicative of the technology used in the manufacture of nails, thus because nail manufacturing technology changed over the course of time, the features are temporally significant.

A standard nail chronology used today is one developed by Lee H. Nelson in 1968 (Nelson 1968). This chronology was severely simplified by Ivor Noël Hume (1972). In his chronology Nelson uses the style (referred to here as "form") of the nail, burrs, and head style to date nails. To use his chronology one compares a nail to those illustrated in the pamphlet to find the closest match. An earlier work, by Henry C. Mercer (1924), is based on samples of nails from several houses in Pennsylvania; however, this pioneering work provides some misinformation. For instance, Mercer shows a photograph of a selection of cut nails that are incorrectly identified as "hammer-headed" (Mercer 1924:9). These nails are completely machine-made by a process that will be discussed later. Mercer does illustrate burrs (1924:7), though his conclusions about the dates of the appearance of these are not necessarily applicable beyond the houses he studied. These chronologies were a good start, based on such information as was available at the time. One of the best attempts at establishing a nail chronology is that by Maureen Phillips (1989). She used nails from dated structures to establish the actual time that a nail type was used. Her nail typology is primarily based on manufacturing features, though it is limited to the houses she studied and may not have a general or regional application.

While cataloging a collection of several thousand nails from a house built in the 18th century and continuously occupied since, the author was faced with nails that could not be matched with any of those illustrated or described by either Nelson or Mercer. In addition, numerous nails that appeared to be hand-made had burrs, presumably a feature of cut nails.

Experiences with the problems of existing nail typologies and chronologies lead the author to collaborate with Jay D. Edwards, of Louisiana State University, in the study of nails. The results of that study were published in a general interest monograph devoted to 19th century-nails in Louisiana (Edwards and Wells 1993). The following article is based in part on research for that publication and on additional research not included in the book. The chronology presented here differs from that published in our book in one respect: the nail designated as Type 9 is replaced with a different nail. The reason for eliminating it is discussed below. The scope of this article is limited to ferrous house nails. The chronology presented here is based heavily on the historical development of nail manufacture, thus a brief technological history is first presented, followed by a general description of the various types of nails produced by methods employed in each stage of technological development of the nail industry. Finally, the Louisiana Nail Chronology is presented. This section briefly discusses the method used to develop the chronology, which can also be applied in other localities. A short lexicon of some technical terms used here is appended.

A Brief History of Nail Manufacturing Technology

Beginning in the late 18th century great changes began in the technology of nail manufacturing. Through the course of the 19th century the American nail industry developed from small, often part-time, cottage-level concerns to large industrial establishments. The technological development of the nail industry closely followed developments in other fields of iron manufacturing technology. Improvements in iron production, synchronized machinery, steam power, iron casting, and eventually steel manufacture were soon followed by changes in nail manufacturing technology. Each stage of nail manufacturing technology has left readily observable, temporally significant evidence on the nails so produced. This evidence is found in the metal used and the characteristic features resulting from the various changes in the production of nails. These pieces of temporally significant evidence may properly be called "features" (from Latin *facere* "to make") rather than "attributes" (*ad* + *tribuere*

"to bestow") because each piece of evidence is characteristic of a stage in the development of nail manufacturing technology rather than a value that is ascribed to aspects of the appearance of a given nail. Identification of the nail types in the Louisiana Nail Chronology is based on these nail features. Historical background is included in a brief review of the evolution of the technology of the nail manufacturing industry.

Metals

Common house nails were made from one of two types of iron: wrought iron or steel. Determining which of these two forms of iron is used and the salient features of each is the first step in establishing the temporal significance of any nail sample. A brief history of 18th and 19th century iron and steel manufacturing technology is presented to introduce the reader to this subject.

Wrought Iron

Wrought iron is a ductile two component metal consisting of almost pure metallic iron and moderate amounts of a siliceous slag (Aston and Story 1939:1). There are traces of other elements which are regarded as contaminants. This form of iron is "wrought," meaning worked rather than cast in its final shape by pouring liquid iron into molds. In the 18th century one of two methods was generally employed to reduce iron ore into metallic iron. These are referred to as the direct method and the indirect method. Which of these two methods was used cannot be discerned in the final product. The entire process, from mining to extraction and refinement, may be found in Georgius Agricola's *De Re Metallica* (Agricola 1950), originally published in 1556.

The roughly consolidated blooms, sometimes called "muck bars," were further refined in the chaffery into "merchant bars" that were next drawn into commonly used stock sizes of bars

FIGURE 1. Surfaces of iron (left) and steel (right) (Edwards and Wells 1993).

bars over and stacking several of these, one on the other, then welding them all together to produce a higher quality, cleaner iron (Mott 1983:28, 35-36).

The last step in whatever process was used was to draw out the iron into stock sizes of bars, flat stock, and rods. Until the 1780s the drawing out process was accomplished by forging the bars using a water powered helve hammer and hand labor, with swedges used to size and shape the stock. In 1784 an English patent was issued for turning out stock using grooved rollers (Mott 1983:37-39). The grooved rollers both consolidated and shaped the hot iron.

When cleaned to bare metal wrought iron can be readily identified by its wood-like grain (Figure 1). The wood-like grain is caused by the silicious slag that could not be removed from the bloom; it was drawn out with the iron, becoming longitudinal glassy veins in the bar. The metallic part of wrought iron is chemically almost pure iron. Typically, a wrought iron bar may have 1% to 3% mixed slag and traces of other impurities (Aston and Story 1939:2, 20-26). Batches of wrought iron may vary considerably in both chemical constituents and their proportions. Even iron samples from the same ores and the same bloomery may differ significantly from bar to bar, depending on the proportions of flux mixed with the ore, the temperature at which the iron was worked, how long it was held at high temperature, and the worker's diligence in the refining processes.

Steel

Steel is an alloy of iron and carbon. A low carbon steel, called mild steel, is usually used for nail manufacture. Steel has a crystalline structure, contains insignificant amounts of slag, and does not have the wood-like grain that is characteristic of wrought iron. Steel may be recognized by its fine uniform surface. When rusty steel is cleaned to bare metal, a surface covered with small circular pits is revealed, in contrast

and plates. Some bars were next sent to the rolling and slitting mill to be made into nail plates and then nail rods.

During the 15th century an additional refining step was added. It involved the reheating of the iron to a welding heat and again hammering it to consolidate the iron better by working out as much of the slag and impurities as possible. Another step in the refining of iron was added in the late 18th century. It consisted of folding the with wrought iron's longitudinal striations (Figure 1).

Though small quantities ███████ have been made for millennia, large sc███ ████ production of steel began in the late 1870s with the adoption of a modified Bessemer process. Until the perfection of the industrial processes steel had been made by carburizing high grade wrought iron. In the late 1880s and 1890s the various ██████er and open hearth methods of steel making were being developed and perfected. Both Bessemer and open hearth processes involved melting pig iron and blowing oxygen through it, generating an extremely high heat that burns out nearly all of the impurities. Carbon content of the steel was controlled by adding it to the molten steel. The molten metal was next poured into ingot molds (Campbell 1940:5-14). The ingots were then sent to rollers to be formed into rods, sheets, or other shapes. By the middle 1890s steel production, being less labor intensive than wrought iron production, began to replace it in most applications, including nail manufacture.

The Manufacture of Nails

Each of the methods of nail manufacture leave readily identifiable features on the nails produced.

FIGURE 2. An eighteenth century rolling and slitting mill (Diderot 1765).

FIGURE 3. Detail of a rolling and slitting machine (Diderot 1765).

These features are indicative of the technology used in the manufacture of nails and because the manufacturing technology changed over the course of time, these features are temporally significant. There are two important divisions of nail manufacturing technology: hand forged and machine made. The earliest of these two, hand forged, will be presented first.

Hand Forged Nails

Hand forged nails were made from iron nail rods. The older way of making nail rods was by drawing out large bars to a smaller size. This was accomplished by the smith, using a hand hammer or with a helve-hammer. This is a rather slow, labor-intensive process, but it continued to be used even after later technological developments had made it obsolete. Its advantage was that no specialized equipment other than basic blacksmith tools was required. Nails made from forged nail rods are generally square in cross section and have evidence of hammering on all sides and the head.

After their development in the 17th century, rolling and slitting mills made most nail rods (Figure 2). In the mills, bars were heated and run through water powered rollers until they had rectangular cross sections and were about one quarter to one half inch thick, according to the size nail rod that was to be produced. These were called nail bars. Each nail bar varied from 6 to 8 in. wide and roughly 12 ft. long. The rectangular nail bar was then sent through the slitter (Kauffman 1966:34-35). This machine consisted of intermeshing hardened disks that cut the nail plate lengthwise into nail rods (Figure 3).

Nail rods made in slitting mills often do not have perfectly square sides; they are often rectangular, rhomboid, or trapezoid in cross section. The rectangular section is the result of feeding a thin plate through the cutters. Rhomboid and trapezoid cross sections are caused by the pulling action of dull cutter disks. As the nailer, the smith who makes nails, draws out the point of a trapezoidal cross section of nail rod, a valley is sometimes formed in the wider face in the upper part of the shaft. A rhomboid cross section will not have marked effect. The cross section of the original nail rod may extend from under the head down the shaft for a quarter of the length of the nail.

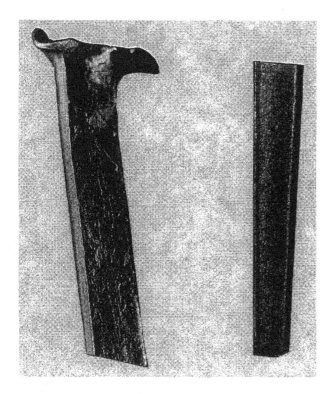

FIGURE 4. Burrs on a forged nail (left) and a cut nail (right).

Hand forged nails may have burrs on the trailing edge of the rod on the same face (Figure 4). The burrs are caused by the cutters dragging a small amount of iron into the slight gap between the cutter disks. The burrs will often be visible on the unmodified part of the shaft below the head and above the tapered part that was drawn to form the point.

Nails were forged using specialized versions of standard blacksmithing tools, including hammer, anvil, and header. The header is a tool that is pierced by a tapered hole that is slightly smaller than the nail rod employed. A standard method used by smiths to forge a nail began with heating the end of a nail rod in the fire. The end was then pointed and the shaft was drawn to a diameter that would slip into the header, a shoulder being left to catch in the header where the head was to be formed. While the rod was still showing color it was nicked above the shoulder and twisted off in the header, leaving the shaft in the hole and a little of the rod projecting above the header. Finally, this projecting piece was "upset," mushrooming it to form the head, completing the nail.

A common feature on nails made from slit stock is a slight depression under the head on one face. This feature suggests an alternative method of heading the nail. Instead of leaving a shoulder to catch in the header, the smith struck the rod on its face, bulging the sides at the place the shaft was to catch the header. The nailer might do this when the nail rod size was the same size or slightly smaller than the hole in the header. On nails made in this way the original unmodified nail rod can be seen between the head and the point taper.

All hand-made nails exhibit hammering on the head and all four sides in the point taper. It is not always possible to tell if a nail is made from forged rods or slit rods, if the nail was drawn from a large slit rod down to a smaller size. This is because the distinct features of the slit rod will be obliterated by the smith's hammering. Shafts often do not taper uniformly from head to point; however, there may be valleys, cold shuts, or other evidence that suggests the use of slit rods. A cold shut is an unconsolidated fold of metal hammered against the shaft. Nails may have burrs or vertical drag marks immediately under the head, the result of seating the nail in a tight header. The heads exhibit hammer marks and are somewhat irregular. There are numerous styles of head which may represent functional types. Head styles and functional types, however, are beyond the scope of this study.

Forged nail technology antedates the colonization of America, and limited numbers of forged nails were still being made well into the 19th century. The use of forged nails became progressively less common as cut nail technology improved. Nails and nail rods were imported into the European colonies from the time of their establishment in the New World and were manufactured in limited numbers in the United States into the 19th century, making forged nails not especially useful for dating. Their presence at a site can only suggest the early 19th century or earlier.

Machine-Made Nails

IRON CUT NAILS

All cut nails are made from strips of iron or steel called nail plates. The length of the nail is determined by the width of the nail plate, and the thickness of the nail is the same as the thickness of the nail plate. The surface of the nail plate is the surface of the nail's face. The body of the nail, the nail blank, is sheared off the end of the nail plate at an angle so the nail blank describes an acute, usually truncated, triangle. The small end is the point and the large end will be upset to form the head. In cutting the blank from the nail plate the shearing action leaves two features on the nail that are of interest here: the cut face and the burr (Figure 5). All cut nails taper on two sides, the cut faces, and have a uniform thickness on the opposite faces below the pinched area. Though cut nails rarely have

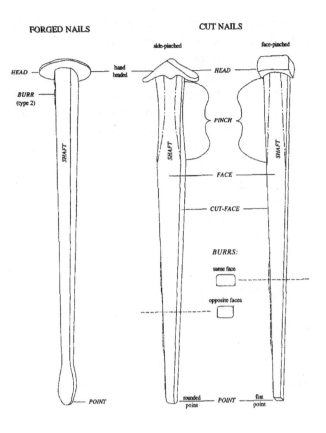

FIGURE 5. Nail nomenclature.

sharp points, some are to be found, usually on early cut nails.

Beginning in the late 18th century, early cut nail manufacture was accomplished in two steps, beginning with the shearing of the nail blank. Then the blank was held in a clamp and headed by hand. The earliest nail cutting machines, like Nathaniel Reed's (Loveday 1983:13, 18), were manually powered and the nail plate was fed into the shear by hand. After the nail blank was cut off it was put in a vice-like header, leaving a short section of the shaft projecting above the header. This device grasped and crushed the cut faces, resulting in a side-pinched nail. The nailer then struck the projecting part of the shaft with a hand hammer to form the head.

The first successful combined cutting and heading machines were developed and used in the northeastern United States in the early 19th century. The factories used water power to drive the machinery rather than human power, thereby increasing the speed of production and uniformity of the product. Some early, fully machine-made, nails can be hard to distinguish from hand-headed cut nails. Both are generally strongly side-pinched, the burr is on opposite faces, both have points that are rounded from front face to back face, and are cross-grained. The heads of machine-headed nails, however, tend to be more

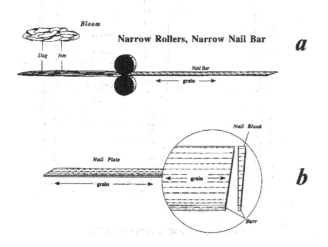

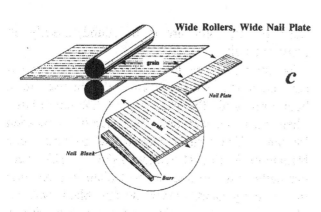

FIGURE 6. Wrought iron grain and methods of making nail plates: *a*, slag in the bloom is drawn out with the iron, narrow rollers form the narrow nail plate with the grain running the length of the bar, nails cut from narrow nail plates are cross-grained; *b*, narrow rollers form the narrow nail plate with the grain running the length of the bar, nails cut from narrow nail plates are cross-grained; *c*, wide rollers produce sheets, which are then sheared across the grain to produce nail plates, nails made from such plates are in-line-grained (after Edwards and Wells 1993).

FIGURE 7. Points of cut nails compared. The top point is that of a nail that was cut from a nail plate which was sheared from a sheet. The bottom point is from a nail cut from a narrow nail plate (Edwards and Wells 1993).

regular and thicker than hand-headed nails, and the shafts tend to be uniform in pinch, shearing angle, and general appearance.

Both hand-headed and machine-headed early cut nails were cross-grained. They were cut from narrow nail plates which were produced by rolling mills using narrow rollers (Figure 6). The grain of the iron in these plates runs the length of the plate so the grain of the nail blank, cut from the end of the nail plate, ran across the nail. The rounded edge of the nail plate usually survives at the point. Nails cut from such plates will have points that are rounded from the front face to the back face (Figure 7).

In the hand-fed nail machines the nail plate had to be repositioned for each cut to produce the necessary angle for the nail blank. The inevitable, though slight, variation in feed angle resulted in nails that are of variable breadth. With the perfection of the automatic feeder came greater uniformity in shaft breadth and taper. Most of the early cut nail types have burrs on opposite faces, evidence that the nail plates were inaccurately repositioned after each cut.

A major drawback of all cross-grained nails is their tendency to break when clinched, bent, or extracted from the wood. This is because wrought iron is laterally weakened by the slag running across the shaft. Cross-grained cut nails break cleanly along the slag inclusions in the grain. The superior performance of grain-in-line nails, such as hand forged nails, was well understood by Jacob Perkins who advertised, in 1795, a machine that he claimed could produce such nails (Phillips 1989:91). That Perkins' nail machines did not dominate the nail market may be ascribed either to the unreliability of the machines or to the expense of making wide plates before the technology had matured. Grain-in-line cut nails dating from before 1834 have not been found in Louisiana, though they may have been used in Boston before the turn of the century (Phillips 1989).

Large scale manufacture of grain-in-line cut nails awaited the full development of other technologies, especially the art of iron casting and steam power. The narrow rollers of the old water-powered rolling mills were unable to produce wide plates and sheet iron. Though wide rollers had been used since the 18th century they were flexible because of their small diameter, limiting their use to the softer non-ferrous metals (Daumas 1964:252). The demand for wide sheet iron for steam engine boilers was met at first by hammering thick narrow plates under a water powered helve hammer until they were sufficiently wide. By 1803 in England, iron casting technology improved enough that large diameter, rigid, wide rollers could be made of cast iron. It was also there that steam power was first applied to drive machinery (Dickinson 1939). After those developments, wide rollers powered by reliable steam engines could economically produce wide plate and sheet iron. These technologies were soon brought to America (Binning 1938:88).

Steam engines provided reliable power, permitting factories to be established away from the falls of the eastern seaboard rivers to the western coal and iron producing areas. There were three advantages realized from the use of steam power. First, factory layout could be directed for manufacturing efficiency rather than being limited by access to the river and the axle that transferred power from the water wheel. Second, power to the machines was no longer limited by the river's flow rate, rate of fall, and seasonal availability of water. And finally, beginning in the early decades of the 19th century, factories could be located in the west where the greatest demand was. In the west, boats communicated with every town in the Mississippi valley, quickly transporting nails for the ever expanding market.

In 1810 a plant in Pennsylvania had water driven rollers 3-4 ft. long and 16-18 in. in diameter; the following year steam power was first used in a Pittsburgh rolling mill (Mackintosh-Hemphill Company 1953:31-32). In 1832 one of the first cut nail factories was established in Wheeling, (West) Virginia, a town that was soon to be the center of the cut nail industry. In this factory, sheets were rolled and cut into nail plates (Heitmann 1989:311). It appears that by 1830 wide roller technology had come into common use by American nail makers to make an improved, in-line-grained nail.

By the second decade of the 19th century some manufacturers were producing nail plates that were cut from sheets or wide plates (Ure 1865:255; Martineau 1866:613). With this new method, wide rolled plates were cut across the grain-producing nail plates that had the grain running across them. Nails cut from the end of cross-grained nail plates had the grain running from point to head. These nails could be successfully clinched without breaking. All nails that were made by this method have flat points with four sharp corners (Figure 7).

In the more technologically advanced machines the angle of the nail blank was established without the necessity of repositioning the plate after each cut. A reciprocating cutter, having two cutting edges, each set at the correct angle, came into use at about the same period as the transition from cross-grained to grain-in-line nails. These machines produced nails having the burrs on the same face. This single feature, however, should not be used by itself for establishing the nail date; there are cross-grained nails that have burrs on the same face.

After the nail blank is cut it is mechanically grasped for heading. Grasping by the header clamp deforms the upper end of the shaft just below where the head will be formed. This is another feature of cut nails referred to as the "pinch" (Edwards and Wells 1993). Most of the later nails are face-pinched, though side-pinched nails have been continuously produced from the beginning of cut nail mass production to the present. The most common in-line-grain nail is face-pinched so the edges of the faces are nearly straight from head to point. The heads are usually small, either square or rectangular when viewed from the top and rather blocky. Two functional types of cut nails do not have a pinch: sprigs, which are left unheaded, and brads, whose heads are cut simultaneously with the shaft.

Heading was done cold or at a low heat, putting great stress on the iron, often resulting in small cracks that run with the grain on the face side of the head. The cracks result from the iron separating along the grain under the force of heading. It is common to find long cracks on the cut faces of all iron cut nails, indicating that the iron was poorly consolidated. As iron producers adopted better iron making techniques, the quality of wrought iron improved so that such cracks are less often seen in nails made after the 1840s.

IRON WIRE NAILS

Wire was made by pulling a rod through successively smaller holes in a draw plate until the desired diameter was reached. At the end of each drawing the leading end of the wire had to be reduced to the next smaller size and started through the hole so it could be grasped by the clamp that pulled the wire (Ferguson 1965:90-94). In iron wire the grain runs the length of the shaft, allowing it to be bent without breaking.

Wire making technology changed little from medieval times until the middle of the 19th century, though water and then steam took the place of human power to pull the wire. Steam was not employed in American wire making until the 19th century (Binning 1938:88-89). Although wrought iron wire had been made for a long time it was not considered suitable for nail making for two main reasons: wrought iron wire could not be made as cheaply as nail plates, and because of their narrow, un-tapered sides, and the softness of iron, wire nails could not be driven into hardwoods without pilot holes. Even so, small iron wire nails called "French points" were made in this country beginning in 1875 with imported French machines. In 1880, the first American wire nail manufacturer began commercial scale operation in Kentucky (The Iron Age 1898).

The manufacture of wire nails begins with feeding the end of a roll of wire into clamps which grasp the length of the shaft with a short length projecting past the clamp. The wire is held in place by teeth in the clamp that make a series of lateral scores found on the upper shaft immediately below the head. The wire projecting from the clamp is mechanically upset to form the head. While still in the clamp, cutter dies squeeze the point on to the shaft, while separating it from the wire roll, then the clamp opens and drops the finished nail; the process begins again as more wire is fed into the machine (Clark 1978:192-193). The same basic design of machine is used in steel wire nail manufacture.

Distinguishing wrought iron wire from steel wire can be difficult. Iron wire for iron wire nails was highly refined and the grain is noticeable only after it has been acid-etched. Recognizing steel wire nails can also be difficult. As steel is drawn through the reducing dies the crystalline structure becomes stretched. This, combined with the minute longitudinal abrasion of the die, often gives the steel a striated appearance similar to that of iron. It is also possible to tell the difference between iron and steel using powerful microscopes, microphotographs, spectral analysis, and other metallurgical techniques.

STEEL CUT NAILS

After the steel making processes were perfected and the price for steel was less than that of wrought iron, cut nail manufacturers began to use steel for nails. From the late 1880s through the 1890s steel gradually replaced wrought iron in the manufacture of cut nails (Heitmann 1989:30). From 1884 through 1886 only 5% of cut nails were made of steel. By 1891 three quarters of all cut nails were made of steel. Before the end of the century all cut nails were made of steel. Steel cut nails are still made in small quantities, some on old machines. The manufacturing process is the same for steel and iron cut nails and because there are styles of steel cut nails that resemble early 19th century-nails, it is necessary to determine whether the nail is made from iron or steel.

STEEL WIRE NAILS

The processes for the manufacture of steel wire nails is essentially the same as that for iron wire nails, though more abrasion resistant materials are now available for use in the dies (Committee of Rod and Drawn Wire Producers 1969:7-9). Though manufacturers began to produce steel wire in the 1860s, the wire was used mostly for telegraphs, seat springs, and crinolines. Steel wire nails do not seem to have been available until the late 1870s (Loveday 1983:136), possibly because of the expense of steel manufacturing of the day. Steel wire nails were not produced in competitive quantities until the late 1880s and early 1890s (Loveday 1983:137). By the turn of the century most nails that were sold were wire nails. By 1920, wire nails had taken over the nail market, leaving cut nails with only 8% of the market.

The Louisiana Nail Chronology

The Louisiana Nail Chronology represents an attempt at establishing a system for dating sites and standing structures using nails as dating tools. One of the problems with existing nail chronologies is that they are form-based: their use requires one to compare a sample nail with illustrations of nails to find one that looks similar. The assumption is that similar form indicates similar dates of manufacture and use. This method can be misleading because nails with the same form have been made for over a century. This problem is slightly ameliorated by the brief descriptions of burr location and grain direction.

Mention should be made here of other systems of categorizing nails. The least useful of these, for dating purposes, is by functional type. Functional types are based on the intended or customary use of a particular kind of nail. Functional types are of little use for establishing dates. Additionally, the actual use of any particular nail cannot be known out of its original context. Functional types may be of limited use in describing some nails, in the same manner and with the same skepticism as "arrow head" or "adz" are used to describe prehistoric stone artifacts.

Closely related to functional types is classification by means of head and point style, which meets with the same objection: style has not proved useful for establishing a chronology, though it may be useful in establishing a nail typology. The English used such classifications as "clout" and "rose head" to describe nails and sometimes this may indicate their use; however, not all such terms need to be discarded. There are useful English terms that have specific and limited use, such as "brad" and "sprig." Such terms may be used to describe the form of specific nail classes. For instance, a sprig is a nail made without an apparent head. Care must be taken because one cannot always be certain that a pointed shaft is a sprig. In the case of "brad," both forged and cut brads have a "7" shape, but modern wire brads have a small round head that slightly overhangs the shaft around its diameter. Although functional types and head and point styles are not reliable temporal indicators, functional types can be valuable for other purposes. Even after having visited and sampled nails from many late 18th and early 19th century-buildings the author can only make very broad generalizations about how any particular functional type was actually used in that period.

The use of "penny" is avoided because of its vagueness. "Penny" can mean the number of nails that could be bought for a penny, the price per pound of a size of nail, or the price, in pence, for a hundred nails. Today the term has been standardized to describe a size of nail. An additional objection is that "penny" is culture-specific; it is an English system not shared by the French or Spanish in Louisiana. For instance, among the supplies requested from France for the colony in 1759 are "twenty *quintals* of double caravel nails; thirty *quintals* of half caravel nails; thirty *quintals* of caravel nails; forty *quintals* of shingling nails, a little longer than half-deck nails." The list goes on to describe a total of seven varieties of nail by using named types. The list, however, also includes "twenty *quintals* of 6-, 7- and 8-inch nails" (Rowland and Sanders 1984:57), a description of nails by length. Interestingly, none of the names of the above types is used by Diderot (1765) to describe nails.

Using patented designs of machines or patent dates for nail machines have been found to be of no use in dating. It is doubtful that it will ever be possible to tell that a particular nail was made by a given machine based on its patent, or even if the machine were built and actually put into service. Many patents were taken out on plausible ideas, often in hopes of making money from litigation against successful manufacturers who could be sued for patent infringement.

Another danger results from using references on the British nail industry for generalizing about nail manufacture in the United States. It should be remembered that throughout the 18th and 19th centuries, the manpower and economic forces of the two countries differed greatly. In Great Britain, and in Europe generally, there was a surplus of manpower. In the U. S. there was a chronic shortage of labor. In England there was considerable resistance, on the part of skilled labor, to the adoption of machinery that could threaten their employment. This resistance retarded the technological development of certain other industries in England, for instance, boots, clothing, and locks. Labor resistance to "labor-saving" machinery has been cited as the chief reason that England continued to produce nails by hand into the late 19th century (Habakkuk 1962:172). In the late 19th century an English nailer could make, by traditional hand forging, about 112 pounds of larger size nails in a day. In a week he earned about 16 shillings ($3.87). At the same time, an American nailer, operating three machines, could produce 54 kegs of 10d nails, and earn $5.00 a day (Schoenhof 1974:226-227).

Historical research may indicate that a particular nail was being manufactured, but how does one tell if it was used in a particular region? Taking Lee Nelson's suggestion that local chronologies be developed, the author and Jay Edwards did just that; however, the nail typology on which the Louisiana Nail Chronology is based depends on the identification of significant features. These features include the physical structure or characteristics of the nails that result from dateable manufacturing technology. Each stage in the history of technological development may be discerned on the nail. The use of iron or steel, grain direction, and so on result from stages in the development of nail manufacture technology and thus, indicate a general date for the manufacture of the nail. This method; however, assumes that earlier technologies were discarded as more efficient technologies were developed.

The nail typology derived from technology-based dates is of general applicability only. Such dates do not allow for the use of nails made from obsolete technologies, differences in trade routes, or old nails used in new structures. In order to obtain dates of actual use specific to Louisiana, another method was used to develop a regional chronology. This method follows that of Mercer (1924) and Maureen Phillips (1989) by using dated standing structures as sources of dateable nails. Technological features were used to establish nail types; however, dates-of-use were determined by sampling dated historic buildings. Nails selected for this study were functional parts of the structure, pulled from original, permanent parts of the building such as the roof truss, knee walls, jack rafters, sills, purlins, and rafters. Roofs may be replaced several times over the lifetime of a building, thus they were not (with one exception) used as sources for nails. Nails from later additions or repairs, unless they were well dated, were not sampled. Thus, structural nails drawn from the original parts of an 1840 house could be assumed to date from 1840 or earlier.

As the historical background research and nail study began to take shape, houses were selected for dates that coincided with documented changes in nail manufacturing technology. This was done to obtain nail samples that would sharpen the transition period from one nail type to another. Of particular interest was the transition from hand-headed cut nails to fully machine-made nails that started near the beginning of the 19th century. Also of special interest was the period of transition from cross-grained nails to grain-in-line nails that took place in the first two decades of the 19th century. Documenting the periods of transition from the use of iron to steel and of cut nails to wire nails was considered less vital because by the late 19th century-interstate transportation made the shipment from factory to carpenter a matter of weeks, if not days. The transition period can be reliably documented by historical research; however, several buildings from the end of the 19th century were sampled to verify the historical evidence.

The resulting data base used to develop the chronology is summarized in Table 1. The name of the building is followed by the date of the building's construction. The date is followed by a letter scale from "A" to "D" designating confidence in the accuracy of that date. An "A" indicates a firm documentary record from the time of construction; "B" is a building dated to within two years by a combination of documentation and other methods; "C" indicates that the

building is dated to within five years by a combination of methods; the scale ends with "D" indicating a building whose construction can be dated to within a decade by a combination of methods. Nails from buildings that could not be dated to within a decade were not used to establish the chronology. Obviously, the "A" buildings are to be preferred as sources for nail samples; however, "A" buildings dating from the years of interest were not always available.

Nail dates based on their use in buildings should be understood to be probabilities; there are abundant opportunities for sample error, especially for the early cut nail dates. Few of the structures built in the 18th century and early 19th century are still standing. Nails from archaeological sites were beyond the scope of the survey. The eventual inclusion of archaeological sites as a source for nail samples may improve the accuracy of the chronology.

How to Determine the Age of a Nail

As many nails as possible (or as many as the owner will allow!) should be sampled to establish the uniformity of the sample and the types used. In addition, nails should be drawn from as many parts of the original structure as possible, again to establish the uniformity of the sample and, eventually, to develop a functional type system based on nail use.

Diagnostic Features

Nails should be cleaned of all oxides to expose the bare metal and in order to reveal the diagnostic features. The important features are: material (iron or steel); general uniformity (or lack of it) of the head and shaft; shaft shape, cross section, and taper; the pinch, if present; shape of the point; burr, if present; cold shuts or cracks; and heading method. No one of these features should be relied on for determining the age of a nail. Except for the use of iron or steel none of these features is, in its self, chronologically significant. When the nail features are used together, one may determine the nail type and its time of use.

DATA BASE

Source of Nail Samples	Nail Types	1	2	3	4	5	6	7	8	9	10	11	12
LaCour (1731 D)		X											
Godchaux-Reserve (1764 D)		X											
St. Gabriel Church (1769 A)	X	X											
Wells (1776 C)	X	X											
Madam John's Legacy (1788 B)	X												
Destrehan (1790 A)	X	X											
Graugnard (1790 C)		X											
Cabildo (1791 A)	X	X											
Magnolia Mound (1791 B)		X	X										
Merieult (1793 A)		X	X										
Pitot (1799 A)		X	X										
Kleinpeter-Knox (1800 C)			X										
Roque (1805 D)		X			X								
Whitney (1805 B)		X	X										
Michael Prudhomme (1809 B)				X									
Magnolia Mound (1810 C)			X	X		X							
Jaque-Duprée (1811 B)									X				
Planter's Cabin (1818 D)					X	X							
Cabildo (1813 A)				X		X							
Bucvalt (1815 D)		X		X		X							
Zeringue (1815 C)		X	X		X								
Kroll (1816 C)			X										
Destrehan, Garconnières (1818 A)					X								
Merieult (1818 A)				X									
Pentagon Barracks, Bldg. B (1819 A)		X	X										
Pentagon Barracks, Bldg. D (1819 A)			X		X								
River Lake (1820 C)					X	X							
Wycliffe (1820 B)		X				X							
Bucvalt (1820 C)								X					
Graugnard (1820 C)								X					
Oakland (1820 D)								X					
Pentagon Barracks, Bldg. B (1823 A)				X	X								
Pentagon Barracks, Bldg. D (1823 A)						X		X					
Aillet (1830 B)					X	X		X					
Moniotte (1830 C)						X							
Estorge (1830 B)						X							
Austerlitz (1832 A)						X							
Evergreen (1832 D)					X								
Riverland (1832 C)								X					
Jackson Barracks, Bldg. 2 (1834 A)				X		X							
Jackson Barracks, Bldg. 4 (1834 A)							X	X					
Live Oak (1835 C)						X							
Lindsey (1835 D)								X					
Kleinpeter (1836 C)			X		X	X							
Bozant-Hart (1836 B)					X	X		X					
Jackson Barracks, Magazine (1837 A)								X					
Kroll (1840 C)								X					
Oaklawn (1840 C)						X		X					
Little Texas (1840 C)								X					
Presbytere (1847 A)							X	X					
Cabildo (1848 A)								X					
Pontalba (1849 A)								X					
Bond (1850 D)								X					
Lobell (1862 C)								X					
Palo Alto, Overseer's (1880 C)								X					
Baytree (1892 D)								X					
Wilbert (1891 B)								X		X		X	
Curole (1891 B)										X			
Curole (1893 A)												X	

Tom Wells

To determine if the nail is iron or steel the distinctive characteristics of iron are important; these include grain and possibly a poorly consolidated structure such as cold shuts and cracks described below. The absence of the typical characteristics of iron probably indicates steel. The transition from the use of iron to steel in the nail industry was not immediate, having begun in the mid-1880s and continued into the 1890s.

Though not itself a dating factor, the general uniformity of the head and shaft, especially in a collection of similar nails from a site, usually indicates improved production methods, and therefore a later date. Heads located eccentrically on the shaft, misshapen heads, and shafts that have several tapers or diameters indicate early nails. The judgment of uniformity can be rather subjective, thus it is desirable to obtain a large nail sample.

The shape of the shaft, its cross section, and taper can be used to distinguish among wire, cut, and hand-made nails. Cut nails have parallel faces but cut faces that taper straight towards the point. Wire nails have parallel sides extending from the head to the point. Hand-made nails, naturally, exhibit the greatest variation in all aspects of shaft form. Generally, hand-made nails tend to taper on all sides to the point and maintain a square cross section, though many such nails have a rectangular cross section, with parallel sides, on the upper one-third to one-half before they gradually taper to the point. Hand-made nails often exhibit hammer marks on the shaft and head, or other evidence of hand work.

Except for sprigs and brads all cut nails are grasped by a clamp at the upper end of the shaft for heading. The clamp leaves a deformation, referred to as the "pinch," under the head. De-

TABLE 2

FEATURES OF LOUISIANA NAIL TYPES

Feature: Nail Type:	1	2	3	4	5	6	7	8	9	10	11	12
Shaft Section:												
square/rect	X	X	X	X	X	X	X	X	X			
square	X	X										
Round											X	X
Material:												
Iron	X	X	X	X	X	X	X	X	X		X	
Steel										X		X
Grain (iron only)												
Cross	X	X	X	X	X	X			X			
In-Line							X	X			X	
Rounded Points			X	X	X							
(cut face view)												
Shaft Shape:												
Four Sides Taper	X	X										
Two Sides Taper		X	X	X	X	X	X	X	X	X		
No Taper											X	X
Burr												
Same Face		X			X	X	X	X		X		
Opposite Faces			X	X					X			
Header Clamp Pinch												
Side-Pinched			X	X	X		X					
Face-Pinched						X		X	X	X		
Hand-Headed	X	X	X									
Used: Beginning	1699	1699	1791	1809	1805	1810	1834	1820	1811	1891	1875	1891
Ending	1805	1820	1836	1834	1836	1840	1847	1891	1812	1893	1880s	present

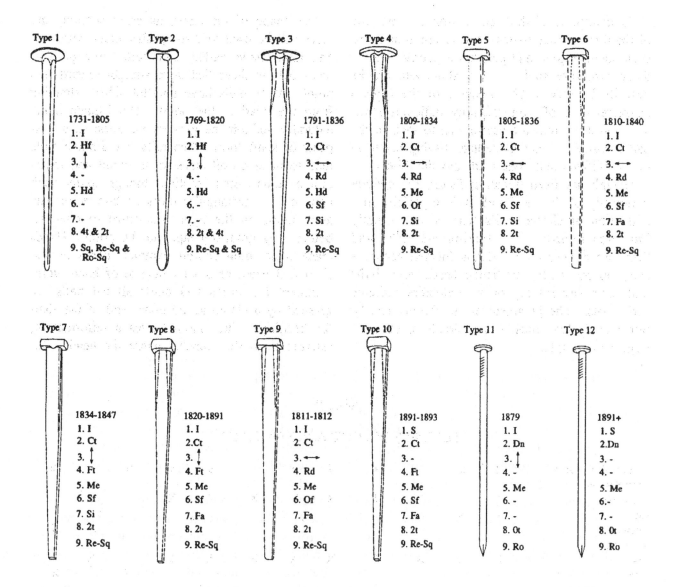

Diagnostic Nail Features

Feature	Symbol	Meaning
1. Metal:	I, S	Iron, Steel
2. Mfg. Method	Hf, Ct, Dn	Hand-forged, Cut, Drawn
3. Grain (iron only)	↕ ↔	In Line, Cross
4. Point (cut only)	Rd, Ft	Round, Flat
5. Head Mfg.	Hd, Me	Hand, Machine
6. Burr (cut only)	Sf, Of	Same faces, Opposite faces
7. Pinch (cut only)	Si, Fa	Side, Face
8. Shaft Taper	4t, 2t, 0t	Taper on: 4 sides, 2 sides, no taper
9. Shaft Section	Sq, Re, Ro	Square, Rectangular, Round

FIGURE 8. Louisiana Nail Types

pending on the length of nail, the pinch usually extends down the shaft, generally for about one-eighth to one-quarter of its length. The pinch is relatively shorter on large nails and longer on small nails. Only cut nails are pinched, thus this feature is useful for establishing the type of nail. The earliest cut nails in Louisiana are pinched on their cut faces (side-pinched). Nails pinched on their faces (face-pinched) began to appear in Louisiana in the 1820s, though there is one face pinched type that was used on a house in 1811. The pinch, however, is not chronologically significant by itself: similar nails were made throughout the 19th century, and are still manufactured, though now they are made of steel.

Variation in the point of wire nails does not appear to be temporally significant, though the point can be of great significance on cut nails. Generally, cut nails have a blunt point: the cut faces form an acute triangle that extends from the head and ends abruptly before meeting. Where the faces end, the flat point, is the edge of the nail plate. The point can indicate whether the nail was made from the early style nail plate or the later nail plates cut from sheets. The points of nails cut from narrow nail plates are slightly rounded from the front face to the back face. Nails made from nail plates that were cut from sheets have four sharp corners at the point. This feature can be used to help distinguish between cross-grained nails and grain-in-line nails, a difference that can be temporally significant. Among hand-made nails there is great variation in point styles. Some hand-made nails have burrs and a rectangular cross section, and can easily be mistaken for early hand-headed cut nails. It is here that the point type can be of use to the archaeologist. The points of cut nails are almost always blunt, while those of hand-made nails are generally either sharply pointed or chisel-shaped. In addition, the point is formed by opposite faces tapering until they meet. Except for distinguishing between cut nails and hand-made nails, these variations do not appear to have any temporal value, though they probably had functional significance.

The burr can cause some unnecessary confusion. Burrs are found on the shafts of cut nails and may be present on some hand-made nails made from slit nail rods. The burr on cut nails indicates whether the cutting of the nail blank from the nail plate was done from the same side or opposite sides. Most of the early nail machines cut the nail blank from the same side of the nail plate, leaving the burr on opposite edges of the nail shaft. Most of the later machines cut the nail from opposite sides of the nail plate, leaving the burrs on the same face of the shaft. Burrs on the same face may indicate a more developed technology: either the nail plate was turned over after each cut or, more likely, the nail plate was fed into a nail machine having a reciprocating cutter with two cutting surfaces. The burr on hand-made nails made from slit stock is often obliterated during the forging of the nail, especially where the shaft is tapered to form the point. Sometimes it may be discerned along the edge as a cold shut, as noted below.

Cracks and cold shuts are characteristic of wrought iron. Cracks result from the fibers of unconsolidated iron opening as the metal is worked. The cracks occur along the grain, where the slag prevented a perfect union of the metal. On cross-grained nails the crack will run across the face, while on grain-in-line nails the cracks will run length-wise on the face. On the cut face of both kinds of nails there may be a crack, or even separation, running length-wise down the shaft. The heads of either kind can be cracked across the top in the direction of the cut faces. Cold shuts are unconsolidated metal folded against the body of the stock. There are numerous causes of cold shuts, but for the purposes of defining nails, they occur on hand-forged nails when the burr is hammered flat against the nail shaft.

All hand-made nails and early cut nails were hand-headed. Hand-formed nail heads are found in a plethora of styles. Though these styles may have a functional significance, they are not useful for establishing temporal significance. For instance, on cut nails, hand-heading indicates an early date of manufacture. Hand-formed nail heads tend not to be uniform and, on cut nails, are usually thinner than machine-formed heads. There will also be evidence of hammering on the head. Caution is advised, however, because the presence of shallow hammer marks on the heads of cut nails may be caused by the carpenter driving the nail rather than the nailer forming the head.

Louisiana Nail Types

Nails are assigned to one of the various types based on their possession of the requisite diagnostic features. The number assigned to any particular type has no significance, though it will be noticed that the first eight numbered types are also in chronological order; this is a reflection only of the evolution in the development of this system. Newly identified types can be added to this list by assigning the next vacant number. The dates of use given should be understood as a general period that a type was used because the dates are based on a limited survey of standing structures. The following list differs from that of Edwards and Wells (1993) by dropping their Type 9 nail. Edwards and the author think that the original Type 9 nail should probably be considered a variant of Type 7 nails. In its place a recently collected nail has been given the designation of Type 9, which is discussed under that heading below.

In the following section descriptions of some of the nail types include elements of the superficial appearance of the nail type. These superficial elements are included to aid the researcher in identifying the nail type to augment, and not to limit, the type description. In the cases in which the type description includes elements about the appearance it must be remembered that superficial elements are merely characteristic of many of the samples observed. In addition, there are some features that may have chronological significance, though these are not representative of technological developments. One of these is the length of pinch on side-pinched nails; the early nails tend to have a rather short

pinched area compared to later nails. The intent is to illustrate a method of establishing a chronologically significant nail typology based on manufacturing and structural features, rather than on the appearance of a nail. Some examples of Louisiana nail types are illustrated in Figure 8.

Type 1. These are hand-made nails made from forged or drawn nail rods. Included in this type are Type 2 nails that do not exhibit burrs and other evidence characteristic of that type. A Type 1 nail is forged from an iron nail rod and exhibits hammer marks on both the shaft and head. The shaft is usually square and tapers evenly on all sides to the point. Heads are generally rather thin and may occasionally bend or even break loose from the shaft if pulled forcefully from the timber. The numerous head and point varieties have no temporal significance other than indicating that the nail is hand made.

Type 2. These nails are similar to the Type 1 except that they are made from slit nail rods and have burrs. Nails of this type are often rectangular from under the head to where the point taper begins. Cold shuts may be present on the shaft. Type 1 and Type 2 nails are found in many varieties, but no temporal value can be attached to the varieties. The technology that produced these nails pre-date the European settlement of Louisiana, so an early date for this type begins with the establishment of the French colony in 1699 at Mobile. Though hand-made nails may have been manufactured well into the 19th century, the latest date of use in Louisiana is 1820.

Type 3. These nails are machine cut and hand-headed. Because they were made from narrow rolled nail plates they are cross-grained and have points that are slightly rounded from the front face to the back face. The shaft is usually strongly side-pinched and the heads are thin. Depending on the size of the nail, the pinch extends only about one-fifth or one-sixth of the way down the length of the shaft from below the head. Burrs are on opposite faces of the shaft.

Within a sample of nails of the same length and thickness from the same building there can be considerable variation in the width of the shaft and its degree of taper. This unevenness is an indication that the nail plate was fed into the shear by hand. The heads are generally a flat disk. Also a common sub-type of Type 3 was manufactured by hammering the heads from two angles, producing a narrow head that overhangs the cut faces, leaving a roof-like peak centered on the shaft. Type 3 use in Louisiana extends from 1791 to 1836.

Type 4. Nails of this type are entirely machine-made cut nails. They are cross-grained and have points that are slightly rounded from front face to back face. Type 4 nails are side-pinched and usually have a flat, discoid head. Some samples of this type are distinguishable from Type 3 nails only by their thicker heads and general uniformity. Burrs are on opposite faces. In Louisiana these nails appear to have been used from 1809 to 1834.

Type 5. These are entirely machine cut nails. They are cross-grained and have points that are slightly rounded from the front face to back face. They are uniformly cut and headed. The heads are roughly square, small, and thick. These are side-pinched nails. The pinch is rather long and shallow, making the upper one-third of the nail appear parallel when viewed from the face. The faces, when viewed from the cut face, bulge slightly. Though not common, these nails saw a rather long use in Louisiana from 1807 to 1836.

Type 6. Nails of this type are cross-grained cut nails and, like the other cross-grained nails, have points that are slightly rounded from the front face to back face. Type 6 nails are face-pinched and, depending on the size, the area deformed by the header extends one-fifth to one-tenth of the length of the nail. Burrs are on the same face. The outline and superficial appearance of these nails is often indistinguishable from that of later Type 7 iron nails and Type 10 steel nails, demonstrating the need for careful attention to the temporally significant features. These nails were used in building construction from 1810 to 1840 in Louisiana.

Type 7. These are side-pinched cut nails; however, the grain runs the length of the shaft, and all four corners of the point are flat. This indicates that the nail blanks were cut from nail plates that were sheared from wide, rolled sheets. Nails in a typical sample of Type 7 nails are uniform, have heads of moderate size, and have a long pinch extending nearly one-half down the shaft. A cross section through the shaft at the pinch describes a square with rounded corners. In Louisiana these nails saw use from 1834 to 1848.

Type 8. These nails are grain-in-line, face-pinched cut nails. Early nails of this type are more often found with cracks or even grain separation on the cut face than later nails. Their form is similar to that of Type 6 nails as well as Type 9 nails. Nails of this type are perfectly uniform and consistent within a sample. There are several styles of head, varying from small and rectangular to large and oval. This is the most common 19th century-nail, seeing long use in Louisiana from 1820 to 1891.

Type 9. This is a cross-grained and face-pinched nail. It exhibits the point rounding common to cross-grained nails. The burrs are on opposite faces, otherwise it is indistinguishable from Type 6 nails. Its head is small, rectangular, and rather thin. This nail type has been found in only one house in Louisiana, dated 1811 or 1812. This is a recently collected type of nail and replaces the former Type 9 nail of Edwards and Wells (1993).

Type 10. These are cut nails made of steel. In general outline this type resembles the earlier face-pinched cut nails (Types 6, 8, and 9). It is distinguishable from the Type 8 only in that it is made of steel rather than iron. The earliest appearance of Type 10 nails in Louisiana is 1891. Steel cut nails are currently available at many hardware stores.

Type 11. These are iron wire nails. The form is indistinguishable from modern steel wire nails. This type is poorly represented in Louisiana, and the provenience of the sample is highly questionable; so far only one house has provided nails of this type, and they were drawn from a roof lath in an 18th century house. Interestingly, this lath also had Type 1, Type 2, and Type 8 nails. The building is believed to have been re-roofed in the late 1870s as a part of a general rebuild of the structure.

Type 12. These are modern steel wire nails. The earliest example found in Louisiana is from 1891.

Conclusion

The establishment of a useful and accurate nail chronology requires a nail typology that is based on readily observable, objective criteria. Each of the evolving methods of nail manufacture leaves readily identifiable features that are indicative of the technology used in the manufacture of nails. The manufacturing technology changed over the course of time, therefore these features are temporally significant. A typology based on these features provides the best basis for the establishment of a nail chronology.

The Louisiana Nail Chronology was developed from samples of nails drawn from houses in southern Louisiana and Natchitoches Parish, Louisiana. The survey provided dates of actual use for the types of nails collected. These data supplemented information derived from historical research into the development of nail manufacturing technology. Investigation further afield indicates that the chronology may have a general applicability to the greater Mississippi and Ohio Valleys. That the Louisiana Nail Chronology can be applied to those areas may be hypothesized, based on the existence of the extensive river-born and coastal trade that linked Louisiana with nail manufacturing centers in Pittsburgh, Wheeling, and elsewhere. The development of similar, locally adjusted, nail chronologies on the East Coast and the Mississippi Valley using the methods outlined here can test this hypothesis.

Nail Terms

*denotes terms developed by the author and Jay Edwards

Alloy: A molecular combination of two or more metals: iron + carbon = steel. Wrought iron is a mixture, not an alloy.

Brad: A forged or cut nail that is "7" shaped. Cut brads do not go through an additional heading step because the head is sheared with the shaft. This type of nail has been made from antiquity, but may be dated on technological features. One of the few traditionally named types included here because it is clearly defined.

Burr: Burrs may be found on cut nails and nails made from slitted rods. The cutting tool leaves a sharp, rough flange of metal on the lower side of the shaft as it cuts through the metal stock. The edge above the burr may be slightly beveled or rounded. Burrs may also be found on hand-made nails. Such burrs are found on nails made from slit nail rods. In some cases, burrs can be left on hand-made nails if they were seated in a poorly fitted header.

Clinch: To bend and hammer the nail's exposed point end flat against the wood; done to prevent its loosening.

Cold shut: An unconsolidated fold caused by hammering the burr against the shaft at a too low heat to weld it to the body of the nail.

Cross-grained nails: Cut nails sheared from the end of a narrow nail plate that has the grain running length-wise. The earliest cut nails are cross grained. See "grain."

Cut face*: The two opposite surfaces of a cut nail that show the dragging of the shear. The upper edge may be slightly rounded where the shear entered the nail plate; lower edge will have the burr. See "face."

Cut nail: A machine-made nail. Cut nails are made by cutting the blank off the end of a long strip of iron or steel. The blank is wider at one end than the other. The wide end is mechanically held and is then headed by hand or by machine. The point is left flat.

Drag marks: Striations below the head of handmade nails caused when being seated in the header. Drag marks are also seen on the cut face of cut nails. These are caused by the shear as it slices through the metal, pulling the metal in the direction of the burr. The burr is also the result of dragging.

Drawn, Draw-out: Blacksmith term for lengthening and narrowing the metal. A point is drawn on a nail shaft by hammering the rod on two sides 90° apart. The opposite of "upset."

Face*: The surface of the shaft that is 90° from the cut face, and is the wider of the two pairs of faces. No distinction is made between front and back faces. See "cut face."

Forged nail: A hand-made nail. The shaft is formed from an iron rod using a hand hammer and an anvil. One end is pointed and then inserted into a header. The head is formed by hammering down on the end of the shaft that projects out of the header.

Grain: Striations in the metal that are characteristic of wrought iron. Iron is strongest when the load is applied across the grain because the slag that forms the grain prevents the metal from having a uniform bond over its whole surface. This is why grain-in-line nails can be clinched reliably and cross grained nails cannot. Steel has no grain because it has a crystalline structure.

Head: That part of a nail that is driven by the carpenter's hammer. Sprigs have no apparent head. Hand-formed heads are usually faceted by the numerous blows made during the heading process. Machine-headed nails will have a flat, smooth surface except for some modern cut nails that have a hemispherical knob centered on the head.

Header: 1. A tool used to form the head of hand forged nails. The most common form of header is a flat bar pierced with a hole the size of the nail shaft. The shaft is inserted into the hole and the header is rested over a hole (the pritchel hole) in the anvil, with the shaft point down. A part of the shaft projects above the header and is hammered down to form the head. 2. A machine or a part of a machine that grasps the shaft of a nail for heading.

Nail bar: A wrought iron strip from which nail rods were slit.

Nail plate: The stock from which cut nails are cut. These were originally produced in the early rolling mills with the grain running their length. Nails cut off these early nail plates are cross grained. Nail plates were later cut from sheet iron in such a way that the grain of the iron of nails cut from them ran the length of the nails. See "grain."

Nail rod: Square or rectangular rods from which some hand-made nails were made. Some nail rods were produced by rolling and slitting mills. Nails made from such rods may exhibit burrs on the same face, between the head and part of the shaft that is drawn out for the point.

Penny, penny weight: English system of nail sizing. It has several meanings: number of nails per pound, price in pence for a hundred nails, number of nails one could get for a "dinar" or penny (hence the abbreviation "d" as in 16d). Today it is standardized to describe the size of a wire nail. Because the term is vague it is not used here.

Pinch*: On cut nails: the area under the head that is grasped for heading. When the unheaded shaft of a cut nail is mechanically held for the heading operation, the part held is deformed on the shaft under the head. Earlier nails are generally deformed on the cut face and are described here as being "side-pinched." Later nails are deformed on the front and back and are described as being "face-pinched."

Point: The end opposite the head. Points may be sharp (all four sides meet), blunt (sides stop abruptly before meeting, forming a square or rectangle when viewed from above), or chisel (two opposite faces meet).

Rolling and slitting: Two stages in the process of making nail rods. The early rollers were about 8-10 in. wide and 10-12 in. thick. By the 1830s rollers were 3 ft. or more wide and over 2 ft. in diameter. To make a flat nail bar the iron ingot was fed into the rollers at a high heat. Slitting follows rolling; it is the longitudinal cutting of the flat nail bar into several long nail rods.

Rose head: English term for a faceted discoid head on a hand-made nail. This term is not used here because it is too vague to be useful for describing the enormous variation in head styles.

Shaft: Body of a nail extending from under the head to the point.

Shear: A cutting tool, usually with one moving edge and a lower stationary edge. Shearing is cutting across the width.

Slit: To cut a bar down its length. A slitter is a machine tool used in the manufacturing of nail rods consisting of an upper and a lower set of interlocking, disk-shaped cutters. The slitter cuts the nail plate longitudinally into nail rods. Though nails made from these rods often exhibit cut faces, they may be distinguished from early machine-made nails by the slitted nail's hand forged heads and grain running the length of the shaft.

Spike: A large nail. Imprecise term standardized too recently to be useful for describing hand-made and cut nails.

Sprig: A headless nail. This term can be defined clearly enough to be useful for describing hand-made and cut nails.

Steel: An iron-carbon alloy, usually having less than 2% carbon. The steel used in nails usually has less than 0.1% carbon. Steel began to supplant wrought iron in nail manufacturing in the 1880s. All modern wire nails are steel. Etched steel shows a very fine crystalline structure.

Upset: Blacksmith term for making the iron shorter and thicker. The head of a hand-headed nail is formed by upsetting the end of the shaft.

Wire nail: Machine-made nails made from round wire. In the 19th century these were called "French Points" and "French nails," after the country in which they were developed.

Wrought iron: Iron/silica amalgam produced by working a lump (bloom) of iron using a silicious flux as a part of the manufacturing process. Wrought iron is soft and more resistant to corrosion than steel. When etched the metal reveals a wood-like grain structure.

REFERENCES

AGRICOLA, GEORGIUS
   1950 *De Re Metallica,* translated and edited by Herbert Clark Hoover and Lou Henry Hoover. Reprint of 1912 edition, originally published in 1556. Dover, New York.

ASTON, JAMES, AND EDWARD B. STORY
   1939 *Wrought Iron.* A. M. Beyers, Pittsburgh.

BINNING, ARTHUR CECIL
   1938 *Pennsylvania Iron Manufacture In the Eighteenth Century.* Pennsylvania Historical Commission, Harrisburg.

CAMPBELL, HARRY L.
   1940 *The Working, Heat Treating, and Welding of Steel.* John Wiley & Sons, New York.

CLARK, DONALD (EDITOR)
1978   *The Encyclopedia of How It's Made.* A & W Publishers, New York.

COMMITTEE OF ROD AND DRAWN WIRE PRODUCERS
1969   *Designer's Handbook: Steel Wire.* American Iron and Steel Institute, New York.

DAUMAS, MAURICE
1964   *A History of Technology and Invention,* Vol. 2, translated by Eileen Hennessy. Crown Publishers, New York.

DICKINSON, H. W.
1939   *A Short History of the Steam Engine.* Cambridge University Press, Cambridge.

DIDEROT, DENIS
1765   *Recueil de Planches, sur les Sciences, les Arts Libéraux, et les Arts Méchaniques, Aves Leur Explication.* Paris.

EDWARDS, JAY D., AND TOM WELLS
1993   *Historic Louisiana Nails: Aids to the Dating of Old Houses.* Geo-Science Publications, Louisiana State University, Baton Rouge.

FERGUSON, EUGENE S. (EDITOR)
1965   Early Engineering Reminiscences (1815-1840) of George Escol Sellers. *Smithsonian Institution, Bulletin* 238. Washington.

HABAKKUK, H. J.
1962   *American and British Technology in the Nineteenth Century: The Search for Labour-Saving Inventions.* Cambridge University Press, Oxford.

HEITMANN, JOHN A.
1989   Peter Shoenberger. In *Iron and Steel in the Nineteenth Century,* edited by Paul Paskoff, pp. 309-311. Facts on File and Bruccoli Clark Layman, New York.

THE IRON AGE
1898   The Pioneer Wire Nail Manufacturer. *The Iron Age* 62(8).

KAUFFMAN, HENRY J.
1966   *Early American Ironware.* Charles E. Tuttle, Rutland, VT.

LOVEDAY, AMOS J., JR.
1983   *The Rise and Decline of the American Cut Nail Industry: A Study in the Relationships of Technology, Business Organization, and Management Techniques.* Greenwood, Westport, CT.

MACKINTOSH-HEMPHILL COMPANY
1953   *Rolling Mills, Rolls, and Roll Making.* Mackintosh-Hemphill, Pittsburgh.

MARTINEAU, R. F.
1866   *Birmingham and Midland Hardware District,* edited by Samuel Timmins. Robert Hardwicke, London.

MERCER, HENRY C.
1924   The Dating of Old Houses. A Paper Read by Dr. Henry C. Mercer, of Doylestown, Pa. at a Meeting of the Bucks County Historical Society, at New Hope, Bucks County, Pa., October 13, 1923. *Bucks County Historical Society Papers,* 5.

MOTT, R. A.
1983   *Henry Cort: the Great Finer,* edited by Peter Singer. The Metals Society, London.

NELSON, LEE H.
1968   Nail Chronology as an Aid to Dating Old Buildings. American Association for State and Local History, *Technical Leaflet* No. 48. Nashville.

NOËL HUME, IVOR
1972   *A Guide to Artifacts of Colonial America.* Alfred Knopf, New York.

PHILLIPS, MAUREEN KATHLEEN
1989   *A Revised Chronology of Cut Nails in New England 1790-1820: A Case Study of the Spencer-Pierce-Little House Addition.* Unpublished Master's thesis, Boston University, Boston.

ROWLAND, DUNBAR, AND A. G. SANDERS
1984   *Mississippi Provincial Archives: French Dominion, 1749-1763,* Vol. 5, revised and edited by Patricia Kay Galloway, Louisiana State University Press, Baton Rouge.

SCHOENHOF, JACOB
1974   *The Economy of High Wages.* Reprint of 1892 edition. Garland, New York.

URE, ANDREW
1865   *A Dictionary of Arts, Manufactures, and Mines,* Vol. 2. D. Appleton, New York.

TOM WELLS
838 AMERICA STREET
BATON ROUGE, LA
70802

PETER J. PRIESS

Historic Door Hardware

The Door

Doors come in a variety of forms, designs, and qualities but they all require two basic features: (1) a means of movement (opening and closing), and (2) a means of being secured (Figure 1a-e). Movement is achieved with some form of hinging device, while security is provided with a variety of different devices including hooks, bolts, latches, and locks.

The objective of this work is to consider the various categories of door hardware; define their basic characteristics of form, material, and manufacture; and present variations of form, design, or technology that may assist in identifying cultural affiliation or date. Attention is also given to items from an archaeological perspective where whole or undistorted objects are seldom the norm. The period covered is generally that of the European presence in North America with emphasis on the 18th and 19th centuries.

Hardware Research

Door hardware, as a component of building hardware, has attracted the interest of a small and varied group of 20th-century researchers. The results of this work have appeared in a variety of published and unpublished sources. Hence, an initial challenge is to determine what is already known about the subject through the work of others. A bibliography by Pruden (1974), followed by an annotated one by Priess (1978), were attempts to provide help for others who might venture into hardware research. The body of available literature has not grown substantially since that time.

The most extensive recent information on various categories of door hardware was provided by Donald Streeter in a series of articles published primarily by the Association for Preservation Technology (Streeter 1954, 1970, 1971, 1973a, 1973b, 1974a, 1974b, 1975a, 1975b, 1976, 1980,

1983). An earlier major effort was that of Sonn (1928), who recorded numerous examples of early building hardware and published an extensive group of illustrations. Other early investigators were Henry C. Mercer and Wallace Nutting. Mercer's area of activity was southeastern Pennsylvania where he documented early structures, collected architectural samples and hardware, and promoted the idea of hardware being a means of interpreting or dating early structures (Amsler 1989b). Nutting's (1921) interest was in the century after 1620, but his information is less detailed and we generally do not know details on provenience of an item (Schiffer et al. 1979).

One of the essential components of shared research is the consistent use of common terminology. There are several sources for building hardware to assist the endeavor. F. J. Butter has produced what is probably the most extensive documentation, beginning with a history of locks (Butter 1931), followed by a glossary (Butter 1948), and culminating in an extensive dictionary (Butter 1968). These are presented from a British perspective and thus differ on some questions such as handedness of doors (on which side do they open), but still provide the most extensive statements on building hardware. Other sources such as Towne (1904) or Eras (1957) have occasionally included more extensive glossaries. A glossary for door locks, using a variety of sources, has been published (Priess 1979) but in a series with only a limited circulation. The frequency with which building hardware is discussed in detail in archaeological reports has not yet forced the issue for consistent terminology.

Material and Manufacture

The predominant material for the manufacture of building hardware into the 19th century was wrought iron, though other materials, often brass, were occasionally used. The principal type of manufacture was hand forging, but casting was an occasional alternate manufacturing type.

Wrought iron is "a two-component metal consisting of high purity iron and iron silicate–a

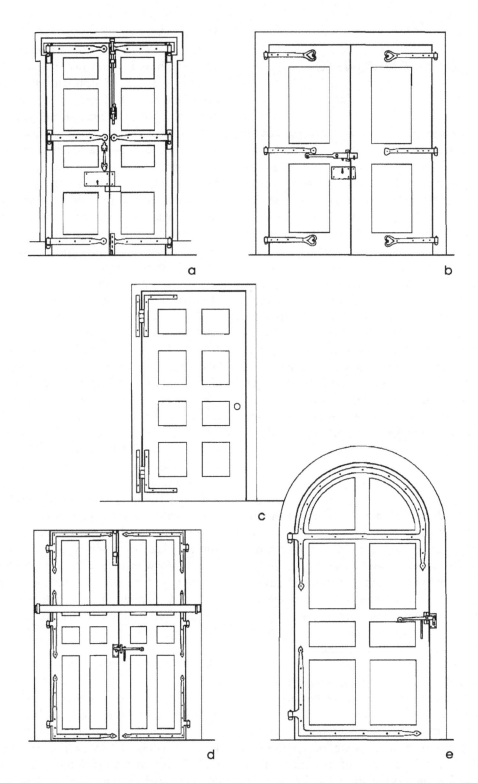

FIGURE 1. Examples of hardware on 18th-century doors: *a,* entrance doors of Independence Hall, Philadelphia, Pennsylvania; constructed 1732 (strap hinges with either driven or plate-mounted pintles, and a combination of sliding bolts, a rim lock, and a thumb latch); *b,* church in Tadoussac, Quebec (strap hinges with some reinforced pintles, and a combination of a rim lock and thumb latch); *c,* Pringle House, Charleston, South Carolina; constructed ca. 1765 (pair of HL hinges); *d,* center doors from Congregational Church, Little Haddam, Connecticut; constructed 1794 (strap and vertical strap hinges, designed to fit around door panels, and a combination of a thumb latch, sliding bolt, and a drop bar); *e,* side door of the Congregational Church (extended and supplemented strap hinges on a driven pintle, and a thumb latch). (After Sonn 1928[2]:Plates 129, 133-135.)

particular type of glass-like slag. The iron and the slag are in physical association, as contrasted to the chemical or alloy relationship that generally exists between the constituents of other metals" (Aston and Story 1939:1). Its advantages are that it resists corrosion, is easy to forge, and is readily forge welded (Aston and Story 1939:59, 65, 78; Gayle and Look 1980:42)

Hand forging involves a variety of techniques, often applied to the metal when hot, to alter the size, shape, and appearance of a piece of metal and, occasionally, to join it to other components to form an object. The end product can be as simple as a nail or as complex as a door lock. Although the techniques and products may be similar, hand forging can be done by an individual blacksmith working in a local community or by a group of smiths working in a manufacturing district producing items for export or trade. The products are basically the same.

A major characteristic of hand forging is the potential for flexibility in design and craftsmanship. Items produced locally can reflect local tastes and the ability of the local craftsman. The smith can produce anything within his capacity and anything that his customers may require. This can mean the rapid adoption of new styles or fashions as well as the perpetuation of previous styles. This can also mean the existence of poor workmanship if no other alternatives exist. Production in a factory setting will likely be less flexible, involving a larger number of smiths, producing for a larger market, probably producing more standardized forms, and possibly producing fewer variations of form. Consumer selection of hardware would be determined more by what was available (being produced) than by personal preference.

The nature of wrought iron also means that repairs or changes can be made locally. A broken or out-of-style item need not be discarded. Repairs can be made, an item can be modified to take on a new form, or it may simply serve as stock for a blacksmith to shape into an entirely different object. For archaeologists, a major consequence of this is that wrought iron objects are often relatively scarce in excavations.

Forged objects may show a variety of features which help to identify the techniques and process

of production. Recognition of many of these is facilitated by corrosion which accentuates the fibrous nature of wrought iron. Forge-welded joints appear as an overlap of two layers of metal. Hammering to change the shape of the metal may be apparent as individual hammer blows, especially on the back of an object where the marks would not be visible when the object was in place. The usual objective for the exposed surfaces of an object would likely have been to make the metal relatively smooth. In an item of wrought iron which has been hammered into shape, the fibers of the metal will follow the shape of the object because they have been deformed to accomplish the shape rather than being cut. A wrought-iron object shaped by machine cutting will have its fibers parallel and running off the edge of the object where they have been cut. Holes in forged objects are often punched rather than drilled. These are recognizable by the deformation of the metal around the hole. The punching operation will drag the metal and produce a raised ridge around the hole on one side. Hand riveting is likely to produce a surface similar to a rose-head nail: a number of facets representing a number of individual hammer blows. Machine riveting, on the other hand, will be smoother and more regular; the riveted surface possibly being completely smooth or having a regular pattern repeated from one example to another.

Casting was initially an infrequent alternate method for producing door hardware. The material could be brass or iron. The use of cast iron had begun by the latter part of the 18th century. Casting involves pouring molten metal into a form to produce the required shape of an object. The cast form can be finished subsequently by drilling, filing, polishing, or other procedures to create the final product. Cast iron is too brittle to be shaped by many of the procedures of hand forging. Neither can it be heated and hammered into another shape, nor forge welded to other components. A broken item of cast iron often cannot be repaired. Items of cast brass are formed by similar processes with some greater flexibility for the final product. Casting is also a process which cannot be as readily carried out locally. Although brass can be melted in a blacksmith's forge fire and, thus, cast into usable objects at a local level, this is not possible with iron.

Peter J. Priess

Cast-iron objects, unless they can be repaired by a few available techniques such as riveting, become discards once broken.

Cast brass may have been used for lock housings and occasionally for other items. Brass can be highly polished and it could have been seen as aesthetically more attractive. Brass is also a non-sparking material and its use in some contexts, such as in areas of gunpowder storage, however, may have been preferable, if not essential. An all-brass door lock or hinge is likely to indicate a special context rather than simply a wish to have a more attractive item. With the increased use of cast iron in the 19th century, brass also became a more common material for the manufacture of some components of lock mechanisms.

Hardware–which at the beginning of European settlement in North America was virtually all hand forged of wrought iron–underwent a number of changes in material and technology from that time until the end of the 19th century. Advances in metal technology in the 18th century allowed a greater use of cast iron. The introduction of rolled plate (shaped by rollers rather than by hand hammering) around the end of the 18th century resulted in changes in the appearance or style of some objects. Mechanization of manufacture during the 19th century resulted in the machine manufacture of many items, the standardization of shapes and sizes, and the reduction of peripheral finishing techniques such as thinning and beveling. Machine or mass production often seems to have emphasized speed at the expense of appearance. Techniques which had been applied in hand forging, partially to reduce the quantity of metal required to make an object, also resulted in objects with greater aesthetic appeal. Techniques to thin, taper, or bevel items were reduced or eliminated with the result that some objects took on a more-massive and less-appealing appearance. Cheaper raw materials became increasingly available as the methods of producing rolled-sheet and bar iron improved, creating a change in the cost relationship between material and labor. "Technically, smiths became less frugal in their use of iron, and work became heavier, with less labour expended to reduce sizes to earlier dimensions" (Streeter 1983:2).

As Sonn (1928[1]:9, 11) has indicated, "there is little if anything in the field of American wrought iron that one might justly claim as being distinctly indigenous or novel in design and execution . . . early American wrought iron is therefore . . . a mixture largely British in character because British colonists generally predominated, but with a dash of the French, Italian, Spanish, Dutch, and German." The hardware of any specific area would depend on the nature of its cultural background, the mixture of cultures, the level of dominance by any one of them, and the level of persistence of the non-English component. Extensive recording and analysis of regional styles has yet to be carried out.

The change in hardware styles through time in North America has also been characterized as a transition from the conspicuous to the concealed (Amsler 1989a). Surface-mounted items provided opportunity and incentive for ornamentation, as well as matching design to a specific application (Figure 1d-e). By the end of the 19th century, however, hinges had virtually disappeared from view and door locks were soon to follow. Both items were relegated to the door edge where they could only be seen when the door was open. Ornamentation continued to be included on some cast hinges, even appearing on areas which would not be visible once the hinges were attached. Although the lock itself disappeared from view, reference to early 20th-century sources will readily demonstrate the extensive effort applied to the ornamentation of such lock accessories as knobs, handles, and back plates (Towne 1904; Sargent 1910). Opportunities for the visible ornamentation of hinges became virtually nonexistent except for the persistence of surface-mounted items in special, public, or monumental circumstances.

Door Hardware Categories

According to tradition, a considerable amount of various sorts of hardware was turned out by individual craftsmen who worked at their own forges in different localities. This usage may largely account for the broad diversity of forms in which certain articles appear. Owing to their general lack of similarity, it is somewhat difficult to make coherent groups of the types of latches, hinges and other products, and the classification can be accomplished only in a broad way (Kelly 1924:197).

Any attempt to offer an overview of door hardware must first acknowledge the enormity of the task and the impossibility of providing anything more than a general overview. For much of the period in question, hand-forged items could be (and often were) produced by local craftsmen responding to a range of local conditions including their own ability or lack of it, the availability of suitable materials, local tastes and preferences, and the acceptable range of creativity. Variations of form and size are possible and likely, especially for public or other substantial buildings. Any attempt to describe or illustrate the total range of any hardware category will only last until the next collection is evaluated and new forms are found. Hence, the descriptions which follow attempt to provide general information on hardware groups based on function and general similarity of form. The assessment of specific collections will still have to rely on descriptions of items which belong to, but do not match, any other items in the same category.

Hinging

Movement of a door is accomplished through the use of hinges. Although it is possible to make a hinge from wood, leather, or other flexible materials, these are not as likely to survive in an archaeological context. They are also likely to be of a simple and basic form, providing little or no substantial information concerning their age or cultural affiliation. Their presence likely implies a makeshift application or limited economics.

A hinge is any device which allows a door to open and close. It has to consist of two basic components; one immovable and attached to the door frame, and another movable and attached to the door. There must also be a joint, a means of connecting the two components and allowing them to move relative to one another. The movement of a door is always perpendicular to the line of the joint. In most cases the joint is vertical and the door moves in a horizontal plane. At least two hinges are required for the operation of a door. Each component, with the exception of pintles, can be referred to as a leaf or flap (Butter 1968:20).

With the exception of a strap hinge, the joint of a hinge consists of two or more loops or "knuckles" (Butter 1968:154) joined by a pin or other system. A hinge can be characterized in terms of the number of knuckles in a complete joint (the knuckles are designated as "parts" and the hinge is described as a 2-part or 3-part, for example). All hinges using knuckles must also have some means of keeping the connecting pin in place. For some cast varieties, this can be accomplished by enclosing the pin completely within the metal. For others, the pin can be (1) riveted at each end, producing a "fast joint" (Russell and Erwin 1865:116), in which case the pin cannot be removed from the joint; (2) held fast in one of the knuckles; or (3) equipped with an enlarged upper end or finial to prevent it from falling out of the joint.

If the pin is riveted into place, the door cannot be removed from its frame without detaching one side of the hinge. Otherwise, the pin can be removed to divide the hinge into two separate leaves. Two-part hinges can also work like a strap hinge and pintle with one leaf being lifted off the other, thus allowing a door to be removed without detaching any part of the hinges. Hinges of this nature have the pin attached permanently in the lower knuckle and are designated as "lift off" (Butter 1968:161), "heave off" (Peabody Essex Museum, Philips Library [hereafter PEM], Volume 2), or "loose joint" (Sargent 1910:517).

Hinges are either mounted on the surface or the edge of a door and the two parts may be symmetrical or not. Surface-mounted hinges are divided into a number of categories based on form. Edge-mounted hinges are considered within the butt-hinge category.

SURFACE MOUNTED HINGES

Early hinges in North America were predominantly, if not exclusively, surface-mounted types, and appeared in a wide variety of sizes and shapes. On a relatively simplistic level, the major categories or subdivisions (based on general similarities of form and mechanism and, where possible, on historical sources) are strap hinges, double-strap hinges, T-strap hinges, and H-type hinges. These categories may differ somewhat from what others have used but represent an attempt to organize a variety of forms into a small number of groups. The analysis of actual hinges in a collection may still require descriptions or illustrations of specific items to illuminate their similarity to and divergence from the common forms.

STRAP HINGES

> The hinges of monumental doors served not only to permit them to swing open and to close, but were a precious means of assembly for the woodwork which frequently consisted of parallel planks held together solely by the ironwork of the hinges. Even where doors were assembled in frames, the hinges were designed to cover the greater part of their surfaces, and their harmonious meanders were generally well studied, with the intention of reinforcing the framework of the doors. In many cases where the hinges themselves were considered insufficient, the smiths made separate pieces of iron, matching or complementing their decorations, and applied them on the doors in the places which needed added strength (Frank 1950:128-129).

A strap hinge consists of a metal strap which extends horizontally across a door and is anchored to the door frame by a pintle. Although it may be more appropriate to designate them as horizontal-strap hinges, to differentiate them from vertical-strap hinges, the more traditional designation of strap hinge is retained here. Their history in North America extends from the beginning of European settlement to the present. They were mostly forged from wrought iron for much of this period. During the 19th century, however, manufacture shifted to machine or mass-production methods, initially using wrought iron and then steel. Strap hinges can be defined in terms of their basic form, but there is considerable variety in shape and size.

A basic requirement of a strap hinge is for it to be relatively long and narrow and oriented horizontally on the door (Figures 2-3). It must have a vertical socket at one end to accommodate the pintle. They can be characterized in terms of the extent of taper from the socket to the end, the nature of the end finish (the presence and form of an ornamental finial or other termination), the presence of thinning toward the finial, the presence of beveling on the edges, the nature of socket manufacture, and

the length of the socket relative to the widest part of the strap.

Strap hinges are generally straight and often taper from the socket to a decorative finial (Figure 2a, d-f). The length of the socket is usually the same as the maximum width of the strap (Figure 2a, d-f). The strap will have a number of holes along its length, including one in the finial, to permit attachment to the door. Attachment could have been either with nails, bolts, or rivets and, when they became more readily available, screws. The major stress on a hinge is near the socket; hence fasteners may be concentrated toward this end and the hinge can be tapered and thinned toward the finial. This also results in a saving of material and produces an object of greater aesthetic appeal. The strap may infrequently have a widening near the socket to provide an area for additional fastening holes (Figure 2b). Called a nailing plate, the widening is often rounded or diamond shaped.

The finial or end is usually a widening of the strap and can have a great variety of shapes (Figure 4). Simple finials may be circular, diamond, or spear shaped. On straps with less taper, if any, the end may be splayed into a fishtail or dovetail shape (Figure 4e-f).

Hand-forged strap hinges may be differentiated to some extent on the basis of cultural affiliation. Dunton (1972:10-12) suggests that English hinges are more likely to have a continuous taper from socket to finial, whereas French hinges frequently have what he calls "compound tapers" (a taper towards the socket as well as the finial, or an extensive untapered section between the socket and finial). It also appears that French hinges are more likely to have little or no taper, ending in a relatively simple splay (Figure 2e-f) (Duhamel du Monceau 1767:Plate 13). Nailing plates are generally considered to be associated with Dutch hinges (Sonn 1928[2]:Plates 137, 139, 140), although they also appear on French examples (Sonn 1928[2]:Plates 140-141). Hinges with widened sections near the socket but with no additional fastening holes appear to be from German contexts (Sonn 1928[2]:Plate 142; Streeter 1983:Figure 16). Finials appear in a variety of shapes. The simple splayed fishtail on an untapered or slightly tapered strap may more commonly be a French feature. A bifurcated

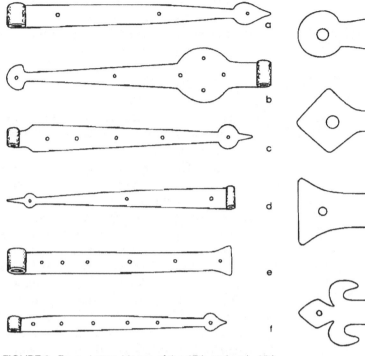

FIGURE 2. Forged strap hinges of the 17th and early 18th centuries: *a*, Bronck House, Greene County, NY, possibly late 17th century; *b*, Youmans House, Greene County, NY, possibly 17th century; *c*, Ensign John Sheldon House, Deerfield, MA, 1698; *d*, Pennsylvania hinge, early 17th century; *e-f*, Fortress of Louisbourg, Nova Scotia. (*a-d*, after Sonn 1928[2]:Plates 137-138; *e-f*, after Dunton 1972:Figures 1, 6.)

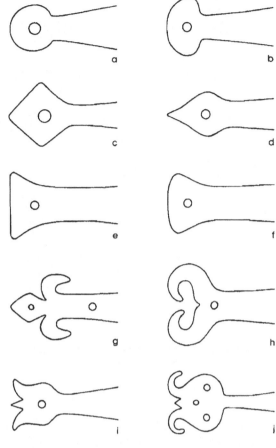

FIGURE 4. Common finials on hinge straps: *a*, round; *b*, bean; *c*, diamond; *d*, spear; *e*, splayed (squared end); *f*, splayed (rounded end); *g*, fleur-de-lis; *h*, bifurcate (the two ends can take on a variety of shapes or convolutions); *i-j*, tulip; both *e* and *f* can also be termed "fishtail" or "dovetail."

curved-scroll finial appears on a French hinge (Sonn 1928[2]:Plate 140), but is also known from 17th-century English examples (Alcock and Hall 1994:22). Circular or ovate finials are more commonly English (Sonn 1928[2]:10), while tulip finials are more frequently associated with Germanic contexts (Sonn 1928[2]:11).

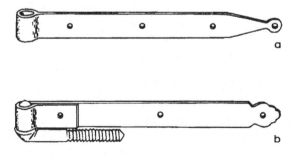

FIGURE 3. Examples of machine-made strap hinges of the 19th and early 20th centuries: *a*, "heavy welded hook hinge;"; *b*, "heavy wrought hook hinge" (*a*, after Russell and Erwin 1865:114; *b*, after Sargent 1910:877.)

Fleur-de-lis finials appear on both English and Continental European hinges (Sonn 1928[1]:74, [2]:Plates 145-146).

Changes in the 19th century–such as the introduction of mass production, the reduction of local hand forging, and a probable shift from the use of strap hinges on houses to outbuildings–resulted in a change in the form and quality of strap hinges. Hinges took on a bulkier appearance as tapering, thinning, and edge beveling received less emphasis. Rather than tapering for their full length, strap hinges tended to be untapered except for a short distance near the finial (the taper allowed for creation of the finial). Thinning and edge beveling appeared less frequently. Locally forged hinges for outbuildings might also be made from old

Peter J. Priess

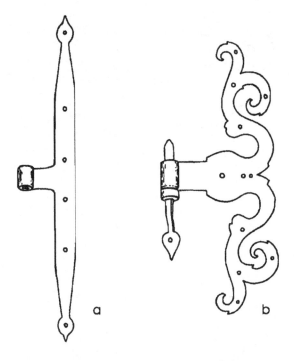

FIGURE 5. Vertical strap hinges: *a,* straight strap with spear finials; *b,* "ram's horn" form. (After Sonn 1928[2]:Plates 129, 177.)

wagon tires, a readily available source of stock, with no attempt to eliminate the rounded edges or the fastening holes. An example of expediency in machine manufacture is a style in which flat stock is simply cut into the required length with one end shaped into a socket. The latter is not welded and the strap end simply has enough overlap with the hinge to allow the first fastening to pass through both layers of material (Figure 3*b*). The cutting may produce an ornamental end on the strap with the mirror image of this ornament appearing on the other end of the strap. There is no other ornamentation, such as a taper or beveling.

VERTICAL STRAP HINGES

Although strap hinges are primarily horizontal, some are vertical. There does not seem to be a good generic term for these hinges in the historical sources. Hence, the term "vertical strap," as suggested by Dunton (1972:13), is proposed here, but without being as all-encompassing as he would have it. The term "side hinge," as used

by Sonn (1928[2]:Plates 175-184) and Streeter (1983:9), is at variance with Moxon (1703:22) and, therefore, is not considered appropriate.

A vertical strap hinge is one which pivots on a pintle and is primarily vertical, or parallel to the line of the pin (Figure 5). There is still a requirement for a short horizontal section for the socket. Some vertical strap hinges may consist of a simple straight strap, possibly with decorative finials (Figure 5*a*), but often they are in the form of two serpentine arms that diverge from a central point to form what is occasionally called a "ram's-horn" (Figure 5*b*) or "stag-horn" hinge or shape (Streeter 1983:Figure 14). This designation can be confusing since the hinge may have little resemblance to an actual ram's horn and may at times be made to look more like the cock's-head hinge discussed below or some other feature. A more generic approach would be to call such shapes "serpentine" with additional descriptive terms used, if necessary, to identify their more-specific form. Vertical strap hinges seem to be hand-forged types, and are more likely to appear in the 18th century or earlier.

COMBINATION STRAP HINGES

Some strap-hinge forms do not fit well into either the strap or vertical-strap category because they have parts oriented in several directions (Figure 6). For want of a better term, it is recommended that these be called combination strap hinges. Such hinges, most of which were probably hand forged, still functioned with a pintle. Because of the range of possible variations in shape, any description of them would have to note the general nature of the various components and their direction or relationship, as well as other information such as the nature of the taper, finial, or other ornamentation.

Combination strap hinges may have been created to provide additional support in specific contexts or to add aesthetic appeal. Sonn (1928[2]:Plates 129, 141, 187) illustrates a number of examples, including some intended for shutters (Sonn 1928[2]:Plate 187). One style is still listed in 1865, by Russell and Erwin (1865:114) as "rolled blind hinges." There are no styles listed for doors.

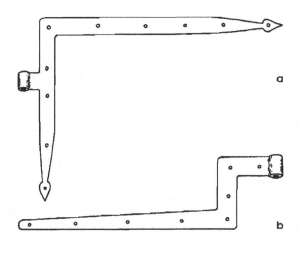

FIGURE 6. Combination strap hinges: *a,* from the center door of the Congregational Church, Little Haddam, Connecticut, 1794; *b,* from St. Paul's Chapel, New York City, 1766. (After Sonn 1928[2]:Plates 129, 141.)

MISCELLANEOUS STRAP HINGES

One occasionally encounters a hinge form that does not readily fit into any of the major strap-hinge categories or any others for that matter. One such (Figure 7), illustrated by Streeter (1983:Figure 12), cannot rightly be considered a strap hinge. It is included here, however, because it requires a pintle, one with a pointed pin. The hinge body consists of a hollow cone with a tapered shank which is driven into the door. The example is from a Spanish context in

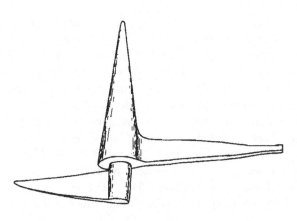

FIGURE 7. A conical hinge and pintle from a Spanish context. (After Streeter 1983:Figure 12.)

San Juan, Puerto Rico, but Streeter (1983:Figure 12) notes that other examples also exist.

PINTLES

Strap hinges generally hang and pivot on a pintle, a pin (generally vertical) that is attached to the door frame. Pintles can be categorized by the method of manufacture or by the means of attachment.

Pintles are produced in one of two ways, and involve one or two pieces of metal. A one-piece pintle is produced from a single piece of metal; one end is forged into a circular pin and the other is formed into a device for attachment (Figure 8*a-d, i-j*). The pin and the attachment are usually at right angles to each other. A two-piece pintle has the pin as a separate piece

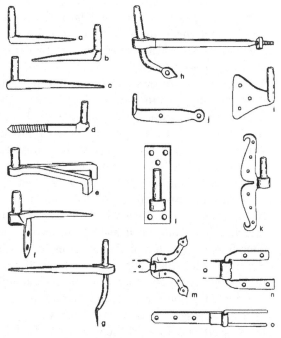

FIGURE 8. Pintle types: *a,* one-piece, driven; *b,* one-piece, driven with dent at heel; *c,* one-piece, driven with reinforced heel; *d,* one-piece, screwed, with additional support for hinge around pin, machine made; *e,* two-piece for masonry; *f,* two-piece, driven with reinforcing on shank; *g,* two-piece, driven with reinforcing on pin; *h,* two-piece, bolted; *i,* one-piece, plate (butterfly) type; *j,* one-piece strap type; *k,* two-piece, vertical strap (serpentine) type; *l,* two-piece, riveted through plate; *m-n,* surface-mounted staple type; *o,* driven-staple type. (*a-b, e-f, i, k,* after Dunton 1972:Figures 21, 24, 26, 27, 33; *c-d, g-h, j, l, n,* after Harris 1971:Figures 30, 37-40; *m,* after Sonn (1928[2]:Plate 147; *o,* after Russell and Erwin 1865:114.)

of metal set into a loop (Figure 8e-h, k-l). This type of construction provides a bearing surface for the hinge around the entire pin whereas in a one-piece pintle the bearing surface is only the relatively narrow section at the bend which connects the pin to the body.

The attachment of a pintle is either in the form of a shank or a plate. A shank is inserted into the frame; a plate is mounted on the surface. Pintles with shanks may be inserted into the frame in several different ways. In the most common, the shank tapers to a point and is driven in like a nail (Figure 8a-c, f-g).

In the 19th century, shanks were also threaded and screwed into pre-drilled holes (Figure 8d). If the back of the frame were accessible, a threaded shank could function like a bolt and be anchored with a nut (Figure 8h). A plain shank could be riveted or held in place with a tapered key.

In the case of stone and brick walls, the shanks are generally mortared into place. To help anchor them, the pintles are usually two-piece with the shank consisting of two arms with bent ends (Figure 8e).

Pintles with shanks are often reinforced, being supported by an arm below the shank. The reinforcement is usually a continuation of the pin (Figure 8g-h), but may also be forged from the shank (Figure 8f). When present, the reinforcement will likely be on a two-piece pintle with the pin continuing through the loop and ending in a finial similar to those on strap hinges (Figure 8g-h). The finial will have one or more fastening holes through it and be attached to the door frame below the pintle. The reinforcement provides additional support for large hinges or heavy doors, but may also be ornamental. Reinforced pintles seem to be more a product of hand-forging (no reinforced types are offered by Russell and Erwin [1865:113-114] in their catalogue).

Pintles attached to a surface are held in place with a mounting plate having holes for nails, screws or, possibly, bolts or rivets. The pintle may be of the one- or two-piece variety, and the plate may be rectangular, a vertical strap, dovetail shaped, or even imitate the strap shape of the hinge. Some types of surface-mounted pintles are of two-piece construction with the shank riveted through an additional mounting plate (Figure 8l).

In their 1865 catalogue, Russell and Erwin (1865:113-114) offer several pintle types. The majority are driven, but there are also plate-mounted, bolt, and screw types while the 1910 offering by Sargent & Company (1910:877, 879) includes only plate-mounted and screw types.

An alternative to a pintle exists in the form of a staple or loop. The associated hinges are still considered strap types because the joint consists of a socket and a pin rather than two or more knuckles held together by a pin. The staple may have tapered shanks and be driven into the door frame, or it may be perforated for surface attachment (Figure 8m-o). Such an arrangement is not easily disassembled since the hinge cannot be detached from the staple and, hence, the staple would have to be detached from the frame. Russell and Erwin (1865:114) offer such an item which is called a "scuttle door" hinge (Figure 8o).

The specific form of pintle used may be influenced by the amount of room available for its attachment. A driven, screwed, or bolted pintle is suited for a narrow frame, while a surface-mounted dovetail plate or strap requires more width.

One feature of pairs of pintles is that one pin may be slightly longer than the other. This allows each hinge to be aligned separately with its pin, one at a time, making it easier to rehang a door. Two pintles with pins of different lengths found together in an archaeological context could represent a pair.

DOUBLE-STRAP HINGES

A double-strap hinge is a surface-mounted hinge in which both sides are some form of strap (generally linear in nature). The term has no historical lineage and is suggested here as a means of differentiating such hinge forms from others and facilitating their description. Hinges considered within this category have generally been included in a "strap hinge" group (Russell and Erwin 1865:112; Sargent 1910:1133) or described as strap hinges with "side members" (Sonn 1928[2]:Plate 154). The hinge may be symmetrical or asymmetrical, depending on the nature of the two leaves. The joint, rather than being a socket and pin as for strap hinges, consists of two or more knuckles held together by a pin, forming a multiple-part joint.

In addition to describing a double-strap hinge as symmetrical (Figure 9*b-c*) or asymmetrical (Figure 9*a*) and describing the type of joint (2-part, 3-part, etc.), the attributes of the two leaves can be described using terms applied to strap hinges. This includes the nature and extent of tapering, thinning, and beveling, and the type of finial.

One form of double-strap hinge is the butterfly type (Figure 9*b*). Such hinges seem to have a more consistent shape, being symmetrical with each strap expanding towards a squared-off end. The ends may be slightly convex to

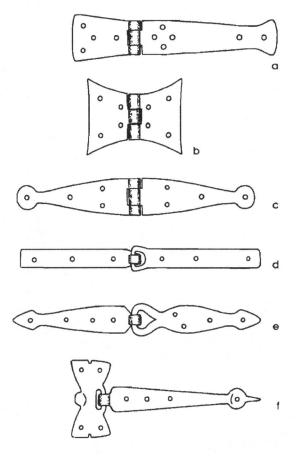

FIGURE 9. Double-strap hinges: *a*, asymmetrical strap, 3-part joint; *b*, symmetrical strap (butterfly), 3-part joint; *c*, symmetrical strap, 3-part joint; *d-e*, symmetrical strap, loop joint; *f*, asymmetrical strap (strap and plate), loop joint. (*a-b, e-f*, after Sonn 1928[2]:Plates 157, 159, 162; *c-d*, after Harris 1971:Figures 30-31.)

impart a less-bulky appearance. Ornamentation may consist of beveled edges or notches filed into the end. Butterfly hinges do not seem to have persisted beyond the hand-forging era (they are not included in the Russell and Erwin [1865] catalogue).

An uncommon joint variant has a socket-and-loop arrangement; the proximal end of the moveable flap has been formed into a socket which encircles a loop on the strap or plate which is attached to the doorframe (Figure 9*d-f*). These have been designated as "wrapped" (Sonn 1928[2]:Plate 155; Streeter 1974b:Figure 5) or "loop pin" joints (Dunton 1972:37), but loop joint is the suggested terminology. The hinge socket for this type of joint is often substantially shorter than the maximum width of the hinge, the hinge having a sharply tapered section adjacent to the socket as well as a gradual taper toward the finial. Unfortunately, the attempt at categorization falls apart somewhat with loop-joint hinges. Some may consist of two symmetrical straps joined by a loop (Figure 9*d-e*), but there are others where the anchor side of the hinge is more like a plate or even a vertical strap (Figure 9*f*). The overall appearance is more like that of a T-strap or cross-garnet hinge, discussed below, but otherwise the hinge does not fit comfortably into the characterization of this hinge category. The options of including such hinges either with double-strap or cross-garnet hinges are equally awkward. It may be preferable to include hinges with a plate or vertical strap anchor and a loop joint in the double-strap category, recognizing that the multiple knuckle joint of a cross garnet would have been more difficult to produce and may have been used more for imported hinges rather than locally made ones.

As with the staple-type joint on a strap hinge, the loop joint cannot be disassembled and a door equipped with them could not be removed without detaching either the hinge or the anchor. Another feature of this joint is that it has considerable play and would likely be too loose for an entry door. It is a type more suited for a crate or trap door although large examples may have functioned on entry doors.

Hand-forged double-strap hinges are less common than strap hinges with pintles. The difference in the amount of effort required to produce them may explain this situation. A double strap also requires a wider frame to accommodate the anchor side of the hinge, even if the anchor is the smaller flap. A symmetrical form with tapered straps and rounded ends is a common machine-made form for the post-1850 era (Russell and Erwin 1865:112).

A hinge may occasionally have more than one joint. In this case the main strap, attached to a door, is segmented, allowing the door to be folded into two or more narrower sections. This may be found on strap hinges but is more likely to appear on double-strap types, either symmetrical or asymmetrical.

T-STRAP OR CROSS GARNET HINGES

A T-strap or cross-garnet hinge has a horizontal strap attached to the door and a vertical strap attached to the doorframe, the two parts connected by a multiple-part joint. The term "cross garnet" has been used historically for a form of this hinge (Moxon 1703:18), but the origin of the designation is unclear. The vertical strap is called the "cross" (Moxon 1703:18). *The Builder's Dictionary* (1981) uses the term "garnets" for a hinge type but provides no further clarification. Butter (1968:41) provides a useful differentiation by limiting the term "cross garnet" to T-shaped hinges in which the joint is "shorter than the length of the vertical flap." Although historically such hinges have also been designated "T hinge" (PEM, Volume 16), Butter's definition will be used here to differentiate between the two major joint sizes.

A cross-garnet hinge may be seen as a combination of a strap hinge and an H-hinge although it is not the contention here that the form developed out of a combination of the two. In fact, it is more likely that the two forms existed side by side until the early 19th century. There are a number of differences which may have historical significance and indicate that the cross garnet had its own line of development. The horizontal strap leaf is similar to that of a strap hinge in that it has the potential for taper, thinning, edge bevel, and an ornamental finial. The finials are similar to what may appear on a strap hinge. The joint end of the horizontal strap is shaped into one or more knuckles which mesh with the knuckles of the vertical strap. For a

3-part joint, the horizontal strap will always have the central knuckle. For cross-garnet hinges, the central knuckle is considerably shorter than the width of the strap (Figure 10*a-b*). This relationship does not persist for T-strap hinge types (Figure 10*c-d*).

The vertical strap component is generally straight (untapered), much like one side of an H-hinge. The ends may have finials like a strap hinge or be ornamented, such as the foliate finials of an H-hinge (Streeter 1974b:Figure 2). The vertical strap usually lacks any ornamentation

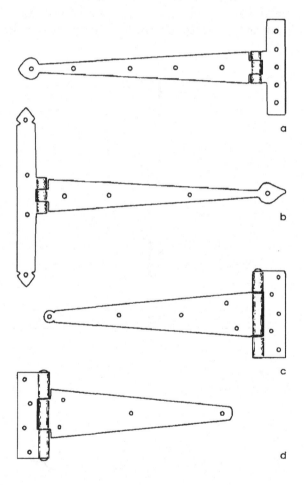

FIGURE 10. Cross-garnet and T-strap hinges: *a,* cross garnet with plain vertical strap, 3-part joint; *b,* cross garnet vertical strap with finials, 3-part joint; *c,* T-strap with plain vertical strap and minimal finial on horizontal strap; *d,* T-strap with plain strap ends. (*a,* after Sonn 1928[2]:Plate 156; *b,* after Streeter 1974b:Figure 4; *c,* after Russell and Erwin 1865:112; *d,* after Sargent 1910:1133.)

regardless of how the horizontal arm is finished, being simply squared at the ends (Figure 10a).

The cross-garnet hinge comes in a variety of sizes. The general indication is that smaller sizes may have been cut and shaped from sheeting or thin plate, but that the larger sizes were forged from flat stock. The joint on the horizontal arm is forged and cut from the same stock as the remainder of the arm. It has been noted, however, that the joint component on the vertical strap is often a separate piece of metal lapped with the strap and forge welded into position (Priess and Streeter 1974:24, 32-33). The knuckles would have been cut and filed to shape after the joint section had been welded, as described by Moxon (1703:20-21). This differs from H-hinges in which the joint always seems to have been formed from the same piece of metal as the remainder of the hinge.

The cross-garnet hinge has a lengthy history in North America and appears to be associated primarily with English contexts. Frank (1950:Plate 41) and d'Allemagne (1924:139) both illustrate hinges of similar form, some of which are presumed to be French, and which d'Allemagne dates to the 15th and 16th centuries. The general configuration is that of a cross garnet but the ornamentation consists of cut-out designs. Similar forms have not been recorded for North American contexts and it is questionable whether the cross garnet was used in French or other non-English contexts.

The 19th century saw the introduction of the machine-made T-strap hinge, one in which the joint extended the full length of the vertical strap. Technology for machine production of hinges was probably introduced by the 1840s. Martineau (1866:610-611) credits the invention to America but a patent was registered in Britain in 1836 (Great Britain, Office of the Commissioners of Patents for Inventions [hereafter GBO] 1873:18). The process involved cutting a blank with tabs or tongues which were then shaped into knuckles using dies. The ends of the tabs butted on the body of the hinge rather than being joined to it, as had been the case with forge welding. Machine production of a hinge is recognizable by the open joint for the knuckles. T-strap hinges, looking much as they do today, are illustrated in the 1865 catalogue of Russell and Erwin (Figure 10c). On these,

the horizontal strap is tapered, and they have an almost imperceptible circular finial. The vertical strap is equally unornamented and the hinge would likely have been intended more for outbuildings. Hinges made during the late 19th century should reflect the general shift from wrought iron to steel.

Both the cross-garnet and T-strap hinges are ideal where only a relatively narrow frame is available for attachment of the vertical strap. Depending on their size, these hinges could be applied to small cupboard doors, as well as to gates, larger room doors, and building doors. Plainer styles, especially those which were available toward the end of the 19th century, were probably more appropriate for outbuildings or gates.

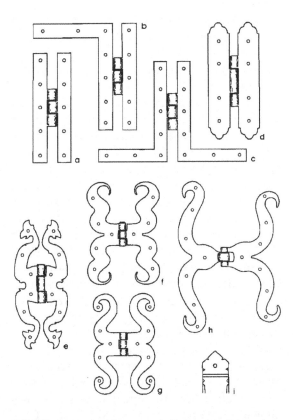

FIGURE 11. H-type hinges: *a*, H-hinge with plain ends; *b*, HL-hinge with plain ends; *c*, HLL-hinge with plain ends; *d*, H-hinge with ornamental ends; *e*, "cockshead" H-hinge; *f-g*, serpentine form of H-hinge; *h*, serpentine form of H-hinge with loop joint; *i*, common form of ornamentation. (After Sonn 1928[2]:Plates 164-165, 167, 169-170.)

Peter J. Priess

H-TYPE HINGES

Shaped like the letter H when opened flat, the H-hinge consists of two vertical "straps" connected by a joint (Figure 11a). In most instances, the joint is separated from the vertical components by a short horizontal strap segment, allowing the hinge attachment to be slightly distanced from the edge of the door and frame. In terms of categories already discussed, an H-hinge could be considered a double vertical-strap hinge.

The HL variation differs only in having a horizontal extension at the end of one of the vertical straps (Figure 11b). This extension may provide an aesthetically more pleasing appearance, but probably also added strength to the door assembly. An uncommon variation is the HLL-hinge in which each flap has a horizontal extension, both at the same end of the hinge (Figure 11c). All such hinges are attached to the surface of a door.

H-type hinges appear to have been in use since the beginning of major European settlement in North America (the 16th or 17th century). Their origin is unknown, but in North America they seem to be associated primarily with the English. D'Allemagne (1924:Plate 139) illustrates several ornamented examples and attributes them to the 15th and 16th centuries. Frank (1950:129, Figure 173), in discussing early French ironwork, illustrates a similar form and considers it to have been "generally" used for room doors. Use of such hinges, however, may not have persisted in French contexts since they do not appear in either Duhamel du Monceau (1767) or the Recueil de planches (1764-1766).

Although the H-type hinge has a basic form which differentiates it from other hinges, there are many variations of form and size. The two leaves—except for the addition of horizontal extensions—are identical. Observations on a small number of examples also suggest that each side is made of a single T-shaped piece of metal. The end of the short horizontal strap is first rolled back to form the joint and then lapped and forge welded to the back of the hinge. It is likely that the gaps which allow the knuckles to mesh are cut out and filed to size at the end of this process. A similar process is described by Moxon (1703:19-22) for the manufacture of a cross garnet and other hinges.

Streeter (1973a:30, 33) notes the existence of examples in which the ends of the knuckles are butted on the hinge, rather than being lapped and welded. Iron H-type hinges commonly have 3-part joints; brass examples are illustrated with 5-part joints (PEM, Volume 6). There do not appear to be examples of H-hinges with loop joints.

Several sample books of the early 19th century (presumably English) illustrate brass HL-hinges from 8 to 12 in. (20 to 30 cm) in length (vertical measure), but also offer that they "may be had of any Size requir'd" (PEM, Volumes 6, 11). The horizontal extension of an HL requires a wide, flat surface for attachment, something not often available on a door frame. The double-L could be used on a folding door where a wide, flat surface would be available on both sides of the hinge joint.

H-type hinges also exhibit variation in ornamentation and shape. Ornamentation of the basic shape is often in the form of decorative ends, such as the foliate shape (Figure 11d), possibly created through forging but often likely created by filing (Figure 11i). If Moxon's (1703:18) description is typical of the production process, the hinge—complete with ornamentation—would be cut out of a sheet of metal and finished by filing. Streeter's (1973a:26) perspective is that decorative finials "did not persist much past the mid-18th century."

A more elaborate variation of the basic H-shape is the so-called "cockshead" hinge. Although it appears in a variety of shapes, the common feature is a serpentine shape to each side, often with a terminal resembling a cock's head (Figure 11e). A more generic description would be "serpentine," to indicate its sinuous nature (Figure 11f-h). The French designation, à moustache (Dubé 1991:Figures 31-32), provides a different perspective, but may be considered as equally generic.

Although the designation of this style as an H-hinge may not suit everyone, it is used here because of a basic similarity between the two. Both are usually symmetrical and composed of two vertical components connected by a much shorter joint section. The joint usually consists of two or more knuckles forming a continuous socket or tube for the pin which holds the two sides together. The pin is usually not attached to either side of the hinge except in the case of a 2-part lift-off joint where the pin has to be fixed in the lower knuckle.

The H-hinge and the cockshead variation appear widely among early North American building hardware. They probably continued in use until replaced by butt hinges during the late 18th and early 19th centuries. If the hinge material is identifiable, it would likely be wrought iron and show some evidence of hand manufacture (forging, filing, etc.). H-type hinges had a variety of applications, depending on their size. The smallest probably functioned on cupboards, but the larger ones may have been used for shutters or doors. A large shutter and a small door might require the same size hinges. Hence, the presence of only a hinge cannot be used as conclusive evidence for a particular type of closure (door or shutter,

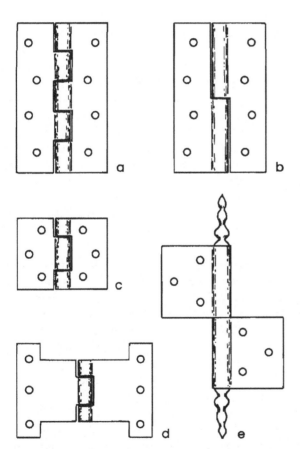

FIGURE 12. Butt hinges: *a*, "fast joint;" *b*, "loose joint" (2-part joint); *c*, "square butt;" *d*, "parliament hinge;" *e*, "French hinge." (*a-b*, after Sargent 1910:517; *c-e*, after PEM, Volumes 3, 12.)

room or cupboard door). The presence of brass examples is suggestive of quality as well as interior use.

BUTT HINGES

Hinges attached to the edge of a door and to the inside surface of the door frame are referred to as "butt" hinges. They are generally symmetrical, and relatively narrow to accommodate the thinness of the door. When opened flat, the hinge is either square or rectangular in outline (Figure 12a-c). The joint consists of two or more knuckles connected by a pin or some other device (a secret joint). Only the joint and possibly a small portion of the leaves are visible on a closed door. Although intended to be attached to a door edge, a butt hinge may also be used on the surface of a door and some hinge types of similar form are, in fact, intended to be used as surface hinges.

The origin of butt hinges is unclear. They are mentioned, without description, in *The Builder's Dictionary* (1734) and are illustrated in a major 18th-century French source: *Recueil de planches* (1764-1766:Plate 343, Figure 9). "Square butts" were offered for sale in Boston in 1756 and 1757 (Dow 1927:230-231). They may not have become popular, however, until a process for casting them in iron was developed during the latter part of the 18th century. The first patent for "casting hinges ready jointed, or with false knuckles or joints and pins, in cast iron" was registered in England in 1775 (Woodcroft 1854:297; GBO 1873:1). The wording of the patent suggests a process for a specific type of joint rather than a new process for producing hinges. Support for this perspective appears in an account of 1866, which explains that the patent was "for joining the two halves or flaps of the hinge in the casting, instead of casting them separately and fitting them together afterwards" (Kendrick 1866:103).

Streeter (1973a:47) discusses the advantage of casting hinges. He sees the process of producing the joint during casting as a major time and labor saver. The process would also allow the large-scale production of identical items, using a common pattern. Casting would have been the only practical method for producing butt hinges until the introduction of machinery to carry out the various cutting and shaping steps. The shift to butt hinges, however, may also have been due to a shift in taste, as suggested by Amsler (1989a:13-14), rather than simply a shift in technology.

Although it is not known when butt hinges were introduced, the appearance of cast-iron examples likely took place during the last quarter of the 18th century. Mercer (1924:178), Hommel (1944:3), and Streeter (1973a:43) all indicate that the use of cast-iron butts began in the United States shortly after the Revolutionary War. Cast-iron butt hinges appear in various English pattern books dating from around the beginning of the 19th century (PEM, Volume 3). Their use persists through the 19th century (Russell and Erwin 1865:116-117) and into the 20th century (Sargent 1910:518-520). Cast-brass examples were also available throughout the same period (Russell and Erwin 1865:117-118; Sargent 1910:524-528).

As discussed for T-strap hinges, the beginning of mechanized production of hinges, initially in wrought iron and brass and more recently in steel, seems to have begun during the second quarter of the 19th century.

Butt hinges are characterized by the number of knuckles in the joint (2-part, 3-part). Hinge dimensions, determined when the specimen is opened flat, are specified as length (parallel to the joint) and width (perpendicular to the joint). The length is often greater than the width.

Commercially produced butt hinges, those appearing in catalogues, are divided into three major categories based on width: narrow, broad (PEM, Volume 9; Russell and Erwin 1865:116), and intermediate (the latter usually has no specific designation but may be referred to as "middle width" [PEM, Volume 15]). Specimens in which the joint is half the hinge's width (each leaf is square) may be referred to as "square butts" (Figure 12c). Hinges with joints substantially shorter than the width were generally intended to be attached on the surface rather than on an edge and should not be designated as butt hinges, even though such hinges are grouped under the general category of butt hinges in some catalogues (Russell and Erwin 1865:115).

A special form of butt hinge is the "shutter" or "parliament" hinge. It is intended to be attached to an edge but is also similar to an H-hinge in its general shape (Figure 12d). Despite the H-shape, they should not be considered as H-hinges. The vertical component of each leaf is relatively narrow compared to the horizontal central section. Fastening holes are limited to the vertical components whose expanded ends provide additional space for them. This design is intended to move the joint away from the point of attachment so that a shutter or door will swing away from the frame and lie flat against the wall when completely opened. The fact that such an action is commonly required of a shutter may explain the designation "shutter hinges." The significance of the "parliament" designation is unknown.

Another special form of butt hinge, in use by the beginning of the 19th century (PEM, Volumes 3, 10, 12), is the "skew joint" or "rising" hinge. This has a 2-part joint in which the abutting surfaces of the two knuckles are at an oblique angle to the line of the joint. In turning, one side of the hinge moves up relative to the other, allowing a door to pass over a carpet or some other obstruction on the floor when opened. The door will also tend to close automatically if not held open (Butter 1968:225). The material of the hinge is thicker than that of other hinges because of the additional stress on the joint. Initially this was achieved by casting the hinges, and later by using thicker plate in mechanized production techniques. Rising hinges were also created by putting a threaded pin in the joint. This was called a "screw rising joint" (PEM, Volume 15).

Cast-iron hinges are often found with impressed marks. These may be as simple as "3 x 3" (indicating the dimensions in inches), but also include such designations as "ASKEW AND PAXSON," "N.ENG.BUTTCo," "BALDWIN PATENT," or "THOS CLARK" (Streeter 1973a:45-46). The latter marks have yet to be identified; neither Baldwin nor Clark have so far been found in patent records.

Cast-iron butt hinges may have been plain initially. Sample books of the early 19th century (PEM, Volumes 2, 3, 5, 6) and catalogues around mid-century (Russell and Erwin 1865:116-117) do not illustrate any other forms. Various forms of surface ornamentation, however, appear slightly later and into the 20th

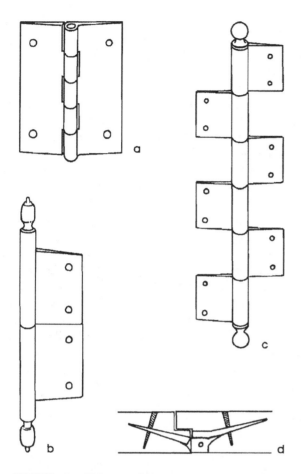

FIGURE 13. *Fiche*-type hinges: *a*, square, butt-hinge shape; *b, fiche à vase; c, fiche à vase*, multiple leaves per side; *d*, method of attaching a *fiche*, cross-section view. (*a-c, e*, after *Recueil de planches* 1764-1766:Plate 32; *d*, after Dunton 1972:Figure 20.)

hinge's presence on the door surface through the use of hinge plates. These are "usually ornamental, adapted for attachment to the surface of a door, fitting at one end against the knuckle of a butt, and intended to give the effect of a strap hinge" (Towne 1904:22). Hinge plates are not included by Russell and Erwin (1865) in their catalogue, possibly because such did not yet exist. By 1904, however, Yale and Towne was offering hinge plates in almost one hundred different designs (Towne 1904:847-869). They were probably used more on public or commercial buildings rather than smaller domestic/residential ones.

A hinge resembling a butt hinge, and designated *fiche*, appears in several 18th-century French references (*Recueil de planches* 1764-1766:Plate 33; Duhamel du Monceau 1767:153, Plate 14). Also referred to as mortised hinges (Dunton 1972:54), they may be found on sites occupied by the French. The hinges generally consist of two perforated, square or rectangular leaves thinned toward the outer edge (Figure 13*a-c*) and intended to be set into slots in the door edge and frame (Figure 13*d*). They may also have more than two leaves (Figure 13*c*). The hinges are held in place by fasteners which pass through the wood and one or two hole in either leaf. Once attached, only the joint (knuckles) and the nails holding the hinge in place would be visible.

There are two basic forms of *fiche*. One is rectangular, like a butt hinge, when opened flat (Figure 13*a*). Duhamel du Monceau (1767:Plate 14, Figures 9-11, 30) illustrates a method for manufacturing this form: a piece of plate is folded-over and sections are cut out to form the knuckles. The second form, more like a hinge and pintle, is composed of two square or rectangular components with one positioned above the other (Figure 13*b*) (Duhamel du Monceau 1767:Plate 14, Figure 6). The lower one holds a pin and serves as the pintle while the upper one has a socket which pivots on the pin. On a closed door, the two components would present to view a long tube or socket. This type of hinge may also have an ornamental finial on either end and is then designated a *fiche à vase* (Figure 13*b-c*) (Duhamel du Monceau 1767:116, 296). These hinges were probably intended pri-

century (Sargent 1910:518-519). The purpose of elaborate surface ornamentation that would not be visible once the hinge was attached or when the door was closed is unclear.

Butt hinges were produced in a great variety of sizes, not all of which would have been appropriate for room doors. Hinges 1 or 1 ½ in. (1.5 to 3.8 cm) in length would have been best suited for smaller cupboard doors. In the absence of the correct size, however, even undersized hinges would have been pressed into use.

Although the introduction and proliferation of the butt hinge during the 19th century relegated door hinges to a less conspicuous role, some attempts were eventually made to maintain the marily for furniture or cabinets (Dunton 1972:54) but if large enough, they would also have been, theoretically at least, suitable for building doors. Duhamel du Monceau (1767:116) notes that they are suitable for light doors but not large gates. They appear on sites with French occupations such as Fort Michilimackinac (Stone 1974:Figure 133) and the Fortress of Louisbourg (Dunton 1972:Figures 12-20). The *Recueil de planches* (1764-1766:Plate 32, Figure 29) illustrates a skew-joint variety of the *fiche à vase* and credits its invention to the author (*de mon invention*).

English manufacturers of the late 18th and early 19th centuries were offering hinges similar to the *fiche à vase* (PEM, Volumes 2, 3, 13, 15), designating them either as "French hinges" (Figure 12e) (PEM, Volumes 3, 15) or "heave out" or "heave off" hinges (PEM, Volumes 2, 13). The illustrations suggest that such hinges were intended to be attached to a surface rather than set into mortises as were the *fiche*. It is further likely that they were intended to be attached to the door edge so that, as with the *fiche* or an ordinary butt hinge, only the joint would show when the door was closed. Specified sizes range from 5 to 7 in. (13 to 17 cm) (PEM, Volume 15), possibly excluding the ornamental finials on the pin, with a smaller size (4 ½ in. [11 cm]) specified for shutters (PEM, Volume 3). Since none has been reported in North American contexts, it is possible that they were not common on this continent.

MISCELLANEOUS HINGES

Simmons and Turley (1980:135-137) describe a hinge which does not easily fit into any of the previous categories. It is called a "snipe," a "staple", or an "eyelet" hinge. "Known in the English seaboard colonies, but . . . used there far less frequently than in the Spanish Southwest" (Simmons and Turley 1980:136), it consists of two eyes or staples hooked together (Figure 14) with one component (leaf) driven into the door frame and the other driven into the door edge. Both may have been driven in an angle so that their ends protruded from the wood and could be clinched. Such a hinge would not be recognizable in an archaeological context if the two components become separated. These hinges are not known to have been pro-

duced by factory methods and likely date to the hand-forged period of an area.

Securing

A door can be secured or held in place, usually in the closed position, by a variety of devices. Their selection is determined by the type of securing and the level of security required. A hook, sliding bolt, or even a door spring will suffice if the intention is simply to hold the door closed. A latch is preferable, however, if operation of the securing device is required equally from both sides of a door. A lock is required if control is to be limited to a select few. Both latches and locks can be further limited to operation from one side of a door. Devices which require a key for part of their operation are dealt with in the locks section even though they may be called latches in historical terminology.

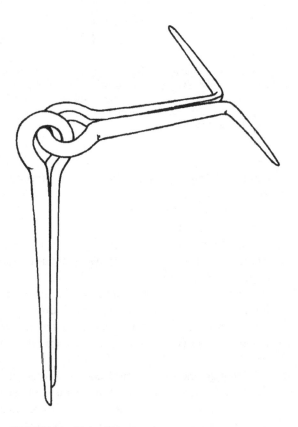

FIGURE 14. "Snipe" hinge.

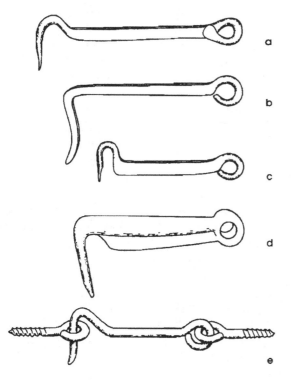

FIGURE 15. Latch hooks: *a*, hand forged with rising hook and lapped and welded eye; *b*, hand forged with non-rising hook and butted eye; *c*, hand forged with rectangular to flat shank, rising hook, and butted eye; *d*, hand forged with flat shank, rising hook, and end perforation, "Hispanic style;" *e*, machine made, wire stock. (*a-b*, after Priess 1972:Figure 3; *c*, after Dunton 1972:Figure 96; *d*, after Simmons and Turley 1980:Chapter 11, Plate 18; *e*, after Sargent 1910:893.)

LATCH HOOKS

Latch hooks, also commonly called gate hooks, have a straight shank with a pivot eye at one end and a hook at the other. The hook engages a second eye or staple, thereby retaining something in position. The most common device for holding a door open or closed (Streeter 1983:Figure 74), latch hooks are generally simple pieces of hardware and, until the ready avail-ability of heavy wire or round bar stock in the 19th century, were forged from square or rectangular stock. The end of the rod forming the eye, which was often forged with a round cross section, either butted on the shank (Figure 15*b-c*) or was lapped and forge welded in place (Figure 15*a*). At the opposite end, the hook either bent down directly from the line of the shank (Figure 15*b*) or, more commonly, rose

slightly above the shank before descending (Figure 15*a, c*). The shanks were generally plain. Ornamentation, when present, usually consisted of twisting along part of the shank.

Latch hooks are anchored at the pivot end with an eye or staple, while the hook end engages another eye or staple (Figure 15*e*). Both are often driven or screwed into wood. Their manufacture parallels that of the latch hook, wire being used when it became available during the 19th century, but previously they were generally forged from square stock. Examples possibly cast in brass are advertised in the late 18th and early 19th centuries and identified as "door stays," "ship hooks," or "ship door hooks" (PEM, Volumes 5, 6, 11, 13). The eyes for these, for both the pivot and hooking, are attached to small plates equipped with fastening holes. The reference to use on ships suggests a non-corroding material such as brass, but this would not preclude use on terrestrial structures as well.

The introduction of wire or round stock for the manufacture of hooks occurred during the 19th century, and the hook and its associated eyes subsequently became relatively plain and simple (Figure 15*e*). Styles offered in the early 20th century (Sargent 1910) consisted of ornamented cast-brass types called "cabin" or "door" hooks, and plain wire types designated as "gate" hooks. The brass types have eyes or staples mounted on plates, whereas the wire types have wire screw eyes.

One form of hook, called a "side hook" by Butter (1968:239), is relatively flat in cross section and, instead of an eye at the pivot end, it has a plate with a perforation for a fastening. The perforation is often countersunk, possibly on both sides, to make the object more versatile. These are intended to be attached with a fastener such as a screw, and can only pivot in one plane. The catch may be a small pin rather than an eye or staple. Such hooks are used on items like boxes and equipment cases where it is preferable to have the hook remain in contact with the surface of the box while pivoting. These hooks are generally small and should not be considered as possible door hardware, although Simmons and Turley (1980:Plate 17) do illustrate a Spanish example used on the door of a wall cabinet.

It has yet to be established if there are significant cultural differences in hand-forged latch hooks. They appear on sites occupied by the English (Priess 1972:Figure 3, 1975:Figure 127), French (Duhamel du Monceau 1767:Plate 13; Dunton 1972:Figures 96, 99; Stone 1974:Figure 145; Dubé 1991:Illustration 4*h*, *i*), and Spanish (Simmons and Turley 1980:Plates 19-20) with no significant differences. Simmons and Turley (1980:142, Plate 18) describe "a distinctive Hispanic-style hook," forged from flat stock (Figure 15*d*). The pivot end is perforated like a side hook and would have been attached with an eye, staple, or nail; the shank is ornamented with stamped designs.

HASPS

A hasp is a latching or locking device generally consisting of a strap or something approximating a strap which pivots at one end and fits over a loop (eye or staple) at the other. A pin or padlock through the loop holds the hasp in place and secures whatever the hasp is attached to. Hasps are used on doors but also appear on various forms of furniture, cupboards, and crates.

A common form of hand-forged hasp is an asymmetrical figure-8 shape fashioned from square or rectangular bar stock (Figure 16*a*). The smaller end has an eye for pivoting, while the larger end has a lenticular slot. The object is produced by bending a bar in the middle to form the pivot eye, lapping and welding the two ends of the bar, and then forming the slot between the bars. The welded end is generally shaped into a simple scroll. Another hand-forged form is made from flat stock with a pivot hole punched at one end and a longitudinal slot cut near the other (Figure 16*c*). This form may have the latching end worked into a scroll, possibly to serve as a grasp, and may also have a latch hook attached to provide a means of closure (Figure 16*b, d, f*). These forms are fairly simple and do not appear to exhibit cultural differences.

An alternate form of hasp has no specific pivot facility but pivots with the door to which it is attached. These are in the form of straps with a slot near one end (Figure 16*d*). They are intended to be fixed rigidly in place with the slotted end projecting past the door edge. The slot passes over a staple in the door frame

as the door is closed. These are generally large and, in fragmentary form, could be mistaken for part of a hinge. They generally have no taper and none has been encountered with finials or other ornamentation. Such fixed hasps may have two additional features. One of these is a handle attached to the strap (Figure 16*d*). The other is a latching pin which drops into the staple when the door is closed. Such an arrangement would be best suited for holding the door of a barn or other outbuilding closed when no one is inside.

Machine-made hasps of the 19th century initially duplicate forms hand-forged from flat stock, and include the use of staples for pivot and catch (Figure 16*e*). They also include forms stamped from thin plate, and are equipped with a multiple-part hinge joint rather than a pivot on a staple (Figure 16*g*). These are referred to as "hinge hasps" (Russell and Erwin 1865:112). In fragmentary form, the latter could also be mistaken for hinges.

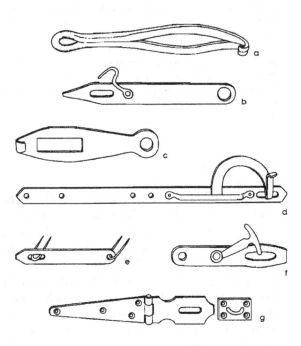

FIGURE 16. Hasps: *a*, common form forged from square or rectangular bar stock; *b*, forged from flat stock with side hook; *c*, forged from flat stock; *d*, forged from flat stock with handle and pivoted latch pin, to pivot with door; *e*, machine-made from flat stock with pivot and catch staple; *f*, machine-made from flat stock with pivoted latch pin; *g*, machine-made "hinge hasp." (*a-b*, unprovenienced; *c-d*, after Harris 1971:Figures 48-49; *e-f*, after Russell and Erwin 1865:144; *g*, after Sargent 1910:1134.)

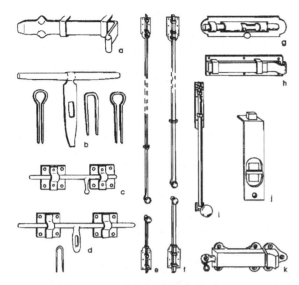

FIGURE 17. Sliding bolts: *a,* forged, flat bolt with staples, mounted directly on door; *b,* forged, round bolt with eyes, attached directly to door, hasp handle; *c,* forged, round bolt with guides, on individual back plates; *d,* forged, round bolt with guides, on individual back plates, hasp handle; *e,* pair of narrow bolts of differing lengths to fit the top and bottom of a door; *f,* pair of wide bolts of differing lengths to fit the top and bottom of a door; *g,* factory-made "barrel" bolt; *h,* factory-made, wrought-iron flat bolt; *i* factory-made, narrow "Canada" bolt; *j,* flush bolt; *k,* chain bolt. (*a,* after Sonn 1928[2]:Plate 116; *b-d,* after Priess 1975:Figures 125-126; *e-f,* after *Recueil de planches* 1764-1766:Plate 34; *g-i, k,* after Russell and Erwin 1865:94-98; *j,* after PEM, Volume 8.)

SLIDING BOLTS

A sliding bolt is a bar which can be attached to a door and slid into a catch on the door frame to hold a door closed. Similar items can also be used on shutters or casement windows. Sliding bolts can be characterized in terms of the method of manufacture, the cross section of the bolt, the methods of controlling its movement, the type of handle, and the method of attaching the bolt to a door. Streeter (1975b:104) summarizes the category as consisting of two types: those secured by staples attached directly to a door, and those affixed to plates nailed or screwed in place. Some of the latter were equipped with springs.

A sliding bolt provides security as it is usually only operable from one side of a door, although Sonn (1928[2]:20, Plate 118) does illustrate a style with a handle that extends through the door and characterizes it as "common to eastern Pennsylvania." Additional security can be achieved by adding some form of lock.

Forged bolts are either rectangular, square, or circular in cross section. A rectangular or square bolt can only slide; a circular bolt can also rotate, thus allowing additional features in its operation.

Bolt handles are quite varied. They may be forged from the end of the bolt, or added to the bolt either at the end or somewhere else along its length. In addition to moving the bolt, the handle may also limit the amount of bolt movement and be a major location for ornamentation. Brass knobs appear to have been used on rectangular bolts by the late 18th century, generally attached to the end of the bolt with a set screw. Ceramic knobs similar to door knobs appear in the 19th century.

The handle may be combined with a hasp (Figure 17*b, d*), thereby providing additional security. Some sliding bolts have long handles which extend well beyond the end of the back plate (Figure 17*e-f*). In fact, some examples have an additional guide and plate attached part way along the handle (Figure 17*e-f*). Such bolts are intended for use at the tops of tall doors, windows, and shutters where the handle has to be brought down within reach of the opera-tor. They appear in the *Recueil de planches* (1764-1766:Plate 34), and Sonn (1928[2]:Plate 122) illustrates an example, from a 1769 Penn-sylvania German context, which is slightly over 5 ft. (1.5 m) in length. If found in related archaeological contexts, sliding bolts which are identical except for their length may comprise a pair, one for the top and the other for the bottom of whatever device they were attached to (Figure 17*e-f*).

The bolt is guided by a number of eyes or staples, generally two, and catches in another, possibly matching, eye or staple. The form of the staple is determined by the cross section of the bolt: round for circular bolts and square for rectangular bolts. In the simplest design, the staples are driven directly into the door and frame (Figure 17*a*). A negative consequence of this is that the bolt slides directly on the wood and may cause wear. Bolts with guides attached directly to a door exist only as forged types. Round bolts without back plates are likely to have their handles attached midway on the bolt, between the two staples (Figure 17*b*). The addition of a back plate (Figure 17*c-d*) eliminates wear on the door and stabilizes the guide staples. It also provides a location for ornamentation, as illustrated by Sonn (1928[2]:Plates 118-120).

A sliding bolt used in a vertical position, especially one shot upwards, must have a means of remaining in that position. With round bolts this can be achieved by rotating the bolt and securing the handle behind or in a catch. This is not an option for four-square bolts, however, so these have a spring between the bolt and the back plate. The spring may be a separate piece of metal attached to the back plate, or be fashioned out of the head of the bolt itself. Machine-made versions also have part of the back plate fashioned into a spring.

The nature of the catch on the door frame is determined by how the bolt is attached to the door. A bolt without a back plate would likely have a matching third staple or eye. The catch for bolts with a back plate may be a simple driven staple or a staple attached to a continuation of the plate. In either case, the catch staple would likely match the guide staples in size and shape.

Examples illustrated by Sonn (1928[2]:Plates 116-122) and Streeter (1975b) reveal that back plates were in use during the late 17th century and throughout the 18th century. The late 18th century saw the introduction of rolled plate and the simplification of the production of back plates. The use of these appears to have become more common during the 19th century and is now universal. The use of hollow brass knobs may have begun in the later 18th century. Such knobs are not included in Sonn (1928[2]:Plates 116-122) who illustrates material primarily from the 17th and 18th centuries.

Most sliding bolts were initially forged of wrought iron. Back plates, when present, may exhibit irregularities as a result of being forged from thicker stock. The ends of the staples, where they have been riveted to the back plate, should be irregular as a result of individual hammer blows rather than impact from a mechanized hammer.

Machine-manufactured bolts of the 19th century exhibit greater consistency in form (e.g., staples machine-riveted to back plates are more regular and uniform), and reveal the eventual introduction of short cuts. These include the production of the back plate and guide staples from a single piece of sheeting. This was done for both rectangular and circular bolts.

The term "barrel bolt" (also "socket bolt") appears in catalogues as early as the beginning of the 19th century (PEM, Volumes 3, 5), and generally designates a round sliding bolt with a tube for a guide (Figure 17g) rather than individual staples (Butter 1968:8). The term should only be used to designate a sub-group within the sliding bolt category.

A "flush bolt" is a specialized sliding bolt, so named because it is designed to be let flush into the edge or surface at the top or bottom of a door. If let into the edge, it is used only on double doors, thereby allowing one door to be secured while the other remains operable. As there is no space for a handle in such a case, it must be recessed in the body of the bolt or consist of a pivoting lever.

Flush bolts consist of a flat or L-shaped plate, often made of polished brass, with a sliding bolt attached to its back (Figure 17j). They exist by the early 19th century, at which time the bolt is shown as being rectangular (PEM, Volumes 5, 6). By 1865, the bolt is round or rectangular (Russell and Erwin 1865:95-96).

Another specialized sliding bolt is the "chain bolt." This consists of a bolt with a beveled head enclosed in a housing (Figure 17k). The bolt, which is held in a thrown or latched position by a spring, is withdrawn by pulling on a chain attached to the bolt's tail. It is not known when this type of bolt was introduced. Russell and Erwin (1865:94) illustrate it in their 1865 catalogue.

Sliding bolts machine manufactured in the 19th century have die-stamped back plates and machine-riveted staples, both of which are generally more regular than hand-forged examples. Furthermore, the plates and bolts would likely have been produced from rolled stock which would be more regular in cross section and surface finish.

It seems that the majority of sliding bolts with rectangular cross sections are set with the wide side against the backing plate. Bolts with this configuration could be called flat or wide (Figure 17h), to contrast them with the few which slide on the narrow side and might be termed narrow (Figure 17e). The latter appear on Canadian sites, possibly in 19th-century contexts. A bolt of similar form is illustrated by Russell and Erwin (1865:96) and called a "Canada Bolt" (Figure 17i), a designation defined by Towne (1904:14) as "a box or other bolt the sliding bar of which is prolonged considerably beyond the back plate and provided with a separate guide near its other end." The Russell and Erwin example fits within Towne's definition in that it has the additional guide. Such bolts are similar to a style illustrated in the *Recueil de planches* (1764-1766:Plate 34), suggesting a French origin for them.

One style of sliding bolt, invariably of the wide variety, has a relatively short bolt with a long back plate (vertical measure). These are hand-forged items with a knob handle attached to the middle of the bolt. The back plates are often highly ornamented with extensive pierced work. These are intended to be used on casement windows or shutters, situations where only relatively narrow frame components are available for their attachment. Hence, the short bolt and narrow back plate. They are unlikely to have been used on doors and should not be interpreted as door hardware unless additional evidence is available to support such a conclusion.

CREMORNE AND ESPAGNOLETTE BOLTS

Both cremorne and espagnolette bolts serve to secure a door, casement window, or other similar feature. A cremorne bolt (Figure 18*a*) is comprised of "up and down sliding bolts extending the full height of the door and operated by a central handle" (Towne 1904:16; Butter 1968:40). This is presumably what Streeter (1983:Figure 34) refers to as "head and foot bolts." Generally, the two bolts interact with the handle in such a way as to move in opposite directions when the handle is turned. The cremorne bolt could be considered a special form of sliding bolt since it essentially consists of two sliding bolts with extended tails which meet at a common point. The term "cremone" is preferred by Butter (1968:40) and used by the French (actually *crémone*) (Duhamel du Monceau 1767:123), but "cremorne" is more commonly used in North America. Bolts of this type are illustrated by both Duhamel du Monceau (1767:Plates 15, 24) and in the *Recueil de planches* (1764-1766:Plate 34), indicating some antiquity for the concept. Operation of the bolts can be with a rack (Figure 18*c*), an eccentric (Figure 18*d*), or possibly some other means.

An espagnolette bolt (Figure 18*b*) differs somewhat from a cremorne but is intended to accomplish a similar purpose. It consists of a

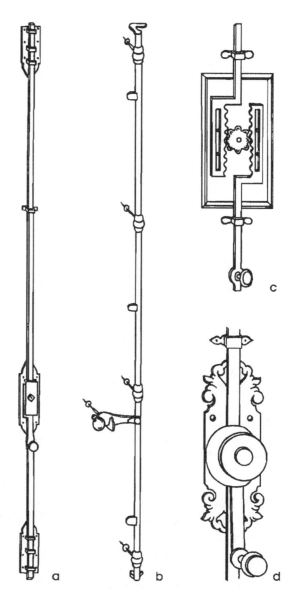

FIGURE 18. Cremorne and espagnolette bolts: *a,* cremorne bolt; *b,* espagnolette bolt; *c,* ratchet method for operating a cremorne bolt; *d,* eccentric method for operating a cremeorne bolt. (*a-b,* after *Recueil de planches* 1764-1766:Plate 34; *c-d,* Duhamel du Monceau 1767:Plates 15, 24.)

single bolt which extends the full height of a door or window and has a hook at either end. When the door or window is almost closed, the bolt is turned by a handle, causing the hooks to engage pins or locking plates on the frame and pulling the door or window completely closed (Butter 1968:64). It may also have "a hinged handle near the center whereby the bar may be rotated to fasten or release the sash [or door] and which also engages with a strike or keeper

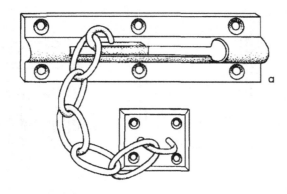

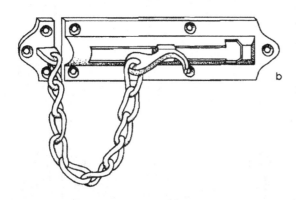

FIGURE 19. Door chains: *a*, early 17th century; *b*, mid-17th century. (*a*, after PEM, Volume 3; *b*, after Russell and Erwin 1865:94.)

which holds the bar in the locked position and further secures the sash [or door] near its center" (Towne 1904:19). Bolts of this type appear in both Duhamel du Monceau (1767:Plate 15) and the *Recueil de planches* (1764-1766:Plate 34), indicating some antiquity for this form of mechanism.

Cremorne and espagnolette bolts are best suited for double doors or windows. No known examples have been recovered from archaeological contexts, and there are presently insufficient data to indicate cultural or temporal differences. Early examples would likely have been forged, with cast and stamped versions probably being introduced some time during the 19th century.

DOOR CHAINS

A door chain is a security device which prevents a door from being opened very far, permitting an assessment of one's callers (Butter 1968:54). One end of the chain is attached to the door frame by means of a small plate, while the other has a fixture which fits into a slotted plate on the door. Such devices have been available since at least the early 19th century (Figure 19*a*). The basic design has changed little since then (Figure 19*b*). Initially forged and then machine made, door chains are presently cast or stamped.

DROP BARS

A simple means of keeping a door closed is to place a stout bar of wood or iron across it (Figure 1*d*). The bar is supported at either end by a staple or L-shaped bracket (Figure 20) driven into the door frame (Streeter 1983:Figure 69). The shanks may be tapered and driven, or bent out and held with fasteners. Using staples is more secure since there is no way to lift the drop bar from the opposite side of the door. Open brackets would be required, however, if there is insufficient room to maneuver the bar into position.

DOOR SPRINGS/DOOR CLOSERS

A door spring or door closer allows a door to close automatically. Streeter (1983:25) describes a type from a late-18th-century context. It consists of a flat spring coiled around a shaft (scroll spring) and enclosed in a housing attached to the door frame. The free end of the spring is attached to an arm which extends horizontally across the door. The end of the arm accommodates a small wheel which rolls along a rectangular plate affixed to the door. When the door is opened, the movement of the arm creates tension on the spring. When the door is released the spring unwinds, exerting pressure on the door, thereby closing it. The roller and plate reduce friction and wear on the door. The same type of door spring is depicted in English hardware sample books around the beginning of the 19th century (Figure 21*a*). A similar type illustrated by Butter (1968:170) is called a "long tail door spring."

The first English patent for a door-closing device (which consisted of a weight and pulleys) was issued in 1786 (GBO 1873:2). The first patent for a device utilizing a spring was issued in 1790 (GBO 1873:3-4), while a patent for the use of a coiled torsion spring within a tube attached to the hinge joint was granted in 1821

FIGURE 20. L-shaped bracket; probable drop-bar support. (After Priess 1975:Figure 128.)

(GBO 1873:9). This may be the first record of such a system, which is similar to modern spring-loaded hinges.

Other examples of door springs include coiled torsion springs (Figure 21c) (Knight 1876:Figure 1688), as well as a simple form consisting of a straight length of heavy wire or rod oriented vertically, with one end attached to the door and the other to the frame (Figure 21b) (Russell and Erwin 1865:375). Opening the door would twist the rod and increase the torsion on it. With the release of pressure, the rod would untwist and close the door. Spring-action door closers combined with a door check system (to prevent the door from slamming) appeared about 1890, first using a pneumatic and then a hydraulic cylinder; the latter was introduced in 1895 (Towne 1904:201-204).

LATCHES

A device for holding a door closed, a latch usually consists of a pivoting bar on the door and a catch on the frame. Unlike a lock, a latch can be operated by anyone who has access to it and it is usually also operable from both sides of a door. It contrasts with a sliding bolt in the manner in which the bolt or bar operates and often also in the complexity of the device. Latches come in a variety of shapes and mechanisms; two major categories are spring latches and thumb latches. Latching components of door locks are discussed in the lock section.

SPRING LATCHES

A spring latch has the various components of the mechanism mounted on a metal plate, with the latch bar held in the latched position by a spring. The latch bar is a pivoting type, often operated with a rotating knob. Butter (1968:15) uses the term "bow latch" for this form. Being attached to the surface of the door, the entire mechanism is exposed to view. Spring latches may be used on doors, but smaller types are also suitable for casement windows or other hinged features.

Two basic mechanisms are illustrated by Streeter (1983:Figures 48-53), each with a differently shaped back or mounting plate. The first mechanism, called a "square spring latch" (Streeter 1983:Figures 48-49), has a knob spindle through the latch-bar pivot (Figure 22c, e). Hence, a turn of the knob (it can only be turned in one direction) is transmitted directly to the latch bar. A handle is attached to the lift bar,

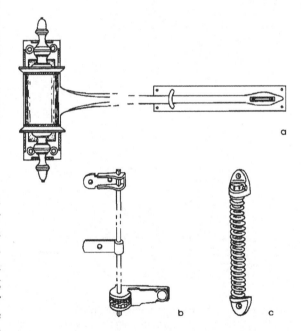

FIGURE 21. Door closures/door springs: *a*, early 17th century, scroll-spring style. (*a*, after PEM, Volume 3); *b-c*, torsion-bar type; *c*, coil-spring type. (after Sargent 1910:556-557.)

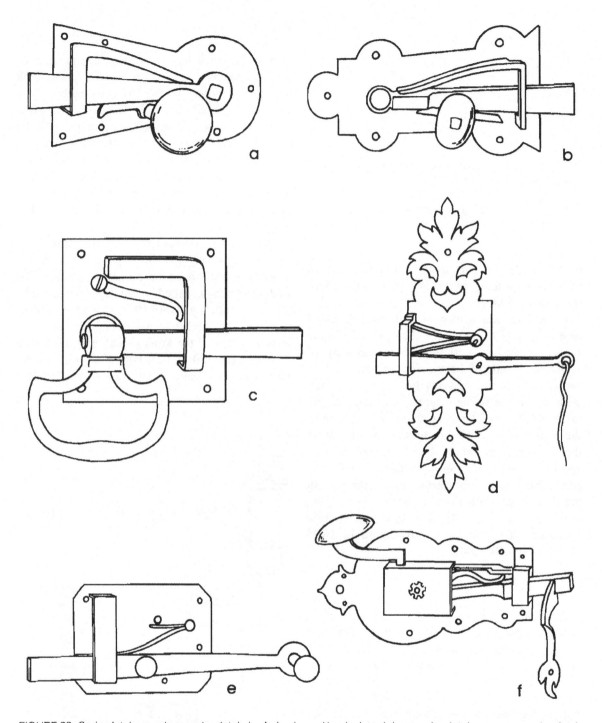

FIGURE 22. Spring latches: *a,* long spring-latch, keyhole-shaped back plate; *b,* long spring-latch; *c,* square spring-latch; *d,* spring latch with vertical back plate; *e,* square spring-latch; *f,* long-latch form from a German context. (*a-c, f,* after Sonn 1928[1]:Plates 98-99, 102; *d,* after Duhamel du Monceau 1767:Plate 15; *e,* after Lunn 1985:Figure 104.)

the mechanisms are relatively short, and the mounting plate is rectangular. Some may have an additional, hand-operated bolt functioning as a night bolt, operable from only one side of the door. The second mechanism, most recently termed a "long spring latch" by Streeter (1983:Figures 50-51), was earlier known as a "wishbone" or "keyhole" latch (Streeter 1954:125). It has the knob spindle passing through a cam positioned under the latch bar

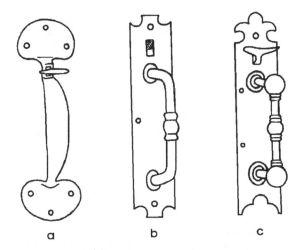

FIGURE 23. Common forms of Suffolk and Norfolk thumb-latch handles: *a*, Suffolk latch with bean-shaped cusps; *b*, Norfolk latch with round cut-out corners; *c*, Norfolk latch with mirror-image ornamentation on the ends of the back plate. (*a-b*, after Priess 1972:Figure 20; *c*, after Sonn 1928[1]:Plate 90.)

(Figure 22*b*). A turn of the knob (it can be turned in either direction) raises one or the other end of the cam which in turn lifts the latch bar. The back plate is relatively long and often has a "keyhole" shape (Figure 22*a*). Both latch mechanisms, including examples with a night bolt, appear in Price's (1856:835) list of available items.

Duhamel du Monceau (1767:Plate 15) and the *Recueil de planches* (1764-1766:Plate 31) illustrate a latch similar in operation to a spring latch, but with a vertical back plate (Figure 22*d*). The latch bar has a pivot near its middle, the pivot point being near the back edge of the back plate. The bar is operated by pulling down on a string attached to a loop at the distal end of the latch bar (the end opposite the catch), thereby lifting the catch end. The use of the string suggests an application beyond the normal reach of a person. A similar latch from a 19th-century Hudson's Bay Company site has a handle instead of the string hole (Figure 22*e*). The specific uses for both forms of these latches are not known, though shutters are a distinct possibility (Duhamel du Monceau 1767:153). It is possible that they were not intended for doors.

Although Butter (1968:Figure 29) illustrates a square spring latch, implying their manufacture

and use well into the 20th century, it appears that both square and long-spring latches, as defined by Streeter, are not common features of 19th-century mass production.

The Germanic variation on a spring latch involves, to some extent, the form of the handle. Latches similar to the long latch, but from German contexts, have a bent handle rather than a knob (Figure 22*f*). This may represent an amalgamation of traditions by North American manufacturers. Other latches from German contexts have the handle and latch bar formed from the same piece of metal, the handle having the scroll or rounded-pad end as found on German locks (Sonn 1928[1]:Plates 98, 100-102).

THUMB LATCHES

A thumb latch consists of a pivoted latch bar attached to one side of a door and operated by a transverse, pivoted lift bar passing through the door. Attached to a handle, the lift bar is pushed down at one end by a thumb or raised at the other end by a finger. The basic components of a thumb latch are a latch bar, lift bar, handle, guide, catch, and occasionally, a latch-bar lock. If security is a factor, a thumb latch may be used in combination with a door lock or other securing device. The inclusion of a latch bar within a door-lock housing obviates the use of two separate hardware items.

Thumb latches exhibit a number of different forms which reflect, in part, changes in technology and have some temporal and/or cultural implications. There are two major categories of forged thumb latches, the main difference between them being the method by which the handle is attached to a door. In the one case, one or both ends of the handle are forged into fastening plates or cusps (Figure 23*a*), while in the other the handle is affixed to a separate plate which can then be attached to a door (Figure 23*b-c*). In English parlance, the former are "Suffolk" latches and the latter are "Norfolk" latches, designations also commonly used in North America. The origin or significance of the names is unknown. The general sense that the Suffolk form preceded the Norfolk and that the latter became popular with the availability of rolled sheet iron is probably an oversimplification.

Volume 2

203

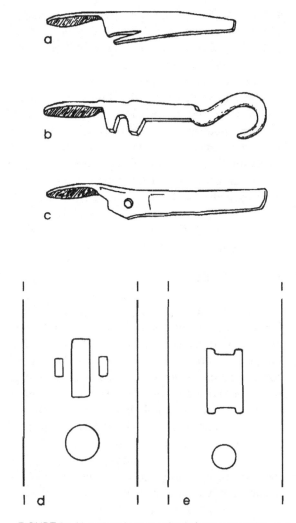

FIGURE 24. Variations in the method of attachment for: *a-c*, lift bars of Suffolk latches, and *d-e*, pivot cheeks on Norfolk thumb-latch back plates. (*a-c*, after Sonn 1928[1]:Plate 93; *d-e*, after Streeter 1971:Figure 6.)

The handle of a Suffolk latch may have perforated plates or cusps at one or both ends. If only one cusp is present, it is always the upper one; the lower end of the handle is formed into a shank which can be driven through the door. This form is uncommon on thumb latches from English contexts. North American examples are illustrated by Sonn (1928[1]:Plates 81-83) and identified as Suffolk. At least some of these have non-English associations, and Sonn (1928[1]:Plates 82-83) illustrates a number of comparative examples from France and Quebec.

There is a great deal of variety in the shape and size of the cusps, though oval, triangular, and bean-shaped forms are fairly common (Sonn 1928[1]; Streeter 1983:Figures 39-40). In many instances, two cusps are mirror images of each other but, if they are different, the upper cusp will be larger and more elaborate. This is more characteristic of German thumb latches (Streeter 1983:Figure 41).

The lift bar of a Suffolk latch either passes through a rectangular opening in the upper cusp, or through a pivot section positioned between the upper cusp and the end of the handle. In the former instance, the bar would likely be held in position by a cleft in the lower edge (Figure 24a) or lugs in the same area (Figure 24b); in the latter case it would have a pin through a pivot hole (Figure 24c). Mercer (1923:140) suggests that the transition to a separate pivot section took place around the middle of the 18th century, but this is only approximate.

The lift bar can either end in a curved handle, or be straight and cut off short so as to barely extend past the latch bar. Opinions on the significance and dating of these differences vary. Nutting (1921:78) states that lift bars were cut short early in the 19th century, whereas Streeter (1983:Figure 40) notes that lift bars were straight and stubby in the 18th century. Based on examples seen by him, Sonn (1928[1]:29-30) provides what appears to be the most rational perspective. He notes that although many early lifts were straight, there were also longer, curved examples, and concludes that the longer examples may simply be a practical solution to the technical problem of opening a door (Sonn 1928[1]:29). He also observes that local variation would have been a factor, with both types of lift bars being produced and preferred, each in its own area (Sonn 1928[1]:30).

On a Norfolk latch, the handle is attached to a back plate which, in turn, is attached to a door. Common back-plate forms are generally relatively simple and symmetrical, with parallel sides and cut corners (Figure 23b), though a range of ornamentation, of the handle as well as the plate, is possible. Streeter (1971:Figure 8) illustrates a variety of forms, including ones which have been sheared, complete with ornamentation, from a continuous strip of stock; consequently, the ornamentation at one end of

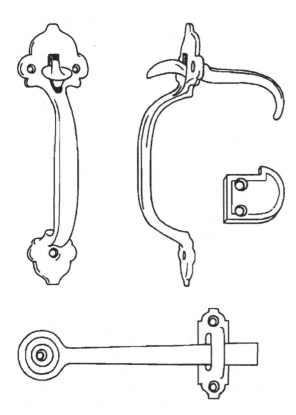

FIGURE 25. Common forms of Blake's-patent cast-iron thumb latch. (After Sonn 1928[1]:Plate 92.)

Norfolk latch became "the standard cheap door latch of its time" and persisted until well after the introduction of cast iron latches (Streeter 1971:19).

Lift bars for Norfolk-type latches are similar to those for Suffolk latches. According to Sonn (1928[1]:28), early lift bars have straight ends. The bars are usually held in place either by a cleft in the lower edge or a pivot pin through a pivot section. The pivot section usually consists of two small plates or cheeks attached at right angles to the main plate immediately above the upper end of the handle (Streeter 1971:17). The cheeks were initially attached by means of three separate slots through the back plate (Figure 24d); this subsequently changed to a single, H-shaped slot (Figure 24e).

The introduction of casting for the production of thumb latches may reflect a broader shift in technology which also saw the introduction of cast-iron hinges in the late 18th century (Streeter 1971:12). Both Suffolk and Norfolk types were offered in cast form (PEM, Volume 3; Stevens 1969; Streeter 1971:12-13, 15), and these found some application in North America (Streeter 1971:Figures 3, 5). Cast-iron thumb latches, however, did not gain in popularity until the arrival of Blake's patent for a cast-iron latch in 1840 (Sonn 1928[1]:216; Stevens 1969:11). Blake's latch (Figure 25) has a distinctive form which persisted into the 20th century. All components–except for the latch bar and possibly its pivot plate–are cast. The handle has an asymmetrical Suffolk-type shape, with a cusp at either end. The upper cusp is larger, but both are invariably the same shape. The lift bar has a jog at the pivot point so that it is held in place by its position in the handle, without resorting to a pivot pin or cleft edge.

Several 18th-century sources suggest a different tradition for French thumb latches (Duhamel du Monceau 1767:Plate 16; *Recueil de planches* 1764-1766:Plate 31). In both instances, the handle has a one-piece back plate, although not symmetrical as would be the norm for Norfolk latches. The handle is not attached permanently to the plate, however. Instead, the handle has tapered shanks at its ends which pass through holes in the back plate (Figure 26a-c) and are driven through the door and clinched. The upper ends of the shanks have a shoulder which

the back plate is a mirror image of that at the other end (Figure 23c).

It is generally claimed that Suffolk latches preceded Norfolk latches. Any specific example may not fit this scenario, however, since Norfolk-type latches and door handles with back plates, but without the lift bar mechanism, were being produced in England several centuries previously (Chamberlain 1928:106). Furthermore, Streeter's (1983:19) contention that Norfolk latches were introduced into North America "in the early 19th century" is an oversimplification. Such latches appear in 17th- and 18th-century contexts on both this continent (Sonn 1928[1]:Plates 24-26, 91) and in England (Alcock and Hall 1994:26). It is likely that the use of Norfolk latches became more common in North America during the early 19th century because of the availability of rolled bar and plate stock (Streeter 1971:19). This simplified their manufacture and made them economically more attractive than Suffolk types. Consequently, the bears on the back plate to hold the latter firmly in place. Specimens from French contexts in North America provide examples of variation of this form. The back plate may relate only to the upper end of the handle, the lower end passing through the door without a plate (Figure 26*e-h*), or there may be a separate, smaller ornamental plate for the lower end of the handle to serve as a washer and to reduce wear on the door (Figure 26*d*). The back plate may also be an integral part of the upper end of the handle (Figure 26*i*). Some of the thumb latches from French contexts also have a lift bar of a different form. The thumb press is a round finial instead of being a flat or curved circular plate (Figure 26*g*).

Other components of a thumb latch–the latch bar, guide staple, and catch–underwent a transition during the late 18th and early 19th centuries. Initially these various components were attached directly to the door. The latch bar had a perforated finial at its pivot end and was

attached to the door with a nail, screw, or other fastener. The guide was a square staple with tapered shanks driven into or through the door. The catch also likely had a tapered shank which was anchored in the door frame. The catch sometimes had a reinforcing tail that ended in a decorative, perforated finial attached to the door frame with a fastening. The major change was to attach each of the components to a backing plate which would then be affixed to the door or frame with fastenings. This is seen as a feature of Norfolk latches, and the result of the ready availability of rolled plate for the production of back plates (Streeter 1971:19). It should not be automatically assumed, however, that any components with a back plate are associated only with Norfolk latches.

Sonn (1928[1]:Plate 98) illustrates a variation attributed to a mid-18th-century Moravian (German) context. In this instance, the latch bar and guide are both attached to a single back plate (Figure 27*a*), much like some lock or spring-latch forms. Information concerning the nature of the handle is not provided. Three other examples presented by Sonn (1928[1]:Plates 53-55) are from the second or third quarter of the 18th century (Figure 27*b*), and are also likely English. Sonn (1928[1]:138, 140, 142, 228) sees this form as being transitional between a latch and a lock.

Late examples of machine-manufactured Norfolk latches include components produced using thinner stock. The catch is formed from such stock bent into a U-shaped cross section, creating the impression of thicker metal and the illusion of greater strength and security. The lift bar may be similarly bent from thin stock. The guide is created by cutting and deforming a single layer of thin metal to provide a slot for the latch bar to pass through and move in. These techniques were used to produce lower-quality materials, but need not have been the only ones used at a particular time.

Although a thumb latch provides little security, it is possible to secure the latch bar. Nutting (1921:78) notes the simple technique of placing a wooden wedge behind the guide staple, above the latch bar, thus making it impossible to raise the latch bar. The more usual arrangement was to place a short latch lock-bar above the

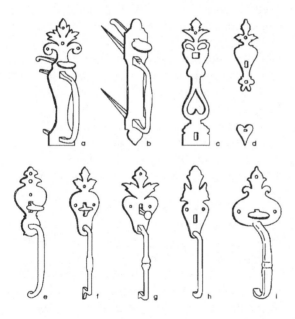

FIGURE 26. Thumb-latch handles or back plates with French or German associations: *a*, mid-17th century; *b*, mid-17th century; *c-d*, probably 18th century; *e*, Quebec, third quarter of the 17th century; *f-g*, France; *h*, early 17th century, Lancaster County, Pennsylvania; *i*, mid-17th century, Moravian. (*a*, after Duhamel du Monceau 1767:Plate 16; *b*, after *Recueil de planches* 1764-1766:Plate 31; *c-d*, after Labonté 1979; *e-i*, after Sonn 1928[1]:Plates 81-83.)

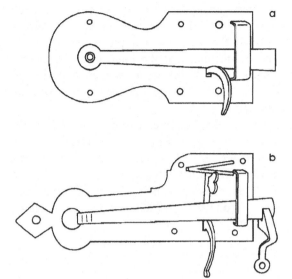

FIGURE 27. Latch bar and guide on back plate: *a*, mid-17th century, Moravian context; *b*, mid-17th century, colonial English context. (After Sonn 1928[1]:Plates 55, 98.)

latch bar. In use, this bar would be positioned vertically above the latch bar, preventing it from being lifted. The lock bar would be positioned on the door so that when not in use it could be pivoted to rest on the guide staple. This was apparently an uncommon feature on thumb latches; it appears on only one of the latch bars illustrated by Sonn (1928[1]:Plate 51). It appears on three latch mechanisms considered to be transitional between latch and lock (Sonn 1928[1]:Plates 53-55). The latch lock-bar on the latter examples is operated with a turn button and held in position by a spring.

BAR LATCHES

A bar latch is a variation that falls between a spring latch and a thumb latch (Streeter 1983:Figures 54-56). The latch bar resembles that of a thumb latch, being pivoted and held down by gravity rather than a spring. Operation of the bar is similar to that of a long spring-latch in that it involves a cam manipulated by a spindle with a knob or handle on one side of the door and a knob attached to the latch bar. In contrast to a spring latch, the various components are mounted on separate back plates (Figure 28), as illustrated by Streeter

(1983:Figures 54-55) and Sonn (1928[1]:Plate 98). These English examples are mostly attributed to the late 18th or early 19th century. They do not appear to persist through the 19th century and are absent from trade catalogues of factory-produced hardware.

RING/KNOCKER LATCHES

A latch bar can also be operated by turning a ring handle on a spindle connected directly or indirectly to the latch bar. According to Sonn (1928[1]:Plates 13-20), there are two basic styles: English (New England) and Dutch. The English style (Figure 29*a*) has a spindle passing through the door and the pivot end of the latch bar. The end of the spindle is split and spread to hold the parts together. The latch bar is guided by a square staple, as for a thumb latch. The Dutch style (Figure 29*b*) is similar, but the end of the spindle engages an asymmetrical cam below the latch bar. A turn of the handle lifts the latch bar, either directly in the English style or indirectly in the Dutch style. In both cases, the ring can only be turned in one direction. The ring may also serve as a knocker but this is not an essential function of the device. Found in an archaeological context, the individual components of a ring/knocker latch, especially the latch bar, may not be recognizable as such since this latch style is similar in its operation to a bar latch. One notable difference is the symmetrical cam of the latter.

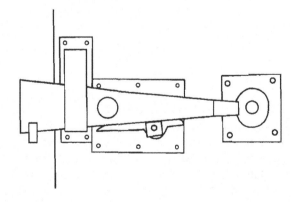

FIGURE 28. Bar latch, late 17th century. (After Streeter 1983:Figure 55.)

Peter J. Priess

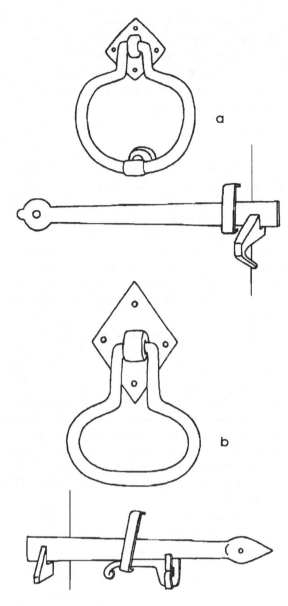

FIGURE 29. Ring/knocker latches: *a*, "English" style; *b*, "Dutch" style. (After Sonn 1928[1]:Plates 14, 16.)

ESCUTCHEON-LIFT LATCHES

On an escutcheon-lift latch (Figure 30), the latch bar and its accessories are the same as for a thumb latch. The difference lies in the nature of the handle and the method of lifting the latch bar. The ends of the handle have tapered shanks which are driven through the

door and clinched. Each shank passes through a slot in a back plate, but does not hold it firmly to the door. A pin protruding from the center of the back of the plate (the escutcheon) extends through the door to the underside of the latch bar. Raising the back plate lifts the latch bar.

Sonn (1928[1]:24) considers this to be "the most unique, and probably the rarest, of the early American latches." A similar latch was recorded in England by Twopeny (1904:Figure 90). The constituent parts, except for the back plate (escutcheon), would not be recognizable individually.

LATCH CATCHES

The most common form of catch for all styles of latches may be characterized as a "figure-4" shape which has a tapered shank to be driven

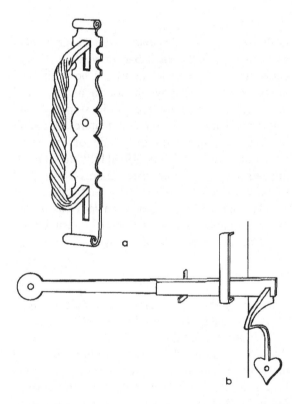

FIGURE 30. Escutcheon-lift latch: *a*, fixed handle with movable escutcheon; *b*, latch bar mechanism. (After Sonn 1928[1]:Plate 22.)

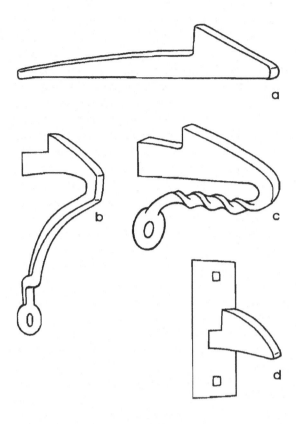

FIGURE 31. Common latch-catch forms: *a,* driven, without reinforcing; *b,* driven, with plain reinforcing; *c,* driven, with twisted-shank reinforcing; *d,* plate mounted. (After Sonn 1928[1]:Plate 94.)

into the door frame (Figure 31*a*). The head or catch end may have a tail depending from it which is also attached to the door frame (Figure 31*b-c*), similar to the reinforcing for a pintle. Since the weight of a latch bar is negligible, however, the tail does not serve a reinforcing function but appears to be largely ornamental. The end of the tail is shaped into a finial, often a simple circle, oval, or point. Further ornamentation might include a twisted shank.

Another form of latch catch has the catch device attached to a plate (Figure 31*d*), similar to the treatment of other parts of the latch mechanism. This apparently became common late in the 18th century.

Although most commonly used for various forms of latches, figure-4 catches would also function for German-style locks with a pivoted latch bar. Hence, the presence of such a catch is not an automatic indication of a latch, and

the presence of a German-style lock can only be inferred if supported by the presence of other diagnostic lock components.

LOCKS

> The subject of locks used on early American buildings is complex, if their historical development were to be traced through the 17th, 18th, and 19th centuries. There were so many different types and so many varied uses, that such an attempt would fail to be more than a superficial review (Streeter 1974a:41).

A lock is any key-operated device attached to a door and equipped with a bolt or other member to keep the door closed (Butter 1968:163). It provides the ultimate in security by limiting operation to the select few who possess the right "key." Additional security can be achieved by using a lock that is operable from only one side of the door.

Door locks can either be portable, such as padlocks, or permanently fixed to a door. The latter may be attached to the door's surface, set into the door's surface, or let into the door's edge. Those attached to the surface have a variety of designations with major categories being "stock locks" and "rim locks." Those let into the surface are termed "flush locks," while locks let into the edge can all be called "mortise locks." The door lock has a lengthy history extending back to the wooden types used in ancient Egypt and elsewhere in the Middle East (Butter 1968:116-117). A number of lock types were available by the time Europeans began settling in North America in the 16th century. These all had metal mechanisms although some types did have wooden housings. They persisted with little change in form into the 19th century, with changes in design and technology being introduced late in the 18th century.

A door lock can be characterized in terms of the nature of its housing, the number of bolts it has, its method of operation, and the composition or complexity of its internal mechanism. Terminology for the various components is extensive and beyond the limits of the present discussion. For an explanation of the various terms, see Towne (1904:11-32b), Butter (1948; 1968), or Priess (1979:46-73).

PADLOCKS

A padlock is a portable lock (Reaumur 1767:216; Butter 1968:200) which consists of a mechanism enclosed in a housing and a curved bow or "shackle" which is passed through a loop such as an eye, hasp, staple, or chain link. The shackle may be: (1) loose and slide into the lock, thereby having both ends secured; (2) held in the housing at one end and allowed to slide or rise for a limited distance without becoming separated from the lock; or (3) pivoted at one end with the free end passing into an opening in the housing where it is secured. Padlocks can be used on doors, as well as for various other applications. Although Jousse (1627:15) characterizes them as easy to make because they do not have many parts and are generally easy to break open, Reaumur (1767:216) states that they can be made as large and as strong as regular locks. They can be characterized in terms of the shape of the housing, the manner in which the housing is assembled, and the manner in which the shackle operates. A number of different forms were used in North America up to the beginning of the 19th century. There do not seem to be definite cultural differences as some shapes appear as readily on English sites as on French ones.

Examples illustrated by Frank (1950:Plate 29) reveal that there were various shapes of

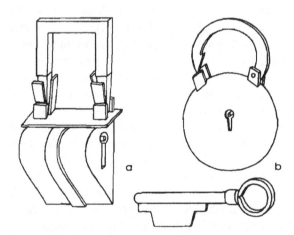

FIGURE 32. Mid-18th-century padlocks: *a*, "half heart" form with key; *b*, ball form. (After *Recueil de planches* 1764-1766:Plate 30.)

padlocks, at least in early French contexts. Some of these probably correspond to the shapes mentioned by Jousse (1627:15): round, heart, square, and triangle. One of these forms, known to have occurred in both English and French contexts, is best characterized as a "half heart" shape (Reaumur 1767:218; Noël Hume 1969:251), based on the cross section of the housing when viewed from the side (Figure 32a). The back of the housing is flat; the front is bowed. The front often has a vertical reinforcing strip, and the openings for the shackle are usually surrounded by additional plates as well. The shackle is a symmetrical U-shape with both ends thinned. One or more springs are attached to each end; Reaumur (1767:218) mentions two springs. When the ends of the shackle are pushed into the housing, the springs are initially compressed but then spring out, preventing removal of the shackle. To open the lock, a simple key is inserted into the keyhole on the right side of the lock and turned to compress the springs, freeing the shackle. The key is a pipe type which fits over a drill pin for alignment and stability, but otherwise there are likely no additional internal obstructions.

Locks of this type are illustrated in both Duhamel du Monceau (1767:Plate 32) and the *Recueil de planches* (1764-1766:Plate 30). Examples illustrated by Frank (1950:Plate 29) are identical and may be of the same time period or earlier. They have been found in 18th-century French contexts such as the Fortress of Louisbourg (Dunton 1972:Figure 77) and Fort Michilimackinac (Stone 1974:233, Figure 143B). Noël Hume (1969:251-252) considers them to be "fairly common" in 18th-century contexts. They appear on sites of the 1730-1820 period, with the earlier examples having a vertical reinforcing on the back as well as the front. These locks are generally small; Noël Hume (1969:252) gives a size range (body length) of $\frac{7}{8}$ to $2\frac{1}{2}$ in. (2.2 to 6.4 cm) The larger examples could have been used on doors, but the smaller ones likely found other applications, such as trunks.

Other early padlocks, such as the triangular, square, or ball-shaped (semi-spherical; Figure 32b) ones illustrated in various sources (*Recueil*

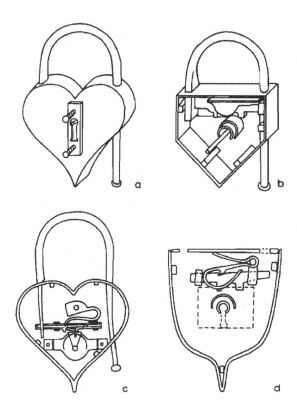

FIGURE 33. Parallel-plate padlocks from French contexts: *a*, heart shaped; *b*, angular; *c*, heart shaped; *d*, rounded-funnel shaped. (*a-b*, after *Recueil de planches* 1764-1766:Plate 30; *c-d*, after Laroche 1988:Figures 17-18.)

de planches 1764-1766:Plate 30; Duhamel du Monceau 1767:Plate 32; Frank 1950:Plate 29), do not appear to be as common in archaeological contexts. Noël Hume (1969:250) indicates that these forms were available in North America during "the first half of the 17th century," with the ball form appearing in contexts as late as the first quarter of the 18th century. These locks, and almost all the other forms yet to be discussed, differ from the half-heart in having a key hole in the front and probably a mechanism with some wards or other obstructions to prevent the use of an incorrect key.

The majority of early padlocks share the characteristic of having their housing constructed of two parallel iron plates joined to a strip of iron by a number of rim rivets (Figure 33*b-d*). The mechanism is attached to the back plate and the keyhole is in the front plate. Variations exist in the shape of the housing (plates) and the nature of the shackle, but in all instances the shackle is secured within the housing. Where only one end of the shackle needs to be secured,

this will invariably be on the left side of the lock (when viewed from the keyhole side). The majority of shackles enter the top of the housing and are secured inside by a horizontal bolt which slides into a notch or slot in the end of the shackle. These shackles are either pivoted on the right side of the lock (Figure 32*b*), or have an extension on the right side that passes through the housing (Figure 33*a-c*). The latter arrangement allows the shackle to rise and fall, moving the free end in and out of the housing. The end of the extension may be enlarged to keep the shackle from falling out of the housing (Figure 33*a-c*).

There are several variations in the shape of the housing, some of which may have cultural affiliations. Two varieties which appear in 18th-century French sources (*Recueil de planches* 1764-1766:Plate 29 Duhamel du Monceau 1767:Plate 32) are heart-shaped (Figure 33*a*), or rectangular with a pointed bottom (Figure 33*b*). Examples of the former are known from Fort Michilimackinac (Stone 1974:Figure 143A) and the Intendant's palace in Quebec City (Laroche 1988:Figures 16-17). A specimen of the latter was found at the Fortress of Louisbourg (Dunton 1972:Figure 77). The Intendant's palace also produced a padlock shaped like a rounded funnel with a small point at the bottom (Figure 33*d*). The nature of its mechanism is unclear, but it may have been a rising shackle with an extended end passing through the housing. Where the mechanism is known, these locks use some form of a one-piece spring and tumbler design as discussed below for French door locks.

Padlocks of similar construction, but with the addition of recognizable ears or lobes at the top, predominate in 18th-century English contexts in North America. Noël Hume (1969:250) indicates they are present "by the late 17th century." They have two lobes, and the housing is usually vertically symmetrical (Figure 34*a*). In all known instances, the bow is pivoted on the right side and the corresponding lobe holds the pivot pin for the shackle. The opposite lobe serves no practical purpose, but provides the symmetry which may have been preferred for aesthetic purposes. In the few instances where the lock is not symmetrical, the upper edge of the housing rises from the right lobe to form a pseudo lobe on the left side (Figure 34*b*). The iron band which joins the front and back plates is a single piece, and begins and ends on the right side at the opening that accommodates the free end of the bow.

Noël Hume (1969:250-251) suggests several trends in shape and design for English locks of the 18th and early 19th centuries. The early locks are supposed to be "bag shaped" (Noël Hume 1969:250); generally rounded and widest near the bottom (Figure 34*b*). A 17th-century form exists which does not fit into this category (Figure 34*a*); plus it has virtually no lobes. On later locks, the widest point has moved up, resulting in a housing which is more circular in appearance (Figure 34*c*). The shape of the lobes varies from near circular (Figure 34*c*) to pointed or arched (Figure 34*e*). Some locks

FIGURE 34. Parallel-plate padlocks from English contexts: *a,* symmetrical housing, 17th-century; *b,* asymmetrical housing, hinged keyhole cover; *c,* symmetrical housing, hinged keyhole cover (incomplete); *d,* asymmetrical housing, pivoted keyhole cover; *e,* symmetrical housing, pivoted keyhole cover; *f,* symmetrical housing, pivoted keyhole cover, late 17th/early 17th century; *g,* symmetrical housing, brass escutcheon and pivoted keyhole cover; *h,* symmetrical housing, brass escutcheon and pivoted keyhole cover. (*a,* after Kenyon 1986:Plate 52; *b-e,* after Priess 1975:Figures 115-116; *f,* after PEM, Volume 3; *g-h,* after Russell and Erwin 1865:106-107.)

from the second or third quarter of the 18th century have a single lobe which provides an attachment point for the pivot pin (Figure 34*b*). This may be an early style which existed along-side double-lobe forms, or it may generally have predated the double-lobe form.

The keyhole cover also changes through time, going from hinged (Figure 34*b, d*) to pivoted (Figure 34*f*) and from iron to brass (Noël Hume 1969:250-251). This is partially at variance, however, with a 17th-century lock from James Bay which has a pivoted cover (Figure 34*a*). The use of brass for keyhole covers is seen as postdating 1840 (Noël Hume 1969:251).

Brass keyhole covers are often stamped and the marks provide an additional means of identifying or dating a lock. The mark may indicate a manufacturer or reveal other pertinent information about the lock type. English locks sometimes exhibit letters which identify the monarch, thus indicating the country of origin as well as providing a date range for the lock. Unfortunately, many of these marks designate Victoria (VR) who reigned from 1837 to 1901, thus limiting their value for dating.

The general shape and construction of padlocks remained the same through much of the 19th century. Most of the locks offered by Russell and Erwin (1865:106-110) are still of the parallel-plate type (Figure 34*g*). The shapes have changed somewhat, however, in that the housing is widest at the lobes and often has a rounded point at the bottom. Other, more elaborate, shapes are also present (Figure 34*h*), and the locks often have a loop and chain attached to the bottom (Russell and Erwin 1865:106-108). Similar shapes are also available in brass housings (Russell and Erwin 1865:108), and many of the locks have brass keyhole escutcheons and keyhole covers. The latter all pivot.

Parallel-plate padlocks persist into the 20th century (Sargent 1910:1039-1048). At the same time, cast-brass and bronze types which imitate the shape of earlier locks are also available (Sargent 1910:1030-1031), as are various other types.

An 18th-century padlock from the Fortress of Louisbourg (Figure 35*a*) resembles other padlocks but is also similar to the embossed door locks discussed below. The lock is square with a housing made of only two plates, the edges of which were apparently riveted together. The back plate is flat, while the front one is embossed (domed) to fit over the mechanism. The right end of the shackle seems to be extended, allowing it to pass into and through the housing as with other padlocks described above. The left end of the shackle is flattened and has a staple-type hasp which fits into a slot in the front plate. The hasp is held in position by a lock bolt inside the lock. The shackle would have to be rotated to remove the hasp from the housing, and the extended right end suggests that it could also rise some distance. The significance of this unusual lock type is presently unknown. Its similarity to the embossed door lock suggests it is French in origin.

A lock style (Figure 35*b-c*) illustrated by Frank (1950) and Simmons and Turley (1980) may be limited to non-English contexts. The housing is a parallel-plate type but, rather than having a moveable shackle, it has a fixed rod attached to the top of the housing. A staple-type hasp slides on this rod and enters the front plate of the housing. A major disadvantage of this arrangement is the possibility that the hasp

may become disassociated and lost. Locks of this form generally tend to be large.

Another style of padlock which appears occasionally has a tubular or barrel housing. The shackle pivots at one end and enters the housing near the other end. The free end of the shackle is held in the housing by various relatively simple systems consisting of a bolt or spring. The lock is opened with a key which simply compresses the spring or pulls back on the bolt (Duhamel du Monceau 1767:Plate 32; Noël Hume 1969:249, Figure 78). Noël Hume (1969:249) presents this type as "the common English padlock of the Middle Ages [which persisted] well into the 18th century." The lock presumably also has French associations as it appears in an 18th-century French technical reference (Duhamel du Monceau 1767:Plate 32) and in the archaeological collections of the Fortress of Louisbourg (Dunton 1972:167, Figure 77).

Early padlocks may not have provided much security. Small locks would have been too fragile to withstand much prying, and the larger locks had more the appearance than the substance of security. The mechanisms are often simple and, as was the case for door locks of the period, did not offer much resistance to picking. The system of internal obstructions (wards) is often simple and the use of variously shaped keyholes provides little advantage. Simple mechanisms, such as the springs to be compressed in half-heart or barrel locks, would likely also not offer any resistance to a determined burglar. Improvements in door-lock technology which began in the late 18th century presumably found their way into padlock manufacture as well. By 1865, padlocks were being offered with tumblers in addition to wards (Russell and Erwin 1865:109).

SURFACE-MOUNTED LOCKS

STOCK LOCKS

A stock lock is a surface-mounted door lock with an iron mechanism set into a wooden housing. The two main subdivisions are "plain" (in which the components of the mechanism are individually attached to the housing) (Figure 36), and "plate" (in which all the parts are first attached to a metal plate which is then affixed

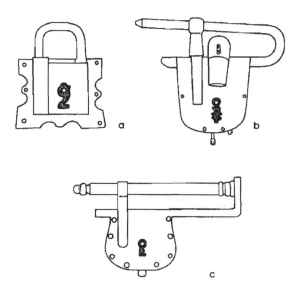

FIGURE 35. Miscellaneous padlocks: *a,* "Embossed" padlock from the Fortress of Louisbourg, probably French; *b,* parallel-plate padlock with hasp, Spanish-American context; *c,* parallel-plate padlock with hasp, possibly French. (*a,* after Dunton 1972:Figure 77; *b,* after Simmons and Turley 1980:Chapter 11, Plate 43; *c,* private collection.)

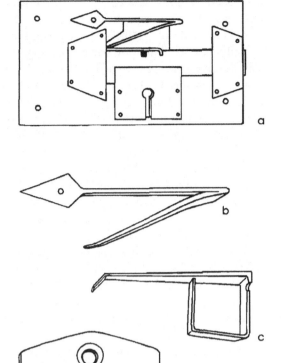

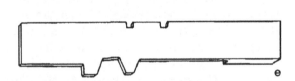

FIGURE 36. Plain stock lock and its constituent parts: *a*, assembled lock; *b*, spring; *c*, tumbler; *d*, main ward; *e*, lock bolt.

ward (Streeter 1970:Figures 9, 11). Other keys (for plate stock locks, rim, or mortise locks) have the collar behind the bit, to contact either the main or cover plate of the lock (Streeter 1970:Figures 9-10).

References to stock locks appear in English documents as early as the 12th century (Hughes 1957:100), suggesting that they could have been used in North America quite early. Streeter (1970:252) contends that stock locks were still being produced in England in 1970. The advantage of a stock lock, especially on an exterior door, appears to be its resistance to weather (Streeter 1970:252).

Stock locks can usually be distinguished from other types in an archaeological context because of their distinctive components. Plain stock locks, which are not likely to be found intact with their wooden housing, have to be recognized from their individual parts. The form of the lock bolt, tumbler, spring, main ward, and possibly also the retaining plates (Figure 36), as well as the distinctive key, is not repeated on other known locks. Hence, the presence of any

to the housing) (Figure 37). They are usually one-bolt (dead bolt) locks (Streeter 1970:251). If a latch were required, it would be provided by a separate mechanism such as a thumb latch. The housing may be ornamented with iron straps (Butter 1968:279; Streeter 1970:Figure 1), and plate stock-locks may have an ornamental brass keyhole escutcheon on the main and cover plates. The escutcheons serve as bearing surfaces since neither of them would have been visible when the lock was attached to a door.

Plain stock locks differ from many other locks in that only the main or bridge ward is available for the attachment of wards and the alignment of the key with the mechanism. The key is kept from passing through the lock by a collar on the shank at the slot in the bit for the main

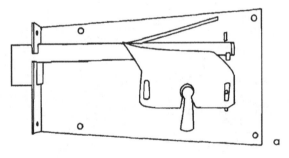

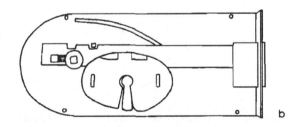

FIGURE 37. Plate stock locks: *a*, common mechanism, trapezoidal main plate; *b*, factory-made, with router-cut housing. (After Priess 1979:Figures 8, 17.)

of these components in a collection reveals the presence of a plain stock lock.

Early plate stock locks also seem to have distinctive, readily recognizable components. The main plate is often trapezoidal, being narrower at the front-plate end. The main plate, even if rectangular, is also recognizable because it will not have any evidence of rim rivets as on rim locks. The lock bolt has a relatively narrow tail, and the cover plate usually has a small spur on an upper corner to hold the lock bolt in place (Figure 37a). The presence of ornamental iron strips (Streeter 1970:Figure 1) at a site may indicate the wooden housing of a stock lock, but other explanations are also possible.

The mechanization of stock-lock production, attributed to the 19th century by Streeter (1970:Figure 8), resulted in several design changes. The lock-bolt tail loses its distinctiveness by becoming wider, with a slot or "lanket hole" (Butter 1968:154, Figure 98) at the end to allow it to ride on a guide, and being held in place with a nut or washer (Figure 37b). This is similar to rim-lock bolts of the period. The cover plate becomes rectangular and loses its spur, and the wards may be of cast brass (Streeter 1970:Figure 8). The main plate is still recognizable because of the absence of rim-rivet holes. Other developments, such as Young's patent of 1825, include the simplification of the creation of the wooden housing by setting the mechanism into a circular rather than a rectangular hole (Price 1856:405-406, Figure 453), the advantage being that the hole could be created with a drill bit rather than a hammer and chisel. The lock mechanism also has a circular main plate rather than the traditional rectangular or trapezoidal one. Similarly, the cut-out for the lock could be done with a router, resulting in a round end on the cut-out and requiring a round end on the main plate (Figure 37b). During the second quarter of the 19th century, a form of stock lock known as Steele's patent (Price 1856:419, Figures 444, 451) was developed wherein the lock mechanism was set into the end of a block of wood, the same as a mortise lock. The lock was intended, however, to be attached to a door's surface and the advantage of the design was that it allowed the lock to be placed on either side of a door without having to turn the lock upside down.

The housing probably did not have ornamental straps on the exterior unless they were added after the lock was attached to a door.

Although stock locks do not appear to have been common in the 19th century, they were still being offered for sale in the United States in 1865 (Russell and Erwin 1865:140) and in England in 1856 (Price 1856:837-843). These sources do not mention any specific advantages of the locks.

RIM LOCKS

The basic requirements for a rim lock are a metal housing and attachment to the surface of a door. The housing minimally consists of a main plate to which the various components are attached, and a rim or sides. Rim locks can be characterized in terms of the method and material of manufacture, the manner in which the housing is assembled, the number of bolts, the manner in which the bolts are operated, the types of obstructions to access, and the proportions of the housing.

The housing is most often made of iron—wrought iron until the 19th century, and then occasionally cast iron. Steel was used later in the 19th century when it became economically feasible. A housing of cast brass could date to the 18th or 19th century. The use of brass for some of the mechanism's components began in the 19th century.

English and French housings are similar to some extent, but possess a few features which often make it possible to differentiate them. On both, the main and front plates are bent from a single piece of iron. The front plate is usually also wider than the other parts of the rim. This allows it to extend onto the edge of the door slightly and provides a means of aligning the lock. On English locks, the back plate is usually also bent from one plate. The English lock then only requires a top and a bottom plate, each of which is a separate strip of iron attached to the main plate with rim rivets. For French locks, as described by Reaumur (1767:160), the three parts of the rim other than the front are made of a single piece of metal bent into a square U and attached to the main plate with rim rivets. Illustrations of 17th- and 18th-century rim locks (Jousse 1627:Figures 25, 28, 31 ,34, 36; Duhamel du

Monceau 1767:Plates 16, 17, 20) show this construction clearly. The ends of the rim may also be bent at right angles and riveted to the front plate (Reaumur 1767:168). Housings assembled in this way can be considered as French in origin and thus, in North America, less likely to date to the 19th or late 18th century. Streeter (1973b:Figure 1) illustrates a "cheap" variation in a housing of probable 19th-century American manufacture in which all parts of the rim are bent from the same sheet of iron.

An English alternative to the all-iron housing was the use of cast brass. The brass housing consists of a shallow box, open on one side, which duplicates the main, front, back, top, and bottom plates of the iron housing. In contrast to iron housings, the equivalent of the front plate is the same width as the remainder of the rim. The mechanism for such locks is similar to that of other rim locks. It is attached to a flat, rectangular iron plate which is dropped into the brass housing and held in place by hooks and set screws in the brass. Brass housings are smaller than those of many iron rim locks, and were usually intended for interior doors.

Locks for powder magazines require non-sparking components and, thus, may be made entirely of non-ferrous materials. Such a lock was recovered from the powder magazine at Coteau du Lac, Quebec (Priess 1972:Figure 11). The lock probably dates from the late 18th century, and has a very simple mechanism of wards. The key may also have been of brass.

Since the door lock is a relatively precise machine requiring the proper interaction of a number of components, it is important that all of the parts are properly fitted to each other. With hand-manufacture technology, this would require shaping each component to fit and work properly in a specific housing. To avoid mixing components from several different locks, all parts for the same lock could be given the same number, marked in Roman numerals with a cold chisel.

Technological changes around the beginning of the 19th century are reflected in the manufacture of contemporary rim lock housings. The introduction of rolled plate by the late 18th century (Streeter 1983:3) made it unnecessary to create the flat components by hand hammering. This reduced the amount of work required to produce a housing, and also meant that the material would be smooth and of uniform thickness. Locks showing evidence of individual hammer blows were produced by forge work and are likely earlier than those having smooth plates of uniform thickness. Bar stock with a triangular or channeled cross section was also introduced. This could be used for the top and bottom plate of the housing, giving it less of a box look.

A rim lock can be characterized by the number of bolts in the mechanism. It minimally requires one bolt–a lock bolt–operated at least partly by a key. Often, however, it has a second bolt–a latch bolt–usually operable from both sides of the door by a knob or lever. Additional security may be provided by a third bolt (often referred to as a night bolt or night latch) which is operable only from the lock side of the door.

English rim locks of the 18th and early 19th centuries often have all three bolts and, to a great extent, the various lock examples are similar to each other. The latch bolt is uppermost in the housing, the lock bolt is below it, and the night bolt is on the bottom. The lock bolt can either be a dead bolt, in which case a key is required to move it in and out of the housing, or it can be a latching lock bolt, in which case the head is beveled and the bolt is kept in the locked position by a spring. The beveling on the head allows the bolt to pass a catch on the door frame and to spring back into a locked position once past the catch. A latching lock bolt has to be operated from at least one side of the door by a key, and it may have a handle or other mechanism to work it from the lock side of the door. The head of the latch bar is always beveled and the bar is kept out by a spring. The night bolt is a dead bolt (it must be moved in both directions manually) and is often operated by a brass handle on the bottom plate of the housing. Variations can occur in any of the major components and thus it is difficult to summarize the characteristics of a lock.

The lock bolt of an English rim lock is generally made of a thick strap with one end folded back a number of times and forged into a rectangular block. The head of the latch bolt may be made in the same manner. The latch-bolt tail often has two bends: one to provide it with a surface to ride on the main plate of the housing, and the second to furnish it with a vertical section to interact with the follower from the knob and spindle. The night bolt is often square and uniform in cross section, and has a L-shaped end for attachment of the handle.

Eighteenth-century French rim locks potentially available in North America are known more from historical references than actual specimens. Illustrated examples (*Recueil de planches* 1764-1766:Plates 23-25; Duhamel du Monceau 1767:Plates 17-23) are either one- or two-bolt locks, the second bolt being either a latch bolt or a night bolt. The lock bolt or the night bolt may have a latching head. Something not seen on English locks is the use of multiple heads for a single lock bolt (*Recueil de planches* 1764-1766:Plates 24; Duhamel du Monceau 1767:Plate 22) and the use of multiple lock bolts. Jousse (1627:Figure 36) illustrates a lock with six bolts and a total of seven heads. In this case, however, all the bolts are moved simultaneously by a single turn of the key, considerably lessening the lock's security potential. Known archaeological examples of probable French locks are one-bolt types with a single head on the bolt (Priess 1975:Figures 109-110; Laroche 1988:Figures 13-14).

German rim locks often differ in several aspects from French and English types. The housing seems to be formed the same way as for French locks; the main and front plate are bent from a single plate and the other three sides are a continuous strap attached with rim rivets (Streeter 1983:Figure 23). The tumbler and spring are of one-piece construction (Nägele and Nägele 1836:Plate 4; Streeter 1983:Figure 24), similar to French locks. When present, latch bolts are often pivoted, rather than sliding, and are operated by a lever on the lock side of the door. The lever may be formed as one piece with the latch bolt and enter the lock housing through the top plate. The end of the lever may be finished with a plate or scroll. Springs in these locks often seem to be of the scroll type (Nägele and Nägele 1836:Plates 5, 6, 8). A night latch operated by a knob may also be present on the bottom plate of the lock (Nägele and Nägele 1836:Plate 5).

In all locks, the lock bolt must have a means of stopping when thrown or moved into the locked position. This is partially accomplished by the limitation of how far the key can actually move it. Additional stops are provided,

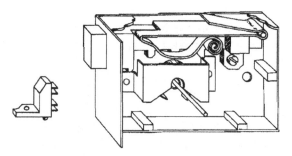

FIGURE 38. French one-bolt rim lock, including detail of a rake ward. (After *Recueil de planches* 1764-1766:Plate 23.)

however. English locks tend to provide this facility somewhere on the bolt tail, either as a widened area or a hook in the end. French locks seem to have a spur on the back of the head (Figure 38). In the case of English locks, the bolt is stopped by an encounter between the mechanism and the bolt tail. On French locks, the encounter is between the bolt head and the housing (front plate). Movement of the lock bolt is usually also restricted by the tumbler catching a notch in the bolt tail up to the early 19th century.

Security in the operation of a lock is provided by several types of obstructions which prevent the use of an incorrect key or the unauthorized movement of the bolt. Lock bolts on early locks, both French and English, have a bar, known as a tumbler, which interferes with the free movement of the bolt. The common tumbler on English locks is a pivoted bar with a lug or "stump" which aligns with one or more lugs on the bolt tail (Figure 39). The tumbler must be lifted out of the way to allow the bolt to move. The tumbler is held in place by a flat, slightly curved spring ("Scotch spring") (Figure 39) which bears on the tumbler near its pivot point. Since it does not move very much, it can be made of iron (Butter 1968:231).

Period illustrations reveal that French locks had two options regarding the form of the mechanism, both of which utilize a combined tumbler and spring. The first option has these two elements in a V-shaped configuration, the upper leg serving as a spring and bearing against the top plate of the housing, with the pivot point being at the apex of the V. Such springs are unknown on North American specimens. The second option utilizes a V-shaped or feather spring. One end of the spring bears against the top plate of the housing, while the other is formed into a rounded or squared P-shaped tumbler (Figure 38). Such spring/tumblers appear on a number of archaeological door locks (Priess 1975:Figures 109-110; Laroche 1988:Figures 13-14), as well as on some padlocks (Laroche 1988:Figures 17-18), and their presence may well indicate the presence of a French lock.

In addition to the tumbler, there are obstructions around the keyhole, theoretically to prevent or hinder the use of an incorrect key. Known collectively as wards, these are often in the form of fixed plates, pins, or other configurations. They are attached to the main and cover plates and a plate known as the bridge ward (Figure 39). The latter is positioned midway between the other two plates, and serves to align the key in the lock and provides another location for the attachment of additional wards. In English rim locks, the bridge ward is held between two vertical plates (cheeks) set perpendicular to the main plate. The cover plate is set on the ends of the cheeks and often held in place with bolts passing into the main plate. The arrangement of cheeks, bridge ward, and cover plate is a relatively rigid structure and provides stability for the operation of the key. In French locks, the bridge ward appears to be attached to the main plate with tabs bent from the end of the ward.

The cover plate is a separate piece with legs and feet straddling the main ward and attached to the main plate (Figure 38). Although Reaumur (1767:163) states that the feet of the cover plate are held in place with screws, they are often attached with rivets, an arrangement that would make it more difficult to remove the cover for repairs. Streeter (1983:13) notes that German locks also had riveted components.

French locks have a number of wards and other obstructions not commonly found on English locks. The ward system often includes a rake ward which consists of a post attached perpendicular to the main plate and has a number of parallel teeth projecting from it (Figure 38). The teeth–the number, spacing, thickness, and length of which vary–interact with slits in the lower edge of the key bit. Additional obstruction was provided by variations in the shape of the keyhole, matched by variations in the cross section of the key bit. A common cross section on French key bits is that of an inverted T, the T being the lower edge of the bit and cut for the rake ward. The cross section of bits on English keys more commonly exhibits straight diverging sides and a rounded end. Additional support for the operation of a key in a French lock may be provided by a tube, often with a round cross section, attached to the cover plate (Duhamel du Monceau 1767:Plate 19, Figures 6,

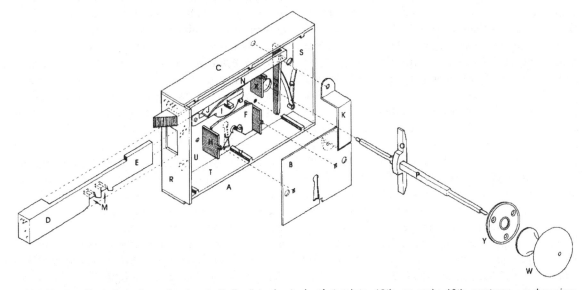

FIGURE 39. Exploded view of a two-bolt English rim lock of the late 18th or early 19th century: *a*, housing (includes main, front, back, top, and bottom plates); *b*, cover plate; *c*, top plate; *d*, lock bolt head; *e*, lock bolt tail; *f*, main/bridge ward; *g*, circle ward; *h*, cheek; *i*, tumbler; *j*, tumbler spring (scotch-spring type); *k*, bolt guide staple; *l*, tumbler stump; *m*, bolt stumps (not visible; behind bolt tail); *n*, latch bolt; *o*, cam/follower; *p*, spindle; *q*, latch bolt spring (feather-spring type); *r*, front plate; *s*, back plate; *t*, bottom plate; *u*, main plate; *v*, rim rivet; *w*, knob; *x*, lock bolt guide; *y*, rose.

9). The tube, which guides the entry of the key into the lock, would extend through the door, its length being approximately equal to the door's thickness. German locks utilized similar tubes (Nägele and Nägele 1836:Plate 5).

A common feature illustrated for French rim locks is the use of a drill pin to guide the key (Duhamel du Monceau 1767:Plate 17, Figure 1, Plate 18, Figure 1). The end of the key is hollow to accommodate the pin. The limitation imposed by this arrangement is that the lock can be operated from only one side. If operation of a lock is required from both sides, it must have a keyhole on either side. These can be aligned so as to access the same mechanism or, as illustrated by Duhamel du Monceau (1767:Plate 22), they can be out of line, thus requiring a separate mechanism (ward system) for either side and involving the use of a drill pin and a pipe key.

Changes in lock security for English locks did not begin to appear until Robert Barron's patent of 1778. One of the initial improvements was the addition of a second tumbler, thereby requiring two parts to be lifted out of the way before the lock bolt could be moved. The second improvement was to introduce a system whereby the tumblers not only had to be lifted to disengage them from the bolt, but they also could not be overlifted. If this were attempted, the tumblers would reengage with other notches in the bolt. A variety of patents followed in an attempt to make locks more secure. The rim locks which had been produced prior to these improvements, however, continued to be manufactured, and seem to be the most common lock found on archaeological sites of the late 18th and early 19th centuries.

Locks resembling the English rim lock were being produced in the United States by the early 19th century (Streeter 1973b:9). A variation from the English design was to shift the latch bolt from above the lock bolt to below it (Streeter 1973b:9). It is further indicated that brass came to be used for some of the parts. Streeter (1973b) also indicates that American-made rim locks are more likely to have marks indicating the manufacturer. English rim locks produced up to the early 19th century do not appear to bear any identifying marks.

Although various lock patents were registered in England and the United States, not all of them caught on. One exception is the 1830 English patent of Carpenter and Young. The

specifications for their lock include a number of security measures with tumblers (Price 1856:423), but the most obvious feature is the use of a pivoting latch bar which is held down with a spring and operated with a spindle and cam or follower. Such a concept was not a new idea, however. Pivoting latch bars had been used in spring latches as well as German locks for a considerable time. The so-called "Carpenter lock" gained considerable popularity, being manufactured into the second half of the 19th century (Trump 1954). These locks generally have a circular brass plate or patent seal attached to the outside of the main plate which provides information on the patent, manufacturer, or some other aspect of the lock. Trump (1954) mentions a number of different markings. They are listed in the Russell and Erwin (1865:22) catalogue as "Carpenter Pattern" with the patent seal marked with an eagle and "RUSSEL ERWIN & Co MANUFACTURERS." The box staple for this type of lock is recognizable by the notch which allows the latch bolt head to pass through and drop into the catch. A heavy brass strip reinforces the edge of the staple and provides a sloping surface to lift the latch bolt head. The strip may also be marked with the manufacturer's name or other similar information.

A major transition in lock manufacture took place in the 19th century. This was the eventual, near-complete change to the use of cast iron which, in North America, was accompanied by changes in design as well. These changes were most likely introduced as a result of American manufacturers becoming the major suppliers of locks at this time. The rationale for the shift has not been established, but it involved the housing as well as various components of the mechanism. A major shift in design was in the use of a full cover plate. This completely closed the housing and allowed either side of the lock to be set against the door, eliminating the need for a separate lock for the right and left side of a door as had been the case. There was also a change in lock orientation during this period, the long axis changing from horizontal to vertical.

A possible early example in this transition is a lock with cast-iron housing, including a full cover plate, a cast lock bolt, and tumbler (the latch bolt is missing). The housing still has the equivalent of rim rivets although in this case they are not necessary to hold the housing together. The fake rivets may appear superfluous but they, in fact, provide points on which the cover plate can rest. The front plate is of the old design (longer than the rest of the rim to fit onto the door edge). Hence, the lock is not reversible.

Streeter (1974a:44-45) has suggested that the manufacture of a door lock begins with the key, the size of which also provides the basic unit of measure for the overall lock size. His examination of English locks led him to the conclusion that, using the length of the keyhole as a unit of measure, the height of a lock was about four units, its length was six to seven units, the thickness was about one unit, and the proportion of length to width ranged from one-and-a-half to one-and-three quarters (Streeter 1974a:45). The extent of the validity of such relationships will have to be confirmed through the continuing examination of greater numbers of relevant locks. The indication is that these figures may be generally valid although greater ranges have been observed. A preliminary impression of French locks is that they can be longer relative to their width. During the 19th century, the orientation of locks, rim and otherwise, underwent a shift. It seems that until some time in that century, door locks were horizontal; their horizontal dimension (length) was considerably greater than their vertical dimension (width). The shift reversed this relationship. The vertical dimension became greater and locks of this nature were designated as "upright." The latter term, as defined by Butter (1968:273), applies to locks in which the handle and keyhole are in the same vertical line. As used by Russell and Erwin (1865:10-11), for example, it also refers to locks without handles.

Streeter (1983:Figure 52) and others describe a style of spring latch which requires a key to operate the bolt from one side of the door. The item is a long-latch style with a keyhole-shaped back plate (Monk 1974:43; Streeter 1983:Figure 52). Details of the mechanism are not provided beyond the fact that the key is of an unusual and distinctive form; rather than being affixed to the side of the round shank, the bit is attached to its end by a pin and is designed to pivot. To enter the lock, the bit forms a straight line with the shank. Once inside, however, it pivots to be at a right angle to the shank and functions as a normal bit. This style of key is not known for any other lock styles. Consequently, its presence in an archaeological collection can be taken to indicate the presence of this particular

lock style. Both Streeter (1983:Figure 52) and Monk (1974:43) attribute it to the 19th century.

The catch for a surface-mounted lock, including stock locks, is traditionally called a staple although this does not describe its most common shape. A square staple driven into the door frame provides the simplest catch for a surface-mounted lock. This is inadequate, however, for locks having both a latch and a lock bolt. In this case, the most common catch is a box, still simply called a staple (PEM, Volume 3). These were constructed, as were the locks, by bending a piece of plate to form a top, bottom, and main plate. The back was a separate strap attached with rim rivets. Two sides of the box, the one facing the lock and the one abutting the door frame, were open. The box could be the same width as the lock, the two appearing to form a single object when seen together on a closed door. Operating a latch bolt placed a strain on the edge of the catch. This was compensated for by strengthening the edge, either by rolling it back or adding a strip of thicker metal, sometimes of brass.

Spindles are operated by either levers, knobs, or rings. For German locks with pivoted latch bolts, levers are the norm, often with an ornamental scroll or pad termination. English locks of the 18th century used brass knobs, usually hollow and round or oval in shape (Figure 40a-b). Such knobs were initially attached by passing the spindle completely through them (Figure 40b); one end of the spindle was riveted to hold the knob and the other was threaded for a nut (Streeter 1974a:51). This arrangement left little room for adjusting a knob's position to

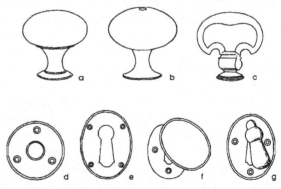

FIGURE 40. Door lock accessories: a, round knob; b, oval knob with hole for through spindle; c, ring handle; d, plain, circular rose; e, plain, oval keyhole escutcheon; f, plain, oval keyhole escutcheon with pivoted oval cover; g, plain, oval keyhole escutcheon with pivoted cover. (After PEM, Volumes 5, 6, 8.)

take up slack on the spindle. The spindle had to be close to the required length, allowing for the thickness of the lock, door, and knobs. Later knobs were sometimes held on the shank with a set screw in the neck of the knob (Streeter 1974a:51). Such brass knobs do not necessarily indicate the presence of a two-bolt door lock, however, since they could also have been used on a number of the latch styles discussed previously.

Ceramic knobs were common during the 19th and early 20th centuries, generally being made in three distinct colors: "porcelain" (white), "jet" (black), and "mineral" (mottled brown) (Towne 1904:168). These were attached to iron necks, and usually held on a spindle by a pin or set screw. Glass knobs, attached to metal necks, were also developed during the 19th century. Towne's (1904:168-169) perspective at the end of the 19th century was that ceramic knobs are "used only with the cheapest grades of locks." Cast iron knobs, although "serviceable," are "rarely attractive." Glass knobs, "if properly made . . . are very handsome," while bronze or brass knobs "constitute the best grade and are always used in buildings of the better class." An alternate for English locks of the 18th and early 19th centuries was a brass ring of a relatively standard shape (Figure 40c). They were intended for use on interior doors.

Abrasion damage to a wooden door through the operation of a latch knob was prevented by placing a rose or bearing plate between the knob and the wood. Initially, these were flat, often circular pieces of brass attached to the door with small nails or pins (Figure 40d). Embossed roses came with the introduction of die stamping toward the end of the 18th century (Streeter (1974a:53). Wear at the keyhole was avoided by a brass escutcheon, often oval, attached with three or four fasteners and possibly also having a pivoted cover (Figure 40e-g). Locks having a tubular key guide did not need a keyhole escutcheon.

Embossed Locks

A type of door lock which appears in 18th-century French references (*Recueil de planches* 1764-1766:Plate 29; Duhamel du Monceau 1767:215, Plate 32, Figure 1) and on sites with French contexts (Dunton 1972:165-166, Figure 75) is used in association with a sliding bolt with a hasp handle (Figure 41). The lock

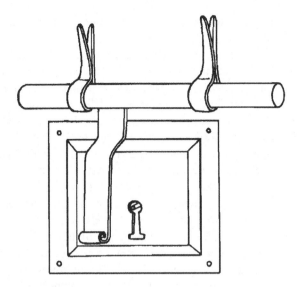

FIGURE 41. Embossed lock. (After Duhamel du Monceau 1767:Plate 32.)

housing consists of two plates: one flat and square; the other also square but embossed with a hollow or depression in the center. The two plates are riveted together to enclose the mechanism, and the housing is attached to the surface of a door. The mechanism appears to be attached to the embossed plate (Duhamel du Monceau 1767:Plate 32, Figure 1). A rectangular slot in this plate permits the entry of a staple-type hasp which serves as the handle for a sliding bolt. The hasp is engaged inside the lock housing by the lock bolt. This type of lock secures the door indirectly since it prevents the sliding bolt from being moved. It differs from an embossed padlock primarily in that it is attached to a door.

Duhamel du Monceau (1767:215) considers the embossed lock to be of great antiquity, usually simply made because it has little value, and seldom used except in the country. Dunton (1972:165) characterizes it as "suitable for cellars." The presence of such a lock in an archaeological collection would suggest a French context predating the mid to late 18th century.

Loquet à la Cordeliere

This is a type of latch which is operated from one side of the door by a specially shaped key (*Recueil de planches* 1764-1766:Plate 31, Figures 151-153; Duhamel du Monceau 1767:136, 138-139, Plate 16, Figures 12-15), hence its inclusion here as a type of lock. The rationale for the name is not clear, but Duhamel du Monceau (1767:136) indicates that they were often used in convent dormitories. The lock bar, guide, and catch may be the same as for a thumb latch. The difference lies in the absence of a handle and thumb-operated lift bar. Instead, the lock bar has a knob attached to its front and a vertical tail affixed to its back. The tail is enclosed in a half tube (Figure 42a) which is attached to the door. From one side, the lock bar is operated by lifting the knob; from the other, it is operated by inserting a key through an escutcheon and lifting it, thereby pushing up on the vertical tail. The shape of the half tube (Figure 42a), the key escutcheon (Figure 42b), and the key (Figure 42c) is quite distinctive, and the presence of any of these components in a collection is conclusive proof of the presence of this type of lock.

English references discuss a lock or latch which, on the basis of key shape, is the same type of lock (Price 1856:Figure 435; Butter 1968:89, Figure 191; Monk 1974:42-43). All the illustrations show the key and keyhole escutcheon, but provide no information concerning the appearance of the latch mechanism. Referred to as a "French latch" (Butter 1968:89) or "French night latch" (Price 1856:Figure 435; Monk 1974:42), it is said to have been invented in 1792 (Butter 1968:89) or "the latter part of the 18th century" (Monk 1974:42) by someone named Odell. This lock type also has English associations although its presence in 19th-century North American contexts is yet to be known. It is known, however, from some probable French contexts (Dubé 1991:Figures 10g, 15f).

MORTISE LOCKS

Mortise locks are set into a mortise on the edge of a door so that only the front plate of the housing is visible. They are similar to rim locks in being one-, two-, or three-bolt locks. The earliest known examples, from the late 18th or early 19th century, have mechanisms similar to those of forged rim locks of the same period.

A major question yet to be answered concerns the inception of the mortise lock. At least one supplier of reproduction hardware claims that a style of mortise lock offered by them has "been used since the early 1700's" (Ball and Ball 1992:77). Neither Moxon (1703:22) nor *The Builder's Dictionary* (1734), however, mention

them in early 18th-century contexts, and Butter (1968:194) notes that mortise-lock makers are not listed in the Birmingham directory prior to 1780. Streeter (1983:11) suggests that they "came into use toward the end of the 18th century," and it is probable that mortise locks found in archaeological contexts do not predate the late 18th century. During the 19th century they were still the less-common lock form, possibly because of the additional work required to cut the mortise. The shift to cast-iron door locks during the 19th century continued to emphasize surface-mounted forms. In 1865, Russell and Erwin (1865) were offering considerably more rim locks than mortise locks. By the beginning of the 20th century, however, mortise locks formed a major portion of the locks offered by such companies as Yale and Towne (Towne 1904:618-673) and Sargent & Company (1910).

As mentioned above, early mortise locks employed the technology and much of the design of rim locks of the same period. The housing is still comprised of a main and back plate bent from a single piece of sheet metal. The top and bottom are attached with rim rivets, and a cover plate is set on the ends of the rim rivets and held down with two or more bolts. The cover plate, however, now completely closes the lock housing. Since it has to be centered on the housing, the front plate is a separate piece of metal, possibly brass. One style, known from various contexts including Price's (1856:Figure 210) listing, is a three-bolt lock type. The bolt arrangement is of the English style with the latch bolt above the lock bolt, but with the

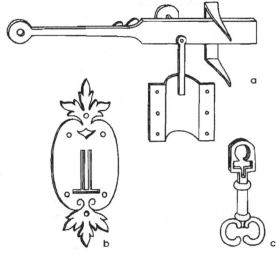

FIGURE 42. *Loquet à la cordeliere:* a, latch bar and half-tube assembly; b, key escutcheon; c, key. (After Duhamel du Monceau 1767:Plate 16.)

night bolt located between them. The night bolt is operated by a knob, spindle, and cam arrangement; the knob is present on only one side of the door. The two spindles and the keyhole are on a single horizontal line, and the knob roses and keyhole escutcheon are a single plate.

FLUSH LOCKS

A flush lock is recessed into an interior surface, and may be used on drawers or the doors of a cupboard or possibly a closet (Butter 1968:85). This means that the lock is usually out of sight when the drawer or door is closed and may, therefore, not be particularly well finished on the exterior. The main and front plate are bent from a single piece of metal. The mechanism, which is attached to the main plate, is generally smaller than the plate. It is often enclosed by and partly attached to a rim comprised of a single strip of metal which forms the sides, as well as a cover plate which is only slightly larger than the mechanism. The smaller mechanism reduces the amount of wood that needs to be removed to install the lock. A similar lock, identified as a drawer lock, is illustrated in the *Recueil de planches* (1764-1766:Plate 25, Figure 82). Its French origin is apparent in the shape of the spring/tumbler combination, as discussed above. Such locks are operable from only one side, probably using a pipe key. Larger examples which could have been used on room or closet doors are rare (Dunton 1972:Figure 75).

Simmons and Turley (1980:156, Plates 39-40) indicate that flush locks are appropriate in New World Spanish contexts. The lock they illustrate has several features in the mechanism which are similar to those in 18th-century French illustrations; specifically, the shape of the spring and tumbler, and the method of attachment for the cover plate. As mentioned above, latches of similar construction are listed for closets and shutters. Most locks of this type are relatively small and more suited for a drawer or a small door, such as on a cupboard. Larger examples may have served as door locks.

Interpretation of Door Hardware

This report provides an overview of the variety of functions and styles of hardware which may be associated with a door. Cultural and temporal differences exist to some extent and allow more detailed identification or interpretation of specific items, assemblages, or contexts. In an archaeological context, the various parts of a door are likely to become separated and scattered, making structural interpretations more difficult. At the most basic level, the presence of door hardware suggests the presence of a door and, depending on the extent of site disturbance, may provide some indication of the location of doors and the layout of a building. Conversely, the absence of door hardware does not mean that doors were not present. Door hardware, like many other metal artifacts, is salvageable and could have been removed after it was no longer required for its original purpose. Once removed, it could have been reused elsewhere, or reworked to suit other, more immediate needs.

The identification of the material, method of manufacture, and style of a piece of door hardware may provide an indication of its date and cultural affiliation. Wrought iron items may date to any time in the historic period, including the late 19th century. Steel items are less likely to be early. Until some time after the middle of the 19th century, this material was more expensive than wrought iron and its use for door hardware was generally impractical. An object made of machine-rolled stock or using various machine processes to shape or assemble it will date no earlier than the late 18th century. Some objects can be identified as likely having a non-English association. This applies to lock components made in the French or Continental European styles, and may apply to latch handles of some forms. Items produced in one cultural tradition, however, may also find their way to other cultures through trade or other means. Hence, the identification of cultural styles may be misleading.

An archaeological site may occasionally produce a large collection of building hardware, much of which may be door hardware. This permits a more thorough interpretation of the structures involved. In attempting to understand the hardware from a building site, it is important to understand the concept of a hierarchy for the items (Nelson 1980:vii; Chappell 1984:2). Hierarchies exist both within and between buildings. Differences in the quality of the hardware may indicate the social or economic level of a building but, within a building, may simply indicate their location. "In general, the level of expense decreases as one moves from the most to the least public places" (Chappell 1984:2). "In the final analysis, the provenance of hardware within any given building [or archaeological context] must be judged individually and compared with other local examples and [available catalogues]" (Nelson 1980:vii). Hence, what may initially appear to be a diverse collection of items may end up providing a reflection of form and function for a specific structure. Nelson (1980:vii) also makes the important point that "many such studies need to be made before a clearer picture emerges."

REFERENCES

ALCOCK, N.W., AND LINDA HALL
1994   Fixtures and Fittings in Dated Houses 1567-1763. Council for British Archaeology, *Practical Handbooks in Archaeology* 11. London, England.

AMSLER, CORY
1989a   Architectural Hardware, 1700-1860: The Mercer Museum Collection. *Mercer Mosaic: Journal of the Bucks County Historical Society* 6(1):3-17.
1989b   Henry Mercer and the Dating of Old Houses. *Mercer Mosaic: Journal of the Bucks County Historical Society* 6(1):18-28.

ASTON, JAMES, AND EDWARD B. STORY
1939   *Wrought Iron: Its Manufacture, Characteristics and Applications.* A. M. Byers, Pittsburgh, PA.

BALL AND BALL
1992   *Hardware Reproductions* [catalogue]. Ball and Ball, Exton, PA.

THE BUILDER'S DICTIONARY
1734   *The Builder's Dictionary: Or Gentleman and Architect's Companion.* Reprinted 1981, Association for Preservation Technology, Ottawa, Ontario.

BUTTER, F. J.
1931   *Locks and Lockmaking*, 2nd edition. Sir Isaac Pitman, London, England.
1948   *Locks and Builders' Hardware Glossary, Design Manufacture and History.* Josiah Parkes, Willenhall, England.
1968   *An Encyclopaedia of Locks and Builders Hardware.* Josiah Parkes, Willenhall, England.

CHAMBERLAIN, SAMUEL
1928   Notes on Old Wrought Iron. *American Architect* 133:101-107.

CHAPPELL, EDWARD
1984   Looking at Buildings. In "Fresh Advices," Research Supplement to the *Colonial Williamsburg Interpreter*, November. Williamsburg, VA.

D'ALLEMAGNE, HENRY RENÉ
1924   *Decorative Antique Ironwork: A Pictorial Treasury.* Reprinted 1968, Dover Publications, New York, NY.

DOW, GEORGE FRANCIS
1927   The Arts and Crafts in New England 1704-1775. Reprinted 1967 as *DaCapo Press Series in Architecture and Decorative Art* 1. New York, NY.

DUBÉ, FRANÇOISE
1991   La quincaillerie d'architecture de Place-Royale. Ministère des Affaires Culturelle, Les Publications du Québec, Collection Patrimoines, *Dossiers* 71. Québec, Québec.

DUHAMEL DU MONCEAU
1767   *Art du serrurier.* Descriptions des arts et Métiers, faitres ou approuvées par messieurs de l'académie royale des sciences, Paris, France.

DUNTON, JOHN
1972   Building Hardware Excavated at the Fortress of Louisbourg. Department of Indian Affairs and Northern Development, National Historic Parks and Sites Branch, *Manuscript Report Series* 97. Ottawa, Ontario.

ERAS, VINCENT J. M.
1957   *Locks and Keys Throughout the Ages.* Vincent J. M. Eras, H. M. Fracsek, Amsterdam, Netherlands.

FRANK, EDGAR B.
1950   *Old French Ironwork.* Harvard University Press, Cambridge, MA.

GAYLE, MARGOT, AND DAVID W. LOOK
1980   A Historical Survey of Metals. Part I of *Metals in America's Historic Buildings*. United States Department of the Interior, Heritage Conservation and Recreation Service, Technical Preservation Services Division, Washington, DC.

GREAT BRITAIN, OFFICE OF THE COMMISSIONERS OF PATENTS FOR INVENTIONS [GBO]
1873   *Abridgements of Specifications Relating to Hinges, Hinge Joints, and Door Springs. A.D. 1775-1866.* Queen's Printer, London, England.

HARRIS, DONALD A.
1971   Building Hardware from Sainte-Scholastique, Quebec. Department of Indian Affairs and Northern Development, National Historic Parks and Sites Branch, *Manuscript Report Series* 103. Ottawa, Ontario.

HOMMEL, RUDOLF
1944   The Secret Joint Hinge. *Early American Industries Association Chronicle* 4(1):3-4.

HUGHES, G. BERNARD
1957   English Domestic Locks. *The Connoisseur Year Book, 1957*, pp. 100-107. London, England.

JOUSSE, MATHURIN
1627   *La fidelle ouverture de l'art de serrurier.* Georges Griveau, La Fleche.

KELLY, J. FREDERICK
1924   *Early Domestic Architecture of Connecticut.* Reprinted 1967, Dover, New York, NY.

KENDRICK, WILLIAM
1866   Cast Iron Hollow-Ware, Tinned and Enameled and Cast Ironmongery. Frank Cass, London, England. Reprinted 1967 in *Birmingham and the Midland Hardware District*, Samuel Timmins, editor, pp. 103-109. Cass, London, England.

KENYON, WALTER A.
1986   The History of James Bay 1610-1686: A Study in Historical Archaeology. Royal Ontario Museum, *Archaeology Monograph* 10. Toronto.

KNIGHT, EDWARD H.
1876   *Knight's American Mechanical Dictionary*. Reprinted 1979 for The Mid-West Tool Collectors Association and The Early American Industries Association. Riverside Press, Cambridge, MA.

LABONTÉ, COLETTE
1979   Serrurerie Traditionelle. Manuscript, Parcs Canada, Région du Québec, Architecture et Genie, Québec, Québec.

LAROCHE, CHRISTINE
1988   Répertoire descriptive des pièces de quincaillerie d'architecture découvertes sur le site archéologique du premier palais de l'intendant à Québec (CeEt30) dans les opérations 1 à 17. Université Laval, Québec, *Hors serie* 1. Québec, Québec.

LUNN, KEVIN
1985   Goods on the Bay: Material Culture from Archaeological Investigations of York Factory Hudson's Bay Company Post, 1788-1957. Canadian Parks Service, *Microfiche Report Series* 347. Ottawa, Ontario.

MARTINEAU, F. E.
1866   *Patent Wrought-Iron Hinges*. Frank Cass, London, England. Reprinted 1967 in *Birmingham and the Midland Hardware District*, Samuel Timmins, editor, pp. 610-612. Cass, London, England.

MERCER, HENRY C.
1923   Notes on Wrought-Iron Door Latches. *Old-Time New England* 13(3):139-142.
1924   The Dating of Old Houses. *Old-Time New England* 14(4):170-190.

MONK, ERIC
1974   *Keys: Their History and Collection*. Shire, Aylesbury, Bucks, England.

MOXON, JOSEPH
1703   *Mechanick Exercises. Or the Doctrine of Handy-Works*. Reprinted 1975, The Early American Industries Association, Scarsdale, NY.

NÄGELE, ADAM, AND FERDINAND NÄGELE
1836   *Darstellung der schönen Schlosser-Profession in ihrem ganzen Umfange*. Herausgeben vom Verfasser der Schmied-Profession, n.p.

NELSON, LEE H.
1980   Introduction. In *Illustrated Catalogue of American Hardware of the Russell and Erwin Manufacturing Company*, pp. iii-xiii. Association for Preservation Technology, Ottawa, Ontario.

NOËL HUME, IVOR
1969   *Artifacts of Colonial America*. Alfred A. Knopf, New York, NY.

NUTTING, WALLACE
1921   *Furniture of the Pilgrim Century 1620-1720, Including Colonial Utensils and Hardware*. Bonanza Books, New York, NY.

PEABODY ESSEX MUSEUM (PEM)
        Sample Book, Volume 2, watermark 1798. 739.4 S19.2, Peabody Essex Museum, Philips Library, Salem, MA.
        Sample Book, Volume 3, watermark 1799. 739.4 S19.2, Peabody Essex Museum, Philips Library, Salem, MA.
        Sample Book, Volume 5, watermark 1800. 739.4 S19.2, Peabody Essex Museum, Philips Library, Salem, MA.
        Sample Book, Volume 6, watermark 1800; 1806 on cover. 739.4 S19.2, Peabody Essex Museum, Philips Library, Salem, MA.
        Sample Book, Volume 8, watermark 1800. 739.4 S19.2, Peabody Essex Museum, Philips Library, Salem, MA.
        Sample Book, Volume 9, watermarks 1803, 1804, 1806. 739.4 S19.2, Peabody Essex Museum, Philips Library, Salem, MA.
        Sample Book, Volume 10, watermark 1804. 739.4 S19.2, Peabody Essex Museum, Philips Library, Salem, MA.
        Sample Book, Volume 11, watermark 1804. 739.4 S19.2, Peabody Essex Museum, Philips Library, Salem, MA.
        Sample Book, Volume 12, undated. 739.4 S19.2, Peabody Essex Museum, Philips Library, Salem, MA.
        Sample Book, Volume 13, watermarks 1812, 1816, 1817. 739.4 S19.2, Peabody Essex Museum, Philips Library, Salem, MA.
        Sample Book, Volume 14, watermark 1814. 739.4 S19.2, Peabody Essex Museum, Philips Library, Salem, MA.
        Sample Book, Volume 15, watermark 1815; dated 1817. 739.4 S19.2, Peabody Essex Museum, Philips Library, Salem, MA.
        Sample Book, Volume 16, watermark 1812; received 1819. 739.4 S19.2, Peabody Essex Museum, Philips Library, Salem, MA.

PRICE, GEORGE
1856   *A Treatise on Fire & Thief-Proof Depositories and Locks and Keys*. Simpkin, Marshall, London, England.

PRIESS, PETER J.
1972   Building Hardware from the Fort at Coteau du Lac, Quebec. National Historic Sites Service, *Manuscript Report Series* 93. Ottawa, Ontario.
1975   Building Hardware. In Hardware from Fort Beausejour, New Brunswick, by Peter J. Priess, J. Michael Shaughnessy, and Barbara J. Wade, pp. 387-576.

Parks Canada, *Microfiche Report Series* 82. Ottawa, Ontario.

1978   An Annotated Bibliography for the Study of Building Hardware. Parks Canada, *History and Archaeology* 21. Ottawa, Ontario.

1979   A Study of Surface-Mounted Door Locks from a Number of Archaeological Sites in Canada. Parks Canada, *History and Archaeology* 25. Ottawa, Ontario.

PRIESS, PETER J., AND DONALD STREETER
1974   Priess and Streeter Correspondence on Hinges. *Association for Preservation Technology, Bulletin* 6(2):24-33.

PRUDEN, THEODORE (EDITOR)
1974   Historic Hardware in the United States and Canada. *Association for Preservation Technology, Newsletter* 3(3):1-26.

REAUMUR, RENÉ ANTOINE FERCHAULT, SEIGNEUR DE
1767   Des serrures de toutes les especes. In *Art du serrurier*, by Duhamel du Monceau, pp. 159-261. Descriptions des arts et Métiers, faitres ou approuvées par messieurs de l'académie royale des sciences, Paris, France.

RECUEIL DE PLANCHES, SUR LES SCIENCES ET LES ARTS
1764   Serrurerie (Vol. 9). Reprinted 1965, Cercle du livre
-1766   précieux, Paris, France.

RUSSELL AND ERWIN MANUFACTURING COMPANY
1865   *Illustrated Catalogue of American Hardware of the Russell and Erwin Manufacturing Company*. Reprinted 1980, Association for Preservation Technology, Ottawa, Ontario.

SARGENT & COMPANY
1910   *Hardware* [catalogue]. Sargent & Company, New Haven, CT.

SCHIFFER, HERBERT, PETER SCHIFFER, AND NANCY SCHIFFER
1979   *Antique Iron Survey of American and English Forms Fifteenth through Nineteenth Centuries*. Schiffer, Exton, PA.

SIMMONS, MARC, AND FRANK TURLEY
1980   *Southwestern Colonial Ironwork*. Museum of New Mexico Press, Santa Fe.

SONN, ALBERT H.
1928   *Early American Wrought Iron*, 3 volumes. Charles Scribner's Sons, New York, NY.

STEVENS, JOHN R.
1969   Early Cast Iron Latches. *Association for Preservation Technology, Bulletin* 1(3):11-13.

STONE, LYLE M.
1974   Fort Michilimackinac 1715-1781: An Archaeological Perspective on the Revolutionary Frontier.

Publications of the Museum, Michigan State University, Anthropological Series 2. East Lansing.

STREETER, DONALD
1954   Early Wrought Iron Hardware: Spring Latches. *Antiques* 66(2):125-127.

1970   Early American Stock Locks. *Antiques* 98(2):351-355.

1971   Early American Wrought Iron Hardware: Norfolk Latches. *Association for Preservation Technology, Bulletin* 3(4):12-30.

1973a   Early American Wrought Iron Hardware: H and HL Hinges, Together with Mention of Dovetails and Cast Iron Butt Hinges. *Association for Preservation Technology, Bulletin* 5(1):22-49.

1973b   Some Signed American Rim Locks. *Association for Preservation Technology, Bulletin* (5)2:9-37.

1974a   Early American Wrought Iron Hardware: English Iron Rim Locks; Late 18th and Early 19th Century Forms. *Association for Preservation Technology, Bulletin* 6(1):40-67.

1974b   Early American Wrought Iron Hardware: Cross Garnet, Side and Dovetail Hinges. *Association for Preservation Technology, Bulletin* 6(2):6-23.

1975a   Wrought Iron Hardware for Exterior Shutters. *Association for Preservation Technology, Bulletin* 7(1):38-56.

1975b   Early American Wrought Iron Hardware: Slide Bolts. *Association for Preservation Technology, Bulletin* 7(4):104-122.

1976   A Signed American Stock Lock from the Manufactory of J. & J. Patterson. *Association for Preservation Technology, Bulletin* 8(2):76-77.

1980   *Professional Smithing*. Charles Scribner's Sons, New York, NY.

1983   The Historic Development of Hand Forged Iron Builders' Hardware. In *The Technology of Historic American Buildings: Studies of the Materials, Craft Processes, and the Mechanization of Building Construction*, H. Ward Jandl, editor. Association for Preservation Technology. Ottawa, Ontario.

TOWNE, HENRY R.
1904   *Locks and Builders Hardware: A Hand Book for Architects*. John Wiley, New York, NY.

TRUMP, ROBERT TOWNSHEND
1954   The Carpenter-type Lock. *Antiques* 66(6):482.

TWOPENY, WILLIAM
1904   *English Metal Work*. Archibald Constable, London, England.

WOODCROFT, BENNET
1854   *Alphabetical Index of Patentees of Inventions*. Reprinted 1969, Augustus M. Kelley, New York, NY.

PETER J. PRIESS
234 CARROLL ROAD
WINNIPEG, MANITOBA R3K 1H6
CANADA

ERICA HILL

Thimbles and Thimble Rings from the circum-Caribbean Region, 1500–1800: Chronology and Identification

ABSTRACT

This paper provides an overview of literature on the subject of thimbles. Particular attention is devoted to the identification of functional categories and determining the gender and age composition of a site using thimbles. Major innovations in construction, decorative patterning, and shape are identified as well. Archaeologically, thimbles are often recovered at European domestic sites, in aboriginal burials, and as trade goods. This omnipresent artifact has considerable potential for general dating and demographic purposes.

Introduction

Although thimbles are often recovered at post-contact sites in the Americas, very little scholarly research is devoted to identification and dating and even less to the gender and age implications of these artifacts. Most information on thimbles has been compiled by collectors, often with impressive attention to historical and archaeological detail, yet these data are circulated among a very specialized audience and are either unknown or unavailable to the professional archaeologist. Due to the specialized nature of the pursuit and the limited number of scholarly publications, an overview of the topic is due. The collections of the Florida Museum of Natural History, primarily those from the Spanish sites of Florida and the circum-Caribbean region, were used to develop a typology and identify key characteristics.

Historical Background

The original purpose of thimbles was to protect the tip of the finger of the tailor or seamstress from injury by the blunt end of the needle. In this regard, some form of thimble has probably been in use since the origins of sewing. Thimble rings—or sewing rings as they are sometimes called—served the same purpose as thimbles, but protected the side of the finger instead of the tip. Their construction and design reflect their use by tailors, who typically sewed using the palm side of the finger to propel the needle through fabric.

Leather thimbles have been documented from the medieval period in Europe (Moorhouse 1971: 60), although such examples rarely are preserved archaeologically. Bone, horn, and wooden thimbles also have been recovered, especially in contexts in which metal was unavailable or undesirable as a construction material. This discussion, however, will focus on thimbles of metal—brass in particular—since this is the type most frequently recovered archaeologically.

The earliest metal thimbles or thimble rings with reliable archaeological provenience have been traced to the site of Corinth (Holmes 1985:19). Over one hundred bronze thimble rings were recovered, all of which date to the 9th through the 12th centuries A.D. (Davidson 1952:178).

While various types of thimbles were probably in use prior to the medieval period, two distinct types with definite regional associations have been identified. The distinctive Hispano-Moresque thimbles, conical in shape and constructed of bronze, are too heavy to have been used for tailoring or mending. Instead, Holmes (1985:20–21) suggests that they were used to make and repair horse trappings. A second early type is the Turkish-style domed thimble suggestive of the onion dome so prominent in architecture of the Near East. Thimble rings of Byzantine origin display a similar rounded shape.

Holmes ([1987b]:1) dates the earliest metal thimbles in England to A.D. 1350, and thimble rings to A.D. 1450, although metal thimbles were in use on the Continent at least a century earlier. This temporal delay is due most likely to the fact that Britain lacked a native brass industry because the island had no workable deposits of copper. An alloy of copper and zinc, brass was imported in sheets in the late Middle Ages (Steane 1984:225).

Erica Hill

TABLE 1
MORPHOLOGICAL CHARACTERISTICS

Time Period	Morphological Characteristics	Manufacturing Technique	Location of Production
Medieval (pre-1500)	Domed, irregular indentations, squat shape	Casting indicated by either a small hole in crown or by four notches in the rim	
1500–1600	Elongated, rectangular indentations, Spiralling punctation around crown	Single-piece casting, annealing indicated by folds of metal near rim	
Late 1500s	Edges folded over	Deep-drawing	Nuremberg
Prior to 1650	"Tonsured" crown (no indentations on crown)		
1650–present	Machine-made indentations that are evenly spaced and sized		
Post-1650	Two-piece assembly crown may be attached separately		
Late 1700s	Edges folded over outside of rim	Deep-drawing	England

By the 1500s, brass thimbles had become a major import to Britain. It was not until the 17th century that Britons began producing sufficient brass to rival the well-developed industries of Germany and the Low Countries (Holmes 1985:37, [1987b]: 1). Primary sources of copper on the Continent included Spain, Bohemia, Saxony, Hanover, and Sweden (Holmes 1985:133).

Although the majority of thimbles recovered archaeologically are of brass, customs records from this period demonstrate that smelted iron was imported to Britain in large quantities for the manufacture of thimbles. However, due to the poor preservation properties of the metal, iron thimbles are rarely recovered archaeologically.

Iron was only one of many types of construction material used to manufacture thimbles. The flow of gold and silver from the Americas into the metals markets of Europe created an exceptional demand for thimbles of these heretofore scarce materials. Although popular as collectibles, thimbles of gold or silver are seldom recovered archaeologically, probably because as expensive and elite goods they were carefully guarded against loss.

Holmes (1985:133) suggests that the increased availability of brass directly contributed to the growth of the thimble-making industry at the end of the 15th century. The hallmark of the medieval thimble is the dome shape. Due to the casting pro-

cess by which they were produced, medieval brass thimbles are frequently squat and heavy with very irregular indentations (Groves 1966:36). A small hole in the top of a domed thimble or four small notches encircling the rim are indications that a thimble has been cast (Holmes 1985:134–135; cf. Greif 1984:28). Since the technique of casting had been refined by the 1500s, such characteristics date thimbles of this type securely within the Middle Ages (Table 1).

Noël Hume (1969:256) has identified additional characteristics of early thimbles. The rim is not rolled, nor are the indentations regularly patterned. Rather, thimbles through A.D. 1600 display uneven punctation, often in a spiralling pattern which terminates before reaching the center of the crown (Noël Hume 1969:256; Holmes [1987b]:2). Thimbles with crowns that have no indentations—"tonsured" thimbles—date prior to A.D. 1650 (Holmes [1987b]:3). Such design may reflect the use of the side of the finger, rather than the tip, to propel the needle through fabric. The disappearance of tonsured thimbles thus suggests not only an alteration in design, but also a change in patterns of usage.

One of the most distinctive characteristics of thimbles produced before A.D. 1600 was single-piece construction. The casting process produced a thimble which, when cooled, was composed of a single piece of brass. A second early construction technique employed hammering and stamping sheet metal into the desired shape. The process involved frequent heating of the cooled metal in order to soften it and thus make it more malleable. This technique, called annealing, often caused the metal to settle in folds, usually near the rim (Holmes 1985:133, 135, [1987b]:2).

By the late 1700s in England, the technique of deep-drawing had become widespread. Deep-drawn thimbles were made by pressing sheet metal, a "form of mechanical stamping" (Holmes [1987b]:2). The edges were then folded over the outside of the rim. In contrast, cast thimbles of this period have edges which project outward but which are solid. In Germany the process of deep-drawing had been in use over two centuries earlier (Greif 1984:12, 29–30; Holmes 1985:26). The city of Nuremberg jealously guarded the means of refining brass and so was the only European producer of deep-drawn thimbles (Greif 1984:28–29). This process is depicted in a 1564 woodcut by Jost Amman (Holmes 1985:27) in which a thimblemaker hammers brass sheets into a mold while a second craftsworker punches indentations into the newly wrought thimbles.

Identification of Thimbles Recovered from circum-Caribbean Sites

Hand-punched indentations are a distinguishing feature of 16th-century thimbles recovered archaeologically from the circum-Caribbean region. A well-dated example from the site of Nueva Cadíz, Venezuela, has evenly spaced elongated indentations which spiral from the rim to the crown (Figures 1, 2). Settled by the Spanish in 1515, Nueva Cadíz was destroyed by an earthquake in 1541 (Deagan 1987:9), securely dating this thimble to the early 16th century.

A second example of the same type was recovered from the site of Convento de San Francisco in the Dominican Republic. Although this site is not as narrowly dated as Nueva Cadíz, the recovered thimble bears a striking resemblance to the one discussed above. The indentations are virtually identical in size and shape to the thimble from

FIGURE 1. Side view of deep-drawn thimbles from Convento de San Francisco (*left*) and Nueva Cadíz (*right*). Note elongated, rectangular indentations. (Courtesy of Florida Museum of Natural History.)

FIGURE 2. Top view of thimbles from Convento de San Francisco (*left*) and Nueva Cadíz (*right*). Note spiralling around crown. (Courtesy of Florida Museum of Natural History.)

Venezuela (Figures 1, 2); however, the indentations are not as evenly spaced nor as finely made. In both examples, the vertical indentations spiral to the crown and terminate in the center.

Despite differential quality in production, both thimbles appear to have been deep-drawn. This process was monopolized by the city of Nuremberg until the late 18th century. Only when the technique of producing metallically pure zinc was acquired by England and the rest of Germany did Nuremberg lose its control of the market for deep-drawn thimbles (Greif 1984:28–30). Therefore, the two thimbles recovered from Venezuela and the Dominican Republic probably were produced in Nuremberg and exported to Spain.

Historical records indicate that trade in thimbles between Spain and Germany developed as early as 1428 (Feldhaus 1931, cited in Holmes 1988), well before links between the two countries were solidified by the Hapsburg presence in 1520. Deagan notes that Spain was unable to supply the increasing demands of its colonies for manufactured goods and thus relied heavily upon imports from Genoa and northern Europe. Goods were shipped first to Seville, then exported to the colonies. As a result, "the material assemblages of the Spanish colonies ought to be of multiple Old World origins from 1503 onward" (Deagan 1987:20). Not surprisingly, then, Nuremberg thimbles appear archaeologically at early Spanish sites throughout the circum-Caribbean region.

The use of nautical archaeology for dating thimbles has been extensively explored by Holmes (1986). A particularly interesting example was recovered from a mid-16th-century Portuguese wreck in the Seychelles. The brass thimble illustrated by Blake and Green (1986:18) displays indentations which are strikingly similar to those of the Nueva Cadíz and Convento sites. Punch marks are unevenly spaced and sized and encircle the crown; indentations are square or rectangular in shape.

A second group of early thimbles, also securely dated archaeologically, have circular or reversed D-shaped indentations. Two examples from Puerto Real, Haiti, display indentations spiralling around the crown. Like the two Nuremberg examples, these thimbles have been hand-punched or drilled. The dates of 1503–1578 for the Puerto Real site (Deagan 1987:8–9) correspond to the period that predates mechanical stamping. A third brass thimble of this type was recovered from Panama la Vieja, Panama (PA-3), 1519–1671 (Deagan 1987). However the hand-made spiralling indentations date this artifact to the 16th century (Figure 3). Like the examples above, indentations are circular in shape, rather than the elongated or rectangular type which characterizes the Nuremberg examples.

By 1620, the technique of hand punching, or

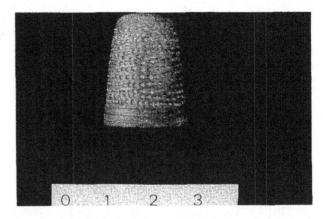

FIGURE 3. Sixteenth-century hand-indented thimble from Panamá la Vieja. (Courtesy of Florida Museum of Natural History.)

drilling, indentations was disappearing with the advent and spread of mechanical knurling—the process of indenting a thimble mechanically rather than by hand. By 1650, virtually all indentations were machine-made (Holmes 1987a:9). Therefore, all thimbles with evenly spaced and sized indentations were manufactured sometime after 1600.

By the beginning of the 17th century, the Nuremberg monopoly on thimble production was in decline. At the same time, the Dutch casting industry was steadily expanding. Large numbers of Dutch thimbles were exported to France and to the Dutch colonies in North America throughout the 1600s (Holmes 1985:135–136; cf. Greif 1984:42).

A tall domed thimble found during an unprovenienced surface collection in Haiti displays several features typical of the Dutch industry (Figure 4). Recovered from the site of En Bas Saline, which was originally a contact-period Taino village, this thimble is cast brass, which distinguishes it from earlier deep-drawn Nuremberg thimbles. Noël Hume (1969:256) noted that thimbles produced until ca. 1650 may be characterized by tonsuring. This example from Haiti displays a bald spot in the very center of the crown. The tonsured crown gradually declined in frequency and entirely disappeared by around 1650 (Holmes [1987b]:3). The high dome and large, regularly shaped circular indentations are characteristic of thimbles produced in the Netherlands during this period.

FIGURE 4. Unprovenienced surface collection from En Bas Saline, Haiti. Note the high, domed shape and large, regularly-shaped circular indentations characteristic of Dutch thimbles. (Courtesy of Florida Museum of Natural History.)

in concentric circles. Indentations on the crown and those encircling the sides may be separated by a ring of unmarked brass or may be distinguished by differential size. Note, for example, the small size of the crown indentations in Figure 4 in comparison to those marking the sides.

In the Spanish examples analyzed for this study, circular indentations spiralling around the crown disappear by the mid-17th century. While thimbles after 1650 may have circular indentations on the crown, they are arranged in rows or concentric circles rather than in a spiral design.

Dutch thimbles of the 17th century are rarely decorated and maintain a simplicity of design thereafter. One possible explanation is the increased popularity of silver thimbles. Attention to design and ornamentation was lavished upon 17th-century silver thimbles, while brass thimbles acquired a reputation as common needleworking tools (Holmes [1987b]:3), useful rather than decorative.

With the apparent exception of the Dutch industry, thimbles were becoming increasingly straight sided by the 1600s (Woodfield 1981:157). The dome shape was gradually abandoned, and thimbles began to acquire the shape which they retain to this day. Excavations at the Jamestown site, inhabited between 1607 and 1699 (Cotter and Hudson 1957:16), yielded both brass and silver thimbles (Cotter and Hudson 1957:50). Several examples have waffle crowns and vertical sides and are undecorated for the most part. Although the dates for the site encompass an entire century, stylistically these thimbles date to the latter part of the 1600s, and probably to the last quarter, ca. 1675–1700.

Two thimbles from the site of Aldgate, London, which have been dated contextually to ca. 1670–1720, also display honeycomb patterning and hatched crowns. Measuring 2.1–2.4 cm, both thimbles are straight sided (Thompson et al. 1984:114–115). Thompson, Grew, and Schofield observe that one thimble was constructed in two separate pieces, the crown being attached to the body. This two-piece construction can be traced to technological change in manufacturing and may parallel the switch to machine-made indentations. Holmes

Thimbles of this type are frequently referred to as "French" (Holthuizen 1984:14–15), perhaps because of the large number exported to that country during the 17th century. Although the Spanish were a formidable presence on Hispaniola in the first half of the 16th century, by the 1600s their settlements were largely abandoned. This Dutch thimble, then, may have originated at a French sugar plantation called Montholon, established in 1650 on the site of the original Taino village.

In contrast to the spiral pattern featured by hand-punched thimbles of the 1500s, thimbles from the 17th century display circular indentations aligned

(1985:137) notes that some 17th-century brass thimbles were constructed in two pieces by applying the crown to the inside rim of the body of the thimble.

Thimbles recovered from Spanish sites dating to the 1700s display a uniformity of shape and design which is unmistakable, and they closely resemble the British thimbles discussed above. The de Hita-Gonzales domestic site (SA 7–4) at St. Augustine, Florida, yielded several brass thimbles. Although artifacts from the 18th through the 20th centuries were recovered, the closed context of the second of two stratigraphic zones has been securely dated to the 1700s (Shephard 1975:20, 32, 1983:71).

Even, honeycomb-patterned indentations characterize thimbles from this period (Figure 5). The indentations encircling the sides of these thimbles are regular and closely spaced. The crowns are distinguished by a hatched waffle pattern spatially distinct from the indented sides. A virtually identical example was recovered from the late 18th- to early 19th-century context of the site of Spaulding's Lower Store (8Pu23) in central Florida. This thimble was probably an item of trade between the Seminole and British colonists. It displays the three primary characteristics of machine-made thimbles of the 18th century: honeycomb indentations, waffle crown, and outwardly rolled rims.

This period of intense production and increased uniformity makes identification more difficult, but not impossible. The two-piece construction of the Aldgate thimble may be an excellent dating feature. At the Second Spanish period domestic site of de León (SA 26–1), St. Augustine, the crown of a thimble was recovered. It had been separately manufactured and attached, since it was fully intact with no evidence of corrosion. Two-piece construction of thimbles originated in the latter half of the 17th century; however, this feature demands further research before a secure date can be determined.

While thimbles of this period usually have rolled edges, the best identifying characteristic of late 17th- to 18th-century thimbles are the even pattern-stamped indentations. The hatched pattern in conjunction with honeycomb indentations originated sometime during the 1600s and has remained fairly consistent.

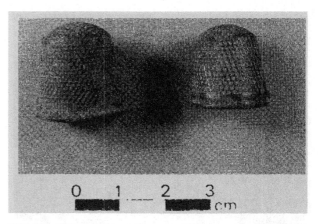

FIGURE 5. Two 18th-century thimbles recovered from the de Hita site (SA 7–4), St. Augustine, Florida. Note the even, honeycomb-patterned indentations, waffle crown, and outwardly-rolled rims. (Courtesy of Florida Museum of Natural History.)

One example from the de Hita site displays evenly spaced indentations, however the pattern begins halfway up the sides of the thimble. The lower portion of the body is not indented, nor are the edges rolled. A similar example was recovered by Hale Smith (1965:114) at the excavation of the town of Santa Rosa Pensacola, 1722–1752. Concentric rings of small circular indentations abruptly end three-quarters of the way down the length of the sides. A series of rings completes the design to the unrolled rim. The settlement of Santa Rosa was destroyed by a tropical storm in 1752 after 30 years of habitation (Smith 1965:4).

The dates for this site dovetail neatly with those of the de Hita site. The historical reconstruction of the genealogy of early St. Augustine families has revealed that, in 1736, Gerónimo José de Hita y Salazar married Juana de Avero and thereafter resided on the de Hita property (Deagan 1983:69). Evidence such as this, which details family composition in terms of both gender and age, can be positively correlated with material remains recovered archaeologically.

Gender and Age Correlation

Fundamentally, historical archaeology contributes to analyses of socially constructed relationships through material remains. Material goods such as sewing implements may potentially be used to address questions of household organization and production, status, and the division of labor (Conkey and Gero 1991:17). McEwan (1991: 34) has noted that "[t]he archaeological correlates of Spanish women are associated mostly with their domestic responsibilities." Sewing, a major occupation of European women in the Spanish colonies, is represented archaeologically in the omnipresence of thimbles at domestic sites. Closely associated with the role of women in household production—at least in European contexts—thimbles have the potential to illuminate both the presence and role of women archaeologically. At historic colonial sites in particular, the correlation of thimbles with the documented residence of women and children confirms their reliability as material indicators of gender and age.

In contrast, open-topped thimble rings, such as those recovered in quantity from the site of Concepción de la Vega, are most often the tool of the tailor. At least two thimble rings were also recovered at Jamestown; both displayed large indentations (Cotter and Hudson 1957:51) more suitable for heavy leather work than for embroidery or fine sewing. Other pursuits which also required thimble rings included harness-making, saddlery, upholstery, and shoemaking (Holmes 1985:163). In European and colonial contexts, at least, these were occupations associated primarily with males.

Less obvious, perhaps, is the correlation which exists between thimbles and the presence of female children. As part of their domestic education and perhaps also as a reflection of their role in household production, young girls were provided with the tools of their mothers and other female relatives in miniature form. Thus, children's thimbles approximating 1 cm in height abound at Spanish colonial sites (Figure 6) (Holmes 1985:169).

Two children's thimbles were recovered from the de Hita site, where five children grew to maturity in the 18th century (Deagan 1983:69). The relative invisibility of children in terms of material culture demands innovation and detailed study of artifacts which may indicate their presence. Greater attention to thimbles as age and gender

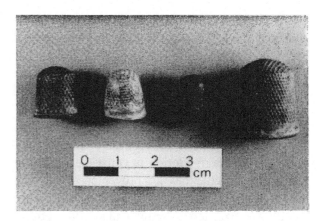

FIGURE 6. Three 18th-century childrens' thimbles (*left*), and an adult's thimble (*right*) for comparison. All thimbles were recovered at the de Hita site with the exception of the second specimen from the right, recovered from Useppa Island, Florida. (Courtesy of Florida Museum of Natural History.)

correlates may help to alleviate this bias in materials recovered archaeologically.

Thimbles Recovered from Native American Sites

Although this discussion has focused on thimbles recovered from Spanish sites in the circum-Caribbean region, thimbles also have been documented in Native American contexts. Beyond the confines of European patterns of use, thimbles as indicators of gender and age are no longer valid. McEwan (1991:34) writes that "Spanish women were important purveyors of Spanish culture among Native American . . . domestics with whom they sustained daily contact." Such culture was material as well as socioreligious. As a result, thimbles are recovered rather frequently in Native American contexts. The impact of trade on the indigenous material assemblage compounded the effects of cultural exchanges occurring within Spanish households.

The use of thimbles as tiny bells by Native American populations has been fairly well documented. Thimble bells of different sizes adorned clothing, bags, and pouches (Holmes 1985:234).

Erica Hill

Noël Hume (1969:256) noted that holes were punched in the crown of trade thimbles, which were then strung on thongs over glass beads. The result was both ornamental and musical. Holmes (1985:234) dates this innovation to the late 18th century.

The design of a waffle-crowned thimble (Figure 6, second from the right) recovered from Useppa Island in southern Florida is consistent with this date. The thimble has no provenience, but was most certainly fashioned as a child's thimble. While the size and patterning place this thimble securely within the 1700s, the tiny circular hole through the center of the crown suggests Native American decorative use rather than an educational purpose in the European tradition.

Another interesting example was recovered from the Philip Mound site, Polk County, central Florida. This Native American burial site was looted; however, a silver thimble was recovered with the crown pierced, probably for suspension (Benson 1967:126).

Conclusion

Thimbles, so often an item of exchange in the historic colonial period, are highly context-specific. Size, indentations, and subsequent alteration of thimbles, when closely observed, may indicate not only patterns of use, such as fine needlework or tailoring, but also the age and gender of the owner. Outside of historic European contexts, thimbles acquired though trade may be used as ornaments.

As an artifact commonly recovered from domestic sites, thimbles are potential date markers. The well-documented history of the thimblemaking industry in Europe, from small medieval workshops where metalsmiths wrought thimbles by hand to the machine-stamping of the 18th century, and the parallel changes in form and design provide a framework for typing and identification of European thimbles recovered archaeologically.

ACKNOWLEDGMENTS

Sincere thanks to Kathleen Deagan for advice and encouragement, and to Elise LeCompte-Baer for her patient assistance. Ryan J. Wheeler gave generously of his time and brought several sources to my attention. I would also like to thank Barbara J. Little for her careful reading and valuable comments.

REFERENCES

BENSON, CARL A.
1967   The Philip Mound: A Historic Site. *Florida Anthropologist* 20(3&4):118–132.

BLAKE, WARREN, AND JEREMY GREEN
1986   A Mid-XVI-Century Portuguese Wreck in the Seychelles. *International Journal of Nautical Archaeology and Underwater Exploration* 15(1):1–23.

CONKEY, MARGARET W., AND JOAN M. GERO
1991   Tensions, Pluralities, and Engendering Archaeology: An Introduction to Women and Prehistory. In *Engendering Archaeology: Women and Prehistory*, edited by Joan M. Gero and Margaret Conkey, pp. 3–30. Basil Blackwell, Oxford.

COTTER, JOHN L., AND J. PAUL HUDSON
1957   *New Discoveries in Jamestown*. National Park Service, Washington, D.C.

DAVIDSON, GLADYS R.
1952   *Corinth*. Vol. 12, *The Minor Objects*. Princeton University Press, Princeton, New Jersey.

DEAGAN, KATHLEEN
1987   *Artifacts of the Spanish Colonies of Florida and the Caribbean, 1500–1800*. Vol. 1, *Ceramics, Glassware, and Beads*. Smithsonian Institution Press, Washington, D.C.

DEAGAN, KATHLEEN (EDITOR)
1983   *Spanish St. Augustine: The Archaeology of a Colonial Creole Community*. Academic Press, New York.

FELDHAUS, FRANZ MARIA
1931   *Die technik der antike und des mittelalters*. Akademische verlagsgesellschaft Athenaion, Wildpark-Potsdam.

GREIF, HELMUT
1984   *Talks about Thimbles: A Cultural Historical Study*. Fingerhutmuseum Creglingen, Klagenfurt, Austria.

GROVES, SYLVIA
1966   *The History of Needlework Tools and Accessories*. Country Life Books, London.

HOLMES, EDWIN F.
1985   *A History of Thimbles*. Cornwall Books, London.
1986   Nautical Archaeology. *Thimble Collector's International Bulletin*, July:2–5.
1987a   Early Brass Thimbles. *Thimble Collector's International Bulletin*, July:3–11.

[1987b]Finds Research Group, 700–1700, Datasheet 9. On file, Archaeology Department, Castle Museum, Norwich, England.

1988 Letter from Edwin F. Holmes to Elise V. LeCompte, 29 October. On file, Florida Museum of Natural History, University of Florida, Gainesville.

HOLTHUIZEN, HENNY
1984 Working Thimbles in Amsterdam, 1550–1700. *De Vingerhoed,* June:13–15. Amstelveen.

McEWAN, BONNIE G.
1991b The Archaeology of Women in the Spanish New World. *Historical Archaeology* 25(4):33–41.

MOORHOUSE, STEPHEN
1971 Finds from Basing House, Hampshire (ca. 1540–1645): Part Two. *Post-Medieval Archaeology* 5:35–76.

NOËL HUME, IVOR
1969 *A Guide to Artifacts of Colonial America.* Knopf, New York.

SHEPARD, STEVEN J.
1975 The Geronimo José de Hita y Salazar Site: A Study of *Criollo* Culture in Colonial St. Augustine. Unpublished M.A. thesis, Department of Anthropology, Florida State University, Tallahassee.

1983 The Spanish *Criollo* Majority in Colonial St. Augustine. In *Spanish St. Augustine: The Archaeology of a Colonial Creole Community,* edited by Kathleen Deagan, pp. 65–97. Academic Press, New York.

SMITH, HALE
1965 Archaeological Excavations at Santa Rosa Pensacola. Florida State University, *Notes on Anthropology* 10. Tallahassee.

STEANE, JOHN
1984 *The Archaeology of Medieval England and Wales.* University of Georgia Press, Athens.

THOMPSON, ALAN, FRANCIS GREW, AND JOHN SCHOFIELD
1984 Excavations at Aldgate, 1974. *Post-Medieval Archaeology* 18:1–148.

WOODFIELD, CHARMAIN
1981 Finds from the Free Grammar School at the Whitefriars, Coventry, ca. 1545–1557/58. *Post-Medieval Archaeology* 15:81–159.

ERICA HILL
DEPARTMENT OF ANTHROPOLOGY
UNIVERSITY OF NEW MEXICO
ALBUQUERQUE, NEW MEXICO 87131

Knee, Garter, Girdle, Hat, Stock, and Spur Buckles from Seven Sites in Portsmouth, New Hampshire

Carolyn L. White

Published online: 17 February 2009

Abstract Material culture studies have begun to take new directions within the field of historical archaeology. Shoe buckles are the most familiar and readily identifiable type of buckle to archaeologists, but there are many other buckles worn as part of a person's dress that may be identified on archaeological sites. Knee, garter, girdle, hat, stock, and spur buckles are regularly recovered. These buckles can be used as an aid to dating archaeological strata and features, and can be employed to understand the kinds of clothing worn by site inhabitants. This paper presents and interprets an assemblage of buckles of assorted types recovered from seven 18th-century domestic sites in Portsmouth, New Hampshire.

Keywords Buckles · Dress · Eighteenth century · Gender · Portsmouth · New Hampshire

Introduction

How far historical archaeology has come since the publication of Ivor Noël Hume's *Artifacts of Colonial America* (1969)! Why is it, then, that this volume remains our most dependable resource for identifying unusual artifacts? Since the 1970s, archaeologists have been content to use a few comprehensive guides (Deagan 1987, 2002; Noël Hume 1969) as well as resources from other fields to interpret many classes of artifacts. Historical archaeologists are beginning to throw enthusiasm behind refining and developing an understanding of material culture beyond its use as a means toward understanding archaeological sites on a broad scale and to examine uncommon artifacts alongside the standard list. To be sure, archaeologists have put their excavated assemblages to work to understand broad questions about landscapes, households, institutions, and communities, but these research directions have largely employed artifacts in a manner that has emphasized typology, identification, and chronology (Cochran and Beaudry 2006).

Archaeologists have sought to learn as much as possible from those artifacts recovered in large amounts on archaeological sites; these classes have been valued for their potential for sensitivity to chronology, reflection of consumption patterns, and the massive amounts of readily retrievable data from a small number of sites. For example, of the twenty artifact-specific articles published in Brauner's *Approaches to Material Culture Research for Historical Archaeologists* (2000), six focus on ceramics, and seven examine glass artifacts. Five articles explore metal objects, and stone and leather artifacts are each examined in one article. These final seven articles represent some of the less novel interests in material culture in recent years.

By and large, following an understanding of temporal and technical change within a given artifact category, archaeologists also use artifacts to understand household change, to date features, and to interpret archaeological sites, large and small, in a general way. Archaeologists have grouped individually meaningful artifacts under broad categories, as they try to use the artifactual data to understand generalized activities, resulting in a diminishment of the interpretive potential of rare sorts of finds (Loren and Beaudry 2006; Beaudry 2002).

There is new interest in studying marginalized artifact categories in order to interpret archaeological sites in a way that combines traditional typological methods with historical archaeology's interest in examining aspects of identity and agency in the archaeological record (see, for example, Beaudry 2007; Loren 2001; Loren and Beaudry 2006; White 2005). This interest in material culture studies can be traced to a variety of influences, with interest in identity at the heart of many approaches (White and Beaudry 2009, provide a detailed examination of these influences and approaches).

This article reflects interest in material culture research as a sensitive tool for accessing the complexity of the past, used to interpret the archaeological record at the scale of the individual as well as at a larger group/community level of scale. Here, as elsewhere (White 2004, 2005), I place personal adornment at the center of study and examine less common types of buckles. Simple identification of the temporal and technical aspects of these atypical—but hardly unknown—objects gives way to understanding their use to assert or affirm gender, class, age, and status. These were visible objects, worn on the body's surface, with a function that permits insight into additional aspects of dress as well as an understanding of the broader social milieu in which they were worn.

"Other" Buckles

Beginning in the seventeenth century, buckles were important elements of dress, serving both functional and decorative purposes on men and women's clothing. Archaeologists encounter shoe buckles most often and they are the most readily identifiable of all buckle types. Buckles were used to fasten all manner of clothing, however, and this article focuses on several less familiar sorts of buckles: knee, boot or garter, girdle, hat, stock, and spur buckles. These buckle forms are regularly recovered on historical sites, but in such small numbers, they have been unrecognized, offered little interpretive attention, or misidentified as more common shoe buckles. This article focuses on buckles recovered in excavations in Portsmouth, New Hampshire.

The assemblage was recovered in excavations undertaken between 1975 and 2000 by the archaeology division of Strawbery Banke Museum. Four of the sites are on the grounds of Strawbery Banke Museum—the Sherburne, Cotton, Rider-Wood, and Shapiro sites—and three are located elsewhere in Portsmouth—the Richard Hart, Hart-Shortridge, and Richard Shortridge sites (Fig. 1). All are domestic sites; the buckles described here were recovered in contexts dating to between 1680 and 1820.

Buckle parts are consistent from one type to the next, and consist of two basic components: the frame (also called the ring) and the chape (Fig. 2). The chape is further subdivided into three elements: the pin, the roll, and the tongue. The pin is set across the underside of the frame, and the ends of the pin taper to fit into holes drilled in the frame. The placement of the pin terminals is a key element for identifying the function of a particular buckle. The roll hinges on the pin. It exhibits considerable variation, and its form is a key element used to determine a buckle's function. Similarly, the tongue, which hinges on the pin and points away from the roll, can take a variety of shapes that make it very useful in diagnosing buckle types. The form of both the frame and chape is instrumental in identifying the particular buckle form one has encountered.

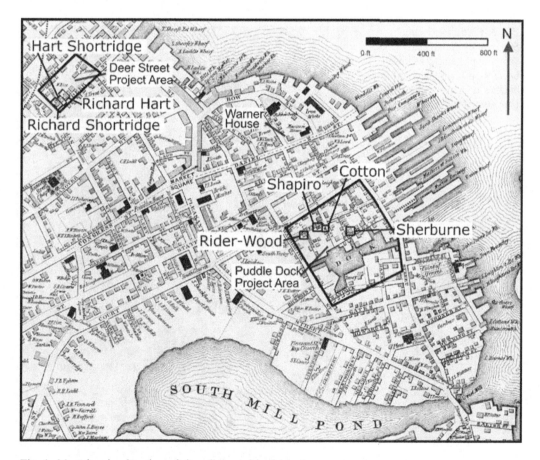

Fig. 1 Map showing location of sites discussed in the text

Fig. 2 Knee buckle parts

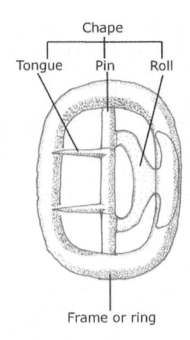

Fig. 3 Portrait of Roger Sherman by Ralph Earl, 1775, showing placement of knee buckles and non-matching shoe buckles (Courtesy Yale University)

Fig. 4 Knee buckle recovered at the Cotton House Site, Portsmouth, New Hampshire (front and back)

Knee Buckles

Knee buckles were placed on the breeches' kneeband and were used to hold the breeches tightly below or above the knee. These buckles had a secondary function of holding up the stockings (Fig. 3; Wright 1990, p. 83).

A knee buckle recovered in excavations at the Cotton House in Portsmouth, New Hampshire, illustrates the two main characteristics of knee buckles (Fig. 4). Knee buckles usually were worn so that the long axis of the buckle was oriented vertically;

Fig. 5 Knee buckle chape

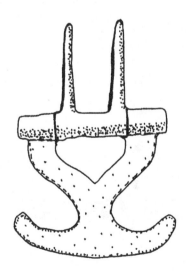

hence the pin terminals are on the short axis of the buckle. This vertical orientation is a key to identification, but it does not definitively mark a buckle as a knee buckle, since vertical orientation is shared by other buckle forms (see hat and stock buckles below). In addition, knee buckles were sometimes oriented horizontally. The Cotton House chape remains attached to the frame, and possesses an anchor-shaped roll with a half-heart cut out and a double tongue. The shape of the chape is a second and more reliable identifying characteristic (Fig. 5). Knee buckle chapes are characterized by their anchor-shaped rolls, which typically have a half-heart cut-out design. The chapes have double or triple tongues, distinguishing them from those anchor chapes used on shoe buckles, which usually have a single tongue (Whitehead 1996, p. 111). The roll was used to hold the knee buckle in place on the kneeband (Fig. 6). It was pushed through a slit in the kneeband, and the buckle was turned 90 degrees. The shape of the roll prevented the buckle from coming out of the slit (Bryant 1988).

An additional key to identifying knee buckles is that they were usually made in flat shapes, and do not have the dramatic convex shape that shoe buckles have to accommodate the shape of the foot (White 2005, p. 45). Despite these diagnostic characteristics, when the frame is recovered without the chape—as is so often the case in archaeological contexts—knee buckles are difficult to identify. It is particularly onerous to distinguish a small shoe buckle from a knee buckle when the chape is missing and the buckle has a horizontal orientation. Further complicating this is the fact that knee buckles were made in the same kinds of shapes and patterns as shoe buckles.

Knee buckles recovered in Portsmouth demonstrate the range of sizes in which knee buckles were made—typically measuring a maximum of 30 × 40 mm (Whitehead 1996, p. 111). A knee buckle recovered at the Sherburne Site measures 18 x 16 mm is an example of a small knee buckle (Fig. 7). On the opposite end of the size spectrum is a knee buckle recovered at the Hart-Shortridge Site, a large knee buckle measuring 35 mm on its longest axis (Fig. 8). The anchor-shaped roll is visible at the back of the buckle.

Dating

There are several temporal shifts in the size and use of knee buckles, which are helpful aids to identification and interpretation. Knee buckles were used to secure

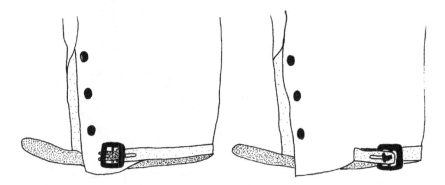

Fig. 6 Placement of knee buckle on breeches kneeband

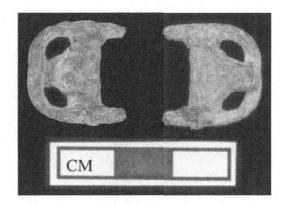

Fig. 7 Knee buckle recovered at the Sherburne Site, Portsmouth, New Hampshire (front and back)

the kneeband beginning around 1735; previously the kneeband buttoned (Cunnington and Cunnington 1972, p. 63). Although buttons continued to be used on breeches along with knee buckles, the kneeband was usually buckled after 1750. It was fashionable to buckle breeches above the knee in the 1750s; by the 1780s breeches were buckled below the knee (Fig. 3; Bryant 1988; Cunnington 1964, p. 103).

The size and shape of knee buckles shifted through the 18th century. In the 1750s knee buckles were small and square in shape. In the next decade their size varied, but by the 1770s knee buckles were relatively large in size (Cunnington and Cunnington 1972, pp. 63, 211) as knee buckles, like most accessories, trended toward increased size (Wallace 1971). In the 1770s both oval and square knee buckles were worn, with neither shape predominant (Cunnington and Cunnington 1972, pp. 63, 211). Excavations at the Sherburne Site recovered a square knee buckle in a 1770s context (Fig. 9).

In the 1780s knee buckles were large and oval and were placed vertically, though square buckles were also worn (Fig. 10). An oval buckle from the Rider-Wood site embodies the most common form in the 1780s and into the 1790s. Later in the 1790s buckles were superseded by the tie, although knee buckles continued to be worn into the early part of the 19th century (Wallace, 1971; Cunnington and Cunnington 1972, pp. 63, 211).

Fig. 8 Knee buckle recovered at the Hart-Shortridge Site, Portsmouth, New Hampshire (front and back)

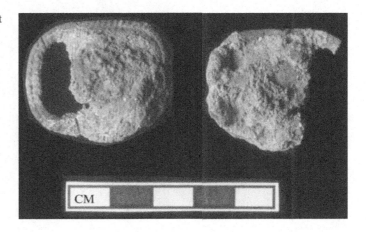

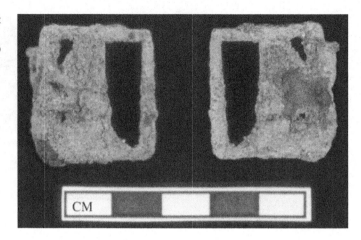

Fig. 9 Knee buckle recovered at the Sherburne Site, Portsmouth, New Hampshire (front and back)

Style

Whether oval or square, large or small, vertically or horizontally oriented, knee buckles exhibited a variety of decoration. Generally, the decoration is fairly restrained, particularly when compared to the intricate embellishment found on shoe buckles (see White 2005, pp. 39–41). Knee buckles often contrasted shoe buckles, which may explain their less ornate appearance. Decorative motifs ranged from scalloped edges (Fig. 10), perhaps the most typical kind of elaboration, molded rope designs (Fig. 8), simple grooves and carved notches (Fig. 11), or no decoration at all. The fanciest knee buckles were set with pastes.

Knee buckles could be purchased individually or in sets with matching shoe buckles. When sold in sets, the knee buckle was a more diminutive version of the larger shoe buckle. Non-matching knee and shoe buckles were worn together in common practice (Fig. 3).

Although knee buckles were a common element of dress, they were not worn by everyone. Knee buckles were less common among people of low socioeconomic means; rather, they secured their kneebands with ties or with buttons (Linda Welters,

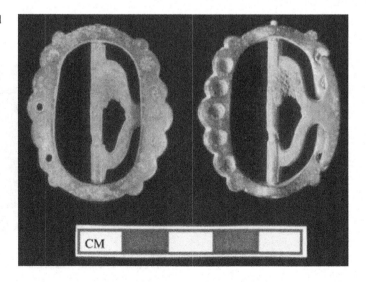

Fig. 10 Knee buckle recovered at the Rider-Wood Site, Portsmouth, New Hampshire (front and back)

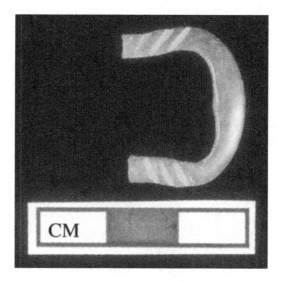

Fig. 11 Knee buckle recovered at the Sherburne Site, Portsmouth, New Hampshire

pers. comm.). In this sense, the presence of knee buckles is an indicator of social class. When worn, buckles reflected the status of the wearer through the material and level of decoration in consort with the rest of the wearer's physical appearance. Since knee buckles were worn on breeches, they also were worn exclusively by men, and are an artifact that reflects male gender and appearance.

Boot or Garter Buckles

Garters kept tall and close-fitting boots from falling down, and buckles were used to fasten the garters (Fig. 12). Top boots, fashionable in the last quarter of the 18th century,

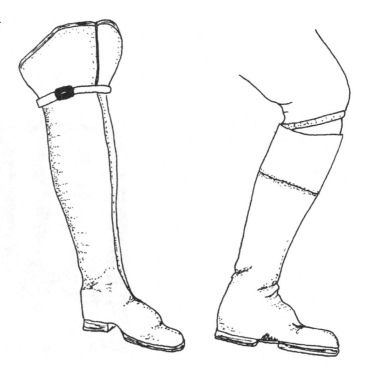

Fig. 12 Tall boot with garter and buckle over boot (left) and top boot with garter and buckle attached to inside posterior of boot (right)

were fastened with a strap that attached to the back of the boot and buckled above the knee. Garters were also used to keep stockings from falling down. Regardless of the function, boot and garter buckles have the same basic form: a rectangular shape measuring less than 25 mm wide. Boot or garter buckles do not posses a roll; they were fixed to the strap with a chape consisting of one to three sharp tongues fixed to the pin. Most boot or garter buckles are tinned copper-alloy and are otherwise undecorated; they may be confused with harness buckles due to their very simple appearance.

Two boot or garter buckles were identified in Portsmouth. The first, found at the Sherburne Site, is rectangular in shape and small in size—a prototypical example of the form of such buckles (Fig. 13). The chape is attached to this buckle, and it has two tongues and no roll. A similar buckle was recovered at the Richard Shortridge Site (Fig. 14). This buckle lacks a diagnostic chape, but its small size suggests its use as a garter or boot buckle.

Like knee buckles, boot and garter buckles were worn exclusively by men, and are a sensitive indicator of male gender. The plain form of these buckles makes it difficult to ascertain further social information as there is little differentiation from one garter or boot buckle to the next.

Girdle Buckles

Girdles were an element of fancy dress, and were fashionable for women beginning around 1740 (Cunnington and Cunnington 1972, p. 143). Girdles were narrow belts made of textiles or leather that fastened in the front of the gown with a bow or a buckle (Cunnington and Cunnington 1972, p. 143). Girdle buckles do not have a characteristic shape, but were quite simple early in the 18th century, often made in two interlocking parts. Later in the 18th century, girdle buckles could be very elaborate, made in an assortment of materials, set with stones and pastes, with fancy baroque patterns as well as gadrooning and interlaced designs (see d'Allemagne 1928, pl. XLII for multiple examples). Alloys were used to make less expensive versions (d'Allemagne 1928; Wallace 1936, p. 824). Girdle buckles could be very valuable and, like many other buckles, were often repaired when they broke.

Fig. 13 Boot or garter buckle recovered at the Sherburne Site, Portsmouth, New Hampshire (front and back)

Fig. 14 Boot or garter buckle recovered at the Richard Short-ridge Site, Portsmouth, New Hampshire

By the early 19th century, the placement of the girdle rose to just below the breasts, and was worn with neo-classical fashions. These were prominent dress embellishments on otherwise simple garments. At this time, girdles commonly were made of leather or velvet and fastened with a simple single or double buckle of metal (Scarisbrick 1994, p. 358). Jewelry pattern books show neo-classical designs with floral and natural motifs, and clasping hands motifs were also favored (Scarisbrick 1994, p. 358).

A single girdle buckle was recovered at the Shapiro Site in an 18th century context (Fig. 15). It is copper alloy with a serrated end and notched decoration on the surface. It would have been plated or tinned when it was worn.

In contrast to the buckles discussed so far, girdle buckles fall into the realm of women's clothing. These are rare archaeological finds, as they are an uncommon element of dress and are often more fragile than other kinds of buckles. These are artifacts that reflect fancy dress, elite status, and female gender.

Hat Buckles

Hat buckles were worn on round hats as well as on tricornered hats (Cunnington and Cunnington 1972, p. 83), and they can be distinguished by their orientation and

Fig. 15 Girdle buckle recovered at the Shapiro Site, Portsmouth, New Hampshire (front and back)

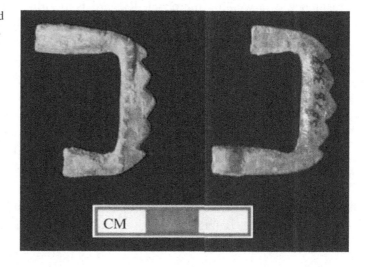

Fig. 16 Hat buckle recovered at the Sherburne Site, Portsmouth, New Hampshire

shape. Hat buckles are oriented vertically and the frames were rectangular, oblong, or octagonal, and were commonly decorated with rococo patterns. Simple nail-head designs were also typical (Cunnington and Cunnington 1972, p. 83; Whitehead 1996, p. 113).

A hat buckle was recovered at the Sherburne Site in a deposit dating to 1800 (Fig. 16). This is a pewter buckle with molded scalloped grooves. The light construction of this buckle suggests its use on a hat, serving as decoration more than as functional fastener.

Hat buckles could be worn by both men and women and, as such, are not gendered artifacts. They are indicative of elevated socioeconomic status since they are an accessory with little functionality, but since inexpensive hat buckles were available, attention to the form and material of these buckles is critical to interpretation.

Stock Buckles

A single fragment of a stock buckle frame was recovered in Portsmouth, at the residence of a wealthy merchant, Richard Hart (Fig. 17). The stock is a neckcloth that wrapped around the neck and buckled or tied in back. Despite the fact that stock buckles were often hidden by clothing or by a person's hair, stock buckles frequently were very fancy. They were made of silver, plated or tinned copper and tin alloys, or pinchbeck, and were worked, plain, and set with gems or pastes. The nail-head design was a common motif used by silversmiths on stock buckles (Fig. 18; Parsons 1983, pp. 27–28). Wigs and hair were sometimes designed or styled specifically to allow others a peek at the buckle. Stock buckles were worn by men as part of male formal dress, and as such they reflect male gender and high socioeconomic status.

Stock buckles can be identified through the shape of the frame, their orientation, and chape. The frame is usually rectangular or oblong and flat. Stock buckles were oriented vertically with the pin terminals on the short side of the frame, although the Sherburne buckle is fragmentary, it exhibits this verticality based on the form of the frame at the point where the buckle has broke. Stock buckles are readily identified

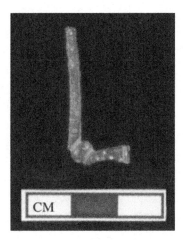

Fig. 17 Stock buckle recovered at the Richard Hart Site, Portsmouth, New Hampshire

by their chape, with its characteristic roll with three or four buttons that fit into corresponding buttonholes on the stock. The chape tongue had, typically, four evenly spaced thin spikes to attach to the stock.

Spur Buckles

Spur buckles were used to fasten spur straps across the boot instep, which held the spurs fast to the wearer's heel. These buckles have narrow frames, sometimes decorated with molded outer edges. The sides of the frame are often pointed or enlarged and the surfaces can be embellished with molded rosettes or floral decorations. The chapes may have hook attachments for the spurs (Whitehead 1996, pp. 81–82; Nöel Hume 1969, p. 85).

Two spur buckles were recovered in the Portsmouth excavations. The first is a copper alloy spur buckle recovered at the Sherburne Site (Fig. 19). This buckle has molded square protrusions at either end of the central pin and has pointed ends. The second spur buckle is a fragment that was recovered at the Richard Hart Site (Fig. 20). It is copper alloy and has angled corners and a raised ridge at the top of the central pin. Both of these would have been tinned or plated at the time when they were worn.

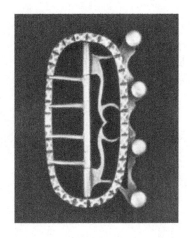

Fig. 18 Stock buckle made by silversmith Mark Nelson (Courtesy Winterthur Museum, Garden, and Library)

Fig. 19 Spur buckle recovered at the Sherburne Site, Portsmouth, New Hampshire

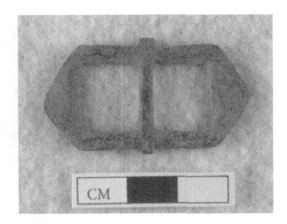

Spur buckles, like many of the buckles discussed here, fall in the realm of male dress and reflect male appearance. They are also associated with fashionable dress, as spurs, beyond their functional equestrian use, were also stylish accessories in the 18th century.

Conclusion

Shoe buckles are readily identified on archaeological sites of the historic period, but buckles were used to fasten myriad other garments and clothing items. Buckles were important items of personal adornment, serving both functional and fashionable purposes on men and women's clothing. Buckles could be valued for their monetary worth, their use as a garment fastener, and for their role in social display. As items of display buckles can be used to understand aspects of class construction as they point to particular pieces of clothing and reflect individual appearance. The quality and fashionability of buckles also point to social class and economic means. Similarly, since particular buckle forms can be associated with distinctive pieces of clothing, buckles are informative artifacts that speak to gender and appearance.

The excavated examples of knee, garter, girdle, hat, stock and spur buckles from Portsmouth are a small sample of the wide variety of forms that existed in 18th century America. There was immense diversity in their form and decoration, which these buckles only begin to demonstrate.

Fig. 20 Spur buckle recovered at the Richard Hart Site, Portsmouth, New Hampshire

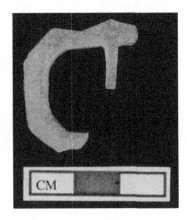

The Historical Archaeology Laboratory Handbook

Acknowledgements A version of this paper was given at the January 2003 Society for Historical Archaeology meetings in Providence, Rhode Island. I would like to thank the support extended to me while conducting this research by the Archaeology Division at Strawbery Banke Museum; Winterthur Museum, Garden, and Library; and the Department of Archaeology at Boston University. I am grateful to Chuck Orser and two anonymous reviewers for their cogent comments on an earlier draft of this paper. Of course, any errors, omissions, and shortcomings are my own.

References

d'Allemagne HR (1928) Les accessoires du costume et du mobilier. Schemit, Paris

Beaudry MC (2002) Re-vision: filling gaps and silences in how we think and write about small finds. Paper presented at the Annual Meeting of the Society for Historical Archaeology, Mobile, Alabama

Beaudry MC (2007) Findings: the material culture of needlework and sewing. Yale University Press, New Haven

Brauner DR (ed) (2000) Approaches to material culture research for historical archaeologists: a reader from historical archaeology. 2nd edn. Society for Historical Archaeology, Tucson

Bryant NO (1988) Buckles and buttons: an inquiry into fastening systems used on eighteenth-century English breeches. Dress 14:27–36

Cochran MD, Beaudry MC (2006) Material culture studies and historical archaeology. In: Hicks D, Beaudry MC (eds) The cambridge companion to historical archaeology. Cambridge University Press, Cambridge, pp 191–204

Cunnington P (1964) Costume in pictures. Studio Vista Limited, London

Cunnington CW, Cunnington P (1972) Handbook of english costume in the eighteenth century. Faber and Faber Limited, London

Deagan K (1987) Artifacts of the Spanish colonies of Florida and the Caribbean, 1500–1800, Vol. 1: ceramics, glassware, and beads. Smithsonian Institution Press, Washington, D. C

Deagan K (2002) Artifacts of the Spanish colonies of Florida and the Caribbean, 1500–1800, Vol. 2: portable personal possessions. Smithsonian Institution Press, Washington, D. C

Loren DD (2001) Social skins: orthodoxies and practices of dressing in the early colonial Lower Mississippi Valley. Journal of Social Archaeology 1(2):172–189

Loren DD, Beaudry MC (2006) Becoming American: small things remembered. In: Hall M, Silliman SW (eds) Historical Archaeology. Blackwell, Oxford, pp 251–271

Nöel Hume I (1969) A guide to artifacts of Colonial America. Knopf, New York

Parsons CS (1983) New Hampshire Silver. A. Brown Co., Exeter, NH

Scarisbrick D (1994) Jewellery in Britain, 1066–1837: a documentary, social, literary, and artistic survey. Michael Russell, Norwich, England

Wallace J (1936) Accessories to masculine fashion. Discovering Antiques 19:448–451

Wallace J (1971) Buttons and buckles. Discovering Antiques 35:821–825

White CL (2004) What the Warners wore: an archaeological investigation of visual appearance. Northeast Historical Archaeology 33:39–66

White CL (2005) American artifacts of personal adornment, 1680–1820: a guide to identification and interpretation. AltaMira Press, Latham

White CL, Beaudry MC (2009) Artifacts and personal identity. In: Majewski T, Gaimster D (eds) International Handbook of Historical Archaeology. Springer, New York

Whitehead R (1996) Buckles: 1250–1800. Greenlight Publishing, Chelmsford, Essex

Wright M (1990) Put on thy beautiful garments: rural new England clothing, 1783–1800. Clothes Press, East Montpelier, VT

A Classification System for Glass Beads for the Use of Field Archaeologists

Kenneth E. and Martha Ann Kidd

Abstract

As a result of examination of numerous collections of glass beads in northeastern North America and elsewhere, and as a result of a study of the procedures used in their manufacture, the authors propose a classification and nomenclature which they hope will permit exact descriptions and a reference base for all beads found in archaeological excavations. New bead types may be added to the system which is expansible to accommodate all possible variations.

Preface

Archaeologists working on sites occupied after the arrival of Europeans in northeastern North America, and indeed in other parts of the continent, frequently encounter glass beads. Describing these beads has proven to be frustrating for most archaeologists, involving the making of fine distinctions as to colour, size, shape and other characteristics between many similar specimens. To date, there has been no completely satisfactory frame of reference, such as has been available in other branches of archaeology, e.g., ceramics. Many classification systems have been set up, but none has proven very useful under field or laboratory conditions, and none has found wide acceptance – a necessary factor if there is to be ready comparison of finds from different sites. It is with some temerity, therefore, that the authors venture to submit one more system of classification to the archaeological community. They do so in the hope that it may be of practical use to those who feel the need of a new system.

Acknowledgements

Research work for this paper was first begun under a John Simon Guggenheim Fellowship which the senior author held in 1951-52 for the general study of trade goods among the American Indians of the Northeast. He was later assisted by a grant from the Corning Museum of Glass, given for the study of glass beads in the same area, and by aid toward clerical assistance from the Canada Council. To each of these agencies he wishes to acknowledge a deep debt of gratitude, for without such help the study could not have been carried to completion.

At the outset, virtually all of the important collections, both in private hands and in public museums in the Northeast, were examined by both authors, notes made upon individual specimens, and numerous photographs and drawings made. At later dates, collections in British and European museums were examined, a visit made to the glassworks at Murano, Italy, and archival and library research carried out.

Both authors wish to thank all those who made their collections available for study. Their names are many, and it would be impossible to list them all here, but special thanks are due to one of them, Mr. Charles F. Wray, of West Rush, New York. Mr. Wray not only made his extensive bead collection available to us for study, but also loaned us the specimens which appear on the cover. His interest in the subject and generosity in imparting his hard-won knowledge greatly enhanced the value of the research.

To Dr. Paul N. Perrot, Director of the Corning Museum of Glass, special thanks are due for encouragement and sound advice. The authors wish to emphasize, however, that they alone are responsible for whatever shortcomings the paper may have, as well as for any errors which may occur.

Kenneth E. and Martha Ann Kidd

1 Drawing a tube for glass beads.

This paper is part of a much more comprehensive investigation on the study of glass beads used for trade with the Indians of northeastern North America. Basic to such a study is the need for a satisfactory terminology and the authors, not finding one ready at hand, decided to try to work one out. After accomplishing this to their satisfaction, they decided not to await the publication of the larger work, but to make the results available to any who might wish to use it. It should be stressed, however, that our firsthand knowledge has been confined largely to specimens from the Northeast, and while the classification scheme should be of worldwide application, our specific knowledge does not extend to all of North America, and there may be many types which we have not seen.

There have always been, of course, terms by which the different kinds of beads have been known and identified. Some of them have referred, however vaguely, to physical characteristics; in this category we would place such terms as "pound," "seed" and "tube." Others, derived from sources now often obscure, are "macca," "cornaline" and "rosetta." None of these has any precise significance, and although they may be useful in the trade, are of no assistance to the archaeologist. The use of such terms as "pony" and "Russian" beads, seemingly not used extensively by dealers but rather by the consumer and by students, are equally valueless. In the Old World, individual types of beads were often called by specific names, but these likewise have no classificatory use. Within the present century, several systems have been devised for bead classification, but so far as the authors are aware, none will permit the identification of each and every glass bead known. The one proposed here will, it is hoped, make good that deficiency, or at least pave the way. It is based on the firsthand study of approximately 500 different types, and has been designed to be infinitely extensible.

This classification is based, in the first instance, upon the processes of manufacture; in the second, upon such physical

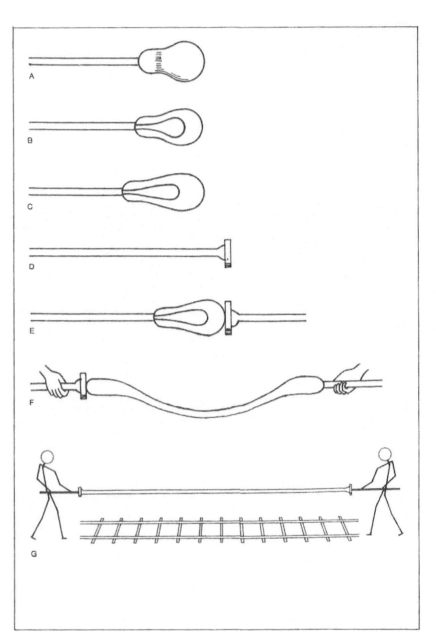

2 Inlay treatment for glass beads.

characteristics as shape, size and colour (including translucency and opacity). The last class of attributes encompasses verifiable entities, for it is possible to subject any given specimen to an examination with regard to them, and to compare said specimen with any other bead with respect to each. Processes of manufacture can also be determined by inspection. It should not be inferred from these remarks that the authors imply any sort of evolutionary development in the making of beads, but it is difficult, nevertheless, to see how some of the procedures used could have come into being except through some developmental process such as is outlined below.

The manufacture of glass beads will be discussed more fully in the book which is in preparation: but in order to understand the function of the classificatory system under discussion, it is necessary to have at least some understanding of how beads are made. To this end, the following extremely brief and condensed synopsis of the various processes is given.

Glass, a complicated substance made from silica, an alkali, a stabilizer and (usually) a colouring agent, is molten when raised to a high temperature, and solid at room temperature. In the molten state it is highly ductile, and while cooling can be manipulated into a vast variety of forms by using appropriate techniques. Beads may be made by two principle methods: (1) by drawing out a bubble of molten or viscid glass into a long, slender tube, and (2) by winding threads of molten glass around a wire which is later withdrawn. A third method, probably often used in conjunction with each of the above, is by molding the beads in two-part molds while the glass is still viscid.

The first method of bead manufacture requires the services of two men (Fig. 1). The first man gathers up a small amount of molten glass on the end of his blowing rod, and by blowing into the rod enlarges it to a bubble. He then puts the bubble into the mass of molten glass to gather up more material. At this time, he may either add more glass of the same colour or glass of

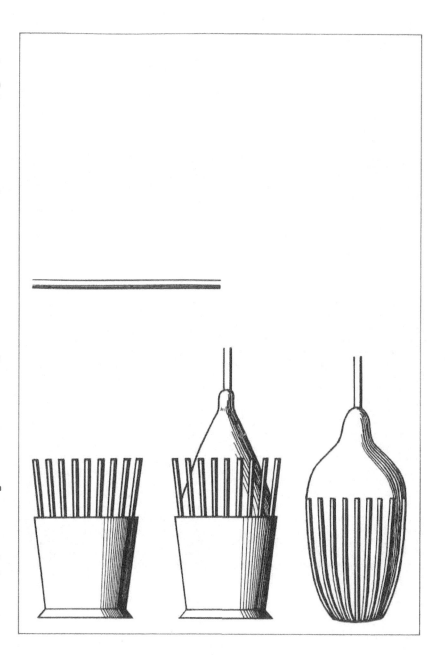

a different colour from another pot. If a different colour is added, the process is called "layering." Two or more colours may be used, and even five or six layers of different colours are not uncommon. If a simple round tube is required, the second man attaches another iron rod to the far end of the glass bubble, the blower hands his end to a servant and both these men then move in opposite directions until the glass becomes cool and will not pull out further. (In practice, neither of the runners, or *tiradors*, is the same man as he who withdraws the glass from the furnace and blows it.) The now rigid tube of glass is laid down on slabs of wood to cool (Fig. 1). When it has cooled sufficiently, it is broken up into short lengths, and these are finally chopped into sizes which will serve as beads. It is necessary to note that during the process of drawing, the proportions at any given point along the length of the tube remain constant. This means that the bore is almost uniform throughout, but it becomes smaller and smaller the more slender the tube becomes. We now have cylindrical beads either of monochrome or polychrome glass, depending upon whether one or more layers have been given to the bubble.

Other treatments than that described above may be given to the bubble. The first of these is the so-called inlay treatment, where "canes" or rods of coloured glass are affixed to it, ultimately producing striped beads. In this process, rods of the required colour are ranged around the inside wall of a pail-like container (Fig. 2). These rods may be themselves either simple or multiple. The bubble is introduced into the centre of the bucket and expanded sufficiently to cause the rods to adhere, whereupon it is re-introduced to the furnace just long enough to cause the rods to coalesce with the surface of the bubble, but not to lose their form. The bubble is then drawn as described above and the resulting tube bears the diminutive remains of the rods on its surface.

Another treatment may be given on the "marver," or board. The bubble, whether it is layered, unlayered, striped, or a com-

bination of these, is laid on the marver, and either flattened slightly, or paddled to make it triangular, square or some other shape in cross-section. If a corrugated marver is used, the bubble is rolled over it to press the corrugations into the sides. The bubble is then drawn in the usual way, and the finished tube will retain the shape, though not the dimensions given it on the marver. (Generally, when the bubble is rolled on the corrugated marver, it is layered in glass of another colour, and the process is repeated until five or six layers, and in some cases up to twelve, have been built up before it is drawn. The resulting bead is the so-called rosetta, star, or chevron.)

While the tube is being drawn, it may also be twisted. This applies not only to simple monochrome tubes drawn from the bubble as blown, but to layered, inset and marvered beads as well; thus it is possible, and indeed it happens, that one finds such complicated forms as beads which have been layered, striped, squared in section, and twisted.

Some beads, especially large ones, like big chevrons, are often ground at the ends and for a short distance along the sides in order to bring out the colour effects in the layering. Most, however, are not given this rather costly treatment.

Imperfectly shaped beads are not uncommon on Indian sites, and their classification poses a slight problem. Even twinned beads sometimes occur. Generally the intended form is easy to see and they are classified accordingly. It would appear that the Indians were not very critical: in fact, one gets the impression that they actually preferred these eccentric specimens.

The diameter of the finished product will depend entirely on the extent to which the bubble has been elongated; it may vary from an eighth of an inch or less to an inch or even more. When the tubes have cooled, they are broken into long pieces which can later be chopped on a block to the desired length; that is, anywhere from a sixteenth of an inch or thereabouts to three or four inches. They may either be left in this condition, or they may be subjected to

further treatment to reduce them to oval or rounded beads.

To effect this shaping, a mixture of ground charcoal and fine sand is worked into the orifices of the beads, and the whole is then placed in a metal container and re-subjected to heat. In order to keep the beads from fusing together while in this heated condition, the container is constantly agitated on an eccentric axle. This action, in conjunction with the heat, reduces the beads to a round shape, while the mixture of sand and charcoal prevents them from sticking together and the orifices from disappearing. When cool, the beads are separated from the mixture, washed, and then agitated for some time in bags of bran to produce a polished surface.

Whether left in tube form or made into round beads, the finished products are sorted, first on a set of sieves of graded sizes, and finally by hand, during which defective examples are removed. They are then strung into hanks, but nowadays this is less often done than packaging in bulk, in which form they are ready for shipment.

Whereas tube beads are mass produced in the sense that thousands may be made from a single bubble or gathering of glass (which, however, is individually fabricated), wire wound beads are made one by one. Wire which has been covered with chalk, or some similar substance to facilitate removal of the final product, is heated at a flame (originally fed by whale oil) and at the same time a cane or solid rod of glass, about as thick as a lead pencil, is heated and a thread started from it. This thread or strand of molten glass, which may be of any colour, is wound around the wire until a bead of the desired size and shape is built up. Indeed, threads of different colours may be introduced to make multicoloured beads; and glass insets of various kinds, such as simple dots, rosettes, or flowers, may be set into the matrix while it is still soft. Such beads, often called *suppialume*, are capable of almost infinite variation and attempts to classify them are consequently no more successful than other individually made, handcrafted products.

Although little is known of the process, it is quite apparent that in the past some beads were molded, and it seems safe to assume that this was accomplished in conjunction with the processes outlined above for the making of both tube and wire wound beads. Certainly there are many examples of beads which have been pinched in two-part molds; the so-called "raspberries," "melons," and facetted types being examples of such molded beads.

There is no problem, obviously, in determining when a bead has been molded, but it is not always quite so easy to decide whether a given specimen has been produced by the drawing method or by wire winding. Close inspection with a hand lens will usually reveal this, however, for in the former, the fibres of glass are arranged side by side longitudinally. This is often more clearly shown in tubular beads which have lain in the soil long enough to disintegrate slightly, at which stage the fibres show up quite clearly. In wire wound beads the fibres are arranged in heliacal fashion, round and round the circumference of the specimen. Such an arrangement is often obvious in the so-called milk glass beads. But perhaps of even greater help in deciding the method of manufacture is the presence of small air bubbles. In both processes, these tiny inclusions of air are bound to occur, and it is seldom that inspection will fail to reveal them. In the case of tube beads, little bubbles, like the fibres of glass, have been drawn out into long, thin shapes, a sure indication of the method used to make them. Just as certainly in the case of wire wound beads, the bubbles are either globular or oval and never elongated.

During the 17th, 18th and 19th centuries, the control of the ingredients was a somewhat haphazard affair for the exact science of chemistry had not yet arisen. The materials which went into the manufacture of glass depended on many variables, but chiefly upon the judgement of the man in charge. It is true that the proportions of the various ingredients which made glass of certain qualities was recognized and followed; but it is equally true that they were not accurately controlled. (A modern analogy would be with a cook who does not follow her recipe exactly in making a cake, but uses her experience and judgement.) Furthermore, the ingredients which went into the glass batch were not chemically pure resulting in considerable variation in the quality of the finished product, some being less stable than others, and so on.

This matter of chemical variation is especially important with regard to colour. It was well understood that certain materials, like copper salts, would produce specific colours; and this knowledge was fully utilized and expanded with increasing experience. But again the colouring chemical was not pure, and slight variations in colour inevitably resulted. Furthermore, the resulting colour could be affected by the nature of the batch into which the chemical was introduced; and if the batch were not uniform in all cases, colour variations could result no matter how pure the pigments were nor how accurately they were measured. All told, therefore, there is room for considerable variation in colour, and 18th century and earlier beads differ considerably in this regard from those made in the 19th and 20th centuries when strict standarization became the rule. In brief, one cannot expect to find consistency of colouring in these early beads; but on the other hand, one does find a rainbow range of beautiful soft colours, very different from the harsh, strident ones so frequently encountered in the modern product.

The Tube Bead Chart

The chart (Fig. 3) illustrating tube beads is divided into four quadrants. Contiguous quadrants can be described as units in themselves but this cannot be done with non-contiguous quadrants. The beads in the lower quadrants (I and III) are all basically tube forms; those in the upper quadrants (II and IV) have been modified to a round form by re-heating. Furthermore, the beads in quadrants I and II are "simple beads"; that is, they are basically monochrome but may have adventitious surface decoration; but those in the two left hand quadrants (III and IV) repeat the classes covered in I and II but are layered, and may therefore be regarded as compound and not simple. The one exception is the class of star beads which is not duplicated in the right quadrant. The chart is not strictly symmetrical because types corresponding to some that appear are hardly conceivable. For instance, there are innumerable beads of the types Id and Id', but their counterparts in quadrant II do not seem possible. The same is true for quadrants III and IV, but the numbers are available for use if the need should arise. All the beads assigned to a quadrant bear the designator for that quadrant (i.e., I, II, III, IV).

It cannot be emphasized too strongly that this chart shows only the most elementary of the possible forms. Examination of the plates will reveal something of the degree of possible elaboration of these basic types.

Class I

All the beads in quadrant I are designated as Tube Beads, Class I (*see* Fig. 5). They are simple monochromes with, in some cases, adventitious surface decoration. Bead Ia is the simplest possible monochrome tube. Bead Ib is made by adding simple or compound stripes of a different colour before drawing to a gathering similar to that from which Ia was made. Bead Ib' was made like Ib except that in drawing it was twisted. Bead Ic is made from a simple gathering which has been squared in section before drawing. Bead Ic' is like Ic

3 Master identification chart for tube beads.

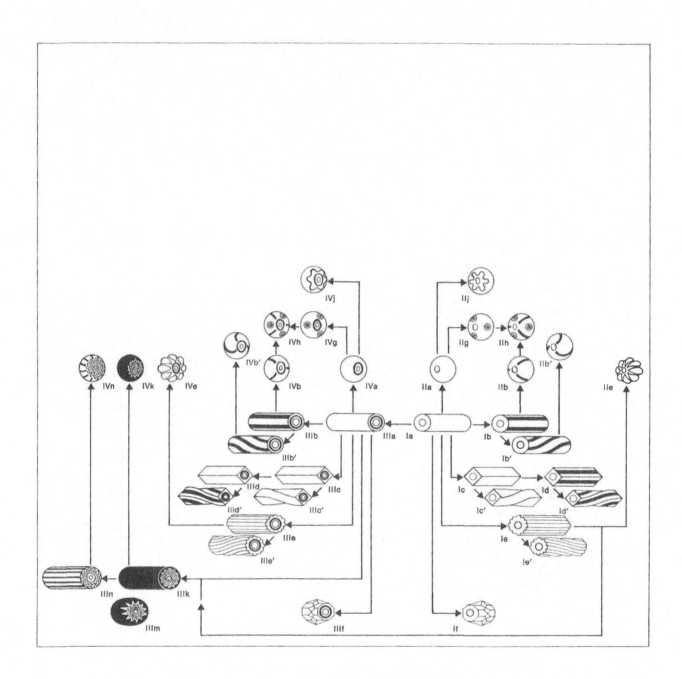

4 Master identification chart for wire wound beads.

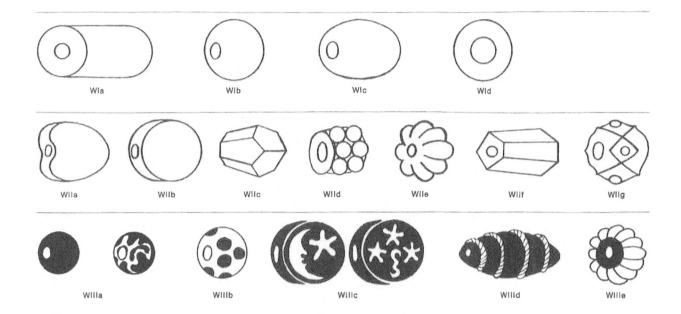

but has been twisted in drawing. The same observations apply to Id and Id' as to Ib and Ib'. Bead Ie is made from a gathering which has been shaped to a ridged form before drawing, while Ie' is the same which has been twisted in drawing. Bead If is a section of tube whose surface has been modified into facets by grinding.

Class II
Beads in the second quadrant are designated as Tube Beads, Class II (see Figs. 6 and 7). Basically, all are theoretically, and probably in practice, derived from Class I types. The essential difference is that, instead of being left in the tube shape, they have been subjected to rounding by re-heating (as previously described). The simplest form is, of course, Bead IIa, which is derived from Ia by re-heating and tumbling the latter until it assumes the round form. Similarly, IIb derives from Ib, IIb' from Ib' and IIe from Ie. Bead IIg is a derivative of IIa, to which round insets or "eyes" have been added, while IIh is a combination of IIb and IIg. Bead IIj is like bead IIa with the addition of two or more wavy lines of a different colour in which the waves may be parallel, crossed or spiralled.

Class III
Beads in the third quadrant are designated as Tube Beads, Class III (see Fig. 7). With the exception of the star beads (IIIm and IIIn), all the beads in this quadrant have analogies in quadrant I, the essential difference being that, whereas the latter are made from the monochrome gathering, those in quadrant III are made from a two- or multilayered gathering. The star beads have up to seven layers of glass, each with twelve ridges, and each alternate layer consisting of an opaque white glass. Bead IIIk is a simple star tube; IIIm is derived from IIIk by grinding down the ends to show the internal design (and is the true star bead); IIIn is similar to IIIk with the addition of three stripes not unlike those in the "b" varieties.

Class IV
Beads in the fourth quadrant of the first chart are designated as Tube Beads, Class IV (see Fig. 8). They derive from the Class III beads in a fashion parallel to the derivation of Class II beads from Class I beads, and are, like the Class III beads, rounded by re-heating. The two beads IVk and IVn have no analogies in the second quadrant, for they are derived from IIIk and IIIn by re-heating.

There are two special cases in the classification of tube beads which require explanation. The first is that in which compound stripes occur. It will be recalled that beads with simple stripes are classed as Ib, IIb, IIIb, and IVb. Similar beads with compound stripes are designated as Ibb, IIbb, and IIIbb and IVbb respectively. The second exception, including beads which look like inferior imitations of the bead IVn, is designated as IVnn.

The Wire Wound Bead Chart
Because they are handcrafted, it is impossible to reduce wire wound beads to a neat classification, but for ease in reference, they have been divided into three groups. All wire wound bead designations are prefaced by the letter W (see Figs. 4 and 9). Group WI comprises beads of simple shapes; i.e., tube, round, oval and doughnut. They are all monochrome. Beads of Group WII are also monochrome but are more elaborately shaped, either by pinching, molding or some other form of manipulation. The so-called "corn" beads, disc, facetted, raspberry, melon and odd-shaped forms occur in this group. Group WIII beads are beads of any of the above shapes which are not monochrome, and which may, and often do, have adventitious surface decorations of contrasting colours.

The numbering system has had to be rather more arbitrary than in the case of the tube beads where some systematic developmental order could be discerned. Hence, the following arrangement is presented as covering more or less adequately the contingencies encountered in this class.

Tubular forms are designated as WIa, round as WIb, oval as WIc and doughnut-shaped beads as WId. The beads of the second group are subdivided as follows: flattened corn-shaped beads, WIIa; disc beads, WIIb; facetted beads, WIIc; raspberry beads, WIId; melon beads, WIIe; cog-shaped or multilateral beads, WIIf; and beads with a pressed design, WIIg.

WIII beads may be any wire wound bead with additional decoration which may be superimposed on or inlaid in the metal. Thus bead WIb, with a surface coating of a different colour or material, becomes WIIIa; WIb with an inlaid decoration becomes WIIIb; WIIb with an inlaid decoration becomes WIIIc; WIc with a spiral overlaid decoration becomes WIIId; and WIIc with a coating of a different material or colour becomes WIIIe.

The taxonomic system outlined above is based essentially on such characteristics as are observable by visual inspection; the only mechanical aids which might be required would be a low-powered hand lens and a millimetre rule. It has not been within the authors' means to employ complicated laboratory tests to determine the chemical nature of the beads concerned, nor is the field archaeologist likely to have either this laboratory equipment or the background training to use it. His determinations will be, for the most part, empirical. The very simplicity makes the system more useful than would be the case if such devices as spectrographic analysis were an integral part. Certainly the desirability of such analyses can not be denied, however. It is greatly to be hoped that in the near future the means and the facilities for carrying out laboratory analyses of beads will be available. When this becomes possible, the inadequacies (and no doubt the errors) of the present system will be smoothed out and it will become more reliable. But till that happy day arrives, perhaps the system suggested here will serve a useful purpose and make the field archaeologist's task a little easier.

14. A Classification System for Glass Beads for the Use of Field Archaeologists

5 Colour plate I.

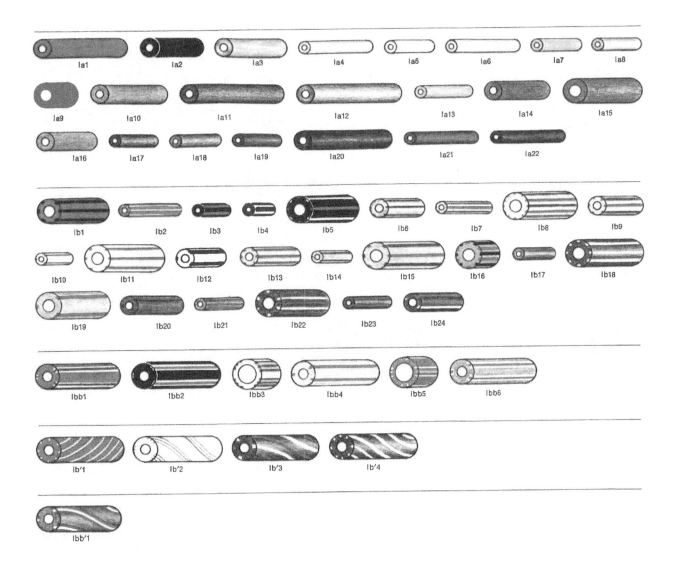

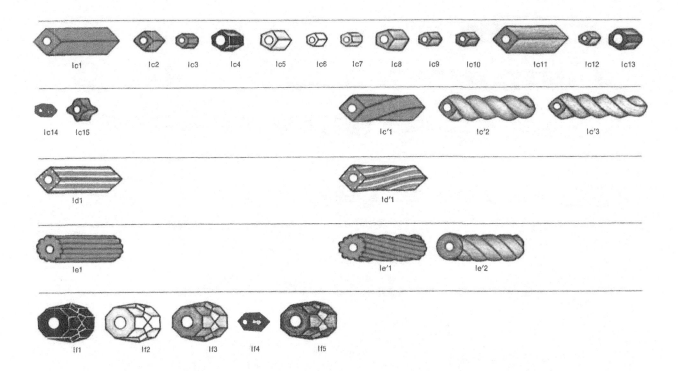

6 Colour plate II.

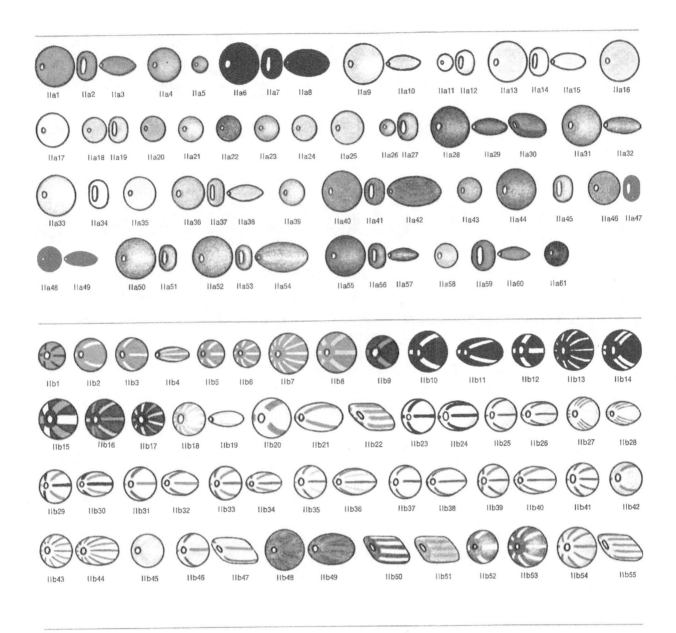

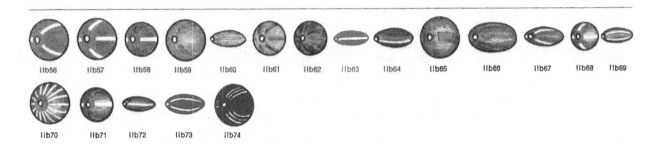

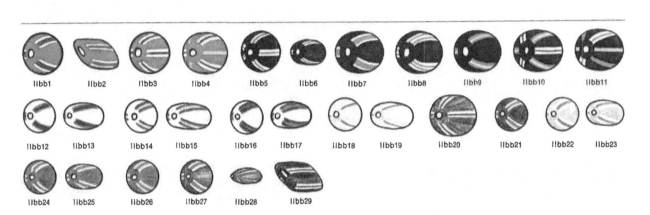

7 Colour plate III.

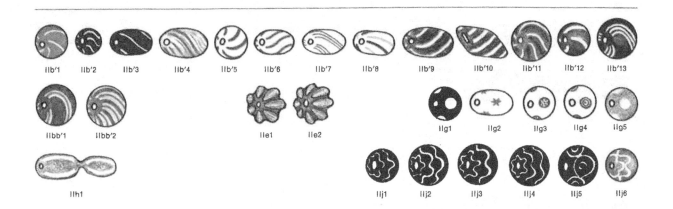

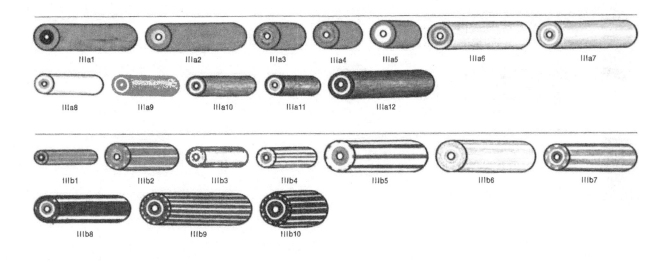

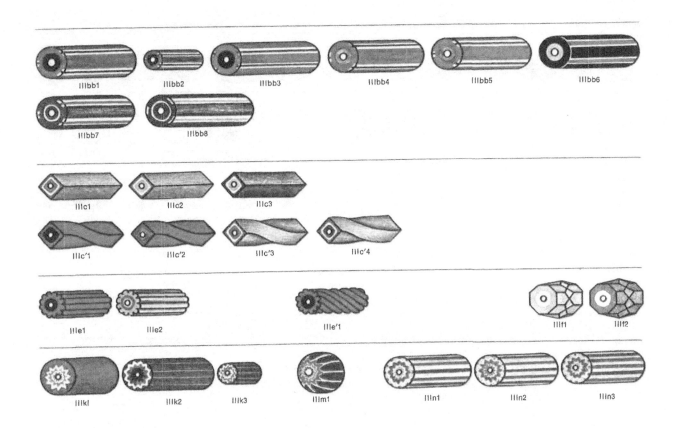

8 Colour plate IV.

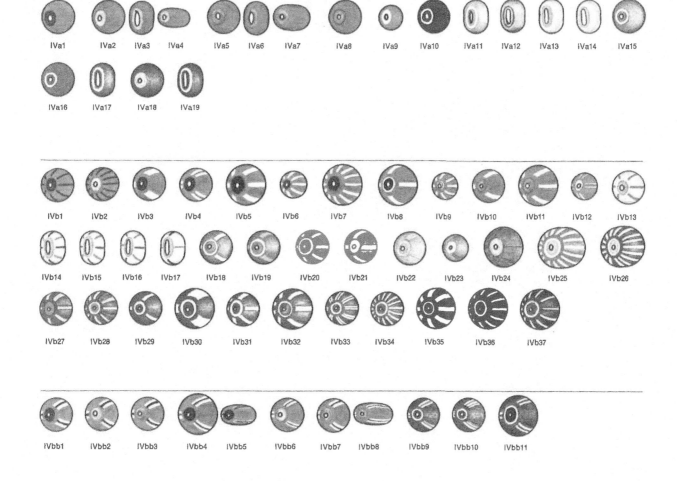

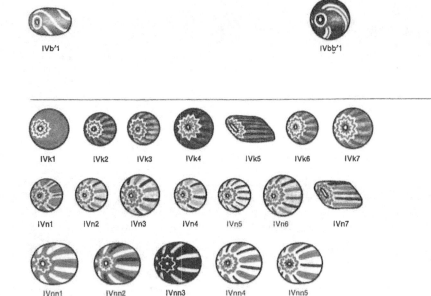

IVb'1　　　　IVbb'1　　　　IVg1

IVk1　IVk2　IVk3　IVk4　IVk5　IVk6　IVk7

IVn1　IVn2　IVn3　IVn4　IVn5　IVn6　IVn7

IVnn1　IVnn2　IVnn3　IVnn4　IVnn5

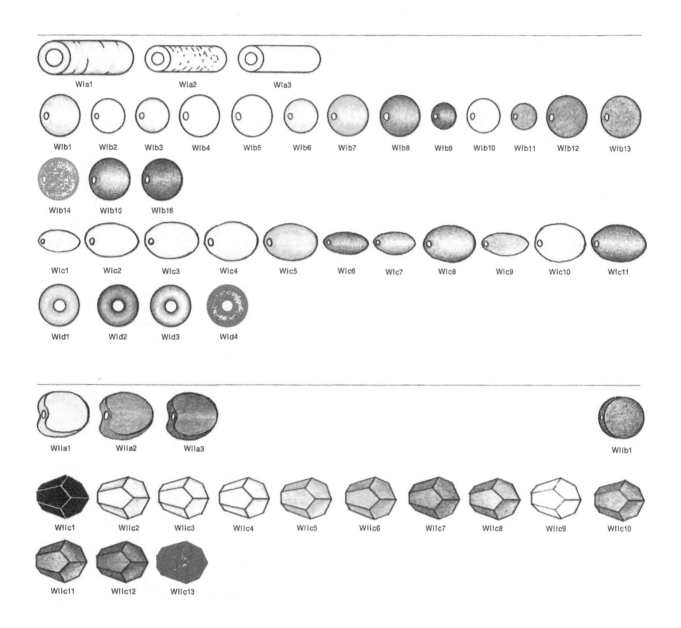

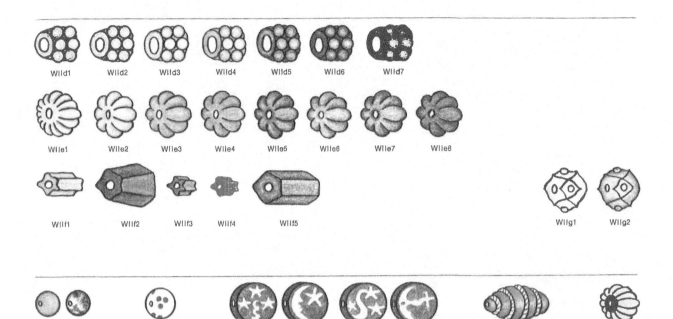

WIId1 WIId2 WIId3 WIId4 WIId5 WIId6 WIId7

WIIe1 WIIe2 WIIe3 WIIe4 WIIe5 WIIe6 WIIe7 WIIe8

WIIf1 WIIf2 WIIf3 WIIf4 WIIf5 WIIg1 WIIg2

WIIIa1 WIIIa2 WIIIb1 WIIIc1 WIIIc2 WIIId1 WIIIe1

How to Use the Classification System to Identify Beads

To identify any bead, it is necessary to consult (a) the Tube Bead chart and the Wire Wound Bead chart; (b) the colour chart of beads already identified (Figs. 5-9); (c) the written description to accompany the bead charts and (d) the table of colours (p. 66). The following steps will be found helpful:

1   Determine whether the bead under examination is a tube or a wire wound bead (*see* section on *Technology of Glass Beads*).

2   If the bead is a tube bead type: (i) consult the tube bead chart to determine whether it follows the tube form or the rounded form; (ii) determine whether it is a Simple Bead (Class I or Class II) or a Layered Bead (Class III or Class IV). For example, in examining a group of tube beads, note those which are simple monochromes; those which are layered; and those which have stripes, eyes, etc. The same technique should be applied to round beads derived from tubes.

3   If the bead is wire wound, consult the wire wound bead chart for its proper placement.

4   Consult the colour illustrations of the individual beads for visual identification.

5   Consult the written descriptions which correspond to the colour illustrations (Figs. 5-9) to determine the precise colour, quality, size and shape classification (a full description of the above appears in Tables 1-6).

If no matching is possible, a new type may have been found; in which case it is desirable that it be reported in order that it may be properly incorporated into the system. If this suggestion meets with general favour, periodic supplements to this paper would be a possibility.

Readers who have found beads on sites in their area are invited to indicate the type or types on separate sheets (*see* sample form) and return them to the authors (Department of Anthropology, Trent University, Peterborough, Ontario). As noted on the sample form, characteristics of size and shape should be added, and new varieties described. By doing so, they will be adding information to what is already known about glass beads in the Northeast, and further afield. When sufficient additional material has been gathered, it will be made available to all interested parties.

Kenneth E. and Martha Ann Kidd

Sample List of Hypothetical
Collection of Beads

Name and Date of Site
_____

Location of Site
_____

Name and Address of Collection
_____

List of Beads Already Recorded:

Ia1–S	IIb2–M	IIIb2–M	IVa12–M	WIb5–L
Ia1–M	IIb11–M	IIIb10–VL	IVa17–M	WIb15–L
Ia2–M	11b18–M	IIIbb3–L	IVa19–M	WIc5–L
Ia18–S	11b21–L	IIIbb5–L	IVb3–M	WId2–L
Ib2–S	IIb31–M	IIIbb7–L	IVb10–L	
Ibb4–M	IIb56–M	IIIc1–L	IVb15–S	WIIa1
Ic12–M	IIb74–L	IIIc'4–L	IVb26–VL	WIIb2
Ic'1–L	IIbb1–L	IIIf2–L	IVb29–M	WIIc4
Ie'1–L	IIbb6–M	IIIk3–S	IVb32–L	WIIc7
If2–L	IIbb11–VL	IIIm1–VL	IVb33–M	WIIc10
	IIb'4–L	IIIn3–M	IVbb7–M	WIIc12
Iia1–S	IIb'6–M		IVbb10–M	WIId2
IIa1–M	IIg3–M	Iva2–M	IVb'1–M	WIId6
IIa6–M	IIj2–L	IVa3–M	IVg1–M	WIIe3
IIa10–S		IVa5–VS	IVk2–M	WIIe8
IIa13–M	IIIa1–M	IVa5–S	IVk4–L	WIIf2
IIa14–S	IIIa2–M	IVa5–M	IVn3–L	WIIf5
IIa29–S	IIIa3–M	IVa5–L	IVnn5–VL	WIIg2
IIa40–S	IIIa7–M	IVa7–M		
IIa40–M	IIIa12–VS	IVa10–M	WIa2–M	WIIIa1
IIa53–S	IIIa12–M	IVa11–M	WIb2–S	WIIIc1

Variations of Beads Already Recorded:

Ia3–L	IIa34–S	IIIa3–L	IVb26–M	WIb3–S
Ia17–M	IIa50–M	IIIa9–M	IVbb7–L	WIb13–M
Ib2–M	IIb4–M	IIIb2–S	IVk4–M	WIb15–M
Ibb6–M	IIbb1–M	IIIbb2–L	IVh3–M	WIc1–M
Ib'4–S	IIg4–L			WIc4–S
Ic13–VL	IIh2–M	IVa10–L	WIa1–S	WIc8–S

New Types of Beads Not Recorded:

Ia –S–tr–Lt. Ivory

Ib –L–tr–Aqua Blue–3 Redwood Stripes & 3 White Stripes

Ibb –M–op–Redwood–3 Black on White Stripes

Ic' –M–tr–Brite Blue–loose twist, four sided

IIa –O–M–op–Pale Blue

IIb –R–M–cl–Brite Copan Blue with 12 Brite Navy Stripes ("Gooseberry" Bead)

IIIa –M–op–Black with Black Core & White Middle Layer

IIIc –L–cl–Turquoise with Redwood Core & White Middle Layer

IIIm –Like IIIm1 except outside layer Teal Green

IVb –O–M–op–Redwood with cl Apple Green Core & 3 White Stripes

IVh –Like IIh1 plus Lt. Gray Core

14. A Classification System for Glass Beads for the Use of Field Archaeologists

Glossary of Terms used in Tables 1-6

Taylor, Helen D., Lucille Knoche & Walter Granville (Eds.)
Descriptive Color Names Dictionary. Container Corporation of America, Chicago.

The colours encountered in the beads seen and studied correspond to those shown on the colour chips in the above publication, numbered and named as below.

6 le	Redwood	op	cl		23 ni	Dk. Palm Green		cl	
8 pc	Ruby		cl		20 ng	Teal Green		cl	
7 pa	Scarlet		cl		17 pa	Turquoise		cl	
p	Lamp Black	op			16 ea	Lt. Aqua Blue	op	cl	tr
c	Lt. Gray		cl		18 gc	Aqua Blue	op		tr
b	Oyster White		cl	tr	16 ic	Robin's Egg Blue	op		tr
a	White	op			16 lc	Brite Blue		cl	tr
15 ca	Pale Blue	op	cl	tr	15 nc	Cerulean Blue		cl	
1 la	Lemon Yellow	op	cl		14 ia	Brite Copen Blue	op	cl	
2 ic	Lt. Gold	op	cl		14 ie	Shadow Blue	op	cl	tr
3 lc	Amber	op	cl		15 ni	Dk. Shadow Blue	op	cl	
3 le	Cinnamon	op	cl		13 la	Brite Dutch Blue	op		
4 ng	Maple		cl		13 pa	Ultramarine		cl	
1 gc	Citron		cl	tr	13 pg	Brite Navy		cl	
2 lg	Mustard Tan	op			14 pi	Dk. Navy		cl	
2 pn	Dk. Brown	op			7 ga	Lt. Cherry Rose	op	cl	
22 ia	Brite Mint Green	op	cl		8 le	Rose Wine		cl	
23 ic	Apple Green	op	cl		11 lc	Amethyst		cl	
22 ie	Surf Green	op		tr	7 pn	Dk. Rose Brown		cl	tr
21 nc	Emerald Green		cl		6 lc	Coral			tr

The abbreviations *op. cl.* and *tr.* after the names indicate whether the colour occurs in *opaque, clear* or *translucent* glass.

Abbreviations Which Occur in Tables

Size:
VS – Very Small, under 2 mm.
 S – Small, 2-4 mm.
 M – Medium, 4-6 mm
 L – Large, 6-10 mm.
VL – Very Large, over 10 mm.

Shape:
R – Round
C – Circular (Ring)
O – Oval
T – Tube
F – Flat
D – Disk

CO – Corn
ME – Melon
RA – Raspberry
ST – Star
FA – Facetted
DO – Donut

Type of Glass:
op – Opaque
cl – Clear
tr – Translucent

Kenneth E. and Martha Ann Kidd

Table 1: Description of Class I Beads (Fig. 5)

Type	Bead Number	Size	Glass	Name of Colour	Type	Bead Number	Size	Glass	Name of Colour
Ia	Ia1	VS	op	Redwood	Ia	Ia9	L	op	Brite Mint Green
		S	op	Redwood		Ia10	M	op	Surf Green
		M	op	Redwood		Ia11	M	tr	Teal Green
		L	op	Redwood		Ia12	M	cl	Turquoise
	Ia2	S	op	Black		Ia13	S	tr	Aqua Blue
		M	op	Black		Ia14	M	op	Robin's Egg Blue
		L	op	Black		Ia15	L	tr	Brite Blue
		VL	op	Black		Ia16	M	op	Shadow Blue
	Ia3	M	cl	Lt. Gray		Ia17	S	cl	Dk. Shadow Blue
	Ia4	S	tr	Oyster White		Ia18	S	cl	Ultramarine
		M	tr	Oyster White			M	cl	Ultramarine
	Ia5	S	op	White		Ia19	S	cl	Brite Navy
		M	op	White			M	cl	Brite Navy
	Ia6	S	op	Lt. Ivory		Ia20	L	cl	Dark Navy
	Ia7	S	op	Lt. Gold		Ia21	S	cl	Rose Wine
	Ia8	S	tr	Citron		Ia22	S	tr	Dk. Rose Brown

Body   **Simple Stripes**

Type	Bead Number	Size	Glass	Name of Colour	Number of Stripes and Name of Colour		
Ib	Ib1	L	op	Redwood	6 Black		
	Ib2	S	op	Redwood	6 White		
	Ib3	S	op	Black	3 Redwood		
		L	op	Black	3 Redwood		
	Ib4	S	op	Black	3 White		
	Ib5	L	op	Black	3 White	3 Redwood	
	Ib6	M	cl	Lt. Gray	6 Ultramarine		
	Ib7	S	tr	Oyster White	3 Redwood	3 Ultramarine	
	Ib8	L	tr	Oyster White	6 Redwood	6 Ultramarine	
	Ib9	M	tr	Oyster White	3 Redwood	3 Dk. Palm Green	
	Ib10	S	op	White	3 Redwood		
	Ib11	L	op	White	6 Redwood		
	Ib12	M	op	White	3 Black		
	Ib13	M	op	Pale Blue	3 Redwood		
	Ib14	S	op	Lt. Gold	3 Dk. Palm Green		
	Ib15	L	op	Lt. Gold	3 Dk. Palm Green	3 Redwood	
	Ib16	M	op	Amber	6 Redwood	6 Black	
	Ib17	S	cl	Apple Green	3 Redwood		
	Ib18	L	cl	Teal Green	8 White		
	Ib19	L	tr	Aqua Blue	3 Redwood		
	Ib20	M	tr	Robin's Egg Blue	3 Redwood		
	Ib21	S	op	Shadow Blue	6 Redwood		
	Ib22	L	cl	Dk. Shadow Blue	6 Redwood	6 White	
	Ib23	S	cl	Brite Navy	3 Redwood		
	Ib24	M	tr	Dk. Rose Brown	2 Redwood	2 White	

Table 1: Description of Class I Beads (Fig. 5) (continued)

				Body	Compound Stripes		
Type	Bead Number	Size	Glass	Name of Colour	Number of Stripes and Name of Their Colours		
Ibb	Ibb1	M	op	Redwood	3 Brite Navy	on White	
		L	op	Redwood	3 Brite Navy	on White	
	Ibb2	S	op	Black	3 Redwood	on White	
		L	op	Black	3 Redwood	on White	
	Ibb3	L	op	White	4 Lt. Gold (Double)	on Maple	
	Ibb4	M	op	Pale Blue	3 White	on Redwood	
	Ibb5	L	op	Brite Mint Green	4 Lemon Yellow	on Scarlet	on White
	Ibb6	S	op	Aqua Blue	3 Redwood	on White	

				Body	Simple Stripes	
Type	Bead Number	Size	Glass	Name of Colour	Number of Stripes and Name of Their Colour	
Ib'	Ib'1	M	op	Redwood	8 White	
	Ib'2	M	op	White	9 Brite Navy (3 groups of 3 fine stripes)	
	Ib'3	M	cl	Dk. Shadow Blue	3 Redwood	3 White
	Ib'4	M	cl	Brite Navy	8 White	

				Body	Compound Stripes	
Type	Bead Number	Size	Glass	Name of Colour	Number of Stripes and Name of Their Colour	
Ibb'	Ibb'1	M	op	Surf Green	3 White	on Redwood

Type	Bead Number	Size	Glass	Name of Colour	Number of Sides
Ic	Ic1	M	op	Redwood	4
		L	op	Redwood	4
	Ic2	S	cl	Ruby	4
	Ic3	VS	cl	Scarlet	6
	Ic4	S	op	Black	6
	Ic5	S	cl	Lt. Gray	5
	Ic6	VS	cl	Oyster White	5
		S	cl	Oyster White	5
	Ic7	VS	cl	Lemon Yellow	6
	Ic8	S	cl	Amber	5
	Ic9	VS	cl	Apple Green	5
		S	cl	Apple Green	5
	Ic10	VS	cl	Turquoise	5
	Ic11	VS	tr	Brite Blue	4
	Ic12	S	cl	Brite Copen Blue	6
		M	cl	Brite Copen Blue	6
	Ic13	M	cl	Brite Navy	6
	Ic14	VS	cl	Brite Navy	5
	Ic15	S	tr	Dk. Rose Brown	4

Table 1: Description of Class I Beads (Fig. 5) (continued)

Type	Bead Number	Size	Glass	Name of Colour	Type of Twist
Ic'	Ic'1	S	op	Redwood	Loose Twist
		M	op	Redwood	Medium Twist
		L	op	Redwood	Tight Twist
	Ic'2	M	cl	Apple Green	Tight Twist
	Ic'3	M	cl	Ultramarine	Tight Twist

Type	Bead Number	Size	Glass	**Body** Name of Colour	**Simple Stripe** Number of Stripes and Name of Their Colour
Id	Id1	M	op	Redwood	8 White (Thin)

Type	Bead Number	Size	Glass	**Body** Name of Colour	**Simple Stripes** Number of Stripes and Name of Their Colour	Type of Twist
Id'	Id'1	M	op	Redwood	8 White (Thin)	Loose Twist

Type	Bead Number	Size	Glass	Name of Colour
Ie	Ie1	L	op	Redwood

Type	Bead Number	Size	Glass	Name of Colour	Type of Twist
Ie'	Ie'1	L	op	Redwood	Medium Twist
	Ie'2	M	cl	Apple Green	Medium Twist

Type	Bead Number	Size	Glass	Name of Colour	Number of Sides
If	If1	L	op	Black	6
	If2	L	cl	Lt. Gray	6
	If3	L	cl	Emerald	6
	If4	S	cl	Turquoise	5
	If5	L	cl	Amethyst	6

14. A Classification System for Glass Beads for the Use of Field Archaeologists

Table 2: Description of Class II Beads (Fig. 6)

Type	Bead Number	Shape	Size	Glass	Name of Colour	Type	Bead Number	Shape	Size	Glass	Name of Colour
IIa	IIa1	R	VS	op	Redwood	IIa	IIa29	O	S	cl	Dk. Palm Green
		R	S	op	Redwood		IIa30	F	L	cl	Dk. Palm Green
		R	M	op	Redwood		IIa31	R	VS	cl	Turquoise
		R	L	op	Redwood			R	M	cl	Turquoise
	IIa2	C	M	op	Redwood			R	L	cl	Turquoise
	IIa3	O	S	op	Redwood		IIa32	O	S	cl	Turquoise
	IIa4	R	M	cl	Redwood		IIa33	R	L	cl	Lt. Aqua Blue
	IIa5	R	VS	cl	Ruby		IIa34	C	M	tr	Lt. Aqua Blue
	IIa6	R	VS	op	Black		IIa35	R	M	op	Lt. Aqua Blue
		R	S	op	Black		IIa36	R	S	op	Aqua Blue
		R	M	op	Black			R	M	op	Aqua Blue
		R	L	op	Black		IIa37	C	S	op	Aqua Blue
		R	VL	op	Black		IIa38	O	S	op	Aqua Blue
	IIa7	C	VS	op	Black		IIa39	R	S	tr	Aqua Blue
		C	S	op	Black		IIa40	R	VS	op	Robin's Egg Blue
		C	M	op	Black			R	S	op	Robin's Egg Blue
	IIa8	O	S	op	Black			R	M	op	Robin's Egg Blue
		O	M	op	Black			R	L	op	Robin's Egg Blue
		O	L	op	Black		IIa41	C	S	op	Robin's Egg Blue
	IIa9	R	L	cl	Lt. Gray		IIa42	O	S	op	Robin's Egg Blue
	IIa10	O	S	cl	Lt. Gray		IIa43	R	VS	tr	Brite Blue
	IIa11	R	VS	tr	Oyster White			R	S	tr	Brite Blue
	IIa12	C	S	tr	Oyster White		IIa44	R	VS	cl	Cerulean Blue
	IIa13	R	VS	op	White			R	M	cl	Cerulean Blue
		R	S	op	White			R	L	cl	Cerulean Blue
		R	M	op	White		IIa45	C	S	cl	Brite Copan Blue
		R	L	op	White		IIa46	R	S	op	Shadow Blue
	IIa14	C	S	op	White			R	M	op	Shadow Blue
	IIa15	O	S	op	White		IIa47	C	S	op	Shadow Blue
		O	M	op	White		IIa48	R	S	op	Dk. Shadow Blue
	IIa16	R	L	op	Pale Blue		IIa49	O	S	op	Dk. Shadow Blue
	IIa17	R	VS	op	Lt. Gold		IIa50	R	S	cl	Dk. Shadow Blue
		R	S	op	Lt. Gold			R	L	cl	Dk. Shadow Blue
		R	M	op	Lt. Gold		IIa51	C	S	cl	Dk. Shadow Blue
	IIa18	R	VS	op	Amber		IIa52	R	M	cl	Ultramarine
		R	S	op	Amber			R	L	cl	Ultramarine
	IIa19	C	S	op	Amber		IIa53	C	S	cl	Ultramarine
	IIa20	R	S	op	Cinnamon		IIa54	O	L	cl	Ultramarine
	IIa21	R	S	tr	Citron		IIa55	R	S	cl	Brite Navy
	IIa22	R	S	op	Mustard Tan			R	L	cl	Brite Navy
	IIa23	R	S	cl	Brite Mint Green		IIa56	C	S	cl	Brite Navy
	IIa24	R	S	op	Apple Green		IIa57	O	S	cl	Brite Navy
	IIa25	R	VS	op	Surf Green		IIa58	R	VS	cl	Lt. Cherry Rose
		R	M	op	Surf Green			R	S	cl	Lt. Cherry Rose
	IIa26	R	VS	cl	Emerald Green		IIa59	C	M	cl	Rose Wine
	IIa27	C	S	cl	Emerald Green		IIa60	O	S	cl	Rose Wine
	IIa28	R	M	cl	Dk. Palm Green		IIa61	R	S	cl	Dk. Rose Brown
		R	L	cl	Dk. Palm Green						

Table 2: Description of Class II Beads (Fig. 6) (continued)

					Body	Simple Stripes		
Type	Bead Number	Shape	Size	Glass	Name of Colour	Number of Stripes / Style of Stripes (Average width unless noted) / Colour of Stripes		
IIb	IIb1	R	S	op	Redwood	6 op Black		
	IIb2	R	M	op	Redwood	3 op White		
	IIb3	R	M	op	Redwood	4 op White		
	IIb4	O	S	op	Redwood	4 op White		
	IIb5	R	S	op	Redwood	6 op White		
	IIb6	R	S	op	Redwood	8 op White		
	IIb7	R	L	op	Redwood	12 op White		
	IIb8	R	L	op	Redwood	6 op Lemon Yellow		
	IIb9	R	M	op	Black	3 op Redwood		
	IIb10	R	S	op	Black	3 op White		
		R	VL	op	Black	3 op White		
	IIb11	O	M	op	Black	3 op White		
	IIb12	R	M	op	Black	4 op White		
	IIb13	R	L	op	Black	10 op White		
	IIb14	R	L	op	Black	3 op Double White		
	IIb15	R	L	op	Black	3 op Broad Redwood	3 Broad White	
	IIb16	R	L	op	Black	3 op Ruby	3 Lt. Cherry Rose	
	IIb17	R	M	op	Black	3 op Redwood	3 White	3 Lemon Yellow
	IIb18	R	S	cl	Lt. Gray	12 op Thin White	These are called "Gooseberry" beads. The stripes may vary from 12 to 15 and colour may vary from very light to dark with occasionally a yellow cast.	
		R	M	cl	Lt. Gray	12 op Thin White		
		R	L	cl	Lt. Gray	12 op Thin White		
	IIb19	O	S	cl	Lt. Gray	12 op Thin White		
	IIb20	R	L	op	White	3 op Redwood		
	IIb21	O	L	op	White	3 op Redwood		
	IIb22	F	L	op	White	8 op Redwood		
	IIb23	R	M	op	White	4 op Black		
	IIb24	O	M	op	White	4 op Black		
	IIb25	R	M	op	White	4 tr Brite Navy		
	IIb26	O	M	op	White	4 tr Brite Navy		
	IIb27	R	L	op	White	9 tr Brite Navy	(3 Groups of 3 Fine Lines)	
	IIb28	O	L	op	White	9 tr Brite Navy	(3 Groups of 3 Fine Lines)	
	IIb29	R	M	op	White	3 op Redwood	3 op Black	
	IIb30	O	M	op	White	3 op Redwood	3 op Black	
	IIb31	R	S	op	White	2 op Redwood	2 tr Brite Navy	
		R	M	op	White	2 op Redwood	2 tr Brite Navy	
	IIb32	O	M	op	White	2 op Redwood	2 tr Brite Navy	
	IIb33	R	M	op	White	3 op Redwood	3 tr Dk. Palm Green	
	IIb34	O	M	op	White	3 op Redwood	3 tr Dk. Palm Green	
	IIb35	R	M	op	White	4 op Lemon Yellow	4 tr Dk. Palm Green	
	IIb36	O	M	op	White	4 op Lemon Yellow	4 tr Dk. Palm Green	
	IIb37	R	M	op	White	2 op Dk. Brown	2 tr Dk. Palm Green	
	IIb38	R	M	op	White	2 op Dk. Brown	2 tr Dk. Palm Green	
	IIb39	R	M	op	White	2 op Redwood	2 Dk. Palm Green	2 Brite Navy

Table 2: Description of Class II Beads (Fig. 6) (continued)

Type	Bead Number	Shape	Size	Glass	Body Name of Colour	Simple Stripes Number of Stripes Style of Stripes Colour of Stripes			
IIb	IIb40	O	M	op	White	2 op Redwood	2	Dk. Palm Green	2 Brite Navy
	IIb41	R	M	op	White	3 tr Dk. Palm Green	3 tr Brite Navy		
	IIb42	R	M	op	Pale Blue	3 op Redwood			
	IIb43	R	M	op	Pale Blue	3 op Redwood	3 tr Brite Navy		
	IIb44	O	M	op	Pale Blue	5 op Redwood	5 tr Brite Navy		
	IIb45	R	M	cl	Lt. Gold	4 op White			
	IIb46	R	M	op	Lt. Gold	2 op Redwood	2 tr Dk. Palm Green		
	IIb47	F	L	op	Lt. Gold	2 op Redwood	2 tr Dk. Palm Green		
	IIb48	R	M	op	Mustard Tan	8 op Redwood			
		R	L	op	Mustard Tan	8 op Redwood			
	IIb49	O	L	op	Mustard Tan	8 op Redwood			
	IIb50	R	L	op	Mustard Tan	8 op White			
	IIb51	F	L	tr	Surf Green	8 op Lt. Gold			
	IIb52	R	M	cl	Emerald Green	4 op White			
	IIb53	R	L	cl	Teal Green	8 op White			
	IIb54	R	L	tr	Lt. Aqua Blue	8 op Redwood			
	IIb55	F	L	tr	Lt. Aqua Blue	8 op Redwood			
	IIb56	R	S	op	Robin's Egg Blue	3 op White			
		R	M	op	Robin's Egg Blue	3 op White			
		R	L	op	Robin's Egg Blue	3 op White			
	IIb57	R	L	op	Robin's Egg Blue	4 op White			
	IIb58	R	M	op	Robin's Egg Blue	2 op Redwood	2 op White		
	IIb59	R	L	tr	Brite Blue	3 op Redwood			
	IIb60	O	S	cl	Brite Copan Blue	12 tr Brite Navy "Gooseberry" Bead			
	IIb61	R	M	op	Shadow Blue	6 op Redwood			
	IIb62	R	M	cl	Dk. Shadow Blue	8 op Redwood			
	IIb63	O	S	cl	Dk. Shadow Blue	2 op White			
	IIb64	O	M	cl	Dk. Shadow Blue	2 op Redwood	2 op White		
	IIb65	R	L	cl	Brite Navy	2 op Broad Redwood			
	IIb66	O	L	cl	Brite Navy	4 op Redwood			
	IIb67	O	S	cl	Brite Navy	3 op White			
		O	L	cl	Brite Navy	3 op White			
	IIb68	R	M	cl	Brite Navy	4 op White			
	IIb69	O	S	cl	Brite Navy	4 op White			
	IIb70	R	L	cl	Brite Navy	16 op Thin White			
	IIb71	R	M	cl	Brite Navy	2 op Redwood	2 op White		
	IIb72	O	S	cl	Brite Navy	2 op Redwood	2 op White		
	IIb73	O	M	tr	Dk. Navy	3 op White			
	IIb74	R	L	tr	Dk. Rose Brown	9 op White (3 Groups of 3 Thin Lines)			

Table 3: Description of Class II Beads (Fig. 7)

Type	Bead Number	Shape	Size	Glass	Body Name of Colour	Compound Stripes Number of Stripes Style of Stripes Colour of Stripes		
IIbb	IIbb1	R	L	op	Redwood	3 Brite Navy	on White	
	IIbb2	F	L	op	Redwood	3 Brite Navy	on White	
	IIbb3	R	L	op	Redwood	4 Brite Navy	on White	
	IIbb4	R	VL	op	Redwood	3 Brite Navy 3 Lt. Gold	on White	
	IIbb5	R	L	op	Black	5 Thin Redwood	on White	
	IIbb6	O	M	op	Black	3 Thin Redwood	on White	
	IIbb7	R	VL	op	Black	3 Broad Redwood	on White	
	IIbb8	R	VL	op	Black	3 Double Redwood	on White	
	IIbb9	R	VL	op	Black	3 Lemon Yellow between Redwood		
	IIbb10	R	VL	op	Black	3 Lemon Yellow between Redwood 3 Fine Brite Navy	on White	
	IIbb11	R	VL	op	Black	2 Fine Redwood 2 Redwood 2 Amber	on White	
	IIbb12	R	M	op	White	3 Brite Navy	on Redwood	
	IIbb13	O	M	op	White	3 Brite Navy	on Redwood	
	IIbb14	R	M	op	White	3 Lemon Yellow	on Brite Navy	(Yellow stripe
	IIbb15	O	M	op	White	3 Lemon Yellow	on Brite Navy	appears green)
	IIbb16	R	M	op	White	3 Redwood	on Dk. Palm Green	
	IIbb17	O	M	op	White	3 Redwood	on Dk. Palm Green	
	IIbb18	R	M	op	Pale Blue	3 Redwood	on White	
	IIbb19	O	M	op	Pale Blue	3 Redwood	on White	
	IIbb20	R	VL	op	Mustard Tan	4 Brite Navy 8 Redwood (In Pairs Between Other Stripes)	on White	
	IIbb21	R	M	op	Teal Green	3 Redwood	on White	
	IIbb22	R	M	op	Lt. Aqua Blue	3 Redwood	on White	
	IIbb23	O	M	op	Lt. Aqua Blue	3 Redwood	on White	
	IIbb24	R	M	op	Robin's Egg Blue	3 Redwood	on White	
	IIbb25	O	M	op	Robin's Egg Blue	3 Redwood	on White	
	IIbb26	R	M	op	Robin's Egg Blue	3 Redwood	on Lemon Yellow	
	IIbb27	R	M	cl	Brite Navy	3 Redwood	on White	
	IIbb28	O	S	cl	Brite Navy	3 Dk. Brown	on White	
	IIbb29	F	L	cl	Dk. Rose Brown	3 Brite Navy	on White	

14. A Classification System for Glass Beads for the Use of Field Archaeologists

Table 3: Description of Class II Beads (Fig. 7) (continued)

Type	Bead Number	Shape	Size	Glass	**Body** Name of Colour	**Simple Stripes** Number of Stripes Colour of Stripes	
IIb'	IIb'1	R	M	op	Redwood	6 White	
	IIb'2	R	S	op	Black	7 White	
	IIb'3	O	M	op	Black	3 White	
	IIb'4	O	L	tr	Oyster White	Numerous irregular stripes–Lt. Gold, Redwood, Ultramarine, Aqua Blue. (Marbled effect)	
	IIb'5	R	M	op	White	6 Redwood	
	IIb'6	O	M	op	White	6 Redwood	
	IIb'7	O	M	op	White	9 Brite Navy (3 Groups of 3 Thin Lines)	
	IIb'8	O	M	op	White	3 Lemon Yellow	3 Brite Navy
	IIb'9	O	L	op	Mustard Tan	6 White	
	IIb'10	F	L	op	Mustard Tan	6 White	
	IIb'11	R	L	op	Robin's Egg Blue	6 Redwood	(6 Stripes which had disappeared)
	IIb'12	R	M	tr	Brite Navy	4 White	
	IIb'13	R	L	cl	Dk. Rose Brown	9 White (3 Groups of 3 Thin Lines)	

Type	Bead Number	Shape	Size	Glass	**Body** Name of Colour	**Compound Stripes** Number of Stripes Colour of Stripes	
IIbb'	IIbb'1	R	L	op	Teal Green	3 Redwood	on Lemon Yellow
	IIbb'2	R	L	op	Robin's Egg Blue	6 Redwood	on Lemon Yellow

Type	Bead Number	Shape	Size	Glass	**Body** Name of Colour	**"Melon" Beads**
IIe	IIe1	R	M	cl	Brite Blue	7 Ridges
	IIe2	R	M	cl	Brite Blue	8 Ridges

Type	Bead Number	Shape	Size	Glass	**Body** Name of Colour	**"Flush Eye" Beads** Name of Decoration Colour
IIg	IIg1	R	M	op	Black	3 White Dots
	IIg2	O	M	op	White	3 Redwood Stars
	IIg3	R	M	op	White	3 Redwood Stars on White Dots on Brite Blue Dots
	IIg4	R	M	op	White	3 Brite Navy Dots each containing 2 White Rings
	IIg5	R	M	op	Shadow Blue	3 Redwood Dots on White Dots

Bead with "Flush Eye" and Stripes
This bead has always appeared as two joined beads

					Body	Decoration
Type	Bead Number	Shape	Size	Glass	Name of Colour	Name of Colours Description
IIh	IIh1	O	M	op	Shadow Blue	3 Redwood Stars on White Dots 3 White Stripes between "Flush Eyes"

"Roman" Beads

					Body	Decoration
Type	Bead Number	Shape	Size	Glass	Name of Colour	Name of Colours Description of Decoration
IIj	IIj1	R	M	op	Black	2 White Parallel Wavy Lines
	IIj2	R	L	op	Black	3 White Alternating Wavy Lines
	IIj3	R	L	op	Black	2 Lemon Yellow Alternating Wavy Lines
	IIj4	R	L	op	Black	1 Lemon Yellow between 2 White Parallel Wavy Lines
	IIj5	R	L	op	Black	2 White Spirals between 2 Lemon Yellow Spirals
	IIj6	R	M	cl	Brite Blue	2 White Alternating Wavy Lines

14. A Classification System for Glass Beads for the Use of Field Archaeologists

Table 4: Description of Class III Beads (Fig. 7)

Type	Bead Number	Size	Glass	Outside Layer Colour Name	Glass	Core Colour Name	Glass	Middle Layer Colour Name
IIIa	IIIa1	M	op	Redwood	op	Black		
	IIIa2	M	op	Redwood	cl	Lt. Gray		
	IIIa3	S	op	Redwood	cl	Apple Green		
		M	op	Redwood	cl	Apple Green		
	IIIa4	M	op	Redwood	cl	Brite Blue		
	IIIa5	M	cl	Scarlet	op	White		
	IIIa6	M	cl	Lt. Gray	cl	Lt. Gray	op	Redwood
	IIIa7	M	cl	Lt. Gray	cl	Lt. Gray	op	White
	IIIa8	S	tr	Oyster White	cl	Lt. Gray		
	IIIa9	S	tr	Shadow Blue	cl	Brite Navy		
	IIIa10	VS	cl	Ultramarine	cl	Ultramarine	op	White
		S	cl	Ultramarine	cl	Ultramarine	op	White
	IIIa11	S	cl	Brite Navy	cl	Lt. Gray	op	White
	IIIa12	VS	cl	Brite Navy	cl	Brite Navy	op	White
		S	cl	Brite Navy	cl	Brite Navy	op	White
		M	cl	Brite Navy	cl	Brite Navy	op	White

Type	Bead Number	Size	Glass	Outside Layer Colour Name	Glass	Core Colour Name	Glass	Middle Colour Name	Simple Stripes Colour Name / Number of Stripes	
IIIb	IIIb1	VS	op	Redwood	op	Black			6 op White	
	IIIb2	M	op	Redwood	cl	Apple Green			6 op White	
	IIIb3	S	cl	Lt. Gray	cl	Lt. Gray	op	White	3 op Black	
	IIIb4	S	tr	Oyster White	cl	Brite Copan Blue			6 Redwood	6 Brite Navy
	IIIb5	L	tr	Oyster White	cl	Brite Copan Blue			4 Redwood	4 Brite Navy
	IIIb6	L	cl	Lt. Aqua Blue	cl	Lt. Aqua Blue	op	White	8 op White	
	IIIb7	M	cl	Shadow Blue	cl	Shadow Blue	op	White	8 op White	
	IIIb8	M	cl	Dk. Shadow Blue	op	Redwood	op	White	3 op White	
	IIIb9	L	cl	Brite Navy	cl	Brite Navy	op	White	15 op White	
	IIIb10	VL	cl	Dk. Navy	cl	Dk. Navy	op	White	16 op White	

Type	Bead Number	Size	Glass	Outside Layer Colour Name	Glass	Core Colour Name	Glass	Middle Colour Name	Compound Stripes Colour Name / Number of Stripes	
IIIbb	IIIbb1	L	op	Redwood	cl	Black			3 op Black	on White
	IIIbb2	S	op	Redwood	op	Black			3 cl Brite Navy	on White
	IIIbb3	L	op	Redwood	op	Black			4 cl Brite Navy	on White
	IIIbb4	L	op	Redwood	cl	Apple Green			3 op Black	on White
	IIIbb5	L	op	Redwood	cl	Apple Green			3 cl Brite Navy	on White
	IIIbb6	L	op	Black	cl	Lt. Gray			3 op Redwood	on White
	IIIbb7	L	cl	Brite Navy	cl	Brite Navy	op	White	3 op Redwood	on White
	IIIbb8	L	cl	Brite Navy	cl	Brite Navy	op	White	3 cl Aqua Blue	on White

Table 4: Description of Class III Beads (Fig. 7) (continued)

Type	Bead Number	Size	Glass	Outside Colour Name	Glass	Core Colour Name	Glass	Middle Layer Colour Name
IIIc	IIIc1	L	cl	Brite Blue	cl	Brite Blue	op	White
	IIIc2	L	tr	Shadow Blue	cl	Lt. Gray	op	White
	IIIc3	L	cl	Brite Navy	cl	Lt. Gray	op	White
IIIc'	IIIc'1	L	op	Redwood	op	Black		
	IIIc'2	L	op	Redwood	cl	Apple Green		
	IIIc'3	L	cl	Turquoise	op	Redwood	op	White
	IIIc'4	L	cl	Turquoise	cl	Brite Navy	op	White
IIIe	IIIe1	M	op	Redwood	op	Black		
	IIIe2	M	cl	Lt. Gray	cl	Lt. Gray	op	Redwood
IIIe'	IIIe'1	M	op	Redwood	op	Black		
IIIf	IIIf1	L	cl	Lt. Gray	tr	Oyster White		
	IIIf2	L	cl	Ultramarine	tr	Lt. Aqua Blue		

Table 4: Description of Class III Beads (Fig. 7) (continued)

Tube "Star" Beads (The Layers are Named from the Outside Inward)

Type IIIk "Star" Tube Bead with Plain Outside Layer

Type	Bead Number	Size	Glass	Outside		2nd		3rd		4th		5th	
IIIk	IIIk1	VL	op	Redwood	op	White	cl	Brite Blue	op	White	cl	Brite Blue	(*1)
	IIIk2	L	cl	Teal Green	op	White	op	Redwood	op	Black			(*2)
	IIIk3	S	cl	Brite Navy	op	White	op	Redwood	op	White	cl	Brite Blue	(*3)

*1 Outside layer very thick. Ends of bead slightly milled.
*2 Outside layer thin so ridges of next layer show through like stripes.
*3 Ends of bead ground to point to show design of inner layers.

Type IIIm True "Star" Bead (Large tube ground down to round or oval form to show ridges of next layer and end design of inner layers). Beads occur in size from Small to Very Large—up to 2½" long.

Type	Bead Number	Glass	Outside		2nd		3rd		4th		5th		6th		7th
IIIm	IIIm1	cl	Brite Blue	op	White	op	Redwood	op	White	cl	Brite Blue	op	White	cl	Brite Blue

Type IIIn "Star" Tube Bead with Stripes Inlayed in Outside Layer

Type	Bead Number	Glass	Outside		2nd		3rd		4th		5th	Stripes		
IIIn	IIIn1	tr	Oyster White	op	White	op	Redwood	op	White	cl	Lt. Gray	6	op	Redwood
												6	cl	Brite Navy
	IIIn2	tr	Oyster White	op	White	op	Redwood	op	White	cl	Brite Blue	6	op	Redwood
												6	cl	Brite Navy
	IIIn3	tr	Oyster White	op	Redwood	op	White	op	White	cl	Brite Blue	4	op	Redwood
												4	cl	Dk. Palm Green
												4	cl	Brite Navy

Table 5: Description of Class IV Beads (Fig. 8)

Type	Bead Number	Shape	Size	Glass	Outside Name of Colour	Glass	Core Name of Colour	Glass	Middle Layer Name of Colour
IVa	IVa1	R	M	op	Redwood	op	Black		
	IVa2	R	VS	op	Redwood	cl	Lt. Gray		
		R	S	op	Redwood	cl	Lt. Gray		
		R	M	op	Redwood	cl	Lt. Gray		
		R	L	op	Redwood	cl	Lt. Gray		
	IVa3	C	M	op	Redwood	cl	Lt. Gray		
	IVa4	O	S	op	Redwood	cl	Lt. Gray		
	IVa5	R	VS	op	Redwood	cl	Apple Green		
		R	S	op	Redwood	cl	Apple Green		
		R	M	op	Redwood	cl	Apple Green		
		R	L	op	Redwood	cl	Apple Green		
	IVa6	C	M	op	Redwood	cl	Apple Green		
	IVa7	O	M	op	Redwood	cl	Apple Green		
	IVa8	R	M	op	Redwood	cl	Brite Blue		
	IVa9	R	VS	cl	Scarlet	op	White		
		R	S	cl	Scarlet	op	White		
	IVa10	R	M	op	Black	op	Black	op	White
	IVa11	C	M	cl	Lt. Gray	cl	Lt. Gray	op	White
	IVa12	C	M	cl	Lt. Gray	cl	Lt. Gray	op	Brite Navy (Bead Appears Blue)
	IVa13	C	S	tr	Oyster White	cl	Lt. Gray		
		C	M	tr	Oyster White	cl	Lt. Gray		
	IVa14	C	M	tr	Oyster White	cl	Lt. Aqua Blue		
	IVa15	R	M	cl	Apple Green	cl	Apple Green	op	White
	IVa16	R	M	op	Robin's Egg Blue	op	Robin's Egg Blue	op	White
	IVa17	C	M	cl	Ultramarine	cl	Ultramarine	op	White
	IVa18	R	M	cl	Brite Navy	cl	Lt. Gray		
	IVa19	C	M	cl	Brite Navy	cl	Brite Navy	op	White

Table 5: Description of Class IV Beads (Fig. 8) (continued)

				Body of Bead						Simple Stripes
Type	Bead Number	Shape	Size	Glass	Outside Colour	Glass	Core Colour	Glass	Middle Colour	Number of Stripes / Colour of Stripes / Type of Glass
IVb	IVb1	R	M	op	Redwood	op	Black			8 op Black
	IVb2	R	M	op	Redwood	cl	Lt. Gray			11 op Black
	IVb3	R	M	op	Redwood	op	Black			3 op Broad White
	IVb4	R	M	op	Redwood	op	Black			6 op White (3 Pairs)
	IVb5	R	L	op	Redwood	op	Black			6 op White
	IVb6	R	S	op	Redwood	op	Black			8 op White
	IVb7	R	L	op	Redwood	op	Black			12 op White
	IVb8	R	L	op	Redwood	op	Black	op	White	4 op White
	IVb9	R	S	op	Redwood	cl	Brite Blue			8 op White
	IVb10	R	M	op	Redwood	cl	Apple Green			3 op White
		R	L	op	Redwood	cl	Apple Green			3 op White
	IVb11	R	L	op	Redwood	cl	Apple Green			6 op White
	IVb12	R	S	cl	Scarlet	op	White			8 op White (4 Pairs)
	IVb13	R	M	op	White	cl	Lt. Aqua			6 op Redwood
	IVb14	C	S	op	White	cl	Lt. Gray			4 op Redwood 4 op Black
	IVb15	C	S	op	White	cl	Lt. Gray			4 op Redwood 4 cl Br. Navy
	IVb16	C	S	op	White	cl	Lt. Aqua Blue			3 op Redwood 3 cl Br. Navy
	IVb17	C	S	op	White	cl	Lt. Gray			2 op Black 2 tr Lt. Aqua Blue
	IVb18	R	M	cl	Apple Green	cl	Apple Green	op	White	3 op White
	IVb19	R	M	cl	Apple Green	cl	Apple Green	op	White	3 cl Lemon Yellow
	IVb20	R	M	cl	Dk. Palm Green	cl	Apple Green	op	White	6 op White
	IVb21	R	M	cl	Teal Green	cl	Lt. Gray			4 op White
	IVb22	R	M	cl	Lt. Aqua Blue	cl	Lt. Aqua Blue	op	Lemon Yellow	3 op Lemon Yellow
	IVb23	R	S	cl	Shadow Blue	cl	Lt. Gray			3 op Redwood
	IVb24	R	L	cl	Dk. Shadow Blue	cl	Lt. Gray			6 op Redwood
	IVb25	R	VL	cl	Ultramarine	cl	Lt. Aqua Blue	op	White	16 op White
	IVb26	R	VL	cl	Brite Navy	cl	Lt. Aqua Blue	op	White	16 op White
	IVb27	R	M	cl	Brite Navy	op	Redwood	op	White	3 op Lemon Yellow 3 op Lt. Cherry Rose
	IVb28	R	M	cl	Brite Navy	op	Redwood	op	White	4 op Redwood 4 op White 4 op Lemon Yellow
	IVb29	R	M	cl	Brite Navy	cl	Brite Navy	op	White	3 op White
	IVb30	R	L	cl	Brite Navy	cl	Brite Navy	op	White	3 op Broad White
	IVb31	R	S	cl	Brite Navy	cl	Brite Navy	op	White	6 op White
		R	M	cl	Brite Navy	cl	Brite Navy	op	White	6 op White
	IVb32	R	L	cl	Brite Navy	cl	Brite Navy	op	White	7 op White
	IVb33	R	M	cl	Brite Navy	cl	Brite Navy	op	White	16 op White (8 Pairs)
	IVb34	R	M	cl	Brite Navy	cl	Brite Navy	op	White	16 op White
	IVb35	R	L	cl	Dk. Navy	cl	Dk. Navy	op	White	8 op White
	IVb36	R	VL	cl	Dk. Navy	cl	Dk. Navy	op	White	12 op White
	IVb37	R	L	cl	Dk. Rose Brown	cl	Dk. Rose Brown	op	White	12 op White

Table 5: Description of Class IV Beads (Fig. 8) (continued)

Type	Bead Number	Shape	Size	Glass	Body of Bead Outside Colour Name	Glass	Core Colour Name	Glass	Middle Colour	Surface Decoration Type Colour Name	
										Compound Stripes	
IVbb	IVbb1	R	M	op	Redwood	op	Black			3 Black	on White
	IVbb2	R	M	op	Redwood	cl	Lt. Gray			3 Black	on White
	IVbb3	R	M	op	Redwood	cl	Apple Green			3 Black	on White
	IVbb4	R	L	op	Redwood	op	Black			3 Brite Navy	on White
	IVbb5	O	S	op	Redwood	op	Black			3 Brite Navy	on White
	IVbb6	R	M	op	Redwood	cl	Lt. Gray			3 Brite Navy	on White
	IVbb7	R	M	op	Redwood	cl	Apple Green			3 Brite Navy	on White
	IVbb8	O	M	op	Redwood	cl	Apple Green			3 Brite Navy	on White
	IVbb9	R	M	cl	Brite Navy	cl	Brite Navy	op	White	3 Redwood	on White
	IVbb10	R	M	cl	Brite Navy	cl	Brite Navy	op	White	3 Redwood Pairs	on White
	IVbb11	R	L	cl	Dk. Rose Brown	op	Black	op	White	3 Brite Navy	on White
										Simple Stripes	
IVb'	IVb'1	O	M	cl	Apple Green	cl	Apple Green	op	White	3 op White	
										Compound Stripes	
IVbb'	IVbb'1	R	L	cl	Brite Navy	cl	Brite Navy	op	White	3 Redwood	on White
										"Flush Eyes"	
IVg	IVg1	O	M	cl	Brite Blue	cl	Brite Blue	op	White	3 Redwood Stars Dots on Brite Blue Dots	on White

Table 5: Description of Class IV Beads (Fig. 8) (continued)

In Recording "Star" Beads the Layers are Named from the Outside Inward

Layers:				Outside		Body of Bead 2nd		3rd		4th	
Type	Bead Number	Size	Glass	Colour Name	Glass	Colour Name	Glass	Colour Name	Glass	Colour Name	
Milled "Star" Beads with Plain Outside Layer											
IVk	IVk1	L	op	Redwood	op	White	cl	Brite Blue	op	White	
	IVk2	M	cl	Brite Navy	op	White	cl	Brite Blue	op	White	
	IVk3	M	cl	Brite Navy	op	White	op	Redwood	op	White	
	IVk4	L	cl	Brite Navy	op	White	op	Redwood	op	White	
	IVk5	F	cl	Brite Navy	op	White	op	Redwood	op	White	
	IVk6	M	cl	Dk. Palm Green	op	White	op	Redwood	op	White	
	IVk7	L	cl	Dk. Palm Green	op	White	op	Redwood	op	White	

Type	Bead Number	Size	Glass	Colour Name	Glass	Colour Name	Glass	Colour Name	Glass	Colour Name
Milled "Star" Beads with Stripes Inlaid in Outside Layer										
IVn	IVn1	M	tr	Oyster White	op	White	op	Redwood	op	White
	IVn2	M	tr	Oyster White	op	White	op	Redwood	op	White
	IVn3	L	tr	Oyster White	op	White	op	Redwood	op	White
	IVn4	M	tr	Oyster White	op	White	op	Redwood	op	White
	IVn5	M	tr	Oyster White	op	White	op	Redwood	op	White
	IVn6	L	tr	Oyster White	op	White	op	Redwood	op	White
	IVn7	F	tr	Oyster White	op	White	op	Redwood	op	White

Type	Bead Number	Size	Glass	Colour Name	Glass	Colour Name	Glass	Colour Name	Glass	Colour Name
Milled "Star" Beads which look like Porcelain Imitations of IVn Beads										
IVnn	IVnn1	VL	op	Redwood	op	White	op	Redwood		
	IVnn2	VL	op	Redwood	op	White	op	Redwood		
	IVnn3	VL	op	Black	op	White	op	Black		
	IVnn4	VL	op	White	op	Redwood	op	White	op	Redwood
	IVnn5	VL	op	White	op	Redwood	op	White	cl	Brite Blue

	5th	**Simple Stripes and Comments about Individual Beads** Number of Stripes and their Colours						
Glass	Colour Name							
cl	Brite Blue	Like IIIk1 but Milled Round						
cl	Lt. Gray	Outside layer very thin making ridges of next layer appear as stripes						
cl	Brite Blue	Outside layer very thin making ridges of next layer appear as stripes						
cl	Brite Blue	Outside layer thick giving a solid blue appearance to surface						
cl	Brite Blue	Like above bead but flattened						
cl	Lt. Gray							
cl	Brite Blue							

Glass	Colour Name	**Simple Stripes**								
cl	Lt. Gray	6	op	Broad Redwood	6	cl	Thin Dk. Palm Green			
cl	Lt. Gray	6	op	Redwood	6	cl	Brite Navy			
cl	Brite Blue	6	op	Redwood	6	cl	Brite Navy			
cl	Lt. Gray	6	cl	Lemon Yellow	6	cl	Brite Navy			
cl	Lt. Gray	6	cl	Dk. Palm Green	6	cl	Brite Navy			
cl	Lt. Gray	4	op	Redwood	4	cl	Dk. Palm Green	4	cl	Brite Navy
cl	Lt. Gray	4	op	Redwood	4	cl	Dk. Palm Green	4	cl	Brite Navy

Simple Stripes					
8	op	White			
6	op	White	6	cl	Brite Navy
8	op	Lt. Gold			
6	op	Broad Redwood	6	cl	Thin Brite Navy
6	op	Broad Redwood	6	cl	Thin Brite Navy

Table 6: Description of Class "W" Beads (Fig. 9)

"Tube"

Type	Bead Number	Shape	Size	Glass	Name of Colour
WIa	WIa1	T	L	cl	Lt. Gray
	WIa2	T	M	cl	Oyster White
	WIa3	T	M	op	White

"Round"

Type	Bead Number	Shape	Size	Glass	Name of Colour
WIb	WIb1	R	L	cl	Lt. Gray
	WIb2	R	VS	op	White
		R	S	op	White
		R	M	op	White
	WIb3	R	M	cl	Pale Blue
	WIb4	R	M	cl	Pale Blue (Opal)
		R	L	cl	Pale Blue (Opal)
		R	VL	cl	Pale Blue (Opal)
	WIb5	R	M	tr	Pale Blue (Alabaster)
		R	L	tr	Pale Blue (Alabaster)
		R	VL	tr	Pale Blue (Alabaster)
	WIb6	R	S	cl	Lt. Gold
		R	M	cl	Lt. Gold
	WIb7	R	VS	cl	Amber
		R	L	cl	Amber
	WIb8	R	L	cl	Maple
		R	VL	cl	Maple
	WIb9	R	S	cl	Dk. Palm Green
	WIb10	R	VS	op	Lt. Aqua Blue
		R	M	op	Lt. Aqua Blue
	WIb11	R	VS	op	Robin's Egg Blue
		R	S	op	Robin's Egg Blue
		R	M	op	Robin's Egg Blue
	WIb12	R	L	op	Brite Blue
	WIb13	R	VS	op	Brite Copan Blue
		R	L	op	Brite Copan Blue
	WIb14	R	VS	op	Brite Dutch Blue
		R	L	op	Brite Dutch Blue
	WIb15	R	L	cl	Ultramarine
	WIb16	R	L	cl	Brite Navy

"Oval"

Type	Bead Number	Shape	Size	Glass	Name of Colour
WIc	WIc1	O	S	op	White
	WIc2	O	L	cl	Pale Blue (Opal)
	WIc3	O	VL	tr	Pale Blue (Marble)
	WIc4	O	L	cl	Lt. Gold
	WIc5	O	L	cl	Amber
	WIc6	O	S	cl	Maple
	WIc7	O	S	cl	Citron
	WIc8	O	L	cl	Turquoise
	WIc9	O	S	op	Aqua Blue
	WIc10	O	L	op	Lt. Aqua Blue
	WIc11	O	L	cl	Ultramarine

"Donut"

Type	Bead Number	Shape	Size	Glass	Name of Colour
WId	WId1	DO	L	cl	Amber
	WId2	DO	L	cl	Maple
	WId3	DO	L	cl	Turquoise
	WId4	DO	L	cl	Amethyst

"Corn Beads"

Type	Bead Number	Glass	Name of Colour
WIIa	WIIa1	cl	Lt. Gold
	WIIa2	op	Surf Green
	WIIa3	cl	Dk. Palm Green

Flat "Disk" Beads

Type	Bead Number	Glass	Name of Colour
WIIb	WIIb1	cl	Ultramarine

Table 6: Description of Class "W" Beads (Fig. 9) (continued)

Facetted "Five Sided" Beads

Type	Bead Number	Glass	Name of Colour
WIIc	WIIc1	op	Black
	WIIc2	cl	Lt. Gray
	WIIc3	cl	Pale Blue (Opal)
	WIIc4	cl	Lt. Gold
	WIIc5	cl	Amber
	WIIc6	cl	Cinnamon
	WIIc7	cl	Teal Green
	WIIc8	cl	Turquoise
	WIIc9	cl	Lt. Aqua Blue
	WIIc10	cl	Brite Copan Blue
	WIIc11	cl	Ultramarine
	WIIc12	cl	Brite Navy
	WIIc13	cl	Amethyst

"Raspberry Beads"

Type	Bead Number	Glass	Name of Colour
WIId	WIId1	cl	Lt. Gray
	WIId2	cl	Pale Blue (Opal)
	WIId3	cl	Lt. Gold
	WIId4	cl	Amber
	WIId5	cl	Ultramarine
	WIId6	cl	Brite Navy
	WIId7	cl	Amethyst

"Melon" Beads

Type	Bead Number	Glass	Name of Colour
WIIe	WIIe1	cl	Lt. Gray
	WIIe2	cl	Lt. Gold
	WIIe3	cl	Amber
	WIIe4	cl	Cinnamon
	WIIe5	cl	Teal Green
	WIIe6	cl	Brite Copan Blue
	WIIe7	cl	Ultramarine
	WIIe8	cl	Brite Navy

"Ridged Tube" Beads

Type	Bead Number	Size	Glass	Name of Colour
WIIf	WIIf1	M	cl	Lt. Gold
	WIIf2	L	cl	Maple
	WIIf3	M	cl	Apple Green
	WIIf4	M	op	Surf Green
	WIIf5	L	cl	Turquoise

Round Bead with Pressed Design

Type	Bead Number	Size	Glass	Name of Colour
WIIg	WIIg1	M	cl	Lt. Gold
	WIIg2	M	cl	Apple Green

Table 6: Description of Class "W" Beads (Fig. 9) (continued)

WIII Type is any Wirewound bead of WI or WII Type with applied Decoration					
	Type	Bead Number	Glass	Colour	Decoration
Solid Plain Glass Overlay	WIIIa	WIIIa1	tr	White	with op Coral Plain Coating
		WIIIa2	tr	White	with cl Amethyst Plain Coating
Plain Glass Overlaid in a Design	WIIIb	WIIIb1	tr	White	with 3 groups of 3 cl Dk. Palm Green Dots
Plain Glass Inlaid in a Design	WIIIc	WIIIc1	cl	Ultramarine	— A Side; 3 five pointed stars and comet — B Side; Man in the moon and five pointed star
		WIIIc2	cl	Ultramarine	— A Side; 3 five pointed stars with "S" growing out of top star — B Side; Crescent Moon connected to cross (Variation of WIIIc1)
Complex Designed Glass Overlay	WIIId	WIIId1	cl	Ruby	Large Oval with fine cane of op White & cl Brite Navy twisted together applied in a spiral around bead
Overlay of Material Other than Glass	WIIIe	WIIIe1	op	Black	"Melon" with Gold Leaf Overlay

List of Beads Recorded by the Authors

Ia1	Ia2	Ia3	Ia4	Ia5	Ia6	Ia7	Ia8	Ia9	Ia10	Ia11
Ia12	Ia13	Ia14	Ia15	Ia16	Ia17	Ia18	Ia19	Ia20	Ia21	Ia22
*	Ib1	Ib2	Ib3	Ib4	Ib5	Ib6	Ib7	Ib8	Ib9	Ib10
Ib11	Ib12	Ib13	Ib14	Ib15	Ib16	Ib17	Ib18	Ib19	Ib20	Ib21
Ib22	Ib23	Ib24	*	Ibb1	Ibb2	Ibb3	Ibb4	Ibb5	Ibb6	*
Ib'1	Ib'2	Ib'3	Ib'4	*	Ibb'1	*	Ic1	Ic2	Ic3	Ic4
Ic5	Ic6	Ic7	Ic8	Ic9	Ic10	Ic11	Ic12	Ic13	Ic14	Ic15
*	Ic'1	Ic'2	Ic'3	*	Id1	*	Id'1	*	Ie1	*
Ie'1	Ie'2	*	If1	If2	If3	If4	If5			
IIa1	IIa2	IIa3	IIa4	IIa5	IIa6	IIa7	IIa8	IIa9	IIa10	IIa11
IIa12	IIa13	IIa14	IIa15	IIa16	IIa17	IIa18	IIa19	IIa20	IIa21	IIa22
IIa23	IIa24	IIa25	IIa26	IIa27	IIa28	IIa29	IIa30	IIa31	IIa32	IIa33
IIa34	IIa35	IIa36	IIa37	IIa38	IIa39	IIa40	IIa41	IIa42	IIa43	IIa44
IIa45	IIa46	IIa47	IIa48	IIa49	IIa50	IIa51	IIa52	IIa53	IIa54	IIa55
IIa56	IIa57	IIa58	IIa59	IIa60	IIa61	*	IIb1	IIb2	IIb3	IIb4
IIb5	IIb6	IIb7	IIb8	IIb9	IIb10	IIb11	IIb12	IIb13	IIb14	IIb15
IIb16	IIb17	IIb18	IIb19	IIb20	IIb21	IIb22	IIb23	IIb24	IIb25	IIb26
IIb27	IIb28	IIb29	IIb30	IIb31	IIb32	IIb33	IIb34	IIb35	IIb36	IIb37
IIb38	IIb39	IIb40	IIb41	IIb42	IIb43	IIb44	IIb45	IIb46	IIb47	IIb48
IIb49	IIb50	IIb51	IIb52	IIb53	IIb54	IIb55	IIb56	IIb57	IIb58	IIb59
IIb60	IIb61	IIb62	IIb63	IIb64	IIb65	IIb66	IIb67	IIb68	IIb69	IIb70
IIb71	IIb72	IIb73	IIb74	*						
IIbb1	IIbb2	IIbb3	IIbb4	IIbb5	IIbb6	IIbb7	IIbb8	IIbb9		
IIbb10	IIbb11	IIbb12	IIbb13	IIbb14	IIbb15	IIbb16	IIbb17	IIbb18		
IIbb19	IIbb20	IIbb21	IIbb22	IIbb23	IIbb24	IIbb25	IIbb26	IIbb27		
IIbb28	IIbb29	*	IIb'1	IIb'2	IIb'3	IIb'4	IIb'5	IIb'6		
IIb'7	IIb'8	IIb'9	IIb'10	IIb'11	IIb'12	IIb'13	*	IIbb'1		
IIbb'2	*	IIe1	IIe2	*	IIg1	IIg2	IIg3	IIg4		
IIg5	*	IIh1	*	IIj1	IIj2	IIj3	IIj4	IIj5	IIj6	
IIIa1	IIIa2	IIIa3	IIIa4	IIIa5	IIIa6	IIIa7	IIIa8	IIIa9		
IIIa10	IIIa11	IIIa12	*	IIIb1	IIIb2	IIIb3	IIIb4	IIIb5		
IIIb6	IIIb7	IIIb8	IIIb9	IIIb10	*	IIIbb1	IIIbb2	IIIbb3		
IIIbb4	IIIbb5	IIIbb6	IIIbb7	IIIbb8	*	IIIc1	IIIc2	IIIc3		
*	IIIc'1	IIIc'2	IIIc'3	IIIc'4	*	IIIe1	IIIe2	*		
IIIe'1	*	IIIf1	IIIf2	*	IIIk1	IIIk2	IIIk3	*		
IIIm1	*	IIIn1	IIIn2	IIIn3						
IVa1	IVa2	IVa3	IVa4	IVa5	IVa6	IVa7	IVa8	IVa9		
IVa10	IVa11	IVa12	IVa13	IVa14	IVa15	IVa16	IVa17	IVa18		
IVa19	*	IVb1	IVb2	IVb3	IVb4	IVb5	IVb6	IVb7		
IVb8	IVb9	IVb10	IVb11	IVb12	IVb13	IVb14	IVb15	IVb16		
IVb17	IVb18	IVb19	IVb20	IVb21	IVb22	IVb23	IVb24	IVb25		
IVb26	IVb27	IVb28	IVb29	IVb30	IVb31	IVb32	IVb33	IVb34		
IVb35	IVb36	IVb37	*	IVbb1	IVbb2	IVbb3	IVbb4	IVbb5		
IVbb6	IVbb7	IVbb8	IVbb9	IVbb10	IVbb11	*	IVb'1	*		
IVbb'1	*	IVg1	*	IVk1	IVk2	IVk3	IVk4	IVk5		
IVk6	IVk7	*	IVn1	IVn2	IVn3	IVn4	IVn5	IVn6		

List of Beads Recorded by the Authors (continued)

IVn7	*	IVnn1	IVnn2	IVnn3	IVnn4	IVnn5		
WIa1	WIa2	WIa3	*	WIb1	WIb2	WIb3	WIb4	WIb5
WIb6	WIb7	WIb8	WIb9	WIb10	WIb11	WIb12	WIb13	WIb14
WIb15	WIb16	*	WIc1	WIc2	WIc3	WIc4	WIc5	WIc6
WIc7	WIc8	WIc9	WIc10	WIc11	*	WId1	WId2	WId3
WId4								
WIIa1	WIIa2	WIIa3	*	WIIb1	*	WIIc1	WIIc2	WIIc3
WIIc4	WIIc5	WIIc6	WIIc7	WIIc8	WIIc9	WIIc10	WIIc11	WIIc12
WIIc13	*	WIId1	WIId2	WIId3	WIId4	WIId5	WIId6	WIId7
*	WIIe1	WIIe2	WIIe3	WIIe4	WIIe5	WIIe6	WIIe7	WIIe8
*	WIIf1	WIIf2	WIIf3	WIIf4	WIIf5	*	WIIg1	WIIg2
WIIIa1	WIIIa2	*	WIIIb1	*	WIIIc1	WIIIc2	*	WIIId1
*	WIIIe1							

Kenneth E. and Martha Ann Kidd

Select Bibliography

For those who may wish to investigate this subject further, the following selected titles are offered. There is not, so far as the authors know, an entirely satisfactory treatment of the making of glass beads in English, and it is necessary to piece the story together from various sources, such as Dillon, Nesbitt and Pellatt, after having first read a general exposition of glass-making such as may be found in Marston. Those who are able to do so may wish to go further afield and examine the writing of some of the more outstanding continental authors. The subject becomes complicated at this point because numerous writers have discussed the manufacture of glass objects (though seldom beads specifically), and some of the more important are of considerable antiquity, e.g., Kunckel, Neri and Theophilus. Unfortunately, these last three are not easily obtainable. The publications of Morazzoni and Pasquato, Pazaurek and Zecchin, however, are recent and perhaps the most satisfactory for the readers of this article.

The Art of Glass-Making 1751-1772
n.d.
A Portfolio of Prints from the Diderot Encyclopedia. Reproduced by Corning Glass Center, Corning Museum of Glass, Corning, N.Y.

Blau, J.
1941
Bead-makers and Bead Glasshouses in the Bohemian Forest. *Glastechnische Berichte*, Vol. 19, No. 3 (Mar.), pp. 89-98.

Bussolin, Dominique
1847
Les célèbres verreries de Venise et de Murano; description historique, technologigue, et statistique.... H. F. Munster, Venise.

Dillon, Edward
1867
Glassworks of Venice and Murano. *Journal of the Royal Society of Arts*, Vol. 15, p. 758.

1907
Glass. Methuen, London.

Haggar, Reginald George
1961
Glass and Glassmakers. Methuen, London.

Haudicquer de Blancourt, Jean
1699
The Art of Glass. Dan Brown, London.

Kunckel, Johann
1679
Ars Vitraria Experimentalis. Johann Bielke, Frankfurt und Leipzig.

Marston, Percival
n.d.
Glass and Glass Manufacture. Pitman, London.

Morazzoni, Giuseppe, and Michelangelo Pasquato
1953
Le conterie veneziane. Società Veneziana Conterie e Cristallerie, Venezia.

Neri, Antonio
1826
The Art of Glass. Trans. by C. M. (Christopher Merret). Typis Medio-Montanis, Worcestershire.

Nesbitt, Alexander
1878
Glass. Chapman and Hall, London.

Pazaurek, Gustav Edmund
1911
Glasperlen und Perlenarbeiten in alter und neuer zeit. A. Koch, Darmstadt.

Pellatt, Apsley
1849
Curiosities of Glass Making: with Details of the Processes and Production of Ancient and Modern Ornamental Glass Manufacture. David Bogue, London.

Pholien, Florent
1899
La verrerie au pays de Liège: étude rétrospective. Aug. Bernard, Liège.

Sleen, W. G. N. van der
1967
A Handbook on Beads. Musée de Verre, Liège. (Publication of the *Journées Internationales du Verre*.)

Solon, M. L.
1919
A Bibliography of Works on Glass Published in all European Countries, Divided into Two Parts.... Abstract in *Journal of the Society of Glass Technology*, Vol. 3.

Theophilus, called also Rugerus
1961
The Various Arts. Trans. from the Latin by C. R. Dodwell. T. Nelson, London.

Zecchin, Luigi
1955
Sulla storia delle conterie veneziane. S. Marco, Venezia.

Trent University,
Peterborough, Ontario

Guide to the Description and Classification of Glass Beads

Karlis Karklins

ABSTRACT

This guide provides information relevant to the classification of glass beads recovered from archaeological sites in Canada. It is partly based on and intended to be used with "A Classification System for Glass Beads for the Use of Field Archaeologists," by Kenneth and Martha Kidd. Material presented includes a critical evaluation of several bead classification schemes, an overview of bead-manufacturing techniques, a descriptive listing of the various classes and types of beads that have been recorded to date, an explication of the physical attributes of a bead, and some interpretative material. Information relevant to entering glass beads in the Parks Canada artifact data base system is also provided.

Submitted for publication 1980, by Karlis Karklins, National Historic Parks and Sites Branch, Parks Canada, Ottawa.

INTRODUCTION

During the past six decades, a number of systems have been proposed for the classification of glass beads. While the majority are elementary in nature and have limited application, four are noteworthy.

The first classificatory scheme for beads was published in 1928 by Horace C. Beck. Comprehensive though it was, his "Classification and Nomenclature of Beads and Pendants" was aimed primarily at Old World researchers and never achieved popularity in North America. Nevertheless, Beck's work remains a valuable research tool and is a classic in its own right.

Little progress was made during the next two decades. Then, in the 1950s, Kenneth E. Kidd formulated a scheme which, with modifications and the collaboration of his wife Martha, was published in 1970 as "A Classification System for Glass Beads for the Use of Field Archaeologists." Utilizing the process of manufacture as the primary criterion for sorting beads and the physical attributes secondarily, the system is most notable for its extensive colour plates illustrating each recorded bead type. Also of note is the extremely well-developed typological flow chart for drawn beads (Kidd and Kidd 1970: 51). Unfortunately, the wound-bead chart (Kidd and Kidd 1970: 52) is not nearly as detailed, and wound-on-drawn, mould-pressed, blown, and moulded beads are not dealt with at all. Furthermore, many of the bead classes and some of the terms are not adequately defined, making the system difficult to use at times. Another drawback centres on the fact that the system, developed using beads derived from early historical period sites in the Northeast, has been found to be of little utility by several researchers in the Pacific Northwest (Ross 1976: 671-73; Sprague 1971: 128-29). In its favour is the fact that it is an open-ended system so that new categories, classes, types and varieties can be added as they are required.

In the same year that the previous report was published, Lyle M. Stone completed his treatise on Fort Michilimackinac. Published four years later, it contains a section on beads wherein the primary sorting is based on function as revealed by relative size. The two pertinent functional categories (necklace beads and seed beads) are each further subdivided into Class (method of manufacture), Series (structure or form), Type (shape), and Variety (colour and diaphaneity). All of the varieties are illustrated in colour photographs.

The main drawback to Stone's approach is that relative size and function do not always equate; not all "large" beads found their use in necklaces and not all "small" beads are seed beads (the latter should have been designated "embroidery beads" as the term "seed bead" is a size designation). There is also the problematic "medium" size group which overlaps both categories. Secondarily, this system, like the previous one, deals only with drawn and wound beads and has not found acceptance on the West Coast.

The final classification system to be dealt with herein appeared in 1976. In that year, Lester A. Ross completed his monograph "Fort Vancouver, 1829-1860: A Historical Archeological Investigation of the Goods Imported and Manufactured by the Hudson's Bay Company" which contains a lengthy and well-illustrated section on glass beads. The specimens are classified using a typological scheme reminiscent of and apparently lightly influenced by that of Kenneth and Martha Kidd (1970). However, the Fort Vancouver typology is much more comprehensive, covering all the major manufacturing types. It is also not as rigid a system as that of the Kidds and there is no coding of the various bead types. While this allows every minor variant to be recorded, it does little to facilitate the inter-site comparison of bead assemblages. Notwithstanding, Ross' scheme is a milestone for a part of the continent where the typical classification "system" has for so long consisted of a loosely ordered list of inadequately described bead types.

Although each of the foregoing systems has its drawbacks, the one that seems to offer the most potential and appears to have found the most universal acceptance is the one devised by Kenneth and Martha Kidd (1970). Consequently, it has been chosen to form the basis for this guide.

The typology for drawn and wound beads that follows is a corrected and expanded version of that proposed by the Kidds (1970). The other manufacturing types are classified using a similar coding system and attribute hierarchy, with the classes and types being defined on the basis of archaeological specimens and several 19th-century bead sample cards and books. While every attempt has been made to make the typology as comprehensive as possible, it is inevitable that new categories will be encountered as more bead assemblages are analysed. Should you record a new class or type, please inform me so that it can be added to the inventory. While instructions for defining varieties are presented for each manufacturing type, no varieties are listed because they are far too numerous. Furthermore, the practicability of recording varieties in a comprehensive classification system becomes doubtful when one considers that well over 100,000 varieties of glass beads have been produced in the world to date (Liu 1975b: 31).

GLASS BEAD CLASSIFICATION

The primary criterion for sorting glass beads into typological categories is the technique of manufacture. Six major types are pertinent to North American researchers: drawn, wound, wound on drawn, mould pressed, blown, and moulded.

Drawn Beads

Also called tube, cane and hollow-cane beads, the appellation "drawn" is preferred because it refers to the production process rather than the form of the finished product. As the process has been described in detail by Kidd and Kidd (1970: 48-49), only a brief survey will be presented here.

In the manufacture of drawn beads, a tube up to 300 yd long was drawn out from a hollow globe of molten glass by two men (Carroll 1917: 7). Depending on what stylistic variation was required, the globe may have been (1) composed of several differently coloured layers, (2) adorned with rods or lumps of coloured glass to form stripes, (3) marvered to create a specific shape, and/or (4) twisted during the drawing process to impart a spiral effect. When cool, the tube was broken into manageable sections which were then sorted according to their diameter. These were subsequently cut into bead lengths by placing them on a sharp iron in the shape of a broad chisel and striking them with a blunt-edged, nearly triangular plate of steel (Anonymous 1825: 120, 1835: 79).

The resultant beads were either left unaltered, save for the possible grinding of facets, or their broken ends were rounded. Before 1817, the latter was accomplished by putting the beads in a large pan with sand and wood ash, or plaster and graphite. The pan was then heated over a charcoal fire and the contents stirred continually with a spatula resembling a hatchet with a round end (Anonymous 1825: 120). Another, much more efficient method came into use in Venice in 1817 (Francis 1979b: 10). It consisted of intermixing the rough beads with plaster and graphite or clay and charcoal dust, and then placing the mixture in an iron drum which was heated and rotated in an oven, a technique commonly referred to as "tumbling" (Orchard 1929: 85). In both processes the heat and agitation rounded the broken ends while the various "packing" mixtures kept the beads from sticking together and prevented their perforations from collapsing as the glass became viscid. Depending on the length of time the beads were treated in this manner, they might range from practically unaltered tube fragments to almost perfect spheroids. After being allowed to cool, the beads were polished and sorted according to size by passing them through a series of graduated sieves.

*Io Hexagonal beads exhibiting an "alternating twist" pattern apparently produced by alternatingly twisting a heated hexagonal tube one way and then the other until a series of undulations have been formed in the body facets

Class II

Non-tubular beads with simple (monochrome) bodies which may exhibit adventitious surface decoration.

IIa Undecorated

IIb Decorated with straight, simple stripes

IIb' Decorated with spiral, simple stripes

IIbb Decorated with straight, compound stripes

IIbb' Decorated with spiral, compound stripes

IIe "Melon" beads (ridged bodies)

*IIf Beads whose surfaces have been modified by the application of ground facets

IIg "Flush eye" beads (decorated with insets)

IIh Decorated with insets and straight, simple stripes

IIj Beads encircled by two or more wavy lines

Class III

Tubular beads with compound (multi-layered) bodies which may exhibit adventitious surface decoration. Cross-sections are round unless otherwise noted.

IIIa Undecorated

IIIb Decorated with straight, simple stripes

*IIIb' Decorated with spiral, simple stripes

IIIbb Decorated with straight, compound stripes

*IIIbb' Decorated with spiral, compound stripes

IIIc Beads with straight, polyhedral bodies

IIIc' Beads with twisted, polyhedral bodies

IIIe Beads with straight, ridged bodies

IIIe' Beads with twisted, ridged bodies

IIIf Beads whose surfaces have been modified by grinding

IIIk "Chevron" beads with plain outer layers

*IIIkk "Semi-chevron" beads (all layers except the core are "starry") with plain outer layers

IIIm "Chevron" beads made by grinding large, multi-layered tubes into round or oval forms to show the ridges of the second layer and the end design of the various layers

IIIn "Chevron" beads decorated with straight, simple stripes on the outer layer

*IIInn "Chevron" beads decorated with straight, simple stripes on the outer layer. These beads resemble porcelain imitations of class IIIn beads and are the tubular counterparts of class IVnn beads

*IIIp "Chevron" beads decorated with straight, simple stripes on the surface of the second layer

*IIIq "Semi-Chevron" beads (all layers except the core are "starry") decorated with straight, simple stripes on the surface of the second layer

Class IV

Non-tubular beads with compound (multi-layered) bodies which may exhibit adventitious surface decoration.

IVa Undecorated

IVb Decorated with straight, simple stripes

IVb' Decorated with spiral, simple stripes

IVbb Decorated with straight, compound stripes

IVbb' Decorated with spiral, compound stripes

IVg "Flush eye" beads (decorated with insets)

IVk "Chevron" beads with plain outer layers

IVn "Chevron" beads decorated with straight, simple stripes on the outer layer

IVnn "Chevron" beads decorated with straight, simple stripes on the outer layer. These beads resemble porcelain imitations of class IVn beads

*IVnn' "Chevron" beads decorated with straight, compound stripes on the outer layer

*IVp "Chevron" beads decorated with straight, simple stripes on the surface of the second layer

*IVq "Semi-chevron" beads (all layers except the core are "starry") decorated with straight, simple stripes on the surface of the second layer

Wound Beads

Wound beads, also termed wire wound and mandrel wound, were produced by winding a viscid rod or a filament drawn therefrom around a rotating metal mandrel one or more times until the desired size and shape were achieved. While still soft, the beads might be decorated with any of a myriad of inlays or appliqués. They might also be pressed with small metal paddles or clamped in tong-like moulds to impart a design or a uniform shape (the latter should not be confused with the "mould-pressed" process [cf.]). When cool, the beads were stripped from the mandrel which is sometimes tapered or covered with chalk, graphite or clay to facilitate this step (Kidd and Kidd 1970: 49; Sprague 1979: 8).

The surfaces of wound beads usually exhibit swirl marks that encircle the axis. Bubbles are either round, or elongate and oriented like the swirl marks. The perforation may taper slightly and have an uneven surface.

The Kidds segregate wound beads into three classes according to their structure (simple or compound) and the relative complexity of their shape. Types are determined on the basis of shape and the general configuration of the decoration, if any, while varieties are based on the colour and diaphaneity of the structural elements.

A listing of the various classes and types recorded to date follows (Fig. 2). Types marked with an asterisk (*) were encountered after the Kidds' classification system was printed. The diversity of the varieties precludes their being listed; see Kidd and Kidd (1970: 86-86) for these.

Class WI

Simple (single-layered), monochrome and polychrome beads with simple shapes.

WIa Cylindrical

WIb Round

WIc Oval

WId Doughnut-shaped

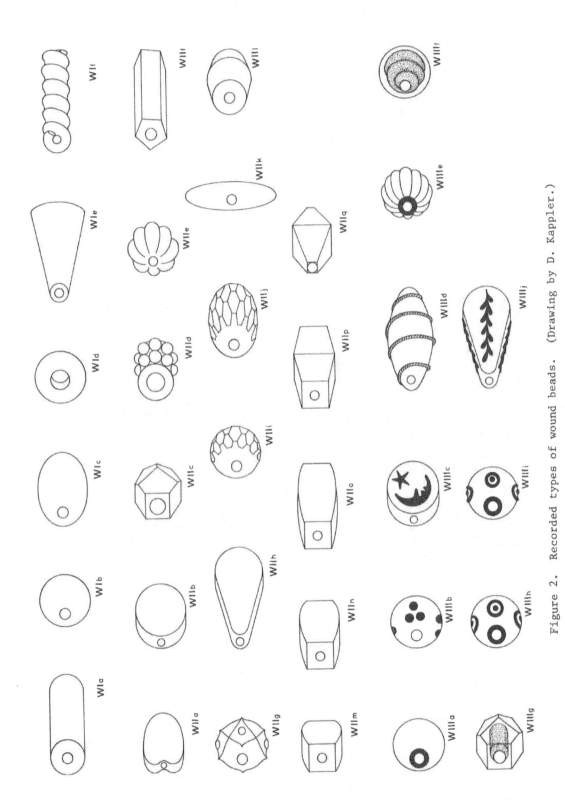

Figure 2. Recorded types of wound beads. (Drawing by D. Kappler.)

*WIe   Conical

*WIf   "Raised spiral" (shaped like a compressed cylindrical spring, this type consists of a glass rod wound in a spiral fashion)

Class WII

Simple (single-layered), monochrome and polychrome beads with relatively elaborate shapes formed by pressing, pinching, moulding, grinding or some other form of manipulation.

WIIa   "Corn" beads (tabular beads in the shape of corn kernels)

WIIb   Flat "disc" beads (tabular beads with circular outlines)

WIIc   Faceted "five sided" beads (each bead has eight or ten, pentagonal, pressed facets)

WIId   "Raspberry" beads (these exhibit several rows of prominent nodes)

WIIe   "Melon" beads (lobed beads resembling melons)

WIIf   "Ridged tube" beads (tubular beads with rectangular pressed facets that extend their entire length)

WIIg   Beads with complex pressed designs

*WIIh   Flattened "teardrop" beads (teardrop-shaped beads pressed flat)

*WIIi   Round-faceted beads (round beads whose surfaces have been modified into facets by grinding)

*WIIj   Ovate-faceted beads (oval beads whose surfaces have been modified into facets by grinding)

*WIIk   Circular convex bicone disc beads (Beck's [1928] type I.A.1.e.)

*WIIl   Standard circular truncated convex bicone beads (type I.C.1.f.)

*WIIm   Short square barrel beads (type IX.B.1.b.)

*WIIn   Standard square barrel beads (type IX.C.1.b.)

*WIIo   Long square barrel beads (type IX.D.1.b.)

*WIIp   Long square truncated convex bicone beads (type IX.D.1.f.)

*WIIq   Standard square bicone beads (type IX.C.2.e)

Class WIII

   Compound (multi-layered) beads with or without adventitious decoration, and simple (single-layered), monochrome and polychrome beads with adventitious decoration.

   WIIIa   Class WI beads with a surface coating of a different colour or material

   WIIIb   Class WI beads with inlaid decoration (incorrectly described in Kidd and Kidd 1970: 86)

   WIIIc   Class WII beads with inlaid decoration

   WIIId   Class WI beads with overlaid decoration

   WIIIe   Class WII beads with a surface coating of a different colour or material (incorrectly described in Kidd and Kidd 1970: 86)

   *WIIIf   Class WI beads with internal decorative elements

   *WIIIg   Class WII beads with internal decorative elements

   *WIIIh   Type WIIIa (multi-layered) beads with inlaid decoration

   *WIIIi   Type WIIIa (multi-layered) beads with overlaid decoration

   *WIIIj   Class WII beads with overlaid decoration

Wound-on-Drawn Beads

   This is a rare type recorded only at one site in the Pacific Northwest (Sprague 1979: 9). It consists of a short section of drawn tubing about which has been wound a layer of contrastingly coloured glass. Having a red exterior and white core, the only variety observed to date is practically indistinguishable from its more common, all-wound counterpart. The only difference is that the cores of the former contain linear bubbles that parallel the axis.
   As only one variety has been observed, it is impossible to do more than make a few suggestions concerning a classifactory scheme for wound-on-drawn beads. Using the wound-bead system as a basis, it is proposed that the wound-on-drawn category (designated WD) be divided into two structural classes:
   Class WDI. Compound (undecorated, multi-layered)
   Class WDII. Composite (decorated, multi-layered)
Types within each class would be designated according to the shape of the beads, and the general configuration of the decoration, if any. Varieties would be based on the colour and diaphaneity of the structural components.

Mould-Pressed Beads

Variously cited in the literature as moulded, pressed, mandrel pressed, and mould pressed, the latter designation is adopted here as it seems to best describe the process of manufacture. Two basic methods were employed to produce the mould-pressed beads found on Canadian sites. In the first, the end of a glass rod was heated over an oil flame until it melted. A piece was then pinched from it and pressed in a tong-like two-piece mould. As the glass was compressed, any excess was forced out at the seam while a moveable pin pierced the glass and formed the perforation.

In the second method, two pieces of viscid glass, one in either half of a two-piece mould, were pressed together to fuse them. This permitted the production of beads with complex coloured patterns that would have been distorted or destroyed in the previous process. The moveable pin that formed the perforation usually extended from one half of the mould to the other in the case of round and oblate beads and across the open face of the mould for flattened and elongated specimens. As a consequence, the beads in the former group have seams about their equators, while those in the latter have seams along their sides and ends.

After the beads were removed from their respective moulds, their mould seams, as well as any facets that might have been present, were frequently ground smooth. If the perforation remained sealed off at one end as in the case of the "mandrel pressed" beads described by Ross (1976: 759), it was punched through.

Mould-pressed beads are usually symmetrical though they may display tiny flattened areas. They may also have pebbled ("orange peel") surfaces, or exhibit mould marks in the form of slight to bold ridges and linear bulges, seams in coloured patterns, or slightly differently coloured linear zones caused by differential light refraction. The perforations sometimes taper distinctly and frequently have crackled surfaces.

Although the manufacturing sub-type might seem to be the ideal criterion for identifying classes within the mould-pressed category, the difficulty in distinguishing the two, unless there are coloured patterns in the glass, precludes this. Instead, the category (designated MP) is divided into four classes on the basis of structure (monochrome and polychrome) and the presence or absence of surface decoration and faceting. Shape determines the type, while varieties are defined according to the colour and diaphaneity of the structural elements, the configuration of the decoration, and the number, shape and type (mould imparted or cut) of facets.

The classes and types recorded to date are listed below and illustrated in Figure 3.

Class MPI

Plain monochrome beads.

MPIa   Round

MPIb   Oval

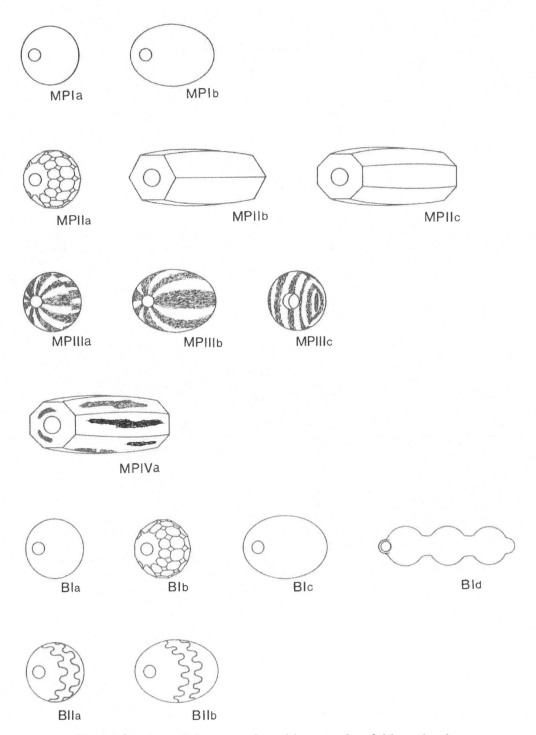

Figure 3. Recorded types of mould-pressed and blown beads.
(Drawing by D. Kappler.)

Class MPII

    Monochrome beads exhibiting faceting and/or surface decoration.

    MPIIa Round-faceted

    MPIIb Long hexagonal barrel (Beck's [1928] type XIII.D.1.b.)

    MPIIc Long octagonal barrel (Beck's type XIV.D.1.b.).

Class MPIII

    Plain polychrome beads.

    MPIIIa Round

    MPIIIb Oval

    MPIIIc Doughnut-shaped

Class MPIV

    Polychrome beads exhibiting faceting and/or surface decoration.

    MPIVa Long octagonal barrel (Beck's type XIV.D.1.b.).

Blown Beads

Three methods have been noted for the manufacture of blown beads. The first entailed fixing a small gather of molten glass on the end of a blowpipe and blowing it into a bubble with a slight hollow projection at either end. When the bubble had cooled, the projections were broken off, creating the perforation, and the jagged edges were usually firepolished. The second method is essentially the same except that the bubble was blown in a two-piece mould, to impart either a design or a special or uniform shape. In the third method, a series of bubbles was blown in a heated glass tube. The latter was then broken into individual or segmented beads whose ends may or may not have been firepolished.

The beads produced by any of the aforementioned methods could be coloured by painting their surfaces or introducing paint, coloured wax, powdered fish scales or metal dust into their interiors (Pazaurek 1911: 2). They were often filled with white wax to render them less fragile (Lardner 1972: 236).

While the ideal criterion for the primary sorting of blown beads would be the manufacturing sub-type, the difficulty in determing the latter in archaeological specimens makes its use impractical. Rather, the category (designated B) is segregated into two classes based on the presence or absence of decorative elements. Types are distinguished according to shape, with the manufacturing sub-type being indicated if determinable. Varieties are defined by the colour and diaphaneity of the structural elements, the nature of the colouration (external, internal, or in the glass itself), and where applicable, the number, shape and type (mould imparted or cut) of facets; the configuration of the decoration; and the number of segments.

The known classes and types of blown beads are listed below and illustrated in Figure 3.

Class BI

Simple (undecorated) beads.

BIa   Round

BIb   Round-faceted

BIc   Oval

BId   Segmented

Class BII

Complex (decorated) beads.

BIIa   Round

BIIb   Oval

Moulded Beads

This manufacturing type was defined by Sprague (1973) and Ross (1974: 18) who termed it "Prosser molded" because of its seeming similarity to the moulding technique for ceramic buttons that was patented by Richard Prosser in 1840. However, as it remains to be determined whether the two techniques are one and the same, the qualifier "Prosser" is deleted here.

While Ross (1974: 22; 1976: 767-70) hypothesizes that the beads were made of molten glass in essentially the same manner as mould-pressed beads, a present-day producer - the Jablonex Foreign Trade Corporation in Jablonec nad Nisou, Czechoslovakia - informs us (1977, pers. com.) that "tile beads" (as they are generically called in the manufacturer's parlance) are "made of glass powder which is moulded and melted." As they would not elucidate, the technological aspects remain a mystery.

Two types of moulded beads have been recorded to date. One is spherical with a broad, raised band about the equator; the other is in the form of a short cylinder. On both, one end is rounded and smooth, while the other is flat and rough or pebbled. The perforation tapers

toward the rounded end. Exterior surfaces range from glazed to dull,
the latter resembling unglazed porcelain.

    As the data base is so limited, it is presently impossible to
formulate a classificatory scheme for moulded beads (designated M).

GLASS BEAD ATTRIBUTES

The following attributes are listed in descending order of their relative importance in the classification of glass beads.

Structure

Structure refers to the physical composition of a bead. There are four structural categories (Stone 1974: 88-89):

Simple - beads composed of a single, undecorated layer of glass.

Compound - beads composed of two or more, undecorated layers of glass.

Complex - simple specimens with adventitious decoration.

Composite - compound specimens with adventitious decoration.

Shape

While the shape nomenclature utilized by the Kidds is basically self-explanatory, a few comments will help elucidate some of the terms.

All tubular beads are assumed to have round cross-sections unless otherwise noted. As they often grade imperceptibly into the circular group, tubular specimens may be segregated using the following criteria. A bead of any length is classified as tubular if it has broken or cut ends that have not been altered by "tumbling." If the ends have been rounded, a bead is tubular if its length exceeds its diameter.

Circular specimens, shaped like little rings, have diameters that are equal to or greater than their lengths.

The round category includes beads not only spheroidal, but also oblate and barrel-shaped. The latter should be designated round (oblate) and round (barrel-shaped), respectively.

Some oval beads are also barrel-shaped and should be recorded as oval (barrel-shaped).

The term doughnut-shaped refers to those beads in the wound category that have extremely oblate bodies and very large perforations (the configuration is much like that of a Life Saver candy). Similarly shaped beads in the drawn category would be termed "circular."

The Kidds use the term flat to define those drawn beads that have been pressed flat parallel to the perforation while the glass was still viscid. As this does not reveal anything about the bead's pre-flattened shape, it is recommended that the term be modified to include this information. For example, a flattened round bead would be recorded as "flat-round."

Other shapes are defined in the Glass Bead Classification chapter of this guide. Should new shapes be encountered, the use of Beck's (1928) system and terminology to designate them is recommended. The hierarchical charts for "regular-rounded" and "regular-faceted" beads are presented in Figures 4-5. For beads with specialized and irregular shapes see Beck (1928). However, as multi-faceted specimens are not adequately covered in the latter, a few comments may be appropriate.

Tubular beads of types If and IIIf that have hexagonal- and heptagonal-sectioned bodies whose corners have been removed by grinding are termed **tubular, cornerless hexagonal** and **tubular, cornerless heptagonal**, respectively. These are the so-called "Russian" beads.

As for beads with more than 21 facets, if the exact shape cannot be determined using Beck, it is suggested that the general form of the bead be given followed by the qualifier "faceted" (for example, round-faceted or elongate-faceted). To this should be appended a description of the type (cut or mould imparted), shape, number and location of the various facets.

Decoration

The adornment encountered on North American beads falls into three major categories:

Overlaid - appliqués of glass or another material which either rest on or protrude noticeably from the surface of the bead (this includes painted decoration).

Inlaid - embedded elements whose surfaces are either flush with or only slightly above the surface of the bead.

Internal - decorative elements, such as coloured cylinders, spiral bands, and metal foil, located within the body of the bead.

Beads may be decorated using multifarious techniques and decorative elements, the most common of which are listed below:

Stripes - the most common design element on drawn beads, stripes may be simple (monochrome) or compound (polychrome), and straight or spiral (Fig. 6a-b).

Wavy lines - undulating lines which may be either simple or compound (Fig. 6c-d).

Interwoven lines - also called "double wave," this design consists of two crossed wavy lines (Fig. 6e).

Rings - stripes in the form of circles that extend about a bead perpendicular to the axis; beads decorated with rings are termed "zone" or "zoned" beads (Fig. 6f).

Combed designs - rings or spiral stripes applied to the surface of a bead are heated until viscid and then have a wire drawn through them to produce a series of scallops, ogees, zigzags, or feather-like patterns (Fig. 6g-j).

Eyes - specimens adorned with simple or compound dots are called "eye beads" (Fig. 6k-m).

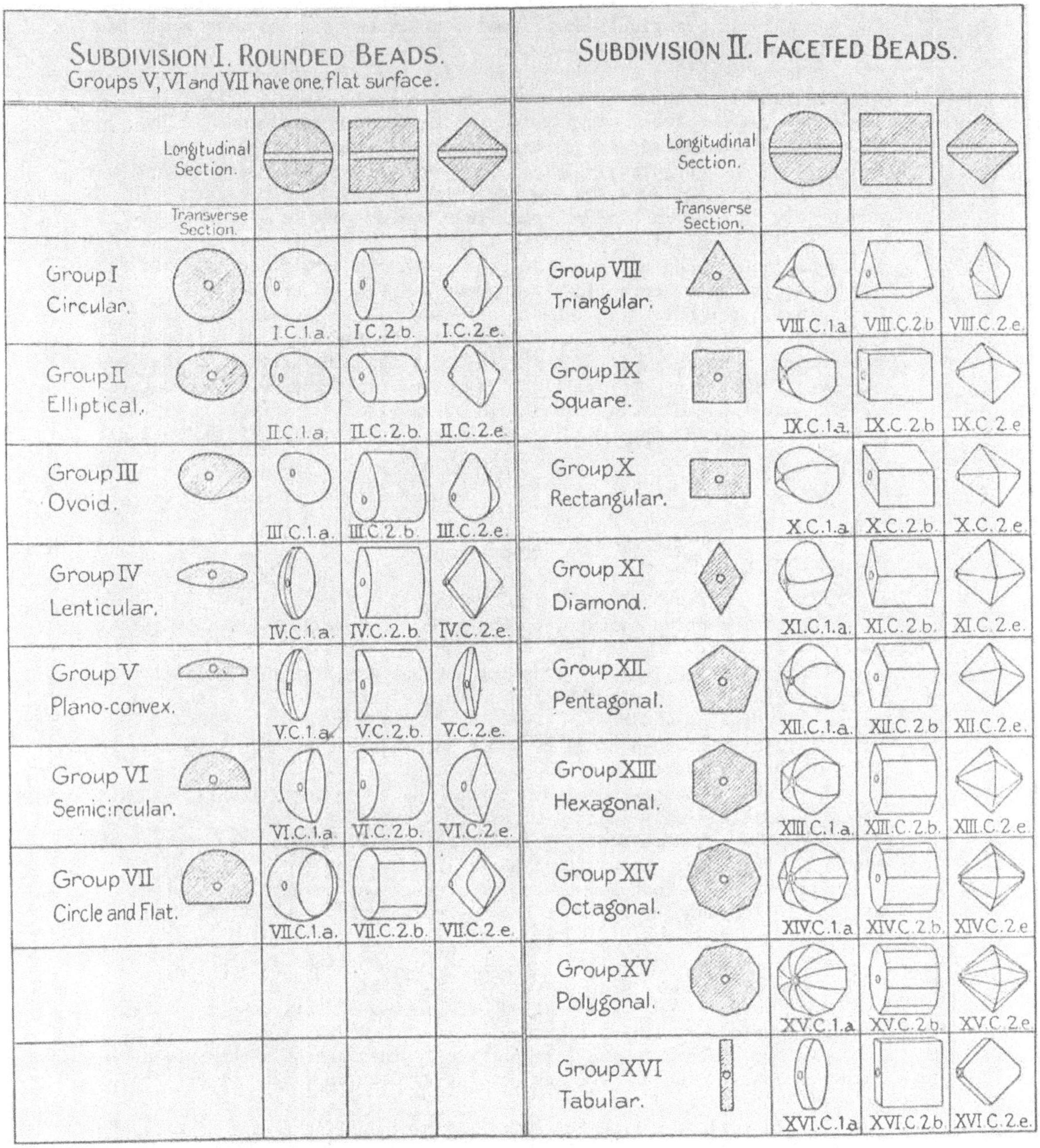

Figure 4. Groups of regular-rounded and regular-faceted beads (Beck 1928: Plate 1).

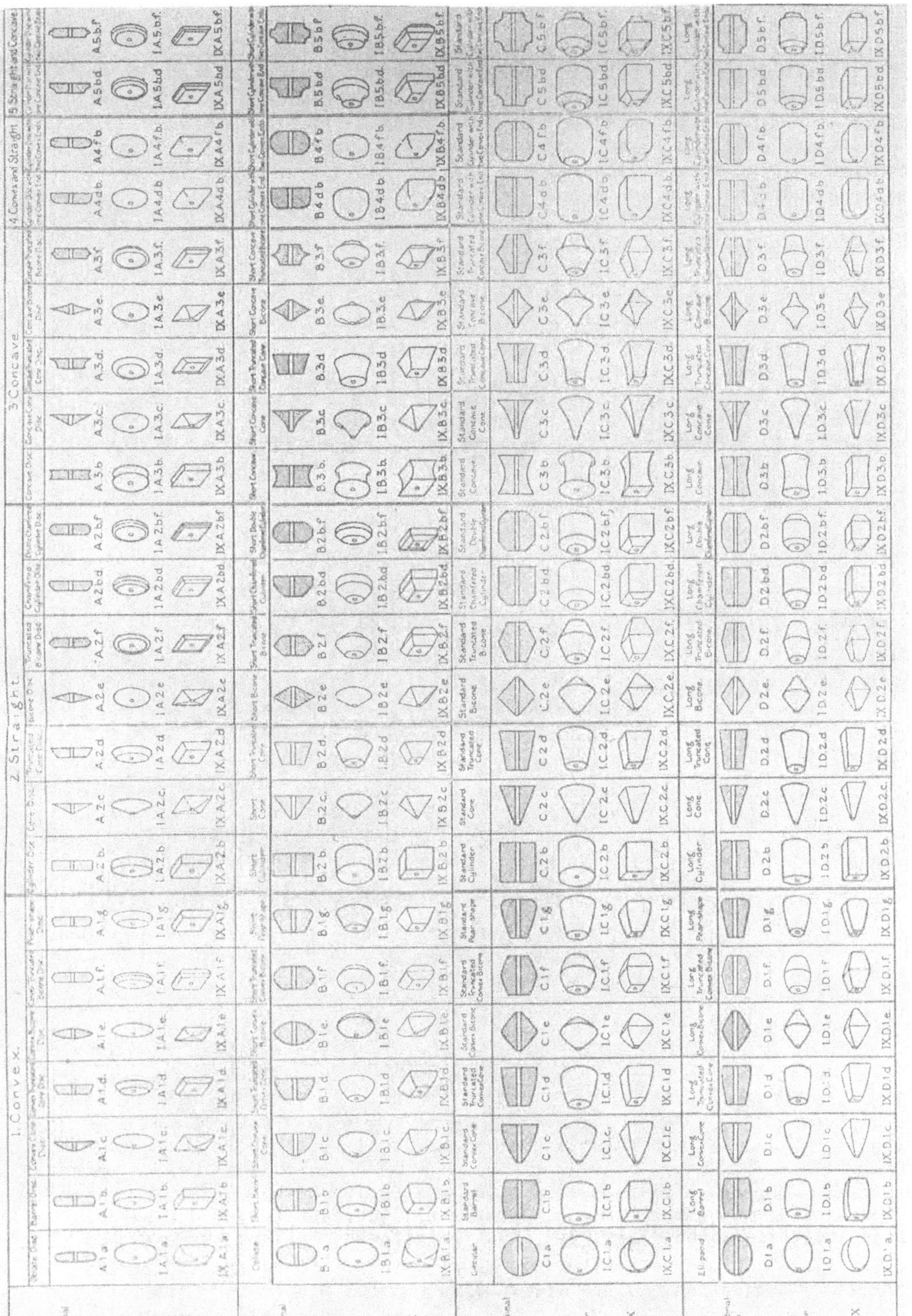

Figure 5. Sub-groups, families and classes of regular-rounded and regular-faceted beads (Beck 1928: Plates 2 and 3).

Floral designs - included in this group are various designs in the form of simple or compound wreaths, flowers, blossoms and plants whose appearance ranges from highly stylized to realistic (Fig. 6n-o).

Crumbs - "crumb beads" are made by embedding small pieces of contrastingly coloured glass in the plastic body of a bead; the crumbs may protrude from the surface or be flush with it (Fig. 6p-q).

Swirls - two or more coloured glasses may be swirled together to ornament the surface of a bead or to form the body thereof (Fig. 6r).

Other forms of decoration that may be encountered are described and illustrated in Beck (1928), van der Sleen (1967) and Francis (1979a).

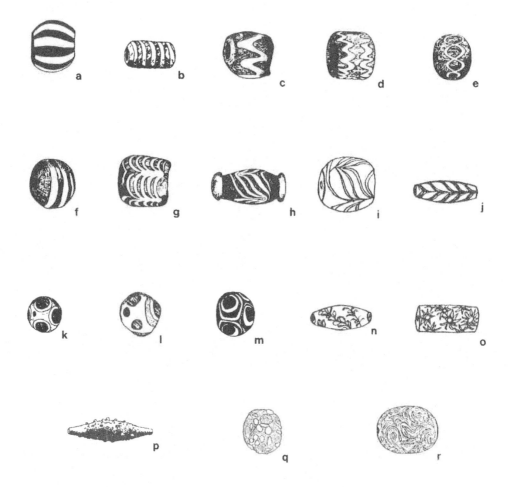

Figure 6. Some common forms of decoration: a-b, stripes; c-d, wavy lines; e, interwoven lines; f, rings; g-j, combed designs; k-m, eyes; n-o, floral designs; p-q, crumbs; r, swirls (Beck 1928; van der Sleen 1967).

Table 1. (Cont'd)

Munsell Code		Color Harmony		Bustanoby Name and Code
		Code	Name	
2.5PB	6/9	14 ia	Bright Copen Blue*	
2.5PB	5/4	14 ie	Shadow Blue*	Sky Blue (H7)
2.5PB	4/6	14 le	Medium Blue	Copenhagen Blue (F8)
2.5PB	3/8	14 pc	Deep Blue	
10.0B	6/3	15 ge	Mist Blue	Brittany Blue (F7)
10.0B	2/4	14 pi	Dark Navy*	
7.5B	8/2	15 ca	Pale Blue*	
7.5B	6/6	15 ic	Sky Blue	
7.5B	6/2	16 ge	Light Gray Blue	
7.5B	4/8	15 nc	Cerulean Blue*	Bluebird (B7)
7.5B	4/4	16 lg	Medium Shadow Blue	
7.5B	3/3	15 ni	Dark Shadow Blue*	
5.0B	8/4	16 ea	Light Aqua Blue*	
5.0B	6/6	16 ic	Robin's Egg Blue*	
5.0B	5/7	16 lc	Bright Blue*	
5.0B	4/6	16 ne	Peacock Blue	Peacock Blue (D9)
5.0B	4/5	16 le	Pale Medium Blue	Gobelin Blue (C11)
5.0B	3/3	16 ni	Dark Gray Blue	Navy Blue (B9)
2.5B	7/2	17 ec	Dusty Aqua Blue	
2.5B	6/7	17 ia	Bright Aqua Blue	
2.5B	6/4	18 gc	Aqua Blue*	Turquoise (D8)
2.5B	5/5	17 le	Med. Turquoise Blue	
10.0BG	4/8	17 pa	Turquoise*	
7.5BG	8/4	19 ea	Light Aqua Green	
7.5BG	6/8	18 la	Bright Turquoise	
7.5BG	6/6	19 ic	Aqua Green	
7.5BG	6/3	19 ge	Dusty Aqua Green	
5.0BG	8/2	19 ba	Ice Blue	
5.0BG	6/3	20 ge	Light Blue Spruce	
5.0BG	4/8	20 nc	Turquoise Green	
5.0BG	3/6	20 ng	Teal Green*	
10.0G	6/6	21 ic	Light Jade Green	
10.0G	5/10	21 nc	Emerald Green*	
10.0G	4/5	21 ng	Dark Jade Green	Emerald Green (F3)
5.0G	5/4	22 ie	Surf Green*	
2.5G	9/2	22 ca	Pale Green	
2.5G	7/8	22 ia	Bright Mint Green*	
2.5G	5/10	22 nc	Bright Green	
2.5G	3/6	22 pi	Dark Green	
2.5G	2/5	22 pl	Bottle Green	Bottle Green (A6)
10.0GY	6/6	23 ic	Apple Green*	
10.0GY	5/10	23 pe	Grass Green	
10.0GY	4/4	23 ni	Dark Palm Green*	
10.0GY	3/5	23 pi	Dark Grass Green	Mint Green (C6)
7.5GY	8/2	24 cb	Celadon Tint	Surf Green (F1)
7.5GY	6/6	24 le	Leaf Green	Jade Green (F2)
7.5GY	4/3	24 li	Sage Green	
5.0GY	5/6	24 ng	Leaf Green	Fern Green (C5)
2.5GY	4/4	24-1/2 ni	Olive Green	Olive Green (E5)
N	9/0	a	White*	
N	8/0	b	Oyster White*	Oyster White (E10)
N	7/0	c	Light Gray*	
N	1/0	p	Lamp Black*	

Diaphaneity

The diaphaneity of beads is described using the terms **opaque** (op.) **translucent** (tsl.) and **transparent** (tsp.). Although the Kidds use "clear" in lieu of "transparent," the latter term is preferred as it is more descriptive. Simply defined, beads that are **opaque** are impenetrable to light except on the thinnest edges. **Translucent** specimens transmit light, yet diffuse it so that the objects viewed through them are indistinct. Objects viewed through **transparent** beads are clearly visible. As bubbles can effect the diaphaneity of a bead, their presence in large numbers should be noted.

Lustre

The appearance of the surface of a bead in reflected light is known as its lustre. The two most common kinds are **shiny** (smooth and bright) and **dull** (not shiny). Others that may be encountered are **metallic** (having a metallic sheen), **greasy** (the appearance of an oiled surface), and **satiny** (characterized by a fibrous structure).

Size

Although the five arbitrary size categories (very small, under 2 mm; small, 2-4 mm; medium, 4-6 mm; large, 6-10 mm; and very large, over 10 mm) preferred by the Kidds are useful in relating relative size, research conducted by Ross (1976: 684-766) and Karklins (1979: 160-61) has revealed that they are too broad to be of any use in establishing historical size groups where the inter-size interval can be as little as 0.2 mm. Measurements are to be made to the nearest tenth of a millimetre using vernier calipers. The pertinent dimensions for most beads are **length** (parallel to the perforation) and **diameter** (perpendicular to the perforation). However, in the case of flattened specimens, they are **length** (parallel to the perforation), **width** (perpendicular to the perforation) and **thickness** (perpendicular to the width). The size of the perforation has not been found to be significant. Where there is more than one specimen per variety, ranges, means and modes should be computed for the sample.

HISTORICAL ARCHAEOLOGICAL INTERPRETATIONS

Origins

Although Venice/Murano, Bohemia and The Netherlands produced the bulk of the glass beads that were exported to the New World, Germany, Austria, England, France and China also appear to have contributed their share (Kidd 1979; Liu 1975a). Unfortunately, there is no routine method to determine the country of origin for any given bead type. While van der Sleen (1967: 108) has proposed that Dutch beads can be distinguished from those of Venetian origin on the basis of chemical composition (Dutch beads supposedly having a high potassium content compared to a high sodium content in Venetian specimens), this supposition seems to have been based on limited evidence and may not hold true. It also totally ignores the chemical make-up of beads manufactured in other countries which must also be high in either potassium or sodium, these being the two standard fluxes utilized in the production of glass.

The problem is further heightened by the notable scarcity of comparative material. Aside from the van der Sleen and van der Made collections of 17th-century Dutch beads in Amsterdam (Karklins 1974; van der Made 1978), there are no recorded assemblages of pre-19th century beads whose manufacture can be attributed with any certainty to a specific country. There is better coverage for the 19th and 20th centuries, but no one has as yet synthesized the data. Clearly much more research needs to be conducted before the question of origins can be resolved.

Chronology

As is the case with most classes of artifacts, no one has as yet worked out a comprehensive chronology for Canadian beads. Fortunately, there are several regional chronologies that will help archaeologists and analysts to date their problematical specimens. Although nothing has been formulated for the Atlantic provinces and the territories, Quebec and Ontario benefit from the proximity of New York state and the Great Lakes. The three most useful works for this area are Pratt (1961), Quimby (1966) and Wray (1973). Several of the volumes in Fenstermaker's *Archaeological Research Booklet* series may also be of use (Fenstermaker, 1974a, b, 1977). The references listed above deal with the period from 1550 to 1820. A sequence for post-1820 beads has yet to be devised.

Researchers in the Prairie provinces should consult Davis (1972), an abbreviated version of which appears in Davis (1973). The reports by

Harris and Harris (1967) and Sudbury (1976) are also recommended. They cover 1700 to 1885.

As for the West Coast, Quimby (1978) presents an overview of the state of the knowledge of beads in the Northwest, while Woodward (1965, 1970) provides generalized dates for some of the more common bead types. For comparative purposes, Ross' (1976) treatise on Fort Vancouver (1829-60) is essential. More comparative information for this and the other regions may be found by checking the index in Karklins and Sprague (1980).

Function

Unless a bead is found in an archaeologically diagnostic context (for example, sewn to clothing, situated at the neck of a burial, or strung on a rosary), it is extremely difficult to assign a specific function to it. Although "little" beads (those under about 6 mm in diameter) were commonly used in embroidery, they were frequently also employed in the formation of necklaces, earrings, nose and hair ornaments, mats, and as decorative inlays in aboriginal pottery. Similarly, "big" beads (those over about 6 mm in diameter) are commonly thought of as necklace components but also served to adorn fringes, baskets, mats, vases and other items. Thus to arrive at the real function of a bead, not only must its size be considered but also the archaeological and ethnohistorical evidence.

Use/Wear Marks

Beads occasionally exhibit use/wear marks that may be useful in establishing their function. Medium to very large specimens are sometimes abraded or battered on the ends, indicating use in necklaces. Abraded surfaces on the same size beads intimate use in such domestic items as mats and table covers. Severe battering or abrasion may denote heirloom pieces utilized over a long period of time.

Popular and Historical Names

Over the years, certain beads have acquired names that are used by dealers, collectors and, to some degree, archaeologists. While some of them are vague or have lost their significance (for example, "pony" and "pound"), others such as "chevron," "Russian" and "Cornaline d'Aleppo" immediately bring to mind specific bead types. This being the case, popular or historical names should be recorded when known.

APPENDIX A.   INSTRUCTIONS FOR COMPLETING PARKS CANADA ARTIFACT DATA BASE
INPUT FORMS FOR GLASS BEADS

        The forms are to be filled out using the terminology set forth in
the preceding guide and the field-specific instructions presented below.
A completed sample form is appended.

Category
Enter PERSONAL/DOMESTIC.

Subcategory
Enter ORNAMENT.

Article
Enter BEAD.

Model
If known, enter the popular or historical name for the specimen.

Type
Enter the appropriate manufacturing category, class and type designation
proffered in the preceding guide, and the Kidd and Kidd (1970) variety
number if applicable. If there is no variety number, append an asterisk
(*) to the code.

Date
If known, enter the temporal range as indicated by the archaeological
context or a regional chronology. The latter should be referenced.

Material
Enter GLASS, and any non-glass elements that may be present as overlays,
inlays or internal decoration.

Manufacture
Enter the appropriate technique of manufacture including the sub-type,
if applicable. Record any marks resulting from manufacture.

Dimensions
Record the measurement as outlined under Size in the attached guide.
Where large quantities of beads are involved, tally the measurements on
the back of the form and enter the range, mean and mode(s) on the
front.

Description
Record the following attributes:
        Structure (simple, compound, complex, or composite).

Shape of body (e.g. tubular, circular or round).
Shape of perforation if other than cylindrical (e.g. square-sectioned, Y-shaped or tapered).
Colour and diaphaneity of body using the Color Harmony name and code or the Munsell code; also note the lustre.
Facets - list their number, shape and location, and how produced (cut, paddle pressed or mould imparted).
Miscellaneous attributes, such as bubbles, patination, striae or swirl marks on or in the glass.

Decoration
Enter the major decorative category (overlaid, inlaid or internal) followed by a detailed description of the various decorative elements including their quantity, colour and diaphaneity, physical appearance, location and orientation.

Condition
Enter COMPLETE or INCOMPLETE, and note if burned, crizzled, solarized, etc.

Comments
Enter use/wear or archaeological data that might help establish function.

	OBJECT CATALOGUE CATALOGUE D'OBJET	2. 0 0 8 Z 0 9 9 A 0 2 3 - 0 0 0 4

Parks Parcs
Canada Canada

3. LOCATION ENDROIT HEADQUARTERS

4. REFERENCE Nº Nº DE RÉFÉRENCE

5. GROUP GROUPE GLASS

6. CATEGORY CATÉGORIE PERSONAL / DOMESTIC

7. SUB CATEGORY SOUS CATÉGORIE ORNAMENT

8. ARTICLE BEAD

9. MODEL MODÈLE CORNALINE D'ALEPPO

10. TYPE GENRE W III b *

11. PATENT Nº Nº DE BREVET

12. SERIAL Nº Nº DE SÉRIE

13. QUANT. 2

14. ASCRIPTION ATTRIBUTION

15. MAKER FABRICANT

16. PERIOD FROM PÉRIODE DU **TO AU**

17. DATE 1852 – 1886 (site date)

18. MATERIAL MATÉRIEL GLASS

19. MANUFACTURE FABRICATION WOUND

20. DIMENSIONS L: 9.3 mm , 8.7 mm
D: 4.6 mm , 4.2 mm

21. DESCRIPTION COMPOSITE; CYLINDRICAL BODY : tsp. scarlet (7 pa) outer layer, op. white (a) core; perforation tapers slightly; shiny surface; distinct wind marks in both layers of glass.

22. DECORATION DÉCORATION Inlaid: a floral wreath of op. bright blue (16 lc) on op. white (a) about the middle, and a ring of op. light gold (2 ic) around either end.

23. MARKS MARQUES

24. CONDITION ÉTAT COMPLETE

25. CONSERVATION

26. MENDS COLLAGES

27. PHOTOS PHOTOGRAPHIES RA-98 W

28. DRAWINGS DESSINS

29. PUBLICATIONS

30. COMMENTS OBSERVATIONS Ends battered

31. CATALOGUER PRÉPOSÉ AU CATALOGUE T.E. LAWRENCE

32. DATE 25 03 80

PC 693 (7-78)

Karlis Karklins

REFERENCES CITED

Anonymous. 1825. "On the Manufacture of Glass Beads." American
    Mechanics' Magazine, Vol. 2, No. 34, p. 120. New York.
---. 1835. "Miscellaneous Communications from an American Naval
    Officer, Travelling in Europe; Forwarded from the Mediterranean, May
    1834." American Journal of Science and Arts, Vol. 27, No. 1,
    pp. 74-84. New Haven.

Beck, Horace C. 1928. "Classification and Nomenclature of Beads and
    Pendants." Archaeologia, Vol. 77, pp. 1-76. Oxford.

Bustanoby, J.H. 1947. Principles of Color and Color Mixing.
    McGraw-Hill, New York.

Carroll, B. Harvey, Jr. 1917. Bead Making at Murano and Venice.
    Unpublished manuscript. General Records of the Department of State
    (RG-59), State Decimal File 1910-1929, File No. 165.184/3, National
    Archives, Washington.

Container Corporation of America. 1958. Color Harmony Manual, 4th ed.
    Chicago.

Davis, Wayne L. 1972. Glass Trade Beads of the Northern Plains - Upper
    Missouri Region. Unpublished Master's thesis. Department of
    Archaeology, University of Calgary, Calgary.
---. 1973. "Time and Space Considerations for Diagnostic Northern
    Plains Glass Trade Bead Types." In Historical Archaeology in
    Northwestern North America, Ronald M. Getty and Knut R. Fladmark,
    eds., pp. 3-52. University of Calgary, Archaeological Association,
    Calgary.

Fenstermaker, Gerald B. 1974a. "Susquehanna, Iroquois Colored Trade
    Bead Chart, 1575-1763." Archaeological Research Booklet, No. 1.
    Lancaster, Pa.
---. 1974b. "Early Susquehanna Iroquois Colored Trade Bead Chart,
    1550." Archaeological Research Booklet, No. 3. Lancaster, Pa.
---. 1977. "Pennsylvania Conoy Colored Trade Bead Chart."
    Archaeological Research Booklet, No. 11. Lancaster, Pa.

Francis, Peter, Jr. 1979a. "A Short Dictionary of Bead Terms and
    Types." World of Beads Monograph Series, No. 4. Lake Placid.
---. 1979b. "The Story of Venetian Beads." World of Beads Monograph
    Series, No. 1, Lake Placid.

Harris, R. King and Inus M. Harris. 1967. "Trade Beads, Projectile
    Points, and Knives." In A Pilot Study of Wichita Indian Archeology
    and Ethnohistory, Robert E. Bell et al., eds., pp. 129-58. Southern
    Methodist University, Anthropology Research Center, Dallas.

Karklins, Karlis. 1974. "Seventeenth Century Dutch Beads." Historical
    Archaeology, Vol. 8, pp. 64-82. Columbia, S.C.
---. 1979. Nottingham House: The Hudson's Bay Company in Athabasca,
    1802-1806. Unpublished Master's thesis. Department of Sociology/
    Anthropology, University of Idaho, Moscow.

Karklins, Karlis and Roderick Sprague. 1980. A Bibliography of Glass
    Trade Beads in North America. South Fork Press, Moscow, Id.

Kidd, Kenneth E. 1979. "Glass Bead-Making from the Middle Ages to the
    Early 19th Century." History and Archaeology, 30. Ottawa.

Kidd, Kenneth E. and Martha A. Kidd. 1970. "A Classification System
    for Glass Beads for the Use of Field Archaeologists." Canadian
    Historic Sites: Occasional Papers in Archaeology and History, No. 1,
    pp. 45-89. Ottawa.

Lardner, Dionysius. 1972. The Manufacture of Porcelain and Glass.
    Noyes Press, Park Ridge, N.J.

Liu, Robert K. 1975a. "Chinese Glass Beads and Ornaments." Bead
    Journal, Vol. 1, No. 3, pp. 13-28. Los Angeles.
---. 1975b. "Early 20th Century Bead Catalogs." Bead Journal, Vol. 2,
    No. 2, pp. 31-32. Los Angeles.

Made, Herman, van der. 1978. "Seventheenth Century Beads from
    Holland." Archaeological Research Booklet, No. 14. Lancaster, Pa.

Munsell Color. 1976. Munsell Book of Color, Glossy Finish Collection.
    Macbeth Division, Kollmorgen Corp., Baltimore.

Orchard, William C. 1929. "Beads and Beadwork of the American
    Indians." Contributions from the Museum of the American Indian, Heye
    Foundation, Vol. 11. New York.

Pazaurek, Gustav E. 1911. Glasperlen und Perlen-Arbeiten in alter und
    neuer Zeit. Alexander Koch, Darmstadt.

Pratt, Peter P. 1961. Oneida Iroquois Glass Trade Bead Sequence,
    1585-1745. Fort Stanwix Museum, Rome.

Quimby, George I. 1966. Indian Culture and European Trade Goods.
    University of Wisconsin Press, Madison.
---. 1978. "Trade Beads and Sunken Ships." In Archaeological Essays
    in Honor of Irving B. Rouse, Robert C. Dunnell and Edwin S. Hall,
    Jr., eds., pp. 231-46. Mouton Publishers, The Hague.

Ross, Lester A. 1974. "Hudson's Bay Company Glass Trade Beads:
    Manufacturing Types Imported to Fort Vancouver (1829-1860)." Bead
    Journal, Vol. 1, No. 2, pp. 15-22. Los Angeles.

———. 1976. Fort Vancouver, 1829-1860: A Historical Archeological Investigation of the Goods Imported and Manufactured by the Hudson's Bay Company. Unpublished manuscript. Fort Vancouver National Historic Site, Vancouver, Wash.

Sleen, W.G.N., van der. 1967. A Handbook on Beads. Musée du Verre, Liège.

Sprague, Roderick. 1971. Review of "Canadian Historic Sites: Occasional Papers in Archaeology and History, No. 1." Historical Archaeology, Vol. 5, pp. 128-29. Lansing.
———. 1973. Molded Ceramic Beads. Paper presented at the 26th Annual Meeting of the Northwest Anthropological Conference, La Grande.
———. 1979. Glass Trade Beads of the Pacific Northwest. Manuscript on file. Department of Sociology/Anthropology, University of Idaho, Moscow.

Stone, Lyle M. 1974. "Fort Michilimackinac, 1715-1781: An Archaeological Perspective on the Revolutionary Frontier." Publications of the Museum, Michigan State University, Anthropological Series, Vol. 2. Lansing.

Sudbury, Byron. 1976. "Ka-3, the Deer Creek Site: An Eighteenth Century French Contact Site in Kay County, Oklahoma." Bulletin of the Oklahoma Anthropological Society, Vol. 24. Oklahoma City.

Woodward, Arthur. 1965. "Indian Trade Goods." Oregon Archaeological Society, Publication No. 2. Portland.
———. 1970. The Denominators of the Fur Trade. Socio-Technical Publications, Pasadena.

Wray, Charles F. 1973. Manual for Seneca Iroquois Archeology. Cultures Primitive, Inc., Honeoye Falls, N.Y.

PHIL DUNNING

Composite Table Cutlery from 1700 to 1930

Introduction

The early manufacturing technology of steel table cutlery has been documented for many years (Ure 1849:385-386; Tomlinson 1854:480-488; Lloyd 1913; Himsworth 1953; Smithurst 1987). As well, there are several publications on fine quality cutlery of the 17th and 18th centuries in museums and private collections (Bailey 1927; Hayward 1957; Victoria and Albert Museum 1979). With few exceptions (Noël Hume 1969:177-180; Kidd 1972; Wade 1982; Moore 1995; Stone 1998), however, cheaper-quality cutlery has been largely ignored. Accordingly, this work focuses on the description (Figure 1) and dating of steel table cutlery with handles of less expensive materials (commonly called "composite cutlery") from ca. 1700, to the rise of stainless steel in the 1920s.

The dating of early examples of composite cutlery depends upon comparison with similar hallmarked silver pieces, pieces with known cutlers' marks, examples from datable archaeological contexts, and iconographic evidence. By the 19th century, trade catalogues, patent records, and mail-order catalogues help to fill out the picture.

Knives and forks with matching handles and steel blades and tines are extremely rare before the third quarter of the 17th century. By the 1660s, they could be found on the tables of the affluent, and handles were of costly materials such as silver, ivory, semiprecious stone, mother-of-pearl, or tortoise shell (Davis 1976:183, No. 196; Victoria and Albert Museum 1979:13, Nos. 40, 43). Extant examples usually have a ferrule of silver between the handle and the blade or tines (Figure 2). The tang is of either the rat-tail or through form (Figure 3).

By the early 18th century, the use of matching knives and forks had become more widespread, and the major manufacturing centers of Sheffield and London were producing cutlery similar in form to their finer wares, but of less-expensive materials. For over 200 years, such cutlery was a popular alternative to silver, silver-plate, or better-quality steel. Recognizing that the old does not give way overnight to the new, it is possible to assign date ranges (with some overlap) to these pieces based on stylistic changes, innovations in manufacturing methods, and new handle materials.

1700-1740

The typical knives and forks of this period have handles of bone or wood. By far the most common form for the handle is the "pistol-grip," so called because the down-curved handle resembles the pistol handle of the period. This shape first appears in the late 17th century. Like better-quality cutlery, knives and forks have rat-tail or through tangs. In place of a silver ferrule, the bolster is heavier and forged as an integral part with the blade and tang (Figure 4).

Steel was more expensive than iron, thus knives of all qualities were made with a steel blade and an iron bolster and tang welded to it. This lapped join often forms a visible mark called a "thumbprint" at the base of the blade (Figure 5). The table knife has a blade with a strongly concave back, a bulbous tip, and convex edge which tapers to the bolster (Figure 4).

One recognizably Continental table knife form (Figure 6) is occasionally found on French-occupation sites in North America (Tremblay 1996:101, 111, Figure 23a, Figure 30b). The blade is narrow, tapering, and turns up at the tip, which is not bulbous like on English knives. The back of the blade has a low hump, and the bolster is very small. Both rat-tail and through tangs were used with this form. Blades of this type were made in cutlery centers all over Continental Europe. The shape appears by about 1700, and is found throughout the period of the French regime, until about 1760. Similar blades do not appear on English or American knives until the 1920s (below). Interestingly, one of the names given them at that time was the "French shape."

It should be noted that knives became stained from acidic foods, and were subject to regular and vigorous polishing and occasional sharpening. These processes can drastically modify the shape of the blade (Figure 7), making dating difficult and creating confusion between Continental and very worn English blades. As mentioned above, Continental blades normally have a very small bolster.

The fork has two long, straight or slightly curved tines and a rounded shoulder. The shank usually narrows to a waist and broadens again to meet the handle. Occasionally the shank is balustroid as in Figure 2, but weaker in form.

1720-1770

By the 1720s, the flat tang began to be used regularly on table cutlery alongside rat-tail and through tangs. Flat-tanged table knives have been found *very* occasionally on late 17th-century French sites (Faulkner and Faulkner 1987:243, Figure 8.18), but do not seem to be associated with English knives and forks until the introduction of the "hump-backed" blade (below). This tang (Figure 3) has the same profile as the complete handle, with two scales riveted to either side. This construction allowed

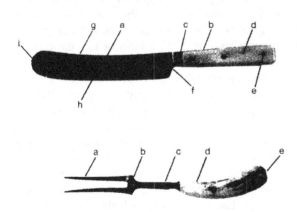

FIGURE 1. Knife terminology: *a,* blade; *b,* handle (in this case with a flat, full or scale tang); *c,* bolster (integral); *d,* scale; *e,* pin; *f,* choil or heel; *g,* blade back; *h,* blade edge; *i,* blade tip. Fork terminology: *a,* tines or prongs; *b,* shoulder; *c,* shank; *d,* handle (in this case with a rat-tail tang); *e,* butt cap.

FIGURE 2. Set of small-size dessert cutlery with mother-of-pearl handles and silver ferrules, ca. 1700-1730. The knife is 19 cm long overall. Less-expensive cutlery followed the same forms with cheaper handle materials, no ferrule, and simplified shaping of the heavier bolster and shank. (Don Carpentier Collection.)

FIGURE 3. Table knives of the late 18th or 19th century. *Top,* flat, full or scale tang (scales would be pinned to either side of the tang); *center,* rat-tail tang (the tang is cemented and/or pinned into the handle); *bottom,* through tang (the tang passes through the length of the handle and is peened over a washer or butt cap).

FIGURE 4. Knife and fork (non-matching) of forms and materials typical of ca. 1700-1740. The knife handle is of wood; the fork handle is of bone. Both are variations of the "pistol-grip" shape. (Fork: Colonial Williamsburg Collection.)

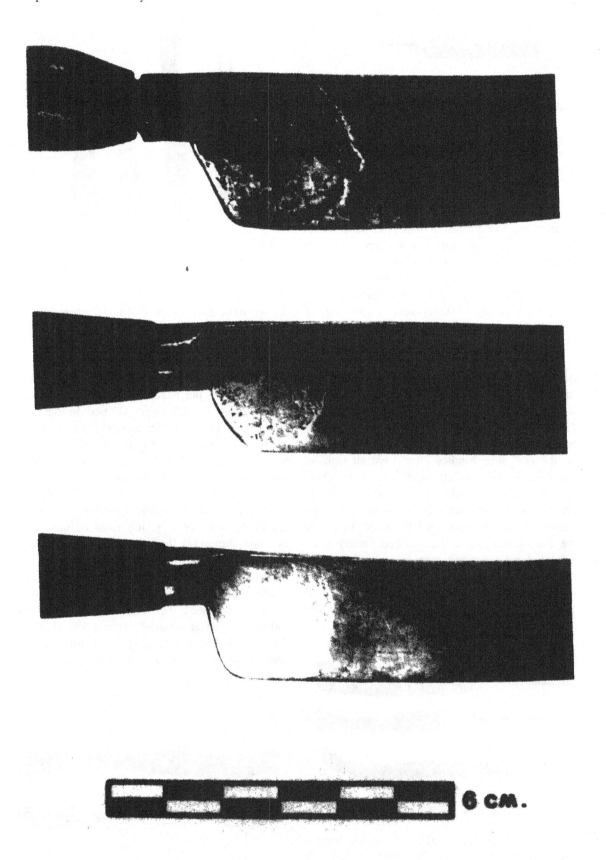

FIGURE 5. Late 18th- or 19th-century knife blades showing the "thumbprint" caused by the lap weld between the steel blade and the iron tang and bolster.

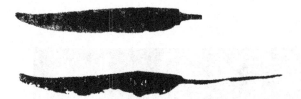

FIGURE 6. Continental European table knife blades, ca. 1700-1760. This form is found on French occupation sites in North America. *Top*, rat-tail tang; *bottom*, through tang.

smaller, thinner pieces of bone, wood or other material to be used with less wastage. Another shape of handle appeared with the new tang: it is wedge-shaped, tapering towards the blade. Bone handles of this form are frequently decorated with rather coarsely scored hatching or cross-hatching (Figure 8). The pistol-grip was also made with the flat tang (Figure 9). It, too, is sometimes heavily scored (Figure 10). Antler (called "stag" or "buck") was used both for scales on a flat tang and as the full handle with a rat-tail tang similar to the (later) fork in Figure 1 (Stone 1974:176, Figure 95*i*). Antler and bone may have the pith or marrow exposed on the end, thus handles often have an iron or, occasionally, a brass butt cap (Figure 11). These caps are attached with two pins which may be present even when the cap has been lost. Full handles of antler continued to be popular into the 20th century, and the attached cutlery must be dated by form and manufacturing methods. Bovine horn was also used. D. Gooking, for example, advertised "Maple, horn & buck haft Table Knives and Forks" in the *Boston News-*

FIGURE 8. Wedge-shaped handles of ca. 1720-1770 with coarsely scored bone scales.

Letter of 1 December 1748. Lighter-colored horn came from oxen and black horn from Indian water buffalo (Dyson 1936:12; Hardwick 1981:135-136). Wood, bone, ivory, and even bovine horn can present a similar and confusing appearance to the naked eye. Bone and ivory, for instance, may become stained brown from burial and resemble some dark, close-grained woods or horn. To add to the problem, bone was often polished to look like ivory, or carved and stained to imitate antler. The latter was called "sham buck" or "forbuck" (Dyson 1936:22). Until the introduction of new materials in the 19th century, the form of the handle is more important than the material for dating purposes.

During the 1720-1770 period, some knife blades acquired a hump on the back close to the bolster (Figure 9). This form is sometimes called "scimitar shaped" today (Noël Hume 1969:178), but the term can be confusing as historically it was used to describe a knife with

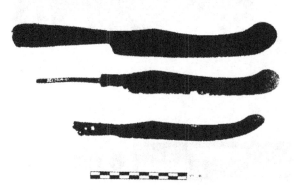

FIGURE 7. *Top*, knife ca. 1770-1820 with the edge of the blade showing minimal wear; *center*, contemporary knife with the edge heavily worn and the choil almost gone; *bottom*, knife so heavily worn that it is impossible to determine whether a choil was originally present.

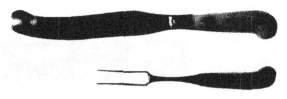

FIGURE 9. Knife and fork ca. 1720-1770 with flat tangs and bone scales in pistol-grip shape.

FIGURE 10. Heavy flat-tang pistol-grip handles ca. 1720-1770 with coarsely scored bone scales.

FIGURE 12. Fork, ca. 1740-1770. Two tines with a pronounced scoop to the rounded shoulder. The handle has a flat tang with scored bone scales.

a simple concave back (Smith 1816; Gordon, MacKay & Co. 1913:389). The term "hump-backed" is used here as it is less prone to confusion.

The tines and shank of the fork continued in form much as they had since the beginning of the century. In the 1740s, however, some forks developed a pronounced scoop to the shoulder (Figure 12). Better-quality forks occasionally have three tines and more strongly modeled balustroid shanks.

1760-1800

Major changes in the forms of both knives and forks took place during the 1760-1800 period. Although the pistol-grip continued to be popular on silver cutlery, by the 1780s it was superseded by a variety of new shapes found on cheaper wares. The wedge-shaped handle

became less broad at the butt with less of a taper towards the blade. The decorative scoring often found on these narrower scales was usually more complex and done with more care than previously (Figure 13). This decoration continued into the third quarter of the 19th century on English cutlery. The narrower wedge was also used on plain handles in bone, wood, ivory, and horn, all with rat-tail tangs (Figures 14, *top and center,* 20). A variation on the wedge-shape has the butt angled rather than straight across (Figure 14, *bottom*). The angled butt was popular until about 1820. Some rat-tail tangs were inserted into the hollow of partially intact metapodial bones of sheep which had been filled with resin or other composition. These were capped on the butt end, but the caps are frequently missing (Figure 15). By the late 1760s, green-stained handles became popular, both in ivory and bone (Figure 14, *bottom*).

FIGURE 11. Domed and flat steel and brass butt caps on antler and bone handles. (***Center,*** Genevieve Duguay Collection).

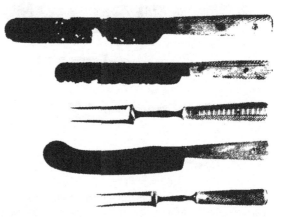

FIGURE 13. Scored decorations on bone scales typical of the late 18th and 19th centuries. The taper to the handle is not as pronounced as on earlier examples.

Phil Dunning

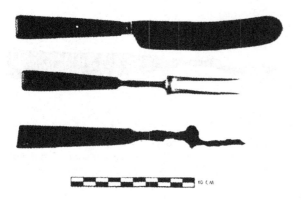

FIGURE 14. *Top and center,* late 18th- or 19th-century knife and fork with rat-tail tangs pinned to wedge-shaped wooden handles; *bottom,* fork ca. 1770-1820 with rat-tail tang and green-stained bone handle with angled butt.

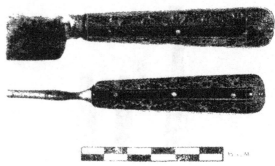

FIGURE 16. Knife and fork with flat tangs and scales of pressed horn with elaborate decoration (late 18th to mid 19th century).

Bovine horn had for many years been decorated by heating and pressing pieces in molds with designs, producing small items such as snuff boxes and, occasionally, cutlery handles. By the end of the 18th century, there was a vast variety of pressed horn handles (Figure 16), and they stayed popular through to the middle of the 19th century. Better-quality knives sometimes had "balance handles." The hole drilled for the rat-tail tang was extended deep enough that a weight could be inserted to counterbalance the blade and prevent it from touching the table when set down (Figure 17). The balance handle continued to be used through the 19th century

(Russell and Erwin Manufacturing Company 1865:357).

During the 1760s, the knife blade developed a choil or heel at the bolster (Figure 18). By the 1780s, some knives had lost the hump-back so that the back and edge of the blade were parallel. By the end of the century, there was a choice of hump-backed, curved, or straight blades on table knives (Figure 19). Stamped marks (Figure 20) such as "BEST CAST STEEL" or "SHEAR STEEL" are found on blades from this period until well into the 19th century. These marks indicate the quality of steel from which the blade was made. Until the 1780s, table knives usually had fairly large blades, averaging 16-18 cm in length including the bolster (dessert knives and forks were smaller, but were

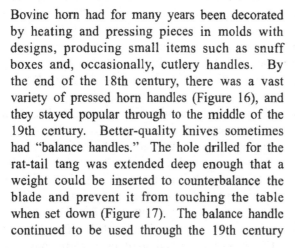

FIGURE 15. Knife and forks of the late 18th to mid 19th century with rat-tail tangs inserted into the hollow of partially intact metapodial bones of sheep which are filled with resin and the butts capped. *Top,* knife missing butt cap; *center,* fork with butt cap and pin inserted into resin to hold it; *bottom,* fork with resin exposed and tines worn short from cleaning.

FIGURE 17. Balance handle of ivory with the counterweight still in place.

The Historical Archaeology Laboratory Handbook

made with ferrules and lighter bolsters [Figure 2]). From the last decades of the 18th century through most of the 19th century, a much wider range of blade sizes was available, varying from about 12.5 cm up to 18 cm in length (Figures 13, 19). Of all the characteristics of knife blades, length is the least reliable for dating.

By about 1770, the shoulder of the fork became squared, retaining the scoop that had appeared a few decades earlier (Figure 12). At the same time, average-quality forks began to be made with three tines, which had previously been found only on fine cutlery (above). A choice of forks "With 2-3 or 4 Prongs" (Smith 1816) was available into the third quarter of the 19th century, when the two-tined fork finally lost favor (Figure 21).

1800-1850

With the exception of the hump-backed blade, which disappeared by about 1820, and the two-tined fork, the forms of knives and forks current at the end of the 18th century continued to be made in Sheffield late into the fourth quarter of the century (Silber and Flemming 1883:74-75; Harrod's Stores 1895:736-738). These forms were the products of a technology that had not changed in England since the 17th century (Ure 1849:385-386; Tomlinson 1854:480-488). English knife blades in the early part of this period were occasionally marked with the initials of the reigning monarch: G R for *Georgius Rex* (18th century to 1830) and W R for *William Rex* (1830-1837). By Queen Victoria's reign (1838-1901), the practice was much more common, and knives marked V R (*Victoria Regina*) are found regularly (Figure 20).

In the United States, the fledgling cutlery industry was introducing manufacturing methods that were to transform both the forms and materials of table cutlery (Greeley et al. 1872:229-238; Taber 1955:32-41; Merriam et al. 1976:8-30). Massachusetts and Connecticut were the centers of production, and the companies there realized that to compete with England they needed to be much more efficient. John Russell of Greenfield, Massachusetts, led the way with many innovations. In the late 1830s and 1840s, he introduced the trip-hammer for forging knives, steam power to augment water power, and a power press for cutting and shap-

ing blades. By 1844, he was making a knife with the blade, bolster, and tang forged from one piece of steel. The cost of the steel for the bolster and tang was more than offset by the speed with which the knives were produced (Greeley et al. 1872:231-232; Taber 1955:36-37). Knives made by this process will not show the distinctive "thumbprint" of joined steel and iron (Figure 5). These processes still utilized the traditional square rods of metal stock to produce knifes and forks. If a knife blade or fork tines and tang were stamped or rolled from sheet steel and a separate bolster attached or "applied," cutlery could be made even more cheaply. Proposals for this process were patented in the United States by 1838 (United States Patent Office 1838), and in England by 1840 (Great Britain, Patent Office 1857). The sheet steel of the period, however, was often too brittle or too weak for cutlery. It was not until the 1850s that the quality of sheet steel began to improve.

1850-1870

Experimentation with stamping and rolling processes for knives and knife blades continued through the 1850s and 1860s. During this period, many knives were still made with steel blades and iron bolsters and tangs, but the parts were formed by mechanized drop-hammers, rather than hand forged, before being welded together. Sheet steel forks were easier to make as they did not need to retain a sharp edge and were subject to less stress and wear than knives. Although table cutlery of sheet steel was being made in the 1850s, it did not account for a large share of the market. As is often the case with wars, the American Civil War (1861-1865) caused an acceleration in both technology and production methods. Much of the output of the New England cutlery makers, however, was directed to wartime needs such as bayonets and utility/butcher knives (Taber 1955:38-41). The cargo of the wrecked steamboat *Bertrand* illustrates this. This vessel sank on the Missouri River in 1865, on its way to the gold mining districts of Idaho and Montana with goods for the miners. Almost all of the butcher knives in the cargo (95 of 106) were made of sheet steel with an applied bolster patented in 1860 by Lamson and Goodnow of Massachusetts (below).

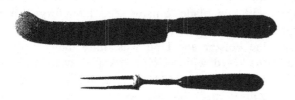

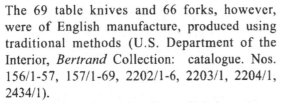

FIGURE 18. Knife and fork ca. 1770-1820. The knife blade retains the hump-back but has a choil or heel. The fork has a squared, scooped shoulder. Both have rat-tail tangs and plain wood handles.

FIGURE 20. English knife blades with stamped "W R" (1830-1837) and "V R" (1838-1901) marks.

The 69 table knives and 66 forks, however, were of English manufacture, produced using traditional methods (U.S. Department of the Interior, *Bertrand* Collection: catalogue. Nos. 156/1-57, 157/1-69, 2202/1-6, 2203/1, 2204/1, 2434/1).

Both war and post-war demands led to numerous patents for bolsters. Joseph Gardiner, an employee of the Lamson and Goodnow Company, invented a stamped bolster in 1860 that had several imitators over the next few years (Figure 22) (United States Patent Office 1860). The most successful form of applied bolster over the long term was the cast-on bolster of tin or tin alloy. A bolster of this type was patented by James Frary in 1866 (United States Patent Office 1866). The tang of the knife or fork was clamped in a mold, often with the scales

in place on the tang. The metal for the bolster was poured into the space left for it and flowed around the tang. The earlier examples with this bolster are fairly simple (Figure 23), sometimes with a butt cap made in the same way (Landers, Frary and Clark 1869:36-41). By the early 1880s, elaborate decoration was added by pressing or cutting designs into the wood scales which would be filled by the molten metal (Figure 24). This decoration was also used with bone scales. To prevent the scales from scorching, the metal used had to have a low melting point and the handles were cooled quickly.

The same principle of casting metal onto the steel tang was in use by 1869, to form the entire handle of cast-iron (Figure 25). These handles were usually japanned black to retard rusting

FIGURE 19. Table-knife blade shapes and lengths available at the end of the 18th century. *Top*, curved blade (with rat-tail-tang and wooden handle; 21 cm long overall); *center*, hump-backed blade (with flat tang and scored bone scales; 23 cm long overall); *bottom*, straight blade (with through tang and horn handle; 26 cm long overall).

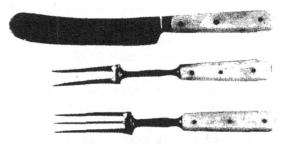

FIGURE 21. Knife with matching two- and three-tined forks with flat tangs and bone scales. Two-, three-, and four-tined forks were available with common cutlery starting in the late 18th century.

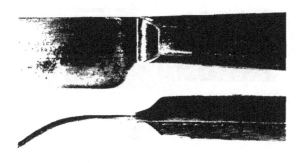

FIGURE 22. Cutlery made with Joseph Gardiner's 1860 patent (Lamson and Goodnow assignees). The bolster is of two separate pieces of stamped sheet steel, pinned onto the tang in the same way as the scales.

FIGURE 24. Knives and forks showing some of the many decorative patterns in cast-on tin alloy, ca. 1880-1920s. *Top*, with bone scales; *bottom*, with wooden scales.

(Landers, Frary and Clark 1869:33). This was some of the cheapest cutlery, and was priced in the same range as sheet-metal knives and forks with no bolsters at all (Figure 26). Cheap, bolsterless cutlery sometimes had a "half-tang" or "slot-tang." Instead of a full-sized flat tang with two scales, a half-length flat tang was inserted into a slot in a wood handle and held with two pins (Figure 26).

Another alternative to scale tangs was the hard or vulcanized rubber handle with a rat-tail tang (Figure 27). Charles Goodyear had discovered in 1839 that the addition of sulfur to natural rubber produced a strong, durable product (Hillman 1986:20). The John Russell Company tried this material in 1853, with little success (Taber 1955:38), but by the 1860s, rubber handles "warranted to stand hot water" (W. A. Currier 1862:7; Landers, Frary and Clark 1869:22) begin

to appear in catalogues.

The major rival to composite cutlery appeared in 1867. In that year, Matthew Chapman, an employee of the John Russell Company, patented table cutlery with the blade or tines and complete handle formed "from one piece of steel" (Figure 28) (United States Patent Office 1867). This solid-steel cutlery could be nickel- or silver-plated depending on the quality (Landers, Frary and Clark 1869:23). It would eventually eclipse earlier types and is the basis for most of the steel cutlery used today. It was many years, however, before it replaced all the competing technologies and forms.

Throughout the second half of the 19th century, England lagged behind the United States in the introduction of new technology. Labor in England was cheap, re-tooling and new machinery expensive, and the old system well

FIGURE 23. Sheet-steel forks. *Top*, with cast-on tin-alloy bolster; *center*, with cast-on bolster and butt plate; *bottom*, with scales missing and bolster and butt plate still attached.

FIGURE 25. Knife and fork of sheet steel with handles of cast iron, late 1860s-1910s. The knife retains the original japanning on the handle to retard rust.

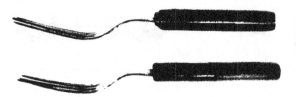

FIGURE 26. Inexpensive bolsterless sheet-steel forks. *Top,* with a flat tang and wooden scales; *bottom,* with a half-tang slotted into a wooden handle.

FIGURE 28. *Top and center,* solid-steel fork and knife made using Chapman's 1867 patent. This fork was offered as a set with the knife from the 1880s onward; *bottom,* this "non-matching" fork was sold as a set with the knife from the late 1860s and, occasionally, into the 1930s.

established (Grayson 1995:5-15, 57-58). For instance, forged knives and forks of English manufacture with handles of antler and buffalo horn (Figure 29) were still offered into the 20th century alongside newer types of cutlery (T. Eaton Co. 1901:157; Hudson's Bay Company 1910:178). It will be obvious from this work that if Sheffield had kept pace with New England in manufacturing methods, some cutlery could be much more closely dated.

1870-1890

This period saw the introduction of an important new handle material, and the increasing use of technologies developed from 1850 to 1870. Rubber handles continued to gain popularity in the 1870s, and by the 1880s, most catalogues carried them (F. A. Walker 1871:42; Francis T. Witte Hardware 1883:14; Merriam et al. 1976:83). The black-colored rubber had a precedent in the ebony and stained-black wood handles that had been made since the 18th century. Cast-on bolsters and butt caps on wood

and bone handles, mentioned above (Figure 24), developed a seemingly infinite variety of simple decorative motifs (Francis T. Witte Hardware 1883:11*a*-13*a*). Other types of applied bolsters for sheet-steel table cutlery disappeared from catalogues by the early 1880s. Bolsterless handles and handles of cast-iron continued to be used for the cheapest cutlery (Montgomery Ward Co. 1884:105).

Around 1870, separate inventors in England and the United States developed a semi-synthetic material based on cellulose (wood dust, linen, paper) and nitric and sulfuric acids. This new substance, cellulose nitrate, resembled ivory in color. It had many trade names including Celluloid, Xylonite, Zylonite, and Ivoride. Cutlery handles were one of the first products made from celluloid in 1872, and were being sold by the John Russell Company in that year (Greeley et al. 1872:235-236; Hillman 1986:21-22). Legal

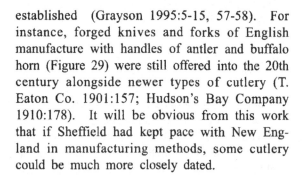

FIGURE 27. Cutlery with hard or vulcanized rubber handles. *Top and center,* knife and fork, 1860s-1910s, with handles impressed "GOODYEARS PATENT MAY 6. 1851". The knife blade is stamped "HARD RUBBER/CUTLERY Co"; *bottom,* knife with slipper-shaped stainless-steel blade, 1920s or 1930s.

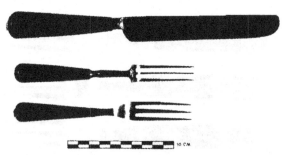

FIGURE 29. Knife and forks with round, tapering horn handles and through tangs. *Top and center,* knife and fork of late-18th-century form and manufacturing methods, but possibly made in Sheffield into the 20th century; *bottom,* sheet-steel fork with cast-on bolster dating from the late 1860s through the 1910s.

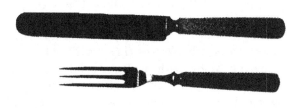

FIGURE 30. Cutlery with celluloid handles, 1880s-1930s.

FIGURE 32. *Top*, stamped mark on a stainless-steel slipper-shaped knife blade, 1920s-1930s; *bottom*, etched mark on a blade of the same material and period.

restrictions, however, limited its use in the 1870s, and it is the 1880s before it becomes common as a handle material (Figure 30) (Francis T. Witte Hardware 1883:14; Hillman 1986:21). In 1883, a method was developed for graining celluloid so that it would better resemble ivory (Figure 31) (Hillman 1986:22).

Also in 1883, a method was patented for etching names and trademarks on knife blades (Figure 32) (Taber 1955:43). Previously names and devices were stamped into blades, and stamping continued to be used by many manufacturers into the 20th century.

The first solid-steel knives of the late 1860s and 1870s were paired with a fork which, to the modern eye, does not appear to match. These forks, often in the "fiddle" or "tipped" pattern (Figure 28), matched the spoons of the period and imitated pieces made by a silversmith rather than a cutler. By the 1880s, solid steel forks that matched the knife rather than the spoon began to appear in catalogues (Merriam et al. 1976:84). The earlier "non-matching" sets, however, continued to be offered by some suppliers well into the 20th century (Montgomery Ward 1926:550; J. H. Ashdown Hardware 1935 [insert of 1937]:C-13 to C-14).

1890-1920

With few exceptions, there is little change in cutlery during the 1890-1920 period. There was a slow increase in the number of synthetic handles being offered, and a gradual decrease in the number of curved knife blades. Even so, the same range of cutlery sold in the 1880s was still available.

From the mid-1890s to the 1910s, cast-iron handles were made with decorations in the casting (Figure 33) (Sears, Roebuck 1897:107; Gordon, MacKay 1910:381; Hudson's Bay Company 1910:178). Cast-iron handles generally disappeared from mail-order catalogues by the 1920s.

About 1900, another semi-synthetic material, made from milk extracts, appeared. This mate-

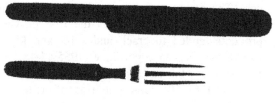

FIGURE 33. Sheet-steel knife and fork with decorated cast-iron handles of the mid-1890s to the 1910s.

FIGURE 31. Celluloid handle showing graining patented in 1883 to more closely resemble ivory.

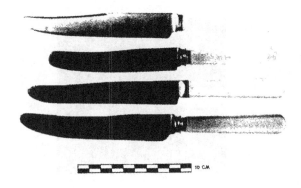

FIGURE 34. Knives of stainless steel with celluloid handles, 1920s-1940s. The knife blades show variations on the "slipper" or "French" shape. The third knife from the top has a slip-on bolster.

rial, commonly called casein, was occasionally used for cutlery handles but was never as widespread as celluloid (Hillman 1986:24). Casein can be difficult to distinguish from celluloid without burning or chemical testing (Katz 1984:146-147).

1920-1930

Several steel alloys that would not rust or stain were developed from about 1910 to World War I. None of them worked well for cutlery, as they tended to be brittle and their manufacture required special equipment and new skills. During the war, the American and British governments took over the production of "stainless" steel for military purposes and, by the war's end, many of the technical problems had been overcome. Most manufacturers, however, still had to change equipment and methods to use the new alloys, and this was costly. As well, the public was suspicious of the new product. The new processes were imperfectly understood by many makers, thus the first post-war products tended to crack and split, and knives would not keep an edge (Taber 1955:47-48). As late as 1927, the same page of the Montgomery Ward (1926:550) catalogue was offering both nickel-plated steel cutlery and "bright, rust-resisting stainless steel." Through the 1920s, stainless steel gradually improved and gained favor. Trade names for the various alloys were

myriad: Norust, Nevastain, Rustproof, Unstainable, and Everclean are but a few (Grayson 1995:57-64).

Along with the new steel, a new blade shape appeared on table knives (Figures 27, 34). This tapering blade with a slightly humped back was called a "slipper" or "French" shape. It is the first of the modern shapes that we still use today. It was originally considered a steak or "meat" knife, and it is shown in catalogues with the standard straight and curved "table" or "dinner" knives (Daniel Low & Co. 1926:91; T. Eaton 1927:223). Within a few years, however, it had gained acceptance for table-knife duties as well.

Knives with stainless-steel slipper-shaped blades sometimes had a bolster that was made separately (Figure 34). These bolsters were slotted to slip over the bare tang and slide up to meet the blade. The handle would then be cemented or molded onto the tang. Such bolsters are found in various metals including tin alloy, nickel-plated brass, and steel. After World War I, aluminum alloys began to be used occasionally as handle material (Montgomery Ward 1922:525), but they were rarely advertised in the 1920s or 1930s.

By the late 1920s, composite cutlery held only a fraction of the market. Although a range of wood, bone, antler, and rubber handles could still be found, most mail-order catalogues offered several pages of inexpensive stamped nickel- and silver-plate compared to a page or less of composite knives and forks (Montgomery Ward 1926:416-419, 550; Sears, Roebuck 1927:754-761). Except for knives and forks with handles of celluloid and the first modern synthetic plastics such as Bakelite (Hillman 1986:24-26), composite table cutlery all but disappeared during the 1930s.

Conclusion

The main features for the dating of table cutlery in the 18th century are stylistic. Some knives acquired humped backs in the 1720s, and choils appeared in the 1760s. By the end of the century, several new blade forms had appeared. Forks acquired a square shoulder around 1770, and three-tined examples become more common about the same time. Little change occurred in the first half of the 19th century, but manufacturing methods being developed in the United States were to have a major impact. In the second half of the 19th century, the main changes were technological. Sheet-steel cutlery was introduced in the 1850s, and was common by the 1860s. Cast-on bolsters were introduced in the 1860s. Hard rubber handles became common at about the same time. Celluloid handles were introduced in the 1870s, and became common in the 1880s. All-steel cutlery was patented in 1867. In the 20th century, stainless steel and the slipper-shaped blade appeared after World War I.

Through all of this change, some cutlery continued to be made using older forms and manufacturing techniques. Although it is sometimes possible to put a *terminus post quem* on cutlery, it is often much more difficult to put a *terminus ante quem* on a style or technology.

REFERENCES

BAILEY, C. T. P.
1927 *Knives and Forks: Selected and Described.* The Medici Society, London, England.

DANIEL LOW & CO.
1926 *Year Book* [catalogue] for 1927. Boston, MA.

DAVIS, JOHN D.
1976 *English Silver at Williamsburg.* Colonial Williamsburg Foundation, Williamsburg, VA.

DYSON, B. RONALD
1936 *A Glossary of Words and Dialect Formerly Used in the Sheffield Trades.* Reprinted 1979, Sheffield Trades Historical Society, Sheffield, England.

F. A. WALKER & CO.
1871 *Illustrated Supplement to Our Catalogue of 1871.* Boston, MA.

FAULKNER, ALARIC, AND GRETCHEN FEARON FAULKNER
1987 *The French at Pentagoet, 1635-1674.* The Maine Historic Preservation Commission and The New Brunswick Museum, Augusta, ME.

FRANCIS T. WITTE HARDWARE CO.
1883 *Hardware, Cutlery and Guns.* New York, NY.

GORDON, MACKAY & CO.
1910 *General Catalogue.* Toronto, Ontario.
1913 *General Catalogue.* Toronto, Ontario.

GRAYSON, RUTH, WITH KEN HAWLEY
1995 *Knifemaking in Sheffield & The Hawley Collection.* Published for Sheffield Hallam University, PAVIC Publications, Sheffield, England.

GREAT BRITAIN, PATENT OFFICE
1857 *Manufacture of Knives and Forks. Greaves' Specification. A.D. 1840, No. 8540.* George Eyre and William Spottiswoode, London, England.

GREELEY, HORACE, LEON CASE, EDWARD HOWLAND, JOHN B. GOUGH, PHILIP RIPLEY, F. P. PERKINS, J. B. LYMAN, ALBERT BRISBANE, AND REV. E. E. HALL
1872 *The Great Industries of the United States.* J. B. Burr and Hyde, Hartford, CT.

HARDWICK, PAULA
1981 *Discovering Horn.* Lutterworth Press, Guilford, Surrey, England.

HARROD'S STORES
1895 *Price List, May, 1895.* Reprinted 1972 as *Victorian Shopping.* David and Charles, Newton Abbot, Devon, England.

HAYWARD, J. F.
1957 *English Cutlery: Sixteenth to Eighteenth Century.* Victoria and Albert Museum, London, England.

HILLMAN, DAVID
1986 A Short History of Early Consumer Plastics. *Journal of the International Institute for Conservation-Canadian Group* 10 and 11:20-27.

HIMSWORTH, J. B.
1953 *The Story of Cutlery: From Flint to Stainless Steel.* Ernest Benn, London, England.

HUDSON'S BAY COMPANY
1910 *Fall and Winter Catalogue 1910-1911.* Reprinted 1977, Watson and Dwyer, Winnipeg, Manitoba.

J. H. ASHDOWN HARDWARE CO. LIMITED
1935 *Ashdown's General Catalog* (containing insert page dated July 1937). Winnipeg, Ontario.

KATZ, SYLVIA
1984 *Classic Plastics.* Thames and Hudson, London, England.

KIDD, KENNETH E.
1972 The Dating of Cutlery Objects for the Use of Archaeologists. Parks Canada, *Microfiche Report Series* 46. Ottawa, Ontario.

LANDERS, FRARY AND CLARK
1869 *Illustrated Catalogue and Price List of Table Cutlery and Hardware.* New Britain, CT.

LLOYD, G. I. H.
1913 *The Cutlery Trades: An Historical Essay in the Economics of Small-Scale Production.* Reprinted 1968, Augustus M. Kelley, New York, NY.

MERRIAM, ROBERT L., RICHARD A. DAVIS, JR., DAVID S. BROWN, AND MICHAEL E. BUERGER
1976 *The History of the John Russell Cutlery Company 1833-1936.* Bete Press, Greenfield, MA.

MONTGOMERY WARD AND CO.
1884   *No. 35, Spring and Summer Catalogue 1884*. Chicago, IL.
1922   *Catalogue No. 97, Fall & Winter 1922-23*. Chicago, IL. Reprinted 1969, H. C. Publishers, New York, NY.
1926   *Catalogue No. 105, Fall and Winter 1926-27*. Baltimore, MD.

MOORE, SIMON
1995   Table Knives and Forks. *Shire Album* 320. Shire Publications, Buckinghamshire, England.

NOËL HUME, IVOR
1969   *A Guide to Artifacts of Colonial America*. Alfred A. Knopf, New York, NY.

RUSSELL AND ERWIN MANUFACTURING COMPANY
1865   *Illustrated Catalogue of American Hardware of the Russell and Erwin Manufacturing Company*. Reprinted 1980, Association for Preservation Technology, Ottawa, Ontario.

SEARS, ROEBUCK AND CO.
1897   *Consumers Guide, Catalogue No 104*. Chicago, IL. Reprinted 1968, Chelsea House, New York, NY.
1927   *1927 Fall and Winter Catalogue*. Chicago, IL. Reprinted 1970, Crown Publishers, New York, NY.

SILBER AND FLEMMING
1883   *The Illustrated Catalogue of Furniture and Household Requisites*. Reprinted 1991 as *The Victorian Catalogue of Household Goods*. Studio Editions, London, England.

SMITH, JOSEPH
1816   *Explanation or Key, to the Various Manufactures of Sheffield, with Engravings of Each Article*. Reprinted 1975, The Early American Industries Association, South Burlington, VT.

SMITHURST, PETER
1987   The Cutlery Industry. *Shire Album* 195. Shire Publications, Buckinghamshire, England.

STONE, LYLE M.
1974   Fort Michilimackinac, 1715-1781: An Archaeological Perspective on the Revolutionary Frontier. *Publications of the Museum, Michigan State University, Anthropological Series* 2. East Lansing.

STONE, ROBERT
1998   The Evolution of the Knife and Fork, 1500-1880. Paper presented at the 27th Annual Meeting of the Association for Living Historical Farms and Agricultural Museums, Waterloo, Ontario.

T. EATON CO.
1901   *Catalogue, Fall and Winter 1901-1902*. Reprinted 1970, Musson, Toronto, Ontario.
1927   *Catalogue, Spring and Summer 1927*. Reprinted 1971, Musson, Toronto, Ontario.

TABER, MARTHA VAN HOESEN
1955   *A History of the Cutlery Industry in the Connecticut Valley*. Department of History of Smith College, Northhampton, MA.

TOMLINSON, CHARLES (EDITOR)
1854   *Cyclopaedia of Useful Arts, Mechanical and Chemical, Manufactures, Mining and Engineering*, Volume 1. George Virtue, London, England.

TREMBLAY, YVES
1996   *Les Ustensiles, les objets de couture et le luminaire de Place-Royale*. Gouvernement du Québec, Québec.

UNITED STATES PATENT OFFICE
1838   *Mode of Making Table Knives and Forks, Letters Patent No. 737, George Ropes, May 10, 1838*. United States Patent Office, Washington, DC
1860   *Table Cutlery, Letters Patent No. 27,357, Joseph W. Gardner, March 6, 1860*. United States Patent Office, Washington, DC. [NB: The Lamson and Goodnow Company were the assignees of this patent.]
1866   *Improvement in Manufacture of Knives and Forks, Letters Patent No. 58,242, James D. Frary, September 25, 1866*. United States Patent Office, Washington, DC.
1867   *Improvement in Table Cutlery, Letters Patent No. 70,525, Matthew Chapman, November 5, 1867*. United States Patent Office, Washington, DC.

URE, ANDREW
1849   *A Dictionary of Arts, Manufactures and Mines*. D. Appleton, New York, NY.

VICTORIA AND ALBERT MUSEUM
1979   *Masterpieces of Cutlery and the Art of Eating*. Victoria and Albert Museum, London, England.

W. A. CURRIER
[1862] *Catalogue. W. A. Currier's Kitchen, House Furnishing and Stove Warehouse*. Haverhill, MA.

WADE, BARBARA J.
1982   Cutlery from the Fort at Coteau-du-Lac, Quebec. Parks Canada, *History and Archaeology* 61. Ottawa, Ontario

PHIL DUNNING
MATERIAL CULTURE RESEARCH
ONTARIO SERVICE CENTRE
PARKS CANADA
1600 LIVERPOOL COURT
OTTAWA, ONTARIO K1A 0M5
CANADA

OLIVE R. JONES

Commercial Foods, 1740–1820

ABSTRACT

Commercial food packaging, in both bulk and unit sizes, can be found in archaeological assemblages. Newspaper advertisements from the ca. 1740 to 1820 period provide information on the shape, size, and contents of wood, metal, glass, ceramic, and fiber containers. The advertisements also show that elements of consumerism, in the form of brand names, distinctive packaging, unit packaging, international markets, fixed prices, ready-made items, and targeted markets, were practiced in the food industry by the early years of the 19th century.

Introduction

Scholarly investigations into the development of consumerism have quite rightly pushed many of its manifestations back into the 18th century, and even earlier (McKendrick et al. 1982; McCracken 1988:11–16). Standard evidence for consumerism—brand name or proprietary products, ready-made items, unit packaging, fixed prices, advertising, credit and cash sales, targeted markets, price-setting by the supplier, frequent changes in style—can be found before the end of the 18th century in considerable quantities and in many different places (Mui and Mui 1989; Palmer 1989: 374–375).

An integral part of the developing consumerism was a complex, carefully structured, worldwide distribution network. Monopolistic companies—like the East India Company, wholesalers, middlemen, city and country merchants, and traders—worked in distribution centers of decreasing size and influence. They were able to bring goods not just to London, New York, and Quebec but also to small towns, settlements, and remote fur trade posts in the interior of North America. The goods could be costly when they reached their final destination but get there they did (Figure 1; Cruikshank 1929:153–155). The trade in foodstuffs was

no exception. The completely self-sufficient household, in Britain or in North America, in terms of food production probably did not exist in the 18th century, at any level of society, in either rural or urban settings. If the capacity existed for nutritional self-sufficiency, the cultural demands of what constituted a meal, or what food should taste like, placed everyone in the position of buying at least some foodstuffs that they had not produced themselves. Through foods such as sugar and salt they became participants in the marketplace.

Evidence for commercial foods can be found on archaeological sites. Unfortunately archaeologists have not really looked for it. Too often glass and ceramic containers are dismissed as storage containers while metal, wood, and fiber artifacts may not even be recognized as containers. Too often serving vessels are simply accepted as tea cups or salts or cruets or dessert glasses without questioning their implications for food consumption practices. Too often the floral and faunal remains are accepted as the only evidence for food choice, food procurement, and food preparation. What can be found?

A great deal of evidence for commercial foodstuffs can be found in the containers discarded at a site. Containers of wood, vegetable and animal fiber, bladders, metal, ceramic, and glass can be used to track goods consumed two hundred years ago. Part of the evidence also lies in historical documents, such as newspaper advertisements, which contain descriptions of foods and their containers. The challenge for the archaeologist is to identify the food/package link by comparing the objects found in the ground with the physical descriptions in the documents.

Newspapers, themselves a product of the growing consumerism, also helped promote the sale of goods. Advertisements make up the bulk of 18th-century newspapers. In the papers examined, two and a half to three of the four pages were devoted to advertisements of various types (cf. Clark and Wetherell 1989:299–303). Advertisements in English, Canadian, and American newspapers attest to the vigorous worldwide trade in food and to the commercialism of that trade. Foreign foods, con-

FIGURE 1. Military and naval officers were sometimes addressed in the newspaper advertisements as potential customers. Their nomadic life-style made army and navy personnel prime consumers of prepared foods. *The Military Adventures of Johnny Newcome, Thomas Rowlandson, 1815.* (Courtesy of Library, Royal Military College, Kingston, Ontario.)

venience foods, unit packaging, retail food outlets, targeted markets, fixed prices, cash and short-term credit sales can all be found in 18th- and early 19th-century newspapers.

The advertisements provide information on food products available in urban areas and, by implication, the hinterlands being serviced by these trading centers—spices of all kinds, fresh, dried and candied fruits, rice, grains, vermicelli and macaroni, scented waters, seeds for garden vegetables, condiments, hams, butter, cheeses, dried beans, potatoes, salt pork and beef, fishes, flour. The lists contain processed foods of many types, staples, and baking and cooking supplies. Modifier terms used to describe foods, such as origin, quality, quantity, and the type of container, provide con-

crete evidence of packaging customs and of the desirable qualities associated with specific foods. Beaudry (1988:43–50) provides an analysis of modifier terms in inventories. A discussion on the newspapers and data bases used for this article is included in Appendix A. Many foods were described by their geographical origins—Yorkshire hams, Cheshire cheese, Durham mustard, Gorgona Anchovies, French olives, Florence oil, Irish pork, beef, and butter—which seem to have acted as a certificate of genuineness and quality. There was no guarantee, of course, that the products actually came from these places. However, their presence in the North American papers indicates that even foods produced here were superseded in desirability by European ones. They also imply that specialized food production in Europe was already scaled to supply more than the local market.

For some foods the traditional containers of the exporting country were used until the product reached its final destination. Olive oil sold in flasks and jars is an example of this product/package link. Other goods were repackaged. For example, the British government controlled the movement of alcoholic beverages through Customs and Excise regulations to protect the revenue it derived from this source. Britain prohibited the large-scale importation of European wines in small packages, the theory being that they were easier to smuggle than larger ones (Francis 1972:146–147.) Consequently European wines were sold in both England and its North American colonies in English bottles, not European ones, as the bulk of archaeological data demonstrates. Sometimes the transfer to bottles took place in England, sometimes in North America (Jones and Smith 1985:9). On the other hand, some of the newspaper advertisements and scattered archaeological evidence suggests that alcoholic beverages such as Florence wine, gin, and brandy may very well have been sold in European-made bottles, such as flasks and square case bottles, to be discussed below (cf. Jones 1989). Containers for other types of products, such as snuff, have been mentioned when the packaging seemed similar to food packaging.

Another common group of modifiers was the container name. The product association could be so strong that phrases such as ''jar raisins,'' ''basket salt,'' or ''firkin butter'' obviously referred to very specific varieties of these goods. Advertisements also mentioned capacities and types of packaging—mustard in quarter-pound bottles, pickles in quart bottles, olive oil by the jar or chest—indicating a variety of packaging and sizes for any given food. Close relationships between size and package also suggest that many foods were regularly shipped in a variety of unit packages, not just in bulk. Standardized terminology for containers and capacities, specialized container shapes, combined with the diversity of package size, material, and shape are evidence of the growing commercialization of the trade in foodstuffs. Consumers had always been able to buy goods in any quantity

FIGURE 2.   Cases, baskets, barrels, and bags appear in this engraving for the Cowie firm. Cowie sold bottled porter, brown stout, Edinburgh and other ale, perry and cider for home consumption and for export. The printer, Edward Gulian, appeared in the *London Directories* at the address on the card between the years 1826 and 1831. (Courtesy of Metropolitan Museum of Art, gift of Bella C. Landauer, 1958.58.544.)

they needed or could afford. Mustard could always have been bought by the ¼ or ½ pound. What *was* new was mustard sold in bottles of a specific size and style (Figures 9, 11).

Wooden Containers

Staved wooden containers (Figure 2)—tierces, kegs, casks, barrels, tubs, drums, puncheons, and hogsheads—contained a host of products, not just foodstuffs. Those for dry goods tended to be made of softer woods, like spruce, and to have metal hoops which were sometimes fastened through the wood. Those for wet goods were made of oak or beech, and had alder hoops. For those designed to be reused, as in the liquor trade, the staves were made flatter, making them easier to ship disassembled. Those used standing on their ends had thicker, sturdier chimes, the part of the stave extending beyond the head (Bradley 1990, pers. comm.).

Staved wooden containers were generally used for shipping and storing large quantities of a specific product. Capacity terms, such as firkin or keg, were well-understood at the time but are now hard to sort out. Sometimes the terms were used comparatively; kegs were always smaller than puncheons, for example. At other times the capacity term was specific to a particular product. Dozens of references to butter in firkins, often with modifiers such as "Irish," "Cork," or "rose," imply that the size was clearly understood. Zupko (1968: 61–62) cites a 1673 statute that required the butter firkin to weigh 8 lbs. and the butter 56 lbs., for a total weight of 64 lbs. One advertisement offered "a choice Parcel of fine Dublin Butter made up in full bound Firkins of about 56 lb. each, after the Cambridge Manner, and equal to it in Quality" (*Daily Advertiser* [*DA*] 6 Aug. 1760:Butter Warehouse). It is not clear if the tallow, lard, tongues, herring, salmon, white bread, and barley also sold in firkins were sold in the same-sized container, or if the term referred to a specific weight. Kegs were used for dried goods such as split peas, barley, crackers, oatmeal, raisins, and rice; for butter, lard, or paint oils; for pickled meats and other pickles; sometimes for alcohol and sometimes for other packaging:

> a large Assortment of Kegs, from one Gallon bigness to Fifteen Do (*Nova-Scotia Gazette and Weekly Chronicle* [*NSG&WC*] 9 Dec. 1783:John Thomson).

> Vinegar in Hogsheads and 10 Gallon Kegs (*NSG&WC* 15 June 1784:Piers and Hill).

> Also Vinegar in 5 gallon Kegs very convenient for Housekeepers (*Quebec Gazette* [*QG*] 20 Sept. 1779:T. Cary).

> Hogs Lard in small kegs from 20 to 28 lbs. each (*QG* 26 May 1785:Richard Dalton).

> Barley in 50 and 25 lb cags (*New-York Mercury* [*NYM*] 26 Jan. 1761:John Alexander and Company).

> best Nantz Brandy in 8 and 4 Gallon Kegs (*NYM* 3 Aug. 1761:Dirck Brinckerhoff).

> Choice French Brandy in Kegs of 5 and 6 Gallons, at five Shillings Halifax per Gallon (*QG* 20 Dec. 1770:John Lees).

> linseed oyl in 10 gallon cags (*NYM* 12 Jan. 1761:Isaac Man).

> 7 Kegs Mustard in 1–4 lb. bottles (*Montreal Herald* [*MH*] 22 Jan. 1820:Macnider, Aird, & Whyte).

It will be difficult to identify the specific contents of staved containers from archaeological sites beyond their use for wet or dry goods.

Boxes of different types (Figure 2)—cases, chests, crates, and boxes—generally held smaller packages or complete objects. They probably had compartments and came in many sizes depending on the commodity. Some terms tended to be used more often with certain types of goods. Crates, for example, were filled with ceramic and glass. Some chests and cases were decorative; made of good woods, with locks and fine fittings, they were used to store tea, medicines, and liquor.

The commercial boxes often held glass and ceramic wares, soap, candles, pipes, medicines, pickles, cordials, toiletry items, or fruits such as lemons, citron, prunellos, plums, and raisins:

> Chocolate by the Box or Dozen (*NYM* 1 June 1761:John Morton).

> A few boxes fresh Durham flour mustard, ¼ lb. bottles (*NSG&WC* 30 June 1789:S. Hart).

> A very fresh, excellent Kind of Poland Starch and Hair Powder in Boxes of ½ Cwt. each in Pound papers (*NSG&WC* 24 May 1785:David Fergusson).

> fine Genoa Vermacelli, at 1s. a Pound, or 14s. a Box, containing seventeen Pounds (*DA* 14 Dec. 1739:Joseph Carbon).

> Lemmons by the Box, Hundred or Dozen (*Boston Gazette & Country Journal* [*BG&CJ*] 14 March 1774:Joseph Hall).

bohea tea by the box, dozen or single pound (*NYM* 23 June 1755:Matheus Sleght).

Chests, also in half and quarter sizes, were used primarily for tea, olive oils, and other Mediterranean goods:

Plain green, superfine, and best Heyson Tea, by the Chest, or Dozen of Pounds (*NYM* 9 July 1759:Wm. Gilliland).

Fine green and hyson teas, by the chest or single pound at 40s., 32s., 28s., and 24s. (*NYM* 4 Oct. 1762:Richard Curson).

Chests containing Bottles of Anchovies, Capers and Olives; also Chests of Florence Oyl, or by the single Bettee (*NYM* 1 Sept. 1760:Gerardus Duyckinck).

Florence Oyl by the Chest, 30 Bottles in a Chest (*QG* 4 July 1765:Daniel Malcom).

Florence Wine in Flasks by the half Chest (*QG* 15 Aug. 1765:Jenkins & Allsopp).

Turky Figs in chests (*QG* 11 April 1782: . . . Shoolbred and Barclay).

Cesalonia Moscatel Wine, at 31.10s. a chest, or 35s. the Half-Chest (*DA* 18 Dec. 1739:Angelo Massa).

Cases were used most often for alcohol—gin, brandy, wines, porter—holding anywhere from one to 10 dozen bottles, for pickles and condiments, and for empty bottles:

Claret of the best quality in hogsheads, tierces, and bottles in cases of four doz . . . best Holland's Gin in cases of twelve bottles (*QG* 11 Oct. 1781:Louis Marchand).

anchovies, olives, capers, mangoes, wall-nuts and gerkins in cases and kegs (*QG* 19 May 1785:Phebe David).

Cases of Pickles 6 Bottles each Case, containing Anchovies, Capers, Mangoes, Walnuts, Girkins and French Olives (*NSG&WC* 14 Dec. 1779:Edward Nichols).

A Small Case Durham Mustard in ½ and ¼ Bottles (*NSG&WC* 23 May 1786:Piers & Hill).

a few 12 Bottle Cases of Capers (*NYM* 9 July 1759:John Waddell).

Cases of 12 and 21 Flasks (*NYM* 19 Jan. 1767:Samuel Verplanck).

cases with bottles, each bottle containing from two to four gallons (*NYM* 6 Jan. 1755:Philip Livingston).

Fiber, Basketry, Bladders

These organic materials have little chance of surviving in most archaeological contexts, aside from their fittings, but they too carried foods of various types. Bags held dry products such as bottle corks, biscuit, flour, coffee, and sometimes ginger, pepper, snuff, and cocoa nuts. The weight of the product was not mentioned. Canvas was rarely mentioned and only in connection with ham. Bales were generally for pepper.

Baskets were used exclusively for salt and cheese. "Basket salt" was such a common phrase that it obviously represented a type of salt; occasionally the phrase was reversed to "salt in baskets," indicating that it was indeed sold in baskets: "Basket Salt is made by boiling away the Water of Salt Springs over the Fire . . . As to the various Kinds of common Salt, the Basket Salt is the mildest and weakest of all; the Sea Salt is of a middle Nature, and the Bay Salt is roughest of all" (Bradley [1770]:120). Examples include:

Cheshire Cheese by the Basket or Single Cheese (*NSG&WC* 14 June 1785:Edward Oxnard).

Gloucester Cheese by the Basket or smaller quantity (*NSG&WC* 23 Feb. 1779:Andrew Thomson).

Hampers mentioned in the *NYM* and *BG&CJ* generally held empty bottles but they also held bottles of beer/porter, cheeses, and once or twice potatoes, wine, or stoneware:

London Bottled Porter in 4 Doz. Hampers,/Ditto bottled Porter in Casks,/Ditto bottled Port Wine in 2, 3, and 4 Doz. Hampers (*NSG&WC* 25 May 1784:Wm. Nixon and Co.).

quart bottles in hampers (*NYM* 7 Sept. 1767:Philip Livingston).

Bladders were often used for snuff and once in a while for hogs' lard, putty, or mustard:

Plain snuff in bladders of 28, 56, and 84 lb. each (*NYM* 24 Dec. 1753:Rip Van Dam).

FIGURE 3. Metal box made of thin, unidentified metal. Extant dimensions are 4 × 4 × 2½ in., minimum of 33 in. (Courtesy of Fortress of Louisbourg National Historic Park [NHP], Nova Scotia.)

fine hogs lard in small bladders (*QG* 9 June 1785:M. Macnider).

Dan French begs Leave to acquaint his Friends and Customers, that he has from the North lately receiv'd a fresh Quantity of Flour of Mustard Seed in Colour, Fineness, and Flavour, as good as any in England, to be sold wholesale or retail at his Warehouse . . . the superfine at 1s.6d. the second sort at 1s. and the third sort at 6d. per Pound, ready made up, and put into Bladders cleaned and scalded for the Purpose, to be paid for, and if return'd sound the Money again . . . (*DA* 22 Dec. 1752:Dan French).

Metal

Metal containers can be found in archaeological assemblages but they may not be recognized as such (Figure 3). Cannisters were used primarily for snuff but the *NYM* regularly advertised tea sold in this container. On the few occasions when the material was noted in the advertisements tin or lead were listed; however, Johnson (1979[1775]) defined cannisters as small baskets or small vessels for holding anything, such as tea or coffee. Later the term was used for preserved meat containers:

Scouchong, Hyson, and Peckoe tea, in pound, half and quarter pound cannisters (*NYM* 14 Aug. 1758:Gerardus Duyckinck).

bohea and congo teas, pound, half and quarter pound tin cannisters (*NYM* 4 Oct. 1762:Richard Curson).

He has likewise a parcel of fine green tea, in pound canisters, at 14s. a canister (*NYM* 29 Dec. 1766:Edward Agar).

Rappee Snuff, in Pound Leaden Cannisters (*NYM* 27 March 1758:Lott and Low).

The meats are prepared in canisters of 4 lb. to 20 lb. weight each . . . Apply to the patentees, Messrs. Donkin, Hall, and Gamble . . . (*The Times* [*Times*] 21 Jan. 1817:Preservation of Meat).

sago round and in cannisters, a large quantity portable soup in canisters 25 lbs each, or pr pound at less than stlg. cost (*Acadian Recorder* 19 Oct. 1816:Samuel Head).

Several times in the 1780s Halifax and Quebec papers lead was noted as a packaging material for cheese; it was also used for snuff:

The best of old Cheshire Cheese cased in lead (*NSG&WC* 2 May 1780:Edward Nichols).

Tin was infrequently mentioned as a packaging material.

Portable Soup, of the best Sorts, made separately from Beef, Veal, Mutton, and Chicken, is sold at 4s. a Dozen in Tin Boxes, which is about equal to 8s. a Pound, excepting the Chicken. Also an inferior Sort made into square Cakes from Beef, is sold by Weight at 5s. a Pound, very handy for Sauces as well as Soups. . . . This Commodity has been made, ever since the late Rebellion, by Mrs. Bennet (whose Name was then Du Bois) and it was at that Time, and ever since, greatly valued by Gentlemen in the Army (*DA* 11 Sept. 1762:Portable Soup . . .).

Ceramics

As a material, ceramics survives well in archaeological contexts, and was made in many different forms (Figures 4–7.) It has, therefore, good potential for identifying commercial food products used at sites. Pots were clearly used both for storage (inks, paints, medicines) and as commercial shipping containers for blacking, pomatum, soap, conserved fruits, honey, and butter. The term obviously covers a wide capacity range and shape:

Gally-pots from 4 lb. to ½ lb./Ditto, from 8 oz. to ½ oz. (*NYM* 26 Oct. 1767:George Ball).

FIGURE 4. Tin-glazed earthenware pots for "confiture," and for pomade (*far right*). Capacity of pot on left is 425 ml; of the center 700 ml. (Courtesy of Fortress of Louisbourg NHP, Nova Scotia.)

FIGURE 5. Coarse earthenware containers. All interiors are glazed. *Left* to *right*: (*a*) Anglo-American, height: ca. 215 mm, capacity: 3,300 ml; (*b*) French, height: 192 mm, capacity: 830 ml; (*c*) Anglo-American, height: 265 mm, capacity: 7,700 ml; (*d*) Anglo-American, height: ca. 195 mm, capacity: 2,700 ml; (*e*) French, height: ca. 245 mm, capacity: 3,000 ml; (*f*) Anglo-American, height: ca. 275 mm, capacity: 8,200 ml. (Courtesy of Fortress of Louisbourg NHP, Nova Scotia.)

FIGURE 6. Coarse stoneware, Normandy, reddish-brown body, unglazed, considered a butter pot. Height: ca. 285 mm, estimated capacity: 5,650 ml. (Courtesy of Fortress of Louisbourg NHP, Nova Scotia.)

Naples Soap, at 5s. a Pot, containing eight Ounces (*DA* 31 Jan. 1740:Joseph Carbon).

A Fine Parcel of New Honey, of this Year's collecting, in glazed Pots, leather'd on the Top, and in Pots from 15 lb. to 35 lb. and to be sold as follows: Single Pots at Fourpence Halfpenny per Pound, and at Forty Shillings per Hundred; and some Allowance to those who take a larger Quantity (*DA* 17 Sept. 1762:To be Sold at the Windmill . . .).

Potted Venison in small Pots at Six-pence per Pot (*DA* 29 July 1760:To be Sold, Fine true Grass fed Venison . . .).

6 [barrels] Pots preserved Peaches of the first quality (*MH* 21 Dec. 1816:Nichols & Sanford).

60 Pots Pickled Oysters (*MH* 5 April 1817:Nichols & Sanford . . . Evening Sale).

Hickson's Prepared Gorgona Anchovies, or Anchovy Paste for Sandwiches, Toast, &c. . . . that all the genuine have Hickson, 170, Strand, printed on the side of every pot, price 2s. each (*Times* 4 Dec. 1818:A Caution . . .).

Stone Butter Potts from 2 gallons to one Quart, in large or Small quantities (*NSG&WC* 14 June 1785:Edward Oxnard).

Potts from 2 to 5 Gallons (*NSG&WC* 5 July 1785:William Kidston).

[stone] pickling and Butter Pots (*QG* 28 Sept. 1769:Woolseys & Bryan).

A few pots and firkins of choice butter for family use (*NYM* 6 Dec. 1762:John Abeel).

damsons, put up in pots without sugar for tarts (*NYM* 6 Dec. 1762:Ann Ramsey).

FIGURE 7. Spanish coarse earthenware containers were made either glazed or unglazed. They were used for a variety of solids and liquids, such as raisins, olive oil, olives, cider, wine, figs, and anchovies, even soap and pitch (James 1988; Gusset 1989, pers. comm.). They were closed with a flat coarse earthenware disc that did not reseal once the jar had been opened, or with cork. The three complete carrot-shaped jars from the Fortress of Louisbourg NHP hold 3,300–4,250 ml and are 403–440 mm in height. The three globular examples are (a) height: 273 mm, capacity: 6,600 ml; (b) height: 272 mm, capacity: 5,000 ml; (c) height: 263 mm, est. capacity: 4,700 ml. (Courtesy of Fortress of Louisbourg NHP, Nova Scotia.)

Some also pickle anchovies in small delf, or earthen pots made on purpose, of two or three pounds weight, more or less, which they cover with plaster, to keep them the better (Rees 1819, 2). [Same information can be found in Savary des Bruslons (1759) and in Postlethwayt (1971[1774])].

Anchovy Butter—This new and excellent Composition is particularly recommended to the admirers of Anchovy Sandwiches, possessing all the genuine flavour of the fish, without the trouble of preparing it, being fit for immediate use, and will spread like butter: officers of the army and navy will find the above a most useful and convenient article, as it will make a most superior fish sauce without the use of flour or butter: it is warranted to keep good in any climate, in pots 1s.6d., 2s.6d., and 4s.6d. each: superior Norfolk pickled eels, a most excellent substitute for pickled salmon, in pots 1s.6d. and 3s. (*Times* 28 March 1817:Anchovy Butter).

The Subscriber has just received a supply of West India Sweetmeats, consisting of Tamarinds, preserved Ginger, Pine Apple Jam. Preserved green Sweetmeats, Currant Jelly, Gooseberry & Raspberry Jam, richly preserved in stone Pots (*MH* 4 Jan. 1817:Sweetmeats . . .).

Jars were used primarily for raisins, oils, pickles, and occasionally honey. Unless the material was specified, it is unlikely that jars in the 18th century were of glass. Although wide-mouthed glass containers were available, they were not called jars (Jones and Smith 1985:61; Jones 1989). In the 19th century jars became used more and more for linseed oil. The term ''jar raisins'' occurred dozens of times between 1740 and 1790 without any other description for size, shape, or material, indicating that it was a well-known package. However, in the early 19th-century papers looked at, including a complete run of the *Montreal Herald* (1814–1820), jar raisins were never listed. Frails—a kind of basket made of rushes—appeared and were added to the boxes, barrels, kegs, and casks mentioned earlier for raisins:

jarr, box and common raisins (*QG* 29 May 1777:Isaac Roberts).

Bloom Raisins in Jars (*QG* 31 Aug. 1780:E. Watts).

Lately landed a curious Parcel of Bloom Sun Raisins, much finer than any in the Jars, in small Boxes about 12 lb. each, to be sold by the Importer . . . at 7s. a Pound. No less Quantity than a Box (*DA* 4 Jan. 1762:Lately landed . . .).

The raisins of the sun, or jar-raisins, so called, because they are imported in jars, are all dried by the heat of the sun . . . (Rees 1819, 29).

Twenty Jars of very fine Lucca Oil, each Jar containing about thirty Gallons, one Jar in each lot (*DA* 21 Nov. 1739:To be sold by Auction . . .).

Fine Lucca Sallad Oil, neat as imported, in whole Jars, Half-Jars, and Quarter-Jars (*DA* 23 May 1740:To be Sold . . .).

Five 40 Gallon Jars of the finest Lucca Oil, [original packages] (*MH* 29 Nov. 1818:Robert Main).

Jar . . . an earthen pot or pitcher, with a big belly, and two handles.
    Jar is used for a sort of measure, or fixed quantity of divers things—The jar of oil is from 18 to 26 gallons: the jar of green-ginger is about 100 pounds weight, of wheat 52 pounds. Jar, a measure of Lucca oil is 25 wine-gallons = 5775 cubic inches . . . (Rees 1819, 18).

He has also for Sale a few Jars Pickled Walnuts and Onions (*NSG&WC* 10 Jan. 1786:Law. Hartshorne).

Anchovies, Girkins, Walnuts in Jars and Bottles (*NSG&WC* 4 May 1784:Andrew Thomson).

Fine green French olives, in kegs, jarrs and bottles; by sending packages they are sold at 7s6 per gallon measured out of the original casks—Any quantity not less than a quart, at the same rate (*QG* 16 Sept. 1784:Lindsay & Macnider).

Linseed oil in 1, 2 or 3 gallon jars (*Halifax Journal* [*HJ*] 28 Oct. 1785:William Lyon & Co.).

white wine vinegar, in jars from 3 ½ to 6 ½ gallons (*Quebec Mercury* [*QM*] 16 Sept. 1811:George Browne).

white wine vinegar in jars containing five and six gallons each (*QG* 6 June 1811:George Browne).

Glass

Like ceramics, glass survives well in the ground, was made in many different shapes, and contained many different types of products (Figures 8–11). Flasks or betties held various types of olive oil, wines, spa waters, and occasionally capers. They often came in chests. Two body shapes were covered by this term—a thin flat-sided body in horizontal cross-section and round in vertical cross-section, or a globular shape without a base. Both were likely covered with osier or leather. Although the term was used frequently in the newspaper advertisements and other documents in North America, flasks of this type are not often found in archaeological excavations. Size was generally not mentioned but extant examples usually hold about a quart, although they can be bigger: "five Quart and two Quart Flasks" (*NYM* 30 March 1761: George Ball). The quart flasks containing wine were likely not of English manufacture.

Bottles were mentioned hundreds of times directly. Their presence was implied by the terms chests, cases, quart, and dozen, particularly when the product was habitually sold in bottles. Most seem to have been of glass as material was rarely mentioned. One exception was "Stone Bottles from 1 Pint to 3 Gallons" (*QG* 28 Sept. 1769:Woolseys & Bryan). Sizes noted were small and large, quart, pint, and half-pint. Products sold by weight, such as snuff and mustard, were sold by the pound,

FIGURE 8. French bottles in blue-green glass (Harris 1978). The shape on the left appears in Chardin paintings with olives in it. The center style continued in production into the middle of the 19th century and may have held capers. The bottle on the right may have held olive oil. (Courtesy of Fortress of Louisbourg NHP, Nova Scotia.)

half-pound, and quarter-pound. In the English glass industry dark green glass was usually used to make bottles holding 6 oz. or more, while a light green or colourless glass was used for the smaller bottles. Glass bottles are found in large numbers on sites in North America. Their capacities, generally a quart or smaller, suggest unit purchases rather than bulk buying. Empty bottles were also sold for home packaging and frequent references to money given for returned bottles indicate that many were reused. Different shapes of bodies, length of neck, and size of mouth on existing bottles, as well as glass manufacturers' records, indicate that 18th-century bottle manufacturers in both Britain and France made specialized glass containers for different products (McKearin and Wilson 1978:246–278; Harris 1979; Jones 1986:11–15, 1989).

Innumerable references to bottled porter/ale/beer and wine echo the quantities of English

FIGURE 9. Flat octagonal bottles with short, wide necks are found regularly in mid- to late 18th-century archaeological contexts. The style was used for mustard (Mc-Kearin and Wilson 1978:263) but may also have been used for snuff. (*a*) Height: 169 mm, est. capacity: 355 ml; (*b*) height: 160 mm; (*c*) height: 155 mm. (Courtesy of Fortress of Louisbourg NHP, Nova Scotia.)

FIGURE 10. Square bottles with straight and tapered bodies are found in pint and quart sizes. In the 19th century the style was strongly identified with snuff but several references in 18th-century documents to square quart bottles for various types of pickles suggest the style had more than one use. Height: 130 mm, est. capacity: 410 ml (Jones and Smith 1985:65, 108).(Courtesy of Artillery Park NHP, Quebec.)

"wine" bottles found on North American sites (Jones 1986:17–26, 73–83). Brandy and gin, cider, punch ingredients such as shrub, lemon or orange juice, perfumed waters (used primarily as medicines but also as flavorings), patent and proprietary medicines, olive oil, snuff, mustard, pickles, and sauces were all sold in bottles. Noticeably absent were bottled inks, blacking, and rum.

Mustard and snuff were sold primarily in bottles holding a half or quarter pound, although sometimes a pound size was mentioned for mustard. In the 1780s one English factory that made dark green bottle glass produced mustard and snuff bottles in 7-, 8-, 14-, and 16-oz. sizes (Jones 1986:12). One bottle style recognized as being for mustard is the flat octagonal bottle with short, wide mouth; one for snuff has a square body (Figures 9, 10; Mc-Kearin and Wilson 1978:259–263). However, square quart bottles also appear to have been used for pickles of different types (Jones and Smith 1985:65, 108). By the early years of the 19th century, a style for London Mustard had appeared (Figure 11; Jones 1983:77–79). Examples include:

> At the same Places are sold, Kirby's new Flower of Mustard-Seed, seal'd up in Six-penny and Three-penny Bottles (*DA* 28 May 1740:To be Sold, Wholesale and Retail).

> Thomas Johnson, The only Preparer of the Flour of Mustard . . . where is continu'd to be sold, for the better Accommodation of his Customers, Johnson's original and much-approv'd Flour of Mustard, which has been sold by the Family upwards of forty Years with Approbation, in Six-penny and Threepenny Bottles, with great Allowances to those that buy Quantities. Each Bottle has Directions pasted thereon. Note, He sells a finer Sort, which far exceeds any yet made, for Colour, Beauty, and Taste, a Tea-Spoonful of which, stirr'd up in the Gravy of Beef, Mutton, Lamb, or Pork, makes the most agreeable Sauce that can be imagin'd; and is most excellent mix'd with Oil and Vinegar in Sallads. . . . Sold in Sixpenny Bottles, or by the Pound. N.B. Mustard ready made, to be had at any time, in any Quantities (*DA* 3 Nov. 1742:Thomas Johnson).

FIGURE 11. London mustard bottle, a small square bottle with chamfered corners embossed LONDON/MUSTARD; the style was introduced in the early 19th century. Height: 135 mm, capacity 120 ml, approximately 2 oz. of dry mustard. (Courtesy of Artillery Park NHP, Quebec.)

Kyan pepper and mustard in ¼ and ½ lb bottles (*Royal Gazette and the Nova-Scotia Advertiser* [*RG&NSA*] 1 Nov. 1791:Mark Mullen).

a few gross of choice quart bottles, and square snuff bottles (*NYM* 30 Nov. 1767:George Traile).

Also a few Bottles of Weston's best Snuff (*NYM* 14 Dec. 1761:John Ernest).

Prepared sauces, fruits, and pickles, made partly as flavorings or condiments, and partly to preserve

foods being shipped over long distances or kept for long-term storage, were also sold in bottles. These are traditionally thought to have been prepared at home and no doubt many were. As the advertisements show, however, pickled and preserved goods were also made commercially. In keeping with other types of consumables—medicines, toiletries, porter, snuff—proprietary food products were in production at least as early as the 1780s; by 1820 there were a number of named sauces—Quins, Sauce Royal, Cherokee, Harvey's, and Burgess' Essence of Anchovies (*Kingston Gazette* 25 Sept. 1810:Romeo Wadsworth; *QG* 6 June 1811:Fras. Durette; *QM* 11 June 1816:George Arnold).

The Cook will have Occasion to recollect what those Things are which serve to give them Flavour, or to eat with them as Additions in Sauce, or such as supply the Place of it. Under this Head come Pickles, and other preserved Things of that Kind. Of these there is a vast Number, but the greater Part of them are prepared at Home. Some we receive from other Countries. . . . These are principally six, Anchovies, Capers, Caviar, Cayan Pepper, Mangoes, and Soy (Bradley [1770]:6).

The best French Olives, at 2s.3d. a large Bottle, or 2s. a Quart Bottle; Lucca Olives, at 1s.6d. a Bottle, or 5s. a Gallon (*DA* 21 March 1740:Joseph Carbon).

Fine French Olives, in large long bottles, at 2s. a bottle (*DA* 24 March 1742:Berto Valle).

French olives in quart at 3s.9d. per bottle/Capers, ditto, per ditto (*Halifax Weekly Chronicle* [*HWC*] 4 June 1791:S. Hart).

French Olives, just imported, of the best quality, at 1s.6d. per pint, or 17s. per dozen; finest Lucca Oils, 5s. per quart; and New Flask Oil, 2s.6d.; the above are all of the best quality, and, if not approved of, the money shall be immediately returned: orders per post duly attended to (*Times* 23 May 1817:French Olives, and New Salad Oil . . .).

Pickled Cucumbers or Girkins in Quart Bottles very cheap (*QG* 15 Aug. 1765:Jenkins & Allsopp).

Pickles, in Quart and Pint Bottles, viz./Capers, Mushrooms, Anchovies, and Melon Mangoes,/Onions, Walnuts, Girkins, Olives, &c. (*HWC* 5 March 1791:Thomas Russell).

Olives, capers, India soy, girkins, walnuts and ketchup in quart, pint and half-pint bottles (*NSG&WC* 2 May 1780: Schwartz and Emerson).

Quin's Fish Sauce (*QG* 13 Oct. 1785:Aylwin & Co).

English pickles, in cases containing 6 bottles (*QM* 16 Sept. 1811:George Browne).

Just landed from the North of England, a fresh Parcel of pickled Mushrooms and Ketchup in Quart Bottles, both exceeding good and fine flavour'd; the Mushrooms at 3s.6d. the Bottle, and the Ketchup at 2s. Bottles included (*DA* 10 Nov. 1750:Sold at the Durham Mustard Warehouse).

the vegetable soups in quart and pint bottles, milk in pints, &c.; also concentrated gravy soup prepared in small bottles, for making quarts, pints, and two-thirds of a pint . . . Donkin, Hall, and Gamble (*Times* 21 Jan. 1817:Preservation of Meat).

About eighteen Dozen Bottles of Fruit, as Gooseberries, Currants, Cherries and Plumbs, fit for a Pastry-Cook (*DA* 23 Jan. 1750:To be Sold cheap . . .).

just landed from New York . . . A Parcel of fine Cranberries, a Fruit greatly esteemed at this Season of the Year, for the Richness of its Flavour in Tarts; to be sold by the Gallon or in single Quart (*DA* 22 Dec. 1750:To be Sold . . .).

Confectionary, consisting of Wet Fruits in bottles (*HJ* 28 Oct. 1785:S. Sparrow).

Excellent for making Punch, A fresh Parcel of Howe's Genuine Acid, Prepared from the Juice of Lemons and Oranges only, A large Tea Spoonful of which is sufficient for a Quart of Punch.
    This Acid is the fittest that can be used for the making of Lemonade, Jellies, and for all other Purposes to which Acid is necessary, upon Trial much Cheaper and more wholesome than the fresh Fruits, as by the process, the Watery and Earthly Particles [*sic*] are taken away and receives no Injury from keeping. . . .
    Sold at Robert Fletcher's at 2s.6d. per Bottle by the Dozen and 3s. each, by the Single Bottle (*NSG&WC* 11 May 1779:Excellent for making Punch . . .).

A few dozen London made Jellies & Preserves (*MH* 18 June 1814:James Fraser).

Olive oil also came in bottles in pint and quart sizes, in shapes other than a flask:

oil in square bottles (*BG&CJ* 3 Jan. 1774:Archibald Cunningham).

Florence oil, in cases containing 12 quart bottles (*QM* 16 Sept. 1811:George Browne).

8 Boxes Sallad Oil in French bottles (*MH* 15 Jan. 1820:John Torrance).

7 cases best sallad Oil in Pint Bottles (*MH* 31 May 1820: Shaw Armour).

Convenience Foods

Packaged prepared foods, such as sauces and bottled fruits, were not the only convenience foods available. In urban centers a host of specialists offered cooked, often hot, "fast" foods to all levels of society. Among their customers were the urban poor. Cooking required money, time for shopping and preparation, utensils, knowledge, and fuel. Hot food could be bought from bakers and street vendors, in taverns and other public places, faster and cheaper than it was to make. Ironically, bread, the modern symbol for home and hearth and for nutritional self-sufficiency, was one of the first foods to be made consistently outside the home. Authorities regarded bread as so crucial to the subsistence of the poor that they set detailed regulations governing its price, weight, and quality (Drummond and Wilbraham 1959:41, 218–219; Wheaton 1983:71–77; Mui and Mui 1988:155–156; Porter in Camporesi 1989:10, 13–14.) Assizes of bread were regularly published in the Canadian papers; sometimes the bakers were required to bake their initials in the bread; if the weight and price were not correct, the offending baker could be found easily:

It is Ordered, That the Six-penny brown Loaf do weigh Four Pounds Eight Ounces, and the Six-penny white Loaf do weigh Three Pounds Six Ounces, and that the Bakers mark the first Letters of their Name distinctly on each Loaf (*QG* 15 May 1777:District of Quebec).

Nor were the poor the only customers for "fast" foods. In the 18th century many meals or parts of meals were prepared or consumed outside the home, particularly by men and always by travellers (Figure 12). Baked goods, foods requiring specialized equipment or unusual ingredients, such as the elaborate desserts required for formal entertaining (Beldon 1983:168), were ordered from commercial establishments. Meals could be delivered:

FIGURE 12.   The Rainbow Tavern, Thomas Rowlandson, London, 1788. (Private collection.)

He begs leave to inform the Ladies, that he has a good Convenience for Baking, in which they may depend on having their Commands duly performed to the greatest Nicety; and hot Mutton Byes every Day (*Nova-Scotia Gazette & Weekly Advertiser* 3 Oct. 1769:John Wills . . . Great Pontac).

where he carries on the Baking business in all its branches, viz: Soft and hard Bread of the best quality, Butter biscuits, and other Cakes. He flatters himself to give universal Satisfaction to all who will favour him with their Custom (*NSG&WC* 25 Nov. 1788:John Fousel).

Will have a good Bill of Fare to furnish every Day on the shortest Notice. Plain Dishes from 1s.6d. to 2s.—Breakfast 1s.—Tea in the Evening 9d.—Supper 1s. . . . Beef Soup or Mutton Broth every Day at 12 o'Clock, from the first of next Month till the Weather grows warm (*NSG&WC* 22 Sept. 1789:Golden Ball).

Renelagh Gardens, For breakfasting, as well as the evening entertainment of Ladies and Gentlemen, are laid out, at a great expense, in a very genteel, pleasing manner, and judged (without exception) to be far the most rural retreat near this city . . . the very best of wine and other liquors, mead, silabubs, &c. with gammon, tongues, alamode beef, tarts, cakes, &c. and on notice given dinners, or other large entertainments, elegantly provided as usual . . . (*NYM* 30 June 1766:Renelagh Gardens).

Mr. Sills, at the London Tavern . . . Dinners drest, and all Sorts of Pastry made, and sent hot to any Part of the Town, on the shortest Notice (*QG* 8 Oct 1767:Sills).

Green Turtle, Dressed In the most perfect Manner every Day this Week at the Pontac. Private Family by sending their Turine's and Dishes between One and Four o'Clock, may be supplyed with it during that Time, in any Quantity (*NSG&WC* 18 July 1786:Green Turtle . . .).

Hartshorn Seville Orange Jellies, fresh every Day, at 3s. a Dozen; Hartshorn and Calves-Foot, at 2s. a Dozen; and Blamanger, at 4s. a Dozen. Four Shillings to be left in Hand till the Glasses are return'd (*DA* 30 Jan. 1752:To be Sold . . .).

The very best Hartshorn Jellies may be had fresh every Day, at Two Shillings a Dozen. Note, Four Shillings per Dozen to be left in Hand for the Glasses til return'd (*DA* 15 Feb. 1751:Tom's Coffee-House).

Physical evidence for the trade in local convenience foods will be difficult to find archaeologically. Bread, the staple food, leaves no traces except in architectural features such as bake ovens. Commercial serving dishes would be the same as those used in ordinary households. One could expect to find an unusually large number of serving dishes, such as dessert glasses, or specialized equipment in establishments offering cooked food for sale.

Conclusion

This sample from newspaper advertisements and of containers from archaeological sites shows that many elements of consumerism were in evidence in the food trade in the 18th century and were firmly established by 1820—proprietary or brand-named products, unit packages often of distinctive character, international trade, stated prices, targeted markets, and prepared foods. The advertisements show that manufacturers addressed the specific needs of certain groups such as cooks and travellers by developing prepared foods for them. Commercial sauces and pickles were designed to save the cook hours of preparation time. Travellers on the road needed food that was quick and easy to prepare and that was compatible with their social position, such as portable soup and the pots of anchovy butter offered to officers in the army and navy.

Both the objects and the advertisements show that many specialized centers of food production, some traditional and some new, supplied the North American market. Spain, France, and Italy supplied olives and olive oils, for example. Ireland specialized in the production of butter and salt beef and pork for the provisioning trade. English manufacturers took the traditional Mediterranean anchovy (or at least a fish which they called anchovy) and reprocessed it into anchovy paste. The West Indies produced not just rum and sugar but also spices and sweetmeats which were originally products grown in the East Indies.

Among the requirements for the successful expansion of food production to serve a wider market were containers to distribute that food. The containers needed to be relatively consistent in size, to be available in a variety of sizes and material, to be made of materials suitable for the product, and to be available in large numbers. Both the documentary and archaeological evidence suggest that by the end of the 18th century the makers of containers were able to meet the bulk of these demands. English dark green glass bottle manufacturers, for example, expanded both the quantity and variety of their production in response to increasing demands. By 1800 glass had become a principal material used in unit packaging.

Prepared commercial foods were also made and distributed locally. The preparation and consumption of food in this period was not confined to the family kitchen or the family dinner table. The reality was far more diverse in terms of location, type of meal, and type of food. Public eating establishments served travelers and people without cooking facilities. Many offered convivial meeting places where men could eat alone or with friends. Even street vendors sold food (Marc LaFrance 1990, pers. comm.) Households used the services of professionals for baked goods and for foods requiring specialized skills, supplies, and equipment.

A romantic stereotyped view of the past, in which each household is thought of as self-sufficient and free from the "taint" of consumerism, does not serve archaeologists well when they are faced with interpreting the foodways of the 18th and early 19th centuries. The evidence from both the documentary and archaeological record points to the determination of the European-derived populations in North America to belong to the "civilized" world at the table. It is time to include food in the growing list of consumer products available to the 18th-century consumer and to study how the commercial foods fit into the daily food choices made by those consumers.

ACKNOWLEDGMENTS

My heartfelt thanks go to Catherine Sullivan, Bernie Walsh, Elizabeth Jorgensen, and Colleen MacIntyre who helped with the mind-numbing task of extracting useful advertisements from the newspapers. Without their work this article could not have been written. I also want to thank Canadian Parks Service staff, Andree Crepeau and the archaeological staff of the Fortress of Louisbourg National Historic Park for providing photographs and information on the artifacts in their collections, Gerard Gusset for his identification of the stoneware and coarse earthenware containers, Chuck Bradley for his comments on casks and barrels, and Marc LaFrance for his help with Quebec foodways.

REFERENCES

Acadian Recorder
1816   Advertisement. *Acadian Recorder*, 19 October.

ATLANTIC CANADA NEWSPAPER SURVEY
1989-   On-line data base, started in 1984, released 1989, present ongoing. Canadian Heritage Information Network, Communications Canada, Ottawa, Ontario.

BEAUDRY, MARY C.
1988   Words for Things: Linguistic Analysis of Probate Inventories. In *Documentary Archaeology in the New World*, edited by Mary C. Beaudry, pp. 43–50. Cambridge University Press, Cambridge, England.

BELDON, LOUISE CONWAY
1983   *The Festive Tradition: Table Decoration and Desserts in America, 1650–1900*. W. W. Norton, New York.

Boston Gazette & Country Journal (BG&CJ)
1774   Advertisements. *Boston Gazette & Country Journal*, 3 January, 14 March.

BRADLEY, MARTHA
[1770]   *The British Housewife: Or, the Cook, Housekeeper's, and Gardiner's Companion* . . . . S. Crowder and H. Woodgate, London.

CAMPORESI, PIERO
1989   *Bread of Dreams, Food and Fantasy in Early Modern Europe*. Preface by Roy Porter, translated by David Gentilcore. Polity Press, Cambridge, England.

CLARK, CHARLES E., AND CHARLES WETHERELL
1989   The Measure of Maturity: *The Pennsylvania Gazette, 1728–1765. William and Mary Quarterly* 96(2): 279–303.

CRUIKSHANK, E. A.
1929   A Country Merchant in Upper Canada, 1800–1812. *Ontario Historical Society, Papers and Records* 252: 145–190.

Daily Advertiser (DA) [London]
1739   Advertisements. *Daily Advertiser*, 21 November, 14 December, 18 December.
1740   Advertisements. *Daily Advertiser*, 31 January, 21 March, 23 May, 28 May.
1742   Advertisements. *Daily Advertiser*, 24 March, 3 November.
1750   Advertisements. *Daily Advertiser*, 23 January, 10 November, 22 December.
1751   Advertisement. *Daily Advertiser*, 15 February.
1752   Advertisements. *Daily Advertiser*, 30 January, 22 December.
1760   Advertisements. *Daily Advertiser*, 29 July, 6 August.
1762   Advertisements. *Daily Advertiser*, 4 January, 11 September, 17 September.

DRUMMOND, J.C., AND ANNE WILBRAHAM
1959   *The Englishman's Food: A History of Five Centuries of English Diet*. Jonathan Cape, London.

FRANCIS, A. D.
1972   *The Wine Trade*. Adam & Charles Black, London.

Halifax Journal (HJ)
1785   Advertisements. *Halifax Journal*, 28 October.

Halifax Weekly Chronicle (HWC)
1791   Advertisements. *Halifax Weekly Chronicle*, 5 March, 4 June.

HARRIS, JANE E.
1979   Eighteenth-Century French Blue-Green Bottles from the Fortress of Louisbourg, Nova Scotia. *History and Archaeology* 29:83–149. Parks Canada, Ottawa, Ontario.

JAMES, STEPHEN, JR.
1988   A Reassessment of the Chronological and Typological Framework of the Spanish Olive Jar. *Historical Archaeology* 22(1):43–66.

JOHNSON, SAMUEL
1979   *A Dictionary of the English Language*. Reprint of 1755 edition. Times Books, London.

JONES, OLIVE R.
1983   London Mustard Bottles. *Historical Archaeology* 17(1):69–84.
1986   *Cylindrical English Wine and Beer Bottles, 1735–1850*. Studies in Archaeology, Architecture and History. Environment Canada-Parks, Ottawa, Ontario.
1989   Squares, Rounds, Octagons, Flasks and Vials; Dark Green Glass Bottles. Ms. on file, Canadian Parks Service, Ottawa, Ontario.

JONES, OLIVE R., AND E. ANN SMITH
1985   *Glass of the British Military, ca. 1755–1820*. Studies in Archaeology, Architecture and History. Environment Canada-Parks, Ottawa, Ontario.

KINGSTON GAZETTE
1810   Advertisement. *Kingston Gazette*, 25 September.

LONDON DIRECTORIES
1800–   *London Directories*, Group II. Guildhall Library,
1855   London. Microfilm.

MCCRACKEN, GRANT
1988   *Culture and Consumption: New Approaches to the Symbolic Character of Consumer Goods and Activities*. Indiana University Press, Bloomington.

MCKEARIN, HELEN, AND KENNETH M. WILSON
1978   *American Bottles & Flasks and Their Ancestry*. Crown, New York.

MCKENDRICK, NEIL, JOHN BREWER, AND J. H. PLUMB
1982   *The Birth of a Consumer Society: The Commercialization of Eighteenth-Century England*. Indiana University Press, Bloomington.

MONTREAL HERALD (MH)
1814   Advertisement. *Montreal Herald*, 18 June.
1816   Advertisement. *Montreal Herald*, 21 December.
1817   Advertisements. *Montreal Herald*, 4 January, 5 April.
1818   Advertisement. *Montreal Herald*, 29 November.
1820   Advertisements. *Montreal Herald*, 15 January, 22 January, 31 May.

MUI, HOH-CHEUNG, AND LORNA H. MUI
1989   *Shops and Shopkeeping in Eighteenth-Century England*. McGill-Queen's University Press, Montreal.

NEWSPAPER ADVERTISEMENTS IN THE PROVINCE OF QUEBEC
1971–   Newspaper Advertisements in the Province of Que-
1972   bec. Notes on file, National Historic Sites Branch, Canadian Parks Service, Ottawa, Ontario.

NEW-YORK MERCURY (NYM)
1753   Advertisement. *New-York Mercury*, 24 December.
1755   Advertisements. *New-York Mercury*, 6 January, 23 June.
1758   Advertisements. *New-York Mercury*, 27 March, 14 August.
1759   Advertisements. *New-York Mercury*, 9 July.
1760   Advertisement. *New-York Mercury*, 1 September.
1761   Advertisements. *New-York Mercury*, 12 January, 26 January, 30 March, 1 June, 3 August, 14 December.
1762   Advertisements. *New-York Mercury*, 4 October, 6 December.
1766   Advertisements. *New-York Mercury*, 30 June, 29 December.
1767   Advertisements. *New-York Mercury*, 19 January, 7 September, 26 October, 30 November.

NOVA-SCOTIA GAZETTE AND WEEKLY ADVERTISER [Halifax]
1769   Advertisement. *Nova-Scotia Gazette and Weekly Advertiser*, 3 October.

NOVA-SCOTIA GAZETTE AND WEEKLY CHRONICLE (NSG&WC) [Halifax]
1779   Advertisements. *Nova-Scotia Gazette and Weekly Chronicle*, 23 February, 11 May, 14 December.
1780   Advertisements. *Nova-Scotia Gazette and Weekly Chronicle*, 2 May.
1783   Advertisement. *Nova-Scotia Gazette and Weekly Chronicle*, 9 December.
1784   Advertisements. *Nova-Scotia Gazette and Weekly Chronicle*, 4 May, 25 May, 15 June.
1785   Advertisements. *Nova-Scotia Gazette and Weekly Chronicle*, 24 May, 14 June, 5 July.
1786   Advertisements. *Nova-Scotia Gazette and Weekly Chronicle*, 10 January, 23 May, 18 July.
1788   Advertisement. *Nova-Scotia Gazette and Weekly Chronicle*, 25 November.
1789   Advertisements. *Nova-Scotia Gazette and Weekly Chronicle*, 30 June, 22 September.

PALMER, RICHARD
1989   Illustrations from the Wellcome Institute Library: Thomas Corbyn, Quaker Merchant. *Medical History* 33:371–376.

POSTLETHWAYT, MALACHY
1971   *The Universal Dictionary of Trade and Commerce*. Reprint of fourth edition (1774). Augustus M. Kelly, New York.

QUEBEC GAZETTE (QG)
1765   Advertisements. *Quebec Gazette*, 4 July, 15 August.
1767   Advertisement. *Quebec Gazette*, 8 October.
1769   Advertisement. *Quebec Gazette*, 28 September.
1770   Advertisement. *Quebec Gazette*, 20 December.
1777   Advertisements. *Quebec Gazette*, 15 May, 29 May.
1779   Advertisement. *Quebec Gazette*, 20 September.
1780   Advertisement. *Quebec Gazette*, 31 August.
1781   Advertisement. *Quebec Gazette*, 11 October.
1782   Advertisements. *Quebec Gazette*, 11 April, 18 December.
1784   Advertisement. *Quebec Gazette*, 16 September.
1785   Advertisements. *Quebec Gazette*, 19 May, 26 May, 9 June, 13 October.
1811   Advertisement. *Quebec Gazette*, 6 June.

QUEBEC MERCURY (QM)
1811   Advertisement. *Quebec Mercury*, 16 September.
1816   Advertisement. *Quebec Mercury*, 11 June.

REES, ABRAHAM
1819   *The Cyclopaedia; or Universal Dictionary of Arts, Science and Literature*. Longman, Hurst, Rees, Orme & Brown, London.

ROYAL GAZETTE AND THE NOVA-SCOTIA ADVERTISER [Halifax]
1791   Advertisement. *Royal Gazette and the Nova-Scotia Advertiser*, 1 November.

SAVARY DES BRUSLONS, JACQUES
1759   *Dictionnaire universel de commerce . . .* , Vol. 1. Revised edition. Claude Philibert, Copenhagen.

The Historical Archaeology Laboratory Handbook

THE TIMES (TIMES) [London]
1817   Advertisements. *The Times*, 21 January, 28 March, 23 May.
1818   Advertisement. *The Times*, 4 December.

WEEKLY CHRONICLE [Halifax]
1791   Advertisement. *Weekly Chronicle*, 5 March, 4 June.

WHEATON, BARBARA KETCHAM
1983   *Savoring the Past: The French Kitchen and Table from 1300 to 1789.* University of Pennsylvania Press, Philadelphia.

ZUPKO, RONALD EDWARD
1968   *A Dictionary of English Weights and Measures from Anglo-Saxon Times to the Nineteenth Century.* University of Wisconsin Press, Madison.

OLIVE R. JONES
CANADIAN PARKS SERVICE
1600 LIVERPOOL COURT
OTTAWA, ONTARIO K1A 0H4
CANADA

Appendix A: The Newspapers and Their Advertisements

The advertisements were collected partly for other projects, partly for this one. The method of gathering them varied. For some papers every issue was looked at; for others a rigid sampling procedure was used (e.g., every second issue or every second week). Because the Canadian newspapers customarily placed new advertisements on the third page, only this page was scanned, not the whole paper. The first and last pages had repeat advertisements. For some papers only a few issues were used, generally because the original search was part of another project. The technique used depended on the time available, the type of paper, and the amount of packaging detail appearing in the advertisements. Consequently, no statistical analysis could be done on the relationships between package type and product. The comparative frequencies of types of package given in the text are based on a private computer data base of 1,200 records from the *Daily Advertiser* (1739–1742), *New-York Mercury* (1753–1767), *Quebec Gazette* (1764–1785), *Nova-Scotia Gazette and Weekly Chronicle* (1773–1789), *Boston Gazette & Country Journal* (1774), covering the period from late

1739 to 1789. Other newspapers searched in detail were the *Daily Advertiser* (1739–1740, 1742, 1750–1753, 1760, and 1762), *The Times* (1817–1818), and the *Montreal Herald* (1814–1820).

Useful individual advertisements were selected from two independent data bases and then the original advertisement was used. The first data base is a card file of advertisements found in 19th-century Quebec papers assembled in the early 1970s by the History Division of the Canadian Parks Service ("Newspaper Advertisements in the Province of Quebec" 1971–1972), and the second is the Atlantic Canada Newspaper Survey (1989–present), a national on-line computer data base of newspaper advertisements from New Brunswick, Nova Scotia, Prince Edward Island, and Newfoundland.

Differences in terminology and in references to certain types of containers occurred in different newspapers. For example, the *New-York Mercury* had far more empty glass and ceramic containers for sale, sold olive oil in betties rather than flasks, and listed tea in cannisters. Cheese cased in lead came from the Nova Scotia and Quebec papers in the early 1780s. The sample is too small to tell if these differences reflect regional or temporal variations. Package details changed from paper to paper and through time in the same paper. For example, the *Daily Advertiser* in the ca. 1740 and ca. 1750 issues contained a great deal of packaging information, but the 1760 and 1762 papers merely listed products. Advertisements in the *Nova-Scotia Gazette and Weekly Chronicle* in the early 1780s, after the influx of United Empire Loyalists from the United States, were long and informative. By 1788, however, commodity advertisements had almost disappeared, replaced by signs of recession—land sales and sales by the sheriff. The 1817–1820 issues of the *Montreal Herald* generally just listed bulk packages although many of these contained smaller packages.

Newspaper searches of this type are never-ending; every new paper lures the optimist into believing that *this* is the paper which will answer all packaging questions. It never is, of course, but the gradual accumulation of information does help to build a picture of the complexities of commercial packaging in the 18th and early 19th centuries.

NANCY KENMOTSU

Gunflints: A Study

ABSTRACT

A study of gunflints was undertaken to determine if a uniform use wear pattern is present on gunflints which would assist in the identification of small rectangular or sub-rectangular lithic artifacts from historic sites as gunflints. The study also sought better to understand how these patterns were formed. Both modern and archaeological specimens were employed in the study. Background information on the history, technology, and use of gunflints is summarized as a key to understanding the use wear patterns.

Introduction

Gunflints are a relatively common artifact recovered at many historic Indian and early European archaeological sites. However, the identification of these artifacts as gunflints, especially those which were native-made, is not always easy. The present study was designed, first, to determine if uniform use wear patterns exist which can assist in identifying small rectangular and sub-rectangular lithic artifacts as gunflints and, second, to understand how these patterns were formed. To achieve these goals a study of gunflint manufacturing and reduction sequences, oral and archival documentation on the history, technology, and use of gunflints, and an examination of used gunflints from modern and archaeological contexts was conducted.

Thirty-eight gunflints from archaeological and modern contexts were utilized in the study. Gunflints from archaeological contexts include five of the 11 gunflints recovered from the Pearson site (41RA5) at Lake Tawakoni Reservoir in Texas and 17 of the 114 recovered from the Gilbert site (41RA13) at nearby Lake Fork Reservoir (Figure 1). The 16 modern gunflints for the study consist of three obtained from black-powder contestants at an annual summer rendezvous in the Cascade Mountains of Washington State in July 1987; six from Leland Bement, an archaeologist and black-powder enthusiast employed by the Texas Archae-

ological Research Laboratory of the University of Texas at Austin; and seven used and unused gunflints purchased from McBride's Guns, a local store in Austin, in June of 1987.

Use wear experimentation studies in the past 20 years have shown that a number of variables affect resulting wear patterns on lithic tools. Given the constraints imposed by the function and size requirements of flintlock guns and the ability of the user to reposition the gunflint in the cock to allow for defects in the shape of the gunflint, a number of these variables (hardness of the material worked, edge angle, edge thickness, etc.) were not considered in this study. Two variables—method of manufacture and duration of tool use—were, however, considered. Methods of tool manufacture may result in microscars that can be mistaken for use wear (Tringham et al. 1974:90), whereas duration of tool use will affect the quantity of use wear evidence (Keeley 1980; Odell and Odell-Vereecken 1980:90).

In order to address the question of tool manufacture, a review of reports describing the history of gunflints and the reduction sequences used in their manufacture was conducted. General information on reduction sequences was also derived from a number of archaeological reports together with considerable advice from lithic specialists. Information gleaned from the literature was also used to determine the length of the time the gunflint was used. In addition, informant data from black powder enthusiasts were gathered.

Once these data were acquired, use wear analysis proceeded with a microscopic inspection of used flints from both modern and archaeological contexts. The results were recorded on a Lithic Analysis Data Sheet (Figure 2) modeled after Ahler (1979:318), and compared to data acquired during literature and oral informant studies of gunflints. It shall be argued that there is a wear pattern that can be associated with gunflints.

The Gunflint Industry: Its History, Development, and Study

This section briefly reviews the history and development of the gunflint industry from 1600 to

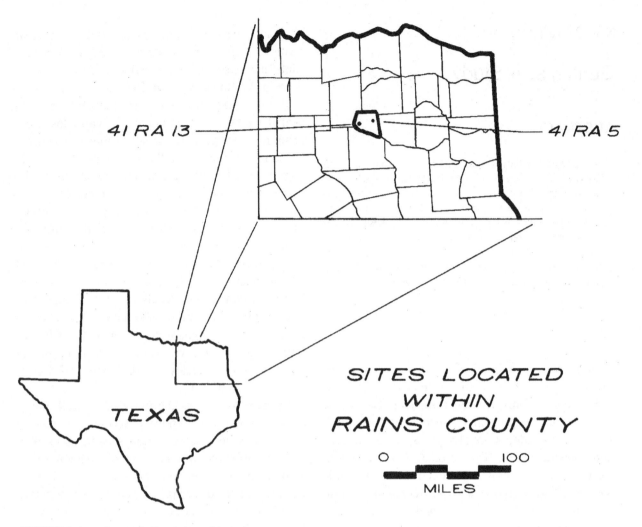

FIGURE 1. Locations of sites referred to in text.

1880, the approximate date when flintlock guns were largely replaced by repeating rifles. The section also provides an overview of the raw material for the gunflints used in Texas and a summary of gunflint manufacturing techniques. Descriptive in nature and taken from a number of other sources, this section is included as necessary background to understanding what manufacturing microscars might be present, how gunflints would have been used, and what wear patterns might be expected.

Gunflints were first employed as the sparking instrument in snaphance guns that were invented around A.D. 1600 (Lenk 1965:29). Much experimentation in gun manufacture and powder ignition

systems followed, and by A.D. 1650 true flintlocks were being manufactured (Chapel 1962:40–45; Rosebush 1962:5–7). This flintlock design was only slightly modified over the next 230 years. Essential to these weapons was the gunflint itself, a small sub-rectangular, wedge-shaped artifact manufactured from flint or chert (Figures 3, 4), a cryptocrystalline silicious rock (Crabtree 1972: 51).

European and North American quarries have been identified as source material for gunflints used in North America and Texas (Hamilton and Emery 1988:210, 235). In France the quarries were generally confined to the Seine and Marne

LITHIC ANALYSIS DATA SHEET: GUNFLINT STUDY

SITE NUMBER _____   ARTIFACT NO. _____   LOT NO._____

DATE _____   ANALYZED BY _____

MAX. LENGTH _____   MAX WIDTH _____   MAX. THICKNESS _____

RAW MATERIAL TYPE _____   SOURCE MATERIAL _____

WEAR NOTED	AREA	COMMENTS
X-Section		
Rounded		
Faceted		
Stepped		
Concave		
Wear Type		
Grinding		
Blunting		
Smooting		
Polishing		
Step Flake		
Crushing		
Flat Flake		
Striation		
Pitting		
Heating		
RESIDUE		
Outline		
Irregular		
Normalized		

Number of working edges:

1   2   3   4   5   6   7   8

FIGURE 2. Lithic Analysis Data Sheet, modeled after Ahler (1979:318).

River valleys in calcareous formations of superimposed horizontal beds of chert nodules of varying quality (Dolomieu [1797] 1960:58). In England the flint is found in the Dover chalk deposits in several thick horizontal strata at depths varying between 3–30 ft. below the surface (Skertchly

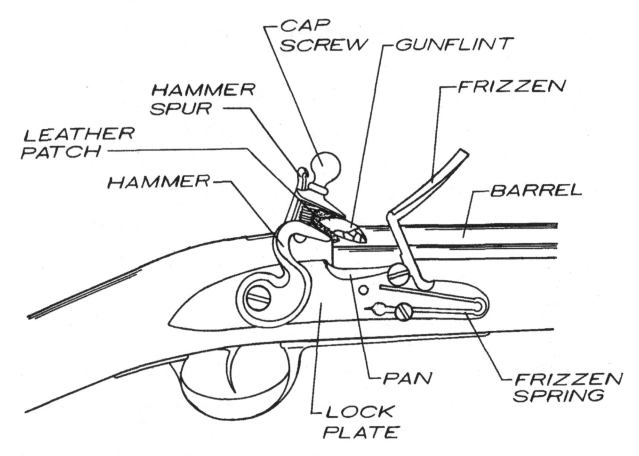

FIGURE 3. Sketch of firing mechanism of flintlock musket.

[1879] 1984:21–22). In the United States historic Indian groups extracted chert from quarries that they also had used as source material for other lithic tools (Hamilton 1960:73).

Gunflints from English, French, and American quarries have two primary distinguishing characteristics: physical qualities of the source material, and the manufacturing technique. Probably the best described source material is from an area centered around Brandon, in Suffolk County, northeast of London. Brandon flint grades from one that is a very dark, nearly black, translucent fine-grained flint to a gray, opaque flint with inclusions. Descriptions of this flint and its variations can be found in Hamilton and Fry (1975) and Skertchly (1984). The sample of Brandon flints purchased from McBride's Guns in Austin reflects this variation (Figure 5).

Until recently it was believed that this dark Brandon flint was quarried from Neolithic to modern times (Woodward 1960:29; Skertchly [1879] 1984:79). Recent research, however, indicates the quarries were not extensively mined for gunflints until the Napoleonic Wars of the 1790s (de Lotbiniere 1984:vii–viii). Presence of black English flints on an archaeological site would indicate a date of later than A.D. 1790. The Pearson sample contains a black musket flint from the Brandon quarries, indicating a terminal date after A.D. 1790. Prior to 1790 the English imported gunflints from France. Others were locally produced from quarries of Southern England. One distinctive brown, banded gunflint from the Pearson site (Figure 8a), identified by Duffield and Jelks (1961: 56) as an English flint, may represent one of these earlier non-Brandon gunflints. It is unique in the

Figure 4. Modern, hand-made flintlock rifle with details of cock plate and gunflint visible; flint is just striking frizzen; note leather pad holding gunflint in jaws of cock.

sample, and similar source material was not found; Jay Blaine (1987, pers. comm.), an historic gun authority from Texas, believes it represents a gunflint manufactured by the British.

French gunflints (Figure 6) are distinguished by a honey-yellow or blond flint which often contains white inclusions and occasionally a whitish chalk cortex. The honey-colored French flints are translucent and fine-grained cherts (Dolomieu [1797] 1960:53). This chert has often been called chalcedony to distinguish it from the fine-grained English flint (Hamilton 1960:73).

French blond gunflints date to at least A.D. 1675 (Hamilton 1960:74). These were the most commonly used gunflints in England, France, and the American colonies prior to A.D. 1800. Witthoft (1966:22) notes, "over 95% of the gunflints found in camps occupied during the American Revolution, including even British camps, are of French origin." Once the Brandon quarries were opened about 1790, however, English gunflints

began to dominate archaeological collections in the United States (Hamilton and Fry 1975:109).

Native American gunflints are less easily distinguished by source materials. These gunflints were knapped from locally available or non-local source material, resulting in substantial source variation. In the present study, it is assumed that all archaeological specimens that could not be typed as French or British were of Native American source material and locally manufactured. This assumption is at odds with some conclusions made by Hamilton and Emery (1988:242–243). Hamilton and Emery state that three Gilbert specimens (120F3, 134F4, and 181F5), which were also used in the present study, are French flakes reworked by the Indians. This may be correct. However, there are a number of other artifacts from Gilbert (not made available to Hamilton and Emery) which were manufactured from the same source materials, suggesting these three were manufactured with local material. Too, the three were concluded by

FIGURE 5. English Brandon gunflints used in this study: a, specimen 41-1, Pearson site; b, specimen 1, Other Modern Gunflints; c, specimen 6, Other Modern Gunflints; d, specimen 10, Other Modern Gunflints; e, specimen 5, Other Modern Gunflints; f, specimen 4, Other Modern Gunflints; g, specimen 9, Other Modern Gunflints; h, specimen 8, Other Modern Gunflints; i, specimen 7, Other Modern Gunflints.

Larry Banks (1988, pers. comm.) to be manufactured from Ouachita Mountains chert. In the absence of petrographic analysis, a North American source designation was given to these specimens for the present study.

Native American manufacture of gunflints began with the introduction of guns into a given region and generally continued until an accepted and reliable source of European gunflints was available. Prior to A.D. 1700 most gunflints on Native American sites were aboriginally knapped and are characterized as being more square than European gunflints, with "all four edges carefully worked to an edge by secondary chipping" (Witthoft 1966: 22). After A.D. 1700 Native American manufac-

ture of gunflints continued in individual tribes until there was an accepted source of European flints. This variable time frame is based upon the archaeological record. For example, the Osage in Missouri continued to manufacture gunflints until about A.D. 1730 (Hamilton 1960:77; Hamilton and Emery 1988:233). In the Upper Missouri River Basin, European flints began to increase around A.D. 1750 (Hamilton 1960:77; Witthoft 1966:22), and at the Tunica Treasure site in Louisiana, dated before A.D. 1740, only one of 44 flints is of native manufacture (Hamilton 1979: 210). Once available and accepted, then, a rapid transition to European gunflints seems to have occurred.

FIGURE 6. French gunflints used in this study: a, specimen 134, Feature 4; b, specimen 27–14, Feature 3; c, specimen 152, Feature 6 (all from the Gilbert site).

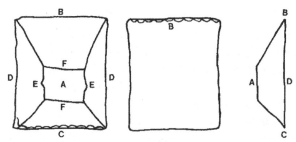

FIGURE 7. Snap-blade gunflint terminology: a, back; b, working edge; c, heel; d, sides; e, aris lip (not always present); f, blade scars.

The other distinguishing characteristic of gunflints is their method of production or reduction. Reduction sequences are used both to date gunflints from a given archaeological context (Hamilton 1964) and to confirm their manufacturing origin and source of trade (Hamilton 1964, 1979). In the present report, reduction sequences were studied to reduce potential errors in the use wear interpretations.

At this juncture it is necessary to briefly discuss standard gunflint terminology. This terminology dates to the 18th century and continues to be used both by contemporary weaponry experts and by authors of archaeological reports describing gunflints. The terminology can be confusing as it sometimes ignores, and at other times contradicts, terms of modern lithic technology. Perhaps most confusing are the terms for two types of European gunflints: gunspalls and gunflints. Gunspalls are wedge-shaped, non-lenticular gunflints (Hamilton 1960:73–79) ancestral to the prismatic gunflint in France and England. The term gunflint is employed to refer to the prismatic gunflints manufactured in Europe through a blade technology. It is also employed to refer to the entire artifact class regardless of when, where, how, or by whom manufactured. In addition to these general terms, there exists a fairly complete nomenclature for the various parts of the body of gunflints and gunspalls. Figure 7 illustrates these terms (face, back, ridge, etc.). In this report the terms of Figure 7 are used

where possible. Use of these terms, when applied to European gunspalls and aboriginally knapped gunflints can be problematical. Therefore, while Skertchly's terms are used, modern lithic terminology has been used or parenthetically added where appropriate.

Gunspalls are produced by removing individual flakes (spalls) from flint nodules or prepared cores through direct percussion (Hamilton 1979:210). They typically have positive bulbs of percussion on the ventral surface, opposed by a relatively flat dorsal surface. The working edge of a gunspall is the roughly straight margin formed on its distal edge. This straight edge is sometimes formed naturally during the reduction process, and sometimes formed by removal of small thinning flakes. The edge of the gunspall opposite the striking edge is called the heel, and it was left unmodified in English gunspalls. In French spalls the heel was "nibbled" or reduced through pressure flaking into a semi-circular form described as "D-form" (Hamilton 1979:211; de Lotbiniere 1984:vi). Sides of English and French gunspalls also tend to have been retouched to form relatively straight, albeit thick, sides.

In the present sample only the British banded flint from Pearson is confidently classified as a European gunspall. One French gunflint from the Gilbert site (Figure 6b) may be a gunspall but has little remaining evidence of the original reduction technique due to subsequent attempts to reduce its thickness through percussion and pressure flaking along its margins.

Gunspall manufacture is believed to have produced greater quantities of waste material than did gunflint manufacture, eventually leading to the demise of the gunspall. In 1836 an English informant described his recollections of the spall production as a "waste of material, and only a small number could be made in a short time" (de Lotbiniere 1984:vii). Often one core would produce only one or two gunspalls. In contrast, with blade technology, large cores are typically used to produce long, slender flakes. Each flake in turn produced a number of flints. Historic documents indicate substantial production increases with gunflint manufacture (Hamilton 1960:74; Woodward 1960:32; Blackmore 1961:138; Skertchly [1879] 1984:33).

The exact date of the introduction of blade technology is unclear. Information gathered from archaeological sites in Canada indicates it had been developed in France by A.D. 1663 (Blanchette 1975) but was probably not perfected until about A.D. 1750. Four blade gunflints were recovered along with 35 "spall or 'wedge-shaped'" gunflints at Chicoutimi, a Canadian site destroyed in 1663 (Blanchette 1975:49). The 44 gunflints from Louisiana's Tunica Treasure site, believed to be occupied from about A.D. 1730 to 1760 (Brain 1979:1), consist of one native made gunflint, 11 French gunflints, and 32 French gunspalls (Hamilton 1979:210). Gunflints from the French Louisbourg Fortress in Canada contained a cache of 541 gunflints, only 20 of which were gunspalls (Hamilton and Fry 1975). While the fortress was occupied from 1713 to 1768, several documents from Louisbourg and France indicate the cache probably relates to a time around A.D. 1740. The documents contain several letters from fortress commanders noting the poor quality of gunflints shipped to them "for the last several years" (Hamilton and Fry 1975:111–113). The presence of both gunflints and gunspalls in the collections from these sites indicates use of both technologies during that period. Further, it would appear that in France blade technology began before A.D. 1663 but was not perfected until some time after A.D. 1740.

Gunflint production consists of removal of a series of fairly long, thick blades from a prepared core using direct percussion. The earliest description of gunflint production were written in France in 1797 (Dolomieu [1797] 1960; Gillet-Laumont [1797] 1960), and a comprehensive English study was made in 1879 by Skertchly ([1879] 1984). The following description of gunflint manufacture has been drawn from these sources. In France, the flint tended to be contained in large nodules of up to 20 pounds (Gillet-Laumont [1797] 1960:62–65). English flint, however, is contained in thick, horizontal beds (see Skertchly [1879] 1984 for illustrations).

Gunflint makers used metal tools with wooden handles for the reduction process. Workers rejected "those which do not have a good color, or which have white inclusions or which contain chalk at the center" (Dolomieu [1797] 1960:65). Critical in the reduction process was removal of a series of long, narrow blades, with the quartering hammer. French and English authors concur that operation requires the "greatest craftsmanship and surest hand" (Dolomieu [1797] 1960:59; Skertchly [1879] 1984:28). The ventral surface of these flakes is slightly convex, tapering to a pointed or rounded distal end (Dolomieu [1797] 1960:60; Skertchly [1879] 1984:29), with one or two dorsal ridges called "single" or "double"-backed. Dorsal ridges were essential to the final forms of the gunflint; flakes without ridges were discarded (Dolomieu [1797] 1960:60) or used for other purposes (Skertchly [1879] 1984:29). For efficiency all flakes were removed until the core was exhausted.

The final process, knapping, was accomplished with the blade resting upon a stake or cutter with the ventral surface up. Several cuts at regular intervals were made along the ventral surface of the blade, producing from one to four gunflints from each blade. The edge and heel were formed by the sides of the long blade. The primary difference between French and British reduction is that French sides and heel were often trimmed by removing small pressure flakes.

In the present sample two French gunflints from the Gilbert site and the English Brandon gunflint from the Pearson site appear to have been manufactured using the blade technology. The black Brandon flint appears to have been the proximal segment of the blade based on the presence of the bulb of percussion resulting from a blow with a hard hammer and the single, irregular dorsal ridge (Figure 8e). A snap fracture from final artifact preparation, as described above, is present on one side. Some light nibbling along one edge appears to represent reverse trimming, produced by rasping the artifact with a hard surface (such as a file) during final gunflint manufacture, and evidenced by the presence of irregular and very small flake scars removed from both surfaces. Based on the side snap fracture, erailluer flake, and dorsal ridge, it is concluded that this is a gunflint rather than a gunspall.

The two French specimens from the Gilbert site are problematical and generally of poor quality (Figure 9o, p). Each appears to have double ridges along its back (dorsal surface), but the ridges are quite close together. In one specimen the ridges have been partially obscured by pressure flaking along the heel. The other specimen has a highly irregular face (ventral surface) produced by removal of several pressure flakes from the sides. However, the two are classified here as gunflints based on the presence of elongated front bevels, lack of bulbs of percussion, and their possible dorsal ridges. The presence of French blade gunflints at Gilbert, together with the absence of any Brandon gunflints among the 114 recovered from the site, suggests a date prior to 1790. In addition both the poor quality of these two gunflints and the presence of a possible French gunspall at the site indicate that a date prior to 1750 may be reasonable.

Native American gunflint production was most similar to that of gunspalls. That is, reduction was initiated by direct percussion to a core, producing a flake subsequently modified to a sub-rectangular form. In the present sample these modifications seem to fall into two groupings. In one group flake modification takes the form of pressure flaking along one or more margins; the remaining ventral and dorsal surfaces are left intact. This type of modification appears in the present sample on five specimens, two from Pearson (Figure 8a,c), and three from Gilbert (Figure 9b, c, d). These specimens were produced from prepared cores struck to

a   b   c

d   e

FIGURE 8. Gunflints used in this study from Pearson site: a, specimen ?-11; b, specimen 87-5; c, specimen 66-1; d, specimen ?-11; e, specimen 47-1.

remove fairly small flakes. Bulbs of percussion are usually evident, and each is plano-convex in form with a roughly wedge shape. One Pearson specimen also has a series of percussion flakes removed from its back (dorsal surface). The specimens also evidence pressure flaking along one or more sides, sometimes bifacially. Both Pearson specimens appear to have been manufactured from different varieties of flint from the Ouachita Mountains, one possibly from Johns Valley Shale (Larry Banks 1988, pers. comm.).

Similar to the Pearson specimens in method of reduction, the Gilbert specimens are lumped with European gunspalls by Blaine and Harris (1967: 81–82), primarily on the basis of their form. In the present study these three are assumed to be native-made from North American source material. One of the three is of the same raw material as several scrapers in the Gilbert collection. Another specimen has bifacial pressure flaking of high quality along two margins, something more typical of Native American than European workmanship. Finally, Larry Banks (1988, pers. comm.) has viewed the specimens and believes they were probably manufactured from several varieties of chert from the Ouachita Mountains.

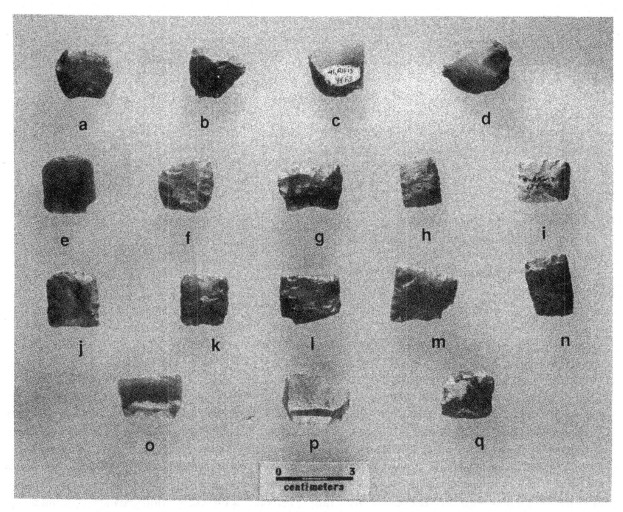

FIGURE 9. Gunflints used in this study from Gilbert site: a, specimen 120, Feature 3; b, specimen 110, Feature 3; c, specimen 94, Feature 3; d, specimen 94, Feature 3; e, specimen 208, Feature 7; f, specimen 9, Feature 15; g, specimen 98, Feature 3; h, specimen 181, Feature 5; i, specimen 134, Feature 4; j, specimen 117, Feature 3; k, specimen 281, Feature 3; l, specimen 29, Feature 3; m, specimen 281, Feature 3; n, specimen 197, Feature 3; o, specimen 27-14, Feature 3; p, specimen 152, Feature 6; q, specimen 134, Feature 4.

The other type of Native American gunflint flake modification is overall bifacial reduction, often followed by careful bifacial retouch along all four sides. Thirteen gunflints in the present sample fall into this grouping. Most initial flake attributes (bulb of percussion, fissures, etc.) have been removed through the reduction process. Typically all four margins are bifacially pressure flaked, and the gunflints are biconvex in cross section with subrectangular outlines. Two contain cortex along one or more surfaces: one has cortex covering its dorsal surface, and one has a small central area containing cortical material. Nine of the specimens appear to be of Ouachita Mountain flints (Larry Banks 1988, pers. comm.).

In summary, the gunflint industry began in the 17th century in response to a need for a more uniform flint for flintlock guns. French gunflints dominated the market in France, England, and North America until the Napoleonic wars of the 1790s. After 1790, English Brandon flint mines began to dominate. Native American gunflints were common on historic Indian sites until an available and accepted source of gunflints was found and tend to reflect the bifacial reduction technology commonly associated with arrowpoint production.

The Sample, the Goals, the Methods

Gunflints from an archaeological context are from the Pearson site (41RA5) at Tawakoni Reservoir and the Gilbert site (41RA13) at Lake Fork Reservoir. Recorded in 1957, the Pearson site consists of about 25 acres in the floodplain of the Sabine River (Johnson 1957:2). In March 1960, the Texas Archaeological Salvage Project conducted machine-aided site excavation, sketch mapping, and an unsystematic surface collection (Duffield 1960; Duffield and Jelks 1961:11–12). The authors conclude Pearson was a late 18th-century Tawakoni village (Duffield and Jelks 1961:68). This conclusion was largely based on a comparison of the Pearson site's native and European artifacts with those from other historic Indian sites in north central Texas.

Eleven gunflints were recovered from the site and analyzed by Dr. Carlyle S. Smith and Mr. C. Malcolm Watkins. The report describes all as rectangular to square in outline, with five of European manufacture and eight "evidently manufactured by the Indians" (Duffield and Jelks 1961:56). Duffield and Jelks note that most of the gunflints show "breakage on one edge" and many evidence secondary retouch on one or more edges. Most gun parts from the site were English, dating from about 1780 to 1835, although some gun fittings could date slightly earlier (Smith, quoted in Duffield and Jelks 1961:77). For the present study, five of the 11 gunflints were selected by the author in a subjective manner. The 11 were placed on a table and five appearing distinct from each other in color and/or physical shape, including two classified by Duffield and Jelks as British, were selected.

The remaining gunflints from an archaeological context were taken from the Gilbert site (41RA13) located on a tributary of the Sabine River (Davis et al. 1967:1). The Gilbert site was first recorded in 1957 and investigated in 1962 by members of the Texas Archaeological Society (TAS). Based on its

similarity to other historic Indian sites, the authors conclude that the site was occupied by Yscani, Tawakoni, or Kichai Indians from about A.D. 1750 to 1775. As at the Pearson site, ethnic affiliation and age of the site was largely reliant upon an artifactual assemblage similar to other sites in north central Texas (Duffield and Jelks 1961:69–75) and upon identification of European artifacts which could be reliably dated.

Among the artifacts, 114 gunflints were recovered at 41RA13. Studied by Jay C. Blaine and R.K. Harris, the gunflints were subdivided into 32 spall, 13 conventional, and 69 native-made gunflints. It is the authors' opinion that Gilbert gunspalls tend to exhibit prepared platforms in the heel area and were produced from prepared cores rather than cobbles (Blaine and Harris 1967:82–83). Blade gunflints were all determined to be French due to the source material, a honey-yellow flint, and rounded heels. The 69 native-made gunflints "were produced from flakes by secondary flaking. Specimens of good workmanship are generally square to rectangular thin and biconvex in cross section; all four sides are usually worked to a fine edge" (Blaine and Harris 1967:84). At least two of the native gunflints were produced from Kay County, Oklahoma, flint and most of the others are from Ouachita Mountain cherts (Larry Banks 1988, pers. comm.).

As with Pearson, the sample of 17 Gilbert site gunflints was chosen subjectively. All gunflints in the collection at the Texas Archeological Research Laboratory were laid out, and an attempt was made to choose a range of specimens representing a variety of source materials and possibly different reduction strategies. Three of the 17 are of French origin. The remainder are considered to have been native made, based on raw material and type of reduction.

Gunflint specimens from non-archaeological contexts also were studied. Seven flints from Brandon, England, were purchased (at $1.00 each) from McBride's Guns in Austin. These seven range in size and purity of the Brandon flint and in quality of the finished product. Three used gunflints were obtained in July 1987 from an informant at the Pine Creek Rendezvous in the Cascade

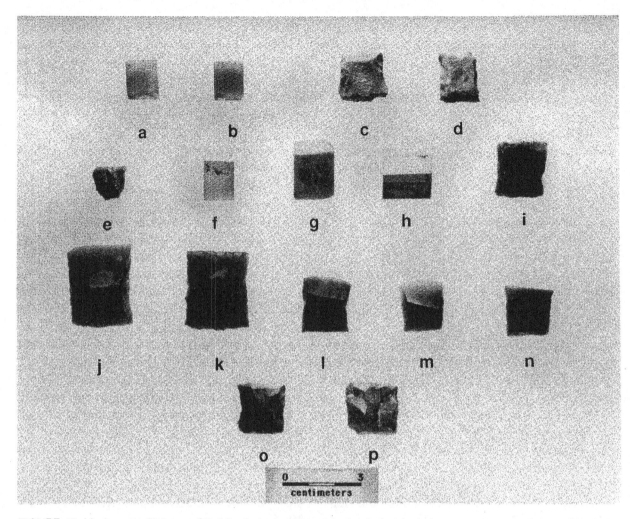

FIGURE 10. Modern gunflints used in this study. Lee Bement specimens include: a, specimen 1; b, specimen 4; c, specimen 2; d, specimen 3; e, specimen 6; f, specimen 5. Pine Creek specimens include: g, specimen 2; h, specimen 3; i, specimen 1. Gunflints purchased from McBride's Guns include: j, specimen 6; k, specimen 10; l, specimen 4; m, specimen 7; n, specimen 8; o, specimen 5; p, specimen 9.

Mountains of Washington State, a shooting competition of black-powder enthusiasts. Six used flints were obtained from Lee Bement, an archaeologist and black-powder enthusiast who provided much valuable information and advice for this study (Figure 10).

It had been hoped that an equal number of used, modern specimens could be obtained. This was not possible for two reasons. First, relatively few black powder enthusiasts use gunflints, most preferring the simpler percussion/cap system. Second, those who use flints are able to maintain a much

longer gunflint life expectancy than was maintained for flints used 300 years ago. Informants in the Pine Creek Rendezvous stated one flint would typically last for an entire meet, about 200 rounds. Lee Bement (1987, pers. comm.) confirmed that flints could last for a substantial number of shots. Historically, however, 20 rounds were considered average. The U.S. Army in 1846 issued one flint per 20 rounds (Chapel 1962:71). One plausible explanation of this difference was suggested, that gunflints with potential flaws can continue to be used without prejudice at a competition; potential flaws in the wilderness or war could mean the difference between life and death (Robert Mallouf 1987, pers. comm.).

As stated in the introduction, the goal of this study was to determine if typical wear patterns on gunflints can be identified and to better understand how those wear patterns are formed. The methods employed to reach the goals are detailed below.

Lithic Reduction Sequences

First, a study of lithic reduction strategies employed in gunflint manufacture was undertaken to ensure that remnants of the manufacturing process were not misidentified as use wear (Cotterell and Kamminga 1987:675–676). Historic accounts of the manufacturing process were sought. These accounts detail how the process changed through time, e.g., from core/flake technique to a blade technology. Second, general sources on lithic technology were reviewed, especially Crabtree (1972), Girard (1982), Patterson (1978), and Cotterell and Kamminga (1987). Other sources pertinent to the study are Bruseth and Perttulla's 1981 report of subsequent investigations at Lake Fork Reservoir and discussions with lithic specialists. Third, characteristics of the reduction strategy for each gunflint were studied and recorded (Appendix A). The table format of Appendix A presents a brief description of each gunflint. The data recorded were then summarized and compared with data from gunflint literature, informant accounts, and Crabtree (1972) and Girard (1982). Much of the reduction data was presented in the preceding section.

Use Wear Analysis

To understand better how gunflint wear patterns are formed, and to attempt to define a "typical" gunflint wear pattern, background research on gunflints and use wear studies was conducted, including a review of pertinent literature. Subsequently wear patterns for each specimen were recorded using a 10–70 power microscope; some patterns were further verified with other lithic analysts.

Informant data offered several variables that needed to be considered during the use wear study. First an informant at the Pine Creek Rendezvous stressed that a relatively uniform and even gunflint working edge presented to the frizzen will ensure its smooth run down the frizzen and will maximize the quantity of sparks reaching the pan. Similarly, Bement (1987, pers. comm.) stressed the need for an equal distribution of force to ensure the greatest quantity of sparks and even wear of the gunflint. To equalize the force, the gunflint should have a relatively flat lower surface, permitting its snug fit in the cock. This does not mean the working edge should be perfectly smooth, as the light serrations created during the knapping process are believed to increase the number of sparks. However, edges with deep (1–2 mm) serrations or irregularly spaced gaps in the working edge can, according to informants, hasten wear of both the gunflint and the frizzen. Likewise the narrower the contact point with the steel frizzen, the more concentrated the force as the gunflint moves down the frizzen. Small irregular projections on the working edge would concentrate that force unevenly and tend to spall off.

The main spring of the flintlock may also be important in this action. Instrumental in producing the firing of a flintlock, these springs can have a tripartite life span (Bement 1987, pers. comm.). New, they can sometimes be tight, driving the cock too forcefully into the frizzen, shattering or causing undue wear on the gunflint. As the spring is used it may gradually loosen and develop an efficient action that ensures predictable movement and spark. Over time the metal of the spring can lose tensile strength and again become unpredictable, subjecting the gunflint to undue wear. Informant data, then, suggest the optimum striking action occurs when the striking edge of the gunflint has only slight irregularity, as would be produced by pressure flake retouch. It also appears that a number of factors influence this optimum.

Another aspect of the sparking action which affects gunflint wear patterns is the overall size and shape of the gunflint itself. Modern gunflint No. 3 (Appendix A) from the Pine Creek Rendezvous informant was considered by him to be exhausted, i.e., no longer effective in producing sparks. He noted the bevel was rather steep and short, and could not be resharpened. Thus, bevel angle and distance from the working edge to the bevel impose some outside limits on gunflints. Bement uses gunflints in a flintlock pistol and noted the length of the gunflint determined whether he used it with its bevel down or up. Too, he noted absolute thickness will be determined by the height allowance within the cock. All of these factors will affect the lifespan of the gunflint and hence the quantity of wear imposed on it. On the other hand some caution should be interjected. Flintlock guns, even when produced in factories, were hand-made. Consequently, individual guns from the same factory vary somewhat. Exact parameters for optimum gunflint size would be difficult to establish and are usually expressed as ranges (Stone 1974: 253, Table 46).

The type and manufacture of the gun is another factor affecting wear patterns. Bement noted there is a shortened strike in pistols simply because of their smaller overall size. Therefore, the first action is one of impacting the frizzen rather than rasping down it. The impact tends to remove flakes from both the top and bottom more quickly than on larger guns. This action may result in more blunting than in large guns. Too, Spanish Miquelets produce a unique wear pattern because of their harsh spring action (Blaine 1987, pers. comm.; Hamilton and Emery 1988: 202). Since the archaeological specimens in this study were likely used in French or British weapons rather than Spanish Miquelets, the potentially heavier wear was not anticipated for this sample.

Pertinent archaeological literature on lithic use wear analysis was also reviewed during this phase of the study. While not exhaustive, most attention was given to articles concerned with tools used in scraping activities (Tringham et al. 1974; Ahler 1979; Odell and Odell-Vereecken 1980; Odell 1981; Girard 1982). From these sources, the background on gunflints and informant data, five expectations of gunflint wear patterns were developed. These are listed below with their rationale.

Expectation No. 1: *The working edge will consistently exhibit crushing and/or heavy step flaking.* Small hinge-terminated, irregular step flaking along an edge has consistently been documented on lithics experimentally used in scraping motions (Ahler 1979:313; Odell and Odell-Vereecken 1980: 99). The material contacted by the flint in the case of gunflints is steel, a material sufficiently hard to be especially resistant to the flint and likely to cause a high incidence of hinge and step fractures (Odell 1981:200). Further, the contact with the steel frizzen is confined to the edge, suggesting scars would be concentrated there, as shown by Tringham et al. (1974:189). Finally, as ignition action is repeated, step flaking should increase until the edge has a crushed appearance. It was thus anticipated that step flaking and crushing would be present.

Expectation No. 2: *The working edge will exhibit a relatively uniform pattern of wear across the margin.* Frison's experiment (1979:264) in bison butchering suggested that any repeated activity with lithic tools would tend to result in a relatively uniform wear pattern across the working margin. Odell and Odell-Vereecken (1981:99) note that transverse scraping use wear tends to occur over a wide area of the tool edge, although projections are worn down first. An informant at the Pine Creek Rendezvous remarked that flints are exhausted when working edges become irregular. His ideal was to achieve a uniform strike down the frizzen surface for two reasons: a uniform edge will provide the largest quantity of sparks, and it will also prevent early deterioration of the frizzen. It was expected, then, that whatever wear pattern was found to be typical, it would be present uniformly across the used edges since the action is repetitive and the artifacts restricted to a single purpose.

Expectation No. 3: *Step flaking will be confined to the upper surface of the working edge; striations, smoothing, or polish will be present on the inferior surface of the working edge of the gunflint.* "Step flaking occurs on tool edge and flake ridge elements. Step flake scars are almost always wider than they are long and terminate in a transverse fracture" (Ahler 1979:309). These types of flake scars have been demonstrated to occur in scraping activities where the scars are concentrated on the upper surface of the tool (Tringham et al.

1974:189; Odell and Odell-Vereecken 1980:99; Odell 1981:200). Girard (1982:268) noted that nearly all use wear on unifaces and unifacially edge-modified spalls at the Deshazo site (41NA27) was unifacial. Based on his replication studies, he concluded that the single margin, edge modified spalls with unifacial wear had been used in scraping motions (Girard 1982:239). Tringham et al. (1974:188) note that these step scars are unifacially formed because "only one surface of the flake [receives] pressure from the worked material." This pressure produces microflakes in a manner similar to intentional retouch (Odell 1980: 198). Given the type of scraping motion involved in the rasping of the gunflint down the frizzen, it was anticipated that step flaking would be unifacial and confined to upper surfaces of working edges. It should be noted that the terms "upper" and "lower" surfaces of a gunflint cannot be equated to the terms "face" or "back" (Figure 7). Gunflints are used today with the bevel up or down, and are frequently turned over. Historic accounts also document variation in gunflint position, especially with regard to whether the bevel is up or down.

At the same time, it was believed that the rasping could result in other types of wear, specifically striations, smoothing, or polish on the inferior surfaces of the working edge. A previous study of the Mayhew site (41NA21) gunflints revealed striations on one surface of two of the five specimens (Kenmotsu 1987). Tringham et al. (1979:189) note that on hard materials "scars do occasionally occur on the surface of the flake nearest the worked material," especially short striations at the immediate edge and oriented perpendicular to the worked edge. Girard (1982:239) notes striations and smoothing present on some inferior surfaces of edge-modified spalls concluded to have been used in a transverse scraping motion. With the rasping of the gunflint down the hard steel frizzen, it was expected that striations and/or smoothing on the inferior surface of the working edge might be present. Since polish is a more intense form of smoothing (Ahler 1979:308), its presence should reflect longer use of the gunflint.

Expectation No. 4: *Blunting will be present on*

the working edge. The first action on Bement's pistol was one of the flint impacting the frizzen. This would cause blunting of the projections of the working edge. Other informants stated that gunflints improperly mounted strike the frizzen too forcefully and shatter. Normal contact with the frizzen, then, should result in blunting defined as "the presence of unpatterned fracturing or pulverization of the worn tool surface" typically found only on flake ridges and edge elements (Ahler 1979:308). Blunting is believed caused by "contact with work material hard enough to produce fracturing of the stone tool, but not necessarily of greater hardness than the stone tool" (Ahler 1979:308). Girard (1982:267) recorded a fairly high proportion of blunting on his Functional Group 5 tools "with steep unifacial marginal retouch and/or use-wear" and inferred they had been used in scraping activities. He noted that blunting often occurred on tools used on hard material (Girard 1982:229). It was therefore anticipated that blunting would be present on the working edges of gunflints.

Expectation No. 5: *Rejuvenation of the gunflint will be evidenced by multiple working edges and edge retouch.* At the Pine Creek Rendezvous two types of gunflint rejuvenation were noted. One informant from Oregon, who used gunflints cut by lapidary saws, stated that he had turned his flint upside down and revolved it 180° that morning in order to use the other available edge. In the other instance, a wooden billet was used lightly to tap the edge of the flat surface of a Brandon flint, removing small thinning flakes on the beveled edge. This was performed with the flint still in the jaws of the cock. Bement's specimens were acknowledged to have multiple working edges; his hand-made specimens tended to have wear along all four edges. Bement's methods of rejuvenation were: (1) revolve the gunflint in the cock, taking advantage of other edges; (2) lightly tap along the edge of the bottom of thinner gunflints with a small chunk of sandstone; and (3) retouch, via percussion, thicker gunflints. Some archaeological and historical reports also document multiple incidents of gunflint rejuvenation (Stone 1974:255; Hanson and Hsu 1975:73). Given this background,

Nancy Kenmotsu

SITE NUMBER: MODERN USED GUNFLINTS

WEAR NOTED X-Section	Total	% of wear on working edge		WEAR NOTED Wear Type	Total	% of wear on working edge
Rounded	0	0		Grinding	0	0
Faceted	6	2 2		Blunting	5	1 9
Stepped	1 4	5 2		Smooting	1 7	6 3
Concave	2	7		Polishing	0	0
				Step Flake	2 7	1 0 0
RESIDUE	1 0	3 7		Crushing	1 2	4 4
				Flat Flake	1 2	4 4
Outline				Striation	3	1 1
Irregular	1 4	5 2		Pitting	0	0
Normalized	2	7		Heating	0	0

Number working edges per gunflint:

1 2 3 4 5 6 7 8	TOTAL
1 4 2 3	27

FIGURE 11. Results of use wear study for modern gunflints; sample size is 17.

it was anticipated that the archaeological specimens in the sample would evidence rejuvenation.

After development of the preceding expectations, all gunflints were studied under a 10-70 power microscope, beginning with the modern specimens. It should be emphasized that the microscopic study of the modern gunflints was critical to all interpretations, because their wear could be orally verified or was observed in the field. While still open to some subjectivity (i.e., hazy remembrances of informants, inaccurate note taking, etc.), the subjectivity was assumed to be less than that which might be imposed on a sample of archaeological specimens only. It was anticipated that wear on modern specimens would be duplicated to a large degree in archaeological specimens. Wear patterns noted during this microscopic inspection were recorded on the Lithic Analysis Data Sheet (Figure 2), adapted from Ahler (1979: 318). Definitions of wear patterns were taken from Ahler and will not be redefined here. Once the

analysis was complete, results were totaled to determine the presence/absence of trends of use wear. In turn, any trends were compared to informant and archival data.

Results of the Analysis

This section presents results of the analysis of wear patterns on 38 gunflints. Figures 11, 12, and 13 present the summary results of the use wear analysis. Each sample has been totaled individually and simple percentages are provided. The figures also provide information on the quantity of working edges for each gunflint. Each expectation described in the preceding section will be discussed, relating how well the data did or did not conform to those expectations. Comparisons to the modern sample will be detailed in these discussions, and relevant informant and archival data noted.

SITE NUMBER: PEARSON SITE 41RA5

WEAR NOTED X-Section	Total	% of wear on working edge		WEAR NOTED Wear Type	Total	% of wear on working edge
Rounded	2	22		Grinding	0	0
Faceted		0		Blunting	0	0
Stepped	5	56		Smooting	6	67
Concave	0	0		Polishing	1	11
				Step Flake	9	100
RESIDUE	4	44		Crushing	2	22
				Flat Flake	1	11
Outline				Striation	0	0
Irregular	1	11		Pitting	0	0
Normalized	0	0		Heating	0	0

Number working edges per gunflint:

1	2	3	4	5	6	7	8	TOTAL
3	2							9

FIGURE 12. Results of use wear study for Pearson site gunflints; sample size is 5.

Expectation No. 1: *The working edge will consistently exhibit crushing and/or heavy step flaking.* The motion of the flint down the frizzen is one of scraping. Scraping activities of experimental tools have been documented to result in step flaking wear patterns (Odell and Odell-Vereecken 1980:99). As the action is repeated, the pattern should intensify. It was thus anticipated that step flaking and crushing would be present.

Step flaking clearly dominated the wear for modern gunflints, being present in 100% of the cases of working edges (Figure 14). In the modern sample, all edges known to have been used as a working edge exhibited step flaking, although intensity varied from very heavy to light. Both Lee Bement and an informant at the rendezvous noted constant wearing of edges as the flint is drawn down the frizzen to release sparks. Similar patterns of step flaking also were present on nine margins of the five gunflints from the Pearson site and 38 margins of the 17 Gilbert site specimens. These margins were concluded to represent working

edges. Stepped cross sections were also fairly well represented on working edges of all three samples, as were irregular outlines. Fourteen (52%) of 27 working edges of modern flints exhibited a stepped cross section and irregular outlines. Five (56%) of the nine Pearson working edges had stepped cross sections and one was irregular in outline. Twenty-five (66%) of 38 Gilbert working edges were stepped in cross section and 17 were irregular in outline. While the samples are quite small and not statistically drawn or valid, it is interesting that the percentages for stepped cross sections of the archaeological specimens so closely approximate those of the modern sample.

Crushing, however, was not as prominent as expected. Fourteen (50%) of the modern sample's working edges had evidence of crushing. In the archaeological sample even less crushing was present: two (22%) of the nine working edges from the Pearson site and four (11%) of 38 working edges from the Gilbert site evidenced crushing. In general, crushing from the gunflint movement

SITE NUMBER: GILBERT 41RA13

WEAR NOTED X-Section	Total	% of wear on working edge
Rounded	7	18
Faceted	0	0
Stepped	25	66
Concave	1	3
RESIDUE	15	39
Outline		
Irregular	17	45
Normalized	5	13

WEAR NOTED Wear Type	Total	% of wear on working edge
Grinding	0	0
Blunting	7	18
Smooting	24	63
Polishing	0	0
Step Flake	38	100
Crushing	4	11
Flat Flake	14	37
Striation	0	0
Pitting	0	0
Heating	0	0

Number working edges per gunflint:

1 2 3 4 5 6 7 8	TOTAL
6 4 4 3	38

FIGURE 13. Results of use wear study for Gilbert site gunflints; sample size is 17.

down the frizzen appears to have a lower incidence than step flaking, especially in the archaeological samples. The lower incidence in the archaeological samples may relate to differences between archival and informant accounts of the average number of shots feasible per flint. Twenty rounds per flint was the U.S. Army estimate in 1846 (Chapel 1962: 71), yet all informants reported modern flints lasted from 50 to 100 rounds. Such a difference in life spans may be sufficient to induce crushing on modern flints but not on archaeological specimens.

Possible reasons for shorter gunflint life spans during historic times are several. Gunflints may have been so cheaply produced, in terms of time and money, that any slight flaw was sufficient to cause its discard. The present sample may represent specimens with inherent material flaws detected during early use. Too crushed edges may have been resharpened, removing evidence of crushing, and subsequently used insufficiently to produce crushing.

Expectation No. 2: *The working edge will exhibit a relatively uniform pattern of wear.* This expectation assumed that whatever wear pattern was found to be typical, it would be present uniformly across the working edges since the action is repetitive and artifacts restricted to a single purpose. During analysis it quickly became apparent that this expectation was poorly defined and hard to quantify. Many unanticipated variables affected the expectation. The gunflint may have been rejuvenated several times, obscuring "uniform wear patterns." At least two Gilbert specimens—one French blade flint and one native made gunflint (Figure 9o and e, respectively)—exhibited fresh pressure flakes along their edges, suggesting they were undergoing rejuvenation, obscuring step flaking and uniform wear patterns when they were discarded or lost. Another problem in qualifying this expectation is that flaws in the raw material could cause small, irregular and deep snap fractures (Figure 9n, l; Figure 10c). These flaws also will confuse the evidence for clear uniform wear

FIGURE 14. Microphotograph of step flaking on upper surface or working edge of modern gunflint; note smoothing of points at the edge of the gunflint; Pine Creek specimen (photo by N. Kenmotsu, 16X).

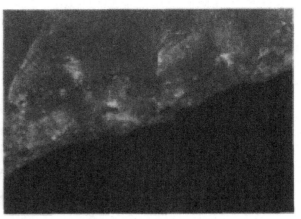

FIGURE 15. Microphotograph of Gilbert specimen 29. Feature 3, with unifacial step flaking and some blunting and smoothing along the edge; dark colored stains represent residue (photo by N. Kenmotsu, 16X).

patterns. In short the expectation was not very helpful and was finally abandoned because it was too broad and inconclusive.

Expectation No. 3: *Step flaking will be confined to the upper surface of the working edge; striations, smoothing, or polish will be present on the inferior surface of the working edge of the gunflint.* Given the type of scraping motion involved in the rasping of the flint down the frizzen, it was anticipated that flaking would be unifacial and confined to the back (upper surface) of the working edge. If present, striations, smoothing, or polish would occur on the face (lower surface) contacting the frizzen.

As expected working edges of all modern specimens exhibited step flaking on their upper surfaces (Figure 14). Archaeological specimens also exhibited unifacial step flaking (Figures 15, 16) in all but one case, and it was concluded that the step flaking represented the upper surfaces of what had been the working edges. One specimen (Figure 8d) from the Pearson site contained some light step flaking on the inferior surface. No clear explanation of this case was found, although it may simply represent turning the flint to obtain a better striking edge on the opposing surface.

Striations were present on three modern gunflints, but none of the archaeological specimens evidenced this attribute. The small sum of incidents of striations may not, however, be unusual. Tringham et al. (1974:189), Odell and Odell-Vereecken (1980:99), and Odell (1981:201) concur that striations are not commonly found on artifacts used in transverse scraping motions, and imply that intensity of use may be involved in creating this wear pattern on inferior surfaces. Hence, its presence on only modern specimens may again relate to a higher intensity of use of those gunflints over archaeological specimens.

Smoothing and polish are related types of abrasive wear (Ahler 1979:308). Smoothing causes a rounded, less coarse appearance of artifact surfaces than the appearance of surfaces with fresh flake scars. Polish is a higher degree of smoothing where light is reflected.

Seventeen (63%) of the 27 working edges in the modern sample exhibited smoothing (Figure 14) while no occurrences of polish were noted. Six (67%) of nine working edges of the Pearson sample exhibited smoothing with one occurrence of polish noted on one specimen (Figure 8d). This specimen is morphologically distinct from all others in the sample and its classification as a gunflint is questionable (see Appendix A). Twenty-four (63%) of the 38 working edges of the Gilbert sample exhibited smoothing; no occurrence of polish

Nancy Kenmotsu

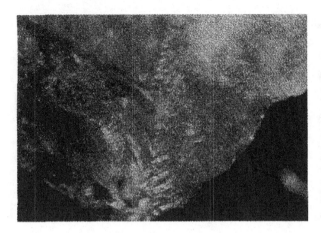

FIGURE 16. Microphotograph of Gilbert specimen 134, Feature 4, with unifacial step flaking on left working edge; bottom of microphoto shows small portion of the burin-like flake removed to rejuvenate the gunflint; the opposing margin of the burin-like flake is very similar to the step flaking on the left margin; left margin's reverse side had burin removed (photo by N. Kenmotsu, 16X).

was recorded. Once again the similarity of the percentages between modern and archaeological samples is striking. Further study of more statistically valid samples would be needed to determine whether this is a fortuitous similarity. Regardless, the results of the analysis tend to suggest a high incidence of smoothing on gunflints. However, the location of this wear pattern is not confirmed by the analysis. Only three of the working edges of the modern sample and one of the Gilbert specimens exhibited smoothing only on inferior surfaces. The remaining occurrences of smoothing were either on both surfaces or on the superior surfaces of the working edges. On reflection, the distinction may be more apparent than real. Evidence for smoothing is along the immediate edge where divisions between superior and inferior are fairly arbitrary. It seems more significant that in all three samples smoothing is second only to step flaking in its occurrence, is located on the working edge, and that the anticipated unifacial step flaking is confirmed in the microscopic inspection of the artifacts. The presence of striations on only three modern specimens and near absence of polish suggests that the intensity of use is generally insufficient to form these wear patterns on gunflints.

Expectation No. 4: *Blunting will be present on the working edge.* The first contact of the gunflint with the frizzen is one of impact. This impact, evidence of blunting from the Deshazo site, 41NA27 (Girard 1982), and use wear studies (Ahler 1979:308) suggested that blunting would be identified on the gunflints inspected microscopically.

Blunting was present, but not to the extent anticipated. Five (19%) working edges of the modern sample evidenced blunting as did seven (18%) of 38 working edges from the Gilbert site (Figure 15). Again the percentages are similar. One modern used gunflint appeared to have blunting on the heel, perhaps due to a loose fit in the cock. Two of the modern occurrences on working edges were from a single specimen. It is possible that the specimen was of a softer chert than the remaining specimens, or that the main spring of the pistol was relatively tight, enhancing the gunflint's impact with the frizzen.

The archaeological occurrences of blunting (Figure 9g, l, o) all appear to have more intense use than the modern sample. Heavy step flaking is present on these specimens on all working edges, and all but one of their working edges is stepped in cross section. All but the French specimen (Figure 9o) have multiple working edges (see Expectation No. 5); several working edges exhibit normalized outlines. This combination of wear attributes is not present in specimens without evidence of blunting. For example, specimens with less intense step flaking do contain evidence of smoothing, but not blunting. On the other hand, crushing is present in the Gilbert sample on two other working edges. If crushing is indicative of intensity of use, then blunting is curiously absent from these two specimens (Figure 9f, m). No simple explanation is offered. It is possible that intensity of use may result in more than one set of wear attributes; or evidence for blunting on the crushed edge may have been missed in the analysis. Nonetheless, each specimen has other working edges with moderate amounts of step flaking (sometimes with smoothing) and yet without evidence for crushing. In sum, while present and apparently not an overly common wear associated with gunflints, blunting

TABLE 1
QUANTITY OF WORKING EDGES PER GUNFLINT

| | No. Working Edges | | | | | | | | |
	1	2	3	4	5	6	7	8	Total
Modern Sample	3	7	2	3					35
Pearson (41RA5)	3		2						9
Gilbert (41RA13)	3	4	4	3					35
Total	9	11	8	6					79

is present in the sample. Blunting may be the result of attributes unique to individual guns, or, as appears to be the case with the archaeological specimens, to reflect the degree and extent of use.

Expectation No. 5: *Rejuvenation of gunflints will be evidenced by multiple working edges and edge retouch*. During the course of this study, modern informants and gunflint literature documented the ease of gunflint rejuvenation. This rejuvenation can occur by turning the gunflint to use another edge, turning the flint over, or edge retouch using a wooden billet or another instrument such as antler, bone or lithic tools, or copper.

Quantity of working edges on the modern gunflints was a known (Table 1). From established wear patterns for these modern specimens, the number of working edges on each archaeological specimen was determined by identifying those with patterns similar to modern specimens. The results indicate a high percentage of rejuvenation by simply revolving the flints in the cock. Three Pearson specimens had evidence of use on one edge; two had evidence of use on three edges. Those from the Pearson site with multiple worked edges are the brown banded English gunspall and one native gunflint, each having three margins that appear to have been used as working edges. At Gilbert three gunflints had only one working edge, four had two working edges, four had three working edges, and three had four working edges. One French and 10 native-made Gilbert specimens contain this evidence of multiple use. The total number of working edges on the 19 archaeological specimens from both sites is 44, suggesting a fairly high incidence of rejuvenation by simply turning the gunflint.

Other types of rejuvenation also are present in the samples. The used French blade flint (Figure 9o) from Gilbert has intermittent pressure flaking along its working edge. These pressure flakes appear to interrupt step flaking formed by use wear and are here concluded to represent resharpening of the working edge. Two other Gilbert specimens (Figure 9e, q) have similar evidence of retouch interrupting step flaking.

Still another type of retouch appears to have been employed as gunflint rejuvenation. Two Gilbert specimens have evidence of burin and burin-like flake removal. One is a native-made gunflint (Figure 16) with two working edges on opposing surfaces, which contains an elongated, narrow flake scar down the lower surface of one working edge. The possible French gunspall (Figure 9q), also contains a burin-like flake removed from the lower surface of one working edge. While not common, burin-type retouch seems to have been employed on inferior surfaces of working edges of relatively thick gunflints and is here tentatively suggested to have been a method of improving the striking action of thicker specimens. It would appear then that there is considerable evidence of gunflint rejuvenation within the three samples.

In addition to the above expectations, two other use attributes of gunflints were discovered through the use of Ahler's analysis sheet: evidence of flat flakes and residue. Flat flakes, confined to the lower surfaces of the working edges and evidenced by wide, flat flakes with feathered or hinged terminations, were present on 14 (38%) of 35 modern working edges. One occurrence (11%) of flat flaking was present in the Pearson sample, and 14 (38%) of 38 working edges in the Gilbert sample contained flat flakes. Photographs in Hamilton and Emery (1988: Figures 46,52) appear to document the removal of flat flakes on the inferior surfaces of working margins as well. Bement (1987, pers. comm.) suggested flat flaking may be related to the shock to the gunflint of the initial impact when striking the frizzen. At any rate, this type of wear, while not ubiquitous, is more frequent than blunting and polishing and appears to be part of overall gunflint wear patterns.

Finally, residue was present on all but three specimens and was identified on all surfaces as well as along edges and sides. Residue falls into three loosely defined types. First there are shiny silver or gold iridescent flecks (visible only at 40+ power under the microscope) on the artifacts. Believed to be metal, these flecks may have resulted from filing of edges performed during terminal stages of manufacture of both modern and European archaeological specimens, or they may be small chips of the steel frizzen. Another type of residue on the gunflints was a black substance sufficiently thick that it is was often visible macroscopically (Figure 17). Although not analyzed, this residue may be fragments of leather used to pad the gunflint in the cock. Informants noted that the gun powder reacts with leather resulting in its moistening. Two of Bement's specimens had this substance, and he identified it as leather.

The third type of residue noted has a very burned, powdery appearance and was especially apparent along edges (Figure 18). Quite distinctive, these may represent hot sparks released from the frizzen which were relatively large and which burned on the gunflint surface. Although outside of the scope of the present inquiry, further analysis would be needed to verify the true nature of the residues. For the purposes of this present study, it is sufficient to note the high incidence of residues which may assist in assessing whether small sub-rectangular lithic tools in an archaeological assemblage are gunflints.

Summary

Gunflints are frequently recovered from historic Indian sites. Since these artifacts are still manufactured and used today, a study was conducted to

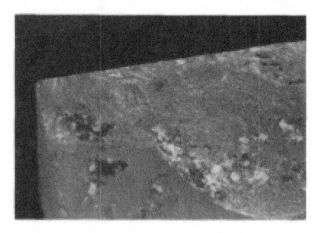

FIGURE 17. Microphotograph of Lee Bernent specimen 1 with flat flake removed from interior surface, dark stains are leather residue (photo by N. Kenmotsu, 64X).

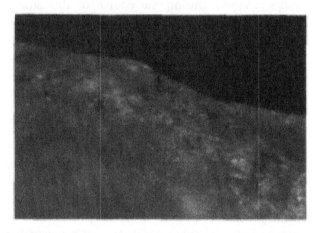

FIGURE 18. Microphotograph of Gilbert site specimen 110, Feature 3, with evidence of light step flaking, unifacial in pattern, and blunting on the central projection; note dark colored area which represents the third type of residue (photo by N. Kenmotsu, 16X).

determine whether typical wear patterns can be established for gunflints to aid in their identification in archaeological assemblages, and to understand better how these patterns formed.

In the course of the study, background data were gathered on the history of gunflints, including data pertinent to methods of manufacture. The gunflint industry began during the 16th century and continues today. French gunflints dominated the market in North America until the Napoleonic wars of the 1790s, when the British began gunflint production at Brandon. These French gunflints were initially manufactured by a core-flake technology whereby each core yielded from one to several flakes suitable for individual gunflints. Commonly called gunspalls, these specimens have a wedge-like shape and often retain a bulb of percussion and exhibit retouch around the heel. Sometime prior to A.D. 1663, the French developed a more efficient blade technology which was perfected by about A.D. 1750. Distinctive from the earlier gunspalls, gunflints are prismatic and a bevel is formed by the blade scars on the dorsal surface. It was this blade technology which was used at Brandon. Brandon quarries dominated the gunflint trade in North America after A.D. 1790. Native American gunflints were common on historic Indian sites until an available and accepted source of commercial gunflints was found. Native-made gunflints tend to reflect the bifacial reduction technology commonly associated with arrowpoint production.

Based on this background 38 gunflints from black-powder enthusiasts in Washington and Texas and from the Gilbert and Pearson archaeological sites in Rains County, Texas, were studied. All specimens were subjected to microscopic inspection to detect wear patterns. The goal was definition of typical wear patterns, and modern specimens were inspected first since their wear could be orally verified or observed. Results of the microscopic study were recorded on the Lithic Analysis Data Sheet (Figure 2) modeled after Ahler (1979). Once complete, the results were totaled and compared with five expectations developed from the background information.

Several expectations of wear patterns were verified by the study, while others were shown to not apply or to be less common for gunflints. Based on these results it appears that a wear pattern for gunflints can at least be outlined at this time. The pattern consists of unifacial step flaking often associated with smoothing of the working edges and some flat flaking on lower surfaces of the working edge. Blunting, while not as common, may be present. Occasional working edges may also exhibit crushing. Rejuvenation is common in the gunflints studied. Lastly, metal and leather residues are characteristically present on gunflint surfaces.

ACKNOWLEDGMENTS

A number of persons have greatly assisted in this study. Dr. Jeremiah Epstein, T. M. Hamilton, and Jay C. Blaine read and offered valuable advice on the direction of the study as well as on constructive changes in the paper, and their assistance is deeply appreciated. Robert Mallouf, James E. Bruseth, and Wayne Bartholomew also provided advice and encouraged completion of the study. Daniel Prikryl and Leland Bement were especially helpful in sharing their knowledge of lithic technology. The source material for native gunflints could not have been accomplished without the help of Larry Banks of the Southwest Region, Corps of Engineers. David Hafernik kindly drafted the map, the gunflint, and the flintlock drawing, and Deborah Smith and Helen Simons graciously edited the manuscript.

Finally, deep appreciation is given to Ray and Jeannie Kenmotsu without whose patience and encouragement nothing would have been accomplished.

REFERENCES

AHLER, STANLEY A.
1979 Functional Analysis of Non-Obsidian Chipped Stone Artifacts: Terms, Variables and Qualification. In *Lithic Use-Wear Analysis*, edited by Brian Hayden, pp. 301–328. Academic Press, New York.

BLACKMORE, H. L.
1961 *British Military Firearms, 1650–1850*. Herbert Jenkins, London.

BLANCHETTE, JEAN-FRANCOIS
1975 Gunflints from Chicoutimi Indian Site (Quebec). *Historical Archaeology* 9:41–54.

BLAINE, JAY C., AND R. K. HARRIS
1967 Guns. In The Gilbert Site, a Norteno Focus Site in Northeastern Texas. *Bulletin of the Texas Archeological Society* 37:33–86. Dallas.

BRAIN, JEFFERY P.
1979 The Tale of the Tunica Treasure. In *Tunica Treasure*, edited by Jeffery P. Brain, pp. 1–32. Papers of the Peabody Museum of Archaeology and Ethnology, Vol. 71. Peabody Museum of Archaeology and Ethnology, Cambridge, Massachusetts.

BRUSETH, JAMES E., AND TIMOTHY K. PERTTULA
1981 *Prehistoric Settlement Patterns at Lake Fork Reservoir*. Southern Methodist University, Dallas.

CHAPEL, CHARLES EDWARD
1962 *U.S. Martial and Semi-Martial Single Shot Pistols*. Coward and McCann, Inc., New York.

COTTERELL, BRIAN, AND JOHAN KAMMINGA
1987 The Formation of Flakes. *American Antiquity* 52: 675–708.

CRABTREE, DON E.
1972 *An Introduction to Flintworking.* Occasional Papers of the Idaho State University Museum 38. Pocatello, Idaho.

DAVIS, E. MOTT, KATHLEEN GILMORE, LOYD HARPER, R. K. HARRIS, EDWARD B. JELKS, AND BILL YANCY
1967 The Site. In The Gilbert Site, a Norteno Focus Site in Northeastern Texas. *Bulletin of the Texas Archeological Society* 37:33–86. Dallas.

DE LOTBINIERE, SEYMOUR
1984 Introduction, Updating Skertchly. In *The Manufacture of Gunflints,* by Sydney B.J. Skertchly, pp. i–viii. Museum Restoration Service, Alexandria Bay, New York.

DOLOMIEU, CITIZEN
1960 Report on the Art of Making Gunflints (Fire-Flint). (Reprint of 1797 article.) *The Missouri Archaeologist* 22:50–61.

DUFFIELD, LATHEL R.
1960 Field Notes. On file at the Texas Archeological Research Laboratory. Balcones Research Center, University of Texas, Austin.

DUFFIELD, LATHEL R., AND EDWARD P. JELKS
1961 The Pearson Site, a Historic Indian Site in Iron Bridge Reservoir, Rains County, Texas. *Archaeology Series No. 4.* Department of Anthropology, University of Texas, Austin.

FRISON, GEORGE C.
1979 Observations on the Use of Stone Tools: Dulling of Working Edges of Some Chipped Stone Tools in Bison Butchering. In *Lithic Use-Wear Analysis,* edited by Brian Hayden, pp. 259–268. Academic Press, New York.

GILLET-LAUMONT, F. P. N.
1960 Extract from a Report by Citizen Salivet on the Making of Gunflints in the Departments of Indre and Loir-et Cher. (Reprint of 1797 article.) *The Missouri Archeologist* 22:62–69.

GIRARD, JEFF SCOTT
1982 The Chipped Stone Collection from the Deshazo Site (41NA27): A Technological, Functional, and Typological Analysis. Unpublished M. A. thesis, Department of Anthropology, University of Texas, Austin.

HAMILTON, T. M.
1960 Additional Comments on Gunflints. *The Missouri Archaeologist* 22:73–79.
1964 Recent Developments in the Use of Gunflints for Dating and Identification. In *Diving into the Past, Theories, Techniques and Applications of Underwater Archaeology,* edited by June D. Holmquist and Ardis H. Wheeler, pp. 52–58. Proceedings of a Conference on Underwater Archaeology. Minnesota Historical Society and the Council of Underwater Archaeology, St. Paul.
1979 Guns, Gunflints, Balls and Shot. In *Tunica Treasure,* edited by Jeffery P. Brain, pp. 206–216. Papers of the Peabody Museum of Archaeology and Ethnology, Vol. 71. Peabody Museum of Archaeology and Ethnology, Cambridge, Massachusetts.

HAMILTON, T. J., AND K. O. EMERY
1988 Eighteenth-Century Gunflints from Fort Michilimackinac and Other Colonial Sites. *Archaeological Completion Report Series* 13. Mackinac Island State Park Commission, Mackinac Island, Michigan.

HAMILTON, T. M., AND BRUCE W. FRY
1975 A Survey of Louisbourg Gunflints. *Occasional Papers in Archaeology and History* 12:101–128. National Historic Parks and Sites Branch, Parks Canada. Ottawa, Canada.

HANSON, LEE, AND DICK PING HSU
1975 Casemates and Cannonballs, Archaeological Investigations at Fort Stanwix, Rome, New York. *Publications in Archaeology 14.* National Park Service, Washington, D.C.

JOHNSON, LEROY, JR.
1957 *Appraisal of the Archeological Resources of Iron Bridge Reservoir, Hunt, Rains and Van Zandt Counties, Texas.* River Basin Surveys, National Park Service, Washington, D.C.

KEELEY, LAWRENCE H.
1980 *Experimental Determination of Stone Tool Uses, a Microwear Analysis.* University of Chicago Press, Chicago.

KENMOTSU, NANCY
1987 The Mayhew Site, 41NA21, a Possible Hasinai Caddo Farmstead in Bayou Loco, Nacogdoches County, Texas. Manuscript on file at the Texas Archeological Research Laboratory, University of Texas, Austin.

LENK, T.
1965 *The Flintlock: Its Origin and Development.* Bramball House, New York.

ODELL, GEORGE H.
1981 The Mechanics of Use-Breakage of Stone Tools: Some Testable Hypotheses. *Journal of Field Archaeology* 8:197–209.

ODELL, GEORGE H., AND FREIDA ODELL-VEREECKEN
1980 Verifying the Reliability of Lithic Use-Wear Assessments by 'Blind Tests': The Low Power Approach. *Journal of Field Archaeology* 7:97–120.

PATTERSON, PATIENCE E.
1978 A Lithic Reduction Sequence, a Test Case in the

North Fork Reservoir Area, Williamson County, Texas. *Bulletin of the Texas Archeological Society* 48:53–82. Austin.

ROSEBUSH, WALDO E.
1962 *American Firearms and the Changing Frontier.* Eastern Washington State Historical Society, Spokane.

SKERTCHLY, SYDNEY B.J.
1984 *The Manufacture of Gunflints.* (Reprint of 1879 edition.) Museum Restoration Service, Alexandria Bay, New York.

STONE, LYLE
1974 *Fort Michilimackinac 1715–1781, an Archaeological Perspective on the Revolutionary Frontier.* Publications of the Museum, Michigan State University, East Lansing.

TRINGHAM, RUTH, GLENN COOPER, GEORGE ODELL, BARBARA VOYTEK, AND ANNE WHITMAN
1974 Experimentation in the Formation of Edge Damage: A New Approach to Lithic Analysis. *Journal of Field Archaeology* 1:171–196.

WITTHOFT, JOHN
1966 A History of Gunflints. *Pennsylvania Archaeologist* 36:12–49.

WOODWARD, ARTHUR
1960 Some Notes on Gunflints. *The Missouri Archaeologist* 22:29–39.

NANCY KENMOTSU
TEXAS HISTORICAL COMMISSION
P.O. BOX 12276
AUSTIN, TEXAS 78711

Appendix A: Gunflint Specimen Descriptions

The following table provides descriptions of individual gunflint specimens. The table format was chosen for easy reference and to reduce bulk. Categories are: specimen number, provenience (if any), length, width, thickness, color, source, and reduction comments. While categories are self explanatory, some explanation of the data presented is in order. Specimen numbers for the Pearson and Gilbert gunflints reflect actual numbers on the artifacts. In both sets of numbers duplicates exist. The only way to compensate for the duplication was to use the same order consistently. Hence the order in the table is mirrored in the photographs of each sample. Numbers for modern flints are arbitrary; all but Bement's will be put on file at the University of Texas at Austin (UT) for future gunflint researchers. Length, width, and thickness are all in millimeters. It should be noted that, contrary to 18th-century practices, the length is the distance from the heel to the working edge, rather than the distance from side to side. Too, for native-made gunflints, length versus width is quite arbitrary, as several margins were often utilized.

Source material for European gunflints is based upon modern purchased samples and upon descriptions and photographs in Hamilton (1960), Witthoft (1966), and Hamilton and Fry (1975). Source material for native-made specimens was determined by comparing each specimen with UT mineralogical samples, and by the assistance of Larry Banks. Where the specimen was concluded to match a sample at UT, the mineralogical sample number is provided below the named source. Although a number of archaeological specimens state "unknown" as their source material, other lithic artifacts in the Gilbert or Pearson site collections on file at UT were produced from the same source material, reinforcing the conclusion that the specimens were native-made.

Reduction comments provide data concerning both overall general methods used to form each gunflint and any evidence of edge retouch. Where possible, percussion versus pressure flaking is noted. When dorsal versus ventral surfaces can be discerned, descriptions use these terms; where indiscernible just the term surface is employed. The term gunflint is restricted to the snap blade specimens, gunspall is restricted to the wedge-shaped English banded flint from Pearson, and flake is used to identify all non-European specimens. While not entirely satisfactory, this system was used to try to reduce confusion.

INDIVIDUAL SPECIMEN DESCRIPTIONS

SPECIMEN	PROVENIENCE	LENGTH (mm)	WIDTH (mm)	THICKNESS (mm)	COLOR	SOURCE	REDUCTION COMMENTS
41RA5 (PEARSON SITE)							
?-11	Surface	23	31	8	Gray with faint white mottling	Ouachita Mountains (Banks 1988, pers. comm.)	Flake from hard hammer percussion; bulb of percussion still evident on heel; no bifacial thinning of original flake; bifacial percussion retouch along irregular working edge; unifacial pressure flaked retouch along dorsal surface of one margin.
87-5	Surface	23	23	7	Buff with reddish inclusions	Ouachita Mountains (Banks 1988, pers. comm.)	Secondary flakes with central channel removed on ventral surface; all but two margins of dorsal surface covered with cortex; one small soft hammer platform present on another margin with only unifacial retouch; remnant bulb of percussion may be present on heel, but evidence is equivocal; may not be gunflint.
66-1	Surface	21	21	7	Tan with gray inclusions	Ouachita Mountains? (Banks 1988, pers. comm.)	Flake produced by percussion with part of bulb of percussion removed from heel; wedge-shaped; sub-rectangular in plan view; margins and working edge bifacially retouched by pressure flaking; size and overall shape may indicate this is a fire flint.
?-11	Surface	18	20	7	Banded tan and gray	English? John's Valley Shale? (Blaine 1987, pers. comm.; Banks 1988, pers. comm.)	Gunspall or flake; wedge-shaped with hard hammer bulb of percussion on ventral surface; relatively flat dorsal surface; unifacial percussion retouch along heel and one thick margin; light irregular pressure retouch along other two margins.

(continued)

INDIVIDUAL SPECIMEN DESCRIPTIONS

SPECIMEN	PROVENIENCE	LENGTH (mm)	WIDTH (mm)	THICKNESS (mm)	COLOR	SOURCE	REDUCTION COMMENTS
47-1	Surface	24	26	7	Black	Brandon, England	Gunflint produced from proximal end of blade; retains hard hammer bulb of percussion with eraillure scar; another margin exhibits snap fracture with hinge; dorsal surface has single ridge or flake scar; heel has small flake scars alternating from dorsal to ventral surface (probably from filing); working edge has no intentional retouch.
41RA13 (GILBERT SITE)							
120	Fea. 3	19	23	7	Blue gray	Ouachita Mountains? (Banks 1988, pers. comm.)	Octagonal shaped flake with overall bifacial reduction; bifacial pressure retouch on all margins; compression rings in central area of ventral surface.
110	Fea. 3	20	23	9	Brown	Ouachita Mountains (Banks 1988, pers. comm.)	Relatively thick flake; roughly triangular in outline and wedge-shaped in cross section; irregular bifacial pressure flaking along margins; hertzian cone, unrelated to gunflint production, present in central area of one surface; no overall bifacial thinning.
94	Fea. 3	20	23	7	Brown	Ouachita Mountains (Banks 1988, pers. comm.)	Flake without bifacial overall thinning; wedge-shaped; irregular bifacial percussion retouch present along all margins and surfaces; two thin margins appear to be working edges and have bifacial pressure retouch.
94	Fea. 3	20	28	8	Tan/gray with white mottling	Ouachita Mountains, possibly from John's Valley Shale (Banks 1988, pers. comm.)	Fairly thick flake with soft hammer platform at one end; bulb mostly removed; oblong in outline; no

							Description
							overall bifacial thinning; relatively flat dorsal surface; unifacial percussion flakes removed from all margins of dorsal surface.
208	Fea. 7	21	22	9	Yellow gray	Georgetown (M41TV1); or Ouachita Mountains (Banks 1988, pers. comm.)	Sub-rectangular flake with overall bifacial thinning; may have old platform on one corner margin; one corner has aborted attempt to remove thick marginal area with a wrap-around flake; all margins bifacially pressure flaked for thinning.
9	Fea. 15	21	23	6	Light gray	Ouachita Mountains (Banks 1988, pers. comm.)	Sub-rectangular thin flake with bifacial retouch along three margins; roughly plano-convex in plan view; one margin is thick and contains evidence of old platform scars unrelated to the removal of this flake from its core.
981	Fea. 3	17	26	7	Gray brown	John's Valley Shale (Banks 1988, pers. comm.)	Sub-rectangular flake; convex in cross section; cortex present along two margins; upper surface exhibits overall percussion reduction with fine, parallel pressure retouch along the two available margins; inferior surface has remnants of large percussion flake removal and fine parallel pressure along the long margin; the other usable margin exhibits single linear wrap-around or burin-like flake removed along entire margin, perhaps in re-sharpening attempt.

(continued)

INDIVIDUAL SPECIMEN DESCRIPTIONS

SPECIMEN	PROVENIENCE	LENGTH (mm)	WIDTH (mm)	THICKNESS (mm)	COLOR	SOURCE	REDUCTION COMMENTS
181	Fea. 5	19	16	4	Tan gray	John's Valley Shale (Banks 1988, pers. comm.)	Sub-rectangular flake with overall bifacial reduction; some evidence of compression rings on one surface; very fine bifacial pressure flaking on all four margins.
134	Fea. 4	17	21	5	White	Ouachita Mountains (Banks 1988, pers. comm.)	Sub-rectangular flake with overall bifacial thinning; some faint compression rings on one surface; all margins bifacially pressure retouched and one margin deliberately rounded (perhaps for a heel?).
117	Fea. 3	23	21	6	White/tan	Ouachita Mountains (Banks 1988, pers. comm.)	Sub-rectangular flake with overall bifacial reduction; rings of compression evident in central portion of one surface; parallel bifacial retouch on all four margins.
281	Fea. 3	22	25	6	Pinkish gray	Ouachita Mountains (Banks 1988, pers. comm.)	Bifacially thinned flake with some faint compression rings on one surface; all margins bifacially pressure retouched; convex, sub-rectangular in outline; one corner has large flake removed, possibly from shovel, based on its relatively fresh appearance.
29	Fea. 3	19	25	6	Blue gray	Ouachita Mountains, possibly John's Valley Shale (Banks 1988, pers. comm.)	Sub-rectangular cortical flake with overall bifacial thinning; heel has brown cortex; other three margins exhibit bifacial pressure retouch.
281	Fea. 3	20	21	11	Gray	Georgetown (M41CM1 or M41CM2); or Ouachita Mountains (Banks 1988, pers. comm.)	Sub-rectangular flake with overall bifacial reduction; some cortex present on one surface, one point of which in center causes the thickness

measurement; all margins bifacially pressure flaked.

No.	Feature				Color	Origin	Description
197	Fea. 7	18	24	6	Gray blue	John's Valley Shale (Banks 1988, pers. comm.)	Sub-rectangular flake with overall bifacial thinning; small area of cortex on central portion of one surface; all margins bifacially pressure retouched with parallel flake removal.
27-14	Fea. 3	18	26	8	Honey-color with chalk heel	France	Probable blade gunflint with what may be two ridges formed by flake scars on dorsal surface; quasi-prismatic in cross section; percussion retouch on heel to form a steep bevel; pressure retouch on ventral surface of working edge.
152	Fea. 6	20	28	8	Honey-color	France	Probable blade gunflint with what may be two ridges formed by flake scars on dorsal surface; quasi-prismatic in cross section; ventral surface covered with percussion flake removals and light pressure flaking along left margin; may have shattered after only one to two firings.
134	Fea. 4	19	20	7	Honey-color with inclusions	France	Thick flake with irregular, bifacial retouch from a punch along margins; one margin has burin; another exhibits attempt to remove another burin; burins may be method of resharpening.

MODERN GUNFLINTS FROM LEE BEMENT

No.	Feature				Color	Origin	Description
1	L. Bement	15	12	5	Clear	Unknown	Pistol gunflint cut with modern lapidary saw.

(continued)

INDIVIDUAL SPECIMEN DESCRIPTIONS

SPECIMEN	PROVENIENCE	LENGTH (mm)	WIDTH (mm)	THICKNESS (mm)	COLOR	SOURCE	REDUCTION COMMENTS
2	L. Bement	19	19	7	Tan	Georgetown Flint	Fairly thick, sub-rectangular flake with thick margins that have been retouched with hard hammer percussion using small quartzitic cobble; one percussion flake removed from ventral surface; knapped by Lee Bement.
3	L. Bement	20	15	9	Gray tan with faint white mottling	Ogallala cobble	Fairly thick, sub-rectangular flake with thick margins; cortex present on one margin, one large compression ring on one surface, percussion retouch used along margins; knapped by Lee Bement.
4	L. Bement	17	11	6	Clear	Unknown	Pistol gunflint cut with modern lapidary saw
5	L. Bement	15	11	5	Clear/gray	Unknown	Pistol gunflint cut with modern lapidary saw
6	L. Bement	15	12	10	Blue gray	Georgetown Flint	Thin interior flake with bulb of percussion on ventral surface along with some concentric rings; both percussion and pressure flaking used on dorsal surface to thin flake and prepare thinner margins; knapped by Lee Bement.

OTHER MODERN GUNFLINTS

SPECIMEN	PROVENIENCE	LENGTH (mm)	WIDTH (mm)	THICKNESS (mm)	COLOR	SOURCE	REDUCTION COMMENTS
1	Pine Creek Rendezvous	22	20	7	Black	Brandon	Conventional rifle gunflint made from snap blade process; one dorsal ridge visible; another may be present but heel percussion retouch obscures the ridge; side margins exhibit manufacturing percussion

retouch and filing largely obscuring snap fractures.

No.	Source				Color	Origin	Description
							retouch and filing largely obscuring snap fractures.
2	Pine Creek Rendezvous	24	16	5	Light brown with tan mottling	Germany	Rifle gunflint cut with modern lapidary saw
3	Pine Creek Rendezvous	17	19	6	Gray/white	Ohio	Modern rifle gunflint manufactured in a mold and cut by lapidary type saw; has narrow medial ridge with two relatively uniform facets.
4	McBride's Guns, Austin	21	19	14	Gray banded	Brandon	Conventional rifle blade gunflint made from snap blade industry; ventral surface has remnant of one compression ring; white inclusion present on corner of margin of working edge; dorsal surface has one irregular ridge; if another ridge present, it has been obscured by pressure retouch along the heel; snap fractures on margins obscured by percussion retouch; impact scar present on one edge of medial ridge.
5	McBride's Guns, Austin	22	20	12	Tan with gray and black inclusions	Brandon	Very thick, irregular rifle gunflint possibly made from blade industry; ventral surface slightly convex; ridges very hard to define on dorsal surface; percussion retouch along all four margins.
6	McBride's Guns, Austin	31	30	16	Gray with tan inclusions	Brandon	Modern musket flint made from snap blade industry; ventral surface slightly convex with very fine pressure retouch along the working edge; side margins and heel of dorsal surface double backed or ridged;

(continued)

INDIVIDUAL SPECIMEN DESCRIPTIONS

SPECIMEN	PROVENIENCE	LENGTH (mm)	WIDTH (mm)	THICKNESS (mm)	COLOR	SOURCE	REDUCTION COMMENTS
							aris lip present on one margin; working edge evidences no retouch.
7	McBride's Guns, Austin	19	17	11	Black	Brandon	Conventional gunflint from snap blade industry; ventral surface slightly convex; dorsal surface with double ridges; heel and side margins' pressure retouch has removed some evidence of snap fractures.
8	McBride's Guns, Austin	22	21	13	Black	Brandon	Conventional gunflint from snap blade industry; ventral surface slightly convex; dorsal surface with double ridges; aris lip on one lateral margin snap; only heel exhibits pressure retouch, possibly to strengthen blade.
9	McBride's Guns, Austin	24	23	17	Black	Brandon	Conventional gunflint from snap blade industry; ventral surface slighly convex; dorsal surface double ridged; aris lip on one marginal snap fracture; white cortex present along one-half the working edge.
10	McBride's Guns, Austin	34	30	16	Black	Brandon	Conventional musket gunflint from snap blade industry; ventral surface slightly convex and with concentric rings; very light retouch along the working edge, ventral surface; dorsal surface is double ridged; heel and two margins have been reduced through pressure retouch; aris lip visible on one marginal snap fracture.

'State of the art' of British gunflint research, with special focus on the early gunflint workshop at Dun Eistean, Lewis

By TORBEN BJARKE BALLIN

SUMMARY: Uncritical use of flawed literature has allowed a number of misunderstandings to affect gunflint terminology and typology, thereby preventing the establishment of a reliable chronology. With reference to the most recent research into the subject, this article discusses gunflint terminology and, on this basis, a gunflint typo-chronology is suggested. As most British gunflint assemblages known from the archaeological literature tend to be late, and most terminological/typological problems in general appear to relate to 16th/17th-century gunflints, the recently discovered early gunflint assemblage from Dun Eistean, Lewis, Western Isles, has been given special attention.

INTRODUCTION

Although gunflints were manufactured in Britain for almost four centuries, the subject has only been dealt with in a relatively small number of papers, in which mainly later (post-1800) gunflints are discussed.[1] Consequently, analyses of British collections have had to rely on presentations of assemblages from Colonial and post-Colonial American excavations,[2] particularly in an effort to cover early (pre-1800) pieces. The inclusion of American papers has generally been helpful, but the joint use of Old and New World literature has also allowed some confusion to creep in, due to factual misunderstandings,[3] unhelpful translations (French to English)[4] and uncritical/circular use of flawed literature.

This has had grave consequences for gunflint terminology and typology, and thereby also for the understanding of gunflint technology, and for the establishment of a reliable gunflint chronology. Some types, for example, appear to be based entirely on misunderstandings,[5] and the distinction between 'French' and 'English' gunflints is at best unclear. Some analysts define the latter two types entirely by raw material colour ('blonde' and 'black'), others by technology ('spall' and 'blade'), whereas yet other analysts identify 'French' and 'English' gunflints by shape (D-shaped and rectangular). In terms of chronology, the competing definitions of 'French' and 'English' gunflints have made it more difficult to establish a reliable temporal sequence, as one view suggests that D-shaped pieces are replaced completely by rectangular pieces, whereas other interpretations indicate considerable overlap.

The main aim of the present paper is therefore to, first, discuss gunflint terminology, and, then, present a gunflint typo-chronology, as suggested by the most recent research into the subject.[6] The focus is mainly on British and Colonial/post-Colonial American gunflints, but will include the effects of the Napoleonic Wars, developments in the New World, and conflicting/overlapping national spheres of interest,[7] as well as continental European gunflints. The recent discovery on Lewis in the Scottish Western Isles of an early gunflint workshop (Dun Eistean) suggests that local formal and technological variation may occur and, in an attempt to explain this phenomenon, the Dun Eistean workshop is given special attention.

Torben Bjark Ballin

It is the author's assumption that some variation amongst local gunflint industries may relate to 'special circumstances', such as varying local raw material availability, differences between central 'proper' industrial production and peripheral cottage industries geared to local needs, as well as the effects of stress in connection with conflict events.[8] It is hoped that this paper, and its discussion/ clarification of terminology and typo-chronology, will prove useful to future research into the topic, in Britain and beyond, as well as to curatorial work on gunflints (correct identification, characterization, dating, display, etc.).

GENERAL GUNFLINT TERMINOLOGY

The discussion of gunflint typology and typo-chronology is based on the correct identification of a gunflint's different elements. This paper follows a terminology mainly adapted from Dolomieu,[9] Blanchette[10] and de Lotbiniere.[11]

A gunflint (Fig. 1) is generally characterized by having two faces, two lateral sides, as well as a rear and a front end. The rear end is usually referred to as 'the heel' (based on the D-shape of many early pieces), and the front (which is the end creating a spark by hitting the 'frizzen' or steel) as the 'the leading edge'. The lateral sides, as well as the heel and leading edge, are usually bevelled. In most cases, the lateral sides and the heel are modified by retouch, whereas the leading edge may be unmodified. However, in many cases the relatively thin leading edge (the working-end of the gunflint) was strengthened by retouching a slight bevel on the lower face of the edge.

Blanchette discusses gunflint terminology at length,[12] not least the various names of the two opposed faces. However, many of the terms for those faces are based on how the gunflint was traditionally inserted into the jaws of the cock, and practices in the Old and New Worlds clearly differed. In Europe (Britain and continental Europe alike) use-wear suggests that gunflints were almost always inserted with the larger face down (see, for example, Fig. 2), whereas in Colonial and post-Colonial America gunflints were usually (although not always) inserted with the larger face up (as indicated by the recovery of corroded flintlock mechanisms with gunflints still *in situ*).[13]

Several of the terms describing the smaller face are highly interpretative, such as 'seat' and 'bed', defining this face in relation to how the gunflint was positioned in the cock-jaws (according to American practice). As gunflints were clearly positioned differently in different parts of the world, it is suggested that these terms are avoided, in favour of the more objective terms 'upper' and 'lower', with the former representing the smaller face (limited in area by the various bevelled edges), and the latter the larger face. In this case, upper and lower simply refer to the manner in which analysts would position a gunflint on the table in front of them during examination, with no reference to its likely orientation during use.

The implementation of a general flint-technological terminology was considered,[14] with the upper face being the dorsal face (characterized by the concave scars of previous blank detachments) and the lower face the ventral face (the convex surface formed when the piece was detached from its parent core), but this practice would not have been workable. Although later (blade) gunflints as a rule have ventral lower faces, earlier

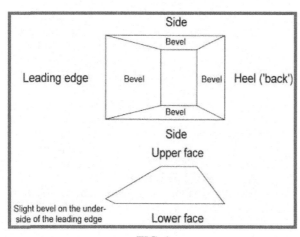

FIG. 1

The descriptive terminology of gunflints: a blade gunflint is used as an example (drawn by T.B. Ballin).

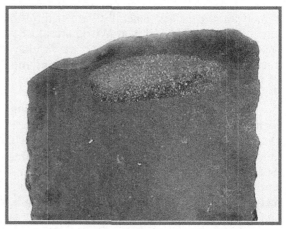

FIG. 2

Lower face of a gunflint from Antrim, Northern Ireland, with 'powder-burn'; this piece measures 32 × 32 × 12mm (see also Figs 21–22).

(spall) gunflints were generally manufactured in a more expedient manner, and their lower faces may be dorsal as well as ventral. The blanks of early gunflints were also frequently struck off the ventral faces of large, thick flakes ('flaked flakes'),[15] occasionally, if not mostly, giving them two opposed ventral faces.[16]

The British way of positioning a gunflint is demonstrated by the use-wear of a gunflint from Antrim in Northern Ireland (Fig. 2).[17] On the lower face, along the leading edge, the piece has a groove characterized by 'micro-crazing' and discolouration (fine white spots on a dark background). This type of wear is frequently associated with a particular form of 'knobbly' polish; micro-crazing, discolouration and/or polish are referred to here as 'powder-burn'.[18]

In general, a gunflint is thought to have had a very short lifespan, and Kenmotsu[19] suggests 20 rounds as a historical average.[20] The groove seen in Figure 2 (as well as the 'polish' observed on other gunflints) is therefore unlikely to have been caused by mechanical wear. Instead, it is suggested that it may have formed as a result of repeated firings, where the igniting powder above and in the hole from the pan to the barrel (the touch-hole) slowly disintegrated the flint (this needs to be tested experimentally).

Rectangular gunflints based on the segmentation of parallel-sided blades occur in two forms, namely pieces with a central (or slightly off-set) arris running from lateral side to lateral side, and pieces with two arrises. The upper face of the latter is characterized by a horizontal surface defined by the various bevels of that face, and this surface is referred to by some as the 'plateau' or 'platform'.[21] It is suggested that the terms 'platform' and 'platform-flakes/-blades' are not used in this manner, as 'platform' is a general flint-technological term referring to a specific reduction technique. In general flint terminology, platform flakes/blades were detached from special cores by hitting a prepared horizontal striking platform; this approach is usually perceived as superior to the less well-controlled bipolar technique, where flakes were detached from lenticular cores by placing nodules/cores on an anvil and then splintering them with a hammer.

The characterization of lithic artefacts in general (not least in connection with the presentation of the Dun Eistean assemblage) is based on consensus regarding the main artefact categories.[22] They are as follows:

Chips: all flakes and indeterminate pieces, the greatest dimension (GD) of which is ≤ 10mm.

Flakes: all lithic artefacts with one identifiable ventral (positive or convex) surface, GD > 10mm and L < 2W (L = length; W = width); in general lithic terminology, 'spall' is now an obsolete term for flakes, but is still accepted for short blanks for gunflints.

Indeterminate pieces: lithic artefacts which cannot be unequivocally identified as either flakes or cores; the problem of identification is generally due to irregular breaks, frost-shattering or fire-crazing.

Blades and microblades: flakes where L ≥ 2W; in the case of blades W > 8mm, and microblades W ≤ 8mm.

Cores: artefacts with only dorsal (negative or concave) surfaces — if three or more flakes have been detached, the piece is a core, if fewer than three flakes have been detached, the piece is a split or flaked pebble.

Tools: artefacts with secondary retouch (modification).

The general difference between blanks produced by platform and bipolar technique is that platform blanks have a small horizontal platform remnant at the proximal (bulbar) end, whereas bipolar flakes have a splintered end where they were struck.

GUNFLINT TYPO-CHRONOLOGY

INTRODUCTION

Gunflint typology — and with it, gunflint chronology — has been confused by errors and circular reasoning. Admittedly, this has mainly caused problems for American gunflint research, but as analysts dealing with early British gunflints occasionally (if not frequently) consult the much richer literature on Colonial and post-Colonial American assemblages, misunderstandings and errors have also affected Old World historical literature.

A number of notable misunderstandings appear to derive from Witthoft,[23] who, in referring to a mid 19th-century source,[24] suggested the following typo-chronology: 1) Nordic gunflints *c.* 1620–75; 2) Dutch gunflints *c.* 1650–1770; 3) French gunflints *c.* 1720–1820; and 4) English gunflints *c.* 1780+. According to Witthoft, Nordic gunflints were manufactured in Jutland, and are square to rectangular, bifacially chipped, and — consequently — pillow-shaped. Dutch gunflints, or gunspalls, are based on flakes struck off pebbles or cobbles, and they are wedge-shaped; French gunflints are prismatic, blade-based pieces; and English gunflints are prismatic, blade-based pieces with a percussion scar/bulb-of-percussion at the centre of each lateral side, where the blade-segments were separated by a hammer strike.

In his paper 'On the origin of gunspalls',[25] White criticizes Witthoft's contribution rigorously. First and foremost, it seems that the concept of Dutch gunflints is based entirely on a misunderstanding, as a reference to Stevensklint in Zeeland must be Stevns Klint on Zeeland, Denmark.[26] Witthoft writes: 'The Low Countries must have been the source. A single early author (Beckman 1846: II-538) mentions the former manufacture of gunflints in the Netherlands, at Stevensklint in Zeeland'.[27] It also appears that the flint-bearing drift in the Netherlands, mentioned by Witthoft,[28] does not exist.[29]

In his discussion of Witthoft's Nordic gunflints, White[30] quotes Hess' paper on the Danish gunflint industry.[31] Despite the fact that the Danes had access to excellent flint, only the gunspall type was produced,[32] and most certainly not bifacial pieces. Witthoft's suggestion that the Nordic gunflints were manufactured in Jutland, Denmark,[33] is slightly puzzling, as the main Danish production was at Stevns Klint on the island of Zeeland, supplemented by activities at neighbouring Møns Klint.[34] The export of Danish gunspalls is thought to have been limited to Danish spheres of influence, such as Norway, Greenland, the Virgin Islands and the African Gold Coast.[35] As Native American gunflints are mostly bifacial pillow-shaped pieces, Witthoft's bifacial Nordic gunflints may generally be Native American in origin.

The 'de-construction' of Witthoft's Nordic and Dutch gunflints leaves two main gunflint forms, namely the so-called French and English types. Both are blade-based, but where the former is mostly D-shaped, the latter is rectangular.

Apparently, the French chose to continue equipping their gunflints with a convex heel after the introduction of blade technology, whereas the British chose to make their blade gunflints rectangular.[36] The advantage of the British approach[37] is that it was possible to turn most of their gunflints in the cock-jaws when the original leading edge was worn down.[38] However, D-shaped and rectangular gunflints were clearly produced in France as well as in Britain.[39] Consequently, it is recommended that the terms 'French' and 'English' should be avoided, and replaced with more objective, descriptive terms.

De Lotbiniere[40] proposes four basic gunflint types produced and used in Britain, namely D-shaped and rectangular gunspalls, and blade-based gunflints with one and two dorsal arrises respectively (Fig. 3). However, the last two are not different gunflint types as such, but simply different qualities, produced within the same industry. Skertchley[41] mentions that pieces with two dorsal arrises were referred to by Brandon knappers as 'bests'; pieces which were too thin or of inferior workmanship or raw material were 'seconds'; whereas pieces with a single dorsal arris were considered 'commons',[42] and of third rate.

In his paper on gunflint recognition[43], de Lotbiniere suggests a basic typo-chronology of gunflints (based mainly on British and other European gunflints from various shipwrecks), which, following the general arguments put forward above, may be adapted into the following approximate chronological sequence:

Early wedges or gunspalls (crude 'do-it-yourself' types)
D-shaped spall gunflints (formerly 'Dutch' gunflints)

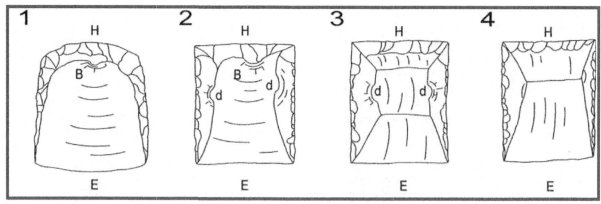

FIG. 3

De Lotbiniere's main gunflint types: 1. D-shaped gunspall; 2. square gunspall; 3. square blade gunflint with two dorsal arrises; 4. square blade gunflint with only one dorsal arris. H = heel; E = leading edge; B = bulb of percussion created when the blank was detached from its parent core; d = 'demicones' from the segmentation of the original blade blank (de Lotbiniere 1984, 206).

Rectangular spall gunflints
D-shaped blade gunflints (formerly 'French' gunflints)
Rectangular blade gunflints (formerly 'English' gunflints)

EARLY WEDGES OR GUNSPALLS: GENERAL

According to de Lotbiniere,[44] the earliest gunflints were crude 'do-it-yourself' items, probably of idiosyncratic shapes and sizes. He suggests that these forms dominated British gunflint production from c. 1550 to c. 1660 when a dawning (probably cottage) industry brought about more regular pieces (below). Unfortunately, there is little information on these first gunflints, and the industry's range of sizes, shapes and applied technologies is almost unknown.

It is possible to gain some insight into the production and use of gunflints at early Aboriginal and Colonial American sites, such as the Indian Chicoutimi site in Québec and various early forts in New England,[45] but most are slightly later, with a date range of c. 1650–1730. By this time gunflint production had already become more-or-less standardized, and most pieces from these sites are D-shaped spall gunflints. However, excavation of the Clarke Site at Plymouth Colony in Massachusetts[46] uncovered information on gunflint manufacture during the period 1620–92, and the site's gunflints clearly differ from assemblages recovered from slightly later Colonial sites.

The excavators of the Clarke Site distinguished between bifacial (probably Native American) pieces, spall gunflints, blade gunflints, and 'advantageous' (or expedient) pieces, with the four categories amounting to c. 6%, 6%, 10% and 78% respectively. It is not possible to determine whether the blade gunflints may represent later intrusion (without carrying out detailed checks of site stratigraphy, contexts, etc.), but 'advantageous' pieces clearly dominate the finds. The excavators define this type as follows:

Advantageous flints result when the knapper working the flint core was most interested in producing quantities of serviceable flints as opposed to quality or 'classic' spall gunflints. The production of advantageous flints can result from either a conscious effort on the part of the knapper to produce as many gunflints as possible from a limited supply of raw material, they may be the result of the inexperience of the knapper in producing gunflints, or they may be a combination of the two

factors. The advantageous flints from the Clarke Site exhibit fine chipping along the match[47] and often the sides, although it is not always present. This chipping is a result of pliers being used to trim the edges to a roughly rectangular shape and to bevel the match. Some of these gunflints appear to be nothing more than a single relatively thin flake struck off the core and trimmed while others are thicker and exhibit a trapezoidal shape in cross-section.[48]

Unfortunately, the report on the Clarke Site does not include detailed information on how the gunflints were produced; for example, whether platform or bipolar technique was applied.

Carovillano describes finds of worked ballast flint from the Den Rock, Massachusetts, dating to the so-called Contact Period (1500–1700).[49] Some are obviously fire-flints (having been struck by steel strike-a-lights), but many are almost certainly 'advantageous' gunflints or, in de Lotbiniere's terminology, early wedges. The illustrations are simple line drawings, and many are difficult to interpret, but apparently platform flakes as well as small cores were used as blanks.

EARLY WEDGES OR GUNSPALLS: THE DUN EISTEAN GUNFLINTS

INTRODUCTION

As information on the earliest British gunflints is exceedingly hard to come by, it was decided to characterize the gunflints from the Dun Eistean 'stack site', as well as the associated industry, in some detail. The site (NGR NB 5355 6501; Fig. 4) was investigated in 2005 by Glasgow University Archaeological Research Department (GUARD). Dun Eistean (an ancestral fort associated with Clan Morrison) is a flat-topped island (a stack) off the north-eastern coast of Lewis, measuring approximately 75 × 50m, and is separated from the mainland by a ravine c. 10–15m broad and of similar depth (Fig. 5).[50]

Along the edge of the ravine are the remains of a strong wall (Structure H), and of a tower (Structure G) at the centre of the stack, surrounded by a ditch. Structure A, towards the south-west, was identified as two rectangular dwellings, with traces of an earlier structure below; a dwelling and conjoining storage cells, Structure B, have been interpreted as a possible gatehouse, controlling access from the mainland; Structure C, a large sub-rectangular building with rounded corners, was identified as a kiln barn. At Structure D, two phases of buildings were revealed, with cellular turf-built structures overlying earlier stone-built

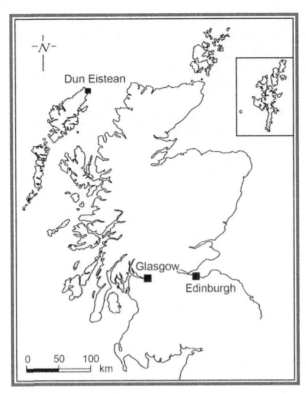

FIG. 4
The location of Dun Eistean, Lewis
(drawn by T.B. Ballin).

ones; and excavations of Structure F revealed two main phases of occupation, as well as a phase of abandonment in which the structure gradually collapsed.[51] During the excavations, a large number of finds were made. They include lithic artefacts, mostly in quartz and flint, as well as, *inter alia*, ceramics, glass and metal objects. A total of 33 radiocarbon dates were obtained, all falling within the period 1465–1670.[52] At a Dun Eistean seminar on Lewis in 2010, specialists presented their interpretations of the various find groups, and all non-lithic categories (pottery, glass, lead projectiles and coins) indicate dates within the above range, mostly in the second half of the period.

As the general size, shape and applied technology of the Dun Eistean gunflints differ substantially from the attributes of traditional gunflints, it is thought that they are contemporary with the site's other finds categories. This view is supported by contextual information.[53] The presentation of the flint assemblage from Dun Eistean is based on a detailed catalogue of all the lithic finds from the site (submitted in Microsoft Access format; available from the National Monuments Record in Edinburgh), and in the present paper the gunflints and implements are referred to by their number (CAT no.) in this catalogue.

In total, 429 flint artefacts were recovered from the excavations at Dun Eistean (Table 1). They are all thought to represent a local gunflint industry. Debitage (or flaked waste) numbers 366 pieces, whereas 21 cores were recovered, in conjunction with 46 tools. The assemblage also includes 173 quartz artefacts, which most likely date to prehistoric times, and are not dealt with in this paper.[54]

RAW MATERIAL

It is difficult to distinguish macroscopically between flint types, particularly when the pieces are relatively small and many are patinated. However, an attempt was made to characterize the raw material of the gunflints, and the following flint types were defined: 1) dark-brown (five pieces); 2) grey (eighteen pieces); 3) marbled black-and-grey (four pieces); and 4) spotted black (one piece).

The dark-brown and the grey flints may have been procured from primary sources in the greater Yorkshire area[55] or south-east England.[56] However, the fact that the cortex of the grey flints is generally abraded and battered suggests that they were obtained either in the form of ballast flint from shores in south-east or east England, or through 'combing' of local shores. The finding of a very large, perfectly formed, 'standard' D-shaped gunflint in dark-brown flint suggests that this flint variety may have been procured from the workshops in south-east England, probably in the form of finished pieces.

The marbled black-and-grey flint is generally more coarse-grained than the grey and dark-brown types, and it is more impure than the site's other flint forms. It corresponds to much of the post-medieval flint discovered in excavations in Scottish ports,[57] for example, and this raw material was almost certainly procured in the form of ballast flint. The solitary gunflint in spotted black flint was probably manufactured from local beach flint.

DEBITAGE AND CORES

The 366 pieces of debitage include 171 chips, 157 flakes, thirteen blades, thirteen microblades and twelve indeterminate pieces. This material is thought to represent waste from the site's gunflint workshops, and it is possible to subdivide it into two technological groups, namely micro-waste and macro-waste. The former includes the chips, whereas the latter includes the flakes, blades, and microblades. The general characterization of the site's larger pieces showed that approximately 85% are bipolar flakes and blades, whereas examination of the chips with a magnifying glass showed that

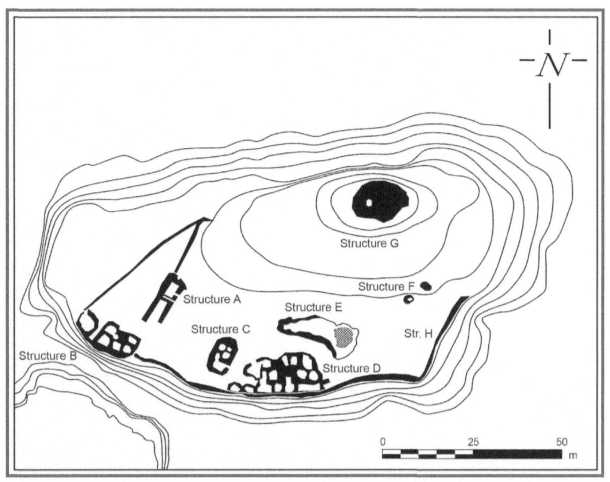

FIG. 5

Plan of the Dun Eistean stack site, with its main structures (A–H). Redrawn after original by C. Francoz, Glasgow University Archaeological Research Division.

they are almost exclusively small hard-hammer (platform) flakes. This fact is crucial to the interpretation of the operational schema responsible for the production of the site's gunflints (below).

Eighteen of the flakes and blades are so-called orange-segment flakes, formed when a pebble was struck on an anvil, usually splitting it into four or five flakes with a triangular cross-section. Orange-segment flakes are highly diagnostic of the bipolar technique (Figs 6 and 7).[58]

Although the assemblage includes 26 blanks defined as blades or microblades, it is important to emphasize that these are 'metric blades' and not 'qualitative blades'. Metric blades are defined simply as flakes which are more than twice as long as they are broad, whereas qualitative blades are defined partly in metrical terms, but they are also characterized by having parallel lateral sides and arrises. The latter is a characteristic of blades detached by the application of soft or hard

percussion (that is, platform techniques), whereas the blades from Dun Eistean are all bipolar. Consequently, they have curved or irregular lateral sides (not straight, parallel sides), and most have a solitary proximal-distal arris, or no complete arrises at all. The indeterminate pieces are predominantly those that have been burnt beyond recognition (54% of this category is burnt), or they may be pot-lid flakes (detached as a result of exposure to heat), or cubic waste.

The 21 cores include six pebbles, four split pebbles, and eleven bipolar cores. The six pebbles were included in this category, as they must represent stored raw material, irrespective of procurement form (obtained from local beaches or in the form of ballast flint). They measure on average 30 × 22 × 16mm, with their greatest dimensions (GD) varying between 20mm and 40mm.

The four split pebbles are early stage bipolar cores, from which fewer than three flakes were

TABLE 1

Flint artefacts from Dun Eistean, Lewis.

Form	No.
Debitage	
Chips	171
Flakes	157
Blades	13
Microblades	13
Indeterminate pieces	12
Subtotal	*366*
Cores	
Pebbles	6
Split pebbles	4
Bipolar cores	11
Subtotal	*21*
Tools	
Gunflints	25
Gunflints?	5
Gunflint chips	3
Fire-flints	6
Retouched pieces	3
Subtotal	*42*
Total	**429**

FIG. 6

Four refitted orange-segment bipolar core flakes from the Norwegian site Lundevaagen 21, SW Norway (photograph by T.B. Ballin).

struck. They measure on average 38 × 28 × 28mm (GD 28–55mm). The eleven bipolar cores proper vary greatly in size and shape. Two are broken-off splintered terminals, and the intact pieces have the following measurements: length 16–50mm; width 10–39mm; and thickness 8–20mm. The smallest bipolar core measures 16 × 10 × 10mm and the largest 50 × 39 × 13mm.

GUNFLINTS AND OTHER TOOLS

The tools include 42 pieces, 33 of which are associated with the production of gunflints (80%). Six are fire-flints (struck by steel strike-a-lights),[59] and three are pieces with simple edge-retouch. Only the gunflints are characterized and discussed here in detail.

The gunflint-related tools include the following specimens: 25 gunflints,[60] five likely gunflints, and three gunflint chips detached either during use or implement rejuvenation. It was possible to subdivide the 25 almost-certain gunflints into a number of subjective formal categories: 1) minimally shaped pieces; 2) D-shaped pieces; 3) straight-backed pieces; 4) thin quadrilaterals; 5) heavily worn ('amorphous') pieces; and 6) larger fragments. Whether these categories have any validity in relation to a larger statistical body of early gunflints from less 'stressed' circumstances (raw material scarcity, possible conflict events) needs to be tested.

As the morphology of most of the Dun Eistean gunflints differs considerably from that of later gunflint forms, the identification of typical gunflint use-wear was crucial to the classification of these implements. In general, a chipped leading edge is a certain determinant in the identification of 'classic' late gunflints, but as this chipping may give an edge an appearance very much like the terminal of a bipolar core or flake, the situation is less straightforward in assemblages based on bipolar reduction (such as the present material). However, it has been possible to identify one type of wear, which is unique to this group of artefacts, namely the so-called 'powder-burn'. This form of wear is usually associated with the leading edge, or the faces or corners of the leading edge. Although it is presently uncertain whether this wear type represents discrete areas of micro-crazing from the exposure to fire, or whether it represents a chemical reaction, a deposit, polish, or a combination of the above, it seems to be an unequivocal attribute of many used gunflints. At Dun Eistean, six gunflints have this type of wear (CAT 79, 84, 101, 161, 295, 308), as well as one gunflint chip (CAT 115).

The 25 gunflints are mostly based on bipolar flakes, although some hard-hammer flakes were also used as gunflint blanks, as well as two bipolar cores (CAT 75, 295). The average dimensions of the site's intact gunflints are 18 × 17 × 7mm (Fig. 8), with the smallest gunflint measuring 11 × 14 × 5mm (CAT 249) and the largest 25 × 23 × 10mm (CAT 318). They are both D-shaped gunflints.

FIG. 7

Exploded bipolar core of four orange-segment flakes from the Norwegian site Lundevaagen 21,
SW Norway (photograph by T.B. Ballin).

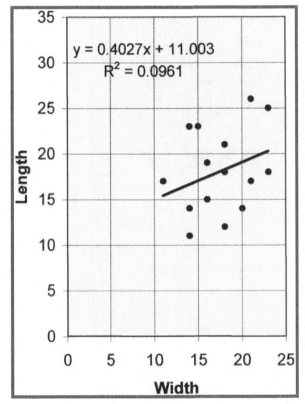

FIG. 8

Dun Eistean: the lengths and widths of all intact
gunflints (in millimetres). A trendline has been inserted
and the line's correlation coefficient calculated
($R^2 = 0.0961$). An R^2 of only 0.0961 indicates that the
Dun Eistean gunflints do not form a morphologically
homogeneous category.

The gunflints include six *minimally shaped
pieces* (CAT 96, 149, 190, 245, 255, 278) (Figs 9 and
10). One rectangular hard-hammer flake is entirely
unmodified (CAT 149), and it was only possible to
identify it as an expedient gunflint by the use-wear
defining its leading edge. A negative bulb-of-
percussion (the negative version of de Lotbiniere's
demicones; Fig. 3) at one end of its right lateral
edge suggests that the piece may have obtained its
rectangular shape partly by snapping off this side.
The other pieces are generally simple flakes shaped
by sporadic retouch or rubbing along their lateral
sides and heel, and CAT 96 has use-wear along its
leading edge. Two pieces have a retouched leading
edge (CAT 190, 255).

CAT 278 is a bipolar flake, which was (deliberately?) split by a blow to one of the blank's
terminals or ends (as the ripples of the two faces
are orientated in perpendicular directions). It is
impossible to determine which edge is an original
terminal and which is an original lateral side); the
leading edge (probably one of the blank's former
lateral sides) is defined by obvious use-wear in
the form of flat spin-offs. The slightly concave
delineation of CAT 255's lateral and leading edges
indicates that this piece may have been used
secondarily as a fire-flint (that is, partially shaped
by being struck by a steel strike-a-light).

Three flake-based pieces have a *D-shaped
outline*, with the curvature of the D forming the
lateral sides and heel, and the straight line of the
D forming the leading edge (Fig. 11). Two of the
D-shaped specimens (CAT 249, 318) are highly
regular, well-executed gunflints, with retouched
leading edges, whereas one is more irregular (CAT
331). The latter forms a misshapen D, and one
lateral side and the heel were shaped by sporadic
retouch and rubbing. CAT 249 and CAT 318 both
have chipped leading edges. Damage to CAT 331's
leading edge appears fresh and may be modern
('trowel retouch'?).

The gunflints also include three *straight-
backed pieces* (CAT 84, 199, 295). CAT 295 is

FIG. 9

Dun Eistean: selection of minimally shaped and 'amorphous' gunflints (CAT 79, 149, 245, 308; photograph by T.B. Ballin).

based on a thin bipolar core, and the lateral sides appear to be defined by the core's two opposed terminals (Fig. 12). Its heel was shaped by sporadic retouch. The category's two flake-based specimens (CAT 84, 199) were formed mainly by a combination of sporadic retouch and rubbing. CAT 199 has a heavily chipped leading edge, and CAT 84 and CAT 295 both display 'powder-burn'. It is possible that CAT 84 acquired its straight heel by snapping a bipolar flake, with the break facet (the heel) subsequently straightened by retouch/rubbing (like

CAT 278, above). There is some overlap between this category and 'minimally shaped pieces'.

Two specimens were defined as *thin quadrilateral pieces* (CAT 150, 158), based on 3mm-thick rectangular flakes (Fig. 13). CAT 150 is intact, and has regular modification along all four sides. However, CAT 158 broke diagonally, detaching its leading edge, although it most likely also had four modified edges. The fact that these pieces are only 3mm thick makes it highly unlikely that they were used as fire-flints — the steel strike-a-light would

FIG. 10

Dun Eistean: selection of minimally shaped and 'amorphous gunflints' (CAT 199, 331, 278, 190;
photograph by T.B. Ballin).

simply have cut deep grooves in the edges of the two pieces had this been attempted.

Five *'amorphous'* pieces (CAT 4, 79, 101, 161, 308) are sufficiently intact to be defined as gunflints, but they are so heavily worn that accurate determination of their original sizes and shapes is impossible (Fig. 9). CAT 161, for example, is missing most edges; it is characterized by distinct 'powder-burn' at one of its proximal corners, suggesting that its leading edge was formed by one of the blank's original lateral sides. The other four pieces were generally shaped by initial crude flaking, followed by a combination of retouch and rubbing of lateral sides and heel. CAT 101 has a retouched leading edge, which is chipped and discoloured by 'powder-burn'. It is almost impossible to identify the leading edge of CAT 308 by morphological analogy, but the location of 'powder-burn' at one corner suggests that a short stretch of chipped edge adjacent to this corner may be a surviving segment of a leading edge. There is no well-defined boundary between this category and the following one.

FIG. 11

Dun Eistean: two D-shaped gunflints (CAT 318, 249; photograph by T.B. Ballin).

A group of *larger gunflint fragments* consists of three lateral halves split from heel to leading edge (CAT 75, 103, 153), two broken-off heels, possibly from D-shaped pieces (CAT 94, 232), and one piece (CAT 132) is either a lateral fragment or a detached heel. These pieces were in the main shaped by a combination of retouch and rubbing.

Five pieces were defined as *likely, but misshapen, gunflints* (CAT 12, 87, 88, 148, 197) on the basis of their size, shape and wear patterns. Apart from CAT 197, which is a small sub-triangular/rectangular flake (13 × 10 × 4mm) with one retouched lateral side and one side blunted by cortex, all pieces are characterized by having been retouched around the entire circumference and by having an uneven outline. Of the latter, the larger specimen (CAT 87) is of sufficient size (18 × 18 × 10mm) to have functioned as a fire-flint, but the three smaller specimens (CAT 12, 88, 148) are only slightly larger than CAT 197, and they do not have enough mass to have functioned in connection with a steel strike-a-light. It is therefore most likely that these pieces are totally exhausted gunflints.

Gunflint chips: three small pieces (CAT 115, 287, 337) are either small waste flakes (average dimensions: 11 × 7 × 2mm) from the production or rejuvenation of gunflints or — just as likely — they were detached from gunflints used in battle.[61] CAT 287 is a piece with a straight lateral retouch and a corticated platform remnant, and CAT 337 is the distal fragment of a thin flake with an angled lateral retouch. Both may be so-called 'Janus flakes', that is, flakes with two ventral faces (detached from the ventral faces of implements), and they both display flat spin-offs (use-wear?) from what is assumed to be their oldest faces. CAT 115 is a small elongated chip detached from the corner of a gunflint, along one of its lateral sides. Its dorsal face is defined by one modified edge and one edge with 'powder-burn' (in this case in the form of 'knobbly' polish; Fig. 14). The examination of gunflints has shown that the detachment of corners is a common occurrence during use, and this piece was probably detached in connection with the discharge of a gun.

FIG. 12

Dun Eistean: straight-backed gunflint based on a bipolar core (CAT 295; photograph by T.B. Ballin).

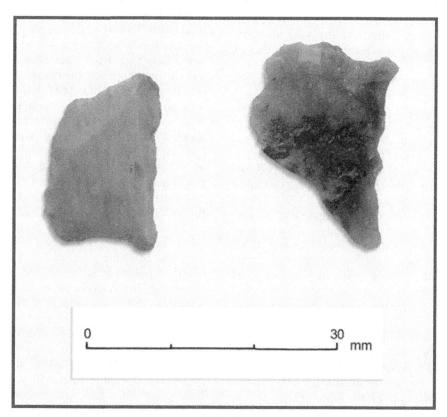

FIG. 13

Dun Eistean: two quadrilateral gunflints (CAT 150, 158; photograph by T.B. Ballin).

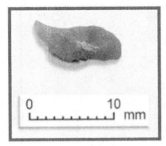

FIG. 14

Dun Eistean: a broken-off gunflint corner with 'powder-burn' ('knobbly' polish; CAT 115; photograph by T.B. Ballin).

Fire-flints: six pieces (CAT 95, 185, 191, 268, 326, 670) form a small heterogeneous group of flakes or flake fragments with concave wear along one or more edges. The concavities were clearly formed by violent, poorly aimed strikes with another tool (a steel strike-a-light?), and the lateral modifications are not regular enough to warrant the use of the term 'retouch'. The blanks are in all cases bipolar or indeterminate flakes, and four specimens are intact (CAT 95, 191, 268, 670). The greatest dimensions of the intact pieces vary between 17mm and 29mm. Three pieces (CAT 185, 191, 326) are relatively thin (Th = 5–6mm), whereas the other three (CAT 95, 268, 670) are somewhat thicker (Th = 10–13mm). Flint strike-a-lights and fire-flints have been discussed in a number of publications.[62]

Pieces with edge-retouch: three implements (CAT 130, 173, 230) are characterized by relatively regular edge-retouch. CAT 230 (24 × 12 × 4 mm) is the proximal fragment of a flake in obviously exotic, homogeneous dark-brown flint. It has regular backing along one lateral side, but unfortunately the opposite lateral side has been snapped off. Most likely, this is the fragment of a backed knife which has lost its cutting-edge. CAT 173 (31 × 16 × 7mm) is a broad flake with a shallow retouched concavity along one of its long edges. This is probably a spoke-shave, plane or concave scraper. CAT 130 (7 × 17 × 2mm) is a small fragment of a thin flake tool. One lateral edge is characterized by crude rubbing, and another edge is notched (chord = 6mm). The function of this specimen is uncertain.

The production of informal flint tools alongside, or as by-products of, gunflint production has been evidenced at a number of locations, such as at the Den Rock site in Massachusetts (1500–1700)[63] and at the Carolina Point slave village in the Danish West Indies (1720–1848).[64] The Carolina Point industry is characterized in the following way by Kidd:[65]

The production of these informal tools seems to indicate a reduction strategy involving hammerstones and anvils, which would account for the large number of bipolar cores and flakes encountered [. . .]. These expedient tools produced from this reduction strategy would most likely have been simple cutting edges and strike-a-lights. Since none of the examples examined revealed extensive reuse it could be suggested that they were intended only as single-use disposable tools.

Simple implements from a presently undated (but probably post-medieval) flint industry based on ballast flint have been recovered from a number of Scottish ports,[66] indicating that post-medieval flint use is not an uncommon phenomenon.

THE OPERATIONAL SCHEMA OF THE DUN EISTEAN GUNFLINT INDUSTRY

The raw material for the Dun Eistean gunflint industry appears to have been obtained partly by selecting suitable pebbles from dumped ballast, and partly by 'combing' the local beaches for rare nodules of flint washed in from outcrops off the Scottish west coast.

At Brandon in Sussex,[67] the production of gunflints was divided into three stages, namely quartering, flaking and knapping. During quartering, nodules were made into cores; during flaking, either flake ('spall') or blade blanks were produced; and during knapping, the blanks were transformed into finished gunflints. At Dun Eistean, quartering was not possible as the beach pebbles available were too small for the production of traditional gunflint cores: the pebbles at hand simply did not have enough mass to be thoroughly prepared (that is, decorticated, crested and trimmed). Instead, gunflint blanks were produced by the application of bipolar technique (Fig. 15), where pebbles were placed on an anvil and 'smashed' by a hammer (in prehistory, this would have been a hammerstone — at Dun Eistean, probably a metal hammer).

The resulting gunflint blanks were therefore mostly bipolar flakes and blades, as well as bipolar cores (Fig. 16). As a consequence, the Dun Eistean gunflints differ considerably from their more southerly, and mostly later, 'cousins'. In some cases, bipolar flakes were modified into the same standard types as those known from southern industries (for example, large and small versions of D-shaped gunflints), but in several cases, Dun Eistean gunflints have lateral sides defined by the two terminals of bipolar flakes, blades and cores (for example, CAT 94, 153, 295). An obvious visible difference between these two types of gunflints

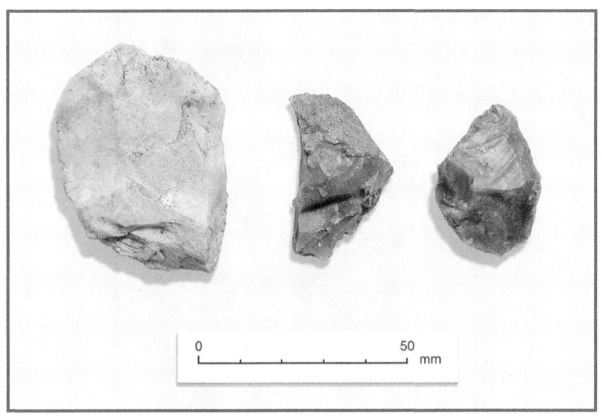

FIG. 15

Dun Eistean: bipolar cores (photograph by T.B. Ballin).

FIG. 16

Dun Eistean: a broken-off terminal of bipolar core, ready to be used as a minimally shaped gunflint (photograph by T.B. Ballin).

is that the former have four-sided (usually trapezoidal) cross-sections and the latter pointed-oval cross-sections. In connection with the identification and orientation of gunflints based on bipolar

blanks, pieces with pointed-oval sections pose a problem, as it may on occasion be difficult to distinguish between their lateral sides (defined by core terminals splintered during primary production) and used leading edges (characterized by detached flat spin-offs, and/or secondary splintering).

Where the pointed-oval pieces (for example, based on bipolar cores) were almost fully formed in connection with the flaking process (creating an overlap between the flaking and knapping stages), pieces with four-sided cross-sections were formed into final gunflints when blanks had their lateral sides and back modified by mostly coarse secondary retouch. This process is evidenced by two sets of attributes, namely series of circular impact scars along the sides and back of the gunflints, and the site's chips, which are mostly small cubic and/or hinge-terminated hard-hammer chips (Fig. 17). The small D-shaped specimen (CAT 249) is a good example of this approach, and it is almost certain that a small pointed steel hammer and an anvil would have been needed to carry out this work.[68]

One consequence of this approach is the formation of a dichotomous operational schema: it includes a flaking stage, characterized by the manufacture of flake, blade and core blanks almost

FIG. 17

Dun Eistean: small hard-hammer chips created in connection with the modification of blanks into final gunflints (photograph by T.B. Ballin).

exclusively in *bipolar technique*, and a knapping stage characterized by the detachment of small *hard-hammer chips* from the various edges of the gunflint blanks. Four-sided as well as pointed-oval specimens would occasionally have had their leading edges modified by fine retouch.

It is presently uncertain whether the technological approach witnessed at Dun Eistean represents a link in the general evolution of British gunflints or a local/temporal aberration.

D-SHAPED SPALL GUNFLINTS (FORMERLY 'DUTCH' GUNFLINTS)

The manufacture of D-shaped spall gunflints (Fig. 3:1) has been discussed by Chandler[69] as well as by McNabb & Ashton,[70] who explained this particular reduction process by the use of a number of detailed diagrams and line drawings. In this case, mostly squat flakes were detached, either directly from unprepared pebbles or, more commonly, from cores referred to as 'flaked flakes'[71] or Kombewa cores.[72] In the 'flaked flake' approach, a thick flake is detached from a large nodule, and this flake then becomes the core. As illustrated by Chandler,[73] decortication flakes were first detached from the 'flaked flake's' lateral sides and dorsal face, and, then, gunflint blanks were detached from the core's ventral face (Fig. 18).

As demonstrated in Figure 19, the gunflint blanks — detached from the ventral face of a 'flaked flake' — tend to be biconvex, that is, they

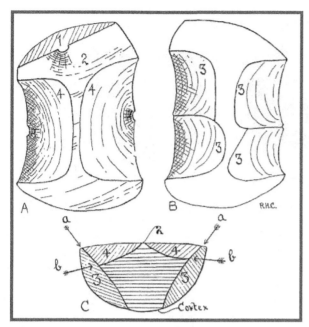

FIG. 18

Reduction of a 'flaked flake': 1. platform remnant with bulb-of-percussion; 2. ventral face of the 'flaked flake'; 3. decortication flakes; 4. gunflint blanks (Chandler 1917, fig. 65, reproduced by courtesy of the Prehistoric Society).

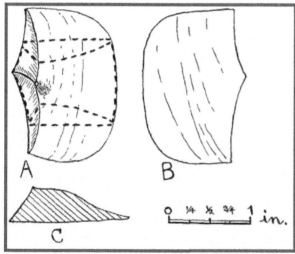

FIG. 19

Gunflint blank detached from a 'flaked flake' at the beginning of the reduction process (Chandler 1917, fig. 66, reproduced by courtesy of the Prehistoric Society).

have two ventral faces (so-called 'Janus-flakes'). This phenomenon is also demonstrated by a number of spall gunflints from Antrim Town (Figs 20–21), most of which have this cross-section.[74]

The D-shaped spall gunflints are called 'wedges' by de Lotbiniere,[75] due to their wedge-shaped profile. This profile is a direct result of the prominent bulb-of-percussion above the heel. De Lotbiniere describes how the D-shape was obtained by trimming the flint's lateral sides and heel from its lower face,[76] whereas the bevel along the leading edge (not visible in Fig. 3) was obtained by reverse trimming from the upper face. These gunflints are associated with the establishment of a craft industry around 1650,[77] and they were produced in Britain until the end of the 18th century.[78]

It is a well-known fact that gunflints vary considerably in size, but Hanson and Hsu suggest, in their presentation of the finds from Fort Stanwix, New York State, that '... this was a late development and that prior to the 19th century there was no standardization into size categories'.[79] However, in his *Story of the English Gunflint*, de Lotbiniere documents the process of standardization as taking place much earlier, probably in the first half of the 18th century.[80] Skertchley lists a number of different gunflint categories and their dimensions (Table 2),[81] and although his work mainly concerns the later gunflint production at Brandon, these gunflint size categories were probably established much earlier.

According to de Lotbiniere,[82] cannon flints were introduced into the Navy *c.* 1757, but they are not mentioned by Skertchley. De Lotbiniere[83] suggests that they must have approximated musket and carbine gunflints in size, since soon after their introduction, a Board Supply Clerk reported that he could provide, from musket and carbine flints already in store, '... whatever extra were needed for Quarter Deck guns',[84] although the flints for 'wall pieces' listed by Skertchley would probably have fitted better. All 2,000+ gunflints from the wreck of HMS *Invincible*, sunk 1758, are D-shaped gunspalls.[85]

RECTANGULAR SPALL GUNFLINTS

Rectangular spall gunflints (Fig. 3:2) are rarely discussed in the archaeological/historical literature, but de Lotbiniere suggests that they were introduced around 1775 in France,[86] along with the first blade gunflints. However, as the first French blade gunflints were D-shaped (unlike the later rectangular British blade gunflints), this is unlikely, and the type's genesis should be researched further. De Lotbiniere mentions that some were recovered alongside contemporary rectangular blade gunflints from the wreck of the British East Indiaman the *Earl of Abergavenny*, which sank in 1805.[87] He suggests that the continued production of rectangular spall gunflints, after the introduction in Britain of the blade technique, may have been due to '... some inadequacies in the size and quality of the only flint nodules then available'. They

FIG. 20

Five gunflints (upper face view) from Antrim Town, Northern Ireland: No. 1 is a blade gunflint; Nos 2 and 4 are rectangular gunspalls; and Nos 3 and 5 are D-shaped gunspalls (photograph by T.B. Ballin).

disappeared soon after, with the increased use of better flint in larger nodules, from more, deeper flint pits at Brandon.

A small collection of gunflints (five pieces) was recovered from excavations in Antrim Town, and the composition of this assemblage indicates that (at least in Britain) rectangular spall gunflints may be a transitional form between the common D-shaped gunspall and the rectangular blade gunflints traditionally produced in this country (see below). The Antrim collection includes two D-shaped gunspalls, two rectangular gunspalls, and one rectangular blade gunflint (Figs 20–21), and the composition of the five gunflints suggested an association with the 1797 Battle of Antrim.[88]

D-SHAPED BLADE GUNFLINTS (FORMERLY 'FRENCH' GUNFLINTS)

There is little doubt that the first blade gunflints were produced in France, but the exact date of the introduction of blade technology is uncertain, with some suggesting a date as early as the mid

17th century.[89] However, the technique was probably not perfected until c. 1740, after which it completely dominated French gunflint production. The production of gunspalls from 'flaked flakes' was most likely replaced by the production of blade gunflints, due to the wasteful character of the former.[90] In most cases, only a couple of gunspalls were produced per core, whereas it was possible to produce numerous gunflints from a large conical blade-core.[91]

The French enjoyed a monopoly over the gunflint market for almost half a century (until just before 1800), after which the British gunflint industry in Kent and around Brandon took over, most probably due to a combination of flint quality (Brandon 'floorstone'), applied technology and gunflint shape. As stated by Woodward, '. . . the French flints were of the honey or taffy coloured types, with rounded heels, thinner and flatter than those of English manufacture'.[92] It is thought that the rectangular shape of the British gunflints may have made them superior, as this allowed them to be turned in the cock-jaws when the original

FIG. 21

Five gunflints (lower face view) from Antrim Town, Northern Ireland: note the ?etched groove on No. 2 ('powder-burn'); No. 4 has faint powder-burn at the right corner of its leading edge (photograph by T.B. Ballin).

leading edge was worn out, after which time the heel became the new leading edge. This effectively prolonged the life of a gunflint by 100%.

In 1986, Queensland Museum participated in an investigation of two shipwrecks, *L'Astrolabe* and *La Bousolle*, the vessels of the French explorer La Pérouse, which were lost in 1788 on reefs in the Solomon Islands. The team recovered 520 gunflints, most of which are typical D-shaped blade gunflints:[93] 16.5% of all gunflints are wedges, and the remainder blade gunflints, and *c.* 90% of all blade gunflints are D-shaped pieces with a single leading edge, with only *c.* 10% being symmetrical pieces with two leading edges.

Although D-shaped blade gunflints are traditionally associated with France, the specimens from the above two vessels clearly demonstrate that some rectangular blade gunflint were produced in that country. An illustration of gunflints from *Le Vieux Fort*, Placentia, Canada shows large numbers of rectangular 'blonde' blade gunflints (with the colour indicating importation from France) mixed with D-shaped spall and blade

gunflints in similar colours.[94] Rectangular blade gunflints were most likely introduced in France at a relatively early stage, and the suggestion in the archaeological literature that all French blade gunflints are D-shaped has an almost mythical character. This point clearly needs further investigation and public discussion.

RECTANGULAR BLADE GUNFLINTS (FORMERLY 'ENGLISH' GUNFLINTS)

It is uncertain exactly when the blade technique was introduced in Britain, but de Lotbiniere suggests that this process took place in Kent soon after 1780 and at Brandon around 1790.[95] Legend has it that the introduction of the blade technique from France was associated with a French prisoner during the Napoleonic Wars, who revealed how production could be increased by the use of a particular pointed ('oval') hammer.[96] However, this does not tally with the proposed date of introduction around 1780. White attributes this technological 'revolution' to a James Woodyer in Kent, who

TABLE 2

Standardized gunflint sizes, according to Skertchley (1879).

	Inches (Skertchley 1879)			Approx. millimetres		
	Length	*Width*	*Thickness*	*Length*	*Width*	*Thickness*
Wall piece	2.0	1.5	0.5	51	38	13
Musket	1.3	1.1	0.4	33	28	10
Carbine	1.2	1.0	0.25	30	25	06
Horse pistol	1.1	0.9	0.3	28	23	08
'Single' (i.e. '-barrelled' sporting guns)	1.0	0.85	0.2	25	22	05
'Double' (i.e. '-barrelled' sporting guns)	1.0	0.7	0.25	25	18	06
Pocket pistol	0.75	0.65	0.2	19	17	05

introduced the technique from France before his death in 1787.[97] Tomlinson reports how the technique was kept a secret by the French,[98] and it was not possible for Dolomieu[99] to write his paper on the French gunflint industry until the secret had been revealed.

By *c.* 1800 the flint industry at Brandon in Sussex was well established,[100] including the procuring of flint from shafts up to 12m deep. Gunflint production involved the use of a number of different hammers, and the individual blades were segmented by cutting opposed notches in their lateral sides, laying them across an iron 'stake', and then striking them to separate the segments. The manufacture of rectangular blade gunflints (Fig. 3:3-4) included a number of stages, such as quartering, flaking and knapping. During quartering, raw nodules were made into conical cores; during flaking, blade blanks were detached from their parent cores; and during knapping, the blades were transformed into finished gunflints (Figs 22 and 23).

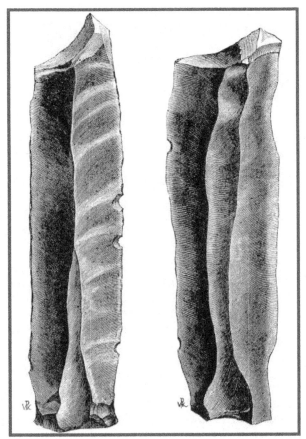

FIG. 23

Blades for gunflint production (Skertchley 1879).

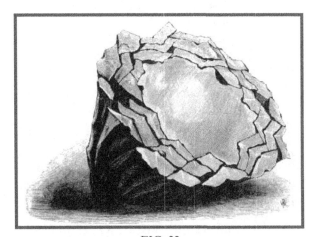

FIG. 22

Blade core for gunflint production (Skertchley 1879).

The gunflints acquired their final form by retouch of their lateral sides and, occasionally, the heel. They were subdivided into two main categories, namely double-backed pieces ('bests', and if slightly too thin or otherwise compromised, 'seconds') and single-backed pieces ('commons'). The pieces referred to as 'bests' would in most cases receive inverse trim of both ends, effectively providing them with two leading edges. It was possible for a good 'flaker' to produce up to 10,000 blades per day, whereas an experienced 'knapper' was able to produce 3,000–4,000 gunflints per day.[101]

At the beginning of the Napoleonic Wars, the Board of Ordnance commissioned nine Brandon gunflint makers to supply 360,000 pieces per month.[102] By 1813, the Board of Ordnance ordered the supply of 1,060,000 flints per month.[103] Although the manufacture of gunflints at Brandon decreased considerably after the Napoleonic Wars, the Turkish Government ordered 11,000,000 gunflints just prior to the Crimean War 1853–56, and in 1868 the output at Brandon was approximately 200,000–250,000 per week.[104]

OTHER GUNFLINTS

Although general gunflint literature indicates that practically all gunflints used in Europe through the 18th and 19th centuries, as well as in most European colonies, were of the well-known standardized types produced in either France or Britain,[105] other countries and regions also produced gunflints. As mentioned above, gunflints were produced in flint-rich Denmark for centuries,[106] although generally in the form of traditional D-shaped gunspalls. In fact, most countries had their own gunflint industries, which would be considered of strategic importance.

A recent paper by Woodall and Chelidonio presents and discusses a regional Italian (Venetian Republic) gunflint industry.[107] They focused on one workshop, the so-called Benedetti Site, where gunflints were produced from discoidal and flat, tabular cores, from which short blades were detached by the application of hard percussion.[108] The raw material is very akin to some forms of French flint, but the actual gunflints were shaped like British rectangular blade gunflints.[109] The date of this industry is uncertain, but the general shape of the gunflints, as well as the operational schema responsible for their production, indicates a date slightly before or after 1800.

A 1996 study of Andalusian gunflint manufacture, by Roncal los Arcos et al.,[110] compared the industries of Andalusia with other European industries. They documented local Andalusian gunspall[111] as well as blade gunflint workshops,[112] where gunflints were manufactured using techniques adapted to local raw materials and traditions. In 1897 Evans illustrated a beautiful Albanian piece,[113] which was, apparently, produced by the application of invasive dorsal retouch, whereas the ventral face seems to have been left untouched.

In the American colonies, bifacial Native American gunflints were particularly common in the so-called Contact Period, and Blanchette suggests that they may dominate many early 17th-century sites.[114] At Plymouth Colony in Massachusetts (1620–92), they amount to c. 6% of all gunflints,[115] and remain common at many American Frontier locations, such as the Gilbert Site in north-east Texas.[116]

Although the well-known French and British gunflints were generally based on a small number of easily recognizable flint types (mostly various browns, greys and blacks), gunflints were also produced in local raw materials throughout the world, such as quartz, chalcedony, agate, and chert.

DISCUSSION

When the evidence for British, French, and American gunflint production and use is examined, it is clear that production was standardized from an early time, probably first in the form of generally preferred well-functioning shapes and sizes, and, later, in the form of government-prescribed shapes and sizes (Table 2). To obtain the intended gunflint forms, proven, or, later, standardized technological approaches were followed, in shaping the gunflint cores and blanks, as well as individual implements. However, it is apparent that, at most times, 'deviant' gunflint forms and technological approaches also existed.

The question is, to what extent a specific assemblage and its typo-technological composition represents a link in a geographically broader evolutionary schema (for example, covering Britain, France, and/or America), or whether it may represent a local branch on the 'evolutionary tree', or even a single event, that is, 'an aberration'. This question is discussed here in the context of the Dun Eistean finds; that is, does the early Dun Eistean assemblage represent general British gunflint evolution or simply local circumstance (e.g. local raw material availability/scarcity, or even a specific conflict event).

The general date of the Dun Eistean finds, in the range 1465–1670,[117] suggests that the site's gunflints are early and belong to the category 'early wedges or gunspalls'. According to de Lotbiniere,[118] the period from 1550 to 1650 is characterized by 'crude do-it-yourself' gunflints, and the distribution of the site's gunflints across several rather plain formal categories indicates that the Dun Eistean gunflints belong to this group. Two pieces (CAT 249, 318) are D-shaped gunspalls, and several fragments may be from D-shaped specimens, but the remainder do not fit any generally recognized formal types. For example, pieces with a straight heel (CAT 84, 199, 295), as well as the so-called 'quadrilaterals' (CAT 150, 158), have nothing in common with the later rectangular gunflints, apart from names suggesting a square to rectangular outline.

Types such as 'minimally shaped pieces' and 'thin quadrilaterals' are less durable than other gunflints, either because they lack strengthening modification of their leading edges, or because of their general thinness. It is possible that they may represent adaptation to a unique historic situation, which required the site's gunflint stocks to be urgently replenished (possibly a conflict event, such as a siege).[119] Their general attributes may be the result of the use of blanks, which would normally have been deemed unsuitable, as well as expedient (i.e. fast) modification. However, although most of the gunflints from this Western Isles location may fit the formal description of 'crude do-it-yourself types', they probably differ significantly from other early British, and presumably also Colonial American, assemblages, in their applied technology. The earliest gunflints from southern Britain, as well as those from the so-called 'Contact Period' in Colonial America, appear to have been based on traditional hard-percussion platform technique.[120] The Dun Eistean gunflints, on the other hand, are based on the splitting of pebbles by the use of an anvil and a hammer (bipolar technique), followed by modification of the resulting irregular blanks by hard percussion.

In prehistoric times,[121] bipolar technique was particularly common along the Scottish west coast, due to the fairly small size of local flint pebbles. It is generally accepted that small pebbles are ill-suited for platform technique.[122] This is because: 1) they do not contain sufficient mass to allow the necessary decortication and preparation of platforms, flaking-fronts and platform-edges; 2) due to their small size and curved exterior, primary blows tend to glance off them; 3) small pebbles have so little mass that a blow tends to move the hand and pebble, rather than detach a flake. This may be the rationale behind the dominance of bipolar technique at Dun Eistean, as the pebbles from this location were also generally small, having been obtained by 'combing' the local beaches, as well as heaps of dumped ballast flint (cf. the collected raw pebbles retained as part of the assemblage). In southern Britain, where better flint was more readily available in the form of larger nodules, there was no reason to apply a technique which is considered less controllable than traditional platform techniques, and it is thought that hard percussion may have been the dominant approach.

It is not possible to determine with certainty whether the application of bipolar technique at Dun Eistean represents adaptation to a conflict event, or whether it represents a technological approach more generally applied at the time along the Scottish western seaboard (where the only available flint was in the form of small pebbles). However, the operational schema of the Dun Eistean gunflint industry does seem to be logically structured, supporting the latter option. The strict technological definition of the schema's main stages, with a first bipolar stage (detaching the blanks) and a second hard-percussion stage (modifying the blanks into gunflints) has the appearance of a tradition, rather than ad hoc, spur-of-the-moment adaptation.

Two possible scenarios are therefore suggested for the Dun Eistean gunflint industry.[123] In the first place, the industry in general, with its well-structured operational schema, may represent a general West of Scotland approach, where the most was made of a scarce resource (a combination of relatively poor beach flint and dumped ballast flint). In the second place, the flimsier, poorly shaped gunflints may owe their physical appearance to a specific conflict event, where blanks were used which would otherwise have been rejected, and where they were modified as speedily as possible.

The assemblage from Fort Argyle in the American Georgia Colony (c. 1730–60) may not be the product of a single conflict event, but it probably does represent a 'stressed' situation, in the sense that regular supplies may have been hampered by the remote location and its status as a Frontier fort.[124] The assemblage of 45 gunflints is clearly dominated by gunspalls, and only one 'French' blade gunflint was recovered (it is uncertain whether it was defined as 'French' by its shape or by the fact that it is in honey-brown flint, or both). All pieces are heavily used and rejuvenated, and illustrated examples indicate that the flints (which appear to be slightly irregular in shape) may have been produced by individual rangers, rather than representing importation from a specialized industry in the 'mother country'.[125] This is also confirmed by the fact that the flint is clearly ballast flint. The existence of a 'stressed' situation at Fort Argyle is further confirmed by the fact that one gunflint is based on a shard of green bottle glass. The author discusses gunflint size at length (generally L = 13–36mm), and suggests that the guns used at the fort must have been surprisingly small, compared with the arsenal of other Colonial American forts of the time.[126] However, it should be borne in mind that in a 'stressed' situation (for example, infrequent supplies) even the smallest flint would have been useful, as it would have been able to produce a spark, thus discharging the weapon.[127] However, at Dun Eistean, the small gunflint sizes probably *do* reflect the local arsenal accurately, as they match the small sizes of recovered lead-shots,[128] indicating that pistols may have been more common at the site than larger firearms.

The interpretation of the Dun Eistean assemblage suggested here, and the impact of a possible 'stressed' situation (partly the scarcity of good flint along the western Scottish seaboard, and partly the effects on gunflint form of a possible conflict event) should be tested when more material is made available by future excavations in the region. However, it is also important that, in general, more early assemblages are made available in national/ international archaeological/historical journals that are more widely accessible than local journals. The study of gunflint production and use in any one country — Britain, France or America — is of importance to the understanding of the wider phenomenon of their development and impact in the Old World as well as in the emerging North Atlantic world.

ACKNOWLEDGEMENTS

The author would like to thank the Society of Antiquaries of Scotland for grant-aiding the Gunflint Project; Dr David Caldwell, Keeper of Scotland and Europe, National Museums Scotland, and Dr Stuart Campbell, Treasure Trove Unit, National Museums Scotland, for advice and comments on the manuscript; Beverley Ballin Smith, Glasgow University Archaeological Research Unit, for permission to use information on the assemblage from Dun Eistean; and Charlotte Francoz, Glasgow University's Archaeological Research Unit, for allowing me to redraw/simplify her site plan of Dun Eistean. The Dun Eistean site archive is held by the NMR for Scotland, RCAHMS, Edinburgh.

NOTES

[1] e.g. Skertchley 1879; Chandler 1917; de Lotbiniere 1977; 1984; Delaney 1989; Fowler 1989; McNabb & Ashton 1990; Whittaker 2001.

[2] e.g. Stone 1974; Blanchette 1975; White 1975; Hanson & Hsu 1975; Kenmotsu 1990; Elliott 1997; Davis *et al.* 1998; PARP 2002; Quinn 2004.

[3] e.g. Witthoft 1966.

[4] e.g. Smith 1960; Blanchette 1975.

[5] e.g. 'Nordic' and 'Dutch' gunflints.

[6] Not least by including important Web-based contributions.

[7] For example, the various colonies and the gunflint trade.

[8] For example, siege or blockade situations and subsequent raw material shortages.

[9] Dolomieu 1960.

[10] Blanchette 1975.

[11] De Lotbiniere 1984.

[12] Blanchette 1975.

[13] e.g. Hanson & Hsu 1975, Fig. 43; Davis *et al.* 1998, fig. 327.

[14] e.g. Inizan *et al.* 1992, 37.

[15] Ashton *et al.* 1991.

[16] McNabb & Ashton 1990, fig. 1.

[17] Ballin 2005.

[18] The author discussed this phenomenon with Dr Stuart Campbell, National Museums Scotland, who commented: 'In precise terms, when the main charge ignites in a flintlock there is a high-pressure bleed-off which exits the touchhole as a high-temperature cloud of gas. This was of sufficient temperature that the 18th century Danish army rather sensibly fitted pan guards to their weapons ... I think this is a very probable cause of the polish or powder-burn'.

[19] Kenmotsu 1990, 103.

[20] Skertchley (1879) noted that 'a good flint will last a gunner about half a day'.

[21] e.g. de Lotbiniere 1984, 206.

[22] See Inizan *et al.* 1992.

[23] Witthoft 1966.

[24] Beckman 1846; this is itself a translation of a text *c.* 50 years earlier.

[25] White 1975.

[26] White 1975, 67.

[27] Witthoft 1966, 26.

[28] Witthoft 1966, 30.

[29] White 1975, 67.

[30] White 1975, 71.

[31] Hess 1968.

[32] See also de Lotbiniere 1984, 209: '... the Danes made wedges only'.

[33] Witthoft 1966, 22.

[34] Hess 1968.

[35] Hess 1968.

[36] cf. White 1975, fig. 1.

[37] De Lotbiniere 1984, 207.

[38] Dr Stuart Campbell, National Museums Scotland, comments on de Lotbiniere's claim: 'While not disregarding the possibility completely, unless there are good first hand accounts of this I suspect this is a retroactive justification. I say this as, by the last half of the 18th century, there is an increasing tendency in the British Army to use lead wraps between flint and cock-jaws to aid the grip. By about 1790, this appears to be universal. A good number of these wraps were designed to be wrapped around the rear of the flint and were not removable after firing'. Dr Campbell's comment is highly relevant, and use-wear analysis

may show whether the most symmetrical rectangular gunflints were turned or not. A used leading edge would almost always show distinct chipping.

[39] e.g. de Lotbiniere 1984, 207; also see Delaney's 1989 account of gunflints from two French 18th-century shipwrecks in the Pacific.

[40] De Lotbiniere 1984, 206.

[41] Skertchley 1879, 47.

[42] A translation of the French term 'ordinaire'; Delaney 1989, 113.

[43] De Lotbiniere 1984, 207.

[44] De Lotbiniere 1984, 207.

[45] Blanchette 1975.

[46] PARP 2002.

[47] By this the author probably means the leading edge; see Fig. 1.

[48] <http://plymoutharch.tripod.com/id71.html> [accessed 28 December 2011].

[49] Carovillano 2002.

[50] Barrowman 2007.

[51] Barrowman 2007.

[52] Outram & Batt 2010.

[53] Ballin forthcoming a.

[54] Ballin forthcoming a.

[55] Ballin 2011.

[56] e.g. Chandler 1917, 360.

[57] Ballin forthcoming b.

[58] Ballin 1999.

[59] cf. Ballin 2005.

[60] Use-wear suggests that some of these may also have been used as fire-flints.

[61] At the site, lead projectiles have been recovered from the turf walls of structures facing the Lewisian mainland: Barrowman forthcoming.

[62] Koch 1990; Mikkelsen 1991; 1994; Stapert & Johansen 1999; Ballin 2005.

[63] Carovillano 2002.

[64] Kidd 2006.

[65] Kidd 2006, 68.

[66] Ballin 2007; forthcoming b.

[67] Davis 1997, 9; Whittaker 2001.

[68] cf. Whittaker 2001.

[69] Chandler 1917.

[70] McNabb & Ashton 1990.

[71] Ashton et al. 1991.

[72] Inizan et al. 1992, 57.

[73] Chandler 1917, fig. 65.

[74] See also McNabb & Ashton 1990, fig. 1.

[75] De Lotbiniere 1984.

[76] De Lotbiniere 1984, 206.

[77] cf. Fowler 1989.

[78] De Lotbiniere 1984, 207.

[79] Hanson & Hsu 1975, 72.

[80] De Lotbiniere 1977, 43.

[81] Skertchley 1879.

[82] De Lotbiniere 1984, 207.

[83] De Lotbiniere 1984, 207.

[84] TNA: PRO WO 47/50, 282.

[85] Bingeman 2004.

[86] De Lotbiniere 1984, 207.

[87] De Lotbiniere 1984, 206.

[88] Ballin 2005.

[89] e.g. Blanchette 1975.

[90] De Lotbiniere 1977, 44.

[91] According to Dolomieu (1960, 60), up to 50 pieces per core.

[92] Woodward 1960, 35.

[93] Delaney 1989, tables 1–2, fig. 7.

[94] Crompton 2004.

[95] De Lotbiniere 1977, 41.

[96] De Lotbiniere 1977, 45.

[97] White 1975, 70.

[98] Tomlinson 1852, 689.

[99] Dolomieu 1960.

[100] Described in great detail by Skertchley 1879.

[101] Skertchley 1879, 30, 33.

[102] de Lotbinniere 1977, 46.

[103] Mason n.d.

[104] Davis 1997.

[105] At least through an almost total neglect of non-French and non-British gunflint industries.

[106] Hess 1968.

[107] Woodall & Chelidonio 2006.

[108] Woodall & Chelidonio 2006, figs 4, 13–14.

[109] Woodall & Chelidonio 2006, fig. 8.

[110] Roncal los Arcos et al. 1996.

[111] Roncal los Arcos et al. 1996, fig. 4.

[112] Roncal los Arcos et al. 1996, fig. 5.

[113] Evans 1897, 21.

[114] Blanchette 1975, fig. 11.

[115] PARP 2002.

[116] Blaine 2001.

[117] Outram & Batt 2010.

[118] De Lotbiniere 1984.

[119] Ballin forthcoming a.

[120] According to de Lotbiniere (1984, 206), it was their prominent bulb-of-percussion which gave them their 'wedge' shape.

[121] e.g. Ballin 1999.

[122] e.g. Finlayson 2000, 105; Callahan 1987, 63.

[123] It should be borne in mind that not all gunflints or waste from the site's gunflint production is necessarily contemporary.

[124] Elliott 1997.

[125] Elliott 1997, fig. 54.

[126] Elliott 1997, 164.

[127] This may be the rationale behind the mid 18th-century note from the Ordnance Board that musket and carbine flints could be used for quarterdeck guns.

[128] Barrowman forthcoming.

BIBLIOGRAPHY

Ashton, N., Dean, P. & McNabb, J. 1991, 'Flaked flakes: what, when and why?', *Lithics* **12**, 1–11.

Ballin, T.B. 1999, 'Bipolar cores in Southern Norway — classification, chronology and geography', *Lithics* **20**, 13–22.

Ballin, T.B. 2005, 'Lithic artefacts and pottery from Townparks, Antrim Town', *Ulster Archaeol. J.* **64**, 12–25.

Ballin, T.B. 2007, 'The lithic assemblage', in Cox 2007, 175–7.

Ballin, T.B. 2011, *Overhowden and Airhouse, Scottish Borders. Characterization and Interpretation of Two Spectacular Lithic Assemblages from Sites near the Overhowden Henge*, Brit. Archaeol. Rep. Brit. Ser. **539**, Oxford: Archaeopress.

Ballin, T.B. forthcoming a, 'The lithic assemblage', in Barrowman forthcoming.

Ballin, T.B. forthcoming b, 'The lithic assemblage', in Cameron forthcoming.

Barrowman, R. 2007, 'Dun Eistean Archaeology Project Excavations 2007: Data Structure Report', Glasgow University Archaeological Research Division unpubl. rep. 2378.

Barrowman R. (ed.) forthcoming, *Dun Eistean — its History and Archaeology*.

Beckman, J. 1846, *A History of Inventions, Discoveries and Origins*, London: Henry G. Bohn.

Bingeman, J.M. 2004, *Gunlocks: their Introduction to the Navy*, <http://www.invincible1758.co.uk/gun_flints.htm> [accessed 31 December 2011].

Blaine, J.C. 2001, *An Eighteenth-Century French Connection in East Texas*, <http://www.texasbeyondhistory.net/gilbert/french.html> [accessed 31 December 2011].

Blanchette, J.-F. 1975, 'Gunflints from Chicoutimi Indian Site (Québec)', *Hist. Archaeol.* **9**, 41–54.

Callahan, E. 1987, *An Evaluation of the Lithic Technology in Middle Sweden during the Mesolithic and Neolithic*, Uppsala: Societas Archaeologica Upsaliensis.

Cameron, A. forthcoming, 'Excavations at the Green, Aberdeen: a Medieval Carmelite House Revealed'.

Carovillano, J.R. 2002, *Worked Ballast Flint at Den Rock*, <http://www.schtick.net/2002/5/03strikea light.htm> [accessed 22 September 2009; now removed from the Internet, but subsequently submitted as a thesis at University of Massachusetts, Boston, USA).

Chandler, R.H. 1917, 'Some supposed gun flint sites', *Proc. Prehist. Soc. East Anglia* **2**, 360–5.

Cox, A. 2007, 'Excavations at Horse Cross, Perth', *Tayside Fife Archaeol. J.* **13**, 112–206.

Crompton, A. 2004, *17th century gunflints found at Le Vieux Fort, Placentia*, <http://www.arts.mun.ca/nahop/image_pages/Gunflints.html> [accessed 31 December 2010].

Davis, R.S. 1997, *Technology in Stone, Notes*, <http://www.coursehero.com/file/2003170/chippedstone/> [accessed 1 September 2010; now only available for a fee].

Davis, R.P.S., Livingood, P.C., Ward, H.T. & Steponatis, V.P. 1998, *Excavating Occaneeshi Town*, Chapel Hill: University of North Carolina Press.

Delaney, W. 1989, 'An examination of gunflints recovered from the La Pérouse shipwrecks, L'Astrolabe and La Boussole, Vanicoro, Solomon Islands', *Int. J. Naut. Archaeol. Underwater Explor.* **18**, 113–22.

De Lotbiniere, S. 1977, 'The story of the English gunflint — some theories and queries', *Arms Armour Soc. J.* **9**, 18–53.

De Lotbiniere, S. 1984, 'Gunflint recognition', *Int. J. Naut. Archaeol. Underwater Explor.* **13**, 206–9.

Dolomieu, T. 1960 [1797], 'Report on the art of making gunflints (fire-flint)', *Missouri Archaeol.* **22**, 50–61 [translation of 'Memoire sur l'art de tailler de pierres à fusil (silex pyromaque)', *Journal de Mines* **6**, 693–712].

Downes, J., & Lamb, R. 2000, *Prehistoric Houses at Sumburgh in Shetland: Excavations at Sumburgh Airport 1967–74*, Oxford: Oxbow Books.

Elliott, D.T. 1997, *Argyle: Historical Archaeological Study of a Colonial Fort in Bryan County, Georgia*, Washington (DC): United States Department of Defense, Legacy Resource Management Program.

Evans, S.J. 1897, *The Ancient Stone Implements, Weapons and Ornaments of Great Britain*, London: Longmans, Green.

Finlayson, B. 2000, 'Chipped stone assemblage', in Downes & Lamb 2000, 104–9.

Fowler, M.J.F. 1989, 'Hampshire gunflint industries', *Hampshire Field Club Archaeol. Soc.*, new ser. **12**, 24–6.

Hanson, L. & Hsu, D.-P. 1975, *Casemates and Cannonballs: Archeological Investigations at Fort Stanwix National Monument, Rome, New York*, Public. Archaeol. **14**, Washington: US Department of the Interior, National Park Service.

Hess, C. 1968, 'De glemte flinthuggere fra Stevns', *Skalk* **1968**:5, 9–15.

Inizan, M.-L., Roche, H. & Tixier, J. 1992, *Technology of Knapped Stone*, Préhistoire de la Pierre Taillée **3**, Meudon: Cercle de Recherches et d'Études Préhistoriques.

Kenmotsu, N. 1990, 'Gunflints: a study', *Hist. Archaeol.* **24**, 92–124.

Kidd, R.S. 2006, 'An Archaeological Examination of Slave Life in the Danish West Indies: Analysis of the Material Culture of a Caribbean Slave Village, Illustrating Economic Provisioning and

Torben Bjark Ballin

Acquisition Preferences', Department of Anthropology, Florida State University Masters thesis.

Koch, E. 1990, 'Fire', *Skalk* **1990**:5, 16–17.

Mason, A. n.d., *From Flint Axe to Gunflint: the Brecks*, Thetford: Ancient House Museum. Also accessible online at <http://www.brecks.org/shared/pdfs/AxetoFlintleaflet.pdf> [accessed 2 January 2012].

McNabb, J. & Ashton, N. 1990, 'Clactonian gunflints', *Lithics* **11**, 44–7.

Mikkelsen, E. 1991, 'Flintmaterialet', in Schia & Molaug 1991, 251–71.

Mikkelsen, E. 1994, *Fangstprodukter i vikingtidens og middelalderens økonomi. Organiseringen av massefangst av villrein i Dovre*, Skrifter, Ny rekke **18**, Oslo: Universitetets Oldsaksamling.

Outram, Z. & Batt, C.M. 2010, 'The Dating Evidence from Dun Eistean, Lewis', School of Life Sciences, Division of Archaeological, Geological and Environmental Sciences, University of Bradford unpubl. rep.

PARP 2002, *Fire-arms in Plymouth Colony*, <http://plymoutharch.tripod.com/id71.html> [accessed 31 December 2011].

Quinn, C. 2004, 'An experimental use-wear and functional analysis of gunflints', *Lambda Alpha J.* **34**, 60–71.

Roncal los Arcos, M.E., Martinez Fernandez, G. & Morgado Rodriguez, A. 1996, 'Las piedras de chispa: una producción lítica olvidada en España', *Munibe Antropologia-Arkeologia* **48**, 105–23.

Schia, E. & Molaug, P.B. (eds) 1991, *De arkeologiske utgravninger i Gamlebyen, Oslo* **8**. *Dagliglivets gjenstander — Del II*, Øvre Ervik: Alvheim & Eide/Akademisk Forlag.

Skertchley, S.B.J. 1879, *On the Manufacture of Gunflints, the Methods of Excavating for Flint, the Age of Palaeolithic Man, and the Connection between Neolithic Art and the Gunflint Trade*, Memoirs of the Geological Survey of England and Wales, London: HMSO.

Smith, C. 1960, 'Two eighteenth century reports on the manufacture of gunflints in France', *Missouri Archaeol.* **22**, 40–50.

Stapert, D. & Johansen, L. 1999, 'Flint and pyrite: making fire in the Stone Age', *Antiquity* **73**:282, 765–77.

Stone, L.M. 1974, *Fort Michilimackinac 1715–1781. An Archaeological Perspective on the Revolutionary Frontier*, East Lansing: The Museum, Michigan State University.

Tomlinson, C. 1852, 'Flint', *The Cyclopaedia of Useful Arts and Manufacturers* **1**, London: John S. Virtue, 688–90.

Weisgerber G. (ed.) 2006, *Stone Age — Mining Age. Proceedings of the VIII International Flint Symposium, Bochum, 1999*, Bochum: Deutsches Bergbau-Museum.

White, S.W. 1975, 'On the origins of gunspalls', *Hist. Archaeol.* **9**, 65–73.

Whittaker, J. 2001, '"The oldest British industry": continuity and obsolescence in a flintknapper's sample set', *Antiquity* **75**, 382–90.

Witthoft, J. 1966, 'A history of gunflints', *Pennsylvania Archaeol.* **36**:1–2, 12–49.

Woodward, A. 1960, 'Some notes on gunflints', *Missouri Archaeol.* **22**, 29–39.

Woodall, J.N. & Chelidonio, G. 2006, 'Gunflint workshop traces in the Lessini Mountains (Verona, Italy). Flintknappers and smugglers at the end of the Venetian Republic', in Weisgerber 2006, 213–26.

ABBREVIATIONS

PARP	Plymouth Archaeological Rediscovery Project
RCAHMS	Royal Commission on Ancient and Historical Monuments of Scotland
TNA: PRO	The National Archives: Public Record Office (Kew)

SUMMARY IN FRENCH, GERMAN, ITALIAN AND SPANISH

RÉSUMÉ
'Etat de l'art' de la recherche sur la pierre à fusil de Grande-Bretagne, avec un intérêt particulier pour l'atelier des premières pierres à fusil de Dun Eistean, Lewis

De nombreux malentendus suscités par une utilisation peu critique de la littérature fallacieuse ont affecté la terminologie et la typologie de la pierre à fusil, prévenant ainsi l'établissement d'une chronologie fiable. Cet article traite de la terminologie de la pierre à fusil à partir des recherches récentes, permettant ainsi de proposer une typo-chronologie. La plupart des assemblages de pierre à fusil connus par la littérature archéologique tendent à être récents et bon nombre des problèmes de terminologie et de typologie semblent en général liés aux pierres à fusil des XVIᵉ–XVIIᵉ siècles. Une attention toute particulière a donc été portée à l'assemblage de pierres à fusil plus anciennes récemment découvert à Dun Eistean, Lewis, Hébrides extérieures (Ecosse).

ZUSAMMENFASSUNG
'Stand der Technik' bei der Untersuchung britischer 'Gunflint' besonders im Hinblick auf frühe Gunflint-Werkstätten in Dun Eistean, Lewis

Unkritischer Gebrauch von fehlerhafter Literatur hat erlaubt, dass eine Reihe von Missverständnissen bei dem Gebrauch des Ausdrucks und der Typologie für „Gunflint", (eine geologische Eisenformation) aufgetreten ist, was die Herstellung einer verlässlichen Chronologie verhindert hat. Dieser Artikel erläutert die Gunflint-Terminologie, indem auf die jüngsten Recherchen dieses Themas hingewiesen und auf dieser Basis eine Gunflint-Typo-Chronologie vorgeschlagen wird. Da die meisten durch die archäologische Literatur bekannten britischen Gunflint-Ansammlungen ein spätes Datum haben, und die meisten terminologisch/ typologischen Probleme hauptsächlich dem 16./17. Jahrhundert zugeordnet sind, ist der jüngst gefundenen, frühen Gruppe von Dun Eistean, Lewis, Western Isles, besondere Aufmerksamkeit gewidmet.

RIASSUNTO
Status quaestionis *della ricerca sugli acciarini, con speciale attenzione agli esordi della bottega di acciarini a Dun Eistean, Lewis*
Un uso acritico di testi inesatti ha portato a numerosi fraintesi che si ripercuotono sulla terminologia e la tipologia degli acciarini, impedendo di conseguenza il raggiungimento di una cronologia affidabile. Facendo riferimento alla più recente ricerca su questo argomento, il presente articolo discute la terminologia usata per gli acciarini, suggerendo, a partire da questa, una tipo-cronologia degli stessi. Poiché la maggior parte dei contesti con la presenza di acciarini noti attraverso la letteratura archeologica sono generalmente tardi, e la maggior parte dei problemi terminologici/tipologici si riferiscono in generale agli acciarini del XVI–XVII secolo, speciale attenzione è stata dedicata al nucleo rinvenuto presso Dun Eistean, a Lewis, Western Isles.

RESUMEN
Un estudio moderno sobre las piedras de fusil británicas, con especial énfasis en el taller temprano de pedernal de Dun Eistean, Lewis
El uso no crítico de algunas publicaciones inexactas ha permitido la difusión de una serie de malentendidos sobre la terminología y la tipología de las piedras de fusil, lo que a su vez ha impedido el establecimiento de una cronología fiable. Este artículo trata de la terminología de las piedras de fusil, sugiriendo una tipo-cronología para las mismas. Ya que la mayoría de los conjuntos británicos publicados tienden a ser tardíos y la mayoría de los problemas de terminología y tipología están relacionados con ejemplares de los siglos XVI y XVII, el conjunto recientemente descubierto en Dun Eistean, Lewis, Hébridas Occidentales, ha recibido especial atención en este estudio.

Lithic Research, Banknock Cottage, Denny, Stirlingshire FK6 5NA, UK
[lithicresearch@btinternet.com]

This paper is published with financial assistance from the Society of Antiquaries of Scotland

DATING EARLY PLAIN BUTTONS BY THEIR FORM

Stanley J. Olsen

Abstract

Very little has been published to date relating to the manufacture of early buttons. This is particularly true of plain, nonmilitary buttons which lack makers' names on their backs. Enough evidence has been assembled from dated garments or excavations to warrant a description of basic button styles, particularly when these styles can be assigned dates of manufacture to aid the archaeologist in the interpretation of his sites.

MILITARY BUTTONS bearing faces with unit or branch insignia, or those having backs with makers' names, can be assigned dates with some certainty (Olsen and Campbell 1962). However, from archaeological sites are recovered many plain buttons that have distinctive patterns, particularly as to the means of attachment, and these can be given approximate dates of manufacture based on their form alone.

This brief contribution deals only with plain 18th- and 19th-century examples, having no face ornamentation or makers' names stamped on their backs. Some of these buttons, however, were worn by the regular armed forces as well as by civilians and militia, and their use will be explained in the discussion.

As a rule early buttons were plain, of cast brass, pewter, or whitemetal with wedge-shaped cast shanks (Fig. 1 a); others had wooden or bone backs overlapped with thin metal fronts, usually of silver (Fig. 1 b). In 1767 the British War Office issued an order to the effect that regimental numbers were to be placed on buttons of officers and men of other ranks. This order was not universally adopted, and some officers as well as civilians continued to wear the plain "gentlemen's" button of bone and silver. Soldiers of the Continental Army followed the same practice from about 1784.

About the time of the French and Indian War, a popular cast button was one of plain whitemetal with an iron-wire shank or eye let into a boss at the button back (Fig. 1 c). This same type of button was also in use by the American and British armies during the Revolution, but differed in having cast unit or branch designations on the button faces.

Spun-back buttons were used by both civilians and the military from about 1760 until the close of the Revolution. Buttons of this type (Fig. 1 d) were cast from whitemetal or brass and with a brass-wire eye set into a boss on the button back. The cast button was held in a chuck and spun, while a tool cut the button back to the desired thickness. A burred edge around the eye and the concentric tool marks usually identify this type. Examination of several pairs of knee-length breeches that were worn during the Revolution revealed that this style of button was used as a fastening device. They were, however, covered with the same material as the trousers.

Plain cast whitemetal buttons with a heavy eye, cast at the same time as the button, were in use from the mid-1700's until well into the 19th century (Fig. 1 e). Many homes of this period had button molds that could produce six or seven buttons from each pouring. The U.S. Army used this style, both plain and with official devices cast on the button face.

Among the first two-piece brass buttons were the "bullet buttons" (named for their shape) of the period of the War of 1812 (Fig. 1 f). They were used by the Army General Staff, dragoons, and surgeons, as well as by the militia. They were still in use after the War of 1812 by many organizations and military bands, but the more recent examples differ from the early buttons by having the makers' names added to the backs, making it an easier matter to assign dates of manufacture. Some manufacturers began the practice of putting their names on the backs about 1800, and it was generally accepted by most companies by the 1820's.

Plain brass or bronze buttons are the most difficult to date because of the long period of their use. The first of these was a plain coin-shaped disc having a simple brass eye fastened to the back (Fig. 1 g). There was so little surface-bearing on the button back that loss of the button due to the breaking off of the eye was common. That this was the case is attested to by the many "eyeless" buttons of this style that are recovered from early house and fort sites, with the imprint of the wire eye still visible on the soldered surface. The design to follow was logically a similar button but one with an eye having bent-over ends to give more fastening surface for the bonding metal (Fig. 1 h). Many of these buttons carry the words "Treble Gilt," "Extra Gilt," "Extra Quality," or similar slogans denoting the button quality, to catch the eye of the purchaser. Not uncommon was the practice of taking these plain-front buttons and at a later date (perhaps much later than that of manufacture) stamping a design on the front by the use of a split die. This latter practice can be identified by the split anvil seam that appears on the backs of these buttons (Fig. 1 h). These last two styles were mainly used by civilians and militia, but they were also used as Indian trade goods and by the military. When used by the regular army, they were worn inside the leather helmets as chinstrap fastenings, or inside trousers.

About the year 1830 the second major change in two-piece, stamped, brass buttons appeared (Fig. 1 i). This button style was well-received by all of the branches of the military as well as by civilians, and is still being manufactured today. When used by the armed forces, the domed face (which was considerably less than that found in the bullet buttons) bore stamped designs of appropriate styles for the various branches or units and, in most instances, makers' names also appeared on the reverse faces. Large quantities of these buttons were manufactured from the time of the Mexican War on through the Civil War. Plain-faced buttons were used by civilians and also issued as trade goods to the Indians. A considerable number of these have been recovered from Indian graves dating from the 1830's and 1840's.

Trouser buttons have been changed little from the time of their introduction, about the mid-1700's, except for the material used in their manufacture. Handmade bone buttons have turned up at many fort sites, and in all stages of construction. Button blanks usually have only the center hole that was used to index the turning tool, which was held in a manner similar to a carpenter's brace and bit. After the blanks were cut, the outside four holes were drilled to hold the button to the garment in the same manner as our present-day fastenings (Fig. 1 j). From about the time of the War of 1812 until the close of the Civil War, a plain-cast whitemetal or lead, four-hole button was commonly used on both civilians' and soldier's trousers (Fig. 1 k). Any fort site that has

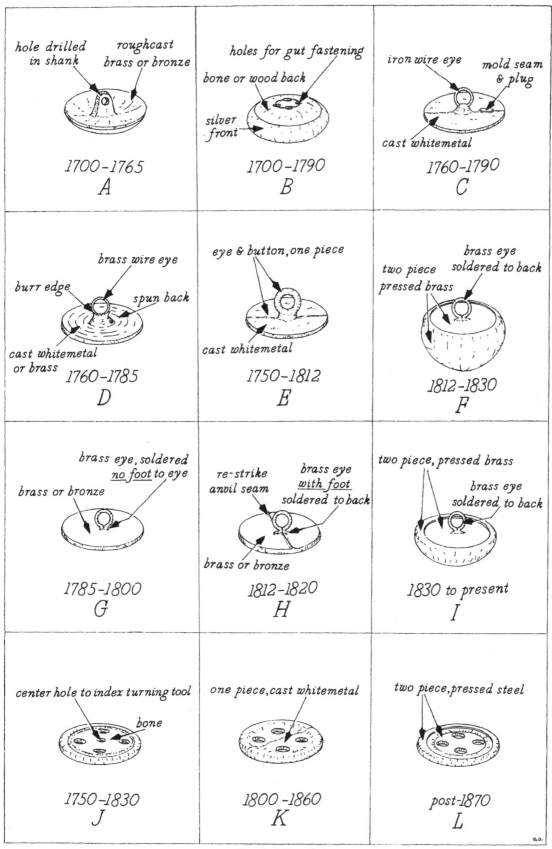

FIG. 1. [OLSEN].

been occupied over a long span of time will have a good many button types present in the soil, as for example, Fort St. Marks, Florida (1680–1875). The last button in Fig. 1 is included because it had its beginning during the Indian wars even though it is little changed from those worn in the 20th century (Fig. 1 l). It is of two-piece, stamped-steel construction with four stamped holes for fastening.

When makers' names appear on the backs of these various types of buttons, or when the button fronts bear military designs, it is an easy matter to narrow down the period of use.

Much more information is needed about these early plain buttons, particularly those worn before 1750. The writer will welcome any information that pertains to archaeological finds from this period.

Acknowledgments. Sincere appreciation and thanks are extended to Col. J. D. Campbell, a noted authority on military and civilian buttons, for his valued assistance in establishing dates for many of these forms.

The courtesies extended me by Dr. Mendel Peterson in permitting me access to the collections in the U. S. National Museum of some civilian buttons taken from dated shipwrecks are deeply appreciated.

Militia uniforms having plain buttons are scattered throughout the museums of the United States. Some fine examples are preserved in the West Point Museum under the care of Col. F. Todd. A buckskin garment (collected by Lewis and Clark) with a full complement of plain buttons was examined at the Peabody Museum, Harvard University, through the courtesy of Dr. J. O. Brew. Some early buttons from a Seminole grave are in the collections of the Florida State Museum in Gainesville, Florida, and this material was generously lent by Dr. R. P. Bullen.

OLSEN, S. J. AND J. D. CAMPBELL
    1962 Uniform Buttons as Interpretive Aids for Military Sites. *Curator*, Vol. V, No. 4, pp. 346–52. New York.

FLORIDA GEOLOGICAL SURVEY
Tallahassee, Florida
September, 1962

Analysis of Buttons from Brunswick Town and Fort Fischer

Stanley South

North Carolina Archives and History

[Florida Anthropologist 17(2):113-133]

From the excavation of the ruins of the homes and shops in Brunswick Town of the period from 1726 to 1830, two hundred and fifty-eight buttons have been recovered. Seventy-eight percent of these were recovered from the six room ruin of the Public House-Tailor Shop. The town was burned in 1776, consequently most of the ruins have a sealed-in context from 1726 to 1776. Two ruins have revealed that they were occupied between 1800 and 1830's, and buttons from this context have been recovered.

Across the Cape Fear River from Brunswick Town, on the site of Civil War Fort Fisher, is located the ruin of the lighthouse keeper's house, which was used as a headquarters by Colonel William Lamb, defender of the fort. This brick house ruin represents the period 1837 to 1865, and is documented through the original construction contract of 1837. From this context, two hundred and forty-nine buttons were recovered, as well as seven sleeve links, making a total from both sites of 507 buttons and sixty sleeve links. With this wealth of material from three isolated contexts, covering a period of one hundred and forty years, an analysis of the button types was undertaken so that some data could be made available which may prove of value to others working in the field of historic site archaeology.

A number of reference sources were examined, but none gave the type of detailed information which would prove of value in a typological analysis such as would be most useful to the archaeologist in an evaluation of buttons from an archaeological context. Apparently late 18th century and early 19th century buttons are considered "early" by some writers on the subject and therefore such studies are of limited use in comparison with buttons from early and middle 18th century contexts. One reason for this situation, is the comparative rarity of button samples from the 18th century. Costumes and museum collections have been examined by some writers on buttons and conclusions as to the button types have been made, but this approach also leaves much to be desired when it comes to comparison with buttons from known [end of page 113] archaeological contexts where percentage relationships based on a relatively large sample can provide valuable comparative typological and temporal data. Historic references and museum collections should be utilized by historic site archaeologists in studies of ceramics,

kaolin pipes, buttons, and other items of material culture, but this data is very limited in its usefulness in the interpretation of an American historic site when it is used without the archaeological data. It is through the archaeological data that the most valuable insights can be had into the material culture of a group once occupying a particular site. The approach of the historic site archaeologist is therefore one in which a synthesis is attempted utilizing the data provided by historic references and archaeological technique, analysis, and interpretation.

In conducting the analysis of the buttons from the ruins at Brunswick Town and Fort Fisher the types were established on the basis of the observable physical characteristics of form and detail. Through this approach a total of 16 button types were described for the period from 1726 to 1776, and 16 types for the period from 1800 to 1865. Three additional types characteristic of sleeve-links were described.

The description of the thirty-five button types is presented first, followed by an analysis and an interpretive summary. Throughout the paper a greater understanding can be had by frequent reference to the analysis chart accompanying the article.

In order to better comprehend the type descriptions some of the terms used should be defined. "Brass" is the term used to refer to the yellow metal composed of copper and zinc and other metals in various proportions, which was used in the manufacture of so many buttons. When the color of the metal was a definite copper color such as in those buttons which had been silverplated, the term "copper" is used. For the brittle metal buttons which have the appearance of white brass, and are made of brass with arsenic added the descriptive term "white brass" is preferred. This hard white metal is sometimes known by the term, tombac. For the soft, cast whitemetal buttons which often have the shank and the disc cast as one piece, the term "whitemetal" has been used. They may be of pewter lead or soft alloys. The buttons indicating that they were once covered with a thin layer of gold are termed "gilt", and those with a silver coating "silverplated". The term "shank" refers to the attachment on the back of the button body or "disc" through which the hole of the "eye" passes. [114]

Volume 2

425

ANALYSIS OF THE BUTTONS FROM THE RUINS AT BRUNSWICK TOWN AND FORT FISHER, N.C. 1726 - 1865

Percentage Relationship of the Button Types

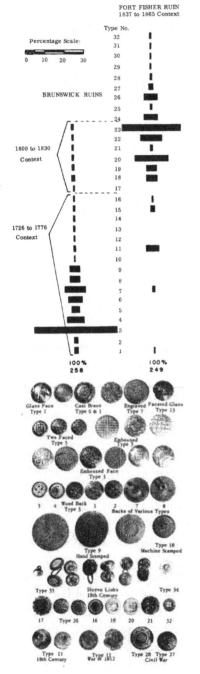

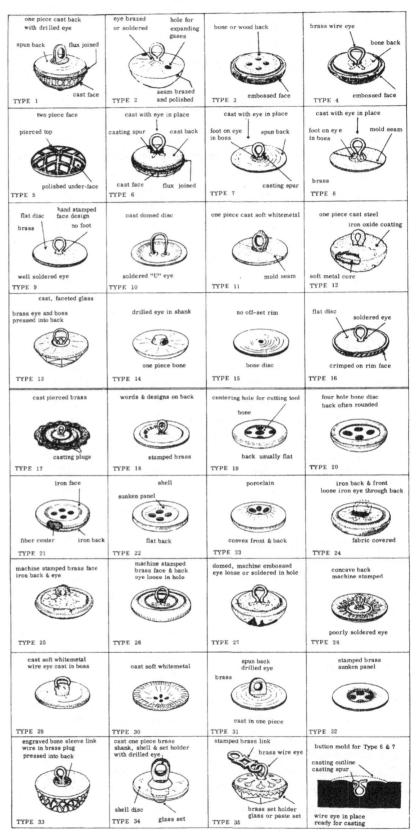

TYPE 1 — one piece cast back with drilled eye, spun back, flux joined, cast face

TYPE 2 — eye brazed or soldered, hole for expanding gases, seam brazed and polished

TYPE 3 — bone or wood back, embossed face

TYPE 4 — brass wire eye, bone back, embossed face

TYPE 5 — two piece face, pierced top, polished under-face

TYPE 6 — cast with eye in place, casting spur, cast back, cast face, flux joined

TYPE 7 — cast with eye in place, foot on eye in boss, spun back, casting spur

TYPE 8 — cast with eye in place, foot on eye in boss, mold seam, brass

TYPE 9 — flat disc, hand stamped face design, brass, no foot, well soldered eye

TYPE 10 — cast domed disc, soldered "U" eye

TYPE 11 — one piece cast soft whitemetal, mold seam

TYPE 12 — one piece cast steel, iron oxide coating, soft metal core

TYPE 13 — cast, faceted glass, brass eye and boss pressed into back

TYPE 14 — drilled eye in shank, one piece bone

TYPE 15 — no off-set rim, bone disc

TYPE 16 — flat disc, soldered eye, crimped on rim face

TYPE 17 — cast pierced brass, casting plugs

TYPE 18 — words & designs on back, stamped brass

TYPE 19 — centering hole for cutting tool, bone, back usually flat

TYPE 20 — four hole bone disc, back often rounded

TYPE 21 — iron face, fiber center, iron back

TYPE 22 — shell, sunken panel, flat back

TYPE 23 — porcelain, convex front & back

TYPE 24 — iron back & front, loose iron eye through back, fabric covered

TYPE 25 — machine stamped brass face iron back & eye

TYPE 26 — machine stamped brass face & back eye loose in hole

TYPE 27 — domed, machine embossed eye loose or soldered in hole

TYPE 28 — concave back machine stamped, poorly soldered eye

TYPE 29 — cast soft whitemetal wire eye cast in boss

TYPE 30 — cast soft whitemetal

TYPE 31 — spun back drilled eye, brass, cast in one piece

TYPE 32 — stamped brass sunken panel

TYPE 33 — engraved bone sleeve link wire in brass plug pressed into back

TYPE 34 — cast one piece brass shank, shell & set holder with drilled eye, shell disc, glass set

TYPE 35 — stamped brass link, brass wire eye, brass set holder glass or paste set

button mold for Type 6 & 7, casting outline, casting spur, wire eye in place ready for casting

N.C. DEPT. of ARCHIVES & HISTORY
South 10/63

THE BUTTON TYPES

Type 1

Cast brass with shank and back cast together. Wedge shaped shank with drilled hole. Two piece construction, with domed cast brass front with relief design. Some have vari-colored domed glass front. Back is cut by tool as it was spun to remove irregularities of casting. The two halves are bonded together with flux after being ground flat on the edges. The two halves form a hollow button with a very neat hairline seam at the edge.

Context: 1726-1776

Comments: The size is 15, 18, or 20mm. across. No flat wedge type disc buttons have been found except in the small sleeve-link size. Front design is often varities [sic] of the Tudor Rose.

Type 2

Domed brass type with halves brazed together to form a sharp smooth edge. Brass wire eye extends through back half and is soldered in place. Hole for expanding gases on each side of eye characterizes this type. Face is usually smooth, but may have face design made during casting.

Context: 1726-1776

Comments: Size is from 12 to 20 mm. across. One example has iron wire eye. This type button was worn by British and French soldiers prior to 1768, when regimental numbers were placed on buttons. (Campbell, ms. p. 7) (Calver & Bolton, p. 229).

Type 3

Domed, thin, embossed brass or copper faces with a wide variety of designs. Frequently gilt or silverplated. The front is crimped over a domed bone or wooden back with four holes. The back has a thinned rim grooved to receive the crimped metal front.

Context: 1726-1776

Comments: Size is about 15 to 30 mm. across. This is the major type recovered from the Brunswick Town ruins, comprising 42 percent of all buttons recovered. Of this type, 16 percent were embossed with imitations of various fabrics, 8 percent were plain, and the remainder were of various designs. Fifty-two percent showed signs of gilt 8 percent were silverplated, and 60 percent [115] were brass or copper, some of which may have originally been covered with gilt. Many of this type are represented only by the embossed face, the wooden back having been destroyed through decay. A number still have the bone backs in place, and several wooden backs have been preserved by action of the copper oxide from the face.

Type 4

Same as Type 3 with the difference lying in the bone back. Instead of four holes there is only one center hole through which a brass wire eye is inserted and bent over. Several bone backs with eye in place but with the front missing have been found. Fronts with no backs attached were included with Type 3.

Context: 1726-1776

Comments: Two related examples have an iron disc back with iron eye.

Type 5

Domed, thin, embossed brass or copper front with pierced areas in the design. Behind this pierced face is a smooth second face providing depth of appearance. Behind these two faces is a bone or wooden back with four holes, or one hole, and an eye of brass wire as in Type 3 and 4.

Context: 1726-1776

Comments: This four piece button is one of the more elaborate forms.

Type 6

Cast brass or copper face with Tudor Rose and other designs. Domed brass or white brass back with brass wire eye extending through back. Eye is fastened in place at the time of casting, with metal from the back conforming to the shape of the eye, producing a "burr" or "spur" on each side of the eye. Back and front halves are ground at edges to insure close fit as in Type 1. Front and back fastened together with adhesive flux. Fine seam around edge where back and front meet.

Context: 1726-1776

Comments: The same basic type as Type 1 with the exception of the eye. Some examples have spun, tooled backs to remove the irregularities of casting. Some have had the spur on each side of the eye removed with a file, the marks of which can be seen. A related example [116] has iron backs and eyes.

Type 7

Brass or white brass discs with brass wire eye fastened to back during casting. The foot and ends of the eye on the button were turned out to form a foot before casting—this foot is usually hidden by the cast boss. The irregularities of the cast back are removed by a cutting tool as the button is held in a chock and turned. The back is slightly concave, flat, or tapering to a high point or boss at the eye. The concentric rings of the cutting tool around the eye are diagnostic. Some eyes are of iron.

Context: 1726-1776

Comments: This type was described by Olsen as having a characteristic burred edge around the eye, however, this burr is not present on the Brunswick buttons as a result of the cutting tool. The Brunswick buttons of this type do, however, have a collar of metal on each side of the wire eye which is a result of the molten metal conforming to the shape of the eye during casting. When the eye is broken off, this part of the cast boss around the eye appears as a double "spur". Faces plain except for one which has fine engraved design. The eye has a turned out foot beneath the boss.

Type 8

Whitemetal, brass, white brass, or copper cast metal disc buttons like Type 7 with the exception of the back, which is not spun and tooled. These buttons were cast in a mold. The raised center boss around the eye is present as in Type 7, but no concentric rings are seen since no cutting tool was used to remove the natural pebbled surface of the casting. The faces are plain, polished smooth, with the exception of one which has a relief design from the casting mold, and two white brass buttons with a Tudor Rose engraved on the face. The size varies from 16 to 27mm. across.

Context: 1726-1776

Comments: On examples where a one-piece face mold was used there is a spur of brass on each side of the eye resulting from the molten metal conforming to the shape of the eye during casting. When two piece face mold was used, the boss was a complete dome without the brass spurs at the base on each side of the eye. The foot is often turned out beneath the boss. [117]

Type 9

Flat coin shaped discs of copper or brass. The brass wire eye is fastened to the back with a drop of solder. The front is often stamped with designs made from several individual dies.

Context: 1726-1776

Comments: The size varies from 14 to 35 mm. across. The larger buttons are those with the more elaborate stamped designs. Two examples of this type had silver-plated faces. It is worthy of note that in other descriptions of this type (Johnson, vol. 1, p. 12, and Olsen, p. 552) a characteristic feature of this type is said to be the tendency of the eye to separate from the button back. Not a single button of this type from the Brunswick ruins was without its securely fastened eye.

Type 10

Cast brass, saucer shaped button with a "U" shaped eye soldered to the concave back. No smoothing of the back was done. The domed face has a small irregular rim.

Context: 1726-1776

Comments: Only one of this type has been recovered from Brunswick Town. It is the type worn by soldiers in the French Army around 1750 (Campbell, ms., p 4)

Type 11

Cast, flat, whitemetal button with eye and disc cast as one piece. Face plain, of with boss where eye comes through, or star in relief. Examples from 19th century context with script "I", "U S", or swirl design. Mold mark visible on back and on eye.

Context: 1726 to 1865

Comments: The buttons of this type from the 1726 to 1776 context were 17 to 24 mm. across, while the "U S" and script "I" types from the 1837 to 1865 context were 13 to 20 mm. across. The 13 mm. were the vest buttons and the 20 mm. were the coat General Service buttons of the militia in the War of 1812, (Calver and Bolton, p 148)

Type 12

Domed whitemetal button with high iron content and an iron wire eye. The oxidation of the iron in the metal has produced a coating of oxide over a soft white-metal core. A solid domed type shaped like Type 2. [118]

Context: 1726-1776

Comments: Only one of this badly preserved type was found.

Type 13

Domed, faceted glass buttons with brass plug in back holding brass wire eye. Color is black, or brown with black spots. Brass back plug with brass wire eye inserted into hot glass while it was still in the mold.

Context: 1726-1776

Comments: Faceted steel buttons were made by the mid-lith [sic] century, and this faceted glass type button probably dates from that same period.

Type 14

Flat bone button with shank and drilled eye in one piece

Context: 1726-1776

Comments: This button, only one of which was recovered from the Brunswick ruins, is an imitation of the cast brass, wedge back buttons with a drilled shank.

Type 15

Bone discs with no tooled rim for receiving the crimped over metal front. These discs have only one central hole. The size varies from 9 to 29 mm. across.

Context: 1726-1865

Comments: These bone button discs were found in some number during the excavation of Fort Michilimackinac, and are dated there from 1750 to 1770. They probably were locally made and may have been covered with fabric with a string eye. None have been found with brass eyes inserted at Brunswick, and

none are shown in the Michilimackinac manuscript illustrations. (Campbell, ms., p. 11).

Type 16

Flat, brass, disc with depressed rim around back to receive crimped front. Front does not cover whole face of button, but only the area around the rim, resulting in a thickened rim on the face. The eye is soldered to the back of the disc.

Context: 1726?-1865

Comments: Only two of this type were found, one in the Brunswick ruins and one at Fort Fisher ruin. [119]

Type 17

Cast brass coated with silver, with pierced pattern around edge. Rope pattern interwoven around edge. Center polished smooth and slightly concave to reflect light. Two additional circular pieces added to build up the center.

Context: 1800-1830

Comments: This is the most elaborate button found at Brunswick. It has two pouring marks on the back made during molding. A brass wire eye is soldered to the back.

Type 18

Brass, flat disc type with brass wire eye soldered to back. Some examples are slightly concave on the back, with a thickened rim on the back. Makers [sic] names, concentric lines, .a wreath motif, and references to the gilding impressed or in relief on the back are characteristic. The front is usually plain, but concentric ring design is found.

Context: 1800-1865

Comments: One included in this type has a plain back, but has an eagle on a cannon with a stack of six balls under the barrel on the front, and the word "CORPS" beneath. This button was used by the enlisted men of the artillery corps between 1814 and 1821. (Johnson, p. 44.) It is also unusual in that the brass wire eye has had the foot bent outward where it joins the button back, thus affording a better footing for the eye. This is one of only two buttons with this type attachment for the eye found in this type. Another button which was included in this type, but is not typical, is one found in the Public House-Tailor Shop at Brunswick, in what is apparently a 1726 to 1776 context. This button would ordinarily be included in Type 9, but on the back, stamped with a die after the button was cut, is the work "GILT". The early context and the style of the button would indicate that this may be an example of the earliest type of marking on the back of buttons, i.e. hand stamped with a die rather than machine stamped or impressed during casting. It should be pointed out here, perhaps, the difference between the disc shaped buttons of the 18th century, represented by Type 9, and Type 18 of the early 19th century other than the wording on the back. The disc buttons of the 18th century are characterized by their flatness and little rounding of the edges. The disc buttons of the early 19th century, besides the frequent use of words, designs etc. on the back, are more rounded at the edges, and do not have the die stamped designs characteristic of the [120] 18th century buttons. The working on the button backs of Type 18 buttons are: "- LORD AND LEES - WARRANTED", "*GILT*", from the 1800-1830 context, and: "TREBLE • GILT • STANDd - COLOUR", "STANDARD • COLOUR", "BEST G", an eagle and ** BEST**, "***LONDON***", "BENEDICT & BORNHAM • EXTRA", as well as various wreath type motifs, and concentric lines, from the 1837-1865 context.

Type 19

Bone buttons with five holes, with the center hole usually larger. The central area of the button face is usually depressed, leaving a thicker rim. The holes are drilled in this depression. The backs show parallel saw marks, and the face shows concentric cutting rings. The size is 16 mm. across, with an occasional one 23 mm., or 13 mm.

Context: 1800-1865

Comments: These have not been found in an 18th century context.

Type 20

Bone buttons with four holes which usually taper both front and back. Made like the five hole buttons, but the backs are often domed, showing concentric rings of a cutting tool used to smooth the back surface as well as the front.

Context: 1800-1865

Type 21

Iron, four hole buttons made in three pieces. The front with a depressed center area is crimped over a thin back disc. A center disc of wood or fiber aids in providing a tight fit of the two metal halves.

Context: 1800-1865

Comments: These buttons are badly preserved, and often are found without the metal back, indicating that other materials than iron may have sometimes been used as a base for the crimped over front. Although this type button is not said to have been introduced before 1870, (Olsen, p. 553) it has been found in an early 19th century context at Brunswick Town, Fort Fisher and elsewhere. The size is from 14 to 18 mm. across.

Type 22

Shell buttons with four holes and a depressed central area for the holes. The size varies from 8 to 13 mm. across. Some have arcs and notches around the rim as a decoration. [121]

Context: 1800-1865
Comments: Two shell buttons of this type, but with only two holes, were found at the Fort Fisher ruin.

Type 23

Porcelain, white, four hole, convex face and back, with depressed area in central portion of the face for the holes. The size is 10 to 11 mm. across, with a few 15 mm.

Context: 1800-1865

Comments: Since only two of these were found in the Brunswick Town context of 1800 to 1830, it is apparent that this type became a major type between 1837 and 1865, as revealed from the Fort Fisher ruin, representing 29 percent of all buttons recovered from this ruin. One green and two blue, four hole buttons, and one blue two hole button were found in the Fort Fisher ruin, and evidently represent rare types during the period.

Type 24

Domed, three piece iron buttons with fabric covering the face. The front domed piece fits over the iron back disc with inserted eye. The pressure of the back disc holds the fabric in place.

Context: 1837-1865

Comments: This type is badly preserved, with only traces of the fabric remaining on the face of the buttons. The eyes frequently pulled out of the iron backing disc.

Type 25
Slightly domed brass front crimped over an iron backing disc with an iron eye. The front is embossed with various decorative patterns and gilded.

Context: 1837-1865

Comments: The iron backs and eyes are very badly preserved, and it is assumed that the iron wire passed through the back disc loosely, as it did with the brass examples of the same period.

Type 26
Slightly domed, three-piece brass buttons with the wire eye passing loosely through a hole in the back piece The back disc often has one or more concentric rings in relief [122] around the eye. The front is pressed over the back disc, and is embossed with various designs and is gilded. The size varies from 9 to 15 mm.

Context: 1837-1865

Comments: These are civilian buttons, counterparts to the military buttons of Type 27.

Type 27
Domed, three-piece brass buttons with the line eagle device on front. Drawn brass wire eye extending through hole in back and loose, or soldered. Back plain, concentric lines in relief, or "SCOVILLS & CO. EXTRA"

Context: 1837-1865

Comments: These buttons were General Service Buttons of the period before and during the Civil War, and no doubt date from the 1865 period of the occupation of Fort Fisher. (Johnson).

Type 28
Disc type, slightly convex on the face with wire eye soldered to back. Stamped brass with the letters "N C" on a lined central area surrounded by a rayed star with

sometimes seven and sometimes eight points. The size is 22 mm. across.

Context: 1860's, during the occupation of Fort Fisher.

Comments: All buttons of this type found have the wire eye broken away from the back.

Type 29
Flat, cast whitemetal button with wire eye set into boss on back. Plain undecorated face. The size is 18 mm. across.

Context: 1837-1865

Comments: Only one of this type was found.

Type 30
Cast whitemetal four hole button with conical shape toward the back, probably from being pulled during use. The size is 17 mm. across.

Context: 1837-1865

Comments: Only one of this type has been found. [123]

Type 31
Flat, cast brass, spun back type with shank and disc cast in one piece. Drilled hole in the shank for the eye.

Context: 1837-1865

Comments: The size is 15 um. across. This type is made like the back of Type 1. None of this type were found in a colonial context except as sleeve links, and only one was found at Fort Fisher.

Type 32
Stamped brass four hole button with a depressed center area. The size is 12 and 16 mm. across.

Context: 1837-1865

Comments: One button of this type is complete in a single piece. Another type has two and probably three parts, a face and a matching back with four matching holes, both stamped. The front piece was pressed over the back piece around the rim with a piece of cardboard probably separating the two halves and helping to

Stanley South

produce a tight fit. This is the same construction as the iron buttons described as Type 21.

SLEEVE LINKS

During the excavation of the ruins at Brunswick and Fort Fisher a total of sixty sleeve links were found. A detailed analysis of these interesting button types will not be presented here, however, three additional types and a general summary is given.

Type 33

Domed bone button with engraved design on the front and a brass eye set into a brass plug in a hole cut into the back of the button.

Context: 1837-1865

Comments: Size is 11 mm. across and 5 mm. thick.

Type 34

Composite button of shell, brass and glass. The shell disc 15 mm. across, with a hole drilled in the center of the back for attachment of the brass shank. The shank is cast brass with a drilled hole for the eye. The shank is attached to the hole with an adhesive Some brass shanks extend through the shell to the front and hold a glass or paste [124] stone which appears as a set on the face of the button. The face of the shell is incised with radial and concentric lines, a geometric or star pattern.

Context: 1726-1776

Comments: The brass shank is often found without the shell disc, and might be difficult to recognize without knowledge of the construction of the complete sleeve link.

Type 35

Domed, hemispheric, round, oval, square or octagon shaped set holders for glass, paste or composition sets. These were made of whitemetal, brass, copper, silver, pewter, or iron. The set was held by crimping the domed back over the edge of the set. The two buttons were held together by brass links of wire or stamped links. The eyes were cast as a part of the set and drilled, or a wire eye was fastened through the holder and soldered, or soldered to the back of the domed holder. The back has embossing on some examples.

Context: 1726-1776

Comments: Many sets without the holder have been recovered as well as the metal holders minus their sets. Sleeve links not of the set holding type can be typed within the same framework as the buttons.

ANALYSIS OF THE BUTTON TYPES

When the buttons were divided into the thirty-two types the percentage relationship between the types was determined with the buttons from Brunswick and Fort Fisher being computed separately. The resulting percentages were plotted as two bar graphs. This graphic data was combined with drawings of the button types and a photograph of various types, into a master analysis chart which illustrated the complied data. From the bar graph it can be seen that types one through sixteen represent the button types from the 1726 to 1776 Brunswick Town context. Types three through nine, however, represent the major types from this context. The most striking part of this graph, of course, is the high percentage of Type 3 buttons represented, indicating that this was a major type used by the residents of Brunswick. As can be seen from the analysis chart Type 3 is an embossed face button crimped over a bone or wood back. Type 4 is virtually the same type with the exception of the brass wire eye through the bone back instead of the four hole back. Type 5 is also basically this same type, having the bone or wood [125] back with four holes or a single hole and a brass wire eye, but with the exception of the two-piece face. When these three types are combined, over fifty-five percent of all buttons recovered from the Brunswick ruins are represented.

Types 6, 7, and 8 are related in that they were cast with a brass wire eye in place in the mold during the casting process. When the wire eye was placed into a hole in the mold and the molten metal poured over it, the metal ran into the slot holding the wire eye, and produced a casting spur on one or both sides of the eye. These spurs are characteristic of Types 6, 7, and 8 except when a two-piece mold was used, producing a mold mark across the back of the button as shown in the drawing of Type 8. In this case the two halves of the mold could be tightly fitted around the wire eye, resulting in the elimination of the casting spur. This method of attaching the eye during the casting process is used with the two-piece cast buttons of Type 6, where the eye passed through the back half. It is also used with Type 7 buttons which are a flat disc but were tooled on the back on a lathe after casting in order to remove irregularities of the cast back surface. The buttons of Type 8 are similar except that they do not have the tooled back surface, but were used as they came from the casting. Types 7 and 8 have the ends of the wire eye bent over to form a foot. This characteristic can seldom be observed due to the fact that the boss of the cast metal around the foot prevents this observation, but the cutting tool used to smooth the back of Type 7 frequently cuts into the wire foot at the edge of the boss, revealing this characteristic.

Types 1, 31, and 34 are related in that the eye is drilled through a cast shank. However, only Type 1 was found as a button in the colonial context. Type 31 was found as a sleeve link type in the colonial context, but no larger buttons of this type were found except in a 19th century context.

Type 2 is a well made button with two domed halves brazed together and polished smooth to produce an almost invisible seam. A hole in the back on each side of the wire eye identifies this type. These holes probably functioned to allow expanding gases created during the brazing process to escape without danger of exploding the button. A number of this type were found during the excavation of Fort Michilimackinac and date from the British occupation of the fort prior to 1768 when numbered buttons began to be used. (Campbell, ms., p. 7-8) Type 10 has been identified as a French button worn by the soldiers around 1750. (Campbell, ms., p. 4) Only one of this type was recovered from the [126] ruins at Brunswick.

Type 9 is of interest in that the face is often stamped by hand with a series of dies to produce a decorative design. These buttons are often quite large, as can be seen from the photograph on the analysis chart. A characteristic of this type button is that the wire eye is well soldered in place, all specimens recovered from the Brunswick ruins having the eye intact, even though only the small ends of the wire eye is all the surface bearing on the button back. This evidence is contrary to that reported by Olsen (Olsen, p. 552) who states that many "eyeless" buttons of this type have been recovered from "early house and fort sites". His date for the type of 1785 to 1800 would indicate that by "early" he means the period not prior to 1785, which would be considered late at Brunswick. The difference in the degree to which the eye of this type is securely fastened to the back is probably related to the period involved. Olsen lists only a fifteen year span for the type, when evidence from Brunswick and Fort Fisher indicates that one hundred years, from the 1760's to 1860's, would be a better estimate of the period involved. This evidence would also indicate that the buttons of this type prior to the Revolution would likely have securely fastened eyes, while those of the 19th century, such as Type 28, would be poorly soldered in place, and frequently broken off and lost.

The analysis chart reveals that the Type 11 buttons, poured into a mold which formed the eye and button disc in the same operation, were used both in the 18th century, and were popular in the early years of the 19th century. Military buttons of the War of 1812 were of this type. One of the differences in this type from the two centuries is that those from the 18th century have the eye complete with a short shank below the eye, while those from the 19th century often lack the shank below the eye, resulting in the eye emerging directly from the back of the button, often as a semi-circle.

Only one button of Type 12 was found in the excavation of these ruins. The relatively soft core and the coating of iron oxide indicate that the material was some sort of steel. With a high whitemetal content. The domed button was cast solid, with an eye of iron held in place during casting. Steel was used as a minor button material from the 1750's. (Perry, p. 268) A similar style button cast in glass is represented by Type 13. This type has a brass eye and circular eye holder or boss pressed into the hot glass, resulting in a small tit of glass pushing up from the button between the two feet of the eye. [127]

Although bone button backs such as found on Type 3 and 4 buttons were a definite part of the button complex of the 18th century context at Brunswick Town, the four and five hole complete bone buttons of Type 19 and 20 have not been found in any context prior to 1800. Olsen reports that the five hole bone button was used as early as 1750, but this has not been found to be the case in the present study. (Olsen, p. 553) However, bone discs with one center hole, and with no off-set rim have been found in the colonial context as well as the 19th century. A number of Type 15 buttons were found at Fort Michilimackinac in a 1750 to 1770 context. (Campbell, ms., p. 11) It is thought that this type was probably covered with fabric. It should be distinguished from the one hole off-set rim backs of Type 4, which were forms or backs for the embossed metal buttons.

Also appearing in the early 19th century context along with the four and five hole bone buttons are the discs of stamped brass frequently having words or concentric lines or a wreath type motif in relief or impressed into the back. The eye of Type 18 buttons is frequently poorly soldered and may be missing. Two of this type had the

Stanley South

ends of the wire eye bent over to form a foot, but this was an exception rather than a rule for the type.

As can be seen from the graph on the analysis chart, buttons of porcelain and shell, for shirts, are major types from the 19th century context. (Type 22 and 23). Type 32 of stamped brass is similar in style, as well as the cast soft whitemetal button of Type 30.

Type 21 is an iron button with four holes made in three parts. The front with a depressed center panel is pressed over an iron back with a fiber center to act to give body and hold pressure on the two iron halves. Buttons of this type are usually badly preserved and are frequently found without the back half. From the evidence from Brunswick Fort Fisher [sic] it would appear that this type button made its appearance during the first quarter of the 19th century. Another type of iron button was made in two parts with a fiber center, but was domed and had an iron wire eye loosely fastened through a hole in the back half. The front half was covered with a fabric. This is Type 24. A variation of this is type 25, which has a stamped brass front and an iron back. Type 26 is also related, but is made with back, front and eye of brass, and consequently this type will be much betterr preserved. Type 25 and 26 relate to the colonial tradition of Types 3 and 4 but the difference is easily seen in the type of embossed face, the stamped relief designs of Type 25 and 26 appearing quite different from the [128] earlier embossed types. This difference can be observed in the photographic plate on the analysis chart.

Type 27 and 28 are of the Civil War period, and are examples of the military buttons of the mid-19th century. Type 28 is the North Carolina star burst pattern with the letters "N C" machine embossed on the face and characterised by a poorly soldered eye. Type 27 is machine embossed with an eagle, and comes in a variety of styles.

Type 29 is a cast soft whitemetal button with a brass wire eye cast into the boss. Although described by Olsen as dating from 1760 to 1790, this type appears only in the context of the 19th century in the present study.

Type 31 is represented by only one button from the 19th century context, but from the typological comparison it would seem to relate to Type 1 of the 18th century. However, this disc type with a drilled eye in the shank was not found to be present in the 18th century ruins at Brunswick. Olsen lists its time span from 1700 to 1765, but this was not verified from the data from the Brunswick Town ruins. However, the type is represented from the Brunswick ruins as a sleeve link, and is the major type shank used on the 18th century sleeve links.

THE SLEEVE LINKS

Of the fifty-three sleeve links found in the Brunswick ruins, sixty-six percent were cast with button and shank in one piece with a drilled hole for the eye. Since only two percent of the vest and coat buttons from the ruins were of this drilled eye type it is remarkable that so many sleeve links were so made. This evidence would tend to indicate that the tradition of drilling the shank on sleeve links was carried on for a much longer time period than it was for the buttons. Finding a sleeve link with a drilled eye, therefore, does not necessarily indicate an earlier context than other types as it might with buttons. Type 34 on the analysis chart illustrates an interesting type sleeve link which constituted 19% of the sleeve links recovered. A cast brass core with a drilled eye also held a disc of shell, and a glass or paste set which appeared on the face of the shell disc. Some of this type did not hold a set, in which case the cast brass core acted only as a shank set into the back of the shell disc. The shell was usually incised in a geometric pattern. All other sleeve link types constituted less than ten percent of the total from the ruins. Some links were stamped from brass as illustrated in Type 35 in the analysis chart, and others were joined by a simple wire [129] link. Type 35 illustrates the set holder type of sleeve link, of which there are a wide variety of styles. Due to the relatively small number of sleeve links recovered a detailed analysis of the type and style variations was not undertaken in the present analysis. Sleeve links, however, will be found to be a relatively frequent artifact to be recovered from colonial English sites of the 18th century. From the Fort Fisher ruin a total of seven sleeve link buttons were recovered. Six of these were of Type 18, with the typical impressed names and designs on the backs. The other was a drilled eye type shown as Type 31 in the analysis chart. An excellent group of 18th century sleeve links are illustrated in various sections of History Written with Pick and Shovel. (Calver & Bolton)

INTERPRETIVE SUMMARY

Although the occupation of the town of Brunswick was during the period 1726 to 1776, with a family or two there as late as the 1830's, the deed records indicate that the houses were built mostly during the 1730's, thus narrowing the time-span for the accumulation of the button sample studied. Another factor to be taken into consideration relative to the time-span represented by the button sample is the following:

The Historical Archaeology Laboratory Handbook

In the early eighteenth century it was made illegal to wear buttons unless they were made of precious metal or covered with textile twists. Metal buttons were then outmoded until this restriction was removed in 1741 bringing about an immediate reversion to metal buttons. Gilded and brass buttons at once became the vogue… From the late 1750's ever-increasing millions of gilt buttons were exported annually for a century to come. (Perry, p. 265-66)

Just how closely this restriction was heeded is not known, but if the statements made here are to be considered, the time-span for the accumulated sample of Brunswick buttons would be narrowed perhaps to the period from 1750 to 1776. Nevertheless, the effect of this restriction would probably be a standard one in the English colonial towns in America, so sites with a similar occupation period would likely show similar button type relationships. It should be kept in mind, however, that the sample probably represents more accurately the third quarter of the eighteenth century.

In order to understand somewhat clearer the relationship between various types described in this report, it might help to examine something of the history of the development [130] of the button industry as it relates to certain types. The trade of button-making was introduced to Birmingham around 1660, and by 1760 there were eighty-three master button-makers there. (Perry, p. 265) The seventeenth century buttons are said to have been cast brass and rather heavy, but by 1680 the lighter brass covered mold button had appeared with a hand hammered face of thin brass shaped to fit snugly over a wood or bone mold. (Perry, p. 268) The solid cast brass type was probably followed by a type in which two domed halves were cast separately and joined by flux as represented in this study by Type 1. Related Type 6 probably also follows in this tradition, as well as the cast disc Types 7 and 8. It is interesting to note an attitude held by some writers on buttons relative to these cast types. As can be seen from the examples illustrated in the analysis chart the designs cast into the face of these buttons are well executed and contain considerable detail. The following statement is relative to this type button with cast designs.

This was a crude and unsatisfactory procedure and because of this was but little used. The mold materials did not permit a clear-cut, detailed design of even the simplest form. Cast buttons had to be turned smooth in a lathe and those with design could not be finished in this manner. (Johnson, vol. I, p. 8)

In studying these fine cast two-piece buttons with the back carefully smoothed by turning a lathe, and the halves carefully ground and matched and fastened together with flux (Type 1 & 6), it is difficult to realize that the above description was meant to apply to this type.

As was mentioned above, the brass covered mold button had appeared by 1680, and in 1769 a patent by Richard Ford was granted for shaping cold button-brass without risk of splitting, thus safely forming the button face and shaping the relief ornament in a hand-press. (Perry, p. 268) This information relates particularly to button Types 3, 4, and 5, and a possible further narrowing of the time for the accumulation of the sample of these types from Brunswick ruins. A comment on this type by an authority on uniform buttons is of interest.

These are of ancient vintage, their origin lying deep in the murk of unremembered and unrecorded events. It seems to have been an aristocrat of excellent and interest [sic] parts, forced to give way to those of more strength and simplicity. [They have] all but disappeared from the face of our [131] careless world. (Johnson, Vol. I, p. 11)

Fortunately, through archaeology, we are now recovering these aristocrats from the murk of unremembered and unrecorded events.

The hand-stamped flat discs of Type 9, whose designs were made by a number of individual dies probably belongs [sic] to the decades just prior to the Revolution. This type is often said to have been the major type used before 1800, but as can be seen from the analysis chart, this does not hold true for Brunswick buttons.

In summarizing the buttons from the colonial period from Brunswick it can be said that they were well made, cast or stamped, pressed and embossed, and were often made of several parts. They by no means fit the description often ascribed to buttons of this period as crude, primitive, poorly made, and simple. They were more often, "aristocrats of excellent and interesting parts".

The 19th century brought into popularity the four and five hole buttons of bone, four hole iron, shell, soft whitemetal, stamped brass and porcelain buttons, as well as the machine stamped brass buttons invented by R. Sanders in 1823 which was the turning of the front piece over the back metal piece. (Johnson, Vol. I, p. 13) Sometimes the back was of brass, but was often of iron. This development is seen in Type 24 through 27. After the invention of the porcelain button in the 1840's, extensive use was made of these and shell buttons for shirts and with the exception of the Sanders Type 26 and 27, the quality of buttons had decreased considerably from the colonial period.

Stanley South

In this study a description of various button types from a pre-Revolutionary and a 19th century context has been undertaken with the aim of presenting data which may prove of value in comparative studies by other archaeologists and students of material culture. As similar data is revealed from other archaeological sites of known context such as contact period Indian villages, and French and English town and fort sites, a more generalized compilation of the evolutionary development of button forms can be undertaken. Historic references are of value to the historic site archaeologist in such problems, but it is to archaeology that archaeologists must continue to look for their most valuable source of data. [132]

BIBLIOGRAPHY

ALBERT, LILLIAN SMITH
    1941   A Button Collector's Second Journal. Hightstown, New Jersey.

CALVER, WILLIAM LOUIS, AND REGINALD PELHAM BOLTON
    1950   History Written with Pick and Shovel. New York Historical Society, New York.

CAMPBELL, J. DUNCAN
    1959   Fort Michilimackinac Excavated Buttons. Unpublished Manuscript on file at the Department of Anthropology, University of Michigan, Ann Arbor.

JOHNSON, DAVID F.
    1948   Uniform Buttons, v. I, II, Century House. Watkins Glen, New York.

OLSEN, STANLEY J.
    1963   "Dating Early Plain Buttons by Their Form", American Antiquity, v. XXVIII, No. 4, April.

PERRY, EDWARD
    1959   "Metal Buttons", Concise Encyclopedia of Antiques, v. IV. Hawthorn Books, Inc. New York.

Made in the USA
Las Vegas, NV
25 April 2024